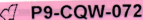

PAGES 98–109
*Street Finder maps
12–13*

PAGES 120–31
*Street Finder maps
4–5, 13*

PAGES 110–19
*Street Finder maps
13–14*

PAGES 132–41
*Street Finder maps
5–6, 13–14*

PAGES 160–71
*Street Finder maps
6–7, 14, 16*

PAGES 142–59
*Street Finder maps
14–16*

Bloomsbury
and
Fitzrovia

Smithfield
and
Spitalfields

Soho and
Trafalgar
Square

Holborn
and the
Inns of Court

The City

Covent
Garden
and the
Strand

R I V E R   T H A M E S

South Bank

Southwark and
Bankside

Whitehall
and
Westminster

PAGES 68–85
*Street Finder maps
13, 20–1*

PAGES 86–97
*Street Finder maps
12–13, 20*

PAGES 184–91
*Street Finder maps
13–14, 21–2*

PAGES 172–83
*Street Finder maps
6, 16*

EYEWITNESS TRAVEL

LONDON

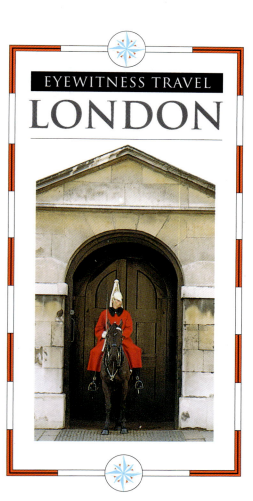

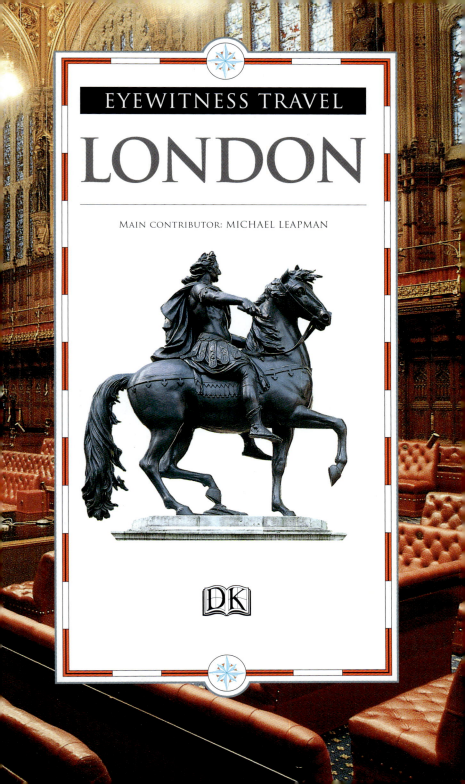

EYEWITNESS TRAVEL

LONDON

Main contributor: MICHAEL LEAPMAN

DK

LONDON, NEW YORK,
MELBOURNE, MUNICH AND DELHI
www.dk.com

PROJECT EDITOR Jane Shaw
ART EDITOR Sally Ann Hibbard
EDITOR Tom Fraser
NORTH AMERICAN EDITORS First Folio Resource Group, Inc.
DESIGNERS Pippa Hurst, Robyn Tomlinson
DESIGN ASSISTANT Clare Sullivan

CONTRIBUTORS
Christopher Pick, Lindsay Hunt

PHOTOGRAPHERS
Max Alexander, Philip Enticknap, John Heseltine, Stephen Oliver

ILLUSTRATORS
Brian Delf, Trevor Hill, Robbie Polley

This book was produced with the assistance of
Websters International Publishers.

Reproduced by Colourscan (Singapore)
Printed and bound by L-Rex Printing Company Limited, China

First American edition 1993
12 13 14 15 10 9 8 7 6 5 4 3 2 1
Published in the United States by
DK Publishing, 375 Hudson Street,
New York, New York 10014

**Reprinted with revisions 1996, 1997, 1999, 2000 (twice),
2001, 2002, 2003, 2004, 2005, 2006, 2007, 2008, 2009, 2010, 2011, 2012**

Copyright 1993, 2012 © Dorling Kindersley Limited, London
A Penguin Company

Published in Great Britain by Dorling Kindersley Limited.

A catalog record of this book is available from the Library of Congress

ISSN 1542-1554
ISBN 978-0-75668-407-5

FLOORS ARE REFERRED TO THROUGHOUT IN ACCORDANCE WITH EUROPEAN
USAGE, I.E., THE "FIRST FLOOR" IS THE FLOOR ABOVE GROUND LEVEL.

Front cover main image: Big Ben

MIX
Paper from
responsible sources
FSC™ C018179
www.fsc.org

**The information in this
DK Eyewitness Travel Guide is checked annually.**
Every effort has been made to ensure that this book is as up-to-date
as possible at the time of going to press. Some details, however,
such as telephone numbers, opening hours, prices, gallery hanging
arrangements and travel information are liable to change. The
publishers cannot accept responsibility for any consequences arising
from the use of this book, nor for any material on third party
websites, and cannot guarantee that any website address in this
book will be a suitable source of travel information. We value the
views and suggestions of our readers very highly. Please write to:
Publisher, DK Eyewitness Travel Guides, Dorling Kindersley,
80 Strand, London, WC2R 0RL, or email: travelguides@dk.com.

◁ **Interior of the House of Lords in Westminster**

CONTENTS

HOW TO USE
THIS GUIDE **6**

Portrait of Sir Walter Raleigh (1585)

INTRODUCING
LONDON

Bedford Square doorway (1775)

The Broadwalk at Hampton Court (c.1720)

Beefeater at the Tower of London

Bandstand in St James's Park

St. Paul's Church: Covent Garden

TRAVELERS' NEEDS

Houses of Parliament

SURVIVAL GUIDE

HOW TO USE THIS GUIDE

This Eyewitness Travel Guide helps you get the most from your stay in London with the minimum of practical difficulty. The opening section, *Introducing London*, locates the city geographically, sets modern London in its historical context, and describes the regular highlights of the London year. *London at a Glance* is an overview of the city's specialties. *London Area by Area* takes you round the city's areas of interest.

It describes all the main sights with maps, photographs, and detailed illustrations. In addition, six planned walking routes take you to parts of London you might otherwise miss.

Well-researched tips on where to stay, eat, shop, and on entertainments are in *Travelers' Needs. Children's London* lists highlights for young visitors, and *Survival Guide* tells you how to do anything from posting a letter to using the Underground (subway).

LONDON AREA BY AREA

The city has been divided into 16 sightseeing areas, each with its own section in the guide. Each section opens with a portrait of the area, summing up its character and history and listing all the sights to be covered. Sights are numbered and clearly located on an *Area Map*. After this comes a large-scale *Street by Street Map* focusing on the most interesting part of the area. Finding your way about the area section is made simple by the numbering system. This refers to the order in which sights are described on the pages that complete the section.

1 The Area Map

For easy reference, sights in each area are numbered and located on an Area Map. *To help the visitor, the map also shows Underground and main line rail stations.*

Photographs of facades and distinctive details of buildings help you to locate the sights.

Color-coding on each page makes the area easy to find in the book.

2 The Street by Street Map

This gives a bird's-eye view of the heart of each sightseeing area. The most important buildings are picked out in stronger color, to help you spot them as you walk around.

A locator map shows you where you are in relation to surrounding areas. The area of the *Street by Street Map* is shown in red.

Sights at a Glance lists the sights in the area by category: Historic Streets and Buildings; Churches; Museums and Galleries; Monuments; Parks and Gardens.

The area covered in greater detail on the *Street by Street Map* is shaded red.

Numbered circles pinpoint all the listed sights on the area map. St. Margaret's Church, for example, is **6**

Travel tips help you reach the area quickly by public transportation.

St. Margaret's Church is shown on this map as well.

Stars indicate the sights that no visitor should miss.

LONDON AT A GLANCE

Each map in this section concentrates on a specific theme: *Remarkable Londoners; Museums and Galleries; Churches; Parks and Gardens; Ceremonies.* The top sights are shown on the map; others are described on the following two pages and cross-referenced to their full entries in the *Area by Area* section.

Each sightseeing area is color-coded.

The theme is explored in greater detail on the pages following the map.

3 **Detailed information on each sight**
All important sights in each area are described in depth in this section. They are listed in order, following the numbering on the Area Map. Practical information is also provided.

4 **London's major sights**
These are given two or more full pages in the sightseeing area in which they are found. Historic buildings are dissected to reveal their interiors; museums and galleries have color-coded floor plans to help you find important exhibits.

The Visitors' Checklist provides the practical information you will need to plan your visit.

PRACTICAL INFORMATION

Each entry provides all the information needed to plan a visit to the sight. The key to the symbols is inside the back cover.

Telephone number

Address

Map reference to Street Finder at back of book

St. Margaret's Church **6** — Sight Number

Parliament Sq SW1. **Map** 13 B5.
Tel 020-7654 4840. 🚇 *Westminster.*
Open 9:30am–3:30pm Mon–Fri,
9:30am–1:30pm Sat, 2–5pm Sun.
⛪ 11am Sun. 🚫 👥 **Concerts.**

Opening hours

Services and facilities available

Nearest Underground station

The façade of each major sight is shown to help you spot it quickly.

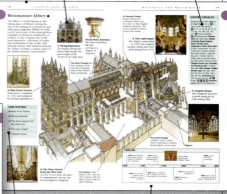

Stars indicate the most interesting architectural details of the building, and the most important works of art or exhibits on view inside.

A timeline charts the key events in the history of the sight.

INTRODUCING
LONDON

FOUR GREAT DAYS IN LONDON

For things to see and do, visitors to London are spoiled for choice. Whether here for a short stay or just wanting a flavor of this great city, you need to make the most of your time. So here are ideas for four days of sightseeing and fun. You'll find

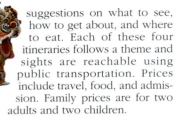

Chinatown dragon

suggestions on what to see, how to get about, and where to eat. Each of these four itineraries follows a theme and sights are reachable using public transportation. Prices include travel, food, and admission. Family prices are for two adults and two children.

Café at the National Portrait Gallery with a view of Trafalgar Square

HISTORY AND CULTURE

- Art at the National Gallery
- Coffee with a view
- Houses of Parliament
- Buckingham Palace

TWO ADULTS allow at least £140

Morning
Start the day by 10am in **Trafalgar Square** *(see p102)*. This is when the **National Gallery** *(see p104)* opens. Give yourself an hour and a half. The gallery is free, but visitors are encouraged to make a donation. After, go for a coffee at the Portrait Restaurant on the top floor of the neighboring **National Portrait Gallery** *(see p102)*, which has a view over Trafalgar Square and Nelson's column. Set off down Whitehall to Parliament Square, a 15-minute walk that may be extended by the passing distractions of Horse Guard's Parade, **Banqueting House** *(see p80)*, and **Downing Street** *(see p75)*. See the **Houses of Parliament** *(see pp72–3)* before visiting the next highlight, the

fabulous **Westminster Abbey** *(see pp76–7)*. There are a number of inexpensive lunch spots around St. James's Park subway station, such as Fuller's Ale and Pie House, 33 Tothill Street. Or go to the more pricey but attractive Inn the Park (must book; 020 7451 9999) by the lake in **St. James's Park** *(see p93)*.

Afternoon
On the far side of St. James's Park is **Buckingham Palace** *(see p94–5)*. The Queen's Gallery has changing exhibitions and you can buy regal souvenirs in its shop. For tea, head up past St. James's Palace to Piccadilly. You may not feel you can afford £40 per person for tea at the Palm Court at the **Ritz** *(see p91)* but there are several cafés and patisseries nearby, such as Richoux at 172 Piccadilly. For the best evening entertainment, get tickets for a West End play or show. These should be booked in advance *(see p343)*, although last-minute tickets are sometimes on sale at the theater box offices.

SHOPPING IN STYLE

- St. James's – shopping with history
- Old Bond Street for style
- Browse in trendy Covent Garden and the Piazza

TWO ADULTS allow at least £55

Morning
Start in Piccadilly and **St. James's Street**, *(see pp88–9)*, home of suppliers to royalty and historic fashion leaders: John Lobb the bootmaker is at No. 9 and Lock the hatter at 6. Turn right into Jermyn Street for high-class men's tailors such as Turnbull & Asser and New Lingwood, outfitters to Eton College. Floris the perfumer at 89 was founded in 1730 and the cheese shop Paxton & Whitfield at 93 has been here since 1740. Walk through Piccadilly Arcade to **Fortnum & Mason** *(see p313)*, where the Fountain Tea Room can provide refreshment before

Historic shopping mall at the Burlington Arcade, Piccadilly

The Queen's House, Greenwich

buying souvenirs. Stop in at **The Royal Academy** *(see p90)* and the **Burlington Arcade** *(see p91)*, before heading up **Old** and **New Bond** streets *(see p322)*, the smartest shopping address in town, with art galleries, antiques, and designer shops. Try South Molton Street for women's fashion and Oxford Street for **Selfridge's** massive department store *(see p321)*.

Afternoon
Head to **Covent Garden** *(see p114)*. Take a look around **London's Transport Museum** *(see p114)*, then wander the Piazza and streets to the north; Floral Street is renowned for high fashion. Check out alternative lifestyles in **Neal's Yard** *(see p115)*. Stop for tea in Paul Bakery and Café at 29 Bedford Street.

THE GREAT OUTDOORS

- Sail to the Cutty Sark
- Ponds and a memorial in the Palace gardens
- Tea at Kensington Palace

TWO ADULTS allow at least £100

Morning
Take a one-hour boat trip from Westminster Millennium Pier to **Greenwich** *(see pp238–43)*. A morning is easily passed at this UNESCO World Heritage Site. There's the Maritime Museum, Royal Observatory, Queen's House, and Cutty Sark. Have a snack

lunch overlooking the river at the historic **Trafalgar Tavern** *(see p242)*.

Afternoon
Return by boat and head to **Kensington Gardens** *(see p210)*. Admire the boats on the Round Pond, and see what's on at the **Serpentine Gallery** *(see p210)*. To the east is the Princess Diana Memorial Fountain. By the Long Water is the delightful statue of Peter Pan. Visit **Kensington Palace** *(see p210)*, Princess Diana's former home. Have tea in the Palace's Orangery Tea Room.

A FAMILY FUN DAY

- Take the kids to the Tower
- Messing about in boats
- Enjoy the undersea world
- Hit Chinatown

FAMILY OF 4 allow at least £300

Predators at the London Aquarium

Morning
Head to the **Tower of London** *(see pp154-7)*, London's top visitor attraction and an

established family favorite. Book tickets to avoid waiting in line. The fascinating castle and Crown Jewels will take at least a couple of hours to explore. For lunch, head across Tower Bridge to **St. Katharine's Dock** *(see p158)* where, among an eclectic collection of boats, there are several attractive places to eat, including the Dickens Inn for snacks or a full meal.

Afternoon
The **London Eye** offers passengers a thrilling ride and spectacular views above the city on the South Bank *(see p189;* phone bookings can be made on: 0870 5000 600).

Nearby there is plenty of other entertainment, especially in **County Hall** *(see p188)*, which was the seat of London's local government for more than 60 years. This leisure complex has the Sea Life London Aquarium. Younger people will enjoy the video games and simulators, bowling alley, and bumper cars in the Namco Station. Afterward, take the subway to **Chinatown** *(see p108)*, situated in and around Gerrard Street, which with its many superb restaurants, colorful shops, and vibrant streetlife, is always lively and interesting. Go for an early Chinese supper of *dim sum*, or small dishes. If the kids are still up for entertainment, end the day at a film in one of the many luxurious movie theaters around Leicester Square.

The gracious sweep of the Diana Memorial Fountain, Hyde Park

Putting London on the Map

London, the capital of the United Kingdom, is a city of over seven million people covering 620 sq miles (1,606 sq km) of southeast England. It is built on the River Thames and is at the center of the UK road and rail networks. From London visitors can easily reach the country's other main tourist attractions.

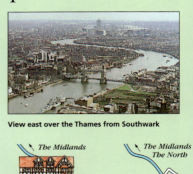

View east over the Thames from Southwark

WESTERN EUROPE

NORWAY
SWEDEN
DENMARK
REPUBLIC OF IRELAND
UNITED KINGDOM
London
NETHERLANDS
GERMANY
BELGIUM
LUXEMBOURG
FRANCE
SWITZERLAND
AUSTRIA
ITALY
SPAIN
PORTUGAL

Western Europe

London is in northwest Europe, on the same latitude as Warsaw. It is Europe's biggest city and the business center of the continent. London has five airports and is about an hour's flying time from Scandinavia, Germany, Holland, and France. It is also linked to the continent by ports and by train via the Eurotunnel.

The Midlands
The Midlands
The North

Stratford-upon-Avon

M40
A43

A40

Thames
Oxford
M40

Chiltern Hills

The West
M4
M4
Reading
Bath
A34

Windsor
M3

Stonehenge
A30
A34
A3

A36
Salisbury

A30
Winchester
So u
Do w

The West

A35
Southampton
M27
A3(M)
A27

Poole
Portsmouth

Isle of Wight

Channel Islands
Cherbourg
St Malo
Cherbourg
Caen
Le Havre

E N G L I S H

Aerial view of central London

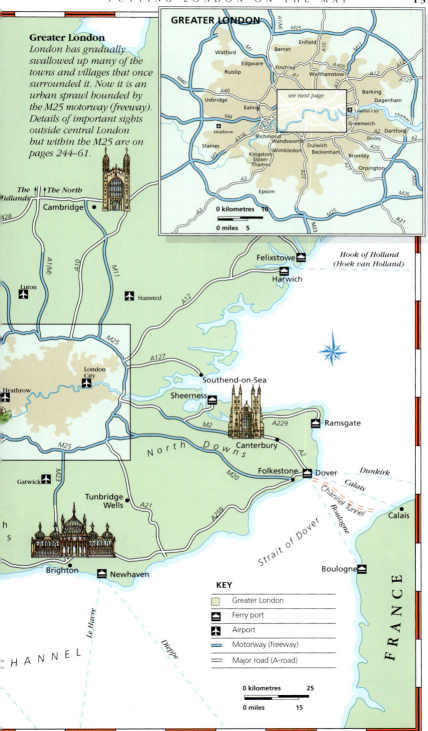

Greater London

London has gradually swallowed up many of the towns and villages that once surrounded it. Now it is an urban sprawl bounded by the M25 motorway (freeway). Details of important sights outside central London but within the M25 are on pages 244–61.

GREATER LONDON

Watford
Barnet
Enfield
Edgware
Finchley
Ruislip
Walthamstow
Uxbridge
Barking
Dagenham
Ealing
London City
Heathrow
Greenwich
Staines
Richmond
Wandsworth
Dartford
Bexley
Kingston Upon Thames
Wimbledon
Dulwich
Beckenham
Bromley
Epsom
Orpington

see next page

0 kilometres 10

0 miles 5

The Midlands
The North

Cambridge

Luton

Stansted

Felixstowe
Harwich

**Hook of Holland
(Hoek van Holland)**

London City

Heathrow

Southend-on-Sea
Sheerness

Ramsgate

North Downs

Canterbury

Gatwick

Folkestone
Dover

Dunkirk
Calais

Channel Tunnel

Boulogne

Calais

Tunbridge Wells

Strait of Dover

Brighton
Newhaven

Boulogne

CHANNEL

Le Havre

Dieppe

FRANCE

KEY

▨	Greater London
⚓	Ferry port
✈	Airport
▬	Motorway (freeway)
═	Major road (A-road)

0 kilometres 25

0 miles 15

Central London

Most of the sights described in this book lie within 14 areas of central London, plus two outlying districts of Hampstead and Greenwich. Each area has its own chapter. If time is short, you may decide to restrict yourself to the five areas that contain most of London's famous sights: Whitehall and Westminster; The City; Bloomsbury and Fitzrovia; Soho and Trafalgar Square; and South Kensington.

Tower of London
For much of its 900-year history the Tower was an object of fear. Its bloody past and the Crown Jewels make it a major attraction (see pp154–7).

National Gallery
This gallery has over 2,300 paintings, and the collection is particularly strong on Dutch, early Renaissance Italian, and 17th-century Spanish painting (see pp104–7).

Natural History Museum
Life on earth and the earth itself are vividly explored at the museum, through a combination of interactive techniques and traditional displays (see pp208–9).

KEY

🟪	Major sight
Ⓔ	Underground station
⇄	Train station
🚢	Riverboat pier
ℹ	Tourist information

0 kilometers   1

0 miles   0.5

Buckingham Palace
The office and home of the monarchy, the palace is also used for state occasions. The State Rooms open to the public in the summer (see pp94–5).

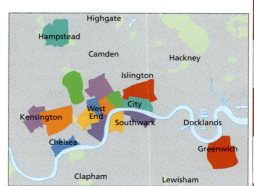

Museum of London
This museum, on the edge of the Barbican complex in the City, provides a lively account of London life from prehistoric times to the present day (see pp166–7).

Houses of Parliament
The Palace of Westminster has been the seat of the two Houses of Parliament, called the Lords and the Commons, since 1512 (see pp72–3).

THE HISTORY OF LONDON

In 55 BC, Julius Caesar's Roman army invaded England, landed in Kent, and marched northwest until it reached the broad River Thames at what is now Southwark. There were a few tribesmen living on the opposite bank but no major settlement. However, by the time of the second Roman invasion 88 years later, a small

The dragon: the City of London's symbol

port and mercantile community had been established here. The Romans bridged the river and built their administrative headquarters on the north bank, calling it Londinium – a version of its old Celtic name.

LONDON AS CAPITAL

London was soon the largest city in England and, by the time of the Norman Conquest in 1066, it was the obvious choice for national capital.

Settlement slowly spread beyond the original walled city, which was virtually wiped out by the Great Fire of 1666. The post-Fire rebuilding formed the basis of the area we know today as the City but, by the 18th century, London enveloped the

settlements around it. These included the royal city of Westminster which had long been London's religious and political center. The explosive growth of commerce and industry during the 18th and 19th centuries made London the biggest and wealthiest city in the world, creating a prosperous middle class who built the fine houses that still grace parts of the capital. The prospect of riches also lured millions of the dispossessed from the countryside and from abroad. They crowded into insanitary dwellings, many just east of the City, where docks provided employment.

By the end of the 19th century, 4.5 million people lived in inner London and another 4 million in its immediate vicinity. Bombing in World War II devastated many central areas and led to substantial rebuilding in the second half of the 20th century, when the docks and other Victorian industries disappeared.

The following pages illustrate London's history by giving snapshots of significant periods in its evolution.

A map of 1580 showing the City of London and, near the lower left corner, the City of Westminster

◁ **A 15th-century manuscript showing the Tower of London with London Bridge in the background**

Roman London

1st-century Roman coin

When the Romans invaded Britain in the 1st century AD, they already controlled vast areas of the Mediterranean, but fierce opposition from local tribes (such as Queen Boudicca's Iceni) made Britain difficult to control. The Romans persevered however, and had consolidated their power by the end of the century. Londinium, with its port, developed into a capital city; by the 3rd century, there were some 50,000 people living here. But, as the Roman Empire crumbled in the 5th century, the garrison pulled out, leaving the city to the Saxons.

EXTENT OF THE CITY

| 125 AD | Today |

Public Baths
Bathing was an important part of Roman life. This pocket-sized personal hygiene kit (including a nail pick) and bronze pouring dish date from the 1st century.

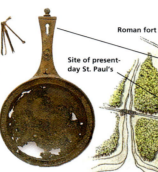

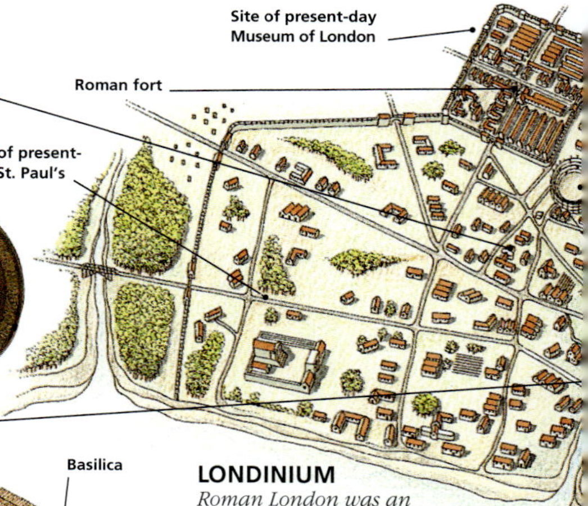

Site of present-day Museum of London

Roman fort

Site of present-day St. Paul's

Basilica

Forum

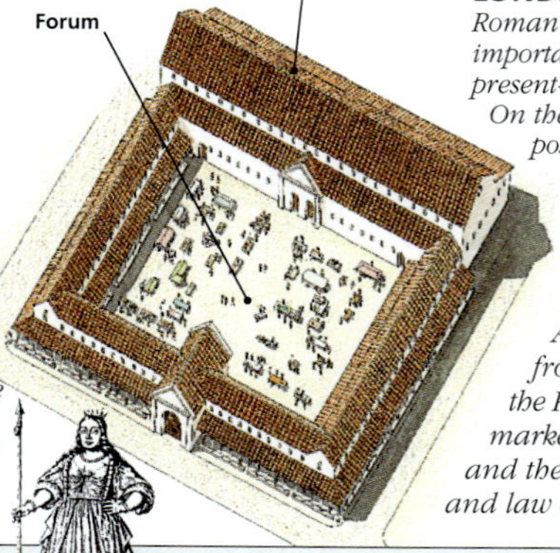

LONDINIUM
Roman London was an important center on the site of the present-day City (see pp142–159). On the Thames, it was in a good position to trade with the rest of the Empire.

Temple of Mithras
Mithras protected the good from evil. This 2nd-century head was in his temple.

Forum and Basilica
About 200 m (600 ft) from London Bridge was the Roman forum (the chief market and meeting place) and the basilica (the city hall and law court).

TIMELINE

55 BC Julius Caesar invades Britain

AD 61 Boudicca rebels

200 City wall built

410 Roman troops begin to leave

| | 100 | 200 | 300 | 400 | 5 |

AD 43 Claudius establishes Roman London and builds the first bridge

London Wall
The tombstone of a Roman legionary was built into the city wall. The writing tablets in his left hand suggest he did clerical work.

Amphitheater
Entertainment was brutal. A popular spectacle was gladiators, dressed like this figurine, fighting to the death.

WHERE TO SEE ROMAN LONDON

Most traces of the Roman occupation are in the City *(see pp142–59)* and Southwark *(pp172–83)*. The Museum of London *(pp166–7)* and the British Museum *(pp126–9)* have extensive collections of Roman finds. There's a Roman pavement in the crypt of All Hallows by the Tower *(p153)*, and in the 1990s an amphitheater was found below the Guildhall *(p159)*. The foundations of the Temple of Mithras are on view near the site on Queen Victoria Street.

This section of the Roman wall, built in the 3rd century to defend the city, can be seen from the Museum of London.

London's best Roman mosaic is this 2nd-century pavement, found in 1869 in the City, now in the Museum of London.

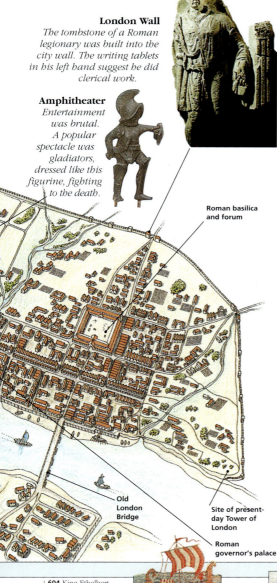

Roman basilica and forum

Old London Bridge

Site of present-day Tower of London

Roman governor's palace

604 King Ethelbert builds first St. Paul's

834 First Viking raids

1014 Norse invader Olaf pulls down London Bridge to take the city

| 600 | 700 | 800 | | 1000 |

871 Alfred the Great becomes king of Wessex

Medieval London

The historic division between London's centers of commerce (the City) and government (Westminster) started in the mid-11th century when Edward the Confessor established his court and sited his abbey (*see pp 76–9*) at Westminster. Meanwhile, in the City, tradesmen set up their own institutions and guilds, and London appointed its first mayor. Disease was rife and the population never rose much above its Roman peak of 50,000. The Black Death (1348) reduced the population by half.

EXTENT OF THE CITY

🔲 *1200*   🔲 *Today*

St. Thomas à Becket
As Archbishop of Canterbury he was murdered in 1170 at the prompting of Henry II with whom he was quarreling. Thomas was made a saint and pilgrims visited his Canterbury shrine.

LONDON BRIDGE
The first stone bridge was built in 1209 and lasted 600 years. It was the only bridge across the Thames in London until Westminster Bridge (1750).

The Chapel of St. Thomas, erected the year the bridge was completed, was one of its first buildings.

Iron railings

Houses and shops projected over both sides of the bridge. Shopkeepers made their own merchandise on the premises and lived above their shops. Apprentices did the selling.

THE HOUSE OF RICHARD WHITTINGTON MAYOR OF LONDON STOOD ON THIS SITE 1423

The piers were made from wooden stakes rammed into the river bed and filled with rubble.

Dick Whittington
The 15th-century trader was thrice mayor of London (see p39).

Stag Hunting
Such sports were the chief recreation of wealthy landowners.

The arches ranged from 4.5 m (15 ft) to 10 m (35 ft) in width.

TIMELINE

1042 Edward the Confessor becomes king

1086 Domesday Book, England's first survey, published

1191 Henry Fitzalwin becomes London's first mayor

1215 King John's Magna Carta gives City more powers

| 1050 | 1100 | 1150 | 1200 | 1250 |

1066 William I crowned in Abbey

1065 Westminster Abbey completed

1176 Work starts on the first stone London Bridge

1240 First parliament sits at Westminster

Chivalry

Medieval knights were idealized for their courage and honor. Edward Burne-Jones (1833–98) painted George, patron saint of England, rescuing a maiden from this dragon.

Geoffrey Chaucer

The poet and customs controller (see p39), is best remembered for his Canterbury Tales *which creates a rich picture of 14th-century England.*

WHERE TO SEE MEDIEVAL LONDON

There were only a few survivors of the Great Fire of 1666 *(see pp24–5)* – the Tower *(pp154–7)*, Westminster Hall *(p72)* and Westminster Abbey *(pp76–9)*, and a few churches *(p46)*. The Museum of London *(pp166–7)* has artifacts, while Tate Britain *(pp82–5)* and the National Gallery *(pp104–7)* have paintings. Manuscripts, including the Domesday Book, are found at the British Library *(p125)*.

The Tower of London was started in 1078 and became one of the few centers of royal power in the largely self-governing City.

A 14th-century rose window is all that remains of Winchester Palace near the Clink on Bankside *(see p182)*.

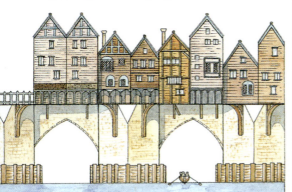

Plan of the Bridge

The bridge had 19 arches to span the river, making it for many years the longest stone bridge in England.

Many 13th-century pilgrims went to Canterbury.

1348 Black Death kills thousands	**1394** Westminster Hall remodeled by Henry Yevele	*The Great Seal of Richard I, who spent most of his 10-year reign fighting abroad*	
1350	**1400**	**1450**	
1381 Peasants' Revolt defeated	**1397** Richard Whittington becomes mayor	**1476** William Caxton sets up first printing press at Westminster	

Elizabethan London

In the 16th century the monarchy was stronger than ever before. The Tudors established peace throughout England, allowing art and commerce to flourish. This renaissance reached its zenith under Elizabeth I as explorers opened up the New World, and English theater, the nation's most lasting contribution to world culture, was born.

EXTENT OF THE CITY

▢ *1561* ▢ *Today*

Curtain

SHAKESPEARE'S GLOBE
Elizabethan theaters were built of wood and only half covered, so plays had to be canceled in bad weather.

A balcony on the stage was part of the scenery.

The apron stage had a trap door for special effects.

Death at the Stake
The Tudors dealt harshly with social and religious dissent. Here Bishops Latimer and Ridley die for so-called heresy in 1555, when Elizabeth's sister, Mary I, was queen. Traitors could expect to be hung, drawn, and quartered.

In the pit, below the level of the stage, commoners stood to watch the play.

Hunting and Hawking
Popular 16th-century pastimes are shown on this cushion cover.

TIMELINE

1536 Henry VIII's second wife, Anne Boleyn, executed

1535 Sir Thomas More executed for treason

1553 Edward dies, succeeded by his sister Mary I

1530

1550

Rat catchers, and other pest controllers, could not prevent epidemics of plague.

1534 Henry VIII breaks with the Roman Catholic church

1547 Henry dies, succeeded by his son Edward VI

The galleries were for rich theater-goers who could watch from the comfort of seats.

Steps allowed tiered seating.

Audience entrance

Elizabeth I
The "Virgin Queen" sat for this portrait to celebrate victory over the Spanish in 1588.

Tilting Spurs
The aim of this high-speed sport, popular among noblemen, was to knock opponents off their horses.

Astronomical Clock
Made in 1540 at Hampton Court, it shows the sun moving round the earth.

WHERE TO SEE ELIZABETHAN LONDON

The Great Fire of 1666 wiped out the City. Fortunately, Middle Temple Hall (*see p139*), Staple Inn (*p141*), and the Lady Chapel inside Westminster Abbey (*pp76–9*) were beyond its reach. The Museum of London (*pp166–7*), Victoria and Albert (*pp202–5*), and Geffrye Museums (*p248*) have fine furniture and artifacts. Farther afield are Hampton Court (*pp254–7*) and Sutton House (*p248*).

Elizabeth I watched *Twelfth Night* by Shakespeare under the hammerbeam roof of Middle Temple Hall in 1603.

The Parr Pot, now in the Museum of London, was made by Venetian craftsmen in London in 1547.

1563 Plague sweeps Europe

1570 Francis Drake makes first voyage to the West Indies

1584 Walter Raleigh's first attempt to colonize America

1588 Drake defeats Spanish Armada

1591 First play by Shakespeare produced

| 1560 | 1570 | 1580 | 1590 |

1558 Mary I's death makes Elizabeth queen

Gloves made from imported silk and velvet

1603 Elizabeth dies, James I accedes

Restoration London

Civil War had broken out in 1642 when the mercantile class demanded that some of the monarch's power be passed to Parliament. The subsequent Commonwealth was dominated by Puritans under Oliver Cromwell. The Puritans outlawed simple pleasures, such as dancing and theater, so it was small wonder that the restoration of the monarchy under Charles II in 1660 was greeted with rejoicing and the release of pent-up creative energies. The period was, however, also marked with two major tragedies: the Plague (1665) and the Great Fire (1666).

EXTENT OF THE CITY

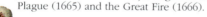

☐ *1680* ☐ *Today*

St. Paul's was destroyed in the fire that raged as far west as Fetter Lane *(map 14 E1).*

London Bridge itself survived, but many of the buildings on it were burned down.

Oliver Cromwell
He led the Parliamentarian army and was Lord Protector of the Realm from 1653 until his death in 1658. At the Restoration, his body was dug up and hung from the gallows at Tyburn, near Hyde Park (see p207).

Charles I's Death
The king was beheaded for tyranny on a freezing day (January 30, 1649) outside Banqueting House (see p80).

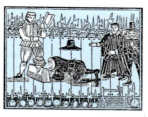

Charles I
His belief in the Divine Right of Kings angered Parliament and was one of the causes of civil war.

TIMELINE

1623 Shakespeare's First Folio published

1625 James I dies, succeeded by his son Charles I

1642 Civil war starts when Parliament defies king

1620

1640

1650

1605 Guy Fawkes leads failed attempt to blow up the King and Parliament

Feathered helmet worn by Royalist cavaliers

1649 Charles I executed, Commonwealth established

Newton's Telescope

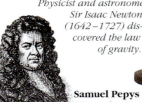

Physicist and astronomer Sir Isaac Newton (1642–1727) discovered the law of gravity.

Samuel Pepys

His exuberant diaries tell us much about courtly life of the time.

The Tower of London was just out of the fire's reach.

WHERE TO SEE RESTORATION LONDON

Wren's churches and his St. Paul's Cathedral *(see p47 and pp148–51)* are, with Inigo Jones's Banqueting House *(p80)*, London's most famous 17th-century buildings. Other fine examples are Lincoln's Inn *(p136)* and Cloth Fair *(p165)*. The Museum of London *(pp166–7)* has a period interior. The British Museum *(pp126–9)* and the V&A *(pp202–205)* have numerous pottery, silver, and textile collections.

Ham House *(p252)* was built in 1610 but much enlarged later in the century. It has the finest interior of its time in England.

THE GREAT FIRE OF 1666

An unidentified Dutch artist painted this view of the fire that burned for 5 days, destroying 13,000 houses.

The Plague

During 1665, carts collected the dead and took them to communal graves outside the city.

Peter Paul Rubens painted the ceiling in 1636 for Inigo Jones's Banqueting House *(p80)*. This is one of its panels.

1664–5 Plague kills 100,000

1666 Great Fire

1685 Charles II dies, Catholic James II becomes king

1692 First insurance market opens at Lloyd's

1660	1670	1690

1660 Monarchy restored under Charles II

A barber's bowl made by London potters in 1681

1688 James ousted in favor of Protestant William of Orange

1694 First Bank of England set up by William Paterson

Georgian London

George I (reigned 1714–27)

The foundation of the Bank of England in 1694 spurred the growth of London and, by the time George I came to the throne in 1714, it had become an important financial and commercial center. Aristocrats with West End estates began laying out elegant squares and terraces to house newly rich merchants. Architects such as the Adam brothers, John Soane, and John Nash developed stylish medium-scale housing. They drew inspiration from the great European capitals, as did English painters, sculptors, composers, and craftsmen.

EXTENT OF THE CITY

☐ 1810　　☐ *Today*

Manchester Square was laid out in 1776–8.

Portman Square was on the town's outskirts when it was started in 1764.

Great Cumberland Place
Built in 1790, it was named after a royal duke and military commander.

Grosvenor Square
Few of the original houses remain on one of the oldest and largest Mayfair squares (1720).

Docks
Purpose-built docks handled the growth in world trade.

TIMELINE

1714 George I becomes king			
1727 George II becomes king		**1759** Kew Gardens established	**1768** Royal Academy of Art established
1720	**1740**		**1760**	**1770**
1717 Hanover Square built, start of West End development	**1729** John Wesley (1703–91) founds the Methodist Church		**1760** George III becomes king

John Nash
Stylish Nash shaped 18th-century London with variations on Classical themes, such as this archway in Cumberland Terrace, near Regent's Park.

GEORGIAN LONDON

The layout of much of London's West End has remained very similar to how it was in 1828, when this map was published.

WHERE TO SEE GEORGIAN LONDON

The portico of the Theatre Royal Haymarket *(see pp344–5)* gives a taste of the style of fashionable London in the 1820s. In Pall Mall *(p92)* Charles Barry's Reform and Travellers' Clubs are equally evocative. Most West End squares have some Georgian buildings, while Fournier Street *(p170)* has good small-scale domestic architecture. The Victoria and Albert Museum (V&A, *pp202–5*) has silver, as do the London Silver Vaults *(p141)*, where it is for sale. Hogarth's pictures, at Tate Britain *(pp82–5)* and Sir John Soane's Museum *(pp136–7)*, show the social conditions.

This English long-case clock (1725), made of oak and pine with Chinese designs, is in the V&A.

Captain Cook
This Yorkshire-born explorer discovered Australia during a voyage round the world in 1768–71.

Berkeley Square
Built in the 1730s and 1740s in the grounds of the former Berkeley House, several characteristic original houses remain on its west side.

Ironwork
Crafts flourished. This ornate railing is on Manchester Square.

Signatories of the American Declaration of Independence

1776 Britain loses American colonies with Declaration of Independence

1802 Stock Exchange formally established

1811 George III goes mad, his son George is made Regent

1820 George III dies, Prince Regent becomes George IV

1830 George IV dies, brother William IV is king

| 1800 | 1810 | 1820 | 1830 |

1829 London's first horse bus

Victorian London

Much of London today is Victorian. Until the early 19th century, the capital had been confined to the original Roman city, plus Westminster and Mayfair to the west, ringed by fields and villages such as Brompton, Islington, and Battersea. From the 1820s these green spaces filled rapidly with terraces of houses for the growing numbers attracted to London by industrialization. Rapid expansion brought challenges to the city. The first cholera epidemic broke out in 1832, and in 1858 came the Great Stink, when the smell from the Thames River became so bad that Parliament had to go into recess. But Joseph Bazalgette's sewerage system (1875), involving banking both sides of the Thames, eased the problem.

Queen Victoria in her coronation year (1838)

EXTENT OF THE CITY

| 1900 | Today |

The building was 1,850 ft (560 m) long and 110 ft (33 m) high.

Nearly 14,000 exhibitors came from all over the world, bringing more than 100,000 exhibits.

Pantomime

The traditional family Christmas entertainment – still popular today (see p344) – started in the 19th century.

Soldiers marched and jumped on the floor to test its strength before the exhibition opened.

Massive elm trees growing in Hyde Park were left standing and the exhibition was erected around them.

The Crystal Fountain was 27 ft (8 m) high.

Carpets and stained glass were hung from the galleries.

TIMELINE

1837 Victoria becomes queen

1851 Great Exhibition

Season ticket for Great Exhibition

A Wedgwood plate in typically florid Victorian style

1861 Prince Albert dies

1860

1836 First London rail terminus opens at London Bridge

1840 Rowland Hill introduces the Penny Post

1863 Metropolitan Railway, world's first subway system, is opened

1870 First Peabody Buildings, to house the poor, built in Blackfriars Road

Railways
By 1900 fast trains, such as this Scotch Express, *were crossing the country.*

Telegraph
Newly invented communications technology, like this telegraph from 1840, made business expansion easier.

Crystal Palace
Between May and October 1851, six million people visited Joseph Paxton's superb feat of engineering. In 1852 it was dismantled and reassembled in south London where it remained until destroyed by fire in 1936.

WHERE TO SEE VICTORIAN LONDON

Grandiose buildings best reflect the spirit of the age, notably the rail termini, the Kensington Museums *(see pp198–213),* and the Royal Albert Hall *(p207).* Leighton House *(p218)* has a well-preserved interior. Pottery and fabrics are in the Victoria and Albert Museum, and London's Transport Museum *(p114)* has buses, trams, and trains.

The Victorian Gothic style suited buildings like the Public Record Office in Chancery Lane.

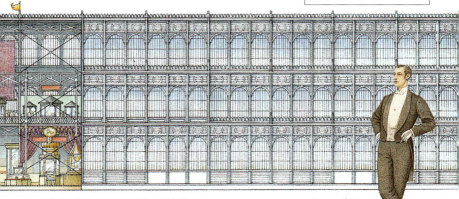

THE GREAT EXHIBITION OF 1851
The exhibition, held in the Crystal Palace in Hyde Park, celebrated industry, technology, and the expanding British Empire.

Formal Dress
Under Victoria, elaborate men's attire was replaced by more restrained evening wear.

A special box for carrying top hats

1889 London County Council (LCC) established

1891 First LCC public housing built, in Shoreditch

1899 First motor buses introduced

1901 Queen Victoria dies, Edward VII accedes

| 1880 | 1890 | 1900 |

1890 First electric subway line, from Bank to Stockwell, opens

Commemorative fan for the Boer War, which ended in 1903

London Between the World Wars

Art Deco china by Clarice Cliff

The society that emerged from World War I grasped eagerly at the innovations of early 20th-century London – the car, the telephone, commuter transportation. The movies brought transatlantic culture, especially jazz and swing music. Victorian social restraints were discarded as people flocked to dance in restaurants, clubs, and dance halls. Many left the crowded inner city for new suburban estates. Then came the 1930s global Depression, whose effects had barely worn off when World War II began.

EXTENT OF THE CITY

🟥 *1938*   🟨 *Today*

Formal evening wear, including hats for both sexes, was still compulsory when going to smart West End night spots.

Commuting
London's new outer suburbs were made popular by the underground railway. In the north was "Metroland," named after the Metropolitan Line which penetrated Hertfordshire.

High Fashion
The sleek flowing new styles contrasted with the fussy elaboration of the Victorians and Edwardians. This tea gown is from the 1920s.

A LONDON STREET SCENE
Maurice Greiflenhagen's painting (1926) captures the bustle of London after dark.

TIMELINE

Medals, like this from 1914, were struck during the campaign for women's votes.

1921 North Circular Road links northern suburbs

1922 First BBC national radio broadcast

1910

1920

1910 George V succeeds Edward VII

Cavalry was still used in the Middle Eastern battles of World War I (1914–18).

Early Movies
London-born Charlie Chaplin (1889–1977), seen here in City Lights, *was a popular star of both silent and talking movies.*

Seven new theaters were built in central London from 1924 to 1931.

George VI
Oswald Birley painted this portrait of the king who became a model for wartime resistance and unity.

Early motor buses had open tops, like the old horse-drawn buses.

Communications
The radio provided home entertainment and information. This is a 1933 model.

Throughout the period newspaper circulations increased massively. In 1930 *The Daily Herald* sold 2 million copies a day.

WORLD WAR II AND THE BLITZ

World War II saw large-scale civilian bombing for the first time, bringing the horror of war to Londoners' doorsteps. Thousands were killed in their homes. Many people took refuge in Underground stations and children were evacuated to the safety of the country.

WOMEN OF BRITAIN
COME INTO
THE FACTORIES

As in World War I, women were recruited for factory work formerly done by men who were away fighting.

Bombing raids in 1940 and 1941 (the Blitz) caused devastation all over the city.

1929 US stock market crash brings world Depression

1939 World War II begins

1930

1927 First talking pictures

1936 Edward VIII abdicates to marry US divorcée Wallis Simpson. George VI accedes

1940 Winston Churchill becomes Prime Minister

Postwar London

Much of London was flattened by World War II bombs. Afterward, the chance for imaginative rebuilding was missed – some badly designed postwar developments are already being razed. But, by the 1960s, London was such a dynamic world leader in fashion and popular music that *Time* magazine dubbed it "swinging London." Skyscrapers sprang up, but some stayed empty as 1980s boom gave way to 1990s recession.

EXTENT OF THE CITY

| ▨ *1959* | ▢ *Today* |

The Beatles
The Liverpool pop group, pictured in 1965, had rocketed to stardom two years earlier with songs of appealing freshness and directness. The group symbolized carefree 1960s London.

Margaret Thatcher
Britain's first woman Prime Minister (1979–90) promoted the market-led policies that fueled the 1980s boom.

Festival of Britain
After wartime, the city's morale was lifted by the Festival, marking the 1851 Great Exhibition's centenary (see pp28–9).

The Royal Festival Hall (1951) was the Festival's centerpiece and is still a landmark *(see p188).*

Telecom Tower (1964), at 620 ft (189 m) high, dominates the Fitzrovia skyline.

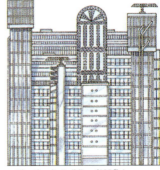

The Lloyd's Building (1986) is Richard Rogers' Post-Modernist emblem *(see p159).*

TIMELINE

1948 Olympic Games held in London

1952 George VI dies; his daughter Elizabeth II accedes

Minis became a symbol of the 1960s; small and maneuverable, they typified the go-as-you-please mood of the decade.

1945	1950	1955	1960	1965	1970	1975	19

1951 Festival of Britain

1945 End of World War II

1954 Food rationing, introduced during World War II, abolished

1963 National Theatre founded at the Old Vic

1971 New London Bridge built

1977 Queen's Silver Jubilee; work starts on Jubilee line underground

1982 Last of the London docks closes

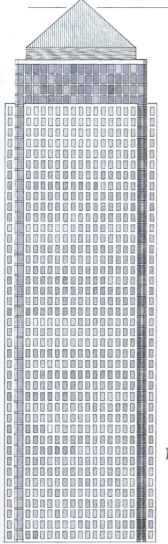

Canada Tower (1991) in Canary Wharf *(see p249)* is no longer London's tallest building.

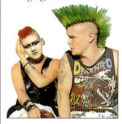

Docklands Light Railway
In the 1980s, new, driver-less trains started to transport people to the developing Docklands.

POST-MODERN ARCHITECTURE

Since the 1980s architects have reacted against the stark shapes of the Mod-ernists. Landmarks like the "Gherkin" by Norman Foster and "The Shard" by Renzo Piano now domi-nate the skyline. Architect Richard Rogers emphasizes structural features, others, like Terry Farrell, adopt a more playful approach using pastiches of Classical features.

Charing Cross (1991) has Terry Farrell's glasshouse on top of the Victorian station *(see p119)*.

(see p249) *(see p119)*

YOUTH CULTURE

With their new mobility and spending power, young people began to influence the development of British popular culture in the years after World War II. Music, fashion and design were increasingly geared to their rapidly changing tastes.

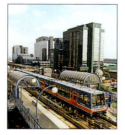

Punks were a phenomenon of the 1970s and 1980s. Their clothes, music, hair, and hab-its were designed to shock.

The Prince of Wales
As heir to the throne, he is outspokenly critical of much of London's modern architecture. He prefers more traditional styles.

| 1984 | 1986 | | 2000 Ken Livingstone | | | | |
| Thames Barrier completed | Greater London Council abolished | *Vivienne Westwood's clothes won prizes in the 1980s and 1990s.* | becomes London's first directly elected mayor | *The observation wheel, the London Eye, was raised during the spring of 2000.* | | | |

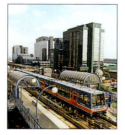

1985	1990	1995	2000	2005	2010	2015	2020

1985 Ethiopi-an famine leads to Live Aid relief campaign

1992 Canary Wharf development opens

1997 Princess Diana's funeral procession brings London to a halt

2005 London shaken by bombs on the public transport system

2012 London hosts the Olympic games

2011 Prince William marries Catherine Middle-ton at Westminster Abbey

Kings and Queens in London

London has been the royal capital of England since 1066, when William the Conqueror began a tradition of holding coronations in Westminster Abbey. Since then, successive kings and queens have left their mark on London and many of the places described in this book have royal associations: Henry VIII hunted at Richmond, Charles I was executed on Whitehall, and the young Queen Victoria rode on Queensway. Royalty is also celebrated in many of London's traditional ceremonies – for more details on these turn to pages 52–5.

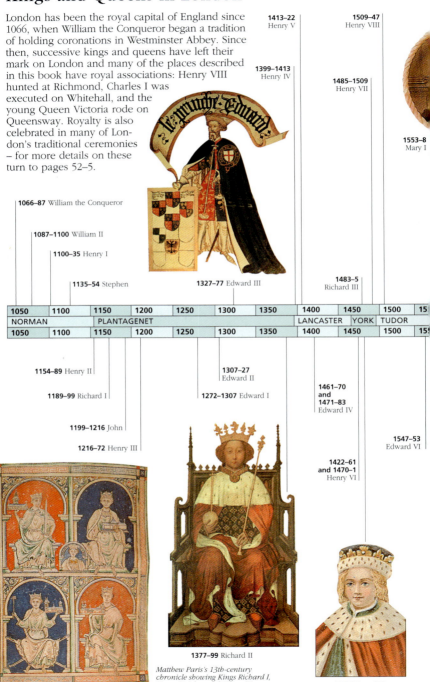

1413–22 Henry V

1509–47 Henry VIII

1399–1413 Henry IV

1485–1509 Henry VII

1553–8 Mary I

1066–87 William the Conqueror

1087–1100 William II

1100–35 Henry I

1135–54 Stephen

1327–77 Edward III

1483–5 Richard III

1050	1100	1150	1200	1250	1300	1350	1400	1450	1500	15
NORMAN		PLANTAGENET					LANCASTER	YORK	TUDOR	
1050	1100	1150	1200	1250	1300	1350	1400	1450	1500	155

1154–89 Henry II

1307–27 Edward II

1189–99 Richard I

1272–1307 Edward I

1461–70 and 1471–83 Edward IV

1199–1216 John

1216–72 Henry III

1547–53 Edward VI

1422–61 and 1470–1 Henry VI

1377–99 Richard II

Matthew Paris's 13th-century chronicle showing Kings Richard I, Henry II, John, and Henry III

1483 Edward V

1685–8 James II

1689–1702 William and Mary

1702–14 Anne

1714–27 George I

1660–85 Charles II

1603–25 James I

1837–1901 Victoria

1727–60 George II

1936 Edward VIII

1901–10 Edward VII

1952– Elizabeth II

1600	1650	1700	1750	1800	1850	1900	1950	2000	2050
STUART		HANOVER				WINDSOR			
1600	1650	1700	1750	1800	1850	1900	1950	2000	2050

1830–37 William IV

1936–52 George VI shown on the George Medal

1649–60 The Commonwealth, established by Oliver Cromwell

1820–30 George IV

1910–36 George V

1625–49 Charles I

1558–1603 Elizabeth I

1760–1820 George III

LONDON AT A GLANCE

There are nearly 300 places of interest described in the Area by Area section of this book. These range from the magnificent National Gallery *(see pp104–7)* to gruesome Old St. Thomas' Operating Theatre *(p176)*, and from ancient Charterhouse *(p164)* to modern Canary Wharf *(p249)*. To help you make the most of your stay, the following 18 pages are a time-saving guide to the best London has to offer. Museums and galleries, churches, and parks and gardens each have a section, and there are guides to remarkable Londoners and ceremonies in London. Each sight mentioned is cross-referenced to its own full entry. Below are the ten top tourist attractions to start you off.

LONDON'S TOP TEN TOURIST ATTRACTIONS

St. Paul's
See pp148–51.

Hampton Court
See pp254–7.

Changing of the Guard
Buckingham Palace, see pp94–5.

British Museum
See pp126–9.

National Gallery
See pp104–7.

Westminster Abbey
See pp76–9.

Madame Tussaud's
See p224.

Houses of Parliament
See pp72–3.

Tower of London
See pp154–7.

Victoria and Albert Museum
See pp202–5.

◁ Big Ben and the Merlin Entertainments London Eye

Remarkable Londoners

Caricature of the Duke of Wellington

London has always been a gathering place for the most prominent and influential people of their times. Some of these figures have come to London from other parts of Britain or from countries farther afield; others have been Londoners, born and bred. All of them have left their mark on London, by designing great and lasting buildings, establishing institutions and traditions, and by writing about or painting the city they knew. Most of them have also had an influence on their times that spread out from London to the rest of the world.

***Venus Venticordia* by Dante Gabriel Rossetti**

ARCHITECTS AND ENGINEERS

John Nash's Theatre Royal Haymarket (1821)

A number of people who built London still have works standing. Inigo Jones (1573–1652), London-born, was the father of English Renaissance architecture. He was also a landscape painter and a stage designer. Jones lived and worked at Great Scotland Yard, Whitehall, then the residence of the royal architect – the post in which he was later succeeded by Sir Christopher Wren (1632–1723).

Wren's successors as the prime architects of London were his protégé Nicholas Hawksmoor (1661–1736) and James Gibbs (1682–1754). Succeeding generations each produced architects who were to stamp their genius on the city: in the 18th century the brothers Robert (1728–92) and James Adam (1730–94), then John Nash (1752–1835), Sir Charles Barry (1795–1860), Decimus Burton (1800–81), and the Victorians Alfred Waterhouse (1830–1905),

Norman Shaw (1831–1912), and Sir George Gilbert Scott (1811–78). The engineer Sir Joseph Bazalgette (1819–91) built London's sewer system and the Thames Embankment.

ARTISTS

Painters in London, as elsewhere, often lived in enclaves, for mutual support and because they shared common priorities. During the 18th century, artists clustered around the court at St. James's to be near their patrons. Thus both William Hogarth (1697–1764) and Sir Joshua Reynolds (1723–92) lived and worked in Leicester Square, while Thomas Gainsborough (1727–88) lived in Pall Mall. (Hogarth's Chiswick house was his place in the country.)

Later, Cheyne Walk in Chelsea, with its river views, became popular with artists, including the masters J. M. W. Turner (1775–1851), James McNeill Whistler (1834–1903), Dante Gabriel Rossetti (1828–82), Philip Wilson Steer, (1860–1942) and the sculptor

HISTORIC LONDON HOMES

Four writers' homes that have been recreated are those of the romantic poet **John Keats** (1795–1821); the historian **Thomas Carlyle** (1795–1881); the lexicographer **Dr. Samuel Johnson** (1709–84); and the prolific and popular novelist **Charles Dickens** (1812–70). The house that the architect **Sir John Soane** (1753–1837) designed for himself remains largely as it was when he died, as does the house where the psychiatrist **Sigmund Freud** (1856–1939) settled after fleeing from the Nazis before World War II.

Dickens Museum

Apsley House, on Hyde Park Corner, was the residence of the **Duke of Wellington** (1769–1852), hero of the Battle of Waterloo. The life and music of Baroque composer **George Frideric Handel** (1685–1759) are on show at his former home in Mayfair. Finally, the rooms of Sir Arthur Conan Doyle's fictional detective **Sherlock Holmes** have been created in Baker Street.

Carlyle's House

PLAQUES

All over London the former homes of well-known figures are marked by plaques. Look out for these, especially in Chelsea, Kensington, and Mayfair, and see how many names you recognize.

No. 3 Sussex Square, Kensington

No. 27b Canonbury Square, Islington

No. 56 Oakley Street, Chelsea

Sir Jacob Epstein (1880–1959). Augustus John (1879–1961) and John Singer Sargent (1856–1925) had studios in Tite Street. John Constable (1776–1837) is best known as a Suffolk painter but lived for a while at Hampstead, from where he painted many fine views of the heath.

WRITERS

Geoffrey Chaucer (c.1345–1400), author of *The Canterbury Tales*, was born in Upper Thames Street, the son of an innkeeper. Both the playwrights William Shakespeare (1564–1616) and Christopher Marlowe (1564–93) were associated with the theaters in Southwark, and may have lived nearby.

The poets John Donne (1572–1631) and John Milton (1608–74) were both born in Bread Street in the City. Donne, after a profligate youth, became Dean of St. Paul's. The diarist Samuel Pepys (1633–1703) was born off Fleet Street.

The young novelist Jane Austen (1775–1817) lived briefly off Sloane Street, near the Cadogan Hotel, where the flamboyant Oscar Wilde (1854–1900) was arrested in 1895 for homosexuality. Playwright George Bernard Shaw (1856–1950) lived at No. 29 Fitzroy Square in Bloomsbury. Later the same house was home to Virginia Woolf (1882–1941) and

George Bernard Shaw

became a meeting place for the Bloomsbury Group of writers and artists, which included Vanessa Bell, John Maynard Keynes, E. M. Forster, Roger Fry, and Duncan Grant.

LEADERS

In legend, a penniless boy named Dick Whittington came to London with his cat seeking streets paved with gold, and later became Lord Mayor. In fact, Richard Whittington (1360?–1423), Lord Mayor three times between 1397 and 1420 and one of London's most celebrated early politicians, was the son of a noble. Sir Thomas More (1478–1535), a Chelsea resident, was Henry VIII's chancellor until they quarreled over the king's break with the Catholic church and Henry ordered More's execution. More was canonized in 1935. Sir Thomas Gresham (1519?–79) founded the Royal Exchange. Sir Robert Peel (1788–1850) established the London police force, who were known as "bobbies" for him.

ACTORS

Nell Gwynne (1650–87) won more fame as King Charles II's mistress than as an actress. However, she did appear on stage at Drury Lane Theatre; she also sold oranges there. The Shakespearean actor Edmund Kean (1789–1833) and the great tragic actress

Sarah Siddons (1755–1831) were more distinguished players at Drury Lane. So were Henry Irving (1838–1905) and Ellen Terry (1847–1928), whose stage partnership lasted 24 years. Charlie Chaplin (1889–1977), born in Kennington, had a poverty-stricken childhood in the slums of London.

In the 20th century, a school of fine actors blossomed at the Old Vic, including Sir John Gielgud (1904–2001), Sir Ralph Richardson (1902–83), Dame Peggy Ashcroft (1907–91), and Laurence (later Lord) Olivier (1907–89), who was appointed the first director of the National Theatre.

Laurence Olivier

WHERE TO FIND HISTORIC LONDON HOMES

London's Best: Museums and Galleries

London's museums are filled with an astonishing diversity of treasures from all over the world. This map highlights 15 of the city's most important galleries and museums whose exhibits cater to most interests. Some of these collections started from the legacies of 18th- and 19th-century explorers, traders, and collectors. Others specialize in one aspect of art, history, science, or technology. A more detailed overview of London's museums and galleries is on pages 42–3.

British Museum
This Anglo-Saxon helmet is part of a massive collection of antiquities.

Wallace Collection
Frans Hals's Laughing Cavalier *is a star attraction in this museum of art, furniture, armor, and* objets d'art.

Royal Academy of Arts
Major international art exhibitions are held here, and the renowned Summer Exhibition, when works are on sale, takes place every year.

Regent's Park and Marylebone

Kensington and Holland Park

South Kensington and Knightsbridge

Piccadilly and St James's

Science Museum
Newcomen's steam engine of 1712 is just one of many exhibits that cater for both novice and expert.

Chelsea

Natural History Museum
All of life is here, with vivid displays on everything from dinosaurs (like this Triceratops skull) to butterflies.

Victoria and Albert
It is the world's largest museum of decorative arts. This Indian vase is 18th century.

0 kilometers	1
0 miles	0.5

41

National Portrait Gallery
Important British figures are document-ed in paintings and photographs. This is Vivien Leigh, by Angus McBean (1954).

National Gallery
The world-famous paintings in its collection are mainly European and date from the 15th to the 19th centuries.

Museum of London
London's history is told through fascinating objects such as this 15th-century reliquary.

Tower of London
The Crown Jewels and a vast collec-tion of arms and armor are here. This suit of armor was worn by a 14th-century Italian knight.

Bloomsbury and Fitzrovia

Holborn and the Inns of Court

Smithfield and Spitalfields

Design Museum
The changing exhibitions here showcase all aspects of design from household prototypes to high fashion garments.

The City

Soho and Trafalgar Square **Covent Garden and the Strand**

Southwark and Bankside

South Bank

Whitehall and Westminster

Tate Modern
Works of the 20th century, such as Dali's Lobster Tele-phone, *are celebrated here.*

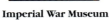

Tate Britain
Formerly the Tate Gallery, this museum showcases an out-standing collection of British art covering the 16th century to the present.

Imperial War Museum
It uses displays, film, and special effects to recreate 20th-century battles. This is one of the earliest tanks.

Courtauld Gallery
Well-known works, such as Manet's Bar at the Folies-Bergère, *line its galleries.*

Exploring Museums and Galleries

London boasts an astonishingly rich and diverse collection of museums. The city's position for centuries at the hub of worldwide trade has been partly responsible for this extraordinarily rich cultural heritage. Britain's rule of a far-flung empire has also played its part. The world-renowned collections are impressive, but find time for the city's range of smaller museums, which are often more peaceful than their grander counterparts. Brimming with character, they cover every imaginable theme from buses and toys to electricity and water power.

Geffrye Museum: Art Nouveau Room

ANTIQUITIES AND ARCHAEOLOGY

Some of the most celebrated artifacts of ancient Asia, Egypt, Greece, and Rome are housed in the **British Museum**. Other antiquities, including books, manuscripts, paintings, busts, and gems, are displayed in **Sir John Soane's Museum**, which is one of the most idiosyncratic to be found in London.

The **Museum of London** contains much of archaeological interest from all periods of the city's history.

Eclectic collection at Sir John Soane's Museum

FURNITURE AND INTERIORS

The Museum of London recreates typical domestic and commercial interiors from the Roman period right up to the present day. The **Victoria and Albert Museum** (or V&A) contains complete rooms rescued from now vanished buildings, plus a magnificent collection of furniture ranging from the 16th century to work by contemporary designers.

Design Museum display of chairs

On a more modest scale, the **Geffrye Museum** consists of fully-furnished period rooms dating from 1600 to the 1990s. Writers' houses, such as the **Freud Museum**, give insights into the furniture of specific periods, while the **Linley Sambourne House** offers visitors a perfectly preserved example of a late Victorian interior.

COSTUME AND JEWELRY

The **V&A's** vast collections include English and European clothes of the last 400 years, and some stunning jewelry from China, India, and Japan. The priceless Crown Jewels, at the **Tower of London**, should not be missed. Here you can also see the world's largest cut diamond, Cullinan I, set in the sovereign's scepter. **Kensington Palace's** Court Dress Collection opens a window on court uniforms and protocol from about 1750. The **British Museum** displays ancient Aztec, Mayan, and African costume.

CRAFTS AND DESIGN

Once again, the **Victoria and Albert Museum** (V&A) is the essential first port of call; its collections in these fields remain unrivaled. The **William Morris Gallery** shows every aspect of the 19th-century designer's work within the Arts and Crafts movement. The **Design Museum** focuses on modern design including products and fashion, while the **Crafts Council Gallery** displays (and sometimes sells) contemporary British craftwork.

MILITARY ARTIFACTS

The **National Army Museum** uses vivid models and displays to narrate the history of the British Army from the reign of Henry VII to the present. The crack regiments of Foot Guards, who are the elite of the British Army, are the main focus of the **Guards Museum**. The **Tower of London** holds part of the national collection of arms and armor; the **Wallace Collection** also has a large and impressive display. The **Imperial War Museum** has recreations of World War I trenches and the 1940 Blitz. The **Florence Nightingale Museum** illustrates the hardships of 19th-century warfare.

TOYS AND CHILDHOOD

Teddy bears, toy soldiers, and dolls' houses are some of the toys that can be seen in **Pollock's Toy Museum.** The collection includes Eric, "the oldest known teddy-bear." The **V&A Museum of Childhood** and the **Museum of London** are a little more formal, but still fun, and illustrate aspects of the social history of childhood with the former offering some interesting children's activities.

SCIENCE AND NATURAL HISTORY

Computers, electricity, space exploration, industrial processes, and transport can all be studied at the **Science Museum.** Transport enthusiasts are also catered for at the **London Transport Museum.** There are other specialized museums such as the **Faraday Museum** concerning the development of electricity, and the **Kew Bridge Steam Museum,** focusing on water power. The **National Maritime Museum** and the **Royal Observatory** in Greenwich chart both maritime history and the creation of GMT, by which the world still sets its clocks.

Samson and Delilah (1620) by Van Dyck at the Dulwich Picture Gallery

The **Natural History Museum** mixes displays of animal and bird life with ecological exhibits. The **Museum of Garden History** is devoted to the favorite British pastime.

Imperial War Museum

VISUAL ARTS

The particular strengths of the **National Gallery** are early Renaissance Italian and 17th-century Spanish painting and a wonderful collection of Dutch masters. **Tate Britain** specializes in British paintings spanning all periods, while **Tate Modern** has displays of international modern art from 1900 to the present day. The **V&A** is strong on European art from 1500–1900 and British art of 1700–1900. The **Royal Academy** and **Hayward Gallery** specialize in major

Stone Dancer (1913) by Gaudier-Brzeska at Tate Britain

temporary exhibitions. The **Courtauld Institute of Art Gallery** contains Impressionist and Post-Impressionist works, while the **Wallace Collection** has 17th-century Dutch and 18th-century French paintings. The **Dulwich Picture Gallery** includes works by Rembrandt, Rubens, Poussin, and Gainsborough, while **Kenwood House** is home to paintings by Reynolds, Gainsborough, and Rubens in fine Adam interiors. The **Saatchi Gallery** is devoted to contemporary, mainly British, art.

WHERE TO FIND THE COLLECTIONS

London's Best: Churches

It is worth stopping to look at London's churches and going in, if they are open. They have a special atmosphere unmatched elsewhere in the city, and they can often yield an intimate glimpse of the past. Many churches have replaced earlier buildings in a steady succession, dating back to pre-Christian times. Some began life in outlying villages beyond London's fortified center, and were absorbed into suburbs as the city expanded from the 18th century. The memorials in the capital's churches and churchyards are a fascinating record of local life, liberally peppered with famous names. A more detailed overview of London churches is on pages 46–7.

All Souls
This plaque comes from a tomb in John Nash's Regency church of 1824.

St. Paul's Covent Garden
Inigo Jones's Classical church was known as "the handsomest barn in England."

Bloomsbury
and Fitzrovia

Regent's Park
and Marylebone

Soho and
Trafalgar
Square

St. Martin-in-the-Fields
James Gibbs's church of 1722–6 was originally thought "too gay" for Protestant worship.

South Kensington
and Knightsbridge

Piccadilly
and St James's

0 kilometers   1

0 miles   0.5

Whitehall a
Westminst

Westminster Cathedral
The Italian-Byzantine Catholic cathedral's red-and-white brick exterior conceals a rich interior of multicolored marbles.

Brompton Oratory
This sumptuous Baroque church was decorated with works by Italian artists.

Westminster Abbey
The famous abbey has the most glorious medieval architecture in London, and highly impressive tombs and monuments.

St. Mary-le-Strand
Now on a traffic island, this ship-like church was built by James Gibbs in 1714–17 to a lively Baroque design. Featuring high windows and rich interior detailing, it was made solid enough to keep out the noise from the street.

St. Mary Woolnoth
The jewel-like interior of Nicholas Hawksmoor's small Baroque church (1716–27) appears larger than the outside.

Holborn and the Inns of Court

Smithfield and Spitalfields

Covent Garden and the Strand

The City

RIVER THAMES

South Bank

Southwark and Bankside

St. Stephen Walbrook
Wren was at his best with this domed interior of 1672–7. Its carvings include Henry Moore's austere modern altar.

St. Paul's
At 360 ft (110 m) high, the dome of Wren's cathedral is the world's second largest after St. Peter's in Rome.

Southwark Cathedral
This largely 13th-century priory church was not designated a cathedral until 1905. It has a fine medieval choir.

Temple Church
Built in the 12th and 13th centuries for the Knights Templar, this is one of the few circular churches to survive in England.

Exploring Churches

The church spires that puncture London's skyline span nearly a thousand years of the city's history. They form an index to many of the events that have shaped the city – the Norman Conquest (1066); the Great Fire of London (1666); the great restoration, led by Wren, that followed it; the Regency period; the confidence of the Victorian era; and the devastation of World War II. Each has had its effect on the churches, many designed by the most influential architects of their times.

St Paul's, Covent Garden

MEDIEVAL CHURCHES

The most famous old church to survive the Great Fire of 1666 is the superb 13th-century **Westminster Abbey**, the scene of royal coronations, with its tombs of British monarchs and heroes. Less well known are the well-hidden Norman church of **St. Bartholomew-the-Great**, London's oldest church, (1123), the circular **Temple Church** founded in 1160 by the Knights Templar, and **Southwark Cathedral**, set amid Vic-torian railway lines and warehouses. **Chelsea Old Church** is a charming village church near the river.

CHURCHES BY JONES

Inigo Jones (1573–1652) was Shakespeare's contemporary, and his works were almost as revolutionary as the great dramatist's. Jones's Classical churches of the 1620s and 1630s shocked a public used to conservative Gothic finery. By far the best-known is **St. Paul's Church** of the 1630s, the centerpiece of Jones's Italian-style piazza in Covent Garden. **Queen's Chapel, St. James's** was built in 1623 for Queen Henrietta Maria, the Catholic wife of Charles I. It was the first Classical church in England and has a magnificent interior but is, unfortunately, usually closed to the public.

CHURCHES BY HAWKSMOOR

Nicholas Hawksmoor (1661–1736) was Wren's most talented pupil, and his churches are among the finest

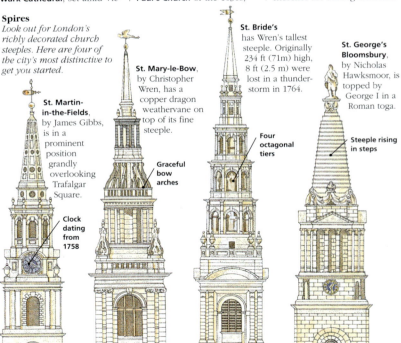

Spires
Look out for London's richly decorated church steeples. Here are four of the city's most distinctive to get you started.

St. Martin-in-the-Fields, by James Gibbs, is in a prominent position grandly overlooking Trafalgar Square.

Clock dating from 1758

St. Mary-le-Bow, by Christopher Wren, has a copper dragon weathervane on top of its fine steeple.

Graceful bow arches

St. Bride's has Wren's tallest steeple. Originally 234 ft (71m) high, 8 ft (2.5 m) were lost in a thunderstorm in 1764.

Four octagonal tiers

St. George's Bloomsbury, by Nicholas Hawksmoor, is topped by George I in a Roman toga.

Steeple rising in steps

Baroque buildings to be found in Britain.

St. George's, Bloomsbury (1716–31) has an unusual centralized plan and a pyramid steeple topped by a statue of King George I. **St. Mary Woolnoth** is a tiny jewel of 1716–27, and further east **Christ Church, Spitalfields** is a Baroque tour-de-force of 1714–29, now being restored.

Among Hawksmoor's East End churches are the stunning **St. Anne's, Limehouse** and **St. Alfege**, of 1714–17, which is across the river in Greenwich. The tower on this temple-like church was added later by John James in 1730.

St. Anne's, Limehouse

CHURCHES BY GIBBS

James Gibbs (1682–1754) was more conservative than his Baroque contemporaries such as Hawksmoor, and he also kept his distance from the Neo-Classical trend so popular after 1720. His idiosyncratic London churches were enormously influential. **St. Mary-le-Strand** (1714–17) is an island church which appears to be sailing down the Strand. The radical design of **St. Martin-in-the-Fields** (1722–6) predates its setting, Trafalgar Square, by a hundred years.

REGENCY CHURCHES

The end of the Napoleonic Wars in 1815 brought a flurry of church building. The need for churches in London's new suburbs fused with a Greek Revival. The results may lack

CHRISTOPHER WREN

Sir Christopher Wren (1632–1723) was leader among the many architects who helped restore London after the Great Fire of 1666. He devised a new city plan, replacing the narrow streets with wide avenues radiating from piazzas. His plan was rejected, but he was commissioned to build 52 new churches; 31 have survived various threats of demolition and the bombs of World War II, although six are shells. Wren's great masterwork is the massive **St. Paul's**, while nearby is splendid **St. Stephen Walbrook**, his domed church of 1672–77. Other landmarks are **St. Bride's**, off Fleet Street, said to have inspired the traditional shape of wedding cakes, **St. Mary-le-Bow** in Cheapside, and **St. Magnus Martyr** in Lower Thames Street. Wren's own favorite was **St. James's, Piccadilly** (1683–4). Smaller gems are **St. Clement Danes** in the Strand, (1680–82) and **St. James, Garlickhythe** (1674–87).

the exuberance of Hawksmoor, but they have an austere elegance of their own. **All Souls, Langham Place** (1822–4), at the north end of Regent Street, was built by the Prince Regent's favorite, John Nash, who was ridiculed at the time for its unusual combination of design styles. Also worth visiting is **St. Pancras**, a Greek Revival church of 1819–22, which is typical of the period.

VICTORIAN CHURCHES

London has some of the finest 19th-century churches in Europe. Grand and colorful, their riotous decoration is in marked contrast to the chaste Neo-Classicism of the preceding Regency era. Perhaps the best of the capital's late Victorian churches is **Westminster Cathedral**, a

Brompton Oratory

stunningly rich, Italianate Catholic cathedral built in 1895–1903, with architecture by J. F. Bentley and *Stations of the Cross* reliefs by Eric Gill. **Brompton Oratory** is a grand Baroque revival, based on a church in Rome and filled with magnificent furnishings from all over Catholic Europe.

WHERE TO FIND THE CHURCHES

London's Best: Parks and Gardens

Since medieval times London has had large expanses of green. Some of these, such as Hampstead Heath, were originally common land, where farmers could graze their animals. Others, such as Richmond Park and Holland Park, were royal hunting grounds or the gardens of large houses; several still have formal features dating from those times. Today you can cross much of central London by walking from St. James's Park in the east to Kensington Gardens in the west. Purpose-built parks, like Battersea, and botanical gardens, like Kew, appeared later.

Hampstead Heath
This breezy, open space is located in the midst of north London. Nearby Parliament Hill offers views of St. Paul's, the City, and the West End.

Kew Gardens
The world's premier botanic garden is a must for anyone with an interest in plants, exotic or mundane.

Kensington Gardens
This plaque is from the Italian Garden, one of the features of this elegant park.

Holland Park
The former grounds of one of London's grandest homes are now its most romantic park.

Richmond Park
The biggest Royal Park in London remains largely unspoiled, with deer and magnificent river views.

Hampstea

Kensington and Holland Park

Sou Kensingt Knightsb

0 kilometers   1

0 miles   0.5

Regent's Park

In this civilized park, surrounded by fine Regency buildings, you can stroll around the rose garden, visit the open-air theater, or simply sit and admire the view.

Greenwich Park

Its focal point is the National Maritime Museum, well worth a visit for its architecture as well as its exhibits. There are also fine views.

Hyde Park

The Serpentine is one of the highlights of a park which also boasts restaurants, an art gallery, and Speakers' Corner.

Regent's Park and Marylebone

Bloomsbury and Fitzrovia

Holborn and the Inns of Court

Smithfield and Spitalfields

The City

Soho and Trafalgar Square

Piccadilly

South Bank

Southwark and Bankside

Whitehall and Westminster

RIVER THAMES

Greenwich and Blackheath

Green Park

Its leafy paths are favored by early-morning joggers from the Mayfair hotels.

St. James's Park

People come here to feed the ducks, or watch the pelicans. A band plays throughout the summer.

Battersea Park

Visitors can hire a rowboat for the best view of the Victorian landscaping around the lake.

Exploring Parks and Gardens

London has one of the the world's greenest city centers, full of tree-filled squares and grassy parks. From the intimacy of the Chelsea Physic Garden to the wild, open spaces of Hampstead Heath, every London park has its own charm and character. For those looking for a specific outdoor attraction – such as sports, wildlife, or flowers – here are some of the most interesting London parks.

Camilla japonica

Embankment Gardens

FLOWER GARDENS

The British are famed for their gardens and love of flowers and this is reflected in several of London's parks. Really keen gardeners will find all they wanted to know at **Kew Gardens** and the **Chelsea Physic Garden**, which is especially strong on herbs. Closer to the center of town, **St. James's Park** boasts some spectacular flower beds, filled with bulbs and bedding plants, which are changed every season. **Hyde Park** sports a magnificent show of daffodils and crocuses in the spring and London's best rose garden is Queen Mary's in

Regent's Park. **Kensington Gardens'** flower walk has an exemplary English mixed border, and there is also a delightful small 17th-century garden at the **Museum of Garden History**.

   Battersea Park also has a charming flower garden, and indoor gardeners should head to the **Barbican Centre**'s well-stocked conservatory.

FORMAL GARDENS

The most spectacular formal garden is at **Hampton Court**, which has a network of gardens from different periods, starting with Tudor. The gardens at **Chiswick House**

remain dotted with their 18th-century statuary and pavilions. Other restored gardens include 17th-century **Ham House**, and **Osterley Park**, whose 18th-century layout was retraced through the art of dowsing. **Fenton House** has a really fine walled garden; **Kenwood** is less formal, with its woodland area. **The Hill** is great in summer. The sunken garden at **Kensington Palace** has a formal layout and **Holland Park** has flowers around its statues.

RESTFUL CORNERS

London's squares are cool, shady retreats but, sadly, many are reserved for key-holders, usually residents of the surrounding houses. Of those open to all, **Russell Square** is the largest and most secluded. **Berkeley Square** is open but barren. **Green Park**, with its shady trees and deck chairs, offers a cool picnic spot right in central London. The Inns of Court provide some really pleasant havens: **Gray's Inn** gardens, **Middle**

Sunken garden at Kensington Palace

GREEN LONDON

In Greater London there are 1,700 parks covering a total of 67 sq miles (174 sq km). This land is home to some 2,000 types of plant and 100 bird species that breed in the trees. Trees help the city to breathe, manufacturing oxygen from the polluted air. Here are some of the species you are most likely to see in London.

The London plane, now the most common tree in London, grows along many streets.

The English oak grows all over Europe. The Royal Navy used to build ships from it.

Temple gardens, and **Lincoln's Inn Fields**. **Soho Square**, which is surrounded by streets, is more urban and animated.

MUSIC IN SUMMER

Stretching out on the grass or in a deck chair to listen to a band is a British tradition. Military and other bands give regular concerts throughout the summer in **St. James's** and **Regent's Parks** and also at **Parliament Hill Fields**. The concert schedule will usually be found posted up close to the bandstand in the park.

Open-air festivals of classical music are held in the summer in several parks *(see p349)*.

WILDLIFE

There is a large and well-fed collection of ducks and other water birds, even including a few pelicans, in **St. James's Park**. Duck lovers will also appreciate **Regent's**, **Hyde**, and **Battersea Parks**, as well as **Hampstead Heath**. Deer roam in **Richmond** and **Greenwich Parks**. For a wide variety of captive animals, **London Zoo** is in **Regent's Park** and there are aviaries or aquariums at several parks and gardens, including **Kew Gardens** and **Syon House**.

Geese in St. James's Park

HISTORIC CEMETERIES

In the late 1830s a ring of private cemeteries was established around London to ease the pressure on the monstrously overcrowded and unhealthy burial grounds of the inner city. Today some of these (notably **Highgate Cemetery** and Kensal Green – Harrow Road W10) are worth visiting for their air of repose and their Victorian monuments. **Bunhill Fields** is earlier; it was first used during the plague of 1665.

Kensal Green cemetery

Boating pond at Regent's Park

SPORTS

Cycling is not universally encouraged in London's parks, and footpaths tend to be too bumpy to allow much rollerskating. However, most parks have tennis courts, which normally have to be reserved in advance with the attendant. Rowboats may be rented at **Hyde, Regent's**, and **Battersea Parks**, among others. Athletics tracks are at both Battersea Park and also **Parliament Hill**. The public may swim at the ponds on **Hampstead Heath** and in the Serpentine in Hyde Park. Hampstead Heath is also ideal kite-flying territory.

The common beech has a close relation, the copper beech, with reddish-purple leaves.

The horse chestnut's hard round fruits are used by children for a game called conkers.

London's Best: Ceremonies

Much of London's rich inheritance of tradition and ceremony centers on royalty. Faithfully enacted today, some of these ceremonies date back to the Middle Ages, when the ruling monarch had absolute power and had to be protected from opponents. This map shows the venues for some of the most important ceremonies in London. For more details on these and other ceremonies please turn to pages 54–5; information on all sorts of events taking place in London throughout the year can be found on pages 56–9.

St. James's Palace and Buckingham Palace
Members of the Queen's Life Guard stand at the gates of these two palaces.

Bloomsbury and Fitzrovia

Soho and Trafalgar Square

South Kensington and Knightsbridge

Piccadilly and St James's

Hyde Park
Royal Salutes are fired by guns of the King's Troop, Royal Horse Artillery, on royal anniversaries and ceremonial occasions.

Whitehall and Westminster

Chelsea

Chelsea Hospital
In 1651 Charles II hid from Parliamentary forces in an oak tree. On Oak Apple Day, Chelsea Pensioners decorate his statue with oak leaves and branches.

Horse Guards
At Trooping the Colour, the most elaborate of London's royal ceremonies, the Queen salutes as a battalion of Foot Guards parades its colors before her.

The City and Embankment
At the Lord Mayor's Show, pikemen and musketeers escort the newly elected Lord Mayor through the City in a gold state coach.

The Cenotaph
On Remembrance Sunday the Queen pays homage to the nation's war dead.

Holborn and the Inns of Court

Covent Garden and the Strand

The City

R I V E R   T H A M E S

South Bank

Southwark and Bankside

| 0 kilometers | 1 |
| 0 miles | 0.5 |

Tower of London
In the nightly Ceremony of the Keys, a Yeoman Warder locks the gates. A military escort ensures the keys are not stolen.

Houses of Parliament
Each fall the Queen goes to Parliament in the Irish State Coach to open the new parliamentary session.

Attending London's Ceremonies

Royalty and commerce provide the two principal sources of London's rich calendar of ceremonial events. Quaint and old-fashioned these events may be, but what may seem arcane ritual has real historical meaning – many of the capital's ceremonies originated in the Middle Ages.

ROYAL CEREMONIES

Although the Queen's role is now largely symbolic, the Guard at Buckingham Palace still patrols the palace grounds. The impressive ceremony of the **Changing of the Guard** – dazzling uniforms, shouted commands, military music – consists of the Old Guard, which forms up in the palace forecourt, going off duty and handing over to the New Guard. The Guard consists of three officers and 40 men when the Queen is in residence, but only three officers and 31 men when she is away. The ceremony takes place in front of the palace. In another changeover ceremony, the Queen's Life Guards travel daily from Hyde Park Barracks to Horse Guards' Parade.

One of the Queen's Life Guards

The **Ceremony of the Keys** at the Tower of London is one of the capital's most timeless ceremonies. After each of the Tower gates has been locked, the last post is sounded by a trumpeter before the keys are secured in the Queen's House.

The Tower of London and Hyde Park are also the scene of **Royal Salutes** which take place on birthdays and other occasions throughout the year. At such times 41 rounds are fired in Hyde Park at noon, and 62 rounds at the Tower at 1pm. The spectacle in Hyde Park is a stirring one as 71 horses and six 13-pounder cannons swirl into place and the roar of the guns begins.

The combination of pageantry, color, and music makes the annual **Trooping the Colour** the high point of London's ceremonial year. The Queen takes the Royal Salute, and after her troops have marched past, she leads them to Buckingham Palace where a second march past takes place. The best place to watch this spectacle is from the Horse Guards Parade side of St. James's Park.

Bands of the Household Cavalry and the Foot Guards stage the ceremony of **Beating the Retreat** at Horse

A Queen's Guard in winter

Guards Parade. This takes place three or four evenings a week in the two weeks leading up to Trooping the Colour.

The spectacular **State Opening of Parliament**, when the Queen opens the annual parliamentary session in the House of Lords – usually in November – is not open to the general public, although it is now televised. The huge royal procession, which moves from Buckingham Palace to Westminster, is, however, a magnificent sight, with the Queen traveling in the highly ornate Irish State Coach drawn by four horses.

MILITARY CEREMONIES

The Cenotaph in Whitehall is the setting for a ceremony held on **Remembrance Sunday**, to give thanks to those who died fighting in any conflict from World War I onwards.

National **Navy Day** is commemorated by a parade down the Mall, followed by a service held at Nelson's Column in Trafalgar Square.

Royal salute, Tower of London

Trooping the Colour

Silent Change ceremony at Guildhall for the new Lord Mayor

CEREMONIES IN THE CITY

November is the focus of the City of London's ceremonial year. At the **Silent Change** in Guildhall, the outgoing Lord Mayor hands over symbols of office to the new Mayor in a virtually wordless ceremony. The following day sees the rumbustious **Lord Mayor's Show**. Accompanying the Lord Mayor in his gold state coach a procession of bands, decorated floats, and military detachments makes its way through the City from Guildhall past the Mansion House to the Law Courts, and back again along the Embankment.

Lord Mayor's chain of office

Many of the ceremonies that take place in the City are linked to the activities of the Livery Companies (see p152). These include the Worshipful Companies of **Vintners' and Distillers'** annual celebration of the wine harvest and the Stationers' **Cakes and Ale Sermon**, held in St. Paul's. Cakes and ale are provided according to the will of a 17th-century stationer.

NAME-DAY CEREMONIES

Every May 21 **King Henry VI**, who was murdered in the Tower of London in 1471, is still remembered by the members of his two famous foundations, Eton College and King's College, Cambridge, who meet for a ceremony at the Wakefield Tower where he was killed. **Oak Apple Day** commemorates King Charles II's lucky escape from the Parliamentary forces of Oliver Cromwell in 1651. The King managed to conceal himself in a hollow oak tree, and today Chelsea Pensioners honor his memory by decorating his statue at Chelsea Royal Hospital with oak leaves and branches. On December 18, the lexicographer **Dr. Johnson** is commemorated in an annual service held at Westminster Abbey.

INFORMAL CEREMONIES

Each July, six guildsmen from the Company of Watermen compete for the prize in **Doggett's Coat and Badge Race**. In the fall, the **Pearly Kings and Queens**, representatives of east London's traders, meet at St. Martin-in-the-Fields. In March children are given oranges and lemons at the **Oranges and Lemons service** at St. Clement Danes church. In February, clowns take part in a service for **Joseph Grimaldi** (1779–1837) at the Holy Trinity Church in Dalston, east London.

Pearly Queen

WHERE TO FIND THE CEREMONIES

Beating the Retreat
Horse Guards p80, date arranged during first two weeks of June.
Cakes and Ale Sermon
St. Paul's pp148–51, Ash Wed.
Ceremony of the Keys
Tower of London pp154–7, 9:30pm daily. Tickets from the Tower, but book well in advance.
Changing of the Guard
Buckingham Palace pp94–5, May–Jul: 11:30am daily; Aug–Apr: alternate days. Horse Guards, Whitehall p80, 11am Mon–Sat, 10am Sun. For details call the London Tourist Board Information Line on 0906 201 5151.
Doggett's Coat and Badge Race
From London Bridge to Cadogan Pier, Chelsea pp192–7, July.
Dr. Johnson Memorial
Westminster Abbey pp76–9, Dec 18.
Joseph Grimaldi Memorial
Holy Trinity Church, Dalston E8, Feb 7.
King Henry VI Memorial
Wakefield Tower, Tower of London pp154–7, May 21.
Lord Mayor's Show
The City pp143–53, second Sat Nov.
Navy Day
Trafalgar Sq p102, Oct 21.
Oak Apple Day
Royal Hospital p197, Thu after May 29.
Oranges and Lemons Service
St. Clement Danes church p138, March.
Pearly Kings and Queens Harvest Festival
St. Martin-in-the-Fields p102, fall.
Remembrance Sunday
Cenotaph p74, Sun nearest Nov 11.
Royal Salutes
Hyde Park p211, royal anniversaries and other state occasions.
Silent Change
Guildhall p159, second Fri Nov.
State Opening of Parliament
Houses of Parliament pp72–3, Oct–Nov. Procession from Buckingham Palace to Westminster.
Trooping the Colour
Horse Guards p80, 2nd Sat Jun (rehearsals on previous two Sats). Tickets from Household Division, Horse Guards.
Vintners' and Distillers' Wine Harvest
St. Olave's Church, Hart St EC3, second Tue Oct.

LONDON THROUGH THE YEAR

Springtime in London carries an almost tangible air of a city waking up to longer days and outdoor pursuits. The cheerful yellow of daffodils studs the parks, and less hardy Londoners turn out for their first jog of the year to find themselves puffing in the wake of serious runners training for the Marathon. As spring turns into summer, the royal parks reach their full glory, and in Kensington Gardens nannies gather to chat under venerable chestnut trees. As autumn takes hold, these same trees are ablaze with red and gold, and Londoners' thoughts turn to afternoons in museums, followed by tea in a café. The year closes with Guy Fawkes and Christmas shopping. The official visitor organization, Visit London, www.visitlondon.com (p362), and the listings magazines (p342) have details of seasonal events.

SPRING

The weather during the spring months may be raw, and an umbrella is a necessary precaution. Druids celebrate the Spring Equinox in a sub-dued ceremony on Tower Hill. Painters compete to have their works accepted by the Royal Academy. Soccer teams close their season in May with the FA Cup Final, while cricketers don their sweaters to begin theirs. Oxford and Cambridge Universities row their annual boat race along the Thames, and Marathon runners pound the streets.

Runners in the London Marathon passing Tower Bridge

MARCH

Chelsea Antiques Fair (2nd week, also Sep), Chelsea Old Town Hall, King's Rd SW3.
Ideal Home Exhibition (17 days from mid-Mar), Earl's Court, Warwick Rd SW5. It is a long-established show with the latest in domestic gadgetry and state-of-the-art technology.
Oranges and Lemons Service, St. Clement Danes (p55). Service for schoolchildren; each child is given an orange and a lemon.
Oxford and Cambridge boat race (late Mar or early Apr), Putney to Mortlake (p355).
Spring Equinox celebration (Mar 21), Tower Hill EC3. Historic pagan ceremony with modern-day druids.

EASTER

Good Friday and following Mon are public holidays.
Easter parades, Battersea Park (p251).
Kite flying, Blackheath (p243).
Easter Kite Festival Hampstead Heath (p234).
Easter procession and hymns (Easter Mon), Westminster Abbey (pp76–9).
London Harness Horse Parade (Easter Mon), Battersea Park (p251).
International Model Railway Exhibition (Easter weekend), Royal Horticultural Hall, Vincent Sq SW1. Of real interest to everyone.

A London park in the spring

APRIL

Head of the River Race (early Apr), more than 400 teams row from Mortlake to Putney.
Queen's Birthday gun salutes (Apr 21), Hyde Park, Tower of London (p54).
London Marathon (Sun in Apr or May), champions and novices run from Greenwich to Westminster (p355).

MAY

First and last Mon are public holidays.
FA Cup Final, soccer season's climax (p354).
Henry VI Memorial (p55).
Beating the Bounds (Ascension Day), throughout the City. Young boys from the City parish beat buildings that mark the parish boundaries.
Oak Apple Day, at the Royal Hospital, Chelsea (p55).
Funfairs (late May public hol weekend), various commons.
Chelsea Flower Show (late May), Royal Hospital, Chelsea.
Beating the Retreat (p54).

AVERAGE DAILY HOURS OF SUNSHINE

Hours

Jan Feb Mar Apr May Jun Jul Aug Sep Oct Nov Dec

Sunshine Chart
London's longest and hottest days fall between May and August. In the height of summer, daylight hours can extend from well before 5am to after 9pm. Daytime is much shorter in the winter, but London can be stunning in the winter sunshine.

SUMMER

London's summer season is packed full of indoor and outdoor events. The weather is unreliable, even at the height of summer, but unless you are notably unlucky there should be enough fine days to sample what is on offer.

The selection includes many traditional events, such as the Wimbledon tennis championships and the cricket test matches at Lord's and the Oval. Well out of view from the general public and prying photographers, the Queen holds garden parties for favored subjects in the splendid grounds of Buckingham Palace. The summer public holiday is also marked with funfairs in some of London's parks.

JUNE

Coronation Day gun salutes *(Jun 2)*, Hyde Park and Tower of London *(p54)*.
International Ceramics Fair, Park Lane Hotel, Park Lane W1.
Fine Art and Antiques fair, Olympia, Olympia Way W14.
Trooping the Colour, Horse Guards Parade *(p54)*.
Duke of Edinburgh's Birthday gun salutes *(Jun 10)*, Hyde Park and Tower of London *(p54)*.
Covent Garden Flower Festival *(mid-Jun)*, Covent Garden WC2 *(pp111–119)*. Floral installations, street performers and fashion shows. Free entry to all.
Wimbledon Lawn Tennis Championships *(two weeks in late Jun; p354)*.
Cricket test match, Lord's Cricket Ground *(p354)*.

Revelers at Notting Hill Carnival

Open-air theater season *(throughout the summer)*, Regent's Park and Holland Park. Shakespeare, Shaw, and others offer the perfect opportunity for a picnic *(p344)*.
Open-air concerts, Kenwood, Hampstead Heath, Crystal Palace, Marble Hill, St. James's Park *(p349)*.
Summer festivals *(late Jun)*, Spitalfields and Primrose Hill. Contact Visit London *(p362)* or see the listings magazines *(p342)* for times and venues of all these events and see July, below.
City of London Festival *(late Jun–mid-July)*, various City venues *(p143)*. Arts and music festival with concerts taking place in some of London's most beautiful historic churches.

JULY

Summer festivals, Greenwich and Docklands, Regent's Park, Richmond, and Soho.
Sales, Price reductions across London's shops *(p321)*.
Doggett's Coat and Badge Race *(p55)*.
Hampton Court Flower Show, Hampton Court Palace *(pp254–7)*.
Capital Radio Jazz Festival, Royal Festival Hall *(p188)*.
Henry Wood Promenade Concerts *(late Jul–Sep)*, Royal Albert Hall *(p207)*.
Royal Academy Summer Exhibition *(Jun–Aug)*, Piccadilly *(p90)*.

AUGUST

Last Monday in August is a public holiday.
Notting Hill Carnival *(late Aug holiday weekend)*. An internationally famous and well attended Caribbean carnival organized by the area's various ethnic communities *(p219)*.
Funfairs *(Aug holiday)*. These tend to run throughout London's parks during the summer months.

Regimental band, St. James's Park

AVERAGE MONTHLY RAINFALL

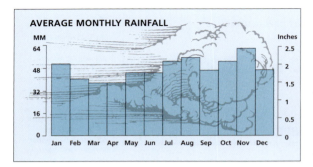

Rainfall Chart
London's average monthly rainfall remains much the same throughout the year. July and August, the capital's warmest months, are also two of its wettest. Rain is less likely in spring, but visitors should be prepared for a shower at any time of year.

AUTUMN

There is a sense of purpose about London in autumn. The build-up to the busiest shopping season, the start of the academic year, and the new parliamentary session, opened by the Queen, inject some life into the colder months. The cricket season ends in mid-September, while food-lovers may be interested in the spectacular displays of fresh fish that are laid out in the vestry of St. Mary-at-Hill, celebrating the harvest of this island nation.

Memories of a more turbulent opening of Parliament are revived on November 5. Bonfires and fireworks across the country commemorate the failed conspiracy, led by Guy Fawkes in 1605, to blow up the Palace of Westminster. A few days later, the dead of any conflict, from World War I onward, are honored at a ceremony held in Whitehall.

Pearly Kings gathering for the harvest festival at St. Martin-in-the-Fields

SEPTEMBER

Mayor Thames Festival, *(mid-Sep).* Entertainment by and on the river between Westminster Bridge and Southwark Cathedral.
Great River Race, Thames.
Last Night of the Proms *(mid-Sep),* Royal Albert Hall *(p207).* Rousing classical hits.
Spitalfields Show *(mid-Sep),* Old Spitalfields Market *(p170).*

OCTOBER

Pearly Harvest Festival *(first Sun),* St. Martin-in-the-Fields.
Punch and Judy Festival Covent Garden WC2. Celebration of puppet duo.
Harvest of the Sea *(second Sun),* St. Mary-at-Hill Church *(p152).*
Horse of the Year Show Wembley Arena *(p353).*
Vintners' and Distillers' Wine Harvest *(p55).*
Navy Day *(p54).*

NOVEMBER

State Opening of Parliament *(p54).*
Guy Fawkes Night *(Nov 5).* Listings magazines give details of firework displays *(p342).*
Remembrance Day Service *(p54).*
Silent Change *(p55).*
Lord Mayor's Show *(p55).*
London to Brighton veteran car rally *(first Sun).*
Christmas lights *(late Nov– Jan 6).* The West End *(p323),* especially Regent's Street, lights up for the festive season.

London-to-Brighton veteran car run

Autumn colors in a London park

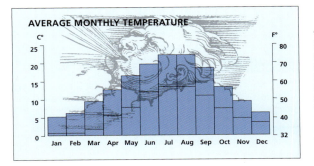

AVERAGE MONTHLY TEMPERATURE

Temperature Chart
The chart shows the average minimum and maximum temperatures for each month. Top temperatures averaging 75° F (22° C) belie London's reputation for year-round chilliness, although November through to February can be icy.

WINTER

Some of the most striking images of London are drawn from winter: paintings of frost fairs in the 17th and 18th centuries, when the River Thames froze over completely; and Claude Monet's views of the river and its bridges.

For centuries thick "pea-souper" fogs were an inevitable part of winter, until the Clean Air Act of 1956 barred coal-burning in open grates.

Christmas trees and lights twinkle everywhere – from the West End shopping streets to construction sites. The scent of roasting chestnuts pervades as street peddlers sell them from glowing mobile braziers.

Seasonal menus feature roast turkey, mince pies, and Christmas pudding. Traditional fare in theaters includes colorful family pantomimes (where the customary cross-dressing between the sexes baffles many visitors – *p344*) and popular ballets such as *Swan Lake* or *The Nutcracker*.

Skaters use open-air ice rinks at Canada Square, Greenwich, Hyde Park, Hampton Court, and at Somerset House *(see p117)*. It is rarely safe to use the parks' frozen lakes.

Winter in Kensington Gardens

DECEMBER

Oxford v Cambridge rugby union match Twickenham *(p355)*.
International Showjumping Championships *(late Dec)*, Olympia. Equestrian competition featuring the cream of riders from around the world.

CHRISTMAS, NEW YEAR

Dec 25–26 and **Jan 1** are public hols. There is no train service on Christmas Day.

Carol services *(leading up to Christmas)*, Trafalgar Square *(p102)*, St. Paul's *(pp148–51)*, Westminster Abbey *(pp76–9)*, and many other churches.
Turkey auction *(Dec 24)*, Smithfield Market *(p164)*.
Christmas Day swim Serpentine, Hyde Park *(p211)*.
New Year's Eve celebrations *(Dec 31)*, Trafalgar Square, St. Paul's.

JANUARY

Sales *(p321)*.
New Year's Day Parade starts at Parliament Sq *(p74)*.
International Boat Show, Earl's Court, Warwick Rd SW5.
International Mime Festival *(mid Jan–early Feb)*, various venues.
Charles I Commemoration *(last Sun)*, procession from St. James's Palace *(p91)* to Banqueting House *(p80)*.
Chinese New Year *(late Jan–mid-Feb)*, Chinatown *(p108)* and Soho *(p109)*.

FEBRUARY

Queen's Accession gun salutes *(Feb 6)*, 41-gun salute Hyde Park; 62-gun salute Tower of London *(p54)*.
Pancake races *(Shrove Tue)*, Lincoln's Inn Fields *(p137)* and Covent Garden *(p112)*.

PUBLIC HOLIDAYS

New Year's Day (Jan 1); **Good Friday; Easter Monday; May Day** (first Monday in May); **Whit Monday** (last Monday in May); **August Bank Holiday** (last Monday in Aug); **Christmas Day and Boxing Day** (Dec 25–26).

Christmas illuminations in Trafalgar Square

A RIVER VIEW OF LONDON

Cruising down the Thames is one of the most interesting ways to experience London. As the country's main commercial artery from the Roman invasion to well into the 1950s, the river is packed with historical references, including the reconstruction of the Elizabethan Globe Theatre, royal palaces and parks, numerous storied bridges, and decommissioned power stations. Now the river is the city's foremost leisure amenity, with the banks accessible via

Decoration on Chelsea Bridge

the Thames Path, numerous riverside pubs and commuters as well as tourists sailing the river. Passenger boat services cover about 30 miles (50 kilometers) of the Thames, from Hampton Court in the west to the Thames Barrier in the east. The most popular and best served section runs through the heart of the city from Westminster to Tower Bridge. Often accompanied by interesting and witty commentary, a cruise along this fascinating stretch of the Thames should not be missed.

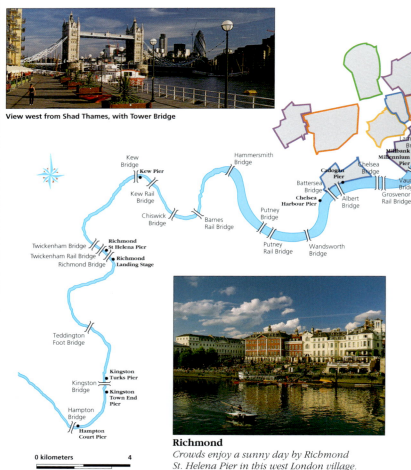

View west from Shad Thames, with Tower Bridge

Kew Bridge
Kew Pier
Kew Rail Bridge
Chiswick Bridge
Barnes Rail Bridge
Hammersmith Bridge
Putney Bridge
Putney Rail Bridge
Wandsworth Bridge
Cadogan Pier
Battersea Bridge
Chelsea Harbour Pier
Albert Bridge
Chelsea Bridge
Grosvenor Rail Bridge
Vauxhall Bridge
Lambeth Bridge
Millbank Millennium Pier

Twickenham Bridge
Twickenham Rail Bridge
Richmond Bridge
Richmond St Helena Pier
Richmond Landing Stage

Teddington Foot Bridge

Kingston Turks Pier
Kingston Bridge
Kingston Town End Pier
Hampton Bridge
Hampton Court Pier

0 kilometers 4
0 miles 2

Richmond
Crowds enjoy a sunny day by Richmond St. Helena Pier in this west London village.

The Thames Barrier
Completed in 1982, the world's second-largest movable flood barrier protects London from rising water levels. The massive steel gates have been raised over 100 times.

Riverside pubs
Beautifully preserved pubs, such as the Prospect of Whitby in Wapping, hug the river's banks.

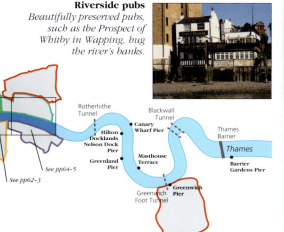

CRUISE OPERATORS

Bateaux London/ Catamaran Cruisers
Tel 020-7695 1800.
www.bateauxlondon.com

City Cruises
Tel 020-7740 0400.
www.citycruises.com

Crown River Cruises
Tel 020-7936 2033.
www.crownriver.com

London Duck Tours
Tel 020-7928 3132.
www.londonducktours.co.uk

Thames Clippers
Tel 0870-781 5049.
www.thamesclippers.com

Thames Executive Charters
Tel 01342-820 600. www.thamesexecutivecharters.com

Thames River Services
Tel 020-7930 4097.
www.thamesriverservices.co.uk

Turks Launches
Tel 020-8546 2434.
www.turks.co.uk

Westminster Passenger Service Association (Upriver) Ltd
Tel 020-7930 2062 or 020-7930 4721.
www.wpsa.co.uk

CRUISE HIGHLIGHTS

Most regular services run from April through September, with some routes having winter schedules. In summer, sailing times are frequent from Westminster and Embankment to Greenwich, with a boat arriving between every half hour and every hour. Commuter river services link Canary Wharf and Chelsea Harbour with some of the city's main termini. Numerous operators cover a variety of routes and a River Thames Boat Service Guide is available at subway stations. Most operators give a third off the ticket price to Travelcard holders *(see p378).*

GREENWICH *(see pp236–43)*
Blessed with frequent service, accessing this area steeped in shipping lore by boat gives a day trip a fitting nautical spin.
Operators: Bateaux London/ Catamaran Cruisers, City Cruises, Thames River Services.
Piers: Westminster, Waterloo, Embankment, Bankside, Tower.
Duration: 1 hr (Westminster).

THAMES BARRIER *(see p249)*
Sail between the nine massive piers that raise the steel gates. Cruises to the barrier also pass the O2 Arena, formerly the Millennium Dome.
Operator: Thames River Services.
Piers: Westminster, Greenwich.
Duration: 30 min (Greenwich).

KEW *(see pp260–61)*
A cruise to Kew leaves the city behind after passing the Battersea Power Station and sailing through Hammersmith.
Operator: WPSA (upriver only).
Piers: Westminster.
Duration: 1.5 hrs (Westminster).

HAMPTON COURT *(see pp254–7)* Arrive at Hampton Court in regal style, but be aware that the round trip from Westminster can take up to eight hours. Consider sailing from one of the piers upriver.
Operator: WPSA (upriver only), Turks Launches.
Piers: Kew, all Richmond and Kingston piers.
Duration: 2 hrs (Kew).

Westminster Bridge to Blackfriars Bridge

Until World War II, this stretch of the Thames marked
the division between rich and poor London. On the
north bank were the offices, shops, luxury hotels, and
apartments of Whitehall and the Strand, the Inns of
Court, and the newspaper district. To the south were
smoky factories and slum dwellings. After the war, the
Festival of Britain in 1951 started the revival of the
South Bank *(see pp184–91)*, which now has some of
the capital's most
interesting modern
buildings.

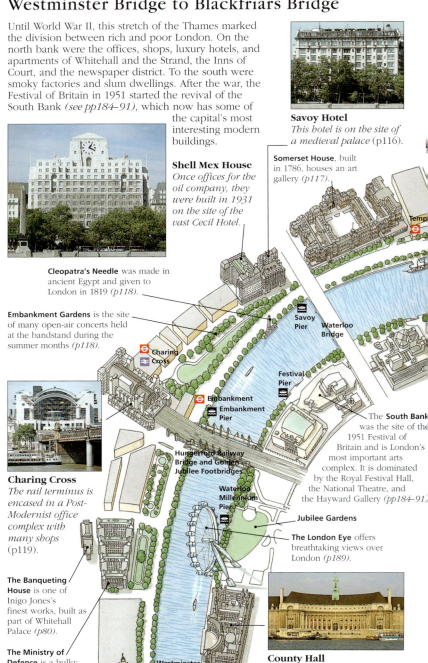

Savoy Hotel
*This hotel is on the site of
a medieval palace (p116).*

Shell Mex House
*Once offices for the
oil company, they
were built in 1931
on the site of the
vast Cecil Hotel.*

Somerset House, built
in 1786, houses an art
gallery *(p117)*.

Temple

Cleopatra's Needle was made in
ancient Egypt and given to
London in 1819 *(p118)*.

Embankment Gardens is the site
of many open-air concerts held
at the bandstand during the
summer months *(p118)*.

Charing
Cross

Embankment

Embankment
Pier

**Savoy
Pier**

**Waterloo
Bridge**

**Festival
Pier**

The **South Bank**
was the site of the
1951 Festival of
Britain and is London's
most important arts
complex. It is dominated
by the Royal Festival Hall,
the National Theatre, and
the Hayward Gallery *(pp184–91)*

**Hungerford Railway
Bridge and Golden
Jubilee Footbridges**

Charing Cross
*The rail terminus is
encased in a Post-
Modernist office
complex with
many shops*
(p119).

**Waterloo
Millennium
Pier**

Jubilee Gardens

The London Eye offers
breathtaking views over
London *(p189)*.

**The Banqueting
House** is one of
Inigo Jones's
finest works, built as
part of Whitehall
Palace *(p80)*.

**The Ministry of
Defence** is a bulky
white fortress
completed in the
1950s.

**Westminster
Pier**

Westminster   **Westminster Bridge**

County Hall
*This is home to the state-of-the-
art London Aquarium and its
350 species of fish.*

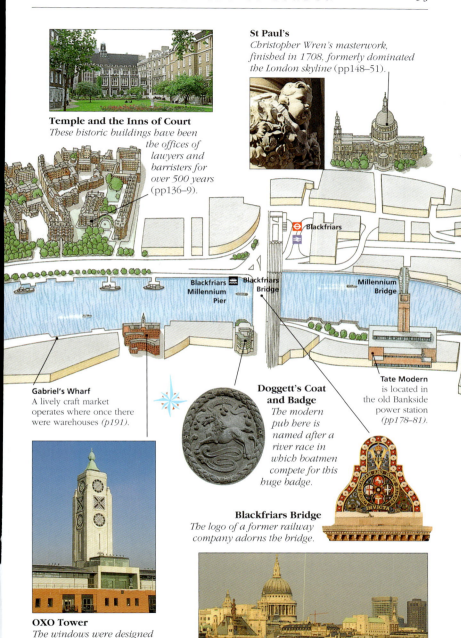

St Paul's
Christopher Wren's masterwork, finished in 1708, formerly dominated the London skyline (pp148–51).

Temple and the Inns of Court
These historic buildings have been the offices of lawyers and barristers for over 500 years (pp136–9).

Blackfriars

Blackfriars Millennium Pier

Blackfriars Bridge

Millennium Bridge

Tate Modern
is located in the old Bankside power station (pp178–81).

Gabriel's Wharf
A lively craft market operates where once there were warehouses (p191).

Doggett's Coat and Badge
The modern pub here is named after a river race in which boatmen compete for this huge badge.

Blackfriars Bridge
The logo of a former railway company adorns the bridge.

OXO Tower
The windows were designed to spell the brand name of a popular meat extract.

KEY

Ⓔ	Underground station
🚆	Train station
⚓	River boat boarding point

St Paul's
The cathedral dominates views from the South Bank.

Southwark Bridge to St. Katharine's Dock

For centuries the stretch just east of London Bridge was the busiest part of the Thames, with ships of all sizes jostling for position to unload at the wharves on both banks. Then, in the 19th century, the construction of the docks to the east eased congestion. Today most landmarks on this section hark back to that commercial past.

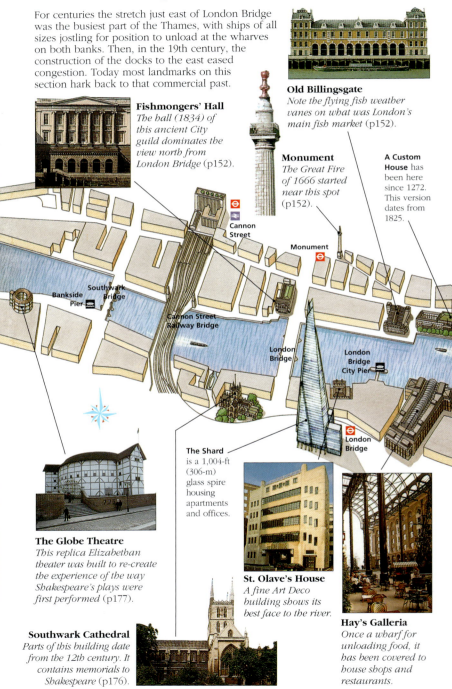

Old Billingsgate
Note the flying fish weather vanes on what was London's main fish market (p152).

Fishmongers' Hall
The hall (1834) of this ancient City guild dominates the view north from London Bridge (p152).

Monument
The Great Fire of 1666 started near this spot (p152).

A Custom House has been here since 1272. This version dates from 1825.

Cannon Street

Monument

Bankside Pier

Southwark Bridge

Cannon Street Railway Bridge

London Bridge

London Bridge City Pier

London Bridge

The Shard is a 1,004-ft (306-m) glass spire housing apartments and offices.

The Globe Theatre
This replica Elizabethan theater was built to re-create the experience of the way Shakespeare's plays were first performed (p177).

St. Olave's House
A fine Art Deco building shows its best face to the river.

Hay's Galleria
Once a wharf for unloading food, it has been covered to house shops and restaurants.

Southwark Cathedral
Parts of this building date from the 12th century. It contains memorials to Shakespeare (p176).

Southwark Wharves
Now there are walkways with river views where ships used to dock.

Tower Bridge
It still opens to let tall ships pass, but not as often as it did when cargo vessels came through (p153).

Tower of London
Look out for Traitors' Gate, where prisoners would be taken into the Tower by boat (pp154–7).

St. Katharine's Dock
The former dock is now a lively attraction for visitors. Its yacht marina is a highlight (p158).

Tower Millennium Pier

Tower Bridge

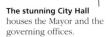 **St. Katharine's Pier**

The stunning City Hall houses the Mayor and the governing offices.

Victorian warehouses on Butlers Wharf have been converted into apartments.

HMS Belfast
This World War II cruiser has been a museum since 1971 (p183).

Design Museum
Opened in 1989, this shiplike building is a shining example of Docklands' renaissance (p183).

Colorful procession of a Guards band ▷

LONDON AREA
BY AREA

WHITEHALL AND WESTMINSTER

Whitehall and Westminster have been at the center of political and religious power in England for a thousand years. King Canute, who ruled at the beginning of the 11th century, was the first monarch to have a palace on what was then an island in the swampy meeting point of the Thames and its vanished tributary, the Tyburn. Canute built his palace beside the church that, some 50 years later, Edward the Confessor would enlarge

into England's greatest abbey, giving the area its name (a minster is an abbey church). Over the following centuries the offices of state were established in the vicinity. All this is still reflected in Whitehall's heroic statues and massive government buildings. But, to its north, Trafalgar Square marks the start of the West End entertainment district.

Horse Guard on Whitehall

SIGHTS AT A GLANCE

Historic Streets and Buildings
Banqueting House ⑪
Big Ben ❷
Blewcoat School ⑰
Cabinet War Rooms and Churchill Museum ⑩
Dean's Yard ❺
Downing Street ❾
Horse Guards Parade ⑫
Houses of Parliament pp72–3 ❶
Jewel Tower ❸
Parliament Square ❼
Queen Anne's Gate ⑭
St. James's Park Station ⑯

Churches, Abbeys, and Cathedrals
Westminster Abbey pp76–9 ❹
St. Margaret's Church ❻
Westminster Cathedral ⑱
St. John's, Smith Square ⑲

Museums and Galleries
Guards' Museum ⑮
Tate Britain pp82–5 ⑳

Theaters
Trafalgar Studios ⑬

Monuments
Cenotaph ❽

GETTING THERE
Rail services and the Victoria, Jubilee, District, and Circle lines all serve the area. Bus numbers 3, 11, 12, 24, 29, 53, 77, 87, 88, 109, 159, 170, and 184 go to Whitehall; 2, 2B, 16, 25, 36A, 38, 39, 52, 52A, 73, 76, 135, 507, and 510 serve Victoria.

KEY

▭	Street by Street map
Ⓔ	Underground station
⇄	Rail station

SEE ALSO

- ***Street Finder,*** maps 13, 20, 21
- ***Where to Stay*** pp278–91
- ***Restaurants, Pubs*** pp292–319

◁ **Looking down Whitehall toward Big Ben**

Street by Street: Whitehall and Westminster

Compared with many capital cities, London has little monumental architecture designed to overawe with pomp. Here, at the historic seat both of the government and of the established church, it most closely approaches the broad, stately avenues of Paris, Rome, and Madrid. On weekdays the streets are crowded with members of the civil service, as most of their work is based in this area. On weekends, however, it is popular with tourists visiting some of London's most famous sights.

Earl Haig, the British World War I chief, was sculpted by Alfred Hardiman in 1936.

Downing Street
British Prime Ministers have lived here since 1732 **9**

Central Hall is a florid example of the Beaux Arts style, built in 1911 as a Methodist meeting hall. In 1946 the first General Assembly of the United Nations was held here.

★ **Cabinet War Rooms and Churchill Museum**
The War Rooms were Winston Churchill's World War II headquarters **10**

★ **Westminster Abbey**
The Abbey is London's oldest and most important church **4**

The Sanctuary was a medieval safe place for those escaping the law.

Richard I's Statue, by Carlo Marochetti (1860), depicts the 12th-century *Coeur de Lion* (Lionheart).

Dean's Yard
Westminster School was founded here in 1540 **5**

KING CHARLES STR

STOREY'S GATE

GREAT GEORGE STREET

BROAD   SANCTUARY

PARLIAMENT SQUARE

ST MARGARET STREET

GREAT COLLEGE STREET

ABINGDON STREET

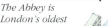

Jewel Tower
Kings once stored their most valuable possessions here **3**

The Burghers of Calais is a cast of Auguste Rodin's original in Paris.

★ Horse Guards
A mounted guard is ceremonially changed here twice a day ⑫

To Trafalgar Square

Dover House, a stately mansion dating from 1787, now houses the Scottish Office.

LOCATOR MAP
See Central London Map pp14–15

★ Banqueting House
Inigo Jones designed this elegant building, which has a Rubens ceiling, in 1622 ⑪

Cenotaph
Edwin Lutyens's war memorial dates from 1920 ⑧

Richmond House
is William Whitfield's prize-winning 1980s building for the Department of Health.

The Treasury
is where the nation's finances are administered.

Norman Shaw Buildings, the Victorian site of New Scotland Yard, the Metropolitan Police headquarters.

Westminster Pier
is a starting point for river excursions.

Westminster station

Boudicca, the British queen who resisted the Romans, was portrayed by Thomas Thornycroft in the 1850s.

STAR SIGHTS

★ Westminster Abbey

★ Houses of Parliament and Big Ben

★ Banqueting House

★ Cabinet War Rooms and Churchill Museum

★ Horse Guards

Parliament Square
Statues of famous statesmen, such as Benjamin Disraeli, Sir Winston Churchill, and Nelson Mandela stand here ⑦

★ Houses of Parliament and Big Ben
These were designed by Barry in 1834 when the Palace of Westminster burned down ① ②

St. Margaret's Church
Society weddings often take place here, in Parliament's church ⑥

KEY

– – – Suggested route

0 meters   100

0 yards   100

Houses of Parliament ❶

Since 1512 the Palace of Westminster has been the seat of the two Houses of Parliament, called the Lords and the Commons. The Commons is made up of elected Members of Parliament (MPs) of different political parties; the party with the most MPs forms the Government, and its leader becomes Prime Minister. MPs from other parties make up the Opposition. Commons' debates can become heated and are impartially chaired by an MP designated as Speaker. The Government formulates legislation which is first debated in both Houses before becoming law.

The mock-Gothic building was designed by Victorian architect Sir Charles Barry. Victoria Tower, on the left, contains 1.5 million Acts of Parliament passed since 1497.

★ Commons' Chamber
The room is upholstered in green. The Government sits on the left, the Opposition on the right, and the Speaker presides from a chair between them.

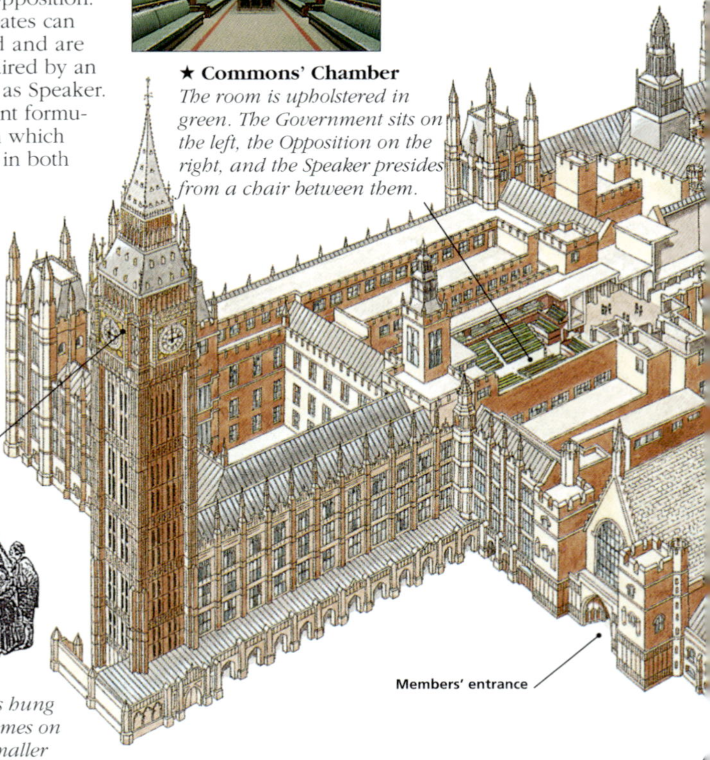

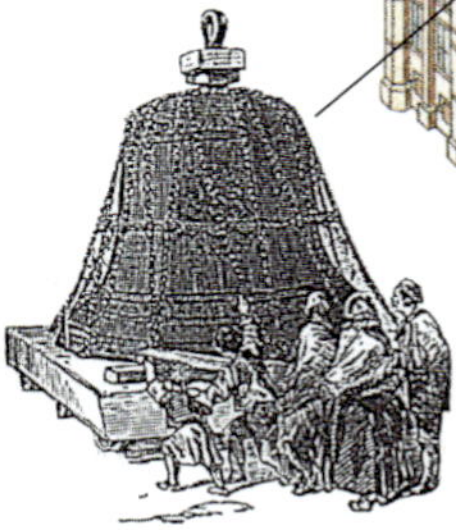

Big Ben
The vast bell was hung in 1858 and chimes on the hour; four smaller ones ring on the quarter hours (see p74).

Members' entrance

STAR FEATURES

★ Westminster Hall

★ Lords' Chamber

★ Commons' Chamber

★ Westminster Hall
The only surviving part of the original Palace of Westminster, it dates from 1097; its hammerbeam roof is 14th century.

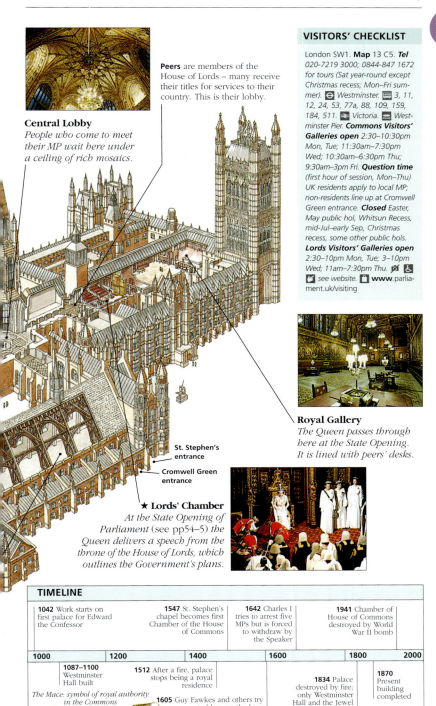

Central Lobby
*People who come to meet
their MP wait here under
a ceiling of rich mosaics.*

Peers are members of the
House of Lords – many receive
their titles for services to their
country. This is their lobby.

VISITORS' CHECKLIST

London SW1. **Map** 13 C5. *Tel
020-7219 3000; 0844-847 1672
for tours (Sat year-round except
Christmas recess; Mon–Fri summer).* ⊖ *Westminster.* 🚌 *3, 11,
12, 24, 53, 77a, 88, 109, 159,
184, 511.* 🚆 *Victoria.* 🚢 *Westminster Pier.* **Commons Visitors'
Galleries open** *2:30–10:30pm
Mon, Tue; 11:30am–7:30pm
Wed; 10:30am–6:30pm Thu;
9:30am–3pm Fri.* **Question time**
*(first hour of session, Mon–Thu)
UK residents apply to local MP;
non-residents line up at Cromwell
Green entrance.* **Closed** *Easter,
May public hol, Whitsun Recess,
mid-Jul–early Sep, Christmas
recess, some other public hols.*
Lords Visitors' Galleries open
*2:30–10pm Mon, Tue; 3–10pm
Wed; 11am–7:30pm Thu.* 🚫 ♿
🎥 *see website.* 📱 **www.**parlia-
ment.uk/visiting

Royal Gallery
*The Queen passes through
here at the State Opening.
It is lined with peers' desks.*

St. Stephen's
entrance

Cromwell Green
entrance

★ **Lords' Chamber**
*At the State Opening of
Parliament (see pp54–5) the
Queen delivers a speech from the
throne of the House of Lords, which
outlines the Government's plans.*

TIMELINE

1042 Work starts on first palace for Edward the Confessor	**1547** St. Stephen's chapel becomes first Chamber of the House of Commons	**1642** Charles I tries to arrest five MPs but is forced to withdraw by the Speaker	**1941** Chamber of House of Commons destroyed by World War II bomb	
1000	1200	1400	1600	1800	2000

| **1087–1100** Westminster Hall built | | **1512** After a fire, palace stops being a royal residence | | **1834** Palace destroyed by fire; only Westminster Hall and the Jewel Tower survive | **1870** Present building completed |

*The Mace: symbol of royal authority
in the Commons*

1605 Guy Fawkes and others try
to blow up the king
and Houses of Parliament

Houses of Parliament **1**

See pp72–3.

Big Ben **2**

Bridge St SW1. **Map** 13 C5.
🚇 *Westminster.*
***Not open** to the public.*

To be pedantic, Big Ben is not the name of the world-famous four-faced clock in the 320-ft (106-m) tower that rises above the Houses of Parliament, but of the resonant 14-ton bell on which the hours are struck. It was named after Sir Benjamin Hall, Chief Commissioner of Works when the bell was hung in 1858. Cast at Whitechapel, it was the second giant bell made for the clock, the first having become cracked during a test ringing. (The present bell also has a slight crack.) The clock is the largest in Britain, its four dials 23 ft (7.5 m) in diameter and the minute hand 14 ft (4.25 m) long, made in hollow copper for lightness. It has kept exact time for the nation more or less continuously since it was first set in motion in May 1859. The deep chimes have become a symbol of Britain all over the world and are broadcast daily on BBC radio.

Jewel Tower **3**

Abingdon St SW1. **Map** 13 B5.
***Tel** 020-7222 2219.* 🚇 *Westminster.*
***Open** Apr–Oct: 10am–5pm;*
*Nov–Mar: 10am–4pm daily. **Closed**
Dec 24–26, Jan 1. **Adm charge.*** 📷
🚻 *ground floor only.* 📱
www.english-heritage.org.uk

This and Westminster Hall *(see p72)* are the only vestiges of the old medieval Palace of Westminster. The tower was built in 1365 as a stronghold for Edward III's treasure and

today houses a fascinating exhibition, *Parliament Past and Present*, that relates the history of Parliament. It includes a display devoted to the history of the Jewel Tower itself.

The tower served as the weights and measures office from 1869 until 1938 and another small display relates to that era. Alongside are the remains of the moat and a medieval quay.

Westminster Abbey **4**

See pp76–9.

Dean's Yard **5**

Broad Sanctuary SW1. **Map** 13 B5.
🚇 *Westminster.* **Buildings not
open** *to the public.*

**Entrance to the Abbey and cloisters
from Dean's Yard**

An arch near the west door of the Abbey leads into this secluded grassy square, surrounded by a jumble of buildings from many different periods. A medieval house on the east side has a distinctive dormer window and backs on to Little Dean's Yard, where the monks' living quarters used to be. Dean's Yard is private property. It belongs to the Dean and Chapter of Westminster and is close to Westminster School, whose famous former pupils include poet John Dryden and playwright Ben Jonson. Scholars are, by tradition, the first to acknowledge a new monarch.

St. Margaret's Church **6**

Parliament Sq SW1. **Map** 13 B5.
***Tel** 020-7654 4840.* 🚇 *Westminster.*
***Open** 9:30am–3:30pm Mon–Fri,
9:30am–1:30pm Sat, 2–5pm Sun.* 🚻
11am Sun. 📷 🚻 *by arrangement.*

**Statue of Charles I overlooking
St. Margaret's doorway**

Overshadowed by the Abbey, this late 15th-century church has long been a favored venue for political and society weddings, such as Winston and Clementine Churchill's. Although much restored, the church retains some Tudor features, notably a stained-glass window commemorating the marriage of King Henry VIII and his first wife, Catherine of Aragon.

Parliament Square **7**

SW1. **Map** 13 B5. 🚇 *Westminster.*

Laid out in the 1840s to provide a more open aspect for the new Houses of Parliament, the square became Britain's first official rotary in 1926. Today it is hemmed in by heavy traffic. Statues of statesmen and soldiers are dominated by Winston Churchill in his greatcoat, glowering at the House of Commons. On the north side Abraham Lincoln sits in front of the Neo-Gothic Middlesex Guildhall, completed in 1913.

Cenotaph **8**

Whitehall SW1. **Map** 13 B4.
🚇 *Westminster.*

This suitably bleak and pale monument, completed in 1920 by Sir Edwin Lutyens to commemorate the dead of World War I, stands in the middle of Whitehall. On Remembrance Day every year – the Sunday nearest November 11 – the monarch and other dignitaries place wreaths of red poppies on the Cenotaph. This solemn ceremony, commemorating the 1918 armistice, honors the victims of World Wars I and II *(see pp54 –5).*

The Cenotaph

Churchill Museum and Cabinet War Rooms ⑩

Clive Steps, King Charles St SW1. **Map** 13 B5. *Tel* 020-7930 6961. ⊖ *Westminster.* **Open** *9:30am–6pm daily (last adm:5pm).* **Closed** *Dec 24–26.* **Adm charge.** ⚬ 🖥 🚻 **www**.iwm.org.uk/cabinet

This intriguing slice of 20th-century history is a warren of rooms below the Government Office Building north of Parliament Square. It is where the War Cabinet – first under Neville Chamberlain, then Winston Churchill – met during World War II when German bombs were falling on London. The War Rooms include living quarters for key ministers and

Telephones in the Map Room of the Cabinet War Rooms

military leaders and a Cabinet Room, where many strategic decisions were taken. They are laid out as they were when the war ended, complete with period furniture, including Churchill's desk, communications equipment, and maps for plotting military strategy. The Churchill Museum is a multimedia exhibit recording Churchill's life and career.

Downing Street ⑨

SW1. **Map** 13 B4. ⊖ *Westminster.* **Not open** *to the public.*

Sir George Downing (1623– 84) spent part of his youth in the American colonies. He was the second graduate from the nascent Harvard College before returning to fight for the Parliamentarians in the English Civil War. In 1680 he

bought some land near Whitehall Palace and built a street of houses. Four of these survive, though they are much altered. George II gave No. 10 to Sir Robert Walpole in 1732. Since then it has been the official residence of the Prime Minister and contains offices as well as a private apartment. In 1989, for security reasons, iron gates were erected at the Whitehall end.

Government policy is decided in the Cabinet Room at No. 10.

No. 12, the Whips' Office, is where Party campaigns are organized.

The famous front door of No. 10

No. 11 is the Chancellor of the Exchequer's official residence.

No. 10 is the official home of the Prime Minister.

The Prime Minister entertains official guests in the State Dining Room.

Westminster Abbey 〇

The Abbey is world-famous as the resting place of Britain's monarchs, and as the setting for coronations and other great pageants such as the marriage of Prince William in 2011. Within its walls can be seen some of the most glorious examples of medieval architecture in London. It also contains one of the most impressive collections of tombs and monuments in the world. Half national church, half national museum, the Abbey is part of the British national consciousness.

★ Flying Buttresses
The massive flying buttresses help transfer the great weight of the 102-ft (31-m) high nave.

North/Main Entrance
The stone-work here, like this carving of a dragon, is Victorian.

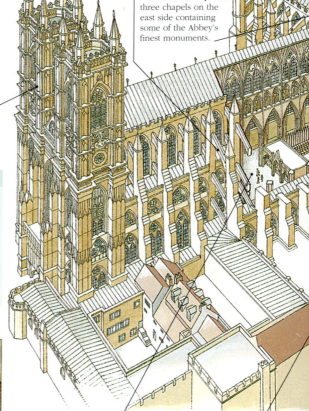

The North Transept has three chapels on the east side containing some of the Abbey's finest monuments.

★ West Front Towers
These towers, completed in 1745, were designed by Nicholas Hawksmoor.

STAR FEATURES

- ★ West Front Towers
- ★ Flying Buttresses
- ★ The Nave viewed from the West End
- ★ The Lady Chapel
- ★ Chapter House

★ The Nave viewed from the West End
At 35 ft (10 m) wide, the nave is comparatively narrow, but it is the highest in England.

The Cloisters, built mainly in the 13th and 14th centuries, link the Abbey church with the other buildings.

St. Edward's Chapel
houses Edward the
Confessor's shrine and
the tombs of other English
medieval monarchs. The
royal Coronation Chair is
located just outside.

★ **The Lady Chapel**
*The chapel, consecrated
in 1519, has a superb
vaulted ceiling and choir
stalls dating from 1512.*

★ **Chapter House**
*This octagonal structure
is worth seeing for its
13th-century tiles.*

The South Transept
contains "Poets' Corner,"
where memorials to famous
literary figures can be seen.

Museum

TIMELINE

1050 New Benedic-tine abbey church begun by Edward the Confessor	**1376** Henry Yevele begins rebuilding the nave	*13th-century tile from the Chapter House*	**1838** Queen Victoria's coronation

1000	1200	1400	1600	1800	2000

1245 New church begun to the designs of Henry of Reyns	**1269** Body of Edward the Confessor moved to new shrine in the Abbey	**1745** West towers completed **1540** Monastery dissolved	**1953** Most recent coronation in the Abbey: Elizabeth II's

A Guided Tour of Westminster Abbey

The Abbey's interior presents an exceptionally diverse array of architectural and sculptural styles. These range from the austere French Gothic of the nave to the stunning complexity of Henry VII's Tudor chapel and the riotous invention of the later 18th-century monuments. Many British monarchs were buried here; some of their tombs are deliberately plain, while others are lavishly decorated. At the same time, there are monuments to a number of Britain's greatest public figures – ranging from politicians to poets – crowded into the aisles and transepts.

② **Nightingale Memorial**
The North Transept chapels contain some of the Abbey's finest monuments – this one, by Roubiliac, is for Lady Elizabeth Nightingale (1761).

Main entrance →

① **The Nave**
The nave is 35 ft (10.5 m) wide and 102 ft (31 m) high. It took 150 years to build.

The Choir houses a gilded 1840s screen, which contains remnants of the 13th-century original.

HISTORICAL PLAN OF THE ABBEY

The first Abbey church was established as early as the 10th century, when St. Dunstan brought a group of Benedictine monks to the area. The present structure dates largely from the 13th century; the new, French-influenced design was begun in 1245 at the behest of Henry III. Because of its unique role as the royal coronation church, the Abbey survived Henry VIII's mid-16th-century onslaught on Britain's monastic buildings.

KEY

■ Built between 1055–1350
■ Added from 1350–1420
□ Built between 1500–1512
□ Towers completed 1745
□ Restored after 1850

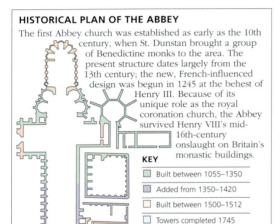

BENEATH THIS STONE RESTS THE BODY
OF A BRITISH WARRIOR
UNKNOWN BY NAME OR RANK
BROUGHT FROM FRANCE TO LIE AMONG
THE MOST ILLUSTRIOUS OF THE LAND
AND BURIED HERE ON ARMISTICE DAY
11 NOV 1920, IN THE PRESENCE OF
HIS MAJESTY KING GEORGE V
HIS MINISTERS OF STATE
THE CHIEFS OF HIS FORCES
AND A VAST CONCOURSE OF THE NATION

THUS ARE COMMEMORATED THE MANY
MULTITUDES WHO DURING THE GREAT
WAR OF 1914–1918 GAVE THE MOST THAT
MAN CAN GIVE LIFE ITSELF
FOR GOD
FOR KING AND COUNTRY
FOR LOVED ONES HOME AND EMPIRE
FOR THE SACRED CAUSE OF JUSTICE AND
THE FREEDOM OF THE WORLD

THEY BURIED HIM AMONG THE KINGS BECAUSE HE
HAD DONE GOOD TOWARD GOD AND TOWARD
HIS HOUSE

The Jericho Parlour, added in the early 16th century, contains some fine paneling. It is closed to the public.

The Jerusalem Chamber has a 17th-century fireplace, fine tapestries, and an interesting painted ceiling. It is closed to the public.

⑧ **Grave of the Unknown Warrior**
The body of an unknown soldier was brought from the battlefields of World War I and buried here in 1920. His grave commemorates all who have lost their lives in war.

The Deanery, home of the Dean of Westminster, was once the monastic abbot's house. It is closed to the public.

CORONATION

The Abbey has been the fittingly sumptuous setting for all royal coronations since 1066. The last occupant of the Coronation Chair was the present monarch, Elizabeth II. She was crowned in 1953 in the first televised coronation.

The Chapel of St. John the Baptist is full of tombs dating from the 14th to the 19th centuries.

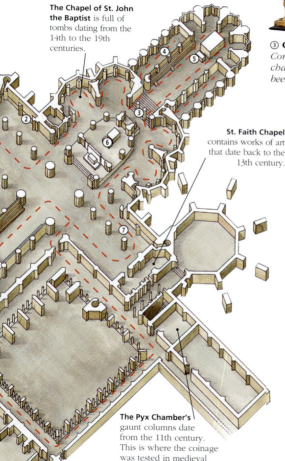

St. Faith Chapel contains works of art that date back to the 13th century.

③ **Coronation Chair**
Constructed in 1301, this is the chair on which monarchs have been crowned since 1308.

④ **Tomb of Elizabeth I**
Inside the Lady Chapel is Elizabeth I's (reigned 1558– 1603) huge tomb. It also houses the body of her half-sister, "Bloody" Mary I.

⑤ **The Lady Chapel**
The undersides of the choir stalls, dating from 1512, are beautifully carved with exotic and fantastic creatures.

⑥ **The Chapel of St. Edward the Confessor**
The shrine of the Saxon king Edward the Confessor and the tombs of many medieval monarchs are here.

The Pyx Chamber's gaunt columns date from the 11th century. This is where the coinage was tested in medieval times.

Dean's Yard entrance

KEY

- - - Tour route

⑦ **Poets' Corner**
Take time to explore the memorials to countless literary giants, such as Shakespeare and Dickens, that are gathered here.

Banqueting House ⓫

Whitehall SW1. **Map** 13 B4. **Tel** 0844-482 7777 (UK) or 020-3166 6000 (outside UK; possible closures – call ahead). 🚇 Charing Cross, Embankment, Westminster. **Open** 10am–5pm Mon–Sat (last adm 4:30pm). **Closed** Sun, public hols, Dec 24–Jan 1; for functions (phone first). **Adm charge.** 🎧 📷 www.hrp.org.uk

This delightful building is of great architectural importance. It was the first in central London to embody the Classical Palladian style that architect Inigo Jones brought back from his travels in Italy. Completed in 1622, its disciplined stone facade marked a startling change from the Elizabethans' fussy turrets and unrestrained external decoration. It was the sole survivor of the fire that destroyed most of the old Whitehall Palace in 1698.

The ceiling paintings by Rubens, a complex allegory on the exaltation of James I, were commissioned by his son, Charles I, in 1630. This blatant glorification of royalty was despised by Oliver Cromwell and the Parliamentarians, who executed King Charles I on a scaffold outside Banqueting House in 1649. Charles II pointedly celebrated his restoration to the throne here 11 years later. The building is used for official functions.

Mounted sentries stationed outside Horse Guards Parade

Horse Guards Parade ⓬

Whitehall SW1. **Map** 13 B4. **Tel** 0906-201 5151. 🚇 Westminster, Charing Cross, Embankment. **Open** 8am–6pm daily. **Changing the Guard** 11am Mon–Sat, 10am Sun. **Dismounting Ceremony** 4pm daily. Times for both are subject to change (phone for details). **Trooping the Colour** see Ceremonial London pp52–5.

Once Henry VIII's tiltyard (tournament ground), nowadays the Changing of the Guard takes place here every morning. The elegant buildings, completed in 1755, were designed by William Kent. On the left is the Old Treasury, also by Kent, and Dover House, completed in 1758 and now used as the Scottish Office.

Nearby is a trace of the "real" (royal) tennis court where Henry VIII is said to have played the ancient precursor of modern lawn tennis. On the opposite side, the view is dominated by the ivy-covered Citadel. This is a bomb-proof structure that was erected in 1940 beside the Admiralty. During World War II it was used as a communications headquarters by the Navy.

Trafalgar Studios ⓭

14 Whitehall SW1. **Map** 13 B3. **Tel** 0844-871 7632. 🚇 Charing Cross. **Open** for performances only. See **Entertainment** pp344–5.

Detail of a Whitehall Theatre box

Formerly the Whitehall Theatre and built in 1930, the plain white front seems to emulate the Cenotaph (see p74) at the other end of the street but, inside, the theater boasts fine Art Deco detailing. The studios comprise two intimate spaces.

Queen Anne's Gate ⓮

SW1. **Map** 13 A5. 🚇 St. James's Park.

The spacious row houses at the west end of this well-preserved enclave date from 1704 and are notable for the ornate canopies over their front doors. At the other end are houses built some 70 years later, sporting blue plaques that record former residents, such as Lord Palmerston, the Victorian Prime Minister. Until recently, the British Secret Service, MI5, was allegedly based in this unlikely spot. A small statue of Queen Anne stands in front of the wall separating Nos. 13 and 15. To the west, situated at the corner of Petty France, Sir Basil Spence's Home Office building (1976)

Panels from the Rubens ceiling, Banqueting House

is an architectural incongruity. Cockpit Steps, leading down to Birdcage Walk, mark the site of a 17th-century venue for the popular, yet blood-thirsty, sport of cockfighting.

Guards Museum ⑮

Birdcage Walk SW1. **Map** 13 A5. **Tel** 020-7414 3428. 🚇 St James's Park. **Open** 10am–4pm daily (last adm: 3:30pm). **Closed** Christmas. **Adm charge** (free for under-16s). 🚫 ♿ 📷 www.theguardsmuseum.com

Entered from Birdcage Walk, the museum is under the parade ground of Wellington Barracks, headquarters of the five Guards regiments. A must for military buffs, the museum uses tableaux and dioramas to illustrate various battles in which the Guards have taken part, from the English Civil War (1642–8) to the present. Weapons and row after row of colorful uniforms are on display, as well as a fascinating collection of models.

St. James's Park Station ⑯

55 Broadway SW1. **Map** 13 A5. 🚇 St. James's Park.

Epstein sculpture outside St. James's Park Station

The subway station is built into Broadway House, Charles Holden's 1929 headquarters for London Transport. It is notable for its sculptures by Jacob Epstein and reliefs by Henry Moore and Eric Gill.

Blewcoat School ⑰

23 Caxton St SW1. **Map** 13 A5. **Tel** 020-7222 2877. 🚇 St. James's Park. **Open** 10am–5:30pm Mon–Fri (and 10am–4pm Sat, Nov 7–Dec 19). 📷

Statue of a Blewcoat pupil above the Caxton Street entrance

A red-brick gem hemmed in by the office towers of Victoria Street, it was built in 1709 as a charity school to teach pupils how to "read, write, cast accounts and the catechism." It remained as a school until 1939, then became an army store during World War II and was bought by the National Trust in 1954. The beautifully proportioned interior now serves as a National Trust gift shop.

Westminster Cathedral ⑱

Ashley Place SW1. **Map** 20 F1. **Tel** 020-7798 9055. 🚇 Victoria. **Open** 7am–7pm Mon–Fri, 8am–7pm Sat & Sun. **Adm charge** for bell tower lift (9:30am–5pm Mon–Fri, 9:30am–6pm Sat & Sun). 🔔 5:30pm Mon–Fri, 10:30am Sat & Sun, sung Mass. ♿ 📷 www.westminstercathedral. org.uk

One of London's rare Byzantine-style buildings, it was designed by John Francis Bentley for the Catholic diocese and completed in 1903 on the site of a former prison. Its 285-ft (87-m) high, red-brick tower, with horizontal stripes of white stone, stands out on the skyline in sharp contrast to the Abbey nearby. A restful piazza on the north side provides a good view of the cathedral from Victoria Street. The rich interior decoration, with marble of varying colors and intricate mosaics, makes the domes above the nave seem incongruous. They were left bare because the project ran out of money.

Eric Gill's dramatic reliefs of the 14 Stations of the Cross, created during World War I, adorn the pier of the nave, which is the widest in Britain. The organ is one of the finest in Europe, and there are often free recitals on Sunday afternoons at 4:45pm.

St. John's, Smith Square ⑲

Smith Sq SW1. **Map** 21 B1. **Tel** 020-7222 1061. 🚇 Westminster. Box office open 10am–5pm Mon–Fri. Not open to public except for concerts. 🚫 ♿ phone first. 🍴 www.sjss.org.uk

Baroque interior of St. John's, Smith Square

Described by artist and art historian Sir Hugh Casson as one of the masterworks of English Baroque architecture, Thomas Archer's plump church, with its turrets at each corner, looks as if it is trying to burst from the confines of the square, and rather overpowers the pleasing 18th-century houses on its north side. Today it is principally a concert hall. It has an accident-prone history: completed in 1728, it was burned down in 1742, struck by lightning in 1773, and destroyed by a World War II bomb in 1941. There is a reasonably priced basement restaurant that is open daily for lunch and on concert evenings.

Tate Britain ⑳

See pp82–5.

Tate Britain ⑳

Tate Britain displays the world's largest collection of British art from the 16th to the 21st century. The international modern art once housed here is now held at Tate Modern *(see pp178–81)*. In the Clore Galleries are works from the magnificent Turner Bequest, left to the nation by the great landscape artist J. M. W. Turner in 1851. The Clore Galleries have their own entrance, giving direct access to the Turner Collection and allowing a full appreciation of Sir James Stirling's Post-Modernist design for the building.

Loan exhibitions covering aspects of British art are installed here and on the lower floor.

Main floor

Lower floor

Manton entrance

The Saltonstall Family *(c.1637)*
David Des Granges's life-size family portrait includes the dead first Lady Saltonstall as the second shows off her new baby.

★ Ophelia *(1851–2)*
Taken from Shakespeare's play Hamlet, *the scene of the drowning of Ophelia by Pre-Raphaelite John Everett Millais is one of the most famous – and popular – paintings at Tate Britain.*

GALLERY GUIDE

Tate Britain is undergoing a building project due for completion in spring 2013. While some rooms are closed for refurbishment, the Collection is being shown in new ways. Highlights from the historic collection fill one gallery, with the modern collection displayed chronologically on either side, and contemporary works in a suite of rooms opposite. More focused individual displays highlight new acquisitions.

KEY TO FLOORPLAN

- ☐ A Walk Through British Art: 1500–2000
- ☐ Contemporary British Art
- ☐ Duveen Sculpture Gallery
- ☐ Clore Galleries
- ☐ Loan Exhibitions
- ☐ Nonexhibition space

Carnation, Lily, Lily, Rose *(1885–6)*
John Singer Sargent (1856–1925) moved to Britain from Paris in 1885 and adopted some of the Impressionist techniques established by his personal friend Claude Monet. The title of this work is taken from a popular song of the time.

THE ART OF GOOD FOOD

The lower floor of Tate Britain boasts a café and an espresso bar, as well as a restaurant. Celebrated murals by Rex Whistler adorn the walls of the restaurant, telling the tale of the mythical inhabitants of Epicuriana and their expedition in search of rare foods. The extensive wine list has won awards. Open for lunch and afternoon tea.

VISITORS' CHECKLIST

Millbank SW1. **Map** 21 B2.
Tel 020-7887 8888. ● Pimlico.
🚌 C10, 36, 87, 88, 159, 185, 436, 507. 🚆 Victoria, Vauxhall.
🚢 Millbank Pier every 40 mins.
Open 10am–5:50pm daily (to 10pm first Fri of month). **Closed**
Dec 24–26. **Adm charge** for special exhibitions only. 🚻 ♿
Atterbury St. 📷 🏠 🍴 🖥 🛍
Lectures, film presentations, exhibitions, children's activities. www.tate.org.uk

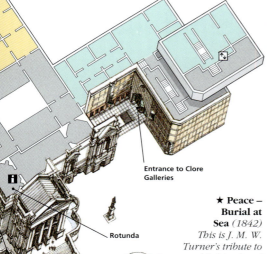

Entrance to Clore Galleries

Rotunda

Millbank entrance

Stairs to lower floor

The Lady of Shalott *(1888)
J. W. Waterhouse's work reflects the Pre-Raphaelite fascination with Arthurian myth.*

★ **Peace – Burial at Sea** *(1842)
This is J. M. W. Turner's tribute to his friend and rival David Wilkie. It was painted in 1842, the year after Wilkie died at sea.*

★ **Three Studies for Figures at the Base of a Crucifixion**
*(c.1944, detail)
Francis Bacon's famous triptych encapsulates an anguished vision of human existence. When first displayed, its savagery deeply shocked audiences.*

STAR PAINTINGS

- ★ Peace – Burial at Sea by Turner

- ★ Ophelia by John Everett Millais

- ★ Three Studies for Figures at the Base of a Crucifixion by Francis Bacon

Exploring Tate Britain

Tate Britain draws its displays from the massive Tate Collection. The variety of works on show, combined with a rigorous program of loan exhibitions and career retrospectives of British artists, results in a selection to suit all tastes – from Elizabethan portraiture to cutting-edge installation. The displays are changed frequently to explore many different aspects of the history and art of Britain from 1500 to the present day.

The Cholmondeley Ladies (c.1600–10), British School

A WALK THROUGH BRITISH ART: 1500–2000

This group of galleries covers a period of dramatic change in British history, from the Tudors and Stuarts through to the age of Thomas Gainsborough. "Hogarth" includes important works by one of Britain's greatest painters, known for his biting satire on the lifestyle and beliefs of his contemporaries. His *Marriage A la Mode* series satirized the marriage contracts of the upper classes. By contrast, "The Grand Manner" shows dramatic large-scale paintings in an idealized style by artists such as Benjamin West and Joshua Reynolds, the head of the newly established Royal Academy. Landscape painting lies at the heart of the revolution in British painting during the nineteenth century, and "British Landscape" shows how images of the countryside changed ideas not only about art, but about what it means to be British. The last

Satan Smiting Job with Sore Boils (c.1826) by William Blake

room in this section is devoted to a series of changing displays about the poet and artist William Blake.

The end of the eighteenth century and the first half of the nineteenth saw dramatic expansion and change in the arts in Britain. New themes began to emerge, and artists started working on a much larger scale as they competed with each other for attention on the walls of public exhibitions. "Romantic Painting in Britain" includes monumental canvases by John Martin, Thomas Lawrence and William Etty, as well as celebrated works by David Wilkie. This is followed by a series of three rooms that tell the story of Victorian art. Storytelling was at the heart of the Victorians' belief in the power of art to convey moral messages, and "Victorian Paintings of Modern Life" includes such important works as Augustus Egg's series *Past and Present*. "Pre-Raphaelites and Painters of the Ideal" brings together work by perhaps the most popular group of artists at Tate Britain: it includes John Everett Millais's *Ophelia*, William Holman Hunt's *Awakening Conscience* and several paintings by Dante Gabriel Rossetti. The last in this sequence of three rooms, "Victorian Spectacle," is a dramatic display of painting and sculpture from the late Victorian period, including John Singer Sargent's haunting *Carnation, Lily, Lily, Rose.*

TURNER AT THE CLORE GALLERIES

The Turner Bequest comprises some 300 oil paintings and about 20,000 watercolors and drawings received by the nation from the great landscape painter J. M. W. Turner after his death in 1851. Turner's will had specified that a gallery be built to house his pictures, and this was finally done in 1987 with the opening of the Clore Galleries. Most of the oil paintings are on view in the main galleries, while the watercolors are the subject of changing displays.

Shipping at the Mouth of the Thames (c.1806–7)

The First Marriage (A Marriage of Styles I) (1962) by David Hockney

CONTEMPORARY BRITISH ART

The modern section of the gallery begins with the early twentieth century. "Modern Figures" looks at artists' fascination with modern cities: cosmopolitan, noisy places with crowded streets, continually changing architecture, and fast, mechanized transport, as well as new places of entertainment. It includes Jacob Epstein's *Torso in Metal from "The Rock Drill,"* a machine-like robot, visored and menacing, that became a symbol of the new age, as well as the work of Wyndham Lewis and his Vorticist group, who saw the artist at the still center of the vortex of modern life.

Recumbent Figure (1938) by Henry Moore

Work by celebrated British sculptors, such as Barbara Hepworth and Henry Moore, can also be seen in this section. Paintings by two of the most famous, and disturbing, modern British artists are also on display here: Francis Bacon, whose *Three Studies for Figures at the Base of a Crucifixion* (c. 1944) depicts three mutant organisms in agony, confined in an apparently hostile and godless world; and Lucian Freud, whose expressive nudes are on display.

From the 1960s, Tate's funding for the purchase of works began to increase substantially, while artistic activity continued to pick up speed, encouraged by public funding. As a result, the Tate Collection is particularly rich on this time period, which means that the frequent rotation of displays is necessary.

There is, however, one room devoted to "Pop," one of the liveliest developments of British art in the 1960s, which focuses in particular on the beginnings of the movement through iconic works by artists such as Sir Peter Blake, Richard Hamilton, the early work of David Hockney, and Gerald Laing, deriving his inspiration for *Skydiver VI* (1964) from mass-produced images of the 1960s.

A revolt against this movement took place at the end of the 1960s, with the emergence of Conceptual artists such as Gilbert & George, known as the Living Sculptures, and Richard Long, who created a whole new approach to landscape painting by importing the land itself into the gallery.

Conceptual art in turn was rejected at the start of the 1980s by the School of London painters, including Howard Hodgkin, Frank Auerbach, and R. B. Kitaj, while Tony Cragg, Richard Deacon, and Antony Gormley pioneered a new kind of sculpture.

The 1990s saw a new surge in British art. Most recent British movements are well represented at Tate Britain. These include the work of the so-called Young British Artists (YBAs), who include Damien Hirst, perhaps the most notorious, as well as the controversial installations and photographic work of Tracey Emin and Sarah Lucas, exhibiting both as a collective and individually. Many contemporary British artists, including Tacita Dean, Douglas Gordon, Sam Taylor-Wood, Steve McQueen, and Jane and Louise Wilson, use film and video as their medium – the subject of a number of special displays at Tate Britain. Works by the four artists shortlisted for the Turner Prize are shown at Tate.

The frequently changing displays at Tate Britain include wider surveys as well as rooms devoted to single artists, and feature important newly acquired works. The Contemporary British Art galleries reflect current developments in British art and are devoted to work by the latest up-and-coming artists.

Skydiver VI (1964) by Gerald Laing

PICCADILLY AND ST. JAMES'S

Piccadilly is the main artery of the West End. Once called Portugal Street, it acquired its present name from the ruffs, or pickadills, worn by 17th-century dandies. St. James's still bears traces of the 18th century, when it surrounded the royal residences, and denizens of the court and society shopped and disported

Buckingham Palace decorative lock

themselves here. Two shops in St. James's Street – James Lock the hatter and Berry Bros. & Rudd vintners – recall that era. Fortnum and Mason, on Piccadilly, has served high-quality food for nearly 300 years. Mayfair to the north is still the most fashionable address in London, while Piccadilly Circus marks the start of Soho.

SIGHTS AT A GLANCE

Historic Streets and Buildings
Piccadilly Circus ❶
Albany ❸
Burlington Arcade ❺
Ritz Hotel ❻
Spencer House ❼
St. James's Palace ❽
St. James's Square ❾
Royal Opera Arcade ❿
Pall Mall ⓫
The Mall ⓮
Marlborough House ⓯
Clarence House ⓱
Lancaster House ⓲
Buckingham Palace pp94–5 ⓳
Royal Mews ㉑
Wellington Arch ㉒
Shepherd Market ㉔

Museums and Galleries
Royal Academy of Arts ❹
Institute of Contemporary Arts ⓬
The Queen's Gallery ⓴
Royal Mews ㉑
Apsley House ㉓
Faraday Museum ㉖

Churches
St. James's Church ❷
Queen's Chapel ⓰

Parks and Gardens
St. James's Park ⓭
Green Park ㉕

GETTING THERE
The Piccadilly subway line serves Hyde Park Corner, Piccadilly Circus, and Green Park – also served by the Jubilee and Victoria lines. The Bakerloo and Northern lines serve Charing Cross. The area is served by buses 6, 9, 15, 23, 139.

KEY
▮ Street by Street map
Ⓤ Underground station
🚉 Rail station

SEE ALSO
- *Street Finder,* maps 12, 13
- *Where to Stay* pp278–291
- *Restaurants, Pubs* pp292–319

◁ **Piccadilly Arcade with its many fine shops**

Street by Street: Piccadilly and St. James's

As soon as Henry VIII built St. James's Palace in the 1530s, the area around it became the center of fashionable London, and it has remained so ever since. The most influential people in the land strut importantly along its historic streets as they press on with the vital business of lunching in their clubs, discussing matters of pith and moment and brandishing their gold cards in the capital's most exclusive stores, or paying a visit to one of the many art galleries.

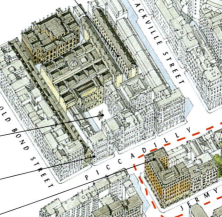

Albany
This has been one of London's smartest addresses since it opened in 1803 ❸

★ **Royal Academy of Arts**
Sir Joshua Reynolds founded the Academy in 1768. Now it mounts large popular exhibitions ❹

★ **Burlington Arcade**
Uniformed beadles discourage unruly behavior in this 19th-century mall ❺

Fortnum and Mason
was founded in 1707 by one of Queen Anne's footmen *(see p321)*.

The Ritz Hotel
Named for César Ritz, and opened in 1906, it still lives up to his name ❻

Spencer House
An ancestor of Princess Diana built this house in 1766 ❼

St. James's Palace
This Tudor palace is still the Court's official headquarters ❽

To The Mall

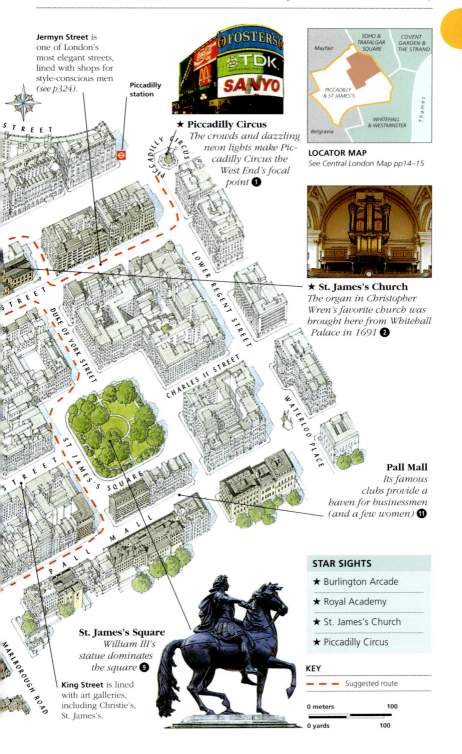

Jermyn Street is one of London's most elegant streets, lined with shops for style-conscious men *(see p324)*.

Piccadilly station

★ **Piccadilly Circus**
The crowds and dazzling neon lights make Piccadilly Circus the West End's focal point ❶

LOCATOR MAP
See Central London Map pp14–15

★ **St. James's Church**
The organ in Christopher Wren's favorite church was brought here from Whitehall Palace in 1691 ❷

Pall Mall
Its famous clubs provide a haven for businessmen (and a few women) ⓫

St. James's Square
William III's statue dominates the square ❾

King Street is lined with art galleries, including Christie's, St. James's.

STAR SIGHTS

★ Burlington Arcade

★ Royal Academy

★ St. James's Church

★ Piccadilly Circus

KEY

– – – Suggested route

| 0 meters | 100 |
| 0 yards | 100 |

Piccadilly Circus ❶

W1. **Map** 13 A3. 🚇 *Piccadilly Circus.*

Alfred Gilbert's statue of Eros

For years people have congregated beneath the symbolic figure of Eros, originally intended as an angel of mercy but renamed for the Greek god of love. Poised delicately with his bow, Eros has become almost a trademark for the capital. It was erected in 1892 as a memorial to the Earl of Shaftesbury, the Victorian philanthropist. Part of Nash's master plan for Regent Street, Piccadilly Circus has been considerably altered over the years and consists for the most part of shops. One shopping mall can be found behind the facade of the London Pavilion (1885), once a popular music hall. The circus has London's gaudiest array of neon advertising signs marking the entrance to the city's lively entertainment district with movie theaters, theaters, night clubs, restaurants, and pubs.

St. James's Church ❷

197 Piccadilly W1. **Map** 13 A3. **Tel** 020-7734 4511. 🚇 *Piccadilly Circus.* **Open** 8am–6:30pm daily. **Craft market** 9am–6pm Wed–Sat, **antiques market** 9am–6pm Tue. 🚻 *access from Jermyn St.* 🖥 **Concerts, talks, events.** www.st-james-piccadilly.org

Among the many churches Wren designed *(see p47)*, this is said to be one of his favorites. It has been altered over the years and was half-wrecked by a bomb in 1940, but it maintains its essential features from 1684 – the tall, arched windows, thin spire (a 1966 fiberglass replica of the original) and a light, dignified interior. The ornate screen behind the altar is one of the finest works of the 17th-century master carver Grinling Gibbons, who also made the exquisite marble font, with a scene depicting Adam and Eve standing by the Tree of Life. Artist and poet William Blake and Prime Minister Pitt the Elder were both baptized here. More of Gibbons's carvings can be seen above the grandiose organ, made for Whitehall Palace chapel but installed here in 1691. Today the church has a full calendar of events, and also houses a popular café.

Albany ❸

Albany Court Yard, Piccadilly W1. **Map** 12 F3. 🚇 *Green Park, Piccadilly Circus.* **Closed** to the public.

These desirable and discreet bachelor apartments, half hidden through an entrance off Piccadilly, were built in 1803 by Henry Holland. Notable residents have included the poet Lord Byron, novelist Graham Greene, two Prime Ministers (William Gladstone and Edward Heath), and the actor Terence Stamp. Married men were admitted in 1878 but could not bring their wives to live with them until 1919. Women are now allowed to live here in their own right.

Byron lived in The Albany

Royal Academy of Arts ❹

Burlington House, Piccadilly W1. **Map** 12 F3. **Tel** 020-7300 8000. 🚇 *Piccadilly Circus, Green Park.* **Open** 10am–6pm Sat–Thu, 10am–10pm Fri. **Closed** Good Fri, Dec 24–25. **Adm charge** some exhibitions. 🚫 ♿ 🚻 🖥 📷 www.royalacademy.org.uk

Michelangelo's *Madonna and Child*

The courtyard in front of Burlington House, one of the West End's few surviving mansions from the early 18th century, is often crammed with people waiting to get into one of the prestigious visiting art exhibitions on show at the Royal Academy (founded 1768). The famous annual summer exhibition, which has now been held for over 200 years, comprises around 1,200 new works by both established and unknown artists. Any artist, established or unknown, may submit work.

The airy Sackler Galleries (1991), designed by Norman Foster, show visiting exhibitions. There are permanent items in the sculpture promenade outside the galleries, notably a Michelangelo relief of the Madonna and Child (1505). The exceptional permanent collection (not all on display) includes one work by each current and former Academician; the highlights are displayed in the Madejski Rooms. Two shops adjacent to the gallery exits sell merchandise inspired by the current exhibitions, as well as a great range of art books.

Burlington Arcade ❺

Piccadilly W1. **Map** *12 F3.* ⊖ *Green Park, Piccadilly Circus. See* **Shops and Markets** *p328.*

This is one of four 19th-century arcades of small shops that sell traditional British luxuries. (The Princes and Piccadilly Arcades are on the south side of Piccadilly, while the Royal Opera Arcade is off Pall Mall.) It was built for Lord Cavendish in 1819 to stop rubbish being thrown into his garden. The arcade is still patrolled by beadles who make sure an atmosphere of refinement is maintained. They have authority to eject anyone who sings, whistles, runs, or opens an umbrella; those powers are infrequently invoked now, perhaps because the dictates of commerce take precedence over those of decorum.

Ritz Hotel ❻

Piccadilly W1. **Map** *12 F3.* **Tel** *020-7493 8181.* ⊖ *Green Park.* **Open** *to nonresidents for tea or restaurant (book ahead).* ♿ *(see p287.)* **www**.theritzlondon.com

César Ritz, the famed Swiss hotelier who inspired the adjective "ritzy," had virtually retired by the time this hotel was built and named after him in 1906. The colonnaded frontal aspect of the imposing château-style building was meant to suggest Paris, where the very grandest and most fashionable hotels were to be

The exquisite Palm Room of Spencer House

found around the turn of the 20th century. It maintains its Edwardian air of opulence and is a popular stop, among those who are suitably dressed (no jeans or sneakers; jacket and tie for men), for afternoon tea, with daily servings in the Palm Court at 11:30am, 1:30, 3:30, and 5:30pm. Champagne tea is served at 7:30pm.

Spencer House ❼

27 St. James's Pl SW1. **Map** *12 F4.* **Tel** *020-7514 1958.* ⊖ *Green Park.* **Open** *10:30am–5:45pm Sun (last adm: 4:45pm). Garden open one Sunday in June 2pm–5pm.* **Closed** *Jan & Aug.* **Adm charge. Children** *not under 10.* 📷 ♿ 🎥 *compulsory.* **www**.spencerhouse.co.uk

This Palladian palace, built in 1766 for the first Earl Spencer, an ancestor of the late Princess of Wales, has been completely restored to its 18th-century splendor (thanks to a $27

million renovation project). It contains some wonderful paintings and contemporary furniture; one of the highlights is the beautifully decorated Painted Room. The house is open to the public for guided tours, receptions, and meetings.

St. James's Tudor gatehouse

St. James's Palace ❽

Pall Mall SW1. **Map** *12 F4.* ⊖ *Green Park.* **Not open** *to the public.* **www**.royal.gov.uk

Built by Henry VIII in the late 1530s on the site of a former leper hospital, it was a primary royal residence only briefly, mainly during the reign of Elizabeth I and during the late 17th and early 18th centuries. In 1952 Queen Elizabeth II made her first speech as queen here, and foreign ambassadors are still officially accredited to "the Court of St. James's." Its northern gatehouse, seen from St. James's Street, is one of London's most evocative Tudor landmarks. Behind it the palace buildings are now occupied by privileged Crown servants.

Afternoon tea served in the opulent Palm Court of the Ritz

Royal Opera Arcade

St. James's Square ⑨

SW1. **Map** 13 A3. 🚇 *Green Park, Piccadilly Circus.*

One of London's earliest squares, it was laid out in the 1670s and lined by exclusive houses for those whose business made it vital for them to live near St. James's Palace. Many of the buildings date from the 18th and 19th centuries and have had many illustrious residents. During World War II Generals Eisenhower and de Gaulle both had headquarters here.

Today No. 10 on the north side is Chatham House (1736), home of the Royal Institute for International Affairs, and in the northwest corner can be found the London Library (1896), a private lending library founded in 1841 by historian Thomas Carlyle *(see p196)* and others. The lovely gardens in the middle contain an equestrian statue of William III, here since 1808.

Royal Opera Arcade ⑩

SW1. **Map** 13 A3. 🚇 *Piccadilly Circus.*

London's first shopping arcade was designed by John Nash and completed in 1818, behind the Haymarket Opera House (now called Her Majesty's Theatre). It beat the Burlington Arcade *(see p91)* by a year or so. The traditional shops that once used to be based here have since moved

on: Farlows, selling shooting and fishing equipment, and the famous Hunter's green Wellington boots, are now nearby, at No. 9 Pall Mall.

Pall Mall ⑪

SW1. **Map** 13 A4. 🚇 *Charing Cross, Green Park, Piccadilly Circus.*

The Duke of Wellington (1842): a frequent visitor to Pall Mall

This dignified street is named for the game of palle-maille – a cross between croquet and golf – which was played here in the 17th century. For more than 150 years Pall Mall has been at the heart of London's clubland. Here, exclusive gentlemen's clubs were formed to provide members with a refuge from their womenfolk.

The clubhouses now amount to a textbook of the most fashionable architects of the era. From the east end, on the left is the colonnaded entrance to No. 116, Nash's United Services Club (1827). This was the favorite club of the Duke of Wellington and

now houses the Institute of Directors. Facing it, on the other side of Waterloo Place, is the Athenaeum (No. 107), designed three years later by Decimus Burton, and long the powerhouse of the British establishment. Next door are two clubs by Sir Charles Barry, architect of the Houses of Parliament *(see pp72–3)*; the Travellers' is at No. 106 and the Reform at No. 104. The clubs' stately interiors are well preserved but only members and their guests are admitted.

Institute of Contemporary Arts ⑫

The Mall SW1. **Map** 13 B3. **Tel** 020-7930 3647. 🚇 *Charing Cross, Piccadilly Circus.* **Open** *noon–11pm Wed, noon–1am Thu–Sat, noon–9pm Sun. (Exhibition space closes 7pm, 9pm Thu, bookshop 9:30pm.)* **Closed** *Dec 24–26, 31, Jan 1, public hols.* **Adm charge.** ♿ *(movie theater and lower gallery) phone first.* 🖥 🍴 🛍 **Concerts, theater, dance, lectures, movies, exhibitions**. *See Entertainment pp350–51.* **www**.ica.org.uk

The Institute (ICA) was established in 1947 in order to offer British artists some of the same facilities as those at The Museum of Modern Art in New York. Originally on Dover Street, it has been situated in John Nash's Classical Carlton House Terrace (1833) since 1968. With its entrance on The Mall, this extensive warren contains a movie theater, auditorium, bookstore, art gallery, bar, and restaurant. It also offers plays, concerts, and lectures. Nonmembers pay a charge.

Institute of Contemporary Arts, Carlton House Terrace

St. James's Park ⓭

SW1. **Map** 13 A4. **Tel** 020-7298
2000. 🚇 *St. James's Park*. **Open**
dawn to dusk daily. 🚻 **Open** *daily*.
♿ **Concerts** *twice daily on summer
weekends in good weather*. **Bird
collection**. www.royalparks.org.uk

In summer, office workers
sunbathe between the dazzling
flower beds of this, the
capital's most ornamental park.
In winter overcoated civil
servants discuss affairs of state
as they stroll by the lake and
eye its ducks, geese, and
pelicans. Originally a marsh,
the park was drained by Henry
VIII and incorporated into his
hunting grounds. Later
Charles II redesigned it for
pedestrian pleasures, with an
aviary along its southern edge
(hence Birdcage Walk, the
street where the aviary was).
It is still a popular place to
take the air, with an appealing
view of Whitehall rooftops. In
the summer there are concerts
on the bandstand.

The Mall ⓮

SW1. **Map** 13 A4. 🚇 *Charing
Cross, Green Park, Piccadilly Circus*.

This broad triumphal approach
to Buckingham Palace was
created by Aston Webb when
he redesigned the front of the
palace and the Victoria Monument in 1911 *(see picture
p96)*. It follows the course of
the old path at the edge of St.
James's Park, laid out in the
reign of Charles II when it
became London's most fashionable promenade. On the
flagpoles down both sides of
The Mall fly national flags of
foreign heads of state during
official visits.

Marlborough
House ⓯

Pall Mall SW1. **Map** 13 A4. **Tel** 020-
7747 6491. 🚇 *St. James's Park, Green
Park*. **Open** *3rd Sat in Sep only (phone
for details)*. 📷 *by appt Tue am*.

Marlborough House was
designed by Christopher
Wren *(see p47)* for the
Duchess of Marlborough,

and finished in 1711. It was
substantially enlarged in the
19th century and used by
members of the Royal Family.
From 1863 until he became
King Edward VII in 1901, it
was the home of the Prince
and Princess of Wales and the
social center of London. An
Art Nouveau memorial in the
Marlborough Road wall of the
house commemorates
Edward's queen, Alexandra.
The building now houses the
Commonwealth Secretariat.

Queen's Chapel ⓰

Marlborough Rd SW1. **Map** 13 A4.
Tel 020-7930 4832. 🚇 *Green Park*.
Open *during services only*. ✝
Easter–July: 8:30am, 11:30am Sun.

This exquisite work of the
architect Inigo Jones was built
for Charles I's French wife,
Henrietta Maria, in 1627, and
was the first Classical church
in England. It was initially

Queen's Chapel

intended to be part of St.
James's Palace but is now
separated from it by Marlborough Gate. George III married
his queen, Charlotte of
Mecklenburg-Strelitz (who
was to bear him 15 children),
here in 1761. The interior of
the chapel, with its wonderful
Annibale Carracci altarpiece
and glorious 17th-century fittings, is open to both regular
worshipers and visitors during
the spring and early summer.

Early summer in St. James's Park

Buckingham Palace ⑲

Buckingham Palace is both office and official London residence of the British monarchy. It is also used for ceremonial state occasions such as banquets for visiting heads of state. About 500 people work at the palace, including officers of the Royal Household and domestic staff.

John Nash converted the original Buckingham House into a palace for George IV (reigned 1820–30). Both he and his brother, William IV (reigned 1830–37), died before work was completed, and Queen Victoria was the first monarch to live at the palace. The present east front, facing The Mall, was added to Nash's conversion in 1913. The State Rooms are open to the public in summer.

Music Room
State guests are presented and royal christenings take place in this room, which boasts a beautiful, original parquet floor by Nash.

The State Dining Room is where meals that are less formal than state banquets are held.

The White Drawing Room is where the Royal Family assemble before passing into the State Dining Room or Ball Room.

The Victorian Ballroom
The Victorian-style ballroom is used for state banquets and investitures.

Blue Drawing Room
Imitation onyx columns, created by John Nash, decorate this room.

The Queen's Gallery
Artworks from the Royal Collection (see p96), such as Canaletto's Rome: The Pantheon, are often on display.

Changing of the Guard
Visitors can witness the Buckingham Palace grounds guard handing over duty regularly throughout the year in a colorful and musical royal military ceremony (see pp52–5).

The garden is a haven for wildlife and is overlooked by most of the lavishly decorated state rooms at the back of the palace. It is also the venue for Royal Garden Parties, where guests enjoy lunches, dinners, and banquets.

The Green Drawing Room is the first of the large and magnificent state rooms entered by all guests of the Queen at royal functions.

VISITORS' CHECKLIST

SW1. **Map** 12 F5. **Tel** 020-7766 7300. ⬛ St. James's Park, Victoria. 🚌 2B, 11, 16, 24, 25, 36, 38, 52, 73, 135, C1. 🚆 Victoria. **State rooms open** end-Jul–end-Sep: 9:30am–5:30pm daily. **Adm charge.** 🚫 www.royalcollection.org.uk **Changing of the Guard:** May–Jul: 11:30am daily; Aug–Apr: alternate days. Tickets not required.

The Throne Room
In a room lit by seven magnificent chandeliers sit the thrones used by the Queen and the Duke of Edinburgh during her coronation.

The Queen's Audience Chamber is one of the Queen's 12 private rooms on the first floor.

The Royal Standard flies when the Queen is in residence.

WHO LIVES IN BUCKINGHAM PALACE?
The palace is the London residence of the Queen and her husband, the Duke of Edinburgh. The Princess Royal, the Duke of York, and the Earl of Wessex also have apartments here. About 50 domestic staff have rooms in the palace. There are more staff homes situated in the Royal Mews *(see p96)*.

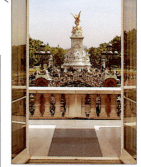

View over The Mall
Traditionally, the Royal Family waves to crowds from the balcony.

Clarence House 🅗

Stable Yard SW1. **Map** 12 F4. **Tel** 020-7766 7303. 🚇 *Green Park, St. James's Park.* **Open** *Aug 1–Sep 30: 10am–5:30pm (further dates may be added).* 🚻 📷 🎫 *mandatory.* **www**.royalcollection.org.uk

Designed by John Nash for William IV in 1827, this is Prince Charles's London home. Once a year, the public can visit the opulent first floor.

Lancaster House 🅘

Stable Yard SW1. **Map** 12 F4. 🚇 *Green Park, St. James's Park.* **Not open** to the public.

Lancaster House

This royal residence was built for the Duke of York by Benjamin Wyatt, architect of Apsley House, in 1825. In 1848 Chopin played here for Queen Victoria, Prince Albert, and the Duke of Wellington. It is now a conference center.

Buckingham Palace 🅙

See pp94–5.

The Queen's Gallery 🅚

Buckingham Palace Rd SW1. **Map** 12 F5. **Tel** 020-7766 7301. 🚇 *St James's Park, Victoria.* **Open** *10am–5:30pm daily (Aug & Sep: 9:30am–5:30pm).* **Closed** *dates vary; call or check website.* **Adm charge.** 🚫 **www**.royalcollection.org.uk

The Royal Family possesses one of the finest and most valuable art collections in the world, rich in the work of Old Masters, including Vermeer and Leonardo. In 2002 the galleries were expanded in the most extensive addition to Buckingham Palace in 150 years, resulting in three and a half times more display space and an impressive entrance gallery with a striking columned portico.

Among the gallery's seven rooms, one is dedicated to a permanent display of some of the royal collection's master-pieces. Changing exhibitions include fine art, jewels, porce-lain, furniture, and manuscripts.

Royal Mews 🅡

Buckingham Palace Rd SW1. **Map** 12 E5. **Tel** 020-7766 7302. 🚇 *St. James's Park, Victoria.* **Open** *end Mar–Oct: 11am–4pm daily (Jul 27–Sep 29: 10am–5pm). Subject to clo-sure at short notice (phone first).* **Adm charge.** 🚻 📷 🎫 **www**.royalcollection.org.uk

Although open for only a few hours each day, the Mews is worth catching for all lovers of horses and of royal pomp. The stables and coach houses, designed by Nash in 1825, accommodate the horses and coaches used by the Royal Family on state occasions. The star exhibit is the gold state coach, built for George III in 1761, with fine panels by Giovanni Cipriani. Among the other vehicles are

Fabergé egg, The Queen's Gallery

the Irish State Coach, bought by Queen Victoria for the State Opening of Parliament; the open-topped royal lan-dau; and the glass coach that was used for royal weddings and for transporting foreign ambassadors. The elaborate horses' harnesses are also on display, and so are some of the fine animals that wear them. The Mews has an exhibition that explains its history and current workings. Visitors may see carriages being prepared for use or limousines in action. A guided route around the mews includes a chance to view the 18th-century riding school where the horses are put through their paces. There is also a shop here selling royal souvenirs, open daily from 9:30am until 5pm.

The Victoria Monument outside Buckingham Palace

Wellington Arch ❷

SW1. **Map** 12 D4. **Tel** *020-7930 2726*. 🚇 *Hyde Park Corner*. **Open** *Apr–Oct: 10am–5pm Wed–Sun & public hols; Nov–Mar: 10am–4pm Wed–Sun.* **Closed** *Dec 24–26, Jan 1.* **Adm charge** *joint ticket with Apsley House available.* 🚻 *limited.* 📷 www.english-heritage.org.uk

After nearly a century of debate about what to do with the patch of land in front of Apsley House, Wellington Arch, designed by Decimus Burton, was erected in 1828. The sculpture, by Adrian Jones, was added in 1912. Before it was installed Jones seated three people for dinner in the body of one of the horses.

The public has access to exhibitions in the inner rooms of the arch. A viewing platform beneath the sculpture has great views over London.

Wellington Arch

Apsley House ❷

Hyde Park Corner W1. **Map** 12 D4. **Tel** *020-7499 5676*. 🚇 *Hyde Park Corner*. **Open** *Apr–Oct: 11am–5pm Wed–Sun & bank hols; Nov–Mar: 11am–4pm Wed–Sun & public hols.* **Closed** *Dec 24–26, Jan 1.* **Adm charge** *joint ticket with Wellington Arch available.* 📷 📷 📷 *pre-booked only.* www.english-heritage.org.uk

Apsley House, on the southeast corner of Hyde Park, was completed by Robert Adam for Baron Apsley in 1778. Fifty years later it was enlarged and altered by the architect Benjamin Dean Wyatt, to provide a grand home for the Duke of Wellington. His dual career as soldier and politician brought him victory against Napoleon at Waterloo (1815), and two terms as Prime Minister

Interior of Apsley House

(1828–30, 1834). Against a sumptuous background of silk hangings and gilt decoration hangs the duke's art collection. Paintings by Goya, Velázquez, Brueghel, and Rubens stand alongside displays of porcelain, silver, and furniture. The duke's memorabilia include swords and medals, but is dominated by Canova's colossal statue of Napoleon, who was Wellington's arch-enemy.

Shepherd Market ❷

W1. **Map** 12 E4. 🚇 *Green Park.*

This attractive and bijou pedestrianized enclave of small shops, restaurants, and outdoor cafés, between Piccadilly and Curzon Street, was named after Edward Shepherd, who built it in the middle of the 18th century. During the 17th century the annual 15-day May Fair (from which the name of the area is derived) took place on this site, and today Shepherd Market is still very much the center of Mayfair.

Green Park ❷

SW1. **Map** 12 E4. **Tel** *020-7930 1793*. 🚇 *Green Park, Hyde Park Corner.* **Open** *all day, year-round.* www.royalparks.org.uk

Once part of Henry VIII's hunting ground, it was, like St. James's Park, adapted for public use by Charles II in the 1660s and is a natural, undulating landscape of grass

and trees (with a good spring show of daffodils). It was a favorite site for duels during the 18th century; in 1771 the poet Alfieri was wounded here by his mistress's husband, Viscount Ligonier, but then rushed back to the Haymarket Theatre in time to catch the last act of a play. Today the park is popular with guests staying at the Mayfair hotels as a place to jog.

Faraday Museum ❷

The Royal Institution, 21 Albemarle St W1. **Map** 12 F3. **Tel** *020-7409 2992*. 🚇 *Green Park.* **Open** *9am–9pm Mon–Fri.* **Closed** *Dec 24–Jan 3.* 📷 🚻 📷 *phone first.* **Lectures**. www.rigb.org

Michael Faraday was a 19th-century pioneer of the uses of electricity. The collections in the Michael Faraday Museum include some of his scientific apparatus and personal effects, as well as the work of other great scientists across the lower three floors.

Michael Faraday

SOHO AND TRAFALGAR SQUARE

Soho has been renowned for pleasures of the table, the flesh, and the intellect ever since it was first developed in the late 17th century. For its first century the area was one of London's most fashionable, and Soho residents of the time have gone down in history for their extravagant parties.

During the later part of the 20th century, Soho consolidated its reputation as a center for entertainment. With a

Clock on Liberty department store

cosmopolitan mix of people, visitors here enjoy the many pleasant bars, restaurants, and cafés – popular with everyone from tourists to locals, office workers, and London's gay community.

Soho is one of London's most multicultural districts. The first immigrants were 18th-century Huguenots from France *(see Christ Church, Spitalfields p170)*. Soho is also famous as a Chinatown; Gerrard Street is lined with Chinese restaurants.

SIGHTS AT A GLANCE

Historic Streets and Buildings
Trafalgar Square ❶
Admiralty Arch ❷
Leicester Square ❻
Shaftesbury Avenue ❽
Chinatown ❾
Charing Cross Road ❿
Soho Square ⓬
Carnaby Street ⓮

Shops and Markets
Berwick Street Market ⓭
Liberty ⓯

Churches
St. Martin-in-the-Fields ❹

Museums and Galleries
National Gallery pp104–7 ❸
National Portrait Gallery ❺
Photographers' Gallery ⓰

Theatres
Palace Theatre ⓫
Theatre Royal Haymarket ❼

GETTING THERE
This area is served by the Central, Piccadilly, Bakerloo, Victoria, and Northern lines. Many buses pass through Trafalgar Square and Piccadilly Circus. Rail services run from Charing Cross.

KEY

🟧	Street by Street map
⊖	Underground station
🚄	Rail station

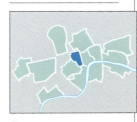

SEE ALSO
- **Street Finder,** maps 11, 12, 13
- **Where to Stay** pp278–291
- **Restaurants, Pubs** pp292–319

◁ **St. Martin-in-the-Fields and Trafalgar Square**

Street-by-Street: Trafalgar Square

This area buzzes both day and night with crowds enjoying the numerous restaurants, movie theaters, and night-clubs. Broad avenues lined with regal office buildings converge at Trafalgar Square. Some of the roads that ring the square have now been pedestrianized, making this already popular meeting place far more accessible.

To Tottenham Court Road station

Charing Cross Road
The stores here are a feast for booklovers ❿

Shaftesbury Avenue
Theaterland's main artery is lined with announcements for current shows ❽

★ Chinatown
An area of Chinese restaurants and stores, this is home to many Chinese-speaking people ❾

The Blue Posts pub stands on the site of a pick-up point for sedan chairs in the 18th century.

The Trocadero's neon and laser-beam deco-rations attract a young crowd to the floors of games, cafés, shops, and movie theaters.

STAR SIGHTS

- ★ National Gallery
- ★ National Portrait Gallery
- ★ St. Martin-in-the-Fields
- ★ Chinatown
- ★ Trafalgar Square

Leicester Square
Film pioneer Charlie Chaplin stands in the traffic-free square ❻

KEY

– – – Suggested route

0 meters   100

0 yards   100

Theatre Royal Haymarket
It is graced by a John Nash portico ❼

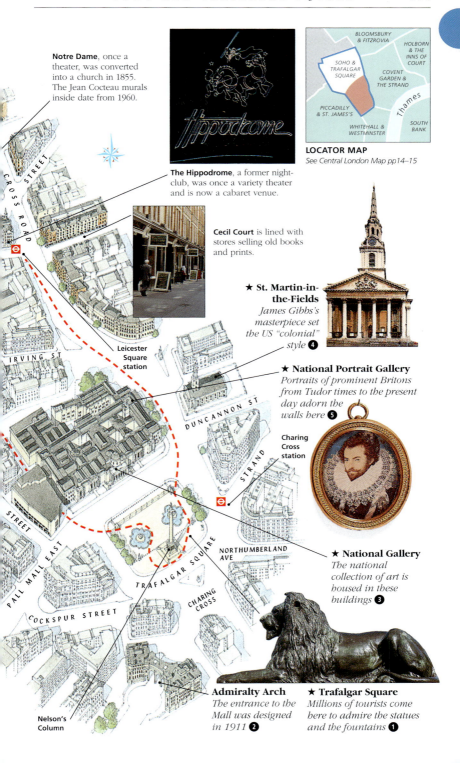

Notre Dame, once a theater, was converted into a church in 1855. The Jean Cocteau murals inside date from 1960.

The Hippodrome, a former nightclub, was once a variety theater and is now a cabaret venue.

Cecil Court is lined with stores selling old books and prints.

LOCATOR MAP
See Central London Map pp14–15

★ **St. Martin-in-the-Fields**
James Gibbs's masterpiece set the US "colonial" style ❹

★ **National Portrait Gallery**
Portraits of prominent Britons from Tudor times to the present day adorn the walls here ❺

Charing Cross station

★ **National Gallery**
The national collection of art is housed in these buildings ❸

Leicester Square station

★ **Admiralty Arch**
The entrance to the Mall was designed in 1911 ❷

★ **Trafalgar Square**
Millions of tourists come here to admire the statues and the fountains ❶

Nelson's Column

Trafalgar Square ❶

WC2. **Map** 13 B3. 🚇 *Charing Cross.*

London's main venue for rallies and outdoor public meetings was conceived by John Nash and was mostly constructed during the 1830s. The 165-ft (50-m) column commemorates Admiral Lord Nelson, Britain's most famous naval captain, who died at the Battle of Trafalgar against Napoleon in 1805. It dates from 1842; 14 stonemasons held a dinner on its flat top before the statue of Nelson was finally installed. Edwin Landseer's four lions were added to guard its base 25 years later. The north side of the square is now taken up by the National Gallery and its annex *(see pp104 – 7)*, with Canada House on the west side, and South Africa House on the east. The restored Grand Buildings on the south side, with their fine arcade, were built in 1880 as the Grand Hotel. The square was partially pedestrianized in 2003, with other refurbishments including an enlarged central staircase descending from the National Gallery.

Nelson's statue over-looking the square

Admiralty Arch ❷

The Mall SW1. **Map** 13 B3. 🚇 *Charing Cross.*

Designed in 1911, this triple archway was part of Aston Webb's scheme to rebuild The Mall as a grand processional route honoring Queen Victoria. The arch effectively seals the eastern end of The Mall, although traffic passes through the smaller side gates, and separates courtly London from the hurlyburly of Trafalgar Square. The central gate is opened only for royal processions, making a fine setting for the coaches and horses trotting through.

Filming *Howard's End* at Admiralty Arch

National Gallery ❸

See pp104–7.

St. Martin-in-the-Fields ❹

Trafalgar Sq WC2. **Map** 13 B3. **Tel** *020-7766 1100.* 🚇 *Charing Cross.* **Open** *daily.* 🕙 *8am, 10am, noon, 5pm, 6:30pm Sun (phone for other days).* ♿ 🔊 🖥 🚻 **London Brass Rubbing Centre Tel** *020-7766 1122.* **Open** *10am–7pm Mon–Wed, 10am–9pm Thu–Sat, 11:30am–6pm Sun (last brass rubbing entry 1 hr before close).* **Concerts** *see* **Entertainment** *pp348–9.* **www**2.stmartin-in-the-fields.org

There has been a church on this site since the 13th century. Many famous people were buried here, including Charles II's mistress, Nell Gwynne, and the painters William Hogarth and Joshua Reynolds. The present church was designed by James Gibbs and completed in 1726. In architectural terms it was one of the most influential ever built; it was much copied in the United States, where it became a model for the Colonial style of church-building. An unusual feature of St. Martin's spacious interior is the royal box at gallery level on the left of the altar.

From 1914 until 1927 the crypt was used as a shelter for homeless soldiers and down-and-outs; during World War II it was an air-raid shelter. Today it helps the homeless by providing a lunchtime soup kitchen for them. It also has a café in the crypt and a religious bookshop as well as the London Brass Rubbing Centre. Lunchtime and evening concerts are held in the church and in the café.

National Portrait Gallery ❺

2 St Martin's Place WC2. **Map** 13 B3. **Tel** *020-7312 2463.* 🚇 *Leicester Sq, Charing Cross.* **Open** *10am–6pm Sat–Wed, 10am–9pm Thu–Fri.* **Closed** *Dec 24–26.* 🚫 ♿ *Orange St entrance.* 🔊 🍴 🖥 🚻 **Lectures.** **www.**npg.org.uk

Too often ignored in favor of the National Gallery next door, this fascinating museum recounts Britain's develop-ment through portraits of its main characters, giving faces to names which are familiar from the history books. There are pictures of kings, queens, poets, musicians, artists, thinkers, heroes, and villains

William Shakespeare portrait on display in the Ondaatje Wing

from all periods since the late 14th century. The oldest works, on the fifth floor, include a Hans Holbein cartoon of Henry VIII and paintings of some of his wives.

The National Portrait Gallery's millennium development project, the Ondaatje Wing, opened in May 2000, allowing it 50 percent more exhibition and public space. It includes a Tudor Gallery, displaying some of the earliest and most important paintings, including one of Shakespeare (by John Taylor in 1651), and the Ditchley portrait of Elizabeth I. A balcony provides an extra display area for portraits from the 1960s to the 1990s.

The gallery has a rooftop restaurant, and a spacious lecture theater in the basement which is also used for drama and movie events.

The gallery also houses temporary exhibitions and has an excellent shop selling books on art and literature, as well as an extensive range of cards, prints and posters featuring pictures from the main collection.

Leicester Square ❻

WC2. **Map** 13 B2. ☻ *Leicester Sq, Piccadilly Circus.*

It is hard to imagine that this, the perpetually animated heart of the West End entertainment district, was once a fashionable place to live. Laid out in 1670 south of Leicester House, a long-gone royal residence, the square's occupants included the scientist Isaac Newton and the artists Joshua Reynolds and William Hogarth. Reynolds made his fortune painting high society in his elegant salon at No. 46. Hogarth's house, in the south-east corner, became the Hôtel de Sablonère in 1801, probably the area's first public restaurant.

In Victorian times several popular music halls were established here, including the Empire (today the movie theater on the same site perpetuates the name) and the Alhambra, replaced in 1937 by the Art Deco Odeon. A booth

selling cut-price theater tickets (*see p344*) sits in the square. There is also a statue of Charlie Chaplin, unveiled in 1981. The Shakespeare fountain dates from 1874.

Regeneration of the southwest corner of the square (to be completed in 2012) will increase public space and include cafés, restaurants, and a state-of-the-art movie theater.

Theatre Royal Haymarket ❼

Haymarket SW1. **Map** 13 A3. **Tel** *0845-481 1870.* ☻ *Piccadilly Circus.* **Open** *performances and guided tours (phone to check).* ♿ **www**.trh.co.uk

The fine frontage of this theater, with its portico of six Corinthian columns, dates from 1821, when John Nash designed it as part of his plan for a stately route from Carlton House to Regent's Park. The interior is equally grand.

Shaftesbury Avenue ❽

W1. **Map** 13 A2. ☻ *Piccadilly Circus, Leicester Sq.*

The main artery of London's theaterland, Shaftesbury Avenue has six theaters and two movie theaters, all on its north side. This street was cut through an area of terrible slums between 1877 and 1886 in order to improve communications across the city's busy West End; it follows the route of a much earlier highway. It is named after the Earl of Shaftesbury (1801–85), whose attempts to improve housing conditions had helped some of the local poor. (The earl is also commemorated by the Eros statue in Piccadilly Circus – *see p90.*) The Lyric Theatre, which was designed by C. J. Phipps, has been open for almost the same length of time as the avenue.

London's West End: the facade of the Gielgud Theatre

National Gallery ❸

Trafalgar Square facade

The National Gallery has flourished since its inception in the early 19th century. In 1824 the House of Commons was persuaded to buy 38 major paintings, including works by Raphael and Rubens, and these became the start of a national collection. Contributions by rich benefactors have today resulted in a collection of 2,300 Western European paintings. The main gallery building was designed in Greek Revival style by William Wilkins and built in 1833–8. To its left lies the Sainsbury Wing, financed by the grocery family and completed in 1991.

Trafalgar Square facade

Stairs and elevator to lower galleries

Education center entrance ♿

Stairs to lower floor

Doge Leonardo Loredan *(1501–2) Giovanni Bellini portrays this Venetian head of state as a serene father figure.*

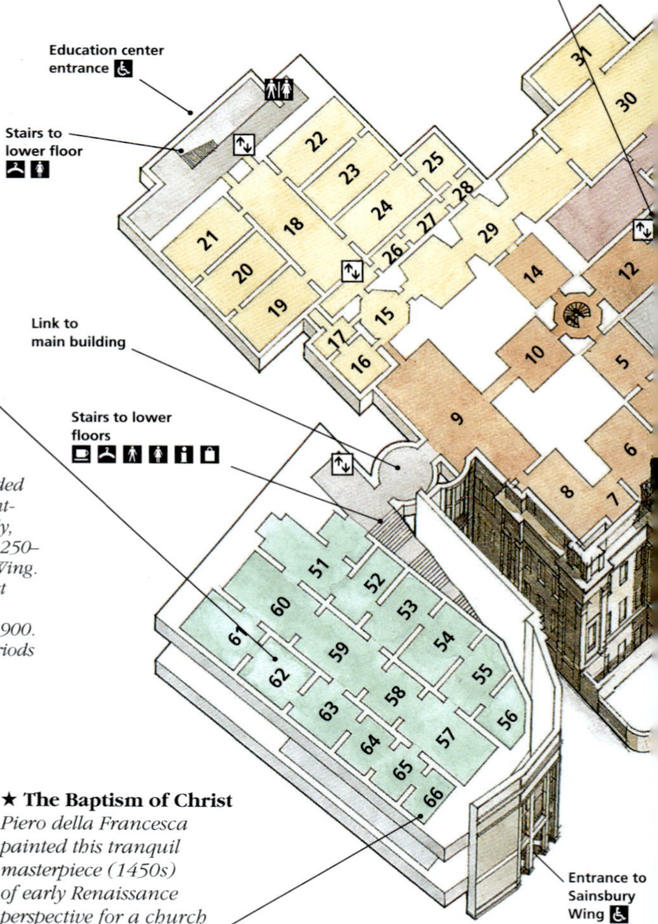

Link to main building

GALLERY GUIDE

Most of the collection is housed on one floor divided into four wings. The paintings hang chronologically, with the earliest works (1250–1500) in the Sainsbury Wing. The North, West, and East Wings cover 1500–1600, 1600–1700, and 1700–1900. Lesser paintings of all periods are on the lower floor.

Stairs to lower floors

★ The Baptism of Christ
Piero della Francesca painted this tranquil masterpiece (1450s) of early Renaissance perspective for a church in his native Umbria.

Entrance to Sainsbury Wing ♿

★ **The Rokeby Venus**
(1647–51) Diego Velázquez painted it to match a lost Venetian nude.

★ **The Hay Wain** *(1821) John Constable brilliantly caught the effect of distance and the changing light and shadow of a typically English cloudy summer day in this famous classic.*

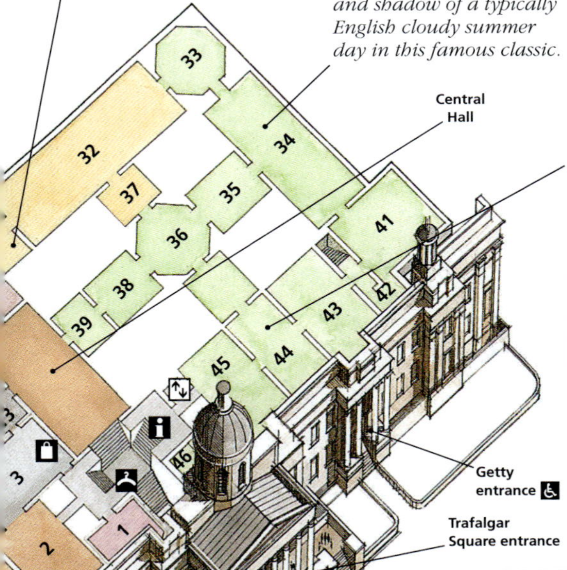

VISITORS' CHECKLIST

Trafalgar Sq WC2. **Map** 13 B3.
Tel 020-7747 2885. ⊖ Charing Cross, Leicester Sq, Piccadilly Circus. 🚌 3, 6, 9, 11, 12, 13, 15, 23, 24, 29, 88, 91, 139, 159, 176, 453.
🚆 Charing Cross. **Open** 10am– 6pm daily (9pm Fri). **Closed** Dec 24–26, Jan 1. 🚫 ♿ Sainsbury Wing and Getty entrances. 🅿
🏠 🛗 🍴 📷 ♿ Sainsbury Wing & temporary exhibitions.
Lectures, film presentations, exhibitions, special events.
www.nationalgallery.org.uk

Central Hall

Getty entrance ♿

Trafalgar Square entrance

At the Theater *(1876–7) Renoir was one of the greatest painters of the Impressionist movement. The theater was a popular subject among artists of the time.*

★ **The Leonardo Cartoon** *(c.1500) The genius of Leonardo da Vinci glows through this chalk drawing of the Virgin and Child with St. Anne and St. John the Baptist.*

STAR PAINTINGS

★ The Baptism of Christ by Piero della Francesca

★ The Leonardo Cartoon by Leonardo da Vinci

★ The Rokeby Venus by Diego Velázquez

★ The Ambassadors by Hans Holbein

★ The Hay Wain by John Constable

KEY TO FLOOR PLAN

- 13th- to 15th-century
- 16th-century
- 17th-century
- 18th- to early 20th-century
- Special exhibitions
- Nonexhibition space

★ **The Ambassadors**
The strange shape in the foreground of this Hans Holbein portrait (1533) is an anamorphic or distorted skull, a symbol of mortality.

Exploring the National Gallery

The National Gallery has over 2,300 paintings, most kept on permanent display. The collection ranges from early works by Cimabue, in the 13th century, to 19th-century Impressionists, but its particular strengths are in Dutch, early Renaissance Italian, and 17th-century Spanish painting. The bulk of the British collections are housed in Tate Britain *(see pp82–5)* while Tate Modern specializes in international modern art *(pp178–81)*.

The Adoration of The Kings (1564) by Pieter Brueghel the Elder

EARLY RENAISSANCE (1250–1500): ITALIAN AND NORTHERN PAINTING

Three lustrous panels from the *Maestà*, Duccio's great altarpiece in Siena cathedral, are among the earliest paintings here. Other Italian works of the period include his outstanding *Madonna*.

The fine *Wilton Diptych* portraying England's Richard II is probably by a French artist. It displays the lyrical elegance of the International Gothic style that swept Europe.

Italian masters of this style include Pisanello and Gentile da Fabriano, whose *Madonna* often hangs beside another, by Masaccio – both date from 1426. Also shown are works by Masaccio's pupil, Fra Filippo Lippi, as well as Botticelli and Uccello. Umbrian paintings include Piero della Francesca's *Nativity* and *Baptism*, and an excellent collection of Mantegna, Bellini, and other works from the Venetian and Ferrarese schools. Antonello da Messina's *St. Jerome in his Study* has been mistaken for a van Eyck; it is not hard to see why, when you compare it with van Eyck's *Arnolfini Portrait*. Important

Netherlandish pictures, including some by Rogier van der Weyden and his followers, are also here, in the Sainsbury Wing.

HIGH RENAISSANCE (1500–1600): ITALIAN, NETHERLANDISH, AND GERMAN PAINTING

Christ Mocked (1490–1500) by Hieronymus Bosch

Sebastiano del Piombo's *The Raising of Lazarus* was painted, with Michelangelo's assistance, to rival Raphael's great *Transfiguration*, which hangs in the Vatican in Rome.

These and other well-known names of the High (or Late) Renaissance are extremely well represented, often with massive works. Look out for Parmigianino's *Madonna and Child with Saints*, Leonardo da Vinci's charcoal cartoon of the *Virgin and Child* (a full-sized drawing used for copying as a painting), and his second version of the *Virgin of the Rocks*. There are also tender and amusing works by Piero di Cosimo, and several Titians, including *Bacchus and Ariadne* – which the public found too bright and garish when it was first cleaned by the gallery in the 1840s.

The Netherlandish and German collections are weaker. Even so, they include *The Ambassadors*, a fine double portrait by Holbein; and Altdorfer's superb *Christ Taking Leave of his Mother*, bought by the gallery in 1980. There is also an Hieronymus Bosch of *Christ Mocked* (sometimes known as *The Crowning with Thorns*), and an excellent Brueghel, *The Adoration of the Kings*.

The Annunciation (c. late 1450s) by Fra Filippo Lippi

THE SAINSBURY WING

Plans for the Sainsbury Wing, opened in 1991, provoked a storm of dissent. An incensed Prince Charles dubbed an early design "a monstrous carbuncle on the face of a much-loved friend." The final building, by Venturi, has drawn criticism from other quarters for being a derivative compromise.

Major changing exhibitions are held here. The wing houses ArtStart, an interactive touch-screen guide to the Collection (also available in the Espresso Bar).

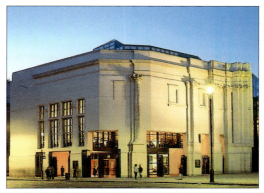

DUTCH, ITALIAN, FRENCH, AND SPANISH PAINTING (1600–1700)

The superb Dutch collection gives two entire rooms to Rembrandt. There are also works by Vermeer, Van Dyck (among them his equestrian portrait of King Charles I), and Rubens (including the popular *Chapeau de Paille*).

From Italy, the works of Carracci and Caravaggio are strongly represented, and Salvatore Rosa has a glowering self-portrait.

French works on show include a magnificent portrait of Cardinal Richelieu by Philippe de Champaigne. Claude's seascape, *The Embarkation of the Queen of Sheba,* hangs beside Turner's rival painting *Dido Building Carthage,* as Turner himself had instructed.

The Spanish school has works by Murillo, Velázquez, Zurbarán, and others.

***Young Woman Standing at a Virginal* (1670–72) by Jan Vermeer**

***The Scale of Love* (1715–18) by Jean-Antoine Watteau**

VENETIAN, FRENCH, AND ENGLISH PAINTING (1700–1800)

One of the gallery's most famous 18th-century works is Canaletto's *The Stonemason's Yard.* Other Venetians here are Longhi and Tiepolo.

The French collection includes Rococo masters such as Chardin, Watteau, and Boucher, as well as landscapists and portraitists.

Gainsborough's early work *Mr. and Mrs. Andrews* and *The Morning Walk* are favorites with visitors; his rival, Sir Joshua Reynolds, is represented by some of his most Classical work and by more informal portraits.

ENGLISH, FRENCH, AND GERMAN PAINTING (1800–1900)

The great age of 19th-century landscape painting is amply represented here, with fine works by Constable and Turner, including Constable's *The Hay-Wain* and Turner's *The Fighting Temeraire,* as well as works by the French artists Corot and Daubigny.

Of Romantic art, there is Géricault's vivid work, *Horse Frightened by Lightning,* and several interesting paintings by Delacroix. In contrast, the society portrait of *Mme Moitessier* by Ingres, though still Romantic, is more restrained and Classical.

Impressionists and other French avant-garde artists are well represented. Among the highlights are *Waterlilies* by Monet, Renoir's *At the Theater,* Van Gogh's *Sunflowers,* not to mention one of Rousseau's famous jungle scenes, *Surprised,* in which a tiger hunts explorers. In Seurat's *Bathers at Asnières* he did not originally use the pointillist technique he was later to invent, but subsequently reworked areas of the picture using dots of color.

***Sunflowers* (1888) by Vincent Van Gogh**

Chinatown 9

Streets around Gerrard St W1.
Map 13 A2. 🚇 *Leicester Sq,
Piccadilly Circus.*

There has been a Chinese
community in London since
the 19th century. Originally it
was concentrated around the
East End docks at Limehouse,
where the opium dens of Victorian melodrama were sited.
As the number of immigrants
increased in the 1950s, many
moved into Soho where they
created an ever-expanding
Chinatown. It contains scores
of restaurants, and mysterious
aroma-filled shops selling oriental produce. Three Chinese
arches straddle Gerrard Street,
where a vibrant, colorful
street festival, held in late
January, celebrates Chinese
New Year *(see p59)*.

Charing Cross Road 10

WC2. **Map** 13 B2. 🚇 *Leicester Sq.
See **Shops and Markets** pp318–19.*

**Antiquarian books from the
shops on Charing Cross Road**

The road is a mecca for booklovers, with a row of second-
hand bookstores south of
Cambridge Circus and, north of
these, a clutch of shops that
between them should be able
to supply just about any recent
volume. Visit the giants: huge
Foyle's and busy Waterstones,
and the smaller, specialist
shops: try Francis Edwards *(see
p330)* for travel and art and
Sportspages for sports. Sadly,
rent rises have put this unique
mix under threat. At the junction with New Oxford Street
rises the 1960s tower, Centre-
point. It lay empty for ten
years after it was built, its
owners finding this more
profitable than renting it out.

At the Palace Theatre in 1898

Palace Theatre 11

Shaftesbury Ave W1. **Map** 13 B2. **Tel
Box office** 0844-755 0016. 🚇
Leicester Sq. **Open** for performances
only. See **Entertainment** pp344–5.
www.palacetheatre.co.uk

Most West End theaters are
disappointingly unassertive.
This one, which dominates
the west side of Cambridge
Circus, is a splendid
exception, with its sparkling
terracotta exterior and opulent
furnishings. Completed as
an opera house in 1891, it
became a music hall the
following year. The ballerina
Anna Pavlova made her
London debut here in 1910.
Now the theater, owned by
Andrew Lloyd Webber whose
own musicals are all over
London, stages hit shows
such as *Spamalot*.

Soho Square 12

W1. **Map** 13 A1. 🚇 *Tottenham
Court Rd.*

Soon after it was laid out in
1681 this square enjoyed a
brief reign as the most fashionable address in London.
Originally it was called King
Square, after Charles II,
whose statue was erected in
the middle. The square went
out of fashion by the late 18th
century and is now surrounded by bland office buildings.
The mock-Tudor garden shed
in the center was added much
later in Victorian times.

Berwick Street Market 13

W1. **Map** 13 A1. 🚇 *Piccadilly
Circus.* **Open** 9am–6pm Mon–Sat.
See **Shops and Markets** p324.

There has been a market here
since the 1840s. Berwick
Street trader Jack Smith introduced grapefruit to London in
1890. Today this is the West
End's best street market, at its
cheeriest and most crowded
during at lunchtime. The
freshest and least expensive
produce for miles around is
to be had here. There are also
some interesting shops,
including Borovick's, which
sells extraordinary fabrics,
and a growing number of
cafés and restaurants. At its
southern end the street nar-
rows into an alley on which
Raymond's Revue Bar (the
comparatively respectable
face of Soho sleaze) has
presented its festival of
erotica since 1958.

Some of London's cheapest produce at Berwick Street Market

Carnaby Street ⓮

W1. **Map** 12 F2. 🚇 *Oxford Circus.*

During the 1960s this street was so much the hub of swinging London that the Oxford English Dictionary recognized the term "Carnaby Street" as meaning "fashionable clothing for young people." Today fashion stores can be found on nearby streets, such as Kingly Court and Fouberts Place.

Liberty ⓯

Regent St W1. **Map** 12 F2. 🚇 *Oxford Circus.* See *Shops and Markets p313.* **www**.liberty.co.uk

Arthur Lasenby Liberty opened his first shop, selling oriental

Liberty's mock-Tudor facade

silks, on Regent Street in 1875. Among his first customers were the artists Ruskin and Rossetti. Soon Liberty prints and designs, by artists such as William Morris, epitomized the Arts and Crafts movement of the late 19th and early 20th centuries. They are still fashionable today.

The present mock-Tudor building with its country-house feel dates from 1925, and was built specifically to house the store.

Today the shop maintains its strong links with crafts of all kinds, including potters, jewelers, and furniture designers.

Photographers' Gallery ⓰

16–18 Ramillies St W1. **Map** 12 F1. 🚇 *Oxford Circus.* **Open** 11am–6pm daily. 🖥 🖼 **www**.photonet.org.uk

Dedicated to photography, this gallery exhibits work from both new and more renowned artists, as well as putting on regular talks and events. The excellent bookstore also sells cameras and prints.

The Heart of Soho

Old Compton Street is Soho's Main Street. Its shops and restaurants reflect the variety of people who have lived in the area over the centuries. These include many great artists, writers, and musicians.

Maison Bertaux is known for producing delicious croissants and coffee and wonderful cakes as good as those found in Paris.

Ronnie Scott's opened in 1959, and nearly all the big names of jazz have played here *(see pp351–3).*

Bar Italia is a coffee shop situated under the room where John Logie Baird first demonstrated television in 1926. As a child, Mozart stayed next door with his family in 1764 and 1765.

The Coach and Horses pub has been a center of bohemian Soho since the 1950s and is still popular.

Algerian Coffee Stores is one of Soho's oldest shops. Delicious aromas of the world's coffees fill the shop.

Patisserie Valerie is a Hungarian-owned café serving delicious pastries *(see pp312–15).*

St. Anne's Church Tower is all that remains after a bomb destroyed the church in 1940.

The French House was frequented by Maurice Chevalier and General de Gaulle.

The Palace Theatre has hosted many successful musicals.

Street labels: WARDOUR STREET, DEAN STREET, FRITH STREET, GREEK STREET, OLD COMPTON STREET, MOOR ST, ROMILLY STREET

COVENT GARDEN AND THE STRAND

The open-air cafés, street enter-tainers, stylish shops, and markets make this area a magnet for visitors. At its center is the Piazza, site of a wholesale market until 1974. Since then, the Georgian and Victorian buildings here and in the surrounding streets have been converted into one of the city's liveliest districts. In medieval times the area was occupied by a convent garden that supplied Westminster Abbey with produce. Then in the 1630s, Inigo Jones laid out the

Piazza as London's first square, with its west side dominated by his St. Paul's Church.

The Piazza was commissioned as a residential development by the Earl of Bedford, owner of one of the mansions that lined the Strand. Before the Embankment was built, the Strand ran along the river.

Dried flowers from the Piazza

SIGHTS AT A GLANCE

Historic Streets and Buildings

The Piazza and Central Market **1**
Neal Street and Neal's Yard **7**
Savoy Hotel **12**
Somerset House **14**
Roman Bath **16**
Bush House **17**
Adelphi **20**
Charing Cross **21**

Museums and Galleries

London's Transport Museum **3**

Churches

St. Paul's Church **2**
Savoy Chapel **13**
St. Mary-le-Strand **15**

Monuments and Statues

Seven Dials **9**
Cleopatra's Needle **18**

Famous Theaters

Theatre Royal Drury Lane **5**
Royal Opera House **6**
Adelphi Theatre **11**
The London Coliseum **22**
Wyndham's Theatre **10**

Parks and Gardens

Victoria Embankment Gardens **19**

Historic Pubs and Shopping Arcades

Lamb and Flag **4**
Thomas Neal's **8**

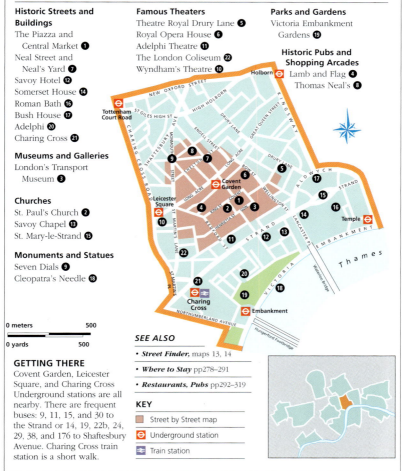

GETTING THERE

Covent Garden, Leicester Square, and Charing Cross Underground stations are all nearby. There are frequent buses: 9, 11, 15, and 30 to the Strand or 14, 19, 22b, 24, 29, 38, and 176 to Shaftesbury Avenue. Charing Cross train station is a short walk.

SEE ALSO

• **Street Finder,** maps 13, 14
• **Where to Stay** pp278–291
• **Restaurants, Pubs** pp292–319

KEY

Street by Street map
Underground station
Train station

0 meters   500
0 yards   500

◁ Enzo Piazotta's statue *The Young Dancer* (1988), opposite the Royal Opera House

Street by Street: Covent Garden

Once an area of decaying streets and
warehouses, Covent Garden came alive
only after dark when the fruit and
vegetable market traders went
about their business. Now it
is completely revitalized.
Day and night, visi-
tors, residents, and
street-entertainers
of every vocation
throng the Piazza,
much as they would
have done several
centuries ago.

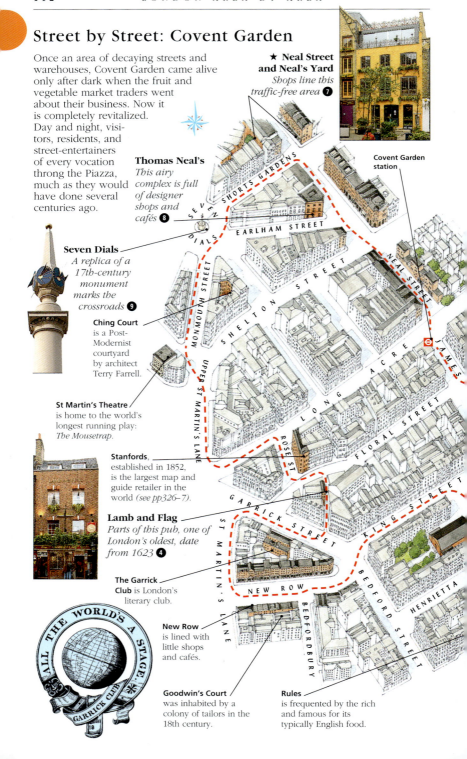

★ **Neal Street
and Neal's Yard**
*Shops line this
traffic-free area* ❼

**Covent Garden
station**

Thomas Neal's
*This airy
complex is full
of designer
shops and
cafés* ❽

Seven Dials
*A replica of a
17th-century
monument
marks the
crossroads* ❾

Ching Court
is a Post-
Modernist
courtyard
by architect
Terry Farrell.

St Martin's Theatre
is home to the world's
longest running play:
The Mousetrap.

Stanfords,
established in 1852,
is the largest map and
guide retailer in the
world *(see pp326–7).*

Lamb and Flag
*Parts of this pub, one of
London's oldest, date
from 1623* ❹

**The Garrick
Club** is London's
literary club.

New Row
is lined with
little shops
and cafés.

Goodwin's Court
was inhabited by a
colony of tailors in the
18th century.

Rules
is frequented by the rich
and famous for its
typically English food.

★ The Piazza and Central Market

Performers of all kinds – jugglers, clowns, acrobats, and musicians – entertain the crowds in the square ❶

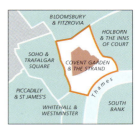

LOCATOR MAP
See Central London Map pp14–15

Royal Opera House

Most of the world's greatest singers and dancers have appeared on its stage ❻

Bow Street Police Station
housed London's first police force, the Bow Street Runners, in the 18th century. It closed in 1992.

★ Theatre Royal Drury Lane

A theater has stood on this site since 1663, making it London's oldest theater. The present theater was built in 1812. It is owned by composer Andrew Lloyd Webber and stages popular musicals ❺

Boswells, now a coffee house, is where Dr. Johnson first met his biographer, Boswell.

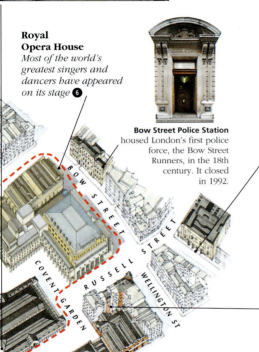

Jubilee Market
sells clothes and bric-à-brac.

★ London's Transport Museum

The history of the city's tube and buses is brought to life in this museum ❸

★ St Paul's Church

Despite appearances, Inigo Jones's church faces away from the Piazza – the entrance is through the churchyard ❷

STAR SIGHTS

- ★ The Piazza and Central Market
- ★ St Paul's Church
- ★ London's Transport Museum
- ★ Theatre Royal
- ★ Neal Street and Neal's Yard

KEY

– – –   Suggested route

0 meters   100

0 yards   100

The Piazza and Central Market ●

Covent Garden WC2. **Map** 13 C2.
🚇 *Covent Garden.* 🚶 *but cobbled streets.* ***Street performers*** *10am–dusk daily. See **Shops and Markets** p333.*

The 17th-century architect Inigo Jones originally planned this area to be an elegant residential square, modeled on the piazza at Livorno, northern Italy. Today the buildings on and around the Piazza are almost entirely Victorian. The covered central market was designed by Charles Fowler in 1833 for fruit and vegetable wholesalers, the glass and iron roof antici-pating the giant rail termini built later in the century – for instance, St. Pancras *(see p130)* and Waterloo *(see p191)*. It now makes a magnificent shell for an array of small shops selling designer clothes, books, arts, crafts, decorative items, and antiques, all surrounded by bustling market stalls that continue south in the neighboring Jubilee Hall, which was built in 1903.

The colonnaded Bedford Chambers, on the north side, give a hint of Inigo Jones's plan, although even they are not original: they were rebuilt and partially modified in 1879.

Street entertainment is a well-loved and now expected tra-dition of the area; in 1662, diarist Samuel Pepys wrote of watching a Punch and Judy show under the portico of St. Paul's Church.

West entrance to St. Paul's

St. Paul's Church ●

Bedford St WC2. **Map** 13 C2. ***Tel*** *020-7836 5221.* 🚇 *Covent Garden.* ***Open*** *8:30am–4:30pm Mon–Fri, 9am–1pm Sun.* 🕀 *11am Sun, 2nd Sun of the month 4pm evensong.* 🚶

Inigo Jones built this church (completed in 1633) with the altar at the west end, so as to allow his grand portico, with its two square and two round columns, to face east into the Piazza. Clerics objected to this unorthodox arrangement, and the altar was moved to its conventional position at the east end. Jones went ahead with his original exterior design. Thus the church is entered from the west, and the east portico is a fake door, used now as an impromptu stage for street entertainers. In 1795 the interior was destroyed by fire but was rebuilt in Jones's airy, uncomplicated style. Today the church is all that is left of Jones's original plan for the Piazza. St. Paul's has long been called "The Actors' Church" and plaques commem-orate distinguished men and women of the theater. A 17th-century carving by Grinling Gibbons, on the west screen, is a memorial to the architect.

Punch and Judy performer

London's Transport Museum ●

The Piazza WC2. **Map** 13 C2.
Tel *020-7379 6344 or 020-7565 7299 (24-hour info line).* 🚇 *Covent Garden.* ***Open*** *10am–6pm Sat–Thu, 11am–6pm Fri (last adm 5:15pm).*
Adm charge. 📷 🍴 🛍 🚶 ✉
book ahead. www.ltmuseum.co.uk

London's Transport Museum

You do not have to be a train spotter or a collector of bus numbers to enjoy this museum. The intriguing collection is housed in the picturesque Victorian Flower Market, which was built in 1872, and features public transportation from the past and present.

The history of London's transportation is in essence a social history of the capital. Bus, tram, and subway route patterns first reflected the city's growth and then pro-moted it: the northern and western suburbs began to develop only after their sub-way connections were built. The museum houses a fine collection of 20th-century commercial art. London's bus and train companies have been, and still are, prolific patrons of contemporary art-ists, and copies of some of the finest posters on display can be bought at the well-stocked museum shop. They include the innovative Art Deco designs of E. McKnight Kauffer, as well as work by renowned artists of the 1930s, such as Graham Sutherland and Paul Nash.

This museum is excellent for children. There are plenty of hands-on exhibits, and these include the opportunity for children to put themselves in the driver's seat of a London bus, or a train from the subway system.

A mid-18th-century view of the Piazza

Lamb and Flag ❹

33 Rose St WC2. **Map** 13 B2.
Tel 020-7497 9504. Covent
Garden, Leicester Sq. **Open** 11am–
11pm Mon–Sat, noon–10:30pm
Sun. See **Restaurants and
Pubs** p317.

There has been an inn here
since the 16th century, making the Lamb and Flag the
oldest tavern in Covent
Garden. Tucked away next
to a narrow alleyway linking
Garrick Street with Floral
Street, the cramped bars are
still largely unmodernized. A
plaque concerns satirist John
Dryden, attacked in the alley
outside in 1679. He was set
upon by hooligans sent by
Charles II to uphold the
honor of the Duchess of
Portsmouth, one of his
mistresses. Dryden had
lampooned her in some of
his verse. The upstairs bar is
also named after Dryden.
   The pub is popular with
both city center workers and
in-the-know tourists, who
spill out into the courtyard.

Theatre Royal Drury Lane ❺

Catherine St WC2. **Map** 13 C2. **Tel**
0844-412 2955. Covent Garden,
Holborn. **Open** for performances and
guided tours (phone to check). **Adm
charge**. See **Entertainment** p344.
www.theatreroyaldrurylane.co.uk

The first theater on this
site was built in 1663 as
one of only two venues
in London where drama
could legally be staged.
Nell Gwynne acted here.
Three of the theaters
built here since then
burned down, including
one designed by Sir
Christopher Wren (see
p47). The present one,
by Benjamin Wyatt, was
completed in 1812 and
has one of the city's largest auditoriums. In the
1800s it was famous for
pantomimes – now it
stages blockbuster musi-
cals. It is called the Theatre Royal Drury Lane
even though its entrance
is on Catherine Street.

The glass Floral Hall, part of the Royal Opera House

Royal Opera House ❻

Covent Garden WC2. **Map** 13 C2.
Tel 020-7304 4000. Covent
Garden. **Open** for performances and
guided tours (phone to check). See
Entertainment p348. 🔟
www.roh.org.uk

Built in 1732, the first theater
on this site staged more spo-
ken drama than music drama,
although many of Handel's
operas and oratorios were
premiered here. Like its
neighbor, the Theatre Royal
Drury Lane, it proved prone
to fire and was destroyed in
1808 and again in 1856. The
present opera house was
designed in 1858 by E. M.
Barry. John Flaxman's portico
frieze, depicting tragedy and
comedy, survived from
the previous building of
1809. The Opera House
has had both high and
low points during its history. In 1892, the first
British performance of
Wagner's Ring was con-
ducted here by Gustav
Mahler. Later, during
World War I, the build-
ing was used as a store-
house by the govern-
ment. Today, it is home
to the Royal Opera and
Royal Ballet Companies
– the best tickets can
cost over £100. An
extensive renovation
project, completed in
1999, added a second
auditorium, along with
rehearsal rooms for its

Royal Opera and Royal Ballet
companies are available, and once a
month visitors can watch
the Royal Ballet attending
its daily class.

Neal Street and Neal's Yard ❼

Covent Garden WC2. **Map** 13 B1.
Covent Garden. See **Shops and
Markets** pp322–3.

A specialist shop on Neal Street

In this attractive street, former
warehouses from the 19th
century can be identified by
the hoisting mechanisms high
on their exterior walls. The
buildings have been converted into a number of shops,
art galleries, and restaurants.
Off Neal Street in Short's
Gardens is Neal's Yard Dairy,
one of London's best cheese
shops, which also sells
delicious breads. Brainchild
of the late Nicholas Saunders,
it, and Neal's Yard itself,
remain an oasis of alternative
values amid the growing
commercialism of the area.

THEATRE ROYAL

St. Mary-le-Strand ⓑ

Strand WC2. **Map** 14 D2. *Tel 020-7836 3126.* ⊖ *Temple.* **Open** 11am–4pm Tue–Sat, 10am–1pm Sun. ✝ 11am Sun, 1:05pm Thu. ⊙ ⬛ www.stmarylestrand.org

Now beached on a road island at the east end of the Strand, this pleasing church was consecrated in 1724. It was the first public building by James Gibbs, who designed St.-Martin-in-the-Fields *(see p102)*. Gibbs was influenced by Christopher Wren, but the exuberant external decorative detail here was inspired by the Baroque churches of Rome, where Gibbs studied. Its multi-arched tower is layered like a wedding cake, and culminates in a cupola and lantern. St.-Mary-le-Strand is now the official church of the Women's Royal Naval Service.

St.-Mary-le-Strand

Roman Bath ⓰

5 Strand Lane WC2. **Map** 14 D2. *Tel 020-7641 5264.* ⊖ *Temple, Embankment, Charing Cross.* **Open** Apr–Sep: 1–5pm most Wed; phone to book. ♿ via Temple Pl.

This little bath and its surround may be seen from a full-length window on Surrey Street, by pressing a light switch on the outside wall. It is almost certainly not Roman, for there is no other evidence

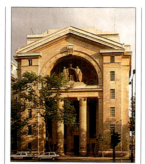

Bush House from Kingsway

of Roman habitation in the immediate area. It is more likely to have been part of Arundel House, one of several palaces which stood on the Strand from Tudor times until the 17th century, when they were demolished for new building. In the 19th century the bath was open to the public for cold plunges, believed to be healthy.

Bush House ⓱

Aldwych WC2. **Map** 14 D2. ⊖ *Temple, Holborn.* **Not open** to the public.

Situated at the center of the Aldwych crescent, this Neo-Classical building was first designed as manufacturers' showrooms by an American, Irving T. Bush, and completed in 1935. It appears especially imposing when viewed from Kingsway, its dramatic north entrance graced with various statues symbolizing Anglo-American relations. Since 1940 it has been used as radio studios, and is the headquarters of the BBC World Service, which is due to be relocated to West London within a few years.

Cleopatra's Needle ⓲

Embankment WC2. **Map** 13 C3. ⊖ *Embankment, Charing Cross.*

Erected in Heliopolis in about 1500 BC, this incongruous pink granite monument is much older than London itself. Its inscriptions celebrate the deeds of the pharaohs of ancient Egypt. It was presented to Britain by the then Viceroy of Egypt, Mohammed Ali, in 1819 and erected in 1878, shortly after the Embankment was built. It has a twin in New York's Central Park, behind the Metropolitan Museum of Art. The bronze sphinxes, added in 1882, are not Egyptian.

In its base is a Victorian time capsule of artifacts of the day, such as the day's newspapers, a rail timetable, and photographs of 12 contemporary beauties.

Victoria Embankment Gardens ⓳

WC2. **Map** 13 C3. ⊖ *Embankment, Charing Cross.* **Open** 7:30am–dusk daily. ♿ ⬛

This narrow sliver of a public park, created when the Embankment was built, boasts well-maintained flower beds, a clutch of statues of British worthies (including the Scottish poet Robert Burns) and, in summer, a season of concerts. Its main historical feature is the water gate at its northwest corner, which was built as a triumphal entry to the Thames for the Duke of Buckingham in 1626. It is a relic of York House, which used to stand on this site and was the home first of the Archbishops of York and then of the Duke. It is still in its original position and although the water used to lap against it, because of the Thames's Embankment the gate is now a good 330 ft (100 m) from the river's edge.

Victoria Embankment Gardens

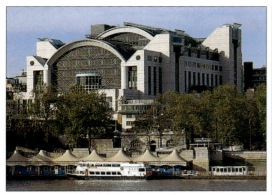

The shopping and office block above Charing Cross

Adelphi ⑳

Strand WC2. **Map** 13 C3. **Tel** 020-7451 6845. ⊖ *Embankment, Charing Cross.* **Not open** to the public.

John Adam Street, Adelphi

The name Adelphi is from *adelphoi*, the Greek word for brothers – this area was once an elegant riverside residential development designed in 1772 by brothers Robert and John Adam. The name now refers to the Art Deco office block, its entrance adorned with N. A. Trent's heroic reliefs of workers at toil, which in 1938 replaced the Adams' much admired Palladian-style apartment complex. That destruction is now viewed as one of the worst acts of 20th-century official vandalism. A number of the Adams' surrounding buildings survive, notably No. 8, the ornate Royal Society for the Encouragement of Arts, Manufactures & Commerce

just opposite (open first Sunday of the month, 10am–12:30pm, not January). In the same exuberant idiom are Nos. 1–4 Robert Street, where Robert Adam lived for a time, and No. 7 Adam Street.

Charing Cross ㉑

Strand WC2. **Map** 13 C3. ⊖ *Charing Cross, Embankment.*

The name derives from the last of the 12 crosses erected by Edward I to mark the funeral route in 1290 of his wife, Eleanor of Castile, from Nottinghamshire to Westminster Abbey. Today a 19th-century replica stands in the forecourt of Charing Cross station. Both the cross and the Charing Cross Hotel, built into the station frontage, were designed in 1863 by E. M. Barry, architect of the Royal Opera House (*see p115*).

Above the station platforms has risen an assertive shopping center and office block, completed in 1991. Designed by Terry Farrell it resembles a giant ocean liner, with portholes looking on to Villiers Street. The building is best seen from the river, where it dominates its neighbors. The railway arches at the rear of the station

have been modernized as a suite of small shops and cafés, as well as a venue for the Players Theatre, the last repository of Victorian music hall entertainment.

The London Coliseum ㉒

St. Martin's Lane WC2. **Map** 13 B3. **Tel** 0871-911 0200. ⊖ *Leicester Sq, Charing Cross.* **Open** performances ♿ 🖥 🔊 **Lectures**. See **Entertainment** *pp348–9*. www.eno.org

London's largest theater and one of its most elaborate, this flamboyant building, topped with a large globe, was designed in 1904 by Frank Matcham and was equipped with London's first revolving stage. It was also the first theater in Europe to have elevators. A former variety house, today it is the home of the English National Opera, and well worth visiting, if only for the Edwardian interior with its gilded cherubs and heavy purple curtains. In 2003, the original glass roof was restored, providing dramatic views over Trafalgar Square.

London Coliseum

BLOOMSBURY AND FITZROVIA

Since the beginning of the 20th century, Bloomsbury and Fitzrovia have been synonymous with literature, art, and learning. The Bloomsbury Group of writers and artists were active from the early 1900s until the 1930s; the name Fitzrovia was invented by writers such as Dylan

Carving in Russell Square

Thomas who drank in the Fitzroy Tavern. Bloomsbury still boasts the University of London, the British Museum, and many fine Georgian squares. But it is now also noted for its Charlotte Street restaurants and the furniture and competitively priced electrical stores lining Tottenham Court Road.

SIGHTS AT A GLANCE

Historic Streets and Buildings
Bloomsbury Square ❷
Russell Square ❹
Queen Square ❺
British Library ❽
St. Pancras International ❾
Woburn Walk ⓫
Fitzroy Square ⓭
Charlotte Street ⓯

Museums
British Museum pp126–9 ❶
Charles Dickens Museum ❻

Foundling Museum ❼
Wellcome Collection ⓬
Pollock's Toy Museum ⓰

Churches
St. George's, Bloomsbury ❸
St. Pancras Parish Church ❿

Pubs
Fitzroy Tavern ⓮

SEE ALSO
• ***Street Finder,*** maps 4, 5, 6, 13

• ***Where to Stay*** pp278–291

• ***Restaurants, Pubs*** pp292–319

KEY

▦	Street by Street map
Ⓤ	Underground station
▤	Train station

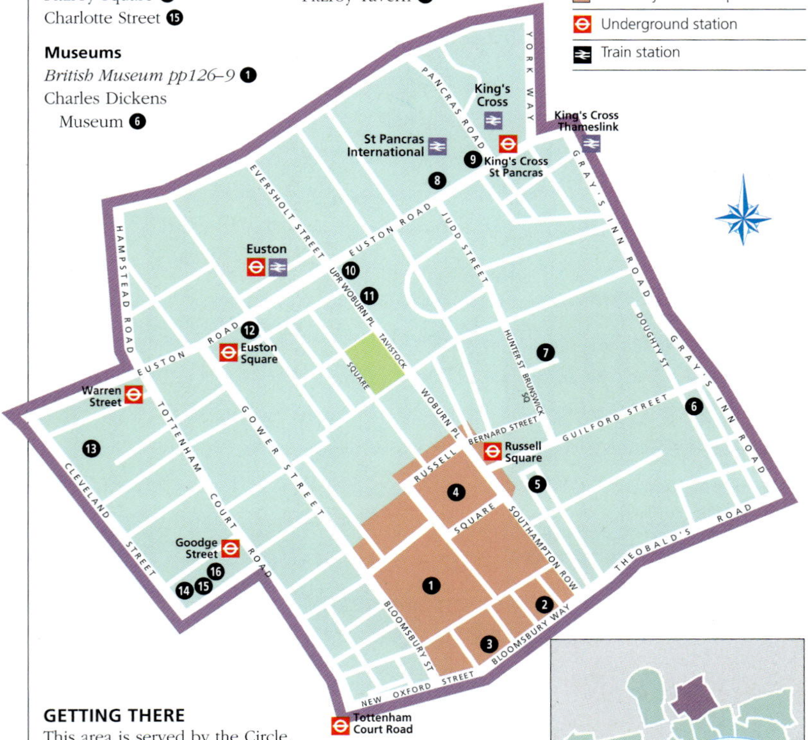

(map of Bloomsbury and Fitzrovia area showing numbered sights, underground and train stations, scale: 0 meters 500, 0 yards 500)

King's Cross
King's Cross Thameslink
St Pancras International
King's Cross St Pancras
Euston
Euston Square
Warren Street
Russell Square
Goodge Street
Tottenham Court Road

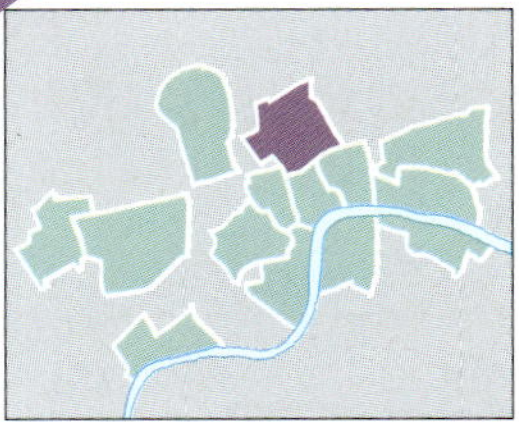

GETTING THERE
This area is served by the Circle, Northern, Piccadilly, Victoria, and Central lines. Useful buses include Nos. 8, 25, 30, 73, and 98. Major railway stations are at Euston, St. Pancras and King's Cross.

◁ **A grand Georgian house in Bedford Square**

Street by Street: Bloomsbury

The British Museum domi-
nates Bloomsbury. Its ear-
nestly intellectual atmo-
sphere spills over into the
surrounding streets, and to
its north lies the main cam-
pus of London University.
The area has been home
to writers and artists, and
is a traditional center of
the book trade. Most of
the publishers have left,
but there are still many
bookstores around.

The Senate House (1932) is
the administrative
headquarters of
the University of
London. It holds a
priceless library.

Bedford Square is one of
London's most complete
Georgian squares. Its
uniform doorways are
fringed in artificial stone.

★ British Museum
*Designed in the mid-19th century, it
is extremely popular and attracts
some five million visitors a year* ➊

STAR SIGHTS

★ British Museum

★ Russell Square

KEY

– – –   Suggested route

0 meters   100

0 yards   100

Museum Street is lined with
small cafés and shops selling
old books, prints, and antiques.

Pizza Express occupies a
charming and little-altered
Victorian dairy.

RUSSELL SQUARE

MALET STREET

GOWER ST

MONTAGUE PLACE

BLOOMSBURY STREET

GREAT MUSEUM

COPTIC ST

LITTL

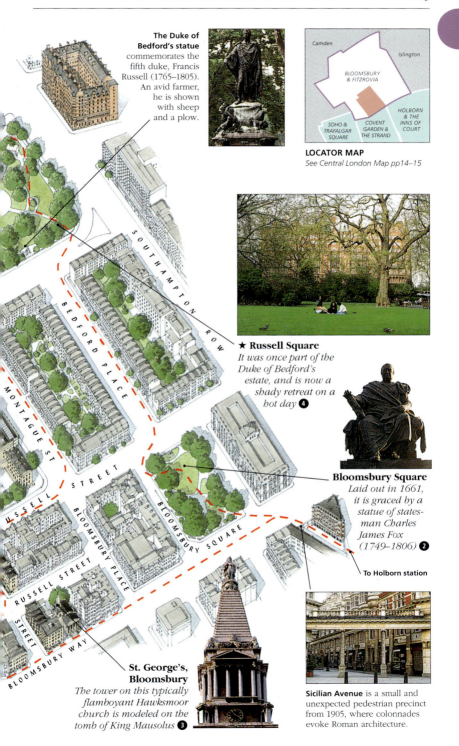

The Duke of Bedford's statue commemorates the fifth duke, Francis Russell (1765–1805). An avid farmer, he is shown with sheep and a plow.

LOCATOR MAP
See Central London Map pp14–15

★ **Russell Square**
It was once part of the Duke of Bedford's estate, and is now a shady retreat on a hot day ❹

Bloomsbury Square
Laid out in 1661, it is graced by a statue of states-man Charles James Fox (1749–1806) ❷

To Holborn station

St. George's, Bloomsbury
The tower on this typically flamboyant Hawksmoor church is modeled on the tomb of King Mausolus ❸

Sicilian Avenue is a small and unexpected pedestrian precinct from 1905, where colonnades evoke Roman architecture.

British Museum ❶

See pp126–9.

Bloomsbury Square ❷

WC1. **Map** 5 C5. *Holborn.*

This is the oldest of the Bloomsbury squares. It was laid out in 1661 by the Earl of Southampton, who owned the land. None of the original buildings survives and its shaded garden is encircled by a busy one-way traffic system. (Unusually for central London, you can nearly always find a space in the parking lot under the square.)

The square has had many famous residents; a plaque commemorates members of the literary and artistic Bloomsbury Group, who lived in the area during the early years of the last century. The group included novelist Virginia Woolf, biographer Lytton Strachey, and artists Vanessa Bell, Duncan Grant, and Dora Carrington. Look out for their individual plaques throughout the area.

A plaque commemorating famous Bloomsbury residents

St. George's, Bloomsbury ❸

Bloomsbury Way WC1. **Map** 13 B1. ***Tel*** *020-7242 1979. Holborn, Tottenham Court Rd, Russell Square.* ***Open*** *1–4pm daily (times may vary – call to check). 1:10pm Wed & Fri, 10:30am Sun.* ***Recitals.*** **www**.stgeorgesbloomsbury.org.uk

A slightly eccentric church, St. George's was designed by Nicholas Hawksmoor, Wren's pupil, and completed in 1730.

The flamboyant Russell Hotel on Russell Square

It was built as a place of worship for the prosperous residents of newly-developed, fashionable Bloomsbury. The layered tower, modeled on the tomb of King Mausolus (the original Mausoleum in Turkey) and topped by a statue of George I, was for a long time an object of derision – the king was thought to be presented too heroically. In 1913, the funeral of Emily Davison, the suffragette who threw herself under King George V's horse, was held here.

Russell Square ❹

WC1. **Map** 5 B5. *Russell Sq.* ***Open*** *7:30am–10pm daily.*

One of London's largest squares, Russell Square is a lively place, with a fountain, café, and traffic roaring around its perimeter. The east side boasts perhaps the best of the Victorian grand hotels to survive in the capital. Charles Doll's Russell Hotel, which was opened in 1900, is a wondrous confection of red terracotta, with colonnaded balconies and prancing cherubs beneath the main columns. The exuberance is continued in the lobby, faced with marble of many colors.

Poet T. S. Eliot worked at the west corner of the square, from 1925 until 1965, in what were the offices of publishers Faber and Faber.

Queen Square ❺

WC1. **Map** 5 C5. *Russell Sq.*

In spite of being named after Queen Anne, this square contains a statue of Queen Charlotte. Her husband, George III, stayed at the house of a doctor here when he became ill with the hereditary disease that drove him mad before his death in 1820. Originally, the north side of the square was left open so that inhabitants had a clear view of Hampstead and Highgate. Today the square is almost completely surrounded by hospital buildings, with early Georgian houses on the west side.

Queen Charlotte's statue in Queen Square

Charles Dickens Museum 6

48 Doughty St WC1. **Map** 6 D4. **Tel** 020-7405 2127. ☻ *Chancery Lane, Russell Sq.* **Open** *10am–5pm daily (last adm: 4:30pm).* **Adm charge.** ☒ *first floor.* ⊘ ☐ **www.**dickensmuseum.com

The novelist Charles Dickens lived in this early 19th-century terraced house for three of his most productive years (from 1837 to 1839). The popular works *Oliver Twist* and *Nicholas Nickleby* were entirely written here, and *Pickwick Papers* was finished. Although Dickens had many London homes throughout his lifetime, this is the only one to have survived. In 1923 it was acquired by the Dickens Fellowship and it is now a well-conceived museum with some of the principal rooms laid out exactly as they were in Dickens's time. Others have been adapted to display a varied collection of articles associated with him, including papers, portraits, and furniture taken from his other homes as well as first editions of many of his best-known works.

The completion of a £3 million restoration project is planned to coincide with the bicentenary of Dickens' birth, in 2012.

Nautical publisher's trade sign, Dickens Museum

Foundling Museum 7

40 Brunswick Square WC1. **Map** 5 C4. **Tel** 020-7841 3600. ☻ *Russell Square.* **Open** *10am–5pm Tue–Sat, 11am–5pm Sun.* **Closed** *Jan 1, Dec 24–26 & 31.* **Adm charge.** ⊘ ☒ ☐ *book ahead.* ☐ ☐ **Coram's Fields** *Guilford St WC1.* **Open** *9am–dusk.* **www.**foundling museum.org.uk

In 1722, Captain Thomas Coram, a retired sailor and shipbuilder recently returned from the Americas, vowed to

Portrait of Captain Coram (1740) by **William Hogarth**

establish a refuge for abandoned children. Horrified by the poverty on London streets, Coram was determined to alter the fate of the city's foundlings by housing and educating them and placing them in private homes. Assisted by his friend, artist William Hogarth, Coram worked tirelessly to raise funds. Finally in 1739, after George II's petitioning, he was granted a Royal Charter to establish a Foundling Hospital. Hogarth donated numerous paintings to the hospital, other artists following suit, effectively creating the first art gallery in Britain. The wealthy were encouraged to view the art and the children at the hospital, in the hope that they would donate.

The original hospital located at the end of Lambs Conduit Street was demolished in the 1920s, but the interiors of two of the 18th-century rooms were saved and relocated to 40 Brunswick Square, the museum's current location. On the first floor, the story of the many children who were cared for in the Foundling Hospital is told. The nationally important collection of 18th-century paintings, sculpture, furniture, and interiors is displayed on the second floor.

Adjacent to the museum,

with its entrance on Guilford Street, is **Coram's Fields**, a central London playground highly popular with children and a convenient pace-changer for families visiting the museums. Dogs are not allowed, and all adults must be accompanied by children.

British Library 8

96 Euston Rd NW1. **Map** 5 B3. **Tel** 0843-208 1144. ☻ *King's Cross St Pancras.* **Open** *9:30am–6pm Mon–Fri (8pm Tue), 9:30am–5pm Sat, 11am–5pm Sun.* **Regular events.** ☒ ⊘ ☐ ☐ ☐ **www.**bl.uk

London's most important building from the late 20th century houses the national collection of books, manuscripts, and maps, as well as the British Library Sound Archive. Designed in red brick by Sir Colin St. John Wilson, it opened in 1997 after nearly 20 years under construction, involving controversial cost overruns, but is now widely admired.

A copy of nearly every printed book in the United Kingdom is held here – more than 16 million – and can be consulted by those with a reader's ticket. There are also exhibition galleries open to all. Visitors may view some of the Library's most precious items, including the Lindisfarne Gospels, with the Turning the Pages system that shows each page on a monitor. Other volumes include a Gutenberg Bible and Shakespeare's First Folio. Running through six floors is a spectacular glass tower holding King George III's library.

Page from the Lindisfarne Gospels

British Museum ❶

The innovatively designed Great Court

The oldest public museum in the world, the British Museum was established in 1753 to house the collections of the physician Sir Hans Sloane (1660–1753), who also helped create the Chelsea Physic Garden *(see p197)*. Sloane's artifacts have been added to by gifts and purchases from all over the world, and the museum now contains innumerable items stretching from the present day to prehistory. Robert Smirke designed the main part of the building (1823–50), but the architectural highlight is Norman Foster's Great Court, with the world-famous Reading Room at its center.

★ Egyptian Mummies
The ancient Egyptians preserved their dead in expectation of an afterlife. Animals that were believed to have sacred powers were also often mummified. This cat comes from Abydos on the Nile and dates from about 30 BC.

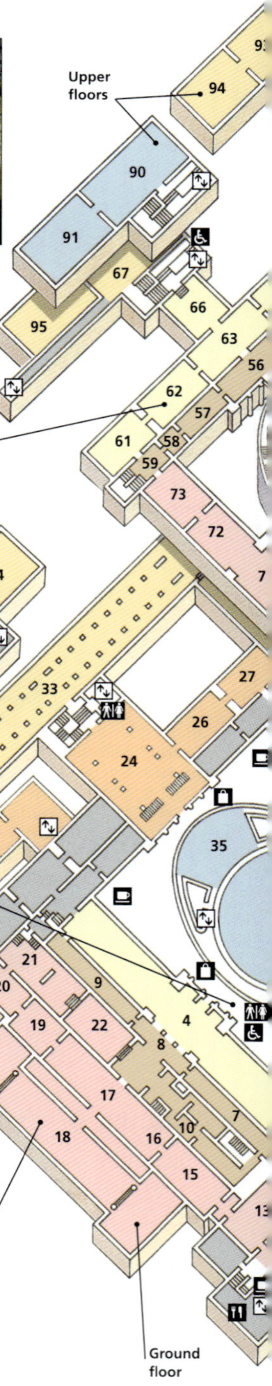

Numerous large-scale sculptures are featured in the Great Court.

Upper floors

94
90
91
95
67
66
63
56
62
57
61 58
59
73
72
7

Montague Place entrance

34
33
27
26
24
35

Ground floor

Lower floor

25
21
20
9
19 22
4
78 77
17
18 16
15
13

KEY TO FLOORPLAN

- ☐ Asia
- ☐ Enlightenment
- ☐ Coins and medals
- ☐ Greece and Rome
- ☐ Egypt
- ☐ Middle East
- ☐ Europe
- ☐ Temporary exhibitions
- ☐ Non-gallery space
- ☐ Africa, Oceania, and the Americas

Lower floor

Ground floor

★ Parthenon Sculptures
These reliefs were brought to England by Lord Elgin from the Parthenon in Athens. The British government purchased them from him in 1816.

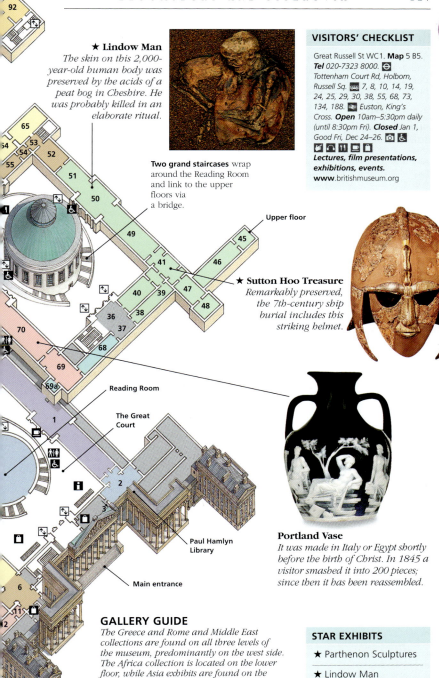

★ Lindow Man
The skin on this 2,000-year-old human body was preserved by the acids of a peat bog in Cheshire. He was probably killed in an elaborate ritual.

Two grand staircases wrap around the Reading Room and link to the upper floors via a bridge.

Upper floor

★ Sutton Hoo Treasure
Remarkably preserved, the 7th-century ship burial includes this striking helmet.

Reading Room

The Great Court

Paul Hamlyn Library

Main entrance

Portland Vase
It was made in Italy or Egypt shortly before the birth of Christ. In 1845 a visitor smashed it into 200 pieces; since then it has been reassembled.

VISITORS' CHECKLIST

Great Russell St WC1. **Map** 5 B5. **Tel** 020-7323 8000. Tottenham Court Rd, Holborn, Russell Sq. 7, 8, 10, 14, 19, 24, 25, 29, 30, 38, 55, 68, 73, 134, 188. Euston, King's Cross. **Open** 10am–5:30pm daily (until 8:30pm Fri). **Closed** Jan 1, Good Fri, Dec 24–26. *Lectures, film presentations, exhibitions, events.* www.britishmuseum.org

GALLERY GUIDE
The Greece and Rome and Middle East collections are found on all three levels of the museum, predominantly on the west side. The Africa collection is located on the lower floor, while Asia exhibits are found on the main and upper floors on the north side of the Museum. The Americas collection is located in the northeast corner of the main floor. Egyptian artifacts are found west of the Great Court and on the upper floors.

STAR EXHIBITS

★ Parthenon Sculptures

★ Lindow Man

★ Egyptian Mummies

★ Sutton Hoo Treasure

Exploring the British Museum's Collections

The Museum's immense hoard of treasure spans two million years of history and culture. The 94 galleries, which stretch 2.5 miles (4 km), cover civilizations from ancient Egypt and Assyria to modern Japan.

Ornamental detail from a Sumerian queen's lyre

PREHISTORIC AND ROMAN BRITAIN

1st-century BC bronze helmet dredged up from the Thames

Relics of prehistoric Britain are on display in six separate galleries. The most impressive items include the gold "Mold Cape," a ceremonial bronze-age cape found in Wales; an antlered headdress worn by hunter-gatherers some 9,000 years ago; and "Lindow Man," a 1st-century AD sacrificial victim who lay preserved in a bog until 1984. Some superb Celtic metalwork is also on show, alongside the silver Mildenhall Treasure and other Roman pieces. The Hinton St. Mary mosaic (4th century AD) features a roundel containing the earliest known British depiction of Christ.

EUROPE

The spectacular Sutton Hoo ship treasure, the burial hoard of a 7th-century Anglo-Saxon king, is on display in Room 41. This superb find, made in 1939, revolutionized our understanding of Anglo-Saxon life and ritual. The artifacts include a helmet and shield, Celtic hanging bowls, the remains of a lyre, and gold and garnet jewelry.

Adjacent galleries contain a collection of clocks, watches, and scientific instruments. Some exquisite timepieces are on view, including a 400-year-old clock from Prague, designed as a model galleon; in its day it pitched, played music, and even fired a cannon. Also nearby are the famous 12th-century Lewis chessmen, and a gallery housing Baron Ferdinand Rothschild's (1839–98) remarkably varied treasures.

The Museum's modern collection includes some Wedgwood pottery, glassware, and a series of Russian revolutionary plates.

Gilded brass late-16th-century ship clock from Prague

ANCIENT NEAR EAST

There are numerous galleries devoted to the Western Asian collections, covering 7,000 years of history. The most famous items are the 7th-century BC Assyrian reliefs from King Ashurbanipal's palace at Nineveh, but of equal interest are two large human-headed bulls from 7th-century BC Khorsabad, and an inscribed Black Obelisk of Assyrian King Shalmaneser III. The upper floors contain pieces from ancient Sumeria, part of the Oxus Treasure (which lay buried for over 2,000 years), and the Museum's collection of clay cuneiform tablets. The earliest of these are inscribed with the oldest known pictographs (c.3300 BC). Also of interest is a skull discovered in Jericho in the 1950s; augmented with shells and lime plaster, the skull belonged to a hunter who lived in the area some 7,000 years ago.

EGYPT

In Room 4 are Egyptian sculptures. These include a fine red granite head of a king, thought to depict Amenophis III, and a colossal statue of King Rameses II. Also on show is the Rosetta Stone, used by Jean-François Champollion (1790–1832) as a primer for deciphering Egyptian hieroglyphs. An extraordinary array of mummies, jewelry, and Coptic art can also be found upstairs. The various instruments that were used by embalmers to preserve bodies before they were entombed are all displayed. Room 61 houses paintings from the lost tomb-chapel of Nebamun.

Part of a colossal granite statue of Rameses II, the 13th-century BC Egyptian monarch

GREECE AND ROME

The Greek and Roman collections include the museum's most famous treasure, the Parthenon sculptures. These 5th-century BC reliefs were once part of a marble frieze that decorated the Parthenon, Athena's temple on the Acropolis in Athens. Much of it was ruined in battle in 1687, and most of what survived was removed between 1801 and 1804 by the British diplomat Lord Elgin, and sold to the British nation. Other highlights include the Nereid Monument

Ancient Greek vase illustrating the mythical hero Hercules's fight with a bull

and sculptures and friezes from the Mausoleum at Halicarnassus. The beautiful 1st-century BC cameo-glass Portland Vase is located in the Roman Empire section.

ASIA

The Chinese collection boasts fine porcelain and ancient Shang bronzes (c.1500–1050 BC). Particularly impressive are the ceremonial ancient Chinese bronze vessels, with their enigmatic animal-head shapes.

The fine Chinese ceramics range from delicate tea bowls to a model pond that is almost a thousand years old. In the Sir Percival David gallery the Chinese ceramics date from the 10th to early 20th centuries.

Adjacent to these is one of the finest collections of Asian religious sculpture outside India. A major highlight is an assortment of sculpted reliefs, which once covered the walls of the Buddhist temple at Amaravati, and which recount stories from the life of the Buddha. A Korean section contains some gigantic works of Buddhist art.

The museum's collection of Islamic art, including a

Statue of the Hindu god Shiva as Nataraja, or Lord of the Dance (11th century AD)

jade terrapin found in a water tank, can be found in Room 34. Rooms 92 to 94 house the Japanese galleries, with a Classical teahouse in Room 92.

AFRICA

An interesting collection of African sculptures, textiles, and graphic art can also be found in Room 25 on the lower floor of the museum. Famous bronzes from the Kingdom of Benin stand alongside modern African prints, paintings, drawings, and colorful fabrics.

THE GREAT COURT AND THE READING ROOM

Surrounding the Reading Room of the former British Library, the £100-million Great Court opened to coincide with the new millennium. Designed by Sir Norman Foster, the Court is covered by a wide-span, lightweight roof, creating London's first indoor public square. The Reading Room has been restored to its original design, so visitors can sample the atmosphere which Karl Marx, Mahatma Gandhi, and George

Bernard Shaw found so agreeable. From the outside, however, it is scarcely recognizable; it is housed in a multilevel construction that partly supports the roof, and which also contains a Centre for Education, temporary exhibition galleries, bookstores, cafés, and restaurants. Part of the Reading Room also serves as a study suite where those wishing to learn more about the Museum's collections have access to information.

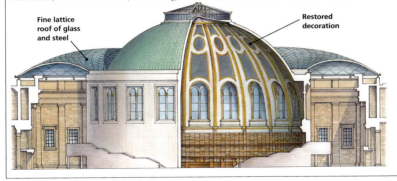

Fine lattice roof of glass and steel

Restored decoration

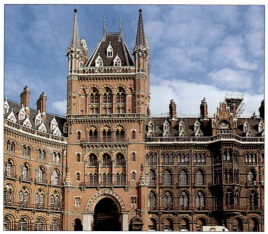
The massive St Pancras Renaissance Hotel above St. Pancras Station

St. Pancras International ❾

Euston Rd NW1. **Map** 5 B2.
Tel 020-7843 7688. ⊖ King's Cross,
St. Pancras. **Open** 5am–11pm daily.
Closed Dec 25. See **Getting to
London** pp372–3.
www.stpancras.com

St. Pancras – the London
terminal for Eurostar services
to continental Europe – is
easily the most spectacular of
the three rail termini along
Euston Road, thanks to its
extravagant frontage, in red-
brick gingerbread Gothic, of
the former Midland Grand
Hotel, opened in 1874 as one
of the most sumptuous hotels
of its time. By 1935 it was too
expensive to run and became
office space. Threatened
with demolition in the 1960s,

Figures on St. Pancras Church

the poet John Betjeman
campaigned to save it (there
is a statue of him on the upper
level). Abandoned in the early
1980s, it has been lavishly
restored as a 5-star hotel, plus
apartments and penthouses.

St. Pancras Parish Church ❿

Euston Rd NW1. **Map** 5 B3. **Tel** 020-
7388 1461. ⊖ Euston. **Open** Mon–
Fri (phone to check). ✝ 8am, 10am
Sun. ♿ **Recitals** 1:15pm Mon–Thu,
evensong 6pm Sun. **www**.
stpancraschurch.org

This is a stately Greek revival
church of 1822 by William
Inwood and his son Henry,
both great enthusiasts for
Athenian architecture. The
design is based on the
Erectheum on the Acropolis
in Athens, and even the
wooden pulpit stands on
miniature Ionic columns of
its own. The long, galleried
interior has a dramatic
severity appropriate to the
church's style. The female
figures on the northern outer
wall were originally taller
than they are now; a chunk
had to be taken out of the
middle of each to make them
fit under the roof they were
meant to be supporting.
    The church hosts a festival
of contemporary church music
in May, and art exhibitions are
sometimes held in the crypt.

Woburn Walk ⓫

WC1. **Map** 5 B4. ⊖ Euston,
Euston Sq.

A well-restored street of bow-
fronted shops, it was
designed by Thomas Cubitt in
1822. The high sidewalk on
the east side was to protect
shop fronts from the mud
thrown up by carriages. The
Irish poet W. B. Yeats lived at
No. 5 from 1895 until 1919.

Wellcome Collection ⓬

183 Euston Rd NW1. **Map** 5 A4.
Tel 020-7611 2222. ⊖ Euston,
King's Cross, Warren St. **Open**
10am–6pm Tue–Sat (to 10pm Thu),
11am–6pm Sun, noon–6pm public
hols. **Closed** Dec 24–26. ♿ ▣ ▣ ▣
www.wellcomecollection.org

Sir Henry Wellcome was a
pharmacist, entrepreneur,
and collector. His passionate
interest in medicine and its
history, as well as ethnography
and archeology, led him to
gather more than one million
objects from around the
world. Wellcome Collection is
a £30-million public venue
used to house his vast
collection as well as explore
the connections between
medicine, art, and the human
condition through events
and exhibitions.
    Exhibits range from the
bizarre to the beautiful, the
ancient to the futuristic. More
than 900 objects are on
permanent display, including
a used guillotine blade and
Napoleon's toothbrush.
Contemporary works include
a DNA sequencing robot and a
sculpture exploring HIV by
Mark Quinn. The Wellcome
library, on the upper floors,
is the world's largest devoted
to the history of medicine.

Fitzroy Square ⓭

W1. **Map** 4 F4. ⊖ Warren St,
Great Portland St.

Designed by Robert Adam in
1794, the square's south and
east sides survive in their
original form, in dignified

Portland stone. Blue plaques record the homes of many artists, writers, and statesmen: George Bernard Shaw and Virginia Woolf both lived at No. 29 – although not at the same time. Shaw gave money to the artist Roger Fry to establish the Omega workshop at No. 33 in 1913. Here young artists were paid a fixed wage to produce Post-Impressionist furniture, pottery, carpets, and paintings for sale to the public.

No. 29 Fitzroy Square

Fitzroy Tavern ⑭

16 Charlotte St W1. **Map** 4 F5. **Tel** 020-7580 3714. Ⓔ Tottenham Court Rd, Goodge St. **Open** 11am–11pm Mon–Sat, noon–10:30pm Sun. Ⓖ See Pubs pp316–19.

This traditional pub was a meeting place between World Wars I and II for a group of writers and artists who dubbed the area around Fitzroy Square and Charlotte Street "Fitzrovia." A basement "Writers and Artists Bar" contains pictures of former customers, including the writers Dylan Thomas and George Orwell, and the artist Augustus John.

Charlotte Street ⑮

W1. **Map** 5 A5. Ⓔ Goodge St.

As the upper classes moved west from Bloomsbury in the early 19th century, a flood of artists and European immigrants moved in, turning the area into a northern appendage to Soho (see pp98–109). The artist John Constable lived and worked for many years at No. 76. Some of the new residents established small workshops

to service the clothing stores on Oxford Street and the furniture stores on Tottenham Court Road. Others set up reasonably-priced restaurants. The street still boasts a great variety of eating places. It is overshadowed from the north by the 620-ft (189-m) Telecom Tower, built in 1964 as a vast TV, radio, and tele-communications aerial (see p32).

Telecom Tower

Pollock's Toy Museum ⑯

1 Scala St W1. **Map** 5 A5. **Tel** 020-7636 3452. Ⓔ Goodge St, Warren St, Tottenham Court Rd. **Open** 10am–5pm Mon–Sat. **Adm charge.** Ⓦ www.pollockstoymuseum.com

Benjamin Pollock was a renowned maker of toy theaters in the late 19th and

early 20th centuries – the novelist Robert Louis Stevenson was an enthusiastic customer. The museum opened in Monmouth Street in Covent Garden in 1956 and relocated to these premises in 1969. The final room is devoted to stages and puppets from Pollock's theaters, together with a reconstruction of his workshop. This is a childsized museum created in two largely unaltered 18th-century houses. The small rooms have been filled with a fascinating assortment of historic toys from all over the world. There are dolls, puppets, trains, cars, construction sets, a fine rocking horse, and a splendid collection of mainly Victorian doll's houses. Parents should beware – the exit leads you through a very tempting toy store.

Pearly king and queen dolls from Pollock's Toy Museum

HOLBORN & THE INNS OF COURT

This area is traditionally home to the legal and journalistic professions. The law is still here, in the Royal Courts of Justice and the Inns of Court, but the national newspapers left Fleet Street in the 1980s. Several buildings here predate the Great Fire of 1666 *(see pp24–5)*. These include the

Royal crest at Lincoln's Inn

superb facade of Staple Inn, Prince Henry's Room, and the interior of Middle Temple Hall. Holborn used to be one of the capital's main shopping districts. Times have changed the face of the area, but the jewelry and diamond dealers of Hatton Garden are still here, as are the London Silver Vaults.

SIGHTS AT A GLANCE

Historic Buildings, Sights and Streets
Dr. Johnson's House **14**
Fleet Street **9**
Gray's Inn **21**
Hatton Garden **18**
Holborn Viaduct **16**
Law Society **5**
Lincoln's Inn **2**
Old Curiosity Shop **4**
Prince Henry's Room **10**
Royal Courts of Justice **7**
Staple Inn **19**
Temple **11**

Museums and Galleries
Sir John Soane's Museum **1**

Churches
St. Andrew, Holborn **15**
St. Bride's **12**
St. Clement Danes **6**
St. Etheldreda's Chapel **17**

Monuments
Temple Bar Memorial **8**

Parks and Gardens
Lincoln's Inn Fields **3**

Pubs
Ye Olde Cheshire Cheese **13**

Shops
London Silver Vaults **20**

KEY

▨	Street by Street map
Ⓔ	Underground station
⮂	Rail station

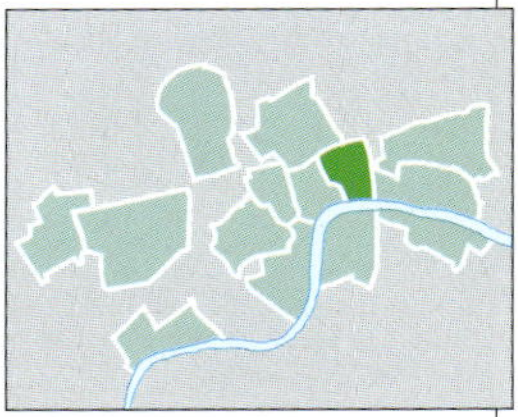

GETTING THERE
This area is served by the Circle, Central, District, Metropolitan, and Piccadilly subway lines. Buses 17, 18, 45, 46, 171, 243, and 259 are among many in the area, and trains run from a number of mainline stations inside or close to the area.

SEE ALSO
- **Street Finder, maps** 6, 13, 14
- **Where to Stay** pp278–91
- **Restaurants, Pubs** pp292–319

◁ **The Royal Courts of Justice on the Strand**

Street by Street: Lincoln's Inn

This is calm, dignified, legal London, packed with history and interest. Lincoln's Inn, adjoining one of the city's first residential squares, has buildings dating from the late 15th century. Dark-suited lawyers carry bundles of briefs between their offices here and the Neo-Gothic Law Courts. Nearby is the Temple, another historic legal district with a famous 13th-century round church.

★ Sir John Soane's Museum
The Georgian architect made this his London home and left it, with his collection, to the nation ❶

To Kingsway

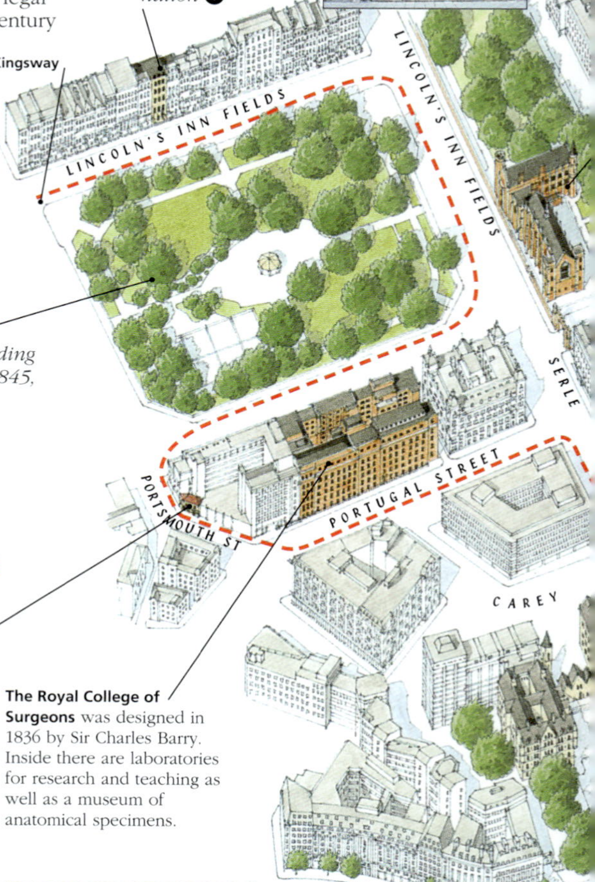

LINCOLN'S INN FIELDS

LINCOLN'S INN FIELDS

SERLE

★ Lincoln's Inn Fields
The mock-Tudor archway, leading to Lincoln's Inn and built in 1845, overlooks the Fields ❸

Old Curiosity Shop
This is a rare 16th-century, pre-Great Fire building which is now a shop ❹

PORTSMOUTH ST

PORTUGAL STREET

CAREY

The Royal College of Surgeons was designed in 1836 by Sir Charles Barry. Inside there are laboratories for research and teaching as well as a museum of anatomical specimens.

STAR SIGHTS

- ★ Sir John Soane's Museum
- ★ Temple
- ★ Lincoln's Inn Fields
- ★ Lincoln's Inn

KEY

− − − Suggested route

| 0 meters | 100 |
| 0 yards | 100 |

Twinings has been selling tea from here since 1706. The door-way dates from 1787 when the shop was called the Golden Lion.

The Gladstone Statue was erected in 1905 to commemorate William Gladstone, the Victorian statesman who was Prime Minister four times.

★ Lincoln's Inn
The Court of Chancery sat here, in Old Hall, from 1835 until 1858. Sir John Taylor Coleridge, nephew of the poet, was a well-known judge of the time ❷

LOCATOR MAP
See Central London Map pp14–15

Royal Courts of Justice
The country's main court for civil cases and appeals was built in 1882. It is made out of 35 million bricks faced with Portland stone ❼

Law Society
Look for the gold lions on the railings of this superb building ❺

Fleet Street
For two centuries this was the center of the national press. Today the newspaper offices are gone ❾

El Vino is a venerable wine bar, where journalists still mingle with lawyers.

Prince Henry's Room
There is an authentic 17th-century room in this former gatehouse ❿

St. Clement Danes
Designed by Wren (1679), it is the Royal Air Force church ❻

Temple Bar Memorial
A dragon marks where the City of London meets Westminster ❽

★ Temple
It was built for the Knights Templar in the 13th century, but today lawyers stroll here ⓫

Wigged barristers on their way to their offices in Lincoln's Inn

Lincoln's Inn ❷

WC2. **Map** 14 D1. **Tel** 020-7405 1393. ⊖ Holborn, Chancery Lane. **Grounds open** 7am–7pm Mon– Fri. **Chapel open** noon–2:30pm Mon–Fri. **Hall** not open to the public. 🔔 www.lincolnsinn.org.uk

Some of the buildings in Lincoln's Inn, the best-preserved of London's Inns of Court, go back to the late 15th century. The coat of arms above the arch of the Chancery Lane gatehouse is Henry VIII's, and the heavy oak door is of the same vintage. Shakespeare's contemporary, Ben Jonson, is believed to have laid some of the bricks of Lincoln's Inn during the reign of Elizabeth I. The chapel is early 17th-century Gothic. Women were not allowed to be buried here until 1839, when the grieving Lord Brougham petitioned to have the rule changed so that his beloved daughter could be interred in the chapel, to wait for him to join her.

Lincoln's Inn has its share of famous alumni. Oliver Cromwell and John Donne,

Sir John Soane's Museum ❶

13 Lincoln's Inn Fields WC2. **Map** 14 D1. **Tel** 020-7440 4263. ⊖ Holborn. **Open** 10am–5pm Tue–Sat, 6–9pm first Tue of month. **Closed** Sun, Mon, bank hols, & Christmas Eve. 🔔 limited – phone first. 📷 Sat 11am; groups book ahead. 🔲 www.soane.org

One of the most surprising museums in London, this house was left to the nation by Sir John Soane in 1837, with a farsighted stipulation that nothing at all should be changed. One of Britain's leading 19th-century architects, responsible for designing the Bank of England, Soane was the son of a bricklayer. After prudently marrying the niece of a wealthy builder, whose fortune he inherited, he bought and reconstructed No. 12 Lincoln's Inn Fields. In 1813 he and his wife moved into No. 13 and later, in 1824, he rebuilt No. 14, extending his museum into the rear of this

building. Today, the collections are much as Soane left them – an eclectic gathering of beautiful, peculiar, and often instructional objects.

The building itself abounds with architectural surprises and illusions. In the main first floor room, with its deep red and green coloring, cunningly placed mirrors play tricks with light and space. The picture gallery is lined with layers of folding panels to increase its capacity. The panels open out to display even more works of art. Among other works here are many of Soane's own exotic designs, including those for Pitzhanger Manor (see p258) and the Bank of England (see p147). Here also is artist William Hogarth's *Rake's Progress* series.

From the center of the low-ceilinged basement an atrium rises up to the roof. A glass dome lights galleries, on every floor, that are laden with Classical statuary.

A glass dome allows light into the basement.

A vast sarcophagus (1300 BC) stands on the floor of the basement.

the 17th-century poet, were both students here, as was William Penn, founder of the state of Pennsylvania.

Lincoln's Inn Fields ❸

WC2. **Map** 14 D1. 🚇 *Holborn.*
Open *dawn–dusk daily.* **Public tennis courts**.

This used to be a public execution site. Under the Tudors and the Stuarts, many religious martyrs, and those suspected of treachery to the Crown, perished here.

When the developer William Newton wanted to build here in the 1640s, students at Lincoln's Inn and other residents made him undertake that the land in the center would remain a public area for ever. Thanks to this early protest, lawyers today play tennis here throughout the summer, or read their briefs in the fresh air. For some years it has also been the site of an evening soup kitchen for some of London's homeless.

Old Curiosity Shop sign

Old Curiosity Shop ❹

13–14 Portsmouth St WC2.
Map 14 D1. 🚇 *Holborn.*

Whether it is or is not the original for Charles Dickens's novel of the same name, this is a genuine 16th-century building and almost certainly the oldest shop in central London. With its overhanging first floor, it gives a rare impression of a London streetscape from before the Great Fire of 1666.

The Old Curiosity Shop maintains its retailing tradition, and currently operates as a handmade shoe store. A preservation order guarantees the building's long-term future.

Law Society ❺

113 Chancery Lane WC2. **Map** 14 E1. **Tel** 020-7242 1222. 🚇 *Chancery Lane.* **Not open** to the public.

The headquarters of the lawyers' professional body is, architecturally, one of the most interesting buildings in the legal quarter. The main part, dominated by four Ionic columns, was completed in 1832. More significant is the northern extension, an early work of Charles Holden, an Arts and Crafts enthusiast who later made his name as a designer of London Underground stations. In his window arches the seated figures depict truth, justice, liberty, and mercy.

The building is on the corner of Carey Street, the site of the bankruptcy court whose name, corrupted to "Queer Street," entered the language to describe a state of destitution.

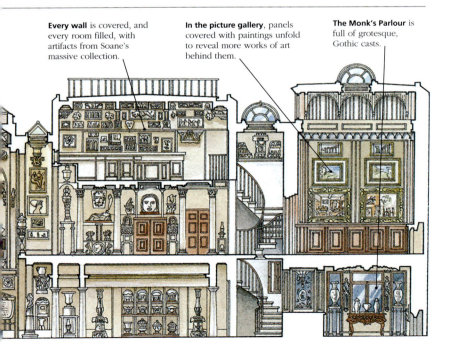

Every wall is covered, and every room filled, with artifacts from Soane's massive collection.

In the picture gallery, panels covered with paintings unfold to reveal more works of art behind them.

The Monk's Parlour is full of grotesque, Gothic casts.

St. Clement Danes ❻

Strand WC2. **Map** 14 D2.
Tel 020-7242 8282. 🚇 Temple.
Open 9am–4pm daily. **Closed**
noon Dec 25–Dec 27, public hols. ✠
12:30am Wed & Fri, 11am Sun.
♿ See **Ceremonial London** p55.

Christopher Wren designed
this wonderful church in 1680.
Its name derives from an earlier church built here by the
descendants of Danish invaders
whom Alfred the Great had
allowed to remain in London
in the 9th century. From the
17th to 19th centuries many
people were buried here, and
their memorials are now in
the crypt. The chain hanging
on the crypt wall was probably used to secure coffin lids
against body snatchers who
stole fresh corpses and sold
them to the teaching hospitals.
   St. Clement Danes sits
proudly isolated on a traffic
island. It is now the Royal Air
Force (RAF) church, and the
interior is dominated
by RAF symbols,

Clock at the Victorian law courts

memorials and monuments.
Outside, to the east, is a
statue (1910) of Dr. Johnson
(see p140), who often came
to services here. The church
bells ring to the tune of the
English nursery rhyme
"Oranges and Lemons" at
9am, noon, 3pm and 6pm
Mon–Sat, and there is an
annual Oranges and
Lemons service
every March.

Royal Courts of Justice (the Law Courts) ❼

Strand WC2. **Map** 14 D2. **Tel** 020-
7947 6000. 🚇 Holborn, Temple,
Chancery Lane. **Open** 9am–4:30pm
Mon–Fri. **Closed** public hols. ♿ ▯
🌐 www.hmcourts-service.gov.uk

Knots of demonstrators and
television cameras can often
be seen outside this sprawling
and fanciful Victorian Gothic
building, waiting for the result
of a contentious case. These
are the nation's main civil
courts, dealing with such
matters as divorce, libel,
civil liability, and appeals.
Criminals are dealt with at
the Old Bailey (see p147),
ten minutes' walk to the east.
The public are admitted to all
the courtrooms and a list tells
you which case is being
heard in which court. The
   massive Gothic building
      was completed in 1882.
   It is said to contain 1,000
rooms and 3.5 miles (5.6 km)
of corridors.

Temple Bar Memorial ❽

Fleet St EC4. **Map** 14 D2.
🚇 Holborn, Temple, Chancery Lane.

The monument in the middle
of Fleet Street, outside the
Law Courts, dates from 1880
and marks the entrance to the
City of London. On state
occasions it is a longstanding
tradition for the monarch to
have to pause here and ask
permission of the Lord Mayor
to enter. Temple Bar, a huge
archway designed by Wren,
stood here until 1878. Depict-
ed on the base of the present
monument, the old archway
was re-erected next to St.
Paul's Cathedral in 2004.

Fleet Street ❾

EC4. **Map** 14 E1. 🚇 Temple,
Blackfriars, St. Paul's.

England's first printing press
was set up here in the late
15th century by William
Caxton's assistant, and Fleet

The dragon, symbol of the City, at the entrance to the City at Temple Bar

William Capon's engraving of Fleet Street in 1799

Street has been a center of London's publishing industry ever since. Playwrights Shakespeare and Ben Jonson were patrons of the old Mitre tavern, now No. 37 Fleet Street. In 1702 the first newspaper, *The Daily Courant*, was issued from Fleet Street – conveniently placed for the City and Westminster which were the main sources of news. Later the street became synonymous with the Press.

The printing presses underneath the newspaper offices were abandoned in 1987, when new technology made it easy to produce papers away from the center of town in areas such as Wapping and the Docklands. Today the newspapers have left Fleet Street and the only remaining agency is the Commonwealth Broadcasting Association.

El Vino wine bar, at the western end opposite Fetter Lane, is a traditional haunt of journalists and lawyers.

Effigies in Temple Church

Prince Henry's Room ⓾

17 Fleet St EC4. **Map** 14 E1. *Tel 020-7332 1097.* ⊖ *Temple, Chancery Lane.* **Open** *check website for details of opening times.* 📷 **www**.cityoflondon.gov.uk

Built in 1610 as part of a Fleet Street tavern, this gets its name from the Prince of Wales's coat of arms and the initials P.H. in the center of the ceiling. They were probably put there to mark the investiture as Prince of Wales of Henry, James I's eldest son, who died before he became king.

The fine half-timbered front, alongside the gateway to Inner Temple, is original and so is some of the room's oak paneling. It contains an exhibition about the diarist Samuel Pepys.

Temple ⓫

Inner Temple, King's Bench Walk EC4. **Map** 14 E2. *Tel 020-7797 8250.* ⊖ *Temple.* **Open** *12:30pm–3pm Mon–Fri (grounds only).* **Middle Temple Hall**, Middle Temple Lane EC4. *Tel 020-7427 4800.* **Open** *10am–11:30, 3–4pm Mon–Fri.* **Closed** *at short notice for functions.* ♿ 📷 *book ahead.* 🏛 **Temple Church** *Tel 020-7353 3470.* **Open** *Wed–Fri; call for times & services.* **www**.templechurch.com

This embraces two of the four Inns of Court, the Middle Temple and the Inner Temple. (The other two are Lincoln's and Gray's Inns, *pp136, 141*.) The name derives from the

Knights Templar, a chivalrous order that used to protect pilgrims to the Holy Land. The order was based here until it was suppressed by the king because its power was viewed as a threat. Initiations probably took place in the crypt of Temple Church, and there are 13th-century effigies of Knights Templar in the nave.

Among some other ancient buildings is the Middle Temple Hall. Its fine Elizabethan interior survives – Shakespeare's *Twelfth Night* was performed here in 1601. Behind Temple, peaceful lawns stretch lazily down toward the Embankment.

St. Bride's ⓬

Fleet St EC4. **Map** 14 F2. *Tel 020-7427 0133.* ⊖ *Blackfriars.* **Open** *8am–6pm Mon–Fri, 10am–6:30pm Sun.* **Closed** *public hols.* ♿ 🔔 *11am & 6:30pm Sun.* 🏛 **Concerts** *check website for details.* **www**.stbrides.com

St. Bride's, church of the Press

St. Bride's is one of Wren's best-loved churches. Its position just off Fleet Street has made it the traditional venue of memorial services for departed journalists. Wall plaques commemorate Fleet Street journalists and printers.

The marvelous octagonal layered spire has been the model for tiered wedding cakes since shortly after it was added in 1703. Bombed in 1940, the interior was faithfully restored after World War II. The fascinating crypt contains remnants of earlier churches on the site, and a section of Roman pavement.

Ye Olde Cheshire Cheese ⓭

145 Fleet St EC4. **Map** 14 E1.
Tel 020-7353 6170. 🔵 Blackfriars.
Open 11am–11pm Mon–Fri,
noon–11pm Sat, noon–7pm Sun.
See **Pubs** pp316–19.

There has been an inn here for centuries; parts of this building date back to 1667, when the Cheshire Cheese was rebuilt after the Great Fire. The diarist Samuel Pepys often drank here in the 17th century, but it was Dr. Samuel Johnson's association with "the Cheese" that made it a place of pilgrimage for 19th-century literati. These included novelists Mark Twain and Charles Dickens.

This is one of the few pubs to have kept the 18th-century arrangement of small rooms with fireplaces, tables, and benches, instead of converting them into larger bars.

Dr. Johnson's House ⓮

17 Gough Sq EC4. **Map** 14 E1.
Tel 020-7353 3745. 🔵 Blackfriars,
Chancery Lane, Temple. **Open** May–
Sep: 11am–5:30pm Mon–Sat;
Oct–Apr: 11am–5pm Mon–Sat.
Closed Dec 24–Jan 3 & public hols.
Adm charge. 📷 small charge.
📷 book ahead. 📱
www.drjohnsonshouse.org

Dr. Samuel Johnson was an 18th-century scholar famous for the many witty (and often contentious) remarks that his

Schoolgirl figure mounted on the facade of St. Andrew's church

biographer, James Boswell, recorded and published. Johnson lived here from 1748 to 1759. He compiled the first definitive English dictionary (1755) in the attic, where six scribes and assistants stood all day at high desks.

The house, built before 1700, is furnished with 18th-century pieces and a small collection of exhibits relating to Johnson and the times in which he lived. These include a tea set belonging to his friend Mrs Thrale and pictures of Johnson and his contemporaries. It also houses replica Georgian costumes for children to try on.

St. Andrew, Holborn ⓯

5 St. Andrew St EC4. **Map** 14 E1. **Tel** 020-7583 7394. 🔵 Chancery Lane. **Open** 8:30am–5pm Mon–Fri. 📱 📱 www.standrewholborn.org.uk

The medieval church here survived the Great Fire of 1666. In 1686 Christopher Wren was, however, asked to redesign it, and the lower part of the tower is virtually all that remains of the earlier church. One of Wren's most spacious churches, it was gutted during World War II but faithfully restored as the church of the London trade guilds. Benjamin Disraeli, the Jewish-born Prime Minister, was baptized here in 1817, at the age of 12. In the 19th century a charity school was attached to the church.

Holborn Viaduct ⓰

EC1. **Map** 14 F1. 🔵 Farringdon, St. Paul's, Chancery Lane.

Civic symbol on Holborn Viaduct

This piece of Victorian ironwork was erected in the 1860s as part of a much-needed traffic scheme. It is best seen from Farringdon Street which is linked to the bridge by a staircase. Climb up and see the statues of City heroes and bronze images of Commerce, Agriculture, Science, and Fine Arts.

St. Etheldreda's Chapel ⓱

14 Ely Place EC1. **Map** 6 E5. **Tel** 020-7405 1061. 🔵 Farringdon. **Open** 8am–7pm daily. 📷 📱 📱 noon–2pm. **www**.stetheldreda.com

This is a rare 13th-century survivor, the chapel and crypt of Ely House, where the Bishops of Ely lived until the

Reconstructed interior of Dr. Johnson's house

Reformation. Then it was acquired by an Elizabethan courtier, Sir Christopher Hatton, whose descendants demolished the house but kept the chapel and turned it into a Protestant church. It passed through various hands and, in 1874, reverted to the Catholic faith.

Hatton Garden ⓲

EC1. **Map** 6 E5. Ⓔ *Chancery Lane, Farringdon.*

Built on land that used to be the garden of Hatton House, this is London's diamond and jewelry district. Gems ranging from the priceless to the mundane are traded from scores of small shops with sparkling window displays, and even from the pavements. One of the city's few remaining pawnbrokers is here – look for its traditional sign of three brass balls above the door.

Staple Inn ⓳

Holborn WC1. **Map** 14 E1. Ⓔ *Chancery Lane.* **Courtyard open** *9am–5pm Mon–Fri.* 📷

This building was once the wool staple, where wool was weighed and taxed. The frontage overlooks Holborn and is the only real example of Elizabethan half-timbering left in central London. Although now much restored, it would still be recognizable by someone who had known it in 1586, when it was built. The shops at street level have the feel of the 19th century, and there are some 18th-century buildings in the courtyard.

London Silver Vaults ⓴

53–64 Chancery Lane WC2. **Map** 14 D1. Ⓔ *Chancery Lane, Holborn.* **Open** *9am–5:30pm Mon–Fri, 9am–1pm Sat.*

These silver vaults originate from the Chancery Lane Safe Deposit Company, established

Staple Inn, a survivor from 1586

in 1885. After descending a staircase you pass through steel security doors and reach a nest of underground shops sparkling with antique and modern silverware. London silver makers have been renowned for centuries, reaching their peak in the Georgian era. The best examples sell for many thousands of pounds but most shops also offer modest pieces at realistic prices.

Coffee pot (1716): Silver Vaults

Gray's Inn ㉑

Gray's Inn Rd WC1. **Map** 6 D5. **Tel** *020-7458 7800.* Ⓔ *Chancery Lane, Holborn.* **Grounds open** *noon–2:30pm Mon–Fri.* 📷 *ask first.* ♿ 💻

This ancient legal center and law school goes back to the 14th century. Like many of the buildings in this area, it was badly damaged by World War II bombs but much of it has been rebuilt. At least one of Shakespeare's plays (*A Comedy of Errors*) was first performed in Gray's Inn hall in 1594. The hall's 16th-century interior screen still survives.

More recently, the young Charles Dickens was employed as a clerk here in 1827–8. Today the garden, once a convenient site for staging duels, is open to lunchtime strollers for part of the year, and typifies the cloistered calm of the four Inns of Court. The buildings may be visited only by prior arrangement.

THE CITY

London's financial district is built on the site of the original Roman settlement. Its full title is the City of London, but it is usually referred to as the City. Most traces of the early City were obliterated by the Great Fire of 1666 and World War II *(see pp24–5 and 33)*. Today glossy modern offices stand among a plethora of banks, with marbled halls and stately pillars. It is the con-

Traditional bank sign on Lombard Street

trast between dour, warren-like Victorian buildings and shiny new ones that gives the City its distinctive character. Though it hums with activity in business hours, few people have lived here since the 19th century, when it was one of London's main residential centers. Today only the churches, many of them by Christopher Wren *(see p47)*, are a reminder of those past times.

SIGHTS AT A GLANCE

Historic Streets and Buildings
Mansion House ❶
Royal Exchange ❸
Old Bailey ❼
Apothecaries' Hall ❽
Fishmongers' Hall ❾
Tower of London *pp154-7* ⓰
Tower Bridge ⓱
Stock Exchange ⓳
Lloyd's of London ㉓

Museums and Galleries
Bank of England Museum ❹
Guildhall Art Gallery ㉔

Historic Markets
Old Billingsgate ⓬
Leadenhall Market ㉒

Monuments
Monument ⓫

Churches and Cathedrals
St. Stephen Walbrook ❷
St. Mary-le-Bow ❺
St. Paul's Cathedral pp148–51 ❻
St. Magnus the Martyr ❿
St. Mary-at-Hill ⓮
St. Margaret Pattens ⓭
All Hallows by the Tower ⓯
St. Helen's Bishopsgate ⓴
St. Katharine Cree ㉑

Docks
St. Katharine's Dock ⓲

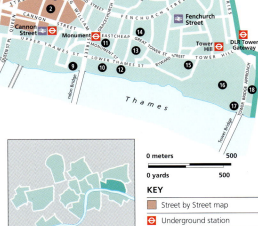

SEE ALSO

• *Street Finder*, maps 14, 15, 16

• *Where to Stay* pp278–291

• *Restaurants, Pubs* pp292–319

GETTING THERE
The City is served by the DLR and the Circle, Central, District, Northern, Metropolitan, Hammersmith and City, and Waterloo and City lines, and numerous bus routes. There are many mainline rail stations.

0 meters   500

0 yards   500

KEY

▢	Street by Street map
⊖	Underground station
⇆	Rail station

◁ **Tower Bridge, a combined bascule and suspension bridge completed in 1894**

Street by Street: The City

This is the business center of London, home to vast financial institutions such as the Stock Exchange and the Bank of England. But in contrast to these 19th- and 20th-century buildings are the older survivors. A walk through the City is in part a pilgrimage through the architectural visions of Christopher Wren, England's most sublime and probably most prolific architect. After the Great Fire of 1666 he supervised the rebuilding of 52 churches within the area, and enough survive to testify to his genius.

St. Mary-le-Bow
Anyone born within earshot of the bells of this Wren church (the historic Bow Bells) is said to be a true Londoner or Cockney ❺

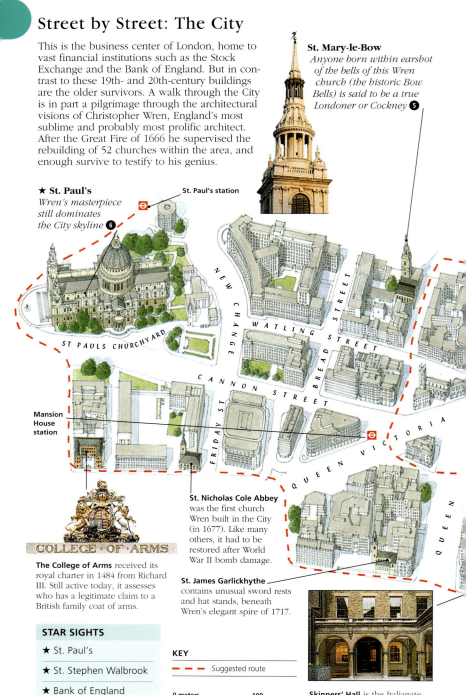

★ **St. Paul's**
Wren's masterpiece still dominates the City skyline ❻

St. Paul's station

Mansion House station

The College of Arms received its royal charter in 1484 from Richard III. Still active today, it assesses who has a legitimate claim to a British family coat of arms.

St. Nicholas Cole Abbey was the first church Wren built in the City (in 1677). Like many others, it had to be restored after World War II bomb damage.

St. James Garlickhythe contains unusual sword rests and hat stands, beneath Wren's elegant spire of 1717.

STAR SIGHTS

★ St. Paul's

★ St. Stephen Walbrook

★ Bank of England Museum

KEY

– – – Suggested route

0 meters　　　100

0 yards　　　100

Skinners' Hall is the Italianate 18th-century guild hall for the leather trade.

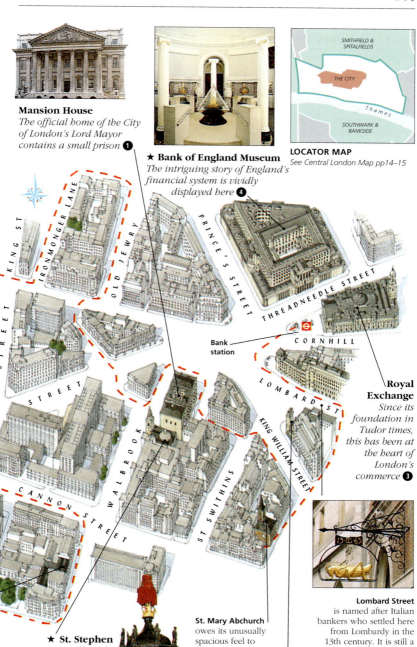

Mansion House
The official home of the City of London's Lord Mayor contains a small prison ❶

★ Bank of England Museum
The intriguing story of England's financial system is vividly displayed here ❹

LOCATOR MAP
See Central London Map pp14–15

SMITHFIELD & SPITALFIELDS

THE CITY

Thames

SOUTHWARK & BANKSIDE

KING ST

IRONMONGER LANE

OLD JEWRY

PRINCE'S STREET

THREADNEEDLE STREET

STREET

STREET

CORNHILL

Bank station

LOMBARD ST

WALBROOK

KING WILLIAM STREET

ST SWITHINS

CANNON STREET

Royal Exchange
Since its foundation in Tudor times, this has been at the heart of London's commerce ❸

Lombard Street
is named after Italian bankers who settled here from Lombardy in the 13th century. It is still a banking center.

★ St. Stephen Walbrook
Experimenting for St. Paul's, Wren created its unique dome. The interior contains original features, such as this font ❷

St. Mary Abchurch owes its unusually spacious feel to Wren's large dome. The altar carving is by Grinling Gibbons.

St. Mary Woolnoth is a characteristically powerful work by Wren's pupil, Nicholas Hawksmoor.

Mansion House ❶

Walbrook EC4. **Map** 15 B2 **Tel** 020-7626 2500. ⊖ Bank, Mansion House. **Open** to group tours only by appt or 2pm Tue on first-come-first-served basis. **www**.cityoflondon.gov.uk

The official residence of the Lord Mayor, it was completed in 1753 to the design of George Dance the Elder, whose work is now in John Soane's Museum (see pp136–7). The Palladian front with its six Corinthian columns is one of the most familiar City landmarks. The state rooms have a dignity appropriate to the office of mayor, one of the most spectacular being the 90-ft (27-m) Egyptian Hall.

Formerly located here, and now in the Museum of London (see pp166–7), were 11 holding cells, a reminder of the building's other function as a magistrate's court; the Mayor is chief magistrate of the City during his year of office. Emmeline Pankhurst, who campaigned for women's suffrage in the early 20th century, was once held here.

Egyptian Hall in Mansion House

St. Stephen Walbrook ❷

39 Walbrook EC4. **Map** 15 B2. **Tel** 020-7626 9000. ⊖ Bank, Cannon St. **Open** 10am–4pm Mon–Fri. ✝ 12:45pm Thu, sung Mass. ◉ **Organ recitals** 12:30pm Fri.

The Lord Mayor's parish church was built by Christopher Wren in 1672–9. Architectural writers consider it to be the finest of his City churches (see p47). The deep, coffered dome, with its ornate plasterwork, was a forerunner of St. Paul's. St. Stephen's airy columned interior comes as a surprise after its plain exterior. The font cover and pulpit canopy are decorated with exquisite carved figures that contrast strongly with the stark simplicity of Henry Moore's massive white stone altar (1987).

However, perhaps the most moving monument of all is a telephone in a glass box. This is a tribute to Rector Chad Varah who, in 1953, founded the Samaritans, a voluntarily staffed telephone helpline for people in emotional need. *The Martyrdom of St. Stephen*, which hangs on the north wall, is by American painter Benjamin West, who became a Royal Academician (see p90) in 1768.

The spire was added in 1717.

The dome makes this small church light and airy.

Wren's original altar and screen are still here.

Wren's pulpit has a delicate canopy.

Henry Moore's polished stone altar was added in 1987.

Royal Exchange ❸

EC3. **Map** 15 C2. **Tel** 020-7623 0444. ⊖ *Bank.* **Shopping center open** *10am–6pm daily.*

Sir Thomas Gresham, the Elizabethan merchant and courtier, founded the Royal Exchange in 1565 as a center for commerce of all kinds. The original building was centered on a vast courtyard where merchants and tradesmen did business. Queen Elizabeth I gave it its Royal title, and it is still one of the sites from which new kings and queens are announced. Dating from 1844, this is the third splendid building on the site since Gresham's.

The building now contains a luxurious shopping center with such designer stores as Cartier, Hermès, and Paul Smith.

The facade of William Tite's Royal Exchange of 1844

Bank of England Museum ❹

Bartholomew Lane EC2. **Map** 15 B1. **Tel** 020-7601 5545. ⊖ *Bank.* **Open** *10am–5pm Mon–Fri, Lord Mayor's Show (p55).* **Closed** *public hols.* ♿ *phone first.* 🎧 📷 **Films, lectures.** **www.**bankofengland. co.uk/education/museum

The Duke of Wellington (1884) opposite the Bank of England

The Bank of England was set up in 1694 to raise money for foreign wars. It grew to become Britain's central bank, and also issues currency notes. Sir John Soane *(see pp136–7)* was the architect of the 1788 bank building on this site, but only the exterior wall of his design has survived. The rest was destroyed in the 1920s and 1930s when the Bank was enlarged. There is now

a reconstruction of Soane's stock office of 1793.

Glittering gold bars, silver plated decoration, and a Roman mosaic floor, discovered during the rebuilding, are among the items on display. The museum illustrates the work of the Bank and the financial system. The gift shop sells paperweights that are made out of used bills.

St. Mary-le-Bow ❺

(Bow Church) Cheapside EC2. **Map** 15 A2. **Tel** 020-7248 5139. ⊖ *St. Paul's, Mansion House.* **Open** *7:30am–6pm Mon–Wed, 7:30am–6:30pm Thu, 7:30am–4pm Fri, 9am–4pm Sat & Sun.* 🔔 *7:30am Tue, 1pm Wed & Fri, 6pm Thu.* ♿ 🍴 **www.**stmarylebow.co.uk

The church takes its name from the bow arches in the Norman crypt. When Wren rebuilt the church (in 1670–80) after the Great Fire, he continued this pattern through the arches on the steeple. The weathervane, dating from 1674, is an enormous dragon.

The church was bombed in 1941, leaving only the steeple and two outer walls standing. It was restored in 1956–62 when the bells were recast and rehung. Bow Bells are important to Londoners: traditionally only those born within earshot of them can claim to be true Cockneys.

St. Paul's ❻

See pp148–51.

Old Bailey ❼

EC4. **Map** 14 F1. **Tel** 020-7248 3277. ⊖ *St. Paul's.* **Open** *10am–1pm, 2–5pm Mon–Fri (but opening hours vary from court to court).* **Closed** *Christmas, New Year, Easter, public hols.* 📷 **www.**cityoflondon.gov.uk

Old Bailey's rooftop Justice

This short street has a long association with crime and punishment. The new Central Criminal Courts opened here in 1907 on the site of the notorious and malodorous Newgate prison (on special days in the legal calendar judges still carry small posies to court as a reminder of those times). Across the road, the Magpie and Stump served "execution breakfasts" until 1868, when mass public hangings outside the prison gates were stopped.

Today, when the courts are in session, they are open to members of the public.

St. Paul's Cathedral ❻

Following the Great Fire of London in 1666, the medieval cathedral of St. Paul's was left in ruins. The authorities turned to Christopher Wren to rebuild it, but his ideas met with considerable resistance from the conservative Dean and Chapter. Wren's 1672 Great Model plan was not at all popular with them, and so a watered-down plan was finally agreed in 1675. Wren's determination paid off though, as can be witnessed from the grandeur of the present cathedral.

Stone urn outside the South Transept

★ **The Dome**
At 360 ft (110 m) high, the dome at St. Paul's is the second biggest in the world after St. Peter's in Rome, as spectacular from inside as outside.

The balustrade along the top was added in 1718 against Wren's wishes.

The pediment carvings, dating from 1706, show the Conversion of St. Paul.

★ **The West Front and Towers**
The towers were not on Wren's original plan – he added them in 1707, when he was 75 years old. Both were designed to have clocks.

Flying buttresses support the nave walls and the dome.

STAR SIGHTS

★ West Front and Towers

★ Dome

★ Whispering Gallery

The West Portico comprises two tiers of columns rather than the single colonnade that Wren intended.

The West Porch, approached from Ludgate Hill, is the main entrance to St. Paul's.

Queen Anne's Statue
An 1886 copy of Francis Bird's 1712 original now stands on the forecourt.

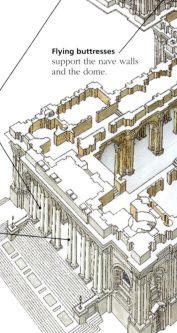

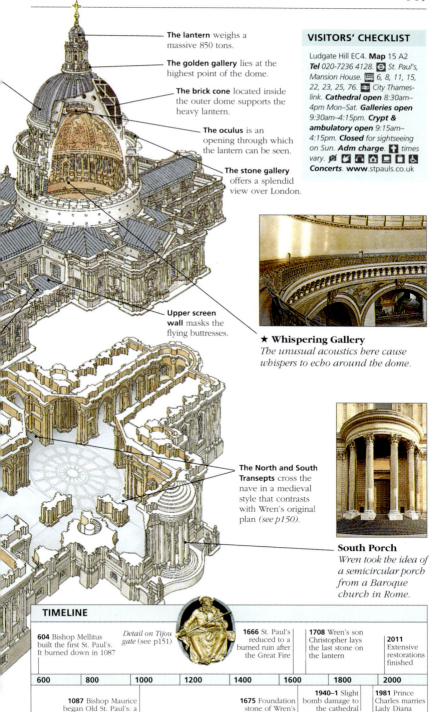

The lantern weighs a massive 850 tons.

The golden gallery lies at the highest point of the dome.

The brick cone located inside the outer dome supports the heavy lantern.

The oculus is an opening through which the lantern can be seen.

The stone gallery offers a splendid view over London.

Upper screen wall masks the flying buttresses.

The North and South Transepts cross the nave in a medieval style that contrasts with Wren's original plan (see p150).

VISITORS' CHECKLIST

Ludgate Hill EC4. **Map** 15 A2
Tel 020-7236 4128. 🚇 St. Paul's, Mansion House. 🚌 6, 8, 11, 15, 22, 23, 25, 76. 🚉 City Thameslink. **Cathedral open** 8:30am–4pm Mon–Sat. **Galleries open** 9:30am–4.15pm. **Crypt & ambulatory open** 9:15am–4.15pm. **Closed** for sightseeing on Sun. **Adm charge.** 🛈 times vary. 🚫 🗗 🖒 🏠 🖼 🛗 🚻 **Concerts.** www.stpauls.co.uk

★ **Whispering Gallery**
The unusual acoustics here cause whispers to echo around the dome.

South Porch
Wren took the idea of a semicircular porch from a Baroque church in Rome.

TIMELINE

604 Bishop Mellitus built the first St. Paul's. It burned down in 1087

Detail on Tijou gate (see p151)

1666 St. Paul's reduced to a burned ruin after the Great Fire

1708 Wren's son Christopher lays the last stone on the lantern

2011 Extensive restorations finished

600	800	1000	1200	1400	1600	1800	2000

1087 Bishop Maurice began Old St. Paul's: a Norman cathedral of stone

1675 Foundation stone of Wren's design laid

1940–1 Slight bomb damage to the cathedral

1981 Prince Charles marries Lady Diana Spencer

A Guided Tour of St. Paul's

The visitor to St. Paul's will be immediately impressed by its cool, beautifully ordered and extremely spacious interior. The nave, transepts, and choir are arranged in the shape of a cross, as in a medieval cathedral, but Wren's Classical vision shines through this conservative floor plan, forced on him by the cathedral authorities. Aided by some of the finest craftsmen of his day, he created an interior of grand majesty and Baroque splendor, a worthy setting for the many great ceremonial events that have taken place here. These include the funeral of Winston Churchill in 1965 and the wedding of Prince Charles and Lady Diana Spencer in 1981.

The mosaics on the choir ceiling were completed in the 1890s by William Richmond.

① **The Nave**
Take in the full glory of the massive arches and the succession of saucer domes that open out into a huge space below the main dome.

② **The North Aisle**
As you walk along the North Aisle, look above: the aisles are vaulted with small domes mimicking those of the nave ceiling.

⑨ **South Aisle**
From here the brave can ascend the 259 steps to the Whispering Gallery and test the acoustics.

Entrance to Whispering Gallery

⑧ **Florence Nightingale's Tomb**
Famous for her pioneering work in nursing standards, Florence Nightingale was the first woman to receive the Order of Merit.

Main entrances

⑦ **Wren's Tomb**
Wren's burial place is marked by a slab. The inscription states: "Reader, if you seek a monument, look around you."

The Geometrical Staircase is a spiral of 92 stone steps giving access to the cathedral library.

KEY

– – – Tour route

③ The Crossing

The climax of Wren's interior is this great open space. The vast dome is decorated with monochrome frescoes by Sir James Thornhill, the leading architectural painter of Wren's time.

Entrance to crypt

④ The Choir

Jean Tijou, a Huguenot refugee, created much of the cathedral's fine wrought ironwork, such as these screens in the choir aisles.

John Donne's memorial, from 1631, was the only monument to survive the Great Fire of 1666 intact. The poet posed for it in his lifetime.

⑤ The High Altar

The canopy over the altar was replaced after World War II. It is based on Wren's original Baroque drawings.

Grinling Gibbons's work can be found on the choir stalls, with typically intricate carvings of cherubs, fruits, and garlands.

T. E. Lawrence, or Lawrence of Arabia, the British World War I hero who earned his nickname by fighting alongside Arab tribes in their resistance to Turkish rule in 1915, is commemorated by this bust in the crypt.

⑥ The Crypt

The tombs of famous figures and such popular heroes as Lord Nelson can be seen in the crypt.

Apothecaries' Hall ⑧

Blackfriars Lane EC4. **Map** 14 F2.
Tel 020-7236 1189. ⊖ *Blackfriars.*
Courtyard open 9am–5pm Mon–Fri.
Closed public hols, end Aug. **Phone Hall** for appt to visit (groups only). ⅙

Apothecaries' Hall, rebuilt in 1670

London has had livery companies, or guilds, to protect and regulate specific trades since early medieval times. The Apothecaries' Society was founded in 1617 for those who prepared, prescribed, or sold drugs. It has some surprising alumni, including Oliver Cromwell and the poet John Keats. Now nearly all the members are physicians or surgeons.

Fishmongers' Hall ⑨

London Bridge EC4. **Map** 15 B3.
Tel 020-7626 3531. ⊖ *Monument.*
Not open to the public. Limited tours by appt only. **www**.fishhall.org.uk

This is one of the oldest livery companies, established in 1272. Lord Mayor Walworth, a member of the Fishmongers' Company, killed Wat Tyler, leader of the Peasants' Revolt, in 1381 *(see p162)*. Today it still fulfills its original role; all the fish sold in the City must be inspected by Company officials.

St. Magnus the Martyr ⑩

Lower Thames St EC3. **Map** 15 C3.
Tel 020-7626 4481. ⊖ *Monument.*
Open 10am–4pm Tue–Fri, 10am–1pm Sun. 🕇 11am Sun. ⅙
www.stmagnusmartyr.org.uk

There has been a church here for over 1,000 years. Its patron saint, St. Magnus, Earl of the Orkney Islands and a renowned Norwegian Christian leader, was brutally murdered in 1116.

When Christopher Wren built this church in 1671–6, it was at the foot of old London Bridge, until 1738 the only bridge across the Thames River in London. Anyone going south from the city would have passed under Wren's magnificent arched porch spanning the flagstones leading to the old bridge.

Highlights of St. Magnus the Martyr include the carved musical instruments that decorate the organ case. Wren's pulpit, with its slender supporting stem, was restored in 1924.

Monument ⑪

Monument St EC3. **Map** 15 C2.
Tel 020-7626 2717. ⊖ *Monument.*
Open 9:30am–5:30pm daily. **Closed** Dec 24–26, Jan 1. **Adm charge.** 📷
www.themonument.info

The column designed by Christopher Wren to commemorate the Great Fire of London, which devastated the original walled city in September 1666, is the tallest isolated stone column in the world. It is 205 ft (62 m) high and is said to be 62 m west of where the fire started in Pudding Lane. It was sited on the direct approach to old London Bridge, which was a few steps downstream from the present one. Reliefs around the column's base

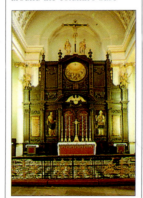

The altar of St. Magnus the Martyr

show Charles II restoring the city. The 311 steps to the top lead to a viewing platform. In 1842 this was enclosed with railings after a suicide. The views are spectacular.

Old Billingsgate ⑫

Lower Thames St EC3. **Map** 15 C3.
⊖ *Monument.* **Not open** to the public.

Fish weathervane at Billingsgate

London's main fish market was based here for 900 years, on one of the city's earliest quays. During the 19th and early 20th centuries 400 tons of fish were sold here every day, much of it delivered by boat. It was London's noisiest market, renowned, even in Shakespeare's day, for foul language. In 1982 the market moved from this building (1877) to the Isle of Dogs.

St. Mary-at-Hill ⑬

Lovat Lane EC3. **Map** 15 C2. *Tel*
020-7626 4184. ⊖ *Monument.*
Concerts. Open 11am–4pm
Mon–Fri. 🕇 1pm Wed, 1:05pm Thu.

The interior and east end of St. Mary-at-Hill were Wren's first church designs (1670–76). The Greek cross design was a prototype for his St. Paul's proposals. Ironically, the delicate plasterwork and rich 17th-century fittings, which had survived both the Victorian mania for refurbishment and the bombs of World War II, were lost in a fire in

1988. The building was then restored to its original appearance, only to be damaged again by an IRA bomb in 1992.

St. Margaret Pattens ⓮

Rood Lane and Eastcheap EC3. **Map** 15 C2. **Tel** 020-7623 6630. ⊖ *Monument.* **Open** *10:30am–4pm Mon–Thu, 7:30am–4pm Fri.* **Closed** *Christmas week.* ⬆ *1:15pm Thu, 11am Sun.* **Concerts and recitals.** ♿

Wren's church of 1684–7 was named after a type of overshoe made near here. Its rendered brickwork and Portland stone contrast with the Georgian stucco storefront in the forecourt. The interior retains 17th-century canopied pews and an ornate font.

All Hallows by the Tower ⓯

Byward St EC3. **Map** 16 D3. **Tel** 020-7481 2928. ⊖ *Tower Hill.* **Open** *8am–6pm Mon–Fri, 10am–5pm Sat & Sun.* **Closed** *Dec 26–Jan 2.* ⬆ *11am Sun.* ♿ 🅿 🕚 📷 **Adm charge** *undercroft museum.* www.allhallowsbythetower.org.uk

The first church on this site was Saxon. The arch in the southwest corner, which contains Roman tiles, dates from that period, as do some crosses in the crypt. There is a Roman pavement in the crypt. William Penn, founder of Pennsylvania, was baptized here in 1644. Most of the interior has been altered, but a limewood font cover, carved by Grinling Gibbons in 1682, survives. John Quincy Adams

Roman tile from All Hallows

married here in 1797 before he was US president. Samuel Pepys watched the Great Fire from the church tower. There are a small museum, brass rubbing center, concerts, and a bookstore.

Tower of London ⓰

See pp154–7.

Tower Bridge ⓱

SE1. **Map** 16 D3. **Tel** 020-7403 3761. ⊖ *Tower Hill.* **The Tower Bridge Exhibition Open** *Apr–Sep: 10am–6:30pm daily; Oct–Mar: 9:30am–6pm daily (open from noon on Jan 1).* **Closed** *Dec 24, 25, & 26.* **Adm charge.** 📷 🅿 ♿ 🕚 www.towerbridge.org.uk

Completed in 1894, this flamboyant piece of Victorian engineering quickly became a symbol of London. Its pinnacled towers and linking catwalk support the mechanism for raising the roadway when big ships have to pass through, or for special and historic occasions. The

bridge now houses The Tower Bridge Exhibition, with interactive displays bringing the bridge's history to life, river views from the catwalk, and a close-up look at the steam engine which powered the lifting machinery until 1976, when the system was electrified.

The walkways, which are now open to the public, afford stunning views along the river.

When raised, the bridge is 135 ft (40 m) high and 200 ft (60 m) wide. In its heyday it was opened five times a day.

There are nearly 300 stairs to the top of the towers.

The Victorian winding machinery was powered by steam until 1976.

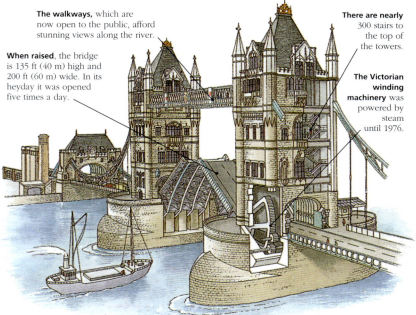

Tower of London ⑯

For much of its 900-year history the Tower was an object of fear. Those who had committed treason or threatened the throne were held within its dank walls. A lucky few lived in comparative comfort, but the majority had to put up with appalling conditions. Many did not get out alive, and some were tortured before meeting violent deaths on nearby Tower Hill.

★ The White Tower
When it was finished, c.1097, it was the tallest building in London – 90 ft (30 m) high.

★ The Jewel House is where the magnificent Crown Jewels are housed *(see p156).*

"Beefeaters"
Thirty-five Yeoman Warders guard the Tower and live here.

Beauchamp Tower
Many high-ranking prisoners were held here, often with their own retinues of servants.

Tower Green was where the aristocratic prisoners were executed, away from the ghoulish crowds on Tower Hill. But only seven people died here – including two of Henry VIII's six wives – hundreds had to undergo public execution on Tower Hill.

STAR BUILDINGS

★ White Tower

★ Jewel House

★ Chapel of St. John

★ Traitors' Gate

Main entrance

Queen's House
This is the official residence of the Tower's governor.

THE RAVENS

The Tower's most celebrated residents are a small colony of ravens. It is not known when they first settled here, but there is a legend that should they desert the Tower, the kingdom will fall. In fact the birds have part of their wings clipped on one side, making flight impossible. The Ravenmaster, one of the Yeoman Warders, looks after the birds.

A memorial in the moat commemorates some of the ravens who have died at the Tower since the 1950s.

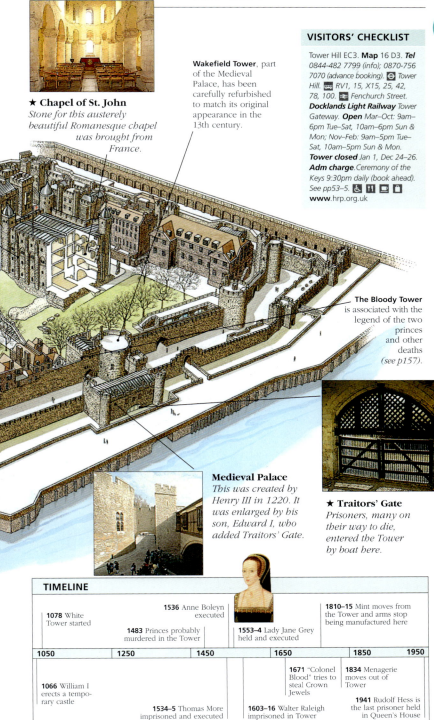

★ **Chapel of St. John**
*Stone for this austerely
beautiful Romanesque chapel
was brought from
France.*

Wakefield Tower, part
of the Medieval
Palace, has been
carefully refurbished
to match its original
appearance in the
13th century.

The Bloody Tower
is associated with the
legend of the two
princes
and other
deaths
(see p157).

Medieval Palace
*This was created by
Henry III in 1220. It
was enlarged by his
son, Edward I, who
added Traitors' Gate.*

★ **Traitors' Gate**
*Prisoners, many on
their way to die,
entered the Tower
by boat here.*

TIMELINE

1050	1250	1450	1650	1850	1950

1078 White
Tower started

1483 Princes probably
murdered in the Tower

1536 Anne Boleyn
executed

1553–4 Lady Jane Grey
held and executed

1810–15 Mint moves from
the Tower and arms stop
being manufactured here

1066 William I
erects a tempo-
rary castle

1534–5 Thomas More
imprisoned and executed

1603–16 Walter Raleigh
imprisoned in Tower

1671 "Colonel
Blood" tries to
steal Crown
Jewels

1834 Menagerie
moves out of
Tower

1941 Rudolf Hess is
the last prisoner held
in Queen's House

Inside the Tower

The Tower has been a tourist attraction since the reign of Charles II (1660–85), when both the Crown Jewels and the collection of armor were first shown to the public. They remain powerful reminders of royal might and wealth.

The Orb, symbolizing the power and empire of Christ the Redeemer

THE CROWN JEWELS

The Crown Jewels comprise the regalia of crowns, scepters, orbs, and swords used at coronations and other state occasions. They are impossible to price but their worth is irrelevant beside their enormous significance in the historical and religious life of the kingdom. Most of the Crown Jewels date from 1661, when a new set was made for the coronation of Charles II; Parliament had destroyed the previous crowns and scepters after the execution of Charles I in 1649. Only a few pieces survived, hidden by the clergy of Westminster Abbey until the Restoration.

The Coronation Ceremony
Many elements in this solemn and mystical ceremony date from the days of Edward the Confessor. The king or queen proceeds to Westminster Abbey, accompanied by objects of the regalia, including the State Sword which represents the monarch's own sword. He or she is then anointed with holy oil, to signify divine approval, and invested with ornaments and royal robes. Each of the jewels represents an aspect of the monarch's role as head of the state and church. The climax comes when St. Edward's Crown is placed on the sovereign's head; there is a cry of "God Save the King" (or "Queen"), the trumpets sound, and guns at the Tower are fired. The last coronation was Elizabeth II's in 1953.

The Imperial State Crown, containing more than 2,800 diamonds, 273 pearls, as well as other gems

The crowns
There are 10 crowns on display at the Tower. Many of these have not been worn for years, but the Imperial State Crown is in frequent use. The Queen wears it at the Opening of Parliament (*see p73*). The crown was made in 1937 for George VI, and is similar to the one made for Queen Victoria. The sapphire set in the cross is said to have been worn in a ring by Edward the Confessor (ruled 1042–66).

The most recent crown is not at the Tower, however. It was made for Prince Charles's investiture as Prince of Wales at Caernarvon Castle in north Wales in 1969, and is kept at the Museum of Wales in Cardiff. The Queen Mother's crown was made for the coronation of her husband, George VI, in 1937. It is the only one to be made out of platinum – all the other crowns on display at the Tower are made of gold.

Other regalia
Apart from the crowns, there are other pieces of the Crown Jewels that are essential to coronations. Among these are three Swords of Justice, symbolizing mercy and spiritual and temporal justice. The orb is a hollow gold sphere encrusted with jewels and weighing about 1.3 kg (3 lbs). The Sceptre with the Cross contains the biggest cut diamond in the world, the 530-carat First Star of Africa. The rough stone it comes from weighed 3,106 carats.

The Sovereign's Ring, sometimes referred to as "the wedding ring of England"

Plate Collection
The Jewel House also holds a collection of elaborate gold and silver plate. The Maundy Dish is still used on Maundy Thursday when the monarch distributes money to selected old people. The Exeter Salt (a very grand salt cellar from the days when salt was a valuable commodity) was given by the citizens of Exeter, in west England, to Charles II; during the 1640s' Civil War Exeter was a Royalist stronghold.

The Sceptre with the Cross (1660), rebuilt in 1910 after Edward VII was presented with the First Star of Africa diamond

The hilt and solid-gold scabbard of the jeweled State Sword, one of the most valuable swords in the world

THE WHITE TOWER

This is the oldest surviving building in the Tower of London, begun by William I in c.1070 and completed before 1100. For centuries it served as an armory, and much of the national collection of arms and armor was held here. In the 1990s many exhibits moved to the Royal Armouries' other museums in Leeds or Portsmouth, but some of the most historic items, especially those connected with the Tower, have remained. The extra space allows the exhibits to be displayed more effectively, and highlights architectural features of the building itself.

The Royal Castle and Armor Gallery

These two chambers on the first floor were the main ceremonial rooms of the original Norman castle. The first one, to the east, is the smaller, probably an antechamber to the Banqueting Hall beyond, and contains exhibits setting out the history of the White Tower. It adjoins St. John's Chapel, a rare surviving early Norman chapel virtually intact, a powerfully solid interior with little ornamentation. Originally the two main rooms were twice their present height; a pitched roof was removed in 1490 to allow extra floors to be built on top. Suits of armor from Tudor and Stuart times are here, including three made for Henry VIII, one covering his horse as well. A suit made in Holland for Charles I is decorated in gold leaf.

Japanese armor presented to James I in 1613

The Ordnance Gallery

This and the temporary exhibition gallery next door were chambers created in 1490 when the roof was raised. They were used chiefly for storage and in 1603 a new floor was installed to allow gunpowder to be kept here: by 1667 some 10,000 barrels of it were stored in the Tower. Among the displays are gilt panels and ornament from the barge of the Master of the Ordnance built in 1700.

The Small Armory and Crypt

The westerly room on the ground floor may originally have been a living area, and has traces of the oldest fireplaces known in England. Pistols, muskets, swords, pikes, and bayonets are mounted on the walls and panels in elaborate symmetrical patterns based on displays in the Tower armories in the 18th and 19th centuries. They were shown in the Grand Storehouse until it burned down in 1841. A collection of weapons taken from the men who planned to assassinate William III in 1696 is on show, and next door is a wooden block made in 1747 for the execution of Lord Lovat – the last public beheading in England. The crypt now houses a shop.

The Line of Kings

The Line of Kings, ten life-size carvings of prominent English monarchs, wearing armor and seated on horseback, originated in Tudor times, when eight such figures adorned the royal palace at Greenwich. Two more had been added by the time they first appeared in the Tower in 1660, celebrating the Restoration of Charles II. In 1688, 17 new horses and heads were commissioned, some from the great carver Grinling Gibbons (the third from the left is reputed to be his work).

Henry VIII's armor (1540)

THE PRINCES IN THE TOWER

Now explored in a display in the Bloody Tower, one of the Tower's darkest mysteries concerns two boy princes, sons and heirs of Edward IV. They were put into the Tower by their uncle, Richard of Gloucester, when their father died in 1483. Neither was seen again and Richard was crowned later that year. In 1674 the skeletons of two children were found nearby.

The yacht haven of the restored St. Katharine's Dock

St. Katharine's Dock ⑱

E1. **Map** 16 E3. **Tel** 020-7488 0555.
🚇 *Tower Hill.* 🚻 🍴 🖥 📷
www.skdocks.co.uk

This most central of all London's docks was designed by Thomas Telford and opened in 1828 on the site of St. Katharine's hospital. Commodities as diverse as tea, marble, and live turtles (turtle soup was a Victorian delicacy) were unloaded here.

During the 19th and early 20th centuries the docks flourished, but by the mid-20th century cargo ships were delivering their wares in massive containers. The old docks became too small and new ones had to be built downstream. St. Katharine's closed in 1968.

St. Katharine's is now one of London's most successful developments, with its commercial, residential, and entertainment facilities, including a hotel and a yacht haven. Old warehouse buildings have shops and restaurants on their first floors, and offices above.

On the north side of the dock is LIFFE Commodity Products, trading in commodities such as coffee, sugar, and oil. There is no public gallery but, if you ask at the door, you may be able to look down from the glass-walled reception area on to the frenzied trading floors. The dock is worth wandering through after visiting the Tower or Tower Bridge *(see pp154–7 and p153)*.

Stock Exchange ⑲

Paternoster Sq EC4. **Map** 15 A1.
🚇 *Bank, Farringdon.* **Not open** to the public.

The first Stock Exchange was established in Threadneedle Street in 1773 by a group of stockbrokers who previously met and did business in nearby City coffee houses. By the 19th century the rules of exchange were laid down, and for a hundred years London's was the biggest stock exchange in the world. Nevertheless, the rise of the American and Japanese economies during the 20th century gradually challenged London's dominance.

In 1986 the deregulation of the UK market, known as the "Big Bang," resulted in the computerization of trades, making the trade floor redundant and setting London's financial markets on a course of rapid growth. Today London has reclaimed its position as the market of choice for companies around the world wishing to raise capital.

St. Helen's Bishopsgate

St. Helen's Bishopsgate ⑳

Great St. Helen's EC3. **Map** 15 C1.
Tel 020-7283 2231. 🚇 *Liverpool St, Bank.* **Open** 9:30am–5pm Mon–Fri. 🕤 1pm Tue & Thu, 10:30am, 6pm Sun. 📷 ♿
www.st-helens.org.uk

The curious appearance of this 13th-century church is due to its origins as two places of worship: one a parish church, the other the chapel of a long-gone nunnery next door. (The medieval nuns of St. Helen's were notorious for their "secular kissing.")

Among its monuments is the tomb of Sir Thomas Gresham, who founded the Royal Exchange *(see p147)*.

St. Katharine Cree ㉑

86 Leadenhall St EC3. **Map** 16 D1.
Tel 020-7283 5733. 🚇 *Aldgate, Tower Hill.* **Open** 10:30am–4pm Mon–Fri. 🕤 1:10pm Wed.
www.london.anglican.org

The organ at St. Katharine Cree

A rare pre-Wren 17th-century church with a medieval tower, this was one of only eight churches in the City to survive the fire of 1666. Some of the elaborate plasterwork on and beneath the high ceiling of the nave portrays the coats of arms of the guilds, with which the church has special links. The 17th-century organ, supported on magnificent carved wooden columns, was played by both Purcell and Handel.

Leadenhall Market ㉒

Whittington Ave EC3. **Map** 15 C2. *Tel* 020-7929 1073. 🚇 *Bank, Monument.* **Open** *7am–4pm Mon–Fri. See* **Shops and Markets** *pp332–41.* **www**.leadenhallmarket.co.uk

There has been a food market here, on the site of the Roman forum *(see pp18–19),* since the Middle Ages. Its name comes from a lead-roofed mansion that stood nearby in the 14th century. The ornate, Victorian covered shopping mall of today was designed in 1881 by Sir Horace Jones, the architect of Billingsgate fish market *(see p152).* Essentially a food market, offering traditional game, poultry, fish, and meat, Leadenhall also has a number of independent shops that sell all kinds of fare from chocolates to wine. The area is busiest during breakfast and lunch times, and is best seen at Christmas when all the stores are decorated. Next door is the Lloyd's of London building.

Lloyd's of London ㉓

1 Lime St EC3. **Map** 15 C2. *Tel* 020-7327 1000. 🚇 *Bank, Monument, Liverpool St, Aldgate.* **Not open** *to the public.* **www**.lloyds.com

Lloyd's was founded in the late 17th century and takes its name from the coffee house where underwriters and shipowners used to meet to arrange marine insurance contracts. Lloyd's soon became the world's main insurers, issuing policies on everything from oil tankers to Betty Grable's legs.

The present building, by Richard Rogers, dates from 1986 and is one of the most interesting modern buildings in London *(see p32).* Its exaggerated stainless steel external piping and high-tech ducts echo Rogers' forceful Pompidou Center in Paris. Lloyd's is a far more elegant building and particularly worth seeing floodlit at night. Nearby is 30 St. Mary Axe, otherwise known as "the Gherkin," one of the most recognizable landmarks on the London skyline.

Leadenhall Market in 1881

Guildhall Art Gallery ㉔

Guildhall Yard EC2. **Map** 15 B1. *Tel* 020-7332 3700. 🚇 *St. Paul's.* **Open** *10am–5pm Mon–Sat, noon–4pm Sun (last adm: 30 mins prior).* **Closed** *Jan 1, Dec 25 & 26.* 📷 *free tours Fri.* 🚫 ♿ 🏛 **Guildhall** *Gresham St EC2.* *Tel* 020-7606 3030. **Open** *phone to check.* **www**.cityoflondon.gov.uk

The Guildhall Art Gallery was built in 1885 to house the art collection of the Corporation of London, but was destroyed

in World War II. The present gallery houses the studio collection of 20th-century artist Sir Matthew Smith, portraits from the 16th century to the present day, a gallery of 18th-century works, including John Singleton Copley's *Defeat of the Floating Batteries at Gibraltar,* and numerous Victorian works.

In 1988, the foundations of a Roman amphitheater were discovered beneath the gallery. Built in 70 AD and capable of holding about 6000 spectators, the arena would have featured animal hunts, executions, and gladiatorial combat. Access to the atmospheric ruins is included with gallery admission.

The adjacent Guildhall itself has been the administrative center of the City for at least 800 years. For centuries the hall was used for trials and many people were condemned to death here, including Henry Garnet, one of the Gunpowder Plot conspirators *(see p24).* Today, a few days after the Lord Mayor's parade *(see pp54–5),* the Prime Minister addresses a banquet here.

Richard Rogers' Lloyd's building illuminated at night

SMITHFIELD AND SPITALFIELDS

The areas just north of the City walls have always been a refuge for those who did not want to come under its jurisdiction, or were not welcome there. These included Huguenots in the 17th century and, in later times, other immigrants from Europe and then Bengal. They founded small industries and brought with them their restaurants and places of worship. The name Spitalfields comes from the medieval priory of St. Mary Spital. Middlesex Street became known as Petticoat Lane in the 16th century, for its clothing stalls; it is still the hub of a popular Sunday morning street market that spreads as far east as Brick Lane, today lined with aromatic Bengali food stores. London's meat market is at Smithfield, and nearby is the Barbican, a late 20th-century residential and arts complex.

Stone dragon in Smithfield Market

SIGHTS AT A GLANCE

Historic Streets and Buildings
Charterhouse **4**
Cloth Fair **5**
Barbican **7**
Whitbread's Brewery **9**
Wesley's Chapel–Leysian Mission **11**
Broadgate Centre **12**
Petticoat Lane **13**
Fournier Street **17**
Spitalfields Centre Museum of Immigration & Diversity **19**
Brick Lane **20**
Dennis Severs House **21**

Museums and Galleries
Museum of London pp166–7 **3**
Whitechapel Gallery **14**

Churches and Mosques
St. Botolph, Aldersgate **2**
St. Bartholomew-the-Great **6**
St. Giles, Cripplegate **8**
Christ Church, Spitalfields **16**
London Jamme Masjid **18**

Cemeteries
Bunhill Fields **10**

Markets
Smithfield Market **1**
Old Spitalfields Market **15**
Columbia Road Market **22**

0 meters   500
0 yards   500

GETTING THERE
This area is served by the Northern, Hammersmith and City, Central, and Circle Underground lines and by rail. The Nos. 8, 15, and many other buses run close by.

SEE ALSO
• *Street Finder,* maps 6, 7, 8, 15, 16
• *Where to Stay* pp278–91
• *Restaurants, Pubs* pp292–319

KEY
■ Street by Street map
⊖ Underground station
▣ Rail Station

◁ **Columbia Road flower and plant market**

Street by Street: Smithfield

This area is among the most historic in London. It contains one of the capital's oldest churches, some rare Jacobean houses, vestiges of the Roman wall (near the Museum of London) and central London's only surviving wholesale food market.

Smithfield's long history is also bloody. In 1381 the rebel peasant leader, Wat Tyler, was killed here by an ally of Richard II as he presented the king with demands for lower taxes. Later, in the reign of Mary I (1553–8), scores of Protestant religious martyrs were burned at the stake here.

The Fat Boy: the Great Fire ended here

The Fox and Anchor pub
is open from 7am for hearty breakfasts, washed down with ale by the market traders of Smithfield.

★ Smithfield Market
A contemporary print shows Horace Jones's stately building for the meat market when it was completed in 1867 ❶

CHARTERHOUSE STREET

LONG

WEST SMITHFIELD

SMITHFIELD STREET

Fat Boy

COCK LANE

SNOW HILL

GILTSPUR STREET

The Saracen's Head, an historic inn, stood on this site until the 1860s when it was demolished to make way for Holborn Viaduct *(see p140)*.

SITE OF THE
SARACEN'S HEAD
INN
DEMOLISHED
1868
THE CITY OF LONDON

St. Bartholomew-the-Less has a 15th-century tower and vestry. Its links to the hospital are shown by this early 20th-century stained glass of a nurse; a gift of the Worshipful Company of Glaziers.

St. Bartholomew's Hospital has stood on this site since 1123. Some of the existing buildings date from 1759.

KEY

— — — Suggested route

0 meters 100

0 yards 100

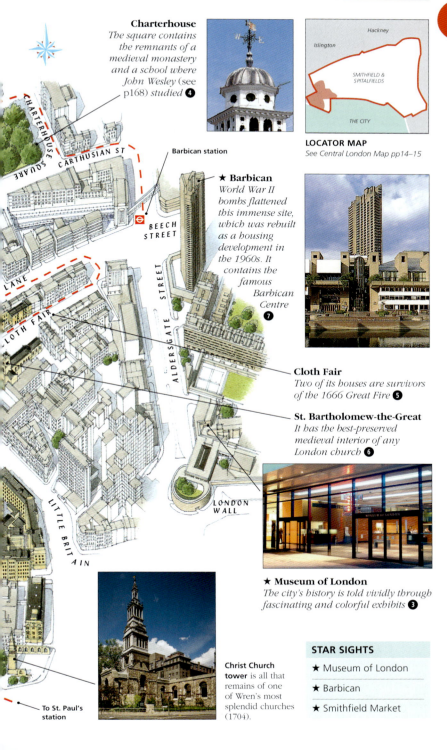

Charterhouse
The square contains the remnants of a medieval monastery and a school where John Wesley (see p168) studied 4

Barbican station

LOCATOR MAP
See Central London Map pp14–15

★ **Barbican**
World War II bombs flattened this immense site, which was rebuilt as a housing development in the 1960s. It contains the famous Barbican Centre 7

Cloth Fair
Two of its houses are survivors of the 1666 Great Fire 5

St. Bartholomew-the-Great
It has the best-preserved medieval interior of any London church 6

★ **Museum of London**
The city's history is told vividly through fascinating and colorful exhibits 3

Christ Church tower is all that remains of one of Wren's most splendid churches (1704).

To St. Paul's station

STAR SIGHTS
★ Museum of London
★ Barbican
★ Smithfield Market

Smithfield Market, now officially known as London Central Markets

Smithfield Market ❶

Charterhouse St EC1. **Map** 6 F5.
⊖ Farringdon, Barbican.
Open 3–9am Mon–Fri. **Closed** public hols. **www**.smithfieldmarket.com

Animals have been traded here since the 12th century, but the site was granted its first official charter in 1400. In 1648 it was officially established as a cattle market and live cattle continued to be sold here until the mid-19th century. It now confines itself to whole-sale trading in dead meat and poultry. It was originally sited in Smithfield outside the city walls. Although moved to its present location in Charter-house Street in the 1850s and called the London Central Meat Market, the original name stuck. The old buildings are by Horace Jones, the Victorian architect, but there are 20th-century additions. Some pubs in the area keep market hours and, from dawn, serve hearty breakfasts. After modernization, Smith-field is now one of the best equipped meat markets in the world. Aim to arrive by 7am.

St. Botolph, Aldersgate ❷

Aldersgate St EC1. **Map** 15 A1.
Tel 020-7606 0684. ⊖ St. Paul's, Barbican, Moorgate. **Open** 1–4pm Tue. ✝ 1pm Tue. ♿

A modest late Georgian exterior (completed in the late 18th century) conceals a flamboyant, well-preserved interior that has a finely decorated plas-ter ceiling, a rich brown wooden organ case and galleries, as well as an oak pulpit resting on a carved palm tree. The original box pews have been kept in the galleries rather than in the body of the church. Some of the memorials come from a 14th-century church that originally existed on the site.

The former church-yard alongside was converted in 1880 into a relaxing green space known as Postman's Park, because it was used by workers from the nearby Post Office head-quarters. In the late 19th century, the Victorian artist G. F. Watts dedicated one of the walls to a quirky collection of plaques that commemorate acts of bravery and self-sacrifice by ordinary people. Some of these plaques are still here and can be viewed. There are three St. Botolph churches in the City; the other two can be found at Aldgate and in Bishopsgate.

Museum of London ❸

See pp166–7.

Charterhouse ❹

Charterhouse Sq EC1. **Map** 6 F5.
Tel 020-7251 5002. ⊖ Barbican.
Open for 👣 only; book well ahead; Apr–Aug: Wed pm.

The Tudor gateway on the north side of the square leads to the site of a former Carthusian monastery, which was dissolved under Henry VIII. In 1611 the buildings were converted into a hospital for poor pensioners, and a charity school – called Charterhouse – whose pupils included John Wesley (see p168), writer William Thackeray, and Robert Baden-Powell, founder of the Boy Scouts. In 1872 the school, which is now a top boarding school, relocated to Godalming in Surrey. Part of the original site was subsequently taken over by St. Bartholomew's Hospital medical school. Some of the old buildings have survived; these include the chapel and part of the cloisters. Today Charterhouse is still home to over 40 pensioners, supported by the charitable foundation.

Charterhouse: stone carving

Cloth Fair ❺

EC1. **Map** 6 F5. 🚇 *Barbican.*

This pretty street is named after the notoriously rowdy Bartholomew Fair, which was the main cloth fair in medieval and Elizabethan England, held annually at Smithfield until 1855. Nos. 41 and 42 are fine 17th-century houses and have distinctive two-storeyed wooden bay windows, although their first floors have since been modernized. The former poet laureate John Betjeman, who died in 1984, lived in No. 43 for most of his life. It has now been turned into a wine bar named after him.

17th-century houses: Cloth Fair

St. Bartholomew-the-Great ❻

West Smithfield EC1. **Map** 6 F5. **Tel** 020-7606 5171. 🚇 *Barbican.* **Open** 8:30am–5pm (4pm in winter) Mon–Fri, 10:30am–4pm Sat, 8:30am–8pm Sun. **Closed** Christmas week. 🔔 9am, 11am, 6:30pm Sun. **Adm charge** ♿ 📷 by appt. 🔔 **Concerts.** www.greatstbarts.com

One of London's oldest churches was founded in 1123 by the monk Rahere, whose tomb is inside. He had been Henry I's courtier until he had a dream in which St. Bartholomew saved him from a winged monster.

The 13th-century arch used to be the door to the church until the nave of that earlier building was pulled down when Henry VIII dissolved the

priory. Today the arch leads from West Smithfield to the burial ground – the gatehouse above it is from a later period. The present building retains the crossing and chancel of the original, with its round arches and other fine Norman detailing. There are also some fine Tudor monuments. The painter William Hogarth was baptized here in 1697.

Parts of the church have been used for secular purposes. In 1725 US statesman Benjamin Franklin worked for a printer in the Lady Chapel. The church also featured in the films *Four Weddings and a Funeral*, *Shakespeare in Love*, and *The Other Boleyn Girl*.

Barbican ❼

Silk St EC2. **Map** 7 A5. **Tel** 0845-120 4141. 📠 020-7638 4141. 🚇 *Barbican, Moorgate.* **Barbican Centre open** 9am–11pm Mon–Sat, noon–11pm Sun, public hols. 🅿 💻 🍴 ⬆ 🚻 ♿ *induction loop.* See **Entertainment** pp342–53. www.barbican.org.uk

An ambitious piece of 1960s city planning, this residential, commercial, and arts complex was begun in 1962 on a site devastated by World War II bombs, and not completed for nearly 20 years. Residential tower blocks surround the Barbican Centre, the arts complex, which also includes an ornamental lake and fountains.

The old city wall turned a corner here and substantial remains are still clearly visible (particularly so from the Museum of London – *see pp166–7*). The word barbican

St. Bartholomew's gatehouse

means a defensive tower over a gate – perhaps the architects were trying to live up to the name when they designed this self-sufficient community with formidable defenses against the outside world. Obscure entrances and raised walkways remove pedestrians from the cramped bustle of the City, but, in spite of the signposts, and yellow lines on the sidewalks, the complex can be difficult to navigate.

As well as two theaters and a concert hall, the Barbican Centre has two movie theaters, two galleries, an excellent library with children's and music sections, and a surprising conservatory. The Guildhall School of Music and Drama is also located in the Barbican.

The well-stocked conservatory at the Barbican Centre

Museum of London ❸

Opened in 1976 on the edge of the Barbican, this museum provides a lively account of London life from prehistoric times to the present day. Reconstructed interiors and street scenes are alternated with displays of original domestic artifacts and items found in the museum's archaeological digs. The museum underwent a huge redevelopment in its lower galleries in 2010, which opened up 25 per cent more gallery space.

★ Marble Head of Serapis
This statue of the Egyptian god of the underworld (2nd–3rd century) was discovered in the temple of Mithras (see p144).

Stairs to Galleries of Modern London

Archaeology in Action

Oliver Cromwell's Death Mask
This plaster copy made from a wax impression acts as a permanent record of how he looked.

Boy's Leather Jerkin
This practical sleeveless jacket (c.1560), decorated with punched hearts and stars, would have been worn over a doublet for extra warmth.

Main entrance

GALLERY GUIDE
The galleries are laid out chronologically, starting on the entrance level with prehistory. Visitors can walk through Roman and medieval London galleries to the War, Plague, and Fire gallery, which includes a special display on the Great Fire. On the lower level, visitors can learn about London from 1666 to the present day, and see the Lord Mayor of London's spectacular State Coach.

Flint Hand Axe
Thousands of these cutting tools (c.350,000–120,000 BC) have been found in the gravels beneath modern London.

KEY

London before London	
Roman London	
Archaeology in Action	
Medieval London	
1550s–1660s: War, Plague, and Fire	
1670s–1850s: Later London	
Victorian Walk	

Sackler Hall	
1850s–1940s: People's City	
1950s–Today: World City	
Inspiring London	
Linbury Gallery	
City Gallery	

STAR EXHIBITS

- ★ Marble Head of Serapis
- ★ Lord Mayor's Coach

Tobacconist
The Victorian Walk uses several original storefronts and objects to recreate the atmosphere of late 19th-century London.

The Expanding City Gallery explores London after the Great Fire.

Ignazio Pluchino Shoes
The Sicilian opened his shoemaking business in London in 1900. He made high-quality shoes for the wealthy.

Selfridges Lift
These bronze and cast iron Brandt Edgar lifts were installed in 1928.

Beatles Dress
Made in 1964, this cotton dress is printed with the Beatles' heads alongside a guitar that features their signatures.

★ **Lord Mayor's Coach**
Finely carved and painted, this gilded coach (c.1757) is paraded once a year during the Lord Mayor's Show (see p55).

St. Giles, Cripplegate ❽

Fore St EC2. **Map** 7 A5. **Tel** 020-7638 1997. 🚇 Barbican, Moorgate. **Open** 11am–4pm Mon–Fri. 🕙 8:30am Mon–Thu, 10am, 4pm Sun. 🎵 2–5pm Tue. ♿ **www**.stgilescripplegate.co.uk

Completed in 1550, this church survived the ravages of the Great Fire in 1666, but was so badly damaged by a World War II bomb that only the tower survived. St. Giles was refurbished during the 1950s to serve as the parish church of the Barbican, and now stands awkwardly amid the Barbican's stark modernity. It is one of the few UK churches to have two complete organs.

Oliver Cromwell married Elizabeth Bourchier here in 1620 and the poet John Milton was buried here in 1674. Well-preserved remains of London's Roman and medieval walls can be seen to the south.

Whitbread's Brewery ❾

Chiswell St EC1. **Map** 7 B5. 🚇 Barbican, Moorgate. **Not open** to public.

In 1736, when he was aged just 16, Samuel Whitbread became an apprentice brewer in Bedford. By the time of his death in 1796, his Chiswell Street brewery (which he had bought in 1750) was brewing

Blake's gravestone at Bunhill Fields

240,200 gal (909,200 liters) a year. The building has not been used as a brewery since 1976 when it was converted into rooms hired out for private functions – they are no longer open to the public. The Porter Tun room, which is now used as a banqueting suite, boasts the largest timber post roof in Europe, and has a huge span of 60 ft (18 m).

The street's 18th-century buildings are well-preserved examples of their period, and are worth a look from the outside. A plaque on one commemorates a visit to the brewery in 1787 by George III and Queen Charlotte.

Bunhill Fields ❿

City Rd EC1. **Map** 7 B4. **Tel** 020-7332 3505. 🚇 Old St. **Open** Apr–Sep: 7:30am–7pm or dusk (Oct–Mar: 7:30am–4pm) Mon–Fri, 9:30am–4pm Sat, Sun, & public hols. **Closed** Dec 25 & 26, Jan 1. ♿ phone first. **www**.cityoflondon.gov.uk/openspaces

This spot was first designated a cemetery after the Great Plague of 1665 (see p25), when it was enclosed by a brick wall and gates. Twenty years later it was allocated to Nonconformists, who were banned from being buried in churchyards because of their refusal to use the Church of England prayer book. The cemetery is situated on the edge of the City, and shaded by large plane trees. There are monuments to the well-known writers Daniel Defoe, John Bunyan, and William Blake, as well as to members of the Cromwell family. John Milton wrote his epic poem *Paradise Lost* while he lived in Bunhill Row, located on the west side of the cemetery. The website has further information on the burial records of Bunhill Fields.

Wesley's Chapel– Leysian Mission ⓫

49 City Rd EC1. **Map** 7 B4. **Tel** 020-7253 2262. 🚇 Old St. **Open** 10am–4pm Mon–Sat, 12:30–1:45pm Sun. **Closed** between Christmas & New Year, public & bank hols (except Good Friday). ♿ not house. 🕙 9:45am (not 1st Sun of month), 11am Sun, 12:45pm Thu. 🎵 groups book ahead. 🖥 **www**.wesleyschapel.org.uk

Wesley's Chapel

John Wesley, the founder of the Methodist church, laid the chapel's foundation stone in 1777. He preached here until his death in 1791, and is buried behind the chapel. Next door is the house where he lived, and today some of his furniture, books, and other assorted possessions can be seen on display there.

The chapel, adorned in a spartan style in accordance with Wesley's austere religious principles, has columns made from ships' masts. Beneath it is a small museum that explores the history of the Methodist church. Baroness Thatcher, the first British woman Prime Minister, in office from 1979 to 1990, was married in the chapel.

St. Giles, Cripplegate

Broadgate Centre ⓬

Exchange Sq EC2. **Map** 7 C5. **Tel** 020-7505 4068 (ice arena; see pp354–5). 🔵 Liverpool St. 🍴 🖥 🛍 ♿

Broadgate Centre skating rink

Situated around Liverpool Street station, the terminal for trains to eastern England, this is one of the most successful shop and office developments of the nineties. Each of the squares has its own distinctive character. Broadgate Arena emulates New York's Rockefeller Center, doubling as a skating rink until the end of March (depending on the weather) and a venue for entertainment in summer.

Among the many sculptures in the complex are George Segal's *Rush Hour Group*, and Barry Flanagan's *Leaping Hare on Crescent and Bell*. Don't miss the spectacular view of Liverpool Street station and its glass-roofed train shed, seen from Exchange Square to the north.

Petticoat Lane ⓭

Middlesex St E1. **Map** 16 D1. 🔵 Aldgate East, Aldgate, Liverpool St. **Open** 10am–2:30pm Mon–Fri, 9am–2pm Sun. See **Shops and Markets** pp332–41.

In Queen Victoria's prudish reign the name of this street, long famous for its market, was changed to the respectable but colorless Middlesex Street. That is still its official designation, but the old name, derived from its many years as a center of the clothing trade,

has stuck, and is now applied to the market held every Sunday morning in this and the surrounding streets. Numerous attempts were made to stop the market, but it was allowed by Act of Parliament in 1936. A great variety of goods is sold but there is still a bias towards clothing, especially leather coats. The atmosphere is noisy and cheerful, with Cockney vendors making use of their wit to attract custom. There are scores of snack bars, and many of these sell traditional Jewish food such as salt beef sandwiches and bagels with smoked salmon.

Whitechapel Art Gallery ⓮

Whitechapel High St E1. **Map** 16 E1. **Tel** 020-7522 7888. 🔵 Aldgate East, Aldgate. **Open** 11am–6pm Tue–Sun (to 9pm Thu). **Closed** Jan 1, Dec 25 & 26. **Occasional adm charge** for exhibitions. ♿ 📷 🖥 🛍 **Wide range of talks & events.** **www.**whitechapel.org

A striking Art Nouveau facade by C. Harrison Townsend fronts this light, airy gallery, founded

Entrance to Whitechapel Gallery

in 1901 and expanded in the 1980s and again in 2007–9. Situated close to Brick Lane and the area's burgeoning art scene, this independent gallery was founded with the aim of bringing great art to the people of East London. Today it enjoys an excellent international reputation for high-quality shows of major contemporary artists. In the 1950s and 1960s the likes of Jackson Pollock, Robert Rauschenberg, Anthony Caro, and John Hoyland all displayed their work here. In 1970 David Hockney's first exhibition was held here.

The gallery has a well-stocked arts bookstore and a café serving a range of appetizing and healthy organic foods in a relaxed atmosphere.

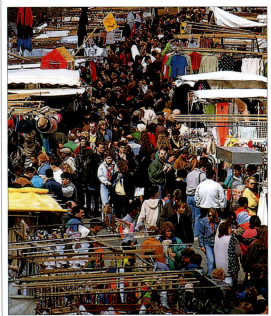

Bustling Petticoat Lane Market

18th-century Fournier Street

Old Spitalfields Market ⓯

Commercial St E1. **Map** 8 E5. 🚇 *Liverpool St.* **Open** *10am–4pm Thu–Fri, 9am–5pm Sun. See* **Shops and Markets** *pp332–41.*

One of the oldest markets in London, Spitalfields started life as a produce market in 1682. Today good quality food, including organic fruit and vegetables, breads, and preserves, can still be purchased here. Although open during the week it is on Sundays that hundreds of people throng the market in search of vintage clothing, bric-a-brac, crafts, and especially innovative fashion by young designers.

Christ Church, Spitalfields ⓰

Commercial St E1. **Map** 8 E5. **Tel** *020-7377 6793.* 🚇 *Liverpool St.* **Open** *11am–4pm Mon–Fri (unless in use as venue, call ahead), 1–4pm Sun.* 🔊 *10:30am Sun.* **Concerts** 🚻 📷 *book ahead.* **www**.spitalfieldsvenue.org

The finest of Nicholas Hawksmoor's six London churches, Christ Church was commissioned by parliament in the Fifty New Churches Act of 1711, aimed at combating the threat of Nonconformism. It was intended to make a powerful statement in an area that was fast becoming a Huguenot stronghold. (The Protestant Huguenots had fled from persecution in Catholic France and came to Spitalfields to work in the local silkweaving industry.)

Completed in 1729, the building was mauled by alterations in the 1850s. By 1960 it was derelict, narrowly escaping demolition. In 1976 the Friends of Christ Church Spitalfields was formed to restore the building to its former glory – a goal achieved in 2004. It is now used as a music venue.

Christ Church still dominates the surrounding streets. The impression of size and strength created by its portico and spire is continued inside by such features as the high ceiling and the gallery.

Fournier Street ⓱

E1. **Map** 8 E5. 🚇 *Aldgate East, Liverpool Street.*

The 18th-century houses on the north side of this street have attics with broad windows that were designed to give maximum light to the silkweaving French Huguenot community who lived here. Even now, the textile trade lives on, in this and nearby streets, still dependent on immigrant labor. Today it is Bengalis who toil at sewing machines in workrooms that are as cramped as they were when the Huguenots used them. Working conditions have improved, however, and many of the sweatshops have been converted into showrooms for companies which now have modern factories away from the town center.

Christ Church, Spitalfields

Bengali sweet factory: Brick Lane

London Jamme Masjid ⓲

59 Brick Lane E1. **Map** 8 E5. 🚇 *Liverpool St, Aldgate East.*

Muslims now worship here, in a building whose life story as a religious site reflects the fascinating history of immigration in the area. Built in 1743 as a Huguenot chapel, it was a synagogue in the 19th century, a Methodist chapel in the early 20th century, and has been a mosque since 1976.

Spitalfields Centre Museum of Immigration & Diversity ⓳

19 Princelet St E1. **Map** 8 E5. **Tel** *020-7247 5352.* 🚇 *Liverpool St.* **Open** *some days & by appt (phone to check).* **www**.19princeletstreet.org.uk

A little Victorian synagogue hidden behind a 1719 Huguenot silk merchant's house with exhibitions celebrating the Jewish and other peoples who arrived as immigrants and settled in London's East End. This historic gem is under constant threat of closure due to lack of funding.

Brick Lane ⓴

E1. **Map** 8 E5. 🚇 *Liverpool St, Aldgate East, Shoreditch.* **Market open** *dawn–noon Sun. See* **Shops and Markets** *pp332–41.*

Once a lane running through brickyards, this is now the busy center of London's

The grand bedroom of Dennis Severs House

Bengali district. Its shops and houses, some dating from the 18th century, have seen waves of immigrants of many nationalities, and most now sell food, spices, silks, and saris. The first Bengalis to live here were sailors who came in the 19th century. In those days it was a predominantly Jewish quarter, and a few Jewish shops remain, including a 24-hour bagel shop at No. 159.

On Sundays a large market is held here and in the surrounding streets, complementing Petticoat Lane *(see p169)*. At the northern end of Brick Lane is the former Black Eagle Brewery, a medley of 18th- and 19th-century industrial architecture, now reflected in, and set off by, a sympathetic mirror-glassed extension.

Dennis Severs House ㉑

18 Folgate St E1. **Map** 8 D5. **Tel** 020-7247 4013. ⊖ *Liverpool St.* **Open** noon–4pm Sun; 6–9pm Mon (book ahead); noon–2pm 1st & 3rd Mon of month; for further dates see website. Private and group bookings welcome. **Adm charge**.
www.dennissevershouse.co.uk

At No. 18 Folgate Street, built

18th-century portrait: Dennis Severs House

in 1724, the late designer and performer Dennis Severs recreated a historical interior that takes you on a journey from the 17th to the 19th centuries. It offers what he called "an adventure of the imagination … a visit to a time-mode rather than … merely a look at a house." The rooms are like a series of *tableaux vivants*, as if the

occupants had simply left for a moment. There is broken bread on the plates, wine in the glasses, fruit in the bowl; the candles flicker and horses' hooves clatter on the cobbles outside. This highly theatrical experience is far removed from more usual museum recreations and is not suitable for the under-12s. Praised by many, including artist David Hockney, it is truly unique. The house's motto is "you either see it or you don't." Around the corner on Elder Street are two of London's earliest surviving terraces, where many of the Georgian redbrick houses have been carefully restored.

Columbia Road Market ㉒

Columbia Rd E2. **Map** 8 D3.
⊖ *Liverpool St, Old St, Bethnal Green.* **Open** 8am–3pm Sun.
See **Shops and Markets** pp332–41.

A visit to this flower and plant market is one of the most delightful things to do on a Sunday morning in London, whether you want to take advantage of the exotic species on offer there or not. Set in a well-preserved street of small Victorian shops, it is a lively, sweet-smelling and colorful event. Aside from the stalls, there are several shops selling, among other things, homemade bread and farmhouse cheeses, antiques, and interesting objects, many of them flower-related. There is also a Spanish delicatessen and an excellent snack bar that sells bagels and welcome mugs of hot chocolate on chilly winter mornings.

Columbia Road flower market

SOUTHWARK AND BANKSIDE

Southwark once offered an escape route from the City, where many forms of entertainment were banned. Borough High Street was lined with taverns: the medieval courtyards that still run off it mark where they stood. The George survives as the only galleried London inn. Among the illicit pleasures that thrived here were brothels in houses by the river, as well as theaters and bear and cock pits, which

Shakespeare window, Southwark Cathedral

were established in the late 16th century. Shakespeare's company was based at the Globe Theatre, which has now been rebuilt close to its original site. Today the south bank of the river has undergone extensive renovation. Riverside attractions range from the Design Museum and Tate Modern, next to the Millennium Bridge, to historic pubs, Borough Market, Southwark Cathedral, and London's tallest building – The Shard.

SIGHTS AT A GLANCE

Historic Streets and Areas
Bermondsey ⑬
Cardinal's Wharf ⑦
Hop Exchange ②
The Old Operating Theatre ⑤

Museums and Galleries
Bankside Gallery ⑧
Clink Prison Museum ⑫
Design Museum ⑮
London Dungeon ⑭
Shakespeare's Globe ⑥

Tate Modern ⑨
Vinopolis ⑪

Cathedrals
Southwark Cathedral ①

Pubs
George Inn ④
The Anchor ⑩

Markets
Borough Market ③

Historic Ships
HMS Belfast ⑯

0 meters 500
0 yards 500

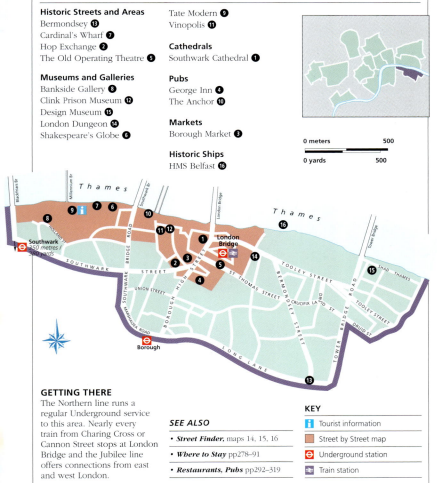

GETTING THERE
The Northern line runs a regular Underground service to this area. Nearly every train from Charing Cross or Cannon Street stops at London Bridge and the Jubilee line offers connections from east and west London.

SEE ALSO
• *Street Finder,* maps 14, 15, 16
• *Where to Stay* pp278–91
• *Restaurants, Pubs* pp292–319

KEY
ℹ Tourist information
▨ Street by Street map
Ⓔ Underground station
▨ Train station

◁ **The Millennium Bridge located opposite Tate Modern**

Street by Street: Southwark

From medieval times until the 18th century, Southwark was a venue for the pursuit of illicit pleasures. Located south of the Thames, it was out of the jurisdiction of the City authorities. The 18th and 19th centuries brought docks, warehouses, and factories. Now Southwark is once again one of London's most exciting boroughs, with the arrival of Tate Modern, a regenerated Borough Market, and the stunning recreation of Shakespeare's Globe Theatre.

BLACKFRIARS BRIDGE

Southwark Bridge was opened in 1912 to replace a bridge of 1819.

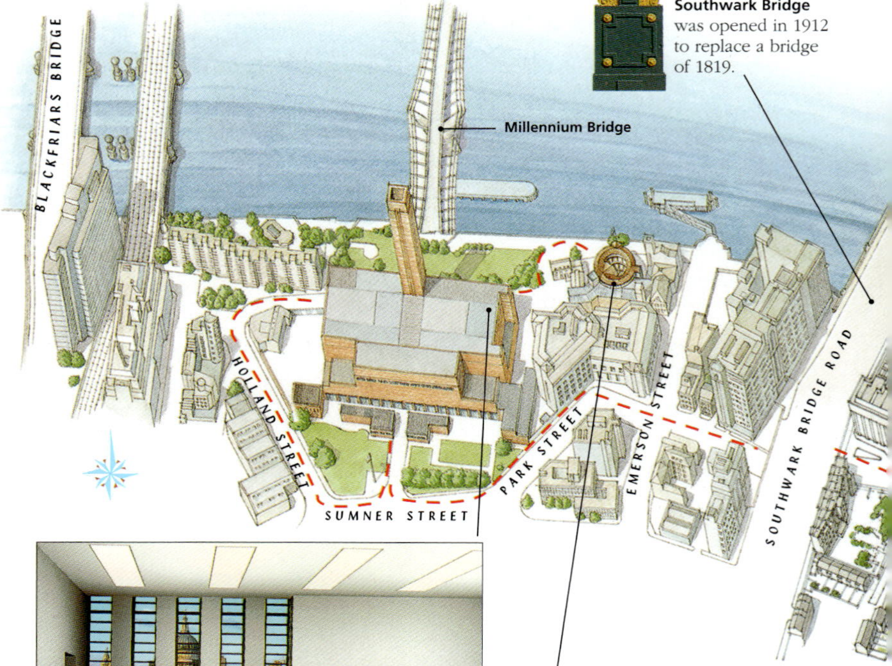

Millennium Bridge

HOLLAND STREET

SUMNER STREET

PARK STREET

EMERSON STREET

SOUTHWARK BRIDGE ROAD

★ Tate Modern
The former Bankside Power Station is now a powerhouse of contemporary art, its spectacular open spaces showing off exhibits to perfection **❾**

★ Shakespeare's Globe
This brilliant recreation of an Elizabethan theater has open-air performances in the summer months and an exhibition open all year round **❻**

STAR SIGHTS

- ★ Southwark Cathedral
- ★ Tate Modern
- ★ Shakespeare's Globe

0 meters 100

0 yards 100

KEY

— — — Suggested route

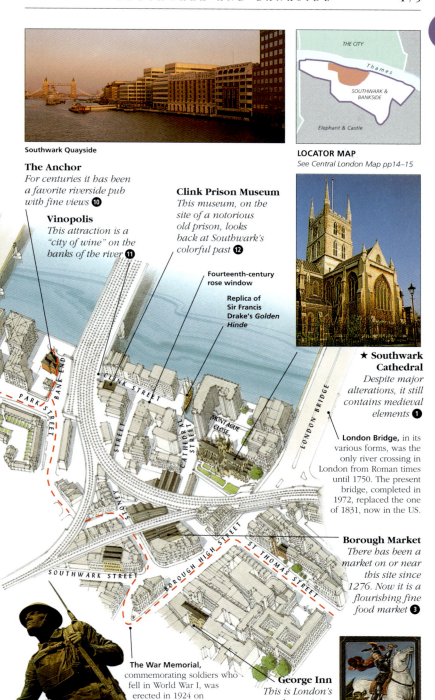

Southwark Quayside

LOCATOR MAP
See Central London Map pp14–15

The Anchor
For centuries it has been a favorite riverside pub with fine views ❿

Vinopolis
This attraction is a "city of wine" on the banks of the river ⓫

Clink Prison Museum
This museum, on the site of a notorious old prison, looks back at Southwark's colorful past ⓬

Fourteenth-century rose window

Replica of Sir Francis Drake's *Golden Hinde*

★ **Southwark Cathedral**
Despite major alterations, it still contains medieval elements ❶

London Bridge, in its various forms, was the only river crossing in London from Roman times until 1750. The present bridge, completed in 1972, replaced the one of 1831, now in the US.

Borough Market
There has been a market on or near this site since 1276. Now it is a flourishing fine food market ❸

The War Memorial, commemorating soldiers who fell in World War I, was erected in 1924 on Borough High Street where it has become a powerful landmark.

George Inn
This is London's only surviving traditional, galleried inn ❹

THE GEORGE

Southwark Cathedral **❶**

Montague Close SE1. **Map** 15 B3.
Tel 020-7367 6700. 🚇 *London
Bridge.* **Open** *8am–6pm Mon–Fri,
8:30am–6pm Sat & Sun.* 🚻 *daily
(check website).* ♿ 🚻 🍴 📷
Concerts. **www**.cathedral.
southwark.anglican.org

This church did not become a
cathedral until 1905. However,
some parts of it date back to
the 12th century, when the
building was attached to a
priory, and many of its medieval features remain. The
memorials are fascinating,
including a late 13th-century
wooden effigy of a knight.
John Harvard, the first benefactor of Harvard University,
was baptized here in 1607
and there is a chapel named
after him.

In 2000 the cathedral was
restored in a multimillion
pound restoration program,
including the addition of new
buildings that house a shop
and a refectory. The exterior
has been landscaped to create
a herb garden and an attractive Millennium Courtyard
that leads to the riverside.

Shakespeare Window in Cathedral

Hop Exchange **❷**

Southwark St SE1. **Map** 15 B4. 🚇
London Bridge. **Not open** *to the public.*

Southwark, with its easy
access to Kent where hops
are grown, was a natural
venue for brewing beer and
trading hops. In 1866 this
building was constructed as
the center of that trade. Now

The George Inn, now owned by the National Trust

a hospitality venue, it retains
its original pediment complete
with carved scenes showing
the hop harvest, and iron
gates with a hop motif.

Borough Market **❸**

8 Southwark St SE1. **Map** 15 B4. 🚇
London Bridge. **Retail market open**
*11am–5pm Thu, noon–6pm Fri,
8am–5pm Sat.*

Borough Market was once an
exclusively wholesale fruit and
vegetable market, which had
its origins in medieval times,
and moved to its current
atmospheric position in 1756,
later beneath the railroad
tracks. A popular fine food
market that sells gourmet foods
from Britain and Europe, as
well as quality fruit and vegetables, and organic meat, fish,
and dairy products.

George Inn **❹**

77 Borough High St SE1. **Map** 15 B4.
Tel 020-7407 2056. 🚇 *London
Bridge, Borough.* **Open** *11am–11pm
Mon–Sat, noon–10:30pm Sun.* 🍴
See **Restaurants and Pubs** *pp316–19.*

Dating from the 17th century,
this building is the only example of a traditional galleried
coaching inn left in London
and is mentioned by Dickens
in *Little Dorrit*. It was rebuilt
after the Southwark fire of
1676 in a style that dates back
to the Middle Ages.

Originally there would have
been three wings around a
courtyard where plays were
staged in the 17th century. In
1889 the north and east wings
were demolished, so there is
only one wing remaining.

The inn, now owned by the
National Trust, is still a restaurant. Perfect on a cold wet
day, the pub has a well-worn,
comfortable atmosphere. In
the summer, the yard fills
with picnic tables and patrons
are occasionally entertained
by actors and morris dancers.

The Old Operating Theatre **❺**

9a St. Thomas St SE1. **Map** 15 B4.
Tel 020-7188 2679. 🚇 *London
Bridge.* **Open** *10:30am–5pm daily.*
Closed *Dec 15–Jan 5.* **Adm charge.**
📷 **www**.thegarret.org.uk

Guy's & St. Thomas' Hospital,
one of the oldest in Britain,
stood here from its foundation
in the 12th century until it was
moved west in 1862. At this
time nearly all of its buildings
were demolished in order to
make way for the railroad.
The women's operating

19th-century surgical tools

theater (The Old Operating Theatre Museum and Herb Garret) survived only because it was located away from the main buildings, in a garret over the hospital church. The UK's oldest operating theater, it dates back to 1822. It lay, bricked up and forgotten, until the 1950s. It has now been fitted out just as it would have been in the early 19th century, before the discovery of either anesthetics or antiseptics. The display shows how patients were blindfolded, gagged, and bound to the wooden operating table, while a box of sawdust underneath was used to catch the blood.

Shakespeare's *Henry IV* (performed at the Globe Theatre around 1600)

Shakespeare's Globe ❻

New Globe Walk SE1. **Map** 15 A3. **Tel** 020-7902 1500. **Tel** box office 020-7401 9919. ⊖ *Southwark, London Bridge.* **Exhibition open** May–Sep: 9am–5:30pm; Oct–Apr: 10am–5:30pm daily. **Adm charge**. 📷 *every 30 mins. (Rose Theatre tours for groups of 15 or more by appt only.)* **Performances** Apr– early Oct. ⬤▣⏸⬜ **www**.shakespeares-globe.org

Built on the banks of the Thames, Shakespeare's Globe is an impressive reconstruction of the Elizabethan theater where many of his plays were first performed. The wooden, circular structure is open in the middle, leaving some of the audience exposed to the elements. Those holding seat tickets have a roof over their heads. The performances are held only in summer, and

seeing a play here is a thrilling experience, with top-quality acting. There is an informative tour for visitors, and groups may book to see the original foundations of the nearby Rose Theatre. Beneath the Globe, and open all year round, is Shakespeare's Globe Exhibition, which brings his work and times to life.

Cardinal's Wharf ❼

SE1. **Map** 15 A3. ⊖ *London Bridge.*

A small group of 17th-century houses still survives here in the shadow of Tate Modern art gallery *(see pp178–81)*. A plaque commemorates Christopher Wren's stay here while St. Paul's Cathedral *(see pp148–51)* was being built. He would have had a particularly fine view of the works. It is thought that the wharf got its name from Cardinal Wolsey who was Bishop of Winchester in 1529.

Bankside Gallery ❽

48 Hopton St SE1. **Map** 14 F3. **Tel** 020-7928 7521. ⊖ *Blackfriars, Southwark.* **Open** 11am–6pm daily. **Closed** Dec 24–26, Jan 1. ♿📷 **Lectures**. **www**.banksidegallery.com

This modern riverside gallery is the headquarters of two historic British societies, namely the Royal Watercolour Society and the Royal Society of Painter-Printmakers. The

View from the Founders' Arms

members of these societies are elected by their peers in a tradition that dates back over 200 years. Their work embraces both established and experimental practices. The gallery's permanent collection is not on show here but there are constantly changing temporary displays of contemporary water colors and original artists' prints. The exhibitions feature the work of both societies and many of the pieces on display are for sale. There is also a superb specialist art shop that sells both books and materials.

There is an unparalleled view of St. Paul's Cathedral from the nearby pub, the Founders' Arms – built on the site of the foundry where the cathedral's bells were cast. South of here, on Hopton Street, is a series of alms-houses that date from 1752.

Row of 17th-century houses on Cardinal's Wharf

Tate Modern ❾

Looming over the southern bank of the Thames, Tate
Modern occupies the converted Bankside power
station, a dynamic space for one of the world's premier
collections of contemporary art. Up until 2000, the Tate
collection was shown at three galleries: Tate St. Ives,
Tate Liverpool and the Tate Gallery, now Tate Britain
(see pp82–85). With the addition of Tate Modern, space
was made for an ever-expanding collection of contemporary art. Tate Modern continually rehangs its collection,
so works and exhibitions may change from those seen
here. A new extension is currently under construction.

★ **Fish (1926)**
*Constantin
Brancusi
attempted to
portray the
"spirit" of a fish
in this abstract
work constructed
from bronze,
metal, and
wood.*

Whaam! *(1963)*
*Roy Lichtenstein took inspiration from
commercial art sources such as comics for
many of his works, of which* Whaam! *is
one of his most famous.*

Quattro Stagioni *(1993–4)*
*Cy Twombly's four paintings
depict the changes of light
and color over the seasons.*

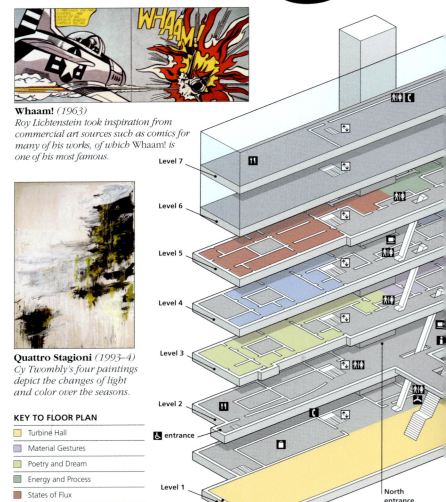

Level 7

Level 6

Level 5

Level 4

Level 3

Level 2

♿ entrance

Level 1

West entrance

North
entrance

KEY TO FLOOR PLAN

- Turbine Hall
- Material Gestures
- Poetry and Dream
- Energy and Process
- States of Flux
- Temporary exhibition space
- Nonexhibition space

★ The Snail (1953)
One of Henri Matisse's final works, The Snail was also one of his largest. It is a cutout, a medium Matisse focused on during his later years where pieces of gouache-painted paper are arranged to form a composition.

VISITORS' CHECKLIST

Bankside, SE1 **Map** 14 F3, 15 A3. **Tel** 020-7887 8888.
🚇 *Blackfriars, Mansion House, Southwark.* 🚌 *45, 63, 100, 344, 381.* **Open** *Sun–Thu 10am–6pm, Fri–Sat 10am–10pm.* **Closed** *Dec 24–26.* **Adm charge** *for special exhibitions only.* 🍴
📷 🚫 📹 🔊 ♿ 📖
www.tate.org.uk

Soft Drainpipe – Blue (Cool) Version (1967)
An advertisement for drainpipes was the inspiration for this sculpture by Pop artist Claes Oldenburg. Like many of his pieces, Soft Drainpipe uses pliable material to represent hard surfaces, and thus renders a familiar object strange.

The "light beam," a two-story glass box, allows light to filter into the upper galleries.

A balcony gives great views of St. Paul's Cathedral (pp148–51) across the river.

GALLERY GUIDE
The main west entrance opens into the expansive, sloped Turbine Hall. From here, a flight of stairs leads to the café and foyer of level 2, or an escalator whisks visitors straight up to gallery level 3. Temporary exhibitions are on level 4, while level 5 is again devoted to galleries. Level 6 is members' access only, but a superb restaurant and spectacular city views can be found on level 7.

★ Spatial Concept "Waiting" (1960)
Cut canvases became a feature of Lucio Fontana's work from 1959, serving to draw the viewer almost inside the work.

The Turbine Hall
The massive scale of this space – it covers 35,520 sq ft (3,300 sq m) – presents an unusual challenge for the artists who install pieces here.

STAR EXHIBITS

★ Fish
by Brancusi

★ The Snail
by Matisse

★ Spatial Concept
"Waiting" by Fontana

Exploring Tate Modern

Tate Modern's displays are arranged into four thematic wings, each of which revolves around a large central room that focuses on a key period of modern art: Cubism, Futurism, and Vorticism; Surrealism; Postwar painting and sculpture; and Minimalism. Around these focal points, smaller, regularly changing displays explore how each movement reflects earlier artistic practice or influenced subsequent developments.

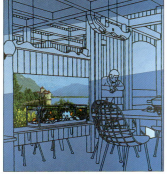

After Lunch (1975) by Patrick Caulfield

MATERIAL GESTURES

The Material Gestures wing is centered around a room committed to painting and sculpture from the 1940s and 1950s which demonstrate how new forms of abstraction and expressive figuration arrived in America and Europe in the aftermath of the Second World War.

The pieces that occupy the surrounding rooms seek to relate the innovative artists of this postwar period to their predecessors, while also illustrating how their ideas have influenced modern artists and inspired the further development of art.

Pieces by the British artist Anish Kapoor and the American Barnett Newman are brought together as an introduction to the wing. A frequent feature of Newman's paintings is a vertical line representative of a column of light. Kapoor has adapted this concept to real space in *Ishi's Light* (2003), a sculptural installation in which a column of light is generated at the centre of the piece.

Subsequent rooms in the wing focus on Mark Rothko, Expressionism, Picasso and Matisse, and the resurgence of painting since the 1990s. However, the most visually arresting room in Material Gestures is perhaps that which brings together works by Claude Monet with pieces by Jackson Pollock, Mark Rothko, and Joan Mitchell. The correlation between Monet's later semiabstract works and those of the Abstract Expressionists is clear to see.

POETRY AND DREAM

The central concept of Poetry and Dream is the process by which modern and contemporary art develops out of what has gone before, while also fueling our understanding of these past movements. Poetry and Dream illustrates this primary concept using the key artists of the Surrealist movement, including Salvador Dalí, René Magritte, and Pablo Picasso. After identifying key Surrealist themes, techniques, and principles, the wing invites visitors to examine works by more modern figures such as Cindy Sherman, Louise Bourgeois, and Francis Bacon and illustrates how these artists invoke the legacy of their Surrealist predecessors. Further rooms focus on the use of film as a Surrealist medium, Cy Twombly and Joseph Beuys, Susan Hiller and her installation piece *From the Freud Museum* (1991–6), and the survival of Realism alongside the burgeoning Surrealist movement using works by André Derain, Max Beckmann, and Diego Rivera.

ENERGY AND PROCESS

"Artists' interest in transformation and natural forces" is the concept behind this sequence of 11 rooms. Room 1 contrasts the work of painter Kasimir Malevich, a pioneer of the early-20th-century avantgarde, and contemporary

BANKSIDE POWER STATION

This forbidding fortress was designed in 1947 by Sir Giles Gilbert Scott, the architect of Battersea Power Station, Waterloo Bridge, and London's famous red telephone boxes. The power station is of a steel-framed brick skin construction, comprising over 4.2 million bricks. The Turbine Hall was designed to accommodate huge oil-burning generators and three vast oil tanks are still in place, buried under the ground just south of the building. The tanks are to be employed in a future stage of Tate Modern development. The power station itself was converted by Swiss architects Herzog and de Meuron who designed the two-story glass box, or lightbeam, which runs the length of the building. This serves to flood the upper galleries with light and also provides wonderful views of London.

The facade, chimney, and light beam of Tate Modern

Summertime: Number 9A (1948) by Jackson Pollock

sculptor Richard Serra, known for his sheet-metal assemblages. Nontraditional approaches to canvas are explored in room 2. Sculptures made from everyday materials are featured in room 3, whereas photography is the focus in room 4, with work from Ana Mendieta. More sculpture follows in room 5 with works by the Italian sculptor Marisa Merz, who applies craft techniques to industrial materials. Room 6 brings together three representatives of the Arte Povera school –Boetti, Fabro, and Pistoletto. Magdalena Abakanowicz's striking, sculptural textiles are found in room 7. Room 8 documents artistic "interventions" in the natural landscape and room 9 highlights a video installation by Brazilian artist Lucia Nogueira. In room 10 you can view an early video art piece – Juan Downey's *Video Trans Americas*. Finally, room 11 has an installation by artists Peter Fischli and David Weiss, whose work recreates cheap, mass-produced objects.

STATES OF FLUX

The States of Flux wing focuses on the ways artists have developed new visual languages to represent the complexity and dynamism of life. The opening room presents a dramatic pairing of works from the first and second halves of the 20th century: Umberto Boccioni's striding figure *Unique Forms of Continuity in Space*, a Futurist vision of speed, strength, and mechanization, alongside Pop artist Roy Lichtenstein's comic-book scene of aerial combat *Whaam!*.

The large central space is devoted to early 20th-century avant-garde. Cubism is represented with major works by figures such as Picasso, Braque, Gris, Lipchitz, and Léger. There are also examples of the Italian Futurist movement and the shortlived British response, Vorticism, with works by Wyndham Lewis, David

Unique Forms of Continuity in Space (1913) by Umberto Boccioni

Bomberg, and Jacob Epstein. An adjoining display, After Impressionism, looks at the very different work of artists working in the same period, with stunning canvases by Matisse, Munch, Vuillard, and Bonnard. Other rooms explore the Fluxus movement and how the innovations of this period influenced experimental film, photography, and design, sometimes with a more pointed political agenda. Displays of collage and Pop Art feature works by Andy Warhol, Jasper Johns, and Claes Oldenburg.

Maman (2000) by Louise Bourgeois

SPECIAL EXHIBITIONS

To complement its permanent collection, Tate Modern presents a program of exhibitions including three large shows a year (retrospectives of modern masters or surveys of important movements). Smaller-scale projects are dotted around, and occasionally outside, the gallery. Once a year Tate Modern challenges an artist to create a work capable of occupying the vast Turbine Hall. Louise Bourgeois was the first artist to install here, with works that included her sculpture *Maman*. Recently, Olafur Eliasson's *The Weather Project* lit the Turbine Hall with a giant glowing sun.

The Bath (1925) by Pierre Bonnard

The Anchor ❿

34 Park St SE1. **Map** 15 A3.
Tel 020-7407 1577. 🚇 *London
Bridge*. **Open** *11am–11pm
Mon–Wed, 11am–midnight Thu–Sat,
noon–10:30pm Sun.* ♿ 🍴

This is one of London's most
famous riverside pubs. It
dates from after the Southwark
fire of 1676, which devastated
the area *(see pp24–5)*. The
present building is 18th
century, but traces of much
earlier hostelries have been
found beneath it. The inn
was once connected with a
brewery across the road that
belonged to Henry Thrale, a
close friend of Dr. Johnson
(see p140). When Thrale died
in 1781, Johnson went to the
brewery sale and encouraged
the bidders with a phrase that
has passed into the English
language: "The potential of
growing rich beyond the
dreams of avarice."

Pub sign at The Anchor Inn

Vinopolis ⓫

1 Bank End SE1. **Map** 15 B3. **Tel**
020-7940 3000. 🚇 *London Bridge*.
Open *noon–10pm Thu–Sat, noon–
6pm Sun (public hols: phone to
check); last adm: 2.5 hrs before close.*
Closed *Dec 25 & 26, Jan 1.* **Adm
charge**. ♿ 🍴 🎧 🎦 📷 www.
vinopolis.co.uk

Vinopolis is a unique attraction
devoted to the enjoyment of
wine. Its blend of interactive
fun and educational exhibits
has made it a popular destination for anyone who
wishes to know more about
making and drinking wine.
Set within cavernous Victorian
railroad arches, Vinopolis

explores the history of
the grape from earliest
times and illuminates
the process of wine-
making from planting
the vines through to la-
beling the bottles.
"Tasting stations" pro-
vide an opportunity to
savor the subject mat-
ter along the way. A
selection of choice vin-
tages can be purchased
from the wine ware-
house after the tour,
while the shop has a
vast assortment of
wine-related merchan-
dise. Cantina Vinopolis
offers good food,
great service, and,
unsurprisingly,
high-quality wines.

Clink Prison Museum ⓬

1 Clink St SE1. **Map** 15 B3. **Tel** 020-
7403 0900. 🚇 *London Bridge*.
Open *Jul–Sep: 10am–9pm daily;
Oct–Jun: 10am–6pm Mon–Fri, 10am–
7:30pm Sat & Sun.* **Closed** *Dec 25.*
Adm charge. 📷 🎧 🎦 *for groups
(phone first).* www.clink.co.uk

Now a macabre museum, the
prison that was once located
here first opened in the 12th
century. It was owned by
successive Bishops of Winchester, who lived in the
adjoining palace just east of
the museum, of which all that
now remains is a lovely rose
window. During the 15th
century, the prison became
known as the "Clink," and
finally closed in 1780.
    The museum illustrates the
history of the prison. Tales of
the inmates are told, including those of the numerous

**Replica Of Civil
War Trooper's Helmet
Made In The Clink**

Antiques stall at Bermondsey Market

prostitutes, debtors, and
priests that were incarcerated
here. Hands-on displays of
instruments of torture leave
little to the imagination and
are not for the fainthearted.

Bermondsey ⓭

SE1. **Map** 15 C5. 🚇 *London Bridge,
Borough*. **Market Open** *4am–1pm
Fri, starts closing noon.* **Fashion and
Textile Museum** *83 Bermondsey St
SE1.* **Tel** *020-7407 8664.* **Open**
11am–6pm Tue–Sat. **Adm charge**.
♿ 🎦 *on request.* 🎧 💻 www.
ftmlondon.org

Bermondsey's winding streets
still hold traces of its historic
past in the form of medieval,
18th-century, and Victorian
buildings. Today it is famous
for its antiques market. Each
Friday at dawn, seriously
committed antiques dealers
trade their latest acquisitions
at Bermondsey. There are
occasional press reports about
long-lost masterworks changing hands here for a song,
and optimists are welcome to
try their luck and test their
judgment. However, trading
starts at the crack of dawn,
and the best bargains tend to
go before most people are
even awake.
    The Fashion and Textile
Museum in Bermondsey
Street re-opened in 2008
and now combines an
education, exhibition, and
visitor center for contemporary
fashion, textiles, and jewelry.
A store sells products by
up-and-coming designers.

London Dungeon ⓮

Tooley St SE1. **Map** 15 C3. 020-7403 7221. London Bridge. **Open** daily Jul–Aug: 9:30am–6:30pm; Sep–Oct: 10am–5:30pm; Nov–Apr: 10:30am–5pm; Apr–Jun: 10am–5:30pm (times may vary slightly so call or check website). **Closed** Dec 25. **Adm charge**. **www**.thedungeons.com

Spooky London Dungeon logo, an indication of the gruesome displays

In effect a much-expanded version of the chamber of horrors at Madame Tussaud's *(see p224)*, this museum is a great hit with children. It illustrates the most bloodthirsty events in British history, with live actors and special effects. It is played strictly for terror, and screams abound with experiences such as Gruesome Goings-on, which includes live actors, a ride, and shows; the Great Plague; the Torture Chamber; and Jack the Ripper.

Eduardo Paolozzi sculpture outside the Design Museum

Design Museum ⓯

Butlers Wharf, Shad Thames SE1. **Map** 16 E4. **Tel** 020-7403 6033. Tower Hill, London Bridge. **Open** 10am–5:45pm daily (last adm: 5:15pm). **Closed** Dec 25 & 26. **Adm charge**. Blueprint Café 020-7378 7031 (booking advised). **www**.designmuseum.org

This museum was the first in the world to be devoted solely to modern and contemporary design when it was founded in 1989. A frequently changing program of exhibitions explores landmarks in modern design history and the most exciting innovations in contemporary design set against the context of social, cultural, economic,

and technological changes. The Design Museum embraces every area of design, from furniture and fashion to household products, cars, graphics, websites, and architecture in exhibitions and new design commissions. Each spring the museum hosts Designer of the Year, a national design prize, with an exhibition at which the public can vote for the winner.

The museum is arranged over three floors, with major exhibitions on the second floor. There is a choice of smaller displays on the third, which also houses an Interaction Space, where visitors can play vintage video games and learn about the designers featured in the museum in the Design at the Design Museum online research archive. The shop and café are on the first floor. On the second floor is the **Blueprint Café** restaurant, which has stunning views of the Thames.

HMS Belfast ⓰

Morgan's Lane, Tooley St SE1. **Map** 16 D3. 020-7940 6300. London Bridge, Tower Hill. **Open** Mar–Oct: 10am–6pm daily; Nov–Feb: 10am–5pm daily (last adm: 1 hr before closing). **Closed** Dec 24–26. **Adm charge**. limited. **www**.hmsbelfast.iwm.org.uk

Originally launched in 1938 to serve in World War II, HMS *Belfast* was instrumental in the destruction of the German battle cruiser, *Scharnhorst*, in the battle of North Cape, and also played an important role in the Normandy Landings.

After the war, the battle cruiser, designed for offensive action and for supporting amphibious operations, was sent to work for the United Nations in Korea. The ship remained in service with the British navy until 1965.

Since 1971, the cruiser has been used as a floating naval museum. Part of it has been recreated to show what the ship was like in 1943, when it participated in sinking the German battle cruiser. Other displays portray life on board during World War II and there are also exhibits relating to the history of the Royal Navy.

As well as being a great family day out, it is also possible for children to take part in educational activity weekends on board the ship.

The now familiar sight of the naval gunship HMS *Belfast* on the Thames

SOUTH BANK

Following the Festival of Britain in 1951, the Southbank Centre grew up around the newly erected Royal Festival Hall. The architecture has been criticized over the years, especially the chunky concrete building that houses The Hayward Gallery, but now appears to be valued as an important part of London's river frontage. The area functions well, and is crowded with culture-seekers most evenings and afternoons. As well as the National Theatre and the Old Vic theater, concert halls, and galleries, the South Bank has the BFI Southbank and London's most striking cinema, the BFI IMAX *(see p347)*. In keeping with Festival of Britain tradition, the South Bank was a focal point for the new millennium, with the raising of the world's highest observation wheel, the London Eye.

SIGHTS AT A GLANCE

Historic Streets and Buildings
Gabriel's Wharf ⑪
Lambeth Palace ⑧
Waterloo Station ⑫

Museums and Galleries
Florence Nightingale
 Museum ⑥
Hayward Gallery ②
Imperial War
 Museum ⑨
Museum of Garden
 History ⑦

Attractions
County Hall ④
The London Eye ⑤

Theaters and Concert Halls
Royal National
 Theatre ①
Royal Festival Hall ③
The Old Vic ⑩

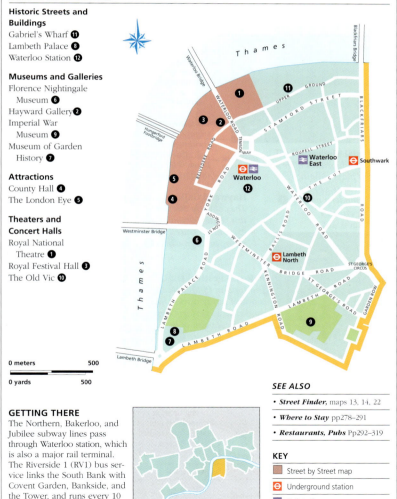

```
0 meters        500
0 yards         500
```

GETTING THERE
The Northern, Bakerloo, and Jubilee subway lines pass through Waterloo station, which is also a major rail terminal. The Riverside 1 (RV1) bus service links the South Bank with Covent Garden, Bankside, and the Tower, and runs every 10 minutes from 6am to midnight.

SEE ALSO

• *Street Finder,* maps 13, 14, 22

• *Where to Stay* pp278–291

• *Restaurants, Pubs* Pp292–319

KEY

▨ Street by Street map

⊖ Underground station

⇌ Rail station

◁ **Riverside walk on the South Bank**

The façade of the Hayward Gallery

National Theatre ❶

South Bank SE1. **Map** 14 D3.
📷 *020-7452 3000*. 🚇 *Waterloo.*
Open *9:30am–10:45pm Mon–Sat.*
Closed *Good Fri, Dec 24, 25, bank hols.* 📷 *during performances.* 🍴
📷 📷 📷 📷 **Concerts** *at 5:45pm,*
exhibitions. *See Entertainment p344.* **www**.nationaltheatre.org.uk

Even if you don't want to see a play, this well-appointed complex is worth a visit. Sir Denys Lasdun's building was opened in 1976 after 200 years of debate about whether there should be a national theater and its location. The company was formed in 1963, under Laurence (later Lord) Olivier, Britain's leading 20th-century actor. The largest of the three theaters is named after him: the others are the Cottesloe and the Lyttleton. In summer, there are sometimes free evening concerts in the foyer.

Festival of Britain: symbol of 1951

Hayward Gallery ❷

South Bank SE1. **Map** 14 D3. **Tel** *0844-875 0073.* 🚇 *Waterloo.*
Open *10am–6pm daily (to 8pm Thu & Fri).* **Closed** *Jan 1, Dec 24–26, between exhibitions.* **Adm charge.**
📷 📷 📷 **www**.southbank centre.co.uk

The Hayward Gallery is one of London's main venues for large art exhibitions. Its slabby grey concrete exterior is too starkly modern for some tastes, but it is also considered by many as an icon of 1960s "Brutalist" architecture. The Waterloo Sunset Pavilion by Dan Graham shows a selection of cartoons and artists' videos.
Hayward exhibitions cover classical and contemporary art, but the work of British contemporary artists is particularly well represented.

Royal Festival Hall ❸

South Bank SE1. **Map** 14 D4.
Tel *0844-875 0073.* 🚇 *Waterloo.*
Open *10am–11pm daily.* **Closed** *Dec 25.* 📷 *during performances.*
🍴 📷 📷 📷 **Pre-concert talks,**
exhibitions, free concerts. *See Entertainment p346.*
www.southbankcentre.co.uk

This was the only structure in the 1951 Festival of Britain *(see p32)* designed for permanence. Sir Robert Matthew and Sir Leslie Martin's concert hall was the first major public building in

London following World War II, and it has stood the test of time so well that many of the capital's major arts institutions have gathered round it. Festival Riverside on level 1 opened in 2004, with restaurants and retail, community, and visitors' facilities. Phase II of the redevelopment began in 2005 and was completed in 2007. The stage has hosted many renowned musicians, including Leonard Bernstein and the cellist Jacqueline du Pré. The organ was installed in 1954. There are cafés and bookstores on the lower floors.

County Hall ❹

Westminster Bridge Rd SE1.
Map 13 C4. **Aquarium Tel** *020-7967 8000.* 🚇 *Waterloo.* **Open** *10am–6pm daily.* **Closed** *Dec 25.*
Adm charge. 📷 📷 📷
www.londonaquarium.co.uk

Shark in a scenic tank at the London Aquarium

Once the home of London's elected government, this imposing building now houses an entertainment complex. The Sea Life London Aquarium, the London Film Museum, and *Namco Station*, a computer games hall, occupy the space alongside two hotels, several restaurants, and a health club.
The Aquarium is home to hundreds of aquatic species from all over the world, including stingrays, turtles, and sea scorpions. Special features include an 82-ft (25-m) glass tunnel through a tropical ocean environment and, for the brave, a Shark Walk across a suspended glass platform.

The London Eye ❺

The London Eye is a 443-ft (135-m) high observation wheel. Erected in 2000 as part of London's millennium celebrations, it immediately became one of the city's most recognizable landmarks, notable not only for its size, but for its circularity amid the block-shaped buildings flanking it. Thirty-two capsules, each holding up to 25 people, take a gentle 30-minute round trip. On a clear day, the Eye affords a unique 25-mile (40-km) view which sweeps over the capital in all directions and on to the countryside and hills beyond.

VISITORS' CHECKLIST

Jubilee Gardens SE1. **Map** 14 D4. **Tel** 0870 5000 600 (information and 24-hour advance booking – recommended as tickets sell out days in advance). 🚇 Waterloo, Westminster. 🚌 11, 24, 211. **Open** daily Oct–Apr: 10am–8pm; May–Jun, Sep: 10am–9pm; Jul–Aug: 10am–9:30pm. **Closed** Dec 25 and mid-Jan for maintenance. **Adm charge**. Pick up tickets at County Hall (adjacent to Eye) at least 30 mins before boarding time. Fast-track tickets are also available. 🖥️ 📷 ♿ www.londoneye.com

The glass capsules are mounted on the outside of the rim, allowing unobstructed 360-degree views.

Houses of Parliament
Seventeen minutes into the "flight," the spectacular aerial view of Westminster should not be missed.

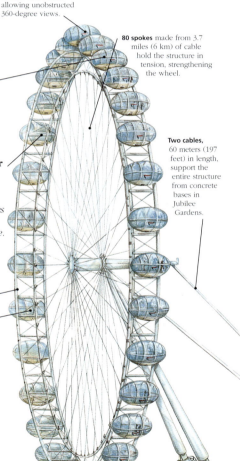

80 spokes made from 3.7 miles (6 km) of cable hold the structure in tension, strengthening the wheel.

Battersea Power Station
After 15 minutes, the distinctive white smokestacks of this old power station are visible.

Two cables, 60 meters (197 feet) in length, support the entire structure from concrete bases in Jubilee Gardens.

The wheel rim was floated down the Thames in sections and then assembled on site.

Buckingham Palace
Ten minutes into the journey, the Queen's official residence glides into view.

The Eye turns continuously and moves slowly enough that the capsules are boarded here while moving. The wheel is halted for those requiring assistance.

Florence Nightingale Museum ❻

2 Lambeth Palace Rd SE1.
Map 14 D5. **Tel** 020-7620
0374. Waterloo, Westminster.
Open 10am–5pm daily (last adm
4:30pm). **Closed** Dec 25 (and
some other dates; call to check).
Adm charge. 🚫 📷 ♿
Videos, lectures. www.florence-
nightingale.co.uk

This determined woman
captured the British
imagination as the "Lady of
the Lamp," who nursed the
wounded soldiers of the
Crimea War (1853–6). She also
founded Britain's first school
of nursing at old St Thomas'
Hospital in 1860.

Obscurely sited near the
entrance to St. Thomas'
Hospital, the museum is
worth finding. It gives a
fascinating account of
Nightingale's career
through displays of
original documents and
personal memorabilia.
They illustrate her life
and the developments
she pioneered in
health care, until
her death in 1910,
aged 90.

Florence Nightingale

Museum of Garden History ❼

Lambeth Palace Rd SE1. **Map** 21 C1.
Tel 020-7401 8865. Waterloo,
Lambeth North, Westminster. **Open**
10:30am–5pm Sun–Fri, 10:30am–
4pm Sat. **Closed** 1st Mon of month;
Dec 22–Jan 1. ♿ 📷 **Library by
appt, lectures, film shows.**
www.museumgardenhistory.org

The world's first museum of
garden history is housed in the
restored church of St. Mary of
Lambeth Palace. In the grounds
are the tombs of John Trades-
cant, father and son who,
as well as being gardeners
to Charles I and Charles II,
were also adventurous plant
hunters and collectors of curiosities. The tomb of William
Bligh of *The Bounty* can also
be seen here.

The Museum of Garden
History consists of a history of

gardening in Britain, illustrated
by a selection of historic garden tools, artifacts, and curiosities. It also runs a program
of exhibitions, events, lectures,
and educational activities.

There is a shop with a stock
of garden-related items for
freshly inspired gardeners.

Lambeth Palace ❽

SE1. **Map** 21 C1. Lambeth
North, Westminster, Waterloo,
Vauxhall. **Not open** to the public.

This palace has housed Archbishops of Canterbury since
the 13th century and today
remains the Archbishop of
Canterbury's official London
residence. The chapel and its
undercroft contain elements
from the 13th century, but a
large part of the rest of the
building is far more
recent. It has been
frequently restored,
most recently by
Edward Blore in 1828.
The Tudor gatehouse,
however, dates from
1485 and is one of
London's most
pleasing and
familiar riverside
landmarks.

Until the first
Westminster Bridge
was built, the horse ferry that
operated between here and
Millbank was a principal river
crossing. The revenues from it
went to the Archbishop, who
received compensation for
loss of business when the
bridge opened in 1750.

The Tudor gatehouse, Lambeth

Imperial War Museum ❾

Lambeth Rd SE1. **Map** 22 E1.
020-7416 5000. Lambeth
North, Elephant & Castle. **Open**
10am–6pm daily. **Closed** Dec 24–26.
📷 ♿ 🍴 📷 📷 **Filmshows,
lectures. www.**iwm.org.uk

In spite of the two colossal
guns that point up the drive
from the main entrance, this
museum is not just concerned
with the engines of modern
warfare. Massive tanks, artillery, bombs, and aircraft are
on show, yet some of the
most fascinating exhibits in
the museum relate more to the
impact on the lives of people
at home than to the business
of fighting. There are displays
about food rationing, air raid
precautions, censorship, and
morale-boosting.

The arts are well represented, with extracts from wartime movies, radio programs,
and literature, plus many
hundreds of photographs,
paintings by Graham

The machinery of war through the ages

Sutherland and Paul Nash, and sculpture by Jacob Epstein. Henry Moore did some evocative drawings of life during the Blitz of 1940, when many Londoners slept in Underground stations in order to protect themselves from falling bombs. There is also a library with a fascinating archive. The Holocaust exhibition is a major permanent display, using historical material and original artifacts to tell its story.

The museum is housed in part of what used to be the Bethlehem Royal Hospital for the Insane ("Bedlam"), built in 1811. In the 19th century, visitors would come for the afternoon to enjoy the antics of the patients. The hospital moved out to new premises in Surrey in 1930, leaving this vast building empty. Its two large, flanking wings were pulled down and this central block converted into the museum, which moved here from its former South Kensington site in 1936.

The memorial to the dead of World War I at Waterloo Station

The Old Vic's façade from 1816

The Old Vic ❿

Waterloo Rd SE1. **Map** 14 E5.
Tel 0844-871 7628. 🔵 *Waterloo.*
Open for performances only. ♿ 🍴
🍸 *See Entertainment pp344–5.*
www.oldvictheatre.com

This splendid building dates back to 1818, when it was opened as the Royal Coburg Theatre. In 1833 the name was changed to the Royal Victoria, in honor of the future queen. Shortly after this the theater became a center for "music hall," the immensely popular Victorian entertainment that included singers,

comedians, and other acts. In 1912 Lillian Baylis became manager and from 1914 to 1923 she staged all of Shakespeare's plays here. In the 1960s the National Theatre *(see p188)* was founded and first based at this site.

In 1997, Sally Greene, with the director Stephen Daldry and others, set up a charitable trust to secure the theatre's future. The Trust set up The Old Vic Theatre Company as a resident company in 2003, with Kevin Spacey as Artistic Director. There are cheap seats for younger people and pantomimes at Christmas.

Gabriel's Wharf ⓫

56 Upper Ground SE1. **Map** 14 E3.
🔵 *Waterloo. See Shops and Markets pp332–41.*

This pleasant enclave of boutiques, craft shops, and cafés was the product of a long and stormy debate over the future of what was once an industrial riverside area. Residents of Waterloo strongly opposed various schemes for office developments before a community association was able to acquire the site in 1984 and build cooperative housing around the wharf.

Adjoining the market is a small garden and a riverside walkway with marvelous views to the north of the City. The OXO Tower to the east, built in 1928 surreptitiously to advertise a meat extract by means of its window shapes, is now the setting for a fine restaurant *(see p302).*

Waterloo Station ⓬

York Rd SE1. **Map** 14 D4.
Tel 08457 484950. 🔵 *Waterloo.*
See Getting to London p372.

The terminal for trains to southwest England, Waterloo station was originally built in 1848 but completely remodeled in the early 20th century, with the addition of a grand formal entrance on the northeast corner. Today the spacious concourse, lined with shops, cafés, and bars, makes it one of the most practical of the London rail terminals.

Toward the end of the 20th century the station was enlarged again to serve as London's first Channel Tunnel rail link to Europe. In the fall of 2007 the Eurostar terminal moved from Waterloo station to its present home at St. Pancras International *(see p130).*

The area around Waterloo has a great community feel and it is worth passing down Lower Marsh with its shops, eateries, and street market.

Illusionistic painting on the buildings around Gabriel's Wharf

CHELSEA

Cow's head outside the Old Dairy on Old Church Street

The showy young shoppers who paraded along the King's Road from the 1960s until the 1980s have more or less gone, along with Chelsea's reputation for extreme behaviour established by the bohemian Chelsea Set of writers and artists in the 19th century. Formerly a riverside village, Chelsea became fashionable in Tudor times. Henry VIII liked it so much that he built a small palace (long vanished) here. Artists, including Turner, Whistler and Rossetti, were attracted by the river views from Cheyne Walk. The historian Thomas Carlyle and the essayist Leigh Hunt arrived in the 1830s and began a literary tradition continued by writers such as the poet Swinburne. Yet Chelsea has always had a raffish element, too: in the 18th century the pleasure gardens were noted for beautiful courtesans and the Chelsea Arts Club has had riotous balls for nearly a century. Chelsea is too expensive for most artists now, but the artistic connection is maintained by many galleries and antique shops.

SIGHTS AT A GLANCE

Historic Streets and Buildings
King's Road ❶
Carlyle's House ❷
Cheyne Walk ❺
Royal Hospital ❽
Sloane Square ❿

Museums
National Army Museum ❼
Saatchi Gallery ❾

Churches
Chelsea Old Church ❸

Gardens
Roper's Garden ❹
Chelsea Physic Garden ❻

GETTING THERE
The District and Circle Underground lines serve Sloane Square; the Piccadilly line passes just outside this area, through South Kensington. Buses 11, 19 and 22 all stop on the King's Road.

SEE ALSO

- **Street Finder**, maps 19, 20

- **Where to Stay** pp278–91

- **Restaurants**, **Pubs** pp292–319

- **Chelsea and Battersea Walk** pp266–7

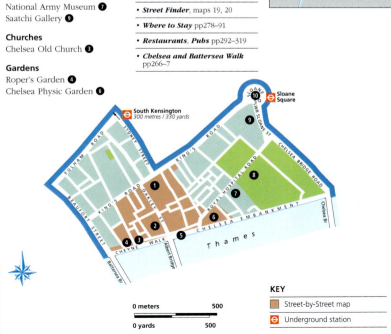

KEY

▨	Street-by-Street map
Ⓔ	Underground station

0 meters   500

0 yards   500

◁ **Picturesque Chelsea residences in a cul-de-sac off the King's Road**

Street by Street: Chelsea

Once a peaceful riverside village, Chelsea has been fashionable since Tudor times when Sir Thomas More, Henry VIII's Lord Chancellor, lived here. Artists, including Turner, Whistler, and Rossetti, were attracted by the views from Cheyne Walk, before a busy main road disturbed its peace. Chelsea's artistic connection is maintained by its galleries and antique shops, while enclaves of 18th-century houses preserve its old village atmosphere.

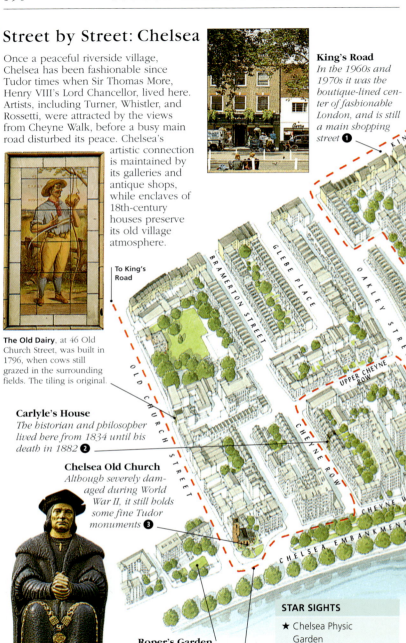

King's Road
In the 1960s and 1970s it was the boutique-lined center of fashionable London, and is still a main shopping street ❶

The Old Dairy, at 46 Old Church Street, was built in 1796, when cows still grazed in the surrounding fields. The tiling is original.

To King's Road

Carlyle's House
The historian and philosopher lived here from 1834 until his death in 1882 ❷

Chelsea Old Church
Although severely damaged during World War II, it still holds some fine Tudor monuments ❸

Roper's Garden
It includes a sculpture by Jacob Epstein who had a studio here ❹

Thomas More, sculpted in 1969 by L. Cubitt Bevis, gazes calmly across the river near where he lived.

BRAMERTON STREET

GLEBE PLACE

OAKLEY STREET

OLD CHURCH STREET

UPPER CHEYNE ROW

CHEYNE ROW

CHEYNE WALK

CHELSEA EMBANKMENT

KING'S

STAR SIGHTS

★ Chelsea Physic Garden

KEY

- - - Suggested route

0 meters   100

0 yards   100

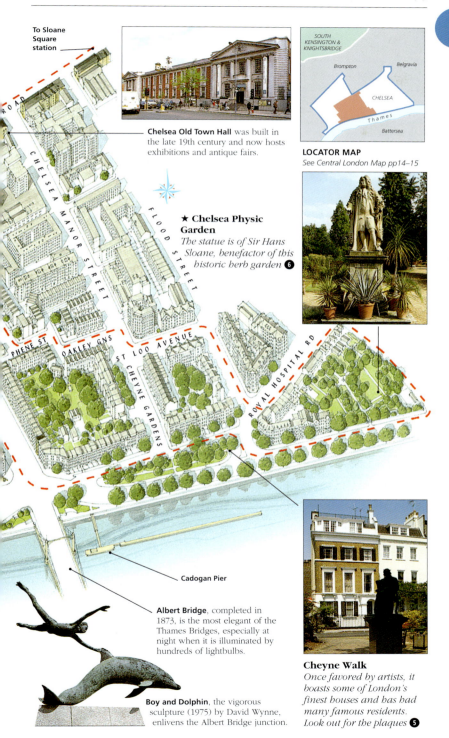

To Sloane Square station

Chelsea Old Town Hall was built in the late 19th century and now hosts exhibitions and antique fairs.

SOUTH KENSINGTON & KNIGHTSBRIDGE

Brompton

Belgravia

CHELSEA

Thames

Battersea

LOCATOR MAP
See Central London Map pp14–15

★ **Chelsea Physic Garden**
The statue is of Sir Hans Sloane, benefactor of this historic herb garden **6**

PHENE ST

OAKLEY GNS

ST LOO AVENUE

CHEYNE GARDENS

ROYAL HOSPITAL RD

CHELSEA MANOR STREET

FLOOD STREET

ROAD

Cadogan Pier

Albert Bridge, completed in 1873, is the most elegant of the Thames Bridges, especially at night when it is illuminated by hundreds of lightbulbs.

Boy and Dolphin, the vigorous sculpture (1975) by David Wynne, enlivens the Albert Bridge junction.

Cheyne Walk
Once favored by artists, it boasts some of London's finest houses and has had many famous residents. Look out for the plaques **5**

The Pheasantry, King's Road

King's Road ❶

SW3 and SW10. **Map** 19 B3.
🚇 *Sloane Square. See **Shops and Markets** pp332–41.*

This is Chelsea's central artery, with its wealth of small fashion shops packed with young people looking for designer fashions. The mini-skirt revolution of the 1960s began here and so have many subsequent style trends, perhaps the most famous of them being punk.

Look out for the Pheasantry at No. 152, with its columns and statuary. It was built in 1881 as the storefront of a furniture maker's premises but now conceals a modern restaurant. Antique-lovers will find three warrens of stalls on the south side of the King's Road: Antiquarius at No. 137, the Chenil Galleries at Nos. 181–3, and the Chelsea Antiques Market at No. 253.

Carlyle's House ❷

24 Cheyne Row SW3. **Map** 19 B4.
Tel 020-7352 7087. 🚇 *Sloane Sq, South Kensington.* **Open** *Mar–Oct: 2–5pm Wed–Fri, 11am–5pm Sat, Sun & public hols (last adm: 4:30pm).* **Adm charge**. 🚫 📷 *tours 11am–12:30pm Wed–Fri (by appt).* **www.** nationaltrust.org.uk/carlylehouse

The historian and founder of the London Library *(see St. James's Square p92)*, Thomas Carlyle moved into this modest 18th-century house in 1834, and wrote many of his best-known books here, notably *The French Revolution* and *Frederick the Great*. His presence made Chelsea more fashionable and the house became a mecca for some great literary figures. The novelists Charles Dickens and William Thackeray, poet Alfred Lord Tennyson, and naturalist Charles Darwin were all regular visitors here. The house has been restored and looks as it did during Carlyle's lifetime.

Chelsea Old Church ❸

64 Cheyne Walk SW3. **Map** 19 A4.
Tel 020-7795 1019. 🚇 *Sloane Sq, South Kensington.* **Open** *2–4pm Tue–Thu.* ♿ 📷 *by appt.* ✝ *8am, 10am, 11am, 12:15pm, 6pm Sun.* **www.** chelseaoldchurch.org.uk

Chelsea Old Church in 1860

Rebuilt after World War II, this square-towered building does not look old from the outside. However, early prints confirm that it is a careful replica of the medieval church that was largely destroyed by World War II bombs.

The glory of this church is its Tudor monuments. One to Sir Thomas More, who built a chapel here in 1528, contains an inscription he wrote (in Latin), asking to be buried next to his wife. Among other monuments is a chapel to Sir Thomas Lawrence, who was an Elizabethan merchant, and a 17th-century memorial to Lady Jane Cheyne, for whose husband Cheyne Walk was named. Outside the church is a statue in memory of Sir Thomas More, "statesman, scholar, saint," gazing piously across the river.

Roper's Garden ❹

Cheyne Walk SW3. **Map** 19 A4.
🚇 *Sloane Square, South Kensington.*

This is a small park outside Chelsea Old Church. It is named for Margaret Roper, Thomas More's daughter, and her husband William, who wrote More's biography. The sculptor Jacob Epstein worked at a studio on the site between 1909 and 1914, and there is a stone carving by him commemorating the fact. The park also contains a figure of a nude woman by Gilbert Carter.

Cheyne Walk ❺

SW3. **Map** 19 B4. 🚇 *Sloane Square, South Kensington.*

Until Chelsea Embankment was constructed in 1874, Cheyne Walk was a pleasant riverside promenade. Now it overlooks a busy road that has destroyed much of its charm. Many of the 18th-century houses remain, though, bristling with blue plaques celebrating some of the famous people who have lived in them. Most were writers and artists, including J. M. W. Turner who lived incognito at No. 119, George Eliot who died at No. 4, and a clutch of writers (Henry James, T. S. Eliot, and Ian Fleming) in Carlyle Mansions.

Thomas More on Cheyne Walk

Chelsea Physic Garden ⑥

66 Royal Hospital Road SW3.
Map 19 C4. *Tel* 020-7352 5646.
🔵 *Sloane Square.* **Open** Apr–Oct:
noon–5pm Tue–Fri, noon–6pm Sun.
Adm charge. 🔇 *call in advance.*
📷 *Gardening school.*
www.chelseaphysicgarden.co.uk

Established by the Society
of Apothecaries in 1673 to
study plants for medicinal
use, this garden was saved
from closure in 1722 by a
gift from Sir Hans Sloane,
whose statue adorns it. Many
new varieties have been
nurtured in its glasshouses,
including cotton sent to the
plantations of the southern
US. Visitors to London's
oldest botanic garden can
see ancient trees and one of
Britain's first rock gardens,
installed in 1772.

Chelsea Physic Garden in autumn

National Army Museum ⑦

Royal Hospital Rd SW3. **Map**
19 C4. *Tel* 020-7730 0717.
🔵 *Sloane Square.* **Open**
10am–5:30pm daily; see
website for celebrity speaker
program. **Closed** Jan 1, Dec
24–26. 🔇 📷 📷 **www**.
national-army-museum.ac.uk

A lively account of
the history of British
land forces from 1485
to the present can be
found here. Tableaux, dioramas, archive film, and interactive displays illustrate major
engagements and give a taste
of life behind the lines. There
are fine paintings of battle
scenes and portraits of soldiers. The store sells a range
of books and model soldiers.

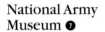
**A Chelsea Pensioner
in uniform**

Royal Hospital ⑧

Royal Hospital Rd SW3. **Map** 20 D3.
Tel 020-7881 5200. 🔵 *Sloane Sq.*
Open 10am–noon, 2–4pm
Mon–Sat, 2–4pm Sun. **Closed** Sun
Oct–Mar, public hols, functions
(check first). 🔇 *limited.* 📷
www.chelsea-pensioners.co.uk

This graceful complex was
commissioned by Charles II

from Christopher Wren in
1682 as a retirement home for
old or wounded soldiers, who
have been known as Chelsea
Pensioners ever since. The
hospital opened ten years later
and is still home to about 330
retired soldiers, whose
distinctive uniforms of
scarlet coats and tricorne
hats date from the 17th
century. Flanking the
northern entrance are
Wren's two main public
rooms: the chapel,
notable for its
wonderful simplicity,
and the paneled Great
Hall, still used as the
dining room. A small
museum explains the
history of the
Pensioners.
A statue of
Charles II by
Grinling Gibbons is to be
found on the terrace outside,
and there is a fine view of the
remains of Battersea Power
Station across the river.

Saatchi Gallery ⑨

Duke of York's HQ, King's Road,
Chelsea. **Map** 19 C3. *Tel* 020-7823
2363. 🔵 *Sloane Square.* **Open**
10am–6pm daily. **Closed** for
private events. 🔇 📷 📷
www.saatchi-gallery.co.uk

The Saatchi Gallery is famous
for presenting the best in
contemporary art and showcasing talent in the UK and
international art world. The
gallery now receives over
600,000 visitors each year.

Many of the featured artists
are unknown when first
exhibited at the gallery but
often rise to fame as a result.
Relocated from its original site
on the South Bank, the Saatchi
Gallery's present home at the
Duke of York's HQ offers an
ideal environment in which
to view contemporary art.
Admire pieces by established
names such as Tracy Emin
and Jenny Saville while also
keeping an eye open for
up-and-coming talent.

Sloane Square ⑩

SW1. **Map** 20 D2. 🔵 *Sloane Square.*

Sloane Square fountain

This pleasant small square
(rectangle to be precise) has
a paved center with a flower
stall and fountain depicting
Venus. Laid out in the late
18th century, it was named
for Sir Hans Sloane, the
wealthy physician and
collector who bought the
manor of Chelsea in 1712.
Opposite Peter Jones, the
1936 department store on
the square's west side, is the
Royal Court Theatre, which
for over a century has
fostered new drama.

SOUTH KENSINGTON AND KNIGHTSBRIDGE

Bristling with embassies and consulates, South Kensington and Knightsbridge are among London's most desirable, and expensive, areas. The proximity of Kensington Palace, a royal residence, means they have remained fairly unchanged. The prestigious shops of Knightsbridge serve their wealthy residents. With Hyde Park to the north, and museums that celebrated Victorian learning at its heart, visitors to this part of London can expect to find a unique combination of the serene and the grandiose.

SIGHTS AT A GLANCE

Historic Streets and Buildings
Royal College of Music ❺
Royal College of Art ❼
Kensington Palace ❿
Speakers' Corner ⓭

Churches
Brompton Oratory ❹

Museums and Galleries
Natural History Museum pp208–9 ❶
Science Museum pp212–13 ❷
Victoria and Albert Museum pp202–5 ❸

Serpentine Gallery ❾

Parks and Gardens
Kensington Gardens ⓫
Hyde Park ⓬

Monuments
Albert Memorial ❽
Marble Arch ⓮

Concert Halls
Royal Albert Hall ❻

Shops
Harrods ⓯

Statue of Peter Pan in Kensington Gardens

GETTING THERE
South Kensington tube station is on the Piccadilly, Circle, and District lines; only the Piccadilly line passes through Knightsbridge station. The No. 14 bus runs from Piccadilly Circus to South Kensington, via Green Park and Knightsbridge.

SEE ALSO
• **Street Finder**, maps 10, 11, 19
• **Where to Stay** pp278–91
• **Restaurants, Pubs** pp292–319

KEY
Street by Street map
Underground station

◁ **The Albert Memorial, opposite the Royal Albert Hall**

Street by Street: South Kensington

A clutch of museums and colleges provide this area with its dignified character. The Great Exhibition of 1851 in Hyde Park was so successful that in the following years smaller exhibitions were held here, just to its south. By the end of the 19th century some of these had become permanent museums, housed in grandiose buildings celebrating Victorian self-confidence.

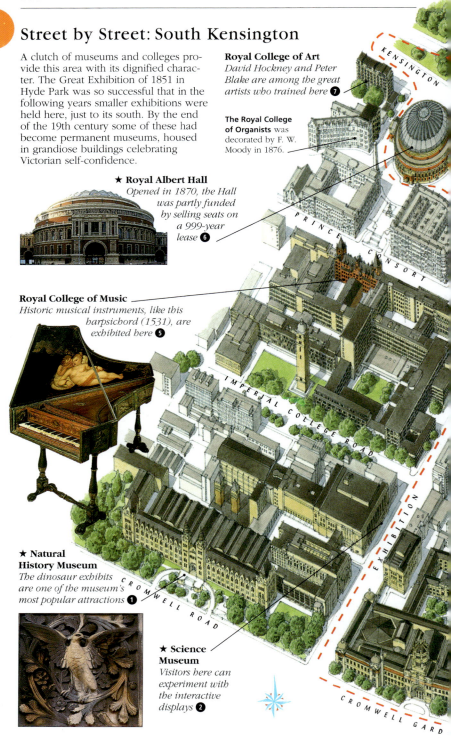

Royal College of Art
David Hockney and Peter Blake are among the great artists who trained here **7**

The Royal College of Organists was decorated by F. W. Moody in 1876.

★ **Royal Albert Hall**
Opened in 1870, the Hall was partly funded by selling seats on a 999-year lease **6**

Royal College of Music
Historic musical instruments, like this harpsichord (1531), are exhibited here **5**

★ **Natural History Museum**
The dinosaur exhibits are one of the museum's most popular attractions **1**

★ **Science Museum**
Visitors here can experiment with the interactive displays **2**

The Albert Hall Mansions, built by Norman Shaw in 1879, started a fashion for red brick.

Albert Memorial
This memorial was built to commemorate Queen Victoria's consort ❽

LOCATOR MAP
See Central London Map pp14–15

KEY

– – – Suggested route

0 meters	100
0 yards	100

The Royal Geographical Society was founded in 1830. Scottish missionary and explorer David Livingstone (1813–73) was a member.

Imperial College, part of London University, is one of the country's leading scientific institutions.

★ Victoria and Albert Museum
A range of objects and a stunning photo gallery illustrate the nation's history of design and decoration ❸

Brompton Oratory
The Oratory was built during the 19th-century Catholic revival ❹

Brompton Square, begun in 1821, established this as a fashionable residential area.

Holy Trinity church dates from the 19th century and is located in a calm backwater among cottages.

To Knightsbridge station

STAR SIGHTS

★ Victoria and Albert Museum

★ Natural History Museum

★ Science Museum

★ Royal Albert Hall

GORE

ALBERT COURT

ROAD

ROAD

PRINCE'S GARDENS

N S

Victoria and Albert Museum ❸

The Glass Gallery

The Victoria and Albert Museum (the V&A) contains one of the world's widest collections of art and design, ranging from early Christian devotional objects to cutting-edge furniture design. Originally founded in 1852 as the Museum of Manufactures to inspire design students, it was renamed by Queen Victoria in 1899 in memory of Prince Albert. The museum is undergoing a dramatic redisplay of some of its collection, including work on a number of galleries and the Sackler Education Centre. To find out if a particular gallery is open, call the reservation office at 020-7942 2211.

British Galleries (1760–1900)
This charming candy box (1770) is one of many pieces on display that were crafted in the workshops of Britain.

Silver Galleries
Radiant pieces such as this Burgess Cup (Britain, 1863) fill these stunning galleries.

★ British Galleries (1500–1760)
Displays of evocative objects, such as this writing desk from King Henry VIII's court, illustrate Britain's fascinating history.

★ Fashion Gallery
In this gallery, European clothing from the mid-1500s to the present day is displayed, such as these famous Manolo Blahnik shoes.

Exhibition Road entrance

KEY TO FLOOR PLAN

- ☐ Level 0
- ☐ Level 1
- ☐ Level 2
- ☐ Level 3
- ☐ Level 4
- ☐ Level 6
- ☐ Henry Cole Wing
- ☐ Nonexhibition space

GALLERY GUIDE

The V&A has a 7-mile (11-km) layout spread over six levels, and the museum incorporates approximately 150 different galleries. The main floor, level 1, houses the China, Japan, and South Asia Galleries, as well as the Fashion Gallery and the Cast Courts. The British Galleries are on levels 2 and 4. Level 3 contains the 20th Century Galleries and displays of silver, ironwork, paintings, and works of 20th-century design. The glass display is also on level 4. The Ceramics Galleries are on level 6. The Henry Cole Wing houses the Sackler Education Centre, RIBA Architecture Study Rooms, and the Prints and Drawings Study Rooms.

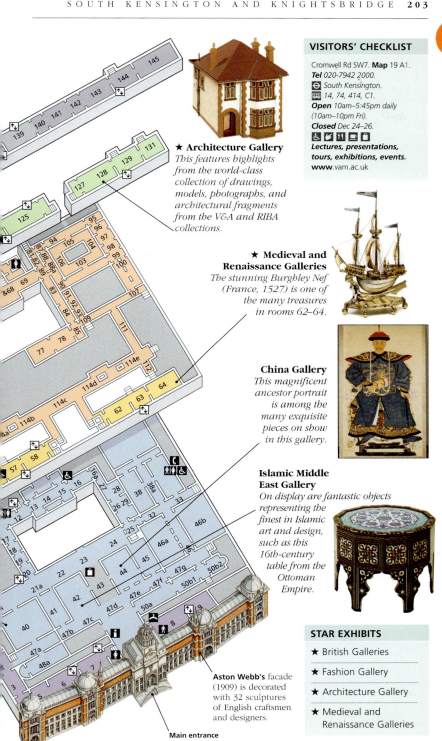

VISITORS' CHECKLIST

Cromwell Rd SW7. **Map** 19 A1.
Tel 020-7942 2000.
🚇 South Kensington.
🚌 14, 74, 414, C1.
Open 10am–5:45pm daily
(10am–10pm Fri).
Closed Dec 24–26.
Lectures, presentations,
tours, exhibitions, events.
www.vam.ac.uk

★ **Architecture Gallery**
*This features highlights
from the world-class
collection of drawings,
models, photographs, and
architectural fragments
from the V&A and RIBA
collections.*

★ **Medieval and
Renaissance Galleries**
*The stunning Burghley Nef
(France, 1527) is one of
the many treasures
in rooms 62–64.*

China Gallery
*This magnificent
ancestor portrait
is among the
many exquisite
pieces on show
in this gallery.*

**Islamic Middle
East Gallery**
*On display are fantastic objects
representing the
finest in Islamic
art and design,
such as this
16th-century
table from the
Ottoman
Empire.*

STAR EXHIBITS

★ British Galleries

★ Fashion Gallery

★ Architecture Gallery

★ Medieval and
 Renaissance Galleries

Aston Webb's facade
(1909) is decorated
with 32 sculptures
of English craftsmen
and designers.

Main entrance

Exploring the V&A's Collections

The sheer size of the V&A means you should plan your visit carefully to avoid missing a highlight or an area of particular interest. One of the joys of the V&A, however, is stumbling across unexpected treasures. Be sure to visit the museum's original refreshment rooms off rooms 11 and 16a (one of which was designed by the then unknown William Morris), now being used once again for their original purpose as a café. The Photography gallery (room 38a) displays the national collection of 300,000 photographs from 1856 to the present.

BRITISH GALLERIES

A sequence of grand rooms starting on level 2 and continuing on level 4 are devoted to the luxurious British Galleries. By presenting design and decorative arts from 1500 to 1900, the galleries chart Britain's rise from obscure island to "workshop of the world." The galleries present the evolution of British high design and the numerous influences, whether technological or aesthetic, absorbed from all over the world.

Beautiful textiles, furniture, costumes, and household objects illustrate the tastes and lifestyles of Britain's ruling classes. Among the highlights are James II's wedding suit, the opulent State Bed from Melville House, and a number of carefully preserved period rooms, including the stunning Rococo Norfolk House Music Room. Discovery Areas give visitors a

Embroidered jacket (1610) in room 56

chance to delve even deeper into the past by sporting a Tudor ruff or viewing 3-D images through a Victorian stereoscope.

CHINA, JAPAN, AND SOUTH ASIA

The Jameel Gallery of Islamic Art was opened in July 2006 and houses more than 400 objects including ceramics, textiles, carpets, metalwork, glass, and woodwork. The exhibits date from the great days of the Islamic caliphate of the 8th and 9th centuries through to the years preceding the First World War.

Middle Eastern art from Syria, Iraq, Iran, Turkey, and Egypt is found in room 42. Beautifully crafted textiles and ceramics illustrate the Islamic influence on fine and decorative arts. A dramatic arc of burnished steel fins, representing the spine of a Chinese dragon, spans the China gallery (room

44). Covering the millennia from 3000 BC to the present, the impressive collection includes a giant Buddha's head from 700–900 AD, a huge yet elegant Ming canopied bed, and rare jade and ceramics.

Japanese art is concentrated in the Japan gallery in room 45, and is particularly notable for lacquer, Samurai armor and woodblock prints.

Gilt copper ice chest (Qing Dynasty, 1700s), room 44

ARCHITECTURE GALLERY

The Architecture Gallery features highlights from the world-class collections of drawings, models, photographs, and architectural fragments of the V&A and the Royal Institute of British Architects (RIBA).

The gallery explores the architecture that shapes our world through five themes. "The Art of Architecture" explores the history and ideas behind architectural styles. A superb collection of artifacts and illustrations is on display, grouped by period and spanning world cultures, including Asian, Spanish Islamic, Classical, Gothic, and Modernist.

THE GREAT BED OF WARE

Made in about 1590 of oak with inlaid and painted decoration, the Great Bed of Ware measures some 3.6 by 3.6 m (12 by 12 ft) and is 2.6 m (8 ft 9 inches) high. It is the V&A's most celebrated piece of furniture. Elaborately carved and decorated, the bed is a superb example of the art of the English woodworker. Its name derives from the town of Ware in Hertfordshire, about a day's ride north of London, where it resided in a number of inns. The Great Bed's enormous size made it an early tourist attraction, and no doubt interest was boosted by Shakespeare's reference to it in *Twelfth Night*, which he wrote in 1601.

Redecorated and refurbished, the bed is located in room 57.

Detail of the Ardabil Carpet (c. 1539–40) from the Jameel Gallery of Islamic Art

"The Function of Buildings" looks at the way in which the design of a building is informed not only by its function but also by the demands of climate.

"Architects and Architecture" examines the team effort involved in designing a building, and how this has evolved over the centuries. A huge range of sketches, models and drawings used by architects supports the theme.

"Structures" examines the different structures needed to create different buildings, from chunky low-rise to tall buildings.

"Buildings in Context" takes a look at the construction of London's Trafalgar Square, from the original maps in 1730 to the present day, in order to explore the relationship that exists between a building and its surroundings.

TWENTIETH CENTURY

Since its foundation in 1852, the V&A has collected examples of contemporary art and design. Two galleries show works exclusively from the 20th century. Art and design are in rooms 70 to 74, and a 20th-century study gallery in rooms 103 to 106 shows the development of furniture design, as well as ceramics, glass, metalwork, and radios. Displays include objects by C. R. Mackintosh, Charles and Ray Eames, and Marcel Breuer.

TEXTILES AND FASHION

Covering 400 years of high fashion, the Fashion gallery in room 40 includes 18th-century courtly dress and 20th-century couturiers, such as Christian Dior and Alexander McQueen. Four huge medieval tapestries, among the museum's greatest treasures, dominate room 94 on level 3. Striking in their detail and depiction of courtly pastimes, they are known as the Devonshire Hunts, despite being made in Flanders. The extensive collection of textiles continues in rooms 95 to 101. The museum's collection of Asian and Middle Eastern carpets is justifiably renowned.

Ruby glass flagon (c. 1858–9)

METALWORK

This group of galleries is located on level 3. In the Silver Galleries, 3,500 pieces from 1400 to the present day are displayed in beautifully refurbished Victorian rooms 65 to 69. Arms and armor, European metalwork from the 1500s to the present, and Islamic brass and bronze can be found in rooms 81, 82, and 87 to 89.

The Sacred Silver and Stained Glass galleries in rooms 83 and 84 display devotional treasures. The highlight of the ironwork

galleries, which are located in rooms 113 to 114e, is the dazzling Hereford Screen designed by Sir George Gilbert Scott in 1862, and displayed at the International Exhibition of that year. The screen became the V&A's largest conservation project.

The Gilbert Collection of gold, silver, micromosaics, and gold boxes, formerly housed at Somerset House, re-opened here in 2009.

GLASS AND CERAMICS

Examples of 2,000 years of glass are exhibited across galleries on level 4. These contain superb porcelain from European china factories, a stunning balustrade by glass artist Danny Lane in room 131. Displays of international contemporary glass are on display in this room as well as in room 129.

The museum holds the world's largest and most comprehensive collection of ceramics. The introductory gallery presents the history and development of ceramics across the world.

Stained glass roundel entitled Susanna and the Elders (c. 1520)

Natural History Museum ❶

See pp208–9.

Relief: Natural History Museum

Science Museum ❷

See pp212–13.

Victoria and Albert Museum ❸

See pp202–205.

Brompton Oratory ❹

Brompton Rd SW7. **Map** 19 A1.
Tel 020-7808 0900. 🚇 South
Kensington. **Open** 6am–8pm daily.
✝ *11am Sun sung Latin Mass (see
website for other times).* ♿ 📷
www.bromptonoratory.com

The Italianate Oratory is a
rich (some think a little too
rich) monument to the English
Catholic revival of the late
19th century. The Oratory was
established by John Henry
Newman (who later became
Cardinal Newman). Father
Frederick William Faber (1814–
63) had already founded a
London community of priests
at Charing Cross. The group
had moved to Brompton, then
an outlying London district,
and this was to be its oratory.
Newman and Faber (both
Anglican converts to Catholi-
cism) were following the
example of St. Philip Neri,
who set up a community of
city-based secular priests
living without vows.

The present church was
opened in 1884. Its facade
and dome were added in the
1890s, and the interior has
been progressively enriched
ever since. Herbert Gribble,
the architect, who was also
a Catholic convert, was
only 29 when he
triumphed in the
highly prestigious
competition to design
it. Inside, all the most
eyecatching treasures
predate the church –
many of them were
transported here
from Italian churches.
Giuseppe Mazzuoli
carved the huge
marble figures of
the 12 apostles for
Siena Cathedral in
the late 17th century.
The beautiful Lady Altar was
originally created in 1693 for
the Dominican church in
Brescia, and the 18th-century

**17th-century viol at the
Royal College of Music**

altar in St. Wilfrid's Chapel
was actually imported from a
church in Rochefort, Belgium.

The Oratory has always
been famous for its splendid
musical tradition.

Royal College of Music ❺

Prince Consort Rd SW7. **Map** 10 F5.
Tel 020-7589 3643. 🚇 Knightsbridge, South Kensington. **Museum
of Instruments Tel** 020-7591 4346.
Open 11:30–4:30pm Tue–Fri
during school or by appointment.
♿ *call 020-7591 4322 before
visit.* 📷 📷 **www**.rcm.ac.uk

Sir Arthur Blomfield
designed the turreted Gothic
palace, with Bavarian over-
tones, that has housed this
distinguished institution
since 1894. The college was
founded in 1882 by
George Grove, who
also compiled the
famous *Dictionary
of Music*; pupils have
included English com-
posers Benjamin
Britten and Ralph
Vaughan Williams.
The Museum of
Musical Instruments
has limited opening
hours; if you do man-
age to get inside,
you will see
instruments from
the earliest times
and from many parts of the
world. Some of the exhibits
were played by such greats
as Handel and Haydn.

The sumptuous interior of Brompton Oratory

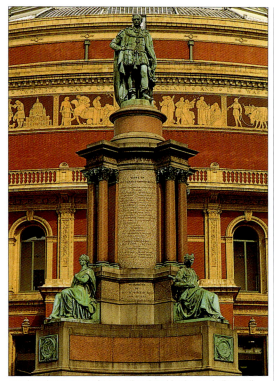

Joseph Durham's statue of Prince Albert (1858) by the Royal Albert Hall

Royal Albert Hall ⑥

Kensington Gore SW7. **Map** 10 F5.
Tel 020-7589 8212. ⊖ *High St
Kensington, South Kensington.* **Open**
for performances. ⊘ ▣ *to book call
0845-401 5045; charge for tour.* ♿
⏰ ▢ *See* **Entertainment** *pp348–9.*
www.royalalberthall.com

Designed by an engineer,
Francis Fowke, and completed
in 1871, this huge concert hall
was modeled on Roman
amphitheaters and is easier on
the eye than most Victorian
structures. On the redbrick
exterior the only ostentation is
a pretty frieze symbolizing the
triumph of arts and science.
In plans the building was
called the Hall of Arts and
Science but Queen Victoria
changed it to the Royal Albert
Hall, in memory of her
husband, when she laid the
foundation stone in 1868.
    The hall is often used for
Classical concerts, most
famously the "Proms," but it
also accommodates other large
gatherings, such as tennis
matches, comedy shows, rock
concerts, circus shows, and
major business conferences.

Royal College of Art ⑦

Kensington Gore SW7. **Map** 10 F5.
Tel 020-7590 4444. ⊖ *High St
Kensington, South Kensington.*
Open *10am–6pm Mon–Fri (phone
first).* ♿ ▣ ⏰ *Lectures, events,
film presentations, exhibitions.*
www.rca.ac.uk

Sir Hugh Casson's mainly
glass-fronted building (1962)
is in stark contrast to the
Victoriana around it. The
college was founded in 1837
as a school of design and
practical art for the manufacturing industries. It became
noted for modern art in the
1950s and 1960s when David
Hockney, Peter Blake, and
Eduardo Paolozzi were there.

Albert Memorial ⑧

South Carriage Drive, Kensington
Gdns SW7. **Map** 10 F5. ⊖ *High St
Kensington, South Kensington.*

This grandiose but dignified
memorial to Queen Victoria's
beloved consort was
completed in 1876, 15 years
after his death. Albert was a
German prince and a cousin
of Queen Victoria. When he
died from typhoid in 1861
he was only 41 and they
had been happily married
for 21 years, producing nine
children. It is fitting that the
monument is near the site of
the 1851 Great Exhibition
(see pp28–9), for Prince Albert
was closely identified with
the Exhibition itself and with
the scientific advances it
celebrated. The larger than
life statue, by John Foley,
shows him with an Exhibition
catalog on his knee.
    The desolate Queen chose
Sir George Gilbert Scott to
design the monument, that
stands 175 ft (55 m) high. It is
loosely based on a medieval
market cross – although many
times more elaborate, with
a black and gilded spire,
multicolored marble canopy,
stones, mosaics, enamels,
wrought iron, and nearly 200
sculpted figures. In October
1998 the regilded statue was
unveiled by Elizabeth II; it
had not been gilded since
1915 when it was painted
black to avoid attracting
attention during World War I.

**Victoria and Albert at the Great
Exhibition opening (1851)**

Natural History Museum ❶

Life on Earth and the Earth itself are vividly explained at the Natural History Museum. Using the latest interactive techniques and traditional displays, exhibits tackle such issues as how human beings evolved and how we can safeguard our planet as well as the Images of Nature exhibit showcasing 350 years of wildlife photography. The vast museum building is a masterwork in itself. It opened in 1881 and was designed by Alfred Waterhouse using revolutionary Victorian building techniques. It is built on an iron and steel framework concealed behind arches and columns, richly decorated with sculptures of plants and animals.

★ Mammals
The life-sized model of a blue whale dwarfs everything else in this vast gallery.

The **Darwin Centre** features an eight-story cocoon in a glass atrium. It is home to 20 million insect and plant specimens, and a research center.

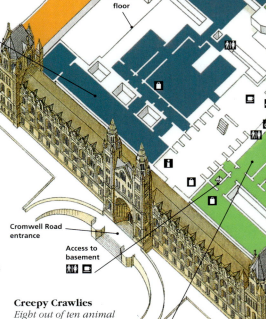

Ground floor

★ Dinosaurs
T Rex, one of the museum's impressively life-like animatronic models, lurches and roars in this hugely popular gallery. More traditional exhibits of fossilized skeletons and eggs are also on display.

Cromwell Road entrance

Access to basement

GALLERY GUIDE
The museum is divided into four sections, the Blue Zone, the Green Zone, the Red Zone, and the Orange Zone.
An 85-ft (26-m) skeleton of the dinosaur Diplodocus dominates the central hall in the Blue Zone – Human Biology, together with Mammals, Dinosaurs, and the Images of Nature are to the left of the hall, while Creepy Crawlies and Ecology are to the right. On the first floor are found Our Place in Evolution and The Vault.
The giant escalator in Visions of Earth leads through a stunning globe to Red Zone highlights The Power Within and Earth's Treasury.

Creepy Crawlies
Eight out of ten animal species are arthropods – insects, crustaceans, centipedes, and spiders, like this tarantula.

KEY TO FLOORPLAN
- Blue Zone
- Green Zone
- Red Zone
- Orange Zone

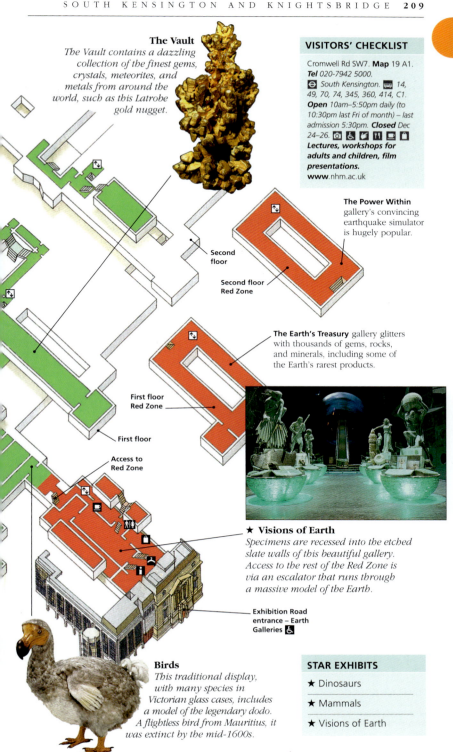

The Vault
The Vault contains a dazzling collection of the finest gems, crystals, meteorites, and metals from around the world, such as this Latrobe gold nugget.

The Power Within gallery's convincing earthquake simulator is hugely popular.

Second floor

Second floor
Red Zone

The Earth's Treasury gallery glitters with thousands of gems, rocks, and minerals, including some of the Earth's rarest products.

First floor
Red Zone

First floor

Access to
Red Zone

★ Visions of Earth
Specimens are recessed into the etched slate walls of this beautiful gallery. Access to the rest of the Red Zone is via an escalator that runs through a massive model of the Earth.

Exhibition Road
entrance – Earth
Galleries

Birds
This traditional display, with many species in Victorian glass cases, includes a model of the legendary dodo. A flightless bird from Mauritius, it was extinct by the mid-1600s.

STAR EXHIBITS

★ Dinosaurs

★ Mammals

★ Visions of Earth

Statue of young Queen Victoria by her daughter Princess Louise outside Kensington Palace

Serpentine Gallery ❾

Kensington Gdns W2. **Map** 11 A4. **Tel** 020-7402 6075. 🚇 *Lancaster Gate, South Kensington.* **Open** *10am–6pm daily.* **Closed** *Jan 1, Dec 24–26 and 31, & between exhibitions.* **Lectures** 🔊 💻 *summer only.* 📷 *art bookshop.* **www**.serpentinegallery.org

The Serpentine Gallery houses temporary exhibitions of major contemporary artists' work. Past exhibitors include Gilbert & George, Rachel Whiteread, and Felix Gonzalez-Torres. This exciting gallery transforms its space to suit the exhibits, sometimes spilling out into the park. Every summer, a temporary pavilion is commissioned from a major architect; this is where you will find the café.

Kensington Palace ❿

Kensington Palace Gdns W8. **Map** 10 D4. **Tel** 0844-482 7777. 🚇 *High St Kensington, Queensway, Notting Hill Gate.* **Open** *Mar–Oct: 10am–6pm daily; Nov–Feb: 10am–5pm daily (last adm: 1 hr earlier).* **Closed** *Dec 24–26.* **Adm charge.** 🎧 🍴 📷 ♿ *partial during building works, no lift to Enchanted Palace.* **Exhibitions.** **www**.hrp.org.uk

Half of this spacious palace is used as royal apartments; the other half, which includes the 18th-century state rooms, is open to the public. When

William III and his wife Mary came to the throne in 1689 they bought a mansion, dating from 1605, and commissioned Christopher Wren to convert it into a royal palace. He created separate suites of rooms for the king and queen.

The palace has seen some important royal events. In 1714 Queen Anne died here from a fit of apoplexy brought on by overeating and, on June 20, 1837, Princess Victoria of Kent was woken at 5am to be told that her uncle William IV had died and she was now queen – the start of her 64-year reign. After the death in 1997 of Diana, Princess of Wales, the gold gates south of the palace became a focal point for mourners in their thousands, who turned the surrounding area into a field of bouquets.

A £12 million renovation project has closed parts of the palace, which is expected to reopen in time for the Olympics and the Queen's Diamond Jubilee in 2012. In place of the usual exhibitions in the state rooms, visitors can now explore the Enchanted Palace. This mysterious wonderland uses modern art and fashion to take visitors on a journey through the stories of past inhabitants, focusing on the seven princesses who once lived here.

Kensington Gardens ⓫

W8. **Map** 10 E4. **Tel** 020-7298 2141. 🚇 *Bayswater, High St Kensington, Queensway, Lancaster Gate.* **Open** *dawn–dusk daily.* 💻 **www**.royalparks.gov.uk

The former grounds of Kensington Palace became a public park in 1841. A small part of it has been dedicated as a memorial playground to Diana, Princess of Wales *(see p219)*. The gardens are full of charm, starting with Sir George Frampton's statue (1912) of J. M. Barrie's Peter Pan, the boy who never grew up, playing his pipes to the bronze fairies and animals that cling to the column below. Often surrounded by parents, nannies, and their charges, the statue stands near the west bank of the Serpentine, not far from where Harriet, wife of the poet Percy Bysshe Shelley, drowned herself in 1816. Just north of here (in Hyde Park) are the ornamental fountains and statues, including Jacob Epstein's *Rima*, at the lake's head. George Frederick Watts's statue of a muscular horse and rider, *Physical Energy*, stands to the south. Not far away is a summerhouse designed by William Kent in 1735, and the Serpentine Gallery.

Detail of the Coalbrookdale gate, Kensington Gardens

The Round Pond, created in 1728 just east of the palace, is often packed with model boats navigated by children and older enthusiasts. In winter it is occasionally fit for skating. In the north, near Lancaster Gate, is a dogs' cemetery, started in 1880 by the Duke of Cambridge while mourning one of his pets.

Hyde Park ⓬

W2. **Map** 11 B3. *Tel 020-7298 2100.* Ⓔ *Hyde Park Corner, Knightsbridge, Lancaster Gate, Marble Arch.* **Open** *5am–midnight daily.* ⬚ **Sporting facilities.** **www**.royalparks.gov.uk

Riding on Rotten Row, Hyde Park

The ancient manor of Hyde was part of the lands of Westminster Abbey seized by Henry VIII at the Dissolution of the Monasteries in 1536. It has remained a royal park ever since. Henry used it for hunting but James I opened it to the public in the early 17th century. The Serpentine, an artificial lake used for boating and bathing, was created when Caroline, George II's queen, dammed the flow of the Westbourne River in 1730.

In its time the park has been a venue for dueling, horse racing, highwaymen, demonstrations, and music. The 1851 Exhibition was held here in a vast glass palace (*see pp28–9*). The Princess Diana Memorial fountain is to the south of the Serpentine.

During the 2012 Olympic Games, the park will be the setting for the triathlon and marathon swimming events.

Speakers' Corner ⓭

Hyde Park W2. **Map** 11 C2. Ⓔ *Marble Arch.*

An 1872 law made it legal to assemble an audience and address them on whatever topic you chose; since then this corner of Hyde Park has become the established venue for budding orators and a fair number of eccentrics. It is well worth spending time here on a Sunday: speakers from fringe groups and one-member political parties reveal their plans for the betterment of humankind while the assembled onlookers heckle them without mercy.

Marble Arch ⓮

Park Lane W1. **Map** 11 C2. Ⓔ *Marble Arch.*

John Nash designed the arch in 1827 as the main entrance to Buckingham Palace. It was, however, too narrow for the grandest coaches and was moved here in 1851. Historically, only senior members of the Royal Family and one of the royal artillery regiments were allowed to pass under it.

The arch stands near the site of the old Tyburn gallows (marked by a plaque), where until 1783 the city's most notorious criminals were hanged in front of crowds of bloodthirsty spectators.

An orator at Speakers' Corner

Harrods ⓯

Knightsbridge SW1. **Map** 11 C5. *Tel 020-7730 1234.* Ⓔ *Knightsbridge.* **Open** *10am–8pm Mon–Sat, 11:30am–6pm Sun.* 🚫 🍴 ⬚ ♿ See **Shops and Markets** *p321.* **www**.harrods.com

London's most famous department store began in 1849 when Henry Charles Harrod opened a small grocery shop nearby on Brompton Road. By concentrating on good quality and impeccable service, the store was soon popular enough to expand.

It used to be claimed that Harrods could supply anything from a packet of pins to an elephant – not quite true today, but the range of stock is still vast. A dress code applies, so shorts, bare midriffs, and flip-flops are not permitted.

Harrods at night, illuminated by 11,500 lights

Science Museum ②

Centuries of continuing scientific and technological development lie at the heart of the
Science Museum's massive collections. The
hardware displayed is magnificent: from
steam engines to aero engines; spacecraft
to the first mechanical computers. Equally
important is the social context of science
– what discoveries and inventions mean
for day-to-day life – and the process of
discovery itself. The high-tech Wellcome
Wing has interactive displays, an IMAX
Cinema, a SimEx simulator and galleries
devoted to new advances in science.

**★ Science and Art
of Medicine**
*A 17th-century
Italian vase for
storing snake bite
treatment is part
of this interesting
collection.*

**Science in the
18th Century**
*The original orrery, a
mechanical model of
the solar system, is one
of many beautiful
scientific instruments
in this gallery.*

Computing
*Babbage's Difference
Engine No. 1 (1832), the
first automatic calculator
and a magnificent example
of precision engineering, is
a highlight of this gallery.*

**Energy: Fueling
the Future** is a new
gallery that explores
how energy powers
every aspect of
our lives.

Challenge of Materials
*Our expectations of materials
are confounded with
exhibits such as a bridge
made of glass and this
steel wedding dress.*

**Stairs to
lower level**

KEY TO FLOOR PLAN

▢	Basement
▢	Ground floor
▢	First floor
▢	Second floor
▢	Third floor
▢	Fourth floor
▢	Fifth floor
▢	Wellcome Wing

Main entrance

★ The Energy Hall
*Dedicated to steam power, this gallery
includes the still-operational Harle
Syke Mill Engine (1903).*

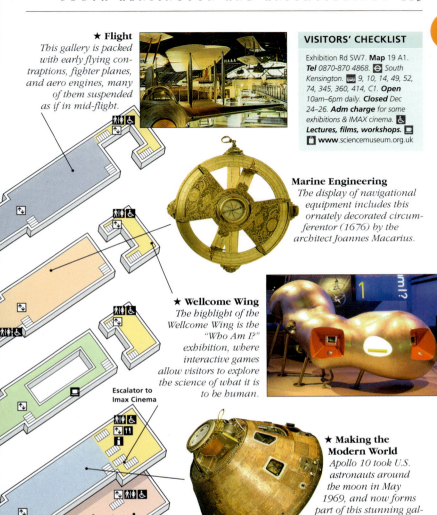

★ Flight
This gallery is packed with early flying contraptions, fighter planes, and aero engines, many of them suspended as if in mid-flight.

VISITORS' CHECKLIST

Exhibition Rd SW7. **Map** 19 A1.
Tel 0870-870 4868. ⊖ South
Kensington. 🚌 9, 10, 14, 49, 52,
74, 345, 360, 414, C1. **Open**
10am–6pm daily. **Closed** Dec
24–26. **Adm charge** for some
exhibitions & IMAX cinema. ♿
Lectures, films, workshops. ▯
🔲 www.sciencemuseum.org.uk

Marine Engineering
The display of navigational equipment includes this ornately decorated circumferentor (1676) by the architect Joannes Macarius.

★ Wellcome Wing
The highlight of the Wellcome Wing is the "Who Am I?" exhibition, where interactive games allow visitors to explore the science of what it is to be human.

Escalator to
Imax Cinema

★ Making the Modern World
Apollo 10 took U.S. astronauts around the moon in May 1969, and now forms part of this stunning gallery of museum highlights.

The hands-on galleries,
including The Garden, prove very popular with children.

STAR EXHIBITS

★ Flight

★ Science and Art of Medicine

★ Making the Modern World

★ The Energy Hall

★ Wellcome Wing

GALLERY GUIDE

The Science Museum is spread over seven floors, balconies, and mezzanine levels. The Wellcome Wing, offering four floors of interactive technology, is at the west end of the museum and is accessible from the ground floor and third floor of the main building. Power dominates the ground floor; here too are Exploring Space and Making the Modern World. The first floor has the Challenge of Materials gallery as well as Weather and Agriculture. On the second floor are such diverse galleries as shipping, mathematics, and computing. The third floor includes Flight, Health Matters, and Launchpad. The fourth and fifth floors (accessible by only one of the elevators) house the medical history galleries.

KENSINGTON AND HOLLAND PARK

The western and northern perimeters of Kensington Gardens are a rich residential area and include many foreign embassies. The stores on Kensington High Street are almost as chic as those in Knightsbridge, and Kensington Church Street is a good source of quality antiques. Around Holland Park are some magnificent late Victorian houses, two of them open to the public. But as you cross into Bayswater and Notting Hill you enter a more vibrant, cosmopolitan part of London. Its stucco terraces are lined with medium-priced hotels and inexpensive restaurants. Westbourne Grove has become increasingly popular with the young, designer-clad

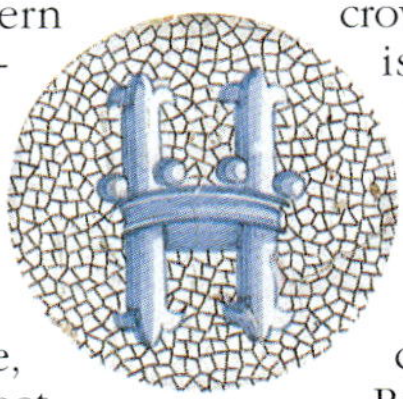

Tiled crest from Holland House

crowd. Whiteleys, in Queensway, is one of the many historic buildings in the area. Built in 1912 by Belcher and Joass as a fashionable department store, it was converted in the 1980s into a vibrant shopping center. To the west, Portobello Road is a popular street market selling anything from food to antiques. Notting Hill is known for its flamboyant Caribbean carnival, which took to the streets in 1965 and has been staged every year since, on the last weekend in August (see p57).

SIGHTS AT A GLANCE

Historic Streets and Buildings
Holland House ❷
Leighton House ❸
Linley Sambourne House ❹
Kensington Square ❻
Kensington Palace
 Gardens ❼
Queensway ❾

Parks and Gardens
Holland Park ❶
Kensington Roof
 Gardens ❺
The Diana, Princess
 of Wales Memorial
 Playground ❽

Markets
Portobello Road ❿

Historic Areas
Notting Hill ⓫

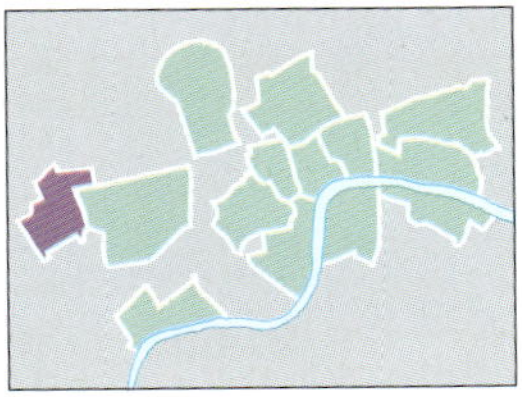

GETTING THERE
The District, Circle, and Central lines serve the area. Bus numbers C1, 9, 10, 27, 28, 31, 49, 52, 70, 73 stop on Kensington High Street; 12, 27, 28, 31, 52, 70, 94 go to Notting Hill Gate; and 7, 12, 15, 23, 27, 36, 70, 94 cross Bayswater.

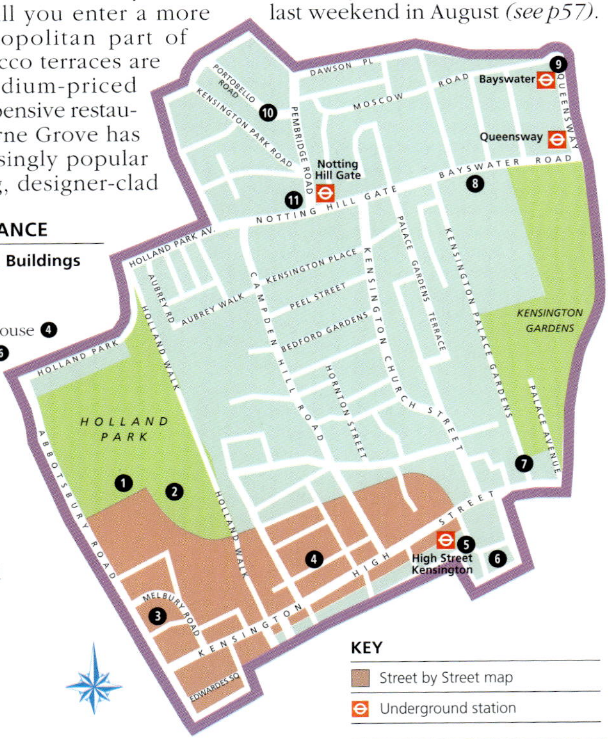

KEY

Street by Street map

Underground station

0 meters 500
0 yards 500

SEE ALSO
- *Street Finder,* maps 9, 17
- *Where to Stay* pp278–91
- *Restaurants, Pubs* pp292–319

◁ **Entrance to a house in Edwardes Square, Kensington**

Street by Street: Kensington and Holland Park

Although now part of central London, as recently as the 1830s this was a country village of market gardens and mansions. Outstanding among these was Holland House; part of its grounds are now Holland Park. The area grew up rapidly in the mid-19th century and most of its buildings date from then – mainly luxury apartments and fashionable stores.

Holland House
The rambling Jacobean mansion, started in 1605 and pictured here in 1795, was largely demolished in the 1950s ❷

★ **Holland Park**
Parts of the old formal gardens of Holland House have been retained to grace this delightful public park ❶

The Orangery, now a restaurant, has parts that date from the 1630s when it was within the grounds of Holland House.

Melbury Road is lined with large Victorian houses. Many were built for fashionable artists of the time.

The Victorian mailbox on the High Street is one of the oldest in London.

★ **Leighton House**
It is preserved as it was when the Victorian painter, Lord Leighton, lived here. He had a passion for Middle Eastern tiles ❸

No. 16 Phillimore Place was home to the author of the children's classic, *The Wind in the Willows*, from 1901 until 1908.

LOCATOR MAP
See Central London Map pp14–15

Church Walk leads to Church Street, which is lined with antiques stores *(see p331)*.

Kensington High Street station

Kensington Civic Centre, an assertive modern building by Sir Basil Spence, was completed in 1976.

Linley Sambourne House
Its carefully preserved late Victorian interior remains intact, complete with original furnishings and draperies ❹

Drayson Mews is one of the quaint alleys that were built behind large town houses for the stabling of horses and coaches. Today most have been converted into small houses.

Sticky Fingers, a lively café on the corner of Phillimore Gardens, is owned by Bill Wyman, former guitarist with the *Rolling Stones* rock group.

STAR SIGHTS

★ Holland Park

★ Leighton House

KEY

— — — Suggested route

0 meters   100

0 yards   100

Holland Park ❶

Abbotsbury Rd W14. **Map** 9 B4.
Tel 020-7361 3003. 🚇 Holland
Park, High St Kensington, Notting Hill
Gate. **Open** dawn–dusk daily (hours
are flexible depending on light).
Closed Dec 25. 🍴 🎭 **Open-air
opera, theater, dance. Tel** 020-
7361 3570. **Art exhibitions** Apr–Oct.
See **Entertainment** pp344–5.

This small but delightful park,
more wooded and intimate
than the large royal parks to
its east (Hyde Park and
Kensington Gardens, see
pp206–7), was opened in
1952 on what remained of the
grounds of Holland House –
the rest had been sold off in
the late 19th century for the
construction of large houses
and terraces to the north and
west. The park still contains
some of the formal gardens,
laid out in the early 19th
century for Holland House.
There is also a Japanese
garden, created for the 1991
London Festival of Japan. The
park has an abundance of
wildlife, including peacocks.

Holland House ❷

Holland Park W8. **Map** 9 B5.
Youth Hostel Tel 020-7937 0748.
🚇 Holland Park, High Street
Kensington.

Original tiling in Holland House

During its heyday in the 19th
century, this was a noted
center of social and political
intrigue. Statesmen such as
Lord Palmerston mixed here
with the likes of the poet
Byron. The remains of the
house are now used as a
youth hostel.
  The outhouses are put to
various uses: exhibitions are
held in the orangery and the
ice house (a forerunner of the
fridge), and the old Garden
Ballroom is now a restaurant.

The café in Holland Park

Leighton House ❸

12 Holland Park Rd W14. **Map** 17 B1.
Tel 020-7602 3316. 🚇 High St Kensington. **Open** 10am–5:30pm Wed–
Mon. **Closed** Jan 1 & 2, Dec 25–28.
Adm charge 🎟 3pm Wed or by
appt for groups. 🎵 **Concerts, exhibitions.** www.rbkc.gov.uk/leighton
housemuseum

Built for respected Victorian
painter Lord Leighton in
1864–79, the house has been
preserved with its opulent
decoration as an extraordinary monument to Victorian
aesthetics. The highlight is the
Arab hall, added in 1879 to
house Leighton's collection of
Islamic tiles, some of which
are inscribed with pieces from
the Qur'an. The best paintings
include some by Edward
Burne-Jones, John Millais,
G. F. Watts, and many works
by Leighton himself.

Linley Sambourne House ❹

18 Stafford Terrace W8. **Map** 9 C5.
Tel 020-7602 3316. 🚇 High St
Kensington. **Open** for guided tours
only, 11:15am, 2:15pm Wed;
11:15am, 1pm, 2:15pm, 3:30pm Sat
& Sun; call 020-7938 1295 to reserve.
Adm charge. 🎵 www.rbkc.gov.
uk/linleysambournehouse

The house, built in about
1870, has received a facelift,
but remains much as Linley
Sambourne decorated and
furnished it, in the Victorian
manner, with china ornaments
and heavy velvet drapes.
Sambourne was a cartoonist

for the satirical magazine *Punch*
and drawings cram the walls.
Some rooms have William
Morris wallpaper *(see p249)*.

Kensington Roof Gardens ❺

99 Kensington High Street W8
(entrance in Derry Street). **Map** 10 D5.
Tel 020-7937 7994. **Open** 9am–5pm
daily (but call ahead, as sometimes
closed for private functions). 🍴

A hundred feet above the
bustle of Kensington High
Street is one of London's best-
kept secrets – a 6,000 square-
meter roof garden. First
planted in the 1930s by the
owners of Derry and Toms
department store below (now
housing many different stores),
the themed gardens are a
lavish flight of fancy and

**Logo for *Punch* magazine
(1841–1992)**

feature a woodland garden, a Spanish garden (with palm trees), and a formal English garden (with a pond, live ducks, and a pair of pink flamingos). Best of all, it's free to wander round, though there is no access when the gardens have been booked for events.

Kensington Square ❻

W8. **Map** 10 D5. 🚇 *High St Kensington.*

This is one of London's oldest squares. It was laid out in the 1680s, and a few early 18th-century houses still remain. (Nos. 11 and 12 are the oldest.) The renowned philosopher John Stuart Mill lived at No. 18, and the Pre-Raphaelite painter and illustrator Edward Burne-Jones at No.41.

Resident's plaque in Kensington Square

Kensington Palace Gardens ❼

W8. **Map** 10 D3. 🚇 *High St Kensington, Notting Hill Gate, Queensway.*

This private road of luxury mansions occupies the site of the former kitchen gardens of Kensington Palace *(see p210)*. It changes its name halfway down: the southern part is known as Palace Green. It is open to pedestrians but closed to cars, unless they have specific business here. Most of the houses are occupied by embassies and their staff. At cocktail hour, you can watch black limousines with diplomatic license plates sweep beneath the raised barriers at each end of the road.

Queensway shop front

The Diana, Princess of Wales Memorial Playground ❽

Kensington Gardens. **Map** 10 E3. **Tel** 020-7298 2141. 🚇 *Bayswater, Queensway.* **Open** *daily, Feb & Oct: 10am–4:45pm; Mar: 10am–5:45pm; Apr & Sep: 10am–6:45pm; May–Aug: 10am–7:45pm; Nov–Jan: 10am–3:45pm.* **Closed** *Dec 25.* 🖥 ♿ www.royalparks.org.uk

The newest of Kensington Gardens' three playgrounds was opened in 2000. Dedicated to the memory of the late Princess Diana, it is located close to the Bayswater Road, on the site of an earlier playground funded by Peter Pan's creator, J. M. Barrie. Diana's innovative adventure playground takes the boy who didn't want to grow up as its theme and is packed with novel ideas and activities including a beach cove with a 50-ft pirates' galleon, a tree house with walkways and ramps, and a mermaid's fountain with a half-submerged slumbering crocodile (careful not to rouse him!). Though all children up to the age of 12 must be accompanied by an adult, staff are on hand to make sure the children are safe. Many features of the playground are accessible to children with special needs.

Queensway ❾

W2. **Map** 10 D2. 🚇 *Queensway, Bayswater.*

One of London's most cosmopolitan streets, Queensway has the heaviest concentration of eating places outside Soho. Newsagents are abundantly stocked with foreign newspapers. At the northern end is Whiteley's shopping center. Founded by William Whiteley, who was born in Yorkshire in 1863, it was probably the world's first department store. The present building dates from 1911.

The street is named for Queen Victoria, who rode here as a princess.

Portobello Road ❿

W11. **Map** 9 C3. 🚇 *Notting Hill Gate, Ladbroke Grove.* **Antiques market Open** *9:30am–4pm Fri, 8am–5pm Sat. See also* **Shops and Markets** *p333.*

There has been a market here since 1837. These days the southern end consists almost exclusively of stalls that sell antiques, jewelry, souvenirs, and many other collectables. The market is extremely popular with tourists and tends to be very crowded on summer weekends. However, it is well worth visiting just to experience its bustling and cheerful atmosphere even if you don't intend to buy anything. If you do decide to buy, be warned – you are unlikely to get a real bargain, since the stallholders have a sound idea of the value of what they are selling.

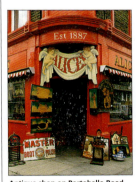
Antique shop on Portobello Road

Notting Hill ⓫

W11. **Map** 9 C3. 🚇 *Notting Hill Gate.*

Now the home of Europe's biggest street carnival, most of this area was farmland until the 19th century.

In the 1950s and 1960s Notting Hill became a center for the Caribbean community, many of whom lived here when they first arrived in Britain. The carnival started in 1966 and takes over the area every August on the bank holiday weekend *(see p57)* when costumed parades flood through the streets.

REGENT'S PARK AND MARYLEBONE

The area south of Regent's Park, incorporating the medieval village of Marylebone, has London's highest concentration of quality Georgian housing. It was developed by Robert Harley, Earl of Oxford, as London shifted west in the 18th century. Terraces by John Nash adorn the southern edge of Regent's Park, the busiest of the Royal Parks, while to its northwest lies St. John's Wood, a smart inner suburb.

GETTING THERE

Regent's Park and Baker Street are the nearest subway stations. Marylebone is served by tube and rail. Buses 13, 139, and 159 run from Trafalgar Square to near Baker Street, and numerous buses run along Oxford St, Baker St, and Gloucester Pl.

0 meters 500
0 yards 500

SIGHTS AT A GLANCE

Historic Streets and Buildings
Harley Street ❹
Portland Place ❺
Broadcasting House ❻
Cumberland Terrace ❶❺

Museums and Galleries
Wallace Collection ❿
Sherlock Holmes Museum ⓫

Churches and Mosques
St. Marylebone Parish Church ❸
All Souls, Langham Place ❼
London Central Mosque ⓬

Parks and Gardens
Regent's Park ❷

Entertainment
Madame Tussauds and the Stardome ❶
Wigmore Hall ❾
London Zoo ⓮

Historic Hotels
Langham Hotel ❽

Historic Waterways
Regent's Canal ⓭

SEE ALSO

• *Street Finder,* maps 3, 4, 12
• *Where to Stay* pp278–91
• *Restaurants, Pubs* pp292–319
• *Regent's Canal Walk* pp264–5

KEY

▢ Street by Street map
⊖ Underground station

◁ St. Andrew's Place, Regent's Park

Street-by-Street: Marylebone

South of Regent's Park lies the medieval village of Marylebone (originally Maryburne, the stream by St. Mary's church). Until the 18th century it was surrounded by fields, but these were built over as fashionable London drifted west. In the mid-19th century, professional people, especially doctors, used the spacious houses to receive wealthy clients. The area has maintained its medical connection and its elegance. Marylebone High Street is full of interesting, high-quality food and clothes stores, bookstores, and cafés.

Tiananmen Square memorial: Portland Place

★ Regent's Park

John Nash laid out the royal park in 1812 as a setting for classically designed villas and terraces ❷

The Royal Academy of Music, England's first music academy, was founded in 1774. The present brick building, with its own concert hall, is from 1911.

★ Madame Tussauds

The wax museum of famous people, historical and contemporary, has been in business since 1835 and remains one of London's most popular attractions. It moved to its present location in 1884 ❶

To Regent's Park

St. Marylebone Parish Church

Poets Robert Browning and Elizabeth Barrett married in this church ❸

KEY

– – – Suggested route

Baker Street station

0 meters	100
0 yards	100

Park Crescent's breathtaking façades by Nash have been preserved, although the interiors were rebuilt as offices in the 1960s. The crescent seals the north end of Nash's ceremonial route from St. James's to Regent's Park, via Regent Street and Portland Place.

LOCATOR MAP
See Central London Map pp14–15

The London Clinic is one of the best-known private hospitals in this medical district.

Regent's Park station

Portland Place
In the center of this broad street stands a statue of Field Marshal Sir George Stuart White, who won the Victoria Cross for gallantry in the Afghan War of 1879 ❺

The Royal Institute of British Architects is housed in a striking Art Deco building designed by Grey Wornum in 1934.

Harley Street
Consulting rooms of eminent medical specialists have been here for more than a century ❹

STAR SIGHTS

★ Madame Tussauds

★ Regent's Park

Madame Tussauds ❶

Marylebone Rd NW1. **Map** 4 D5.
📞 0871-894 3000. 🚇 Baker St.
Open 9:30am–5:30pm Mon–Fri,
9am–6pm Sat & Sun. **Closed** Dec 25.
Adm charge. 📷 🖥 🚻 ♿ phone
first. **www**.madametussauds.co.uk

Madame Tussaud began her
wax-modeling career rather
morbidly, taking death masks
of many of the best-known
victims of the French
Revolution. In 1835 she set
up an exhibition of her work
in Baker Street, not far from
the collection's present site.

The collection still uses
traditional wax-modeling
techniques to recreate politicians, royals, movie and
television actors, rock stars,
and sporting heroes.

The main sections of the
exhibition are "Blush," where
visitors get to feel what it is
like to be at a celebrity "A-list"
party; "Premiere Night," devoted
to giants of the entertainment
world such as Marilyn Monroe

**Traditional wax-modeling at
Madame Tussauds**

and Charlie Chaplin; and the
"World Leaders," containing a
collection of statesmen and
world leaders, writers, and
artists. Where else could
Shakespeare, Lenin, Martin
Luther King Jr., and Madonna
all rub shoulders?

The Chamber of Horrors
is the most renowned part
of Madame Tussauds and
features an interactive area
called "Scream". It includes
recreations of the most
gruesome episodes in the

grim catalogue of crime and
punishment: the murderer
Dr. Crippen; Vlad the Impaler;
and the chill gloom of an east
London Victorian street during
Jack the Ripper's time in the
late 19th century.

The "Spirit of London" is
the finale. Visitors travel in
stylized London taxicabs and
participate in momentous
events of the city, from the
Great Fire of 1666 to
1960s Swinging
London.

Ticket prices
include entry to
temporary exhib-
itions featuring
media icons of
the moment.
There are also
educational tours
designed for
groups and
schools – check
website for
further
information.

**Waxwork of
Elizabeth II**

Tulip time at Queen Mary's Gardens in Regent's Park

Regent's Park ❷

NW1. **Map** 3 C2. **Tel** 020-7486 7905.
🚇 Regent's Park, Baker St, Great
Portland St. **Open** 5am–dusk daily.
♿ 🖥 **Open air theater** see **Enter-
tainment** pp344–5. **Zoo** see p227.
Sports facilities.
www.royalparks.gov.uk

This area of land became
enclosed as a park in 1812.
John Nash designed the
scheme and originally envis-
aged a kind of garden suburb,

dotted with 56 villas in a
variety of Classical styles, with
a pleasure palace for the
Prince Regent. In the event
only eight villas – but no
palace – were built inside the
park (three survive round the
edge of the Inner Circle).

The boating lake, which has
many varieties of water birds,
is marvelously romantic,
especially when music drifts
across from the bandstand in
the distance. Queen Mary's
Gardens are a mass of

wonderful sights and smells
in summer, when visitors
can enjoy Shakespeare
productions at the **Open Air
Theater** nearby.

Nash's master plan for the
park continues just beyond its
northeastern edge in Park
Village East and West. These
elegant stucco buildings date
from 1828.

The park is also renowned
for its excellent sports facilities.

St. Marylebone Parish Church ❸

Marylebone Rd NW1. **Map** 4 D5. **Tel**
020-7935 7315. 🚇 Regent's Park.
Open phone to check. ♿ 🚻 11am
Sun. 🖥 **www**.stmarylebone.org.uk

This is where the poets
Robert Browning and
Elizabeth Barrett were
married in 1846 after eloping
from her strict family home
on nearby Wimpole Street.
The large, stately church by
Thomas Hardwick was
consecrated in 1817 after the
former church, where Lord
Byron was christened in 1778,

had become too small. Hardwick was determined that the same should not happen to his new church – so everything is on a grand scale.

Commemorative window in St. Marylebone Parish Church

Harley Street ❹

W1. **Map** 4 E5. 🚇 *Regent's Park, Oxford Circus, Bond St, Great Portland St.*

The large houses on this late 18th-century street were popular with successful physicians and specialists in the mid-19th century when it was a rich residential area. The doctors' practices stayed and lend the street an air of hushed order, unusual in central London. There are very few private houses or apartments here now, but Prime Minister William Gladstone lived at No. 73 from 1876 to 1882.

Portland Place ❺

W1. **Map** 4 E5. 🚇 *Regent's Park, Oxford Circus.*

The Adam Brothers, Robert and James, laid this street out in 1773. Only a few of the original houses remain, the best being 27 to 47 on the west side, south of Devonshire Street. John Nash added the street to his processional route from Carlton House to Regent's Park and sealed its northern end with Park Crescent.

The building of the Royal Institute of British Architects (1934) at No. 66 is adorned with symbolic statues and reliefs. Its bronze front doors depict London's buildings and the Thames River.

Broadcasting House ❻

Portland Place W1. **Map** 12 E1. 🚇 *Oxford Circus.* **Open** *Sun for guided tours only. Reservations essential; call 0370-901 1227.* **Tel** *0870-603 0304.* 🚇 *White City.* **Adm charge.** ♿ 🎫 *No children under 12.*

Broadcasting House was built in 1931 as a suitably modern Art Deco headquarters for the brand-new medium of broadcasting. Its front, curving with the street, is dominated by Eric Gill's stylized relief of Prospero and Ariel. As the invisible spirit of the air, Shakespeare's Ariel was considered an appropriate personification of broadcasting. The character appears in two other sculptures on the western frontage, and again over the eastern entrance in "Ariel Piping to Children."

Broadcasting House is now occupied by management, as some radio studios moved to west London in the 1990s. Fascinating tours of Broadcasting House (and also of BBC TV Centre in White City) are available. Each tour is unique, as the itinerary depends on programming and events of the day.

In partnership with English Heritage, a major refurbishment in 2011 opened a public piazza, a BBC store, a café, and an exhibition/interactive area.

Relief on the Royal Institute of British Architects on Portland Place

All Souls, Langham Place ❼

Langham Place W1. **Map** 12 F1. **Tel** *020-7580 3522.* 🚇 *Oxford Circus.* **Open** *9:30am–6pm Mon–Fri, 9am–3pm, 5:30–8:30pm Sun.* 🕐 *9:30, 11:30am, 6:30pm Sun.* ♿ 🎫 *Sun.* **www**.allsouls.org

John Nash designed this church in 1824. Its quirky round frontage is best seen from Regent Street. When it was first built, the spire was ridiculed as it appeared too slender and flimsy.

The only Nash church in London, it had close links with the BBC, based opposite at Broadcasting House, and ten years ago used to double as a recording studio for the daily broadcast church service.

Langham Hotel ❽

1 Portland Place W1. **Map** 12 E1. **Tel** *020-7636 1000.* 🚇 *Oxford Circus. See* **Where to Stay** *p288.* **www**.langhamhotels.com

This was London's grandest hotel after opening in 1865. The writers Oscar Wilde and Mark Twain and composer Antonin Dvořák were among its many distinguished guests. It was, for a time, used by the BBC as a record library and as a venue for recording shows. It has since been restored, bringing it boldly into the 21st century with its luxurious guest rooms, chic Artesian bar, and The Landau restaurant.

All Souls, Langham Place (1824)

Wigmore Hall ⑨

36 Wigmore St W1. **Map** 12 E1. *Tel*
020-7935 2141. ⊖ *Bond St, Oxford
Cir.* 🚻 ⚟ *See* **Entertainment**
p349. **www**.*wigmore-hall.org.uk*

This appealing little concert
hall for chamber music was
designed by T. E. Collcutt,
architect of the Savoy Hotel
(see p290), in 1900. At first it
was called Bechstein Hall
because it was attached to the
Bechstein piano showroom:
the area used to be the heart
of London's piano trade.
Opposite is the Art Nouveau
emporium built in 1907 as
Debenham and Freebody's
department store – now
Debenham's on Oxford Street.

Wallace Collection ⑩

Hertford House, Manchester Sq W1.
Map 12 D1. 📞 *020-7563 9500.*
⊖ *Bond St, Baker St.* **Open** *10am–
5pm daily.* **Closed** *Dec 24–26.*
Lectures. 🚻 📷
www.*wallacecollection.org*

Late 18th-century Sèvres porcelain
vase at the Wallace Collection

This is one of the world's
finest private collections of art.
It has remained intact since it
was bequeathed to the British
government in 1897 with the
stipulation that it should go on
permanent public display with
nothing added or taken away.
The product of passionate
collecting for four generations
of the Hertford family, it is a

must for anyone with even a
passing interest in the progress
of European art up to the late
19th century. In 2000 four
more galleries were opened
so that even more of the
collection could be shown.
　Among the 70 masterworks
are Frans Hals's *The Laughing
Cavalier,* Titian's *Perseus and
Andromeda,* and Rembrandt's
Titus. There are superb portraits by Reynolds, Gainsborough, and Romney. Other
highlights include Sèvres
porcelain and sculpture by
Houdon and Roubiliac. The
fine European and Oriental
armor collection is the second
largest in the UK.

Sherlock Holmes Museum ⑪

221b Baker St NW1. **Map** 3 C5.
Tel 020-7224 3688. ⊖ *Baker St.*
Open *9:30am–6pm daily.* **Closed**
25 Dec. **Adm charge.** 📷
www.*sherlock-holmes.co.uk*

Sir Arthur Conan Doyle's
fictional detective lived at
221b Baker Street. This
building, dating from 1815,
has been converted to
resemble Holmes's flat, and is
furnished exactly as described
in the books. Visitors are
greeted by Holmes's
"housekeeper" and shown to
his recreated rooms on the
first floor. The shop sells the
novels and deerstalker hats.

The Mosque on the edge of Regent's Park

London Central Mosque ⑫

146 Park Rd NW8. **Map** 3 B3.
Tel 020-7725 2213. ⊖ *Marylebone,
St. John's Wood, Baker St.* **Open**
dawn–dusk daily. 🚻 **Lectures.**

Surrounded by trees on the
edge of Regent's Park, this
large, golden-domed mosque
was designed by Sir Frederick
Gibberd and completed in
1978. Built to cater for the
increasing number of Muslim
residents and visitors in
London, the mosque is capable
of holding 1,800 worshipers.
The main hall of worship is a
plain square chamber with a
domed roof and a magnificent
carpet. Visitors must remove
their shoes before entering the
mosque, and women should
remember to cover their heads.

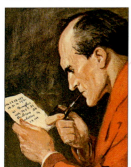

Conan Doyle's Sherlock Holmes

Regent's Canal ⑬

NW1 & NW8. **Map** 3 C1. *Tel 020-7482 2660 (waterbus).* Camden Town, St. John's Wood, Warwick Ave. **Canal towpaths open** dawn–dusk daily. See **Six Guided Walks** pp264–5.

A boat trip on Regent's Canal

John Nash was extremely enthusiastic about this waterway, opened in 1820 to link the Grand Junction Canal, which ended at Little Venice in Paddington in the west, with the London docks at Limehouse in the east. He saw it as an added attraction for his new Regent's Park, and originally wanted the canal to run through the middle of that park. He was persuaded out of that by those who thought that the bargees' bad language would offend the genteel residents of the area. Perhaps this was just as well – the steam tugs that hauled the barges were dirty and sometimes dangerous.

In 1874 a barge carrying gunpowder blew up in the cutting by London Zoo, killing the crew, destroying a bridge, and terrifying the populace and the animals. After an initial period of prosperity the canal began to be hit by increasing competition from the new railroads and so gradually slipped into decline.

Today it has been revived as a leisure amenity; the towpath is paved as a pleasant walkway and short boat trips are offered between Little Venice and Camden Lock, where there is a thriving crafts market. Visitors to the zoo can use the landing stage that is situated alongside it.

London Zoo ⑭

Regent's Park NW1. **Map** 4 D2. 020-7722 3333. Camden Town. **Open** 10am–5:30pm (4:30pm Nov–Mar) daily. **Closed** Dec 25. **Adm charge.** www.zsl.org

Opened in 1828, the Zoo has been one of London's biggest tourist attractions ever since, and is also a major research and conservation center. London Zoo has over 600 species of animal, from Sumatran tigers and sloth bears to Mexican red-kneed bird-eating spiders. Exhibits include the

London Zoo's aviary designed by Lord Snowdon (1964)

Web of Life which takes you through the vast range of life forms found in Earth's major habitats. There are also plenty of interactive activities.

Cumberland Terrace ⑮

NW1. **Map** 4 E2. Great Portland St, Regent's Park, Camden Town.

James Thomson is credited with the detailed design of this, the longest and most elaborate of the Nash terraces around Regent's Park. Its imposing central block of raised Ionic columns is topped with a decorated triangular pediment. Completed in 1828, it was designed to be visible from the palace Nash planned for the Prince Regent (later George IV). The palace was never built because the Prince was too busy with his plans for Buckingham Palace (*see pp94–5*).

Nash's Cumberland Terrace, dating from 1828

HAMPSTEAD

Hampstead has always stayed aloof from London, looking down from its site on the high ridge north of the metropolis. Today it is essentially a Georgian village. The heath separating Hampstead from Highgate reinforces its appeal, isolating it further from the hurly-burly of the modern city. A stroll around the charming village streets, followed by a tramp across the Heath, makes for one of the finest walks in London.

SIGHTS AT A GLANCE

Historic Streets and Buildings
Flask Walk and Well Walk ①
Church Row ⑤
Downshire Hill ⑥
Vale of Health ⑬

Museums and Galleries
Burgh House ②
Fenton House ④
Keats House ⑦
Kenwood House ⑩

Parks and Gardens
Hampstead Heath ⑧
Parliament Hill ⑨
The Hill Garden ⑫

Pubs and Restaurants
Old Bull and Bush ③
Spaniards Inn ⑪

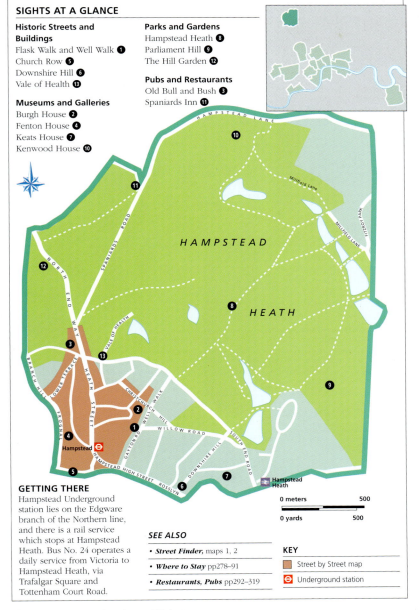

GETTING THERE

Hampstead Underground station lies on the Edgware branch of the Northern line, and there is a rail service which stops at Hampstead Heath. Bus No. 24 operates a daily service from Victoria to Hampstead Heath, via Trafalgar Square and Tottenham Court Road.

SEE ALSO

• *Street Finder,* maps 1, 2

• *Where to Stay* pp278–91

• *Restaurants, Pubs* pp292–319

KEY

▨ Street by Street map

🚇 Underground station

0 meters   500
0 yards   500

◁ **View across Hampstead Heath toward Highgate**

Street by Street: Hampstead

Perched awkwardly on a hilltop, with its broad heath to the north, Hampstead has kept its villagey atmosphere and sense of being aloof from urban pressures. This has attracted artists and writers since Georgian times and made it one of London's most desirable residential areas. Its mansions and town houses are perfectly maintained and a stroll through Hampstead's narrow streets is one of London's quieter pleasures.

Old Bull and Bush
This pub on the edge of the Heath was a former haunt for writers and artists ❸

★ Hampstead Heath
A welcome retreat from the city, its broad open spaces include bathing ponds, meadows, and lakes ❽

Whitestone Pond takes its name from the old white milestone nearby. It is 4.5 miles (7 km) from Holborn *(see pp132–41)*.

Grove Lodge was home to novelist John Galsworthy (1867–1933), author of the *Forsyte Saga*, for the last 15 years of his life.

Admiral's House dates from about 1700. Built for a sea captain, its name derives from its exterior maritime motifs. No admiral ever actually lived in it.

STAR SIGHTS

★ Burgh House

★ Hampstead Heath

★ Fenton House

★ Church Row

KEY

– – – Suggested route

0 meters   100

0 yards   100

★ Fenton House
Summer visitors should seek out this late 17th-century house and its exquisite walled garden, which are well hidden in the jumble of streets near the Heath ❹

★ **Burgh House**
*Built in 1702 but much
altered since, the house
contains an intriguing
local history museum and
a café overlooking the
small garden* **❷**

LOCATOR MAP
See Central London Map pp14–15

The New End Theatre
produces rare but significant
work. The building used to
be a morgue.

No. 40 Well Walk is where
artist John Constable lived
while working on his many
Hampstead pictures.

Flask Walk and Well Walk
*An alley of charming
specialist shops broadens
into a residential village
street* **❶**

**Hampstead
station**

**The
Everyman
Cinema**
has been an
art movie theater
since 1933.

★ **Church Row**
*The tall houses are
rich in original detail.
Notice the superb iron-
work on what is probably
London's finest
Georgian street* **❺**

Old Bull and Bush in 1900

Flask Walk and Well Walk ❶

NW3. **Map** 1 B5. ⊖ *Hampstead.*

Flask Walk is named after the Flask pub. Here, in the 18th century, therapeutic spa water from what was then the separate village of Hampstead was put into flasks and sold to visitors or sent to London. The water, rich in iron salts, came from nearby Well Walk where a disused fountain now marks the site of the well. The Wells Tavern, almost opposite the spring, used to be a hostelry that specialized in accommodating those who engaged in the illicit liaisons for which the spa became notorious.

In later times, there have been many notable residents of Well Walk including artist John Constable (at No. 40), writers D. H. Lawrence and J. B. Priestley, and the poet John Keats, before he moved to his better-known house in what is now Keats Grove.

Site of the well on Well Walk

At the High Street end, Flask Walk is narrow and lined with old shops. Beyond the pub (note the Victorian tiled panels outside) it broadens into a row of Regency houses, one of which used to belong to the novelist Kingsley Amis.

Burgh House ❷

New End Sq NW3. **Map** 1 B4. *Tel* 020-7431 0144. ⊖ *Hampstead.* **Open** noon–5pm Wed–Sun (Sat ground-floor art gallery & café only), 2–5pm public hols. **Closed** Christmas week. 📷 ♿ 🖥 🏠 *Music recitals.* **www**.burghhouse.org.uk

The last private tenant of Burgh House was the son-in-law of the writer Rudyard Kipling, who visited here occasionally in the last years of his life until 1936. After a period under the ownership of Hampstead Borough Council, the house was let to the independent Burgh House Trust. Since 1979 the Trust has run it as the Hampstead Museum, which illustrates the history of the area and concentrates on some of its most celebrated residents.

One room is devoted to the life of John Constable, who painted an extraordinary series of studies of clouds from Hampstead Heath. The house also has sections on Lawrence, Keats, the artist Stanley Spencer and others who lived and worked in the area. There is a display about Hampstead as a spa in the 18th and 19th centuries, which is also worth a visit. Burgh House often has exhibitions by contemporary local artists.

The house itself was built in 1703 but is named after a 19th-century resident, the Reverend Allatson Burgh. It has been much altered inside, and today the marvelously carved staircase is a highlight of the interior. Also worth seeing is the music room which was reconstructed in 1920, but contains good 18th-century pine paneling from another house. In the 1720s Dr. William Gibbons, chief physician to the then thriving Hampstead spa, lived here. A licensed café serves delicious food and has a terrace overlooking the pretty garden.

Burgh House staircase

Old Bull and Bush ❸

North End Rd NW3. **Map** 1 A2. *Tel* 020-8905 5456. ⊖ *Golders Green.* **Open** 11am–11pm Mon–Sat, 11am–10:30pm Sun. ♿ 🍴

This pub, one of London's oldest and most famous, dates back to 1645, when it was a farmhouse. It received its license to sell ale in 1721 and quickly became a haunt for artists and literary figures, including the famous artist William Hogarth *(see p259)* and the writer Austin Dobson. It is reputed that Hogarth planted a tree in the pub's garden. Located next to Hampstead Heath, the pub serves food at lunchtime and in the evening, and has barbecues in the summer in the garden. The interior is comfortably furnished.

Fenton House ❹

20 Hampstead Grove NW3. **Map** 1
A4. *Tel 01494-755563.* 🚇 *Hampstead.* **Open** *Mar–Oct: 11am–5pm Wed–Sun & public hols (2–5pm some Thu due to lunchtime concerts).* **Adm charge.** ♿ *first floor only.* 📷 *book ahead.* 🌐 **www**.national trust.org.uk/fentonhouse

Built in 1686, this splendid William and Mary house is the oldest mansion in Hampstead. It contains two specialized exhibitions that are open to the public during the summer: the Benton-Fletcher collection of early keyboard instruments, which includes a harpsichord dating from 1612, said to have been played by Handel; and a fine collection of porcelain. The instruments are kept in full working order and are actually used for concerts held in the house. The porcelain collection was largely accumulated by Lady Binning who, in 1952, bequeathed the house and its contents to the National Trust.

Church Row ❺

NW3. **Map** 1 A5. 🚇 *Hampstead.*

The row is one of the most complete Georgian streets in London. Much of its original detail has survived, notably the ironwork.

At the west end is St. John's, Hampstead's parish church, built in 1745. The iron gates are earlier and come from Canons Park in Edgware. Inside the church is a bust of John Keats. John Constable's grave is in the churchyard, and many Hampstead luminaries are buried in the adjoining cemetery.

Downshire Hill ❻

NW3. **Map** 1 C5. 🚇 *Hampstead.*

A beautiful street of mainly Regency houses, it lent its name to a group of artists, including Stanley Spencer and Mark Gertler, who would gather at No. 47 between the two World Wars. That same

house had been the meeting-place of Pre-Raphaelite artists, among them Dante Gabriel Rossetti and Edward Burne-Jones. A more recent resident, at No. 5, was the late Jim Henson, the creator of the television puppets, *The Muppets.*

The church on the corner (the second Hampstead church to be called St. John's) was built in 1823 to serve the Hill's residents. Inside, it still has its original box pews.

Keats House ❼

Keats Grove NW3. **Map** 1 C5.
📞 *020-7332 3868.* 🚇 *Hampstead, Belsize Park.* **Open** *Apr–Oct: 1–5pm Tue–Sun, Nov–Apr: 1–5pm Fri–Sun.* **Closed** *Good Fri, Christmas week.* **Adm charge.** ♿ *ground floor only.* 🎭 *Poetry readings, lectures.* **www**.cityoflondon.gov.uk/keats

Lock of Fanny Brawne's hair

Originally two semi-detached houses built in 1816, the smaller one became Keats's home in 1818 when a friend persuaded him to

St. John's, Downshire Hill

move in. Keats spent two productive years here: *Ode to a Nightingale,* perhaps his most celebrated poem, was written under a plum tree in the garden. The Brawne family moved into the larger house a year later and Keats became engaged to their daughter, Fanny. However, the marriage never took place because Keats died of consumption in Rome before two years had passed. He was only 25 years old.

A copy of one of Keats's love letters to Fanny, the engagement ring he offered her, and a lock of her hair are among the mementos that are exhibited at the house – it was first opened to the public in 1925. Visitors are also able to see facsimiles of some of Keats's manuscripts, part of a collection that serves as an evocative and memorable tribute to his life and work.

Fenton House's 17th-century facade

View over London from Hampstead Heath

Hampstead Heath ❽

NW3. **Map** 1 C2. **Tel** 020-7332 3322. ⊜ Belsize Park, Hampstead. **Open** 24hrs daily. **Special walks** on Sundays. ♿ phone for disability buggies. 💻 **Concerts, some children's activities** in summer. **Sports facilities, bathing ponds. Sports bookings Tel** 020-7332 3774.

The best time to stride across these broad 3 sq miles (8 sq km) is Sunday afternoon, when the local residents walk off their roast beef lunches, discussing the contents of the Sunday papers. Separating the hilltop villages of Hampstead and Highgate (see p246), the Heath was made from the grounds of several, formerly separate, properties and embraces a variety of landscapes – woods, meadows, hills, ponds, and lakes. It remains uncluttered by the haphazard buildings and statues that embellish the central London parks, and its open spaces have become increasingly precious to Londoners as the areas around it get more crowded. There are ponds for bathing and fishing and, on three holiday weekends – Easter, late spring, and late summer – the southern part of the Heath is taken over by a funfair (see pp56–9).

Parliament Hill ❾

NW5. **Map** 2 E4. **Tel** 020-7332 3773. ⊜ Belsize Park, Hampstead. ♿ **Concerts, children's activities** in summer. **Sporting facilities.** 💻

An unlikely but romantic explanation for the area's name is that it is where Guy Fawkes's fellow-plotters gathered on November 5, 1605 in the vain hope of watching the Houses of Parliament blow up after they had planted gunpowder there (see p24). More probably it was a gun emplacement for the Parliamentary side during the Civil War 40 years later. The gunners would have enjoyed a

Kenwood House ❿

Hampstead Lane NW3. **Map** 1 C1. **Tel** 020-8348 1286. ⊜ Highgate, Archway. **Open** 11:30am–4pm daily. **Closed** Jan 1, Dec 24–26. 🚫 **Lakeside concerts** in summer. **Regular events.** ♿ first floor only. 💻 📷 See **Entertainment** pp348–9. **www**.english-heritage.org.uk

This is a magnificent Adam mansion, filled with Old Master paintings, including works by Vermeer, Turner, and Romney (who lived in Hampstead). It is situated in landscaped grounds high on the edge of Hampstead Heath. There has been a house here since 1616 – the present one was remodeled by Robert Adam in 1764 for the Earl of Mansfield. Adam refitted existing rooms and added to the original building. Most of his work has survived, the highlight being the library. A Rembrandt self-portrait is the star attraction of the collection, and there are also works by Van Dyck, Hals, and Reynolds.

The orangery is now used for occasional concerts and recitals.

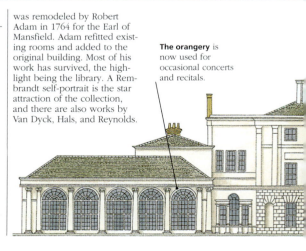

broad view across London: even today, when tall buildings intervene, it provides one of the most spectacular views over the capital. From here the dome of St. Paul's is prominent. Parliament Hill is also a popular place for flying kites and sailing model boats on the boating pond.

Spaniards Inn ⓫

Spaniards Rd NW3. **Map** 1 B1. **Tel** 020-8731 8406. ⊖ Hampstead, Golders Green. **Open** 11am–11pm Mon–Fri, 10am–11pm Sat, 10am–10:30pm Sun. ⓴ See **Restaurants and Pubs** pp292–319.

The historic Spaniards Inn

Dick Turpin, the notorious 18th-century highwayman, is said to have frequented this pub. When he wasn't holding up stagecoaches on their way to and from London, he stabled his horse, Black Bess, at the Kenwood stables. The building certainly dates from

Turpin's time and, although the bar downstairs has been altered frequently, the small upstairs Turpin Bar is original. A pair of guns over the bar were reputedly taken from anti-Catholic rioters, who came to Hampstead to burn the Lord Chancellor's house at Kenwood during the Gordon Riots of 1780. The landlord detained them by offering pint after pint of free beer and, when they were drunk, disarmed them.

Among the pub's noted patrons have been the poets Shelley, Keats, and Byron, the actor David Garrick and the artist Sir Joshua Reynolds.

The toll house has been restored; it juts into the road so that, in the days when tolls were levied, traffic could not race past without paying.

The Hill Garden ⓬

North End Way NW3. **Map** 1 A2. ⊖ Hampstead, Golders Green. **Open** 9am–one hour before dusk daily.

This charming garden was created by the Edwardian soap manufacturer and patron of the arts, Lord Leverhulme. It was originally the grounds to his house, and is now part of Hampstead Heath. It boasts a raised pergola walkway, best seen in summer when the plants are in flower; the garden also has a beautiful formal pond.

Pergola walk at The Hill Garden

Vale of Health ⓭

NW3. **Map** 1 B4. ⊖ Hampstead.

This area was famous as a distinctly unhealthy swamp before it was drained in 1770; until then it was known as Hatches Bottom. Its newer name may derive from people fleeing here from cholera in London at the end of the 18th century. Alternatively, the name could have been the hype of a property developer, when it was first recorded in 1801.

The poet James Henry Leigh Hunt put it on the literary map when he moved here in 1815, and played host to Coleridge, Byron, Shelley, and Keats.

D. H. Lawrence lived here briefly and Stanley Spencer painted in a room above the Vale of Health Hotel, demolished in 1964.

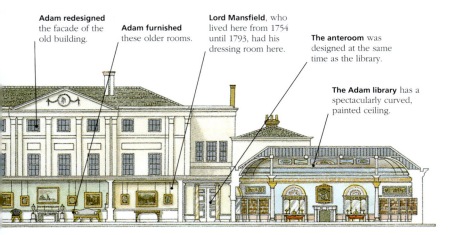

Adam redesigned the facade of the old building.

Adam furnished these older rooms.

Lord Mansfield, who lived here from 1754 until 1793, had his dressing room here.

The anteroom was designed at the same time as the library.

The Adam library has a spectacularly curved, painted ceiling.

GREENWICH AND BLACKHEATH

Best known as the place from which the world's time is measured, Greenwich marks the historic eastern approach to London by land and water. Home to the National Maritime Museum and the Queen's House, Greenwich remains an elegant oasis of bookstores, antique shops and markets. Blackheath lies just to the south.

SIGHTS AT A GLANCE

Historic Streets and Buildings
Queen's House ❷
Old Royal Naval College ❼
Royal Observatory
  Greenwich ❾
Croom's Hill ⓬

Museums
National Maritime Museum ❶
Fan Museum ⓭

Wernher Collection ❹

Churches
St. Alfege Church ❸

Parks and Gardens
Greenwich Park ❿
Blackheath ⓫

Walkway
Greenwich Foot
  Tunnel ❻

Pubs and Restaurants
Trafalgar Tavern ❽

Ships
Cutty Sark ❺

KEY

▨	Street-by-Street map
⊖	Underground station
⇌	Train Station

0 meters ———— 500
0 yards ———— 500

GETTING THERE

The best way is by rail from Charing Cross or London Bridge, or by the DLR. The 188 bus goes five times an hour to Greenwich from Euston. There are also numerous river boats *(pp60–65)*.

SEE ALSO

• *Street Finder*, maps 23, 24
• *Where to Stay* pp278–91
• *Restaurants, Pubs* pp292–319

◁ **View north across the Thames from Greenwich Park, overlooking Queen's House**

Street by Street: Greenwich

This historic town marks the eastern approach to London and is best visited by river *(see pp60–5)*. In Tudor times it was the site of a palace much enjoyed by Henry VIII, near a fine hunting ground and his naval base. The old palace is gone, leaving Inigo Jones's exquisite Queen's House, built for James I's wife. Museums, book and antiques stores, markets, Wren's architecture and the magnificent park make Greenwich an enjoyable day's excursion. Greenwich has also been awarded UNESCO World Heritage Site status.

Greenwich Foot Tunnel, *leading to the Isle of Dogs, is one of two tunnels built solely for pedestrians* **6**

Greenwich Pier provides a boarding point for boat services to Westminster and the Thames Barrier.

Cutty Sark
Clipper ships such as this once traded across the oceans. The Cutty Sark is being restored following a fire. Her figurehead can be seen in the visitors' center **5**

Greenwich Market
Selling crafts, antiques, and books, this market is popular on Sundays.

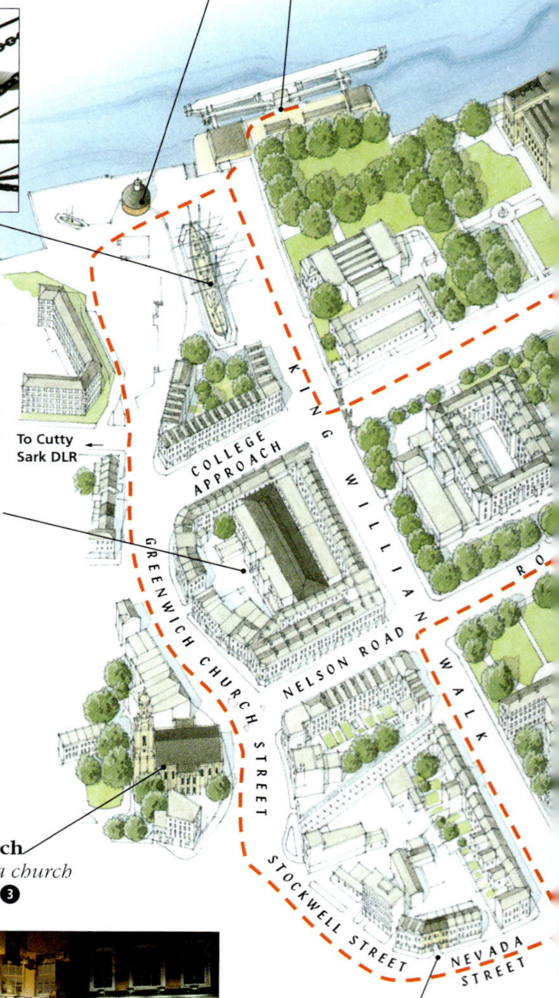

To Cutty Sark DLR

COLLEGE APPROACH

KING WILLIAM WALK

GREENWICH CHURCH STREET

NELSON ROAD

STOCKWELL STREET

NEVADA STREET

St. Alfege Church
There has been a church here since 1012 **3**

Spread Eagle Yard
Once a stopping point for horse-drawn carriages. The Spread Eagle restaurant is next to the site of the ticket office.

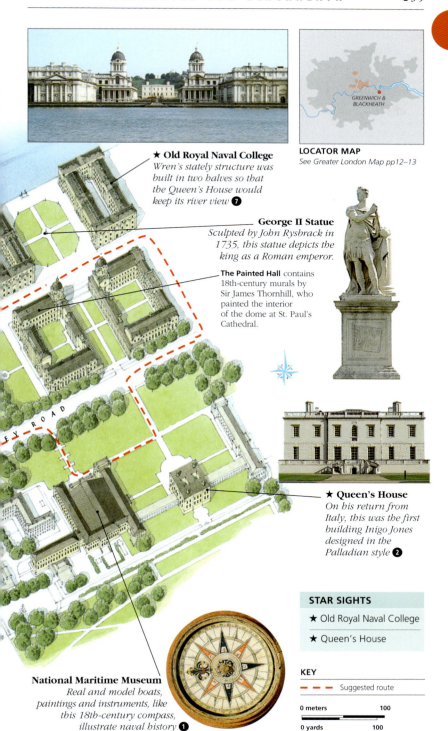

LOCATOR MAP
See Greater London Map pp12–13

GREENWICH & BLACKHEATH

★ Old Royal Naval College
*Wren's stately structure was
built in two halves so that
the Queen's House would
keep its river view* 🄣

George II Statue
*Sculpted by John Rysbrack in
1735, this statue depicts the
king as a Roman emperor.*

The Painted Hall contains
18th-century murals by
Sir James Thornhill, who
painted the interior
of the dome at St. Paul's
Cathedral.

EY ROAD

★ Queen's House
*On his return from
Italy, this was the first
building Inigo Jones
designed in the
Palladian style* 🄤

National Maritime Museum
*Real and model boats,
paintings and instruments, like
this 18th-century compass,
illustrate naval history* 🄠

STAR SIGHTS

★ Old Royal Naval College

★ Queen's House

KEY

– – – Suggested route

| 0 meters | | 100 |
| 0 yards | | 100 |

National Maritime Museum ❶

Romney Rd SE10. **Map** 23 C2.
Tel 020-8858 4422. 🚇 Cutty
Sark DLR. 🚉 Greenwich. **Open**
10am–5pm daily (last adm: 30 mins
before close). **Closed** Dec 24–26.
Adm charge special
exhibitions. 🚫 ♿ 🖥 🏪
Lectures. www.nmm.ac.uk

The sea has always played an
extremely important role in
British history as a means of
both defense and expansion,
and this museum celebrates
the "island nation's" seafaring
heritage. Exhibits tell the story
of explorers, from early
Elizabethan times through the
development of passenger
lines to the modern day.
There are sections devoted to
trade and empire, the
exploratory expeditions of
Captain Cook and Sir Ernest
Shackleton, and the
Napoleonic Wars.

One of the star exhibits is
the uniform that Lord Horatio
Nelson was wearing when he
was fatally shot at the Battle
of Trafalgar in October 1805:
you can easily see the bullet
hole and the bloodstains.

Rather more spectacular,
however, is the royal barge
that was built for Prince
Frederick, father of King
George III, in 1732, decorated
with gilded mermaids, shells,
garlands, and his Prince of
Wales's feathers on the stern.
Throughout the museum,
(built in the 19th century
as a school for sailors'
children), are scores of finely
crafted models of ships and
historic paintings.

St. Alfege's altar with rails attributed to Jean Tijou

Queen's House ❷

Romney Rd SE10. **Map** 23 C2. **Tel**
020-8858 4422. 🚇 Cutty Sark DLR.
🚉 Greenwich. **Open** 10am–5pm
daily (last adm: 4:30pm). Closes early
some Fri & Sat for special events –
phone to check. **Closed** Dec 24–26.
🚫 ♿ 🍴 🖥 🏪 www.nmm.ac.uk

The house was
designed by Inigo
Jones and was com-
pleted in 1637. It was
originally meant to be
the home of Anne of
Denmark, wife of James
I, but she died while it was
still being built and it was
finished for Charles I's
queen, Henrietta Maria. She
fell in love with it and called
it her house of delights. After
the Civil War it was briefly
occupied by Henrietta as
dowager queen, but was not
much used by the royal
family after that.

The building has been
refurbished, and in 2001 the
house opened with galleries
displaying the art collection of

the National Maritime
Museum. On the first floor is
a permanent exhibition,
Historic Greenwich, which
includes two models showing
how the house looked in
17th-century Greenwich. The
paintings on show include
early views of Greenwich and
portraits of historical figures
associated with the house,
including Inigo Jones. Visitors
can also see the spiral "tulip
staircase," which curves
sinuously upward without a
central support.

St. Alfege Church ❸

Greenwich Church St SE10.
Map 23 B2. **Tel** 020-8853 0687.
🚇 Cutty Sark DLR. **Open** 11:30am–
4pm Sat, 12–4pm Sun. ⛪ 8am,
10am Sun. ♿ if accompanied.
Concerts. www.st-alfege.org

This is one of Nicholas
Hawksmoor's most distinctive
and powerful designs, with
its gigantic columns and

**Prince Frederick's barge at the
National Maritime Musueum**

pediments topped by urns. It was completed in 1714 on the site of an older church which marked the martyrdom of St. Alfege, the then Archbishop of Canterbury, killed on this spot by Danish invaders in 1012. A second church here was the site of Henry VIII's baptism in 1491 and of 16th-century composer and organist Thomas Tallis's burial in 1585. Today a stained-glass window commemorates Thomas Tallis.

Some of the carved wood inside is by Grinling Gibbons, but much of it was badly damaged by a World War II bomb and has been restored. The wrought iron of the altar and gallery rails is original, attributed to Jean Tijou.

Wernher Collection ❹

Ranger's House, Chesterfield Walk, Greenwich Park SE10. **Map** 23 C4. **Tel** 020-8853 0035. Ⓔ *Cutty Sark DLR.* ⌖ *Blackheath.* **Open** *Apr–Sep by guided tour only Sun–Wed.* **Adm charge.** ⬛ *guided tours by appointment: call for details.* ♿ ▯
www.english-heritage.org.uk

Opal-set lizard pendant at the Wernher Collection

The Wernher Collection is located in Ranger's House (1688), an elegant building southeast of Greenwich Park *(see p243)*. It is an enchanting array of over 650 pieces accumulated by South African mine owner Sir Julius Wernher in the late 19th century. The collection is displayed in 12 rooms and includes paintings, jewelry, furniture, and porcelain. Highlights include Renaissance masterworks by Hans Memling and Filippo Lippi, over 100 Renaissance jewels, and an opal-set lizard pendant jewel. Other curiosities include enameled skulls.

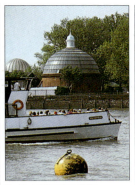

The domed terminal of the Greenwich Foot Tunnel

Cutty Sark ❺

King William Walk SE10. **Map** 23 B2. **Tel** 020-8858 2698. Ⓔ *Cutty Sark DLR.* ⌖ *Greenwich Pier.* **Open** *Currently closed to the public, due to re-open in spring 2012; call or check website for details.* **Adm charge.** ⓞ *restricted.* **www**.cuttysark.org.uk

This majestic vessel is a survivor of the clippers that crossed the Atlantic and Pacific Oceans in the 19th century. Launched in 1869 as a tea carrier, it was something of a speed machine in its day, winning the annual clippers' race from China to London in 1871 in a time of 107 days. It made its final voyage in 1938 and was put on display here in 1957. In 2006 the Cutty Sark was closed to visitors for renovation work, which suffered a major setback in May 2007 when the ship was severely damaged by fire. It is due to re-open in spring 2012, fully restored.

Greenwich Foot Tunnel ❻

Between Greenwich Pier SE10 and Isle of Dogs E14. **Map** 23 B1. Ⓔ *Island Gardens, Cutty Sark DLR.* ⌖ *Greenwich Pier.* **Open** *24hrs daily.* **Elevators open** *7am–7pm Mon–Sat, 10am–5:30pm Sun.* ⓞ ♿ *when elevators open.*

This 1,200-ft (370-m) long tunnel was opened in 1902 to allow south London laborers to walk to work in Millwall

Docks. Today it is worth crossing for the wonderful views, across the river, of Christopher Wren's Royal Naval College and of Inigo Jones's Queen's House.

Matching round redbrick terminals, with glass domes, mark the top of the elevator shafts on either side of the river. The tunnel is about 9 ft (2.5 m) high and is lined with 200,000 tiles. Both ends of the tunnel are close to stations on the Docklands Light Railway (DLR), with trains to Canary Wharf *(see p249)*, Limehouse, East London, Tower Hill, and Lewisham. Although there are security cameras, the tunnel can be eerie at night.

A late 19th-century figurehead in the Cutty Sark

Old Royal Naval College ❼

King William Walk SE10. **Map** 23 C2.
📞 020-8269 4747. 🖲 *Cutty Sark,*
Greenwich. 🚆 *Greenwich, Maze Hill.*
Open *10am–5pm daily.* **Closed** *Dec*
24–26 & some Sat. **Grounds open**
8am–6pm daily. **Chapel open** *10am–*
5pm Mon–Sat, 12:30am–5pm Sun.
📷 🎫 *call 020-8269 1799 to*
reserve. 🔧 🍴 📷 🔧
www.oldroyalnavalcollege.org

These ambitious buildings by
Christopher Wren were built
on the site of the old 15th-
century royal palace, where
Henry VIII, Mary I, and Elizabeth I were born. Only the
chapel, the hall, and the visitors' center are open to the
public. The west front was
completed by Vanbrugh.

Wren's chapel was
destroyed by fire in 1779. The
present Greek Revival interior,
by James Stuart, is light and
airy. The Painted Hall was
opulently decorated by Sir
James Thornhill in the early
18th century. The ceiling
paintings are supported by his
illusionistic pillars and friezes.
There is an informative
Discover Greenwich Visitor
Centre on the grounds.

Trafalgar Tavern ❽

Park Row SE10. **Map** 23 C1. **Tel**
020-8858 2909. 🖲 *Greenwich.*
Open *noon–11pm Mon–Thu,*
noon–midnight Fri & Sat, noon–
10:30pm Sun. 🔧 *See* **Restaurants**
and Pubs *pp315–19.*

This charming paneled pub
was built in 1837 and quickly
became established, along

Thornhill's painting of King William III in the Hall of the Naval College

with other waterside inns in
Greenwich, as a venue for
"whitebait dinners." Government ministers, legal luminaries, and the like would arrive
from Westminster and Charing
Cross by water on celebratory
occasions and feast on the
tiny fish. The last such meeting of government ministers
was held here in 1885. Whitebait still features, when they
are in season, on the menu at
the pub's restaurant, although
they are no longer fished
from the Thames.

This was another of Charles
Dickens's haunts. He drank
here with one of his novels'
most famous illustrators,
George Cruickshank.

In 1915 the pub became an
institution for old merchant
seamen. It was restored in
1965 after a spell of being
used as a social club for
working men.

Royal Observatory Greenwich ❾

Greenwich Park SE10. **Map** 23 C3.
Tel *020-8858 4422.* 🖲 *Cutty Sark*
DLR. 🚆 *Greenwich.* **Open** *10am–*
5pm daily (last adm: 4:30pm).
Closed *Dec 24–26.* **Adm charge** *for*
Planetarium shows (last adm 4pm).
🚫 🔧 📷 **www.**nmm.ac.uk

The meridian (0° longitude)
that divides the Earth's eastern
and western hemispheres
passes through here, and
millions of visitors have taken
the opportunity of being
photographed standing with a
foot on either side of it. In
1884, Greenwich Mean Time
became the basis of time
measurement for most of the
world, following an important
international agreement.

The original building,
Flamsteed House, was
designed by Christopher
Wren. Above one of the
building's two turrets is a ball
on a rod that has dropped at
1pm every day since 1833, so
that sailors on the Thames,
and makers of chronometers
(navigators' clocks), could set
their clocks by it. The house
now contains a display of
John Harrison's marine time-
keepers and an intriguing
exhibition about Greenwich
Mean Time. Flamsteed was
the first Astronomer Royal,
appointed by Charles II, and

Trafalgar Tavern viewed from the Thames

this was the official government observatory from 1675 until 1948. By then the lights of London had become too bright and the astronomers moved to darker Sussex.

A state-of-the-art planetarium, the only one in London, opened here in 2007.

A rare 24-hour clock at the Royal Observatory Greenwich

Greenwich Park ⓾

SE10. **Map** 23 C3. **Tel** 020-8858 2608. ⊖ ⤢ *Greenwich, Blackheath, Maze Hill.* **Open** *6am–dusk daily.* 🖳 🚻 **Children's shows, sports facilities.** www.royalparks.gov.uk **Ranger's House**, Chesterfield Walk, Greenwich Park SE10. **Map** 23 C4. www.english-heritage.co.uk *see also* **Wernher Collection**, *p241.*

Originally the grounds of a royal palace and still a Royal Park, Greenwich Park was enclosed in 1433 and its brick wall built in the reign of King James I. Later, in the 17th century, the French royal landscape gardener André Le Nôtre, who laid out the gardens at Versailles and Fontainebleau, was invited to design one at Greenwich. The broad avenue, rising south up the hill, was part of Le Nôtre's plan.

There are great river views from the hilltop and on a fine day most of London can be seen. In 2012, the park is hosting Olympic equestrian events.

To the south-east of the park, and on the edge of the park's rose garden, is the Ranger's House (1688), which now houses the art collection of Julius Wernher *(see p241).*

From here the walk to the charming village of Blackheath is flat, compared with the steep walk down to the village of Greenwich at the bottom of the hill.

Blackheath ⓫

SE3. **Map** 24 D5. ⤢ *Blackheath.*

This open heath used to be a rallying point for large groups who were entering London from the east, including Wat Tyler's band of rebels at the time of the Peasants' Revolt in 1381.

Blackheath is also the place where King James I of England (who was also King James VI of Scotland) introduced the game of golf from his native Scotland, to the then largely skeptical English.

Today the heath is well worth exploring for the stately Georgian houses and terraces that surround it. In the prettily-named Tranquil Vale to the south, there are stores selling books, prints, and antiques. The heath will host the 2012 Olympic and Paralympic equestrian events.

Ranger's House in Greenwich Park

Croom's Hill ⓬

SE10. **Map** 23 C3. ⤢ *Greenwich.*

This is one of the best kept 17th- to early 19th-century streets in London. The oldest buildings are at the southern end, near Blackheath: the original Manor House of 1695; near it, No. 68, from about the same date; and No. 66 the oldest of all. Famous residents of Croom's Hill include Irish actor Daniel Day Lewis.

Fan Museum ⓭

12 Croom's Hill SE10. **Map** 23 B3. **Tel** 020-8305 1441. ⤢ *Greenwich.* **Open** *11am–5pm Tue–Sat, noon–5pm Sun.* **Closed** *Jan 1, Dec 24–26.* **Adm charge.** 📷 *no flash.* 🎦 *by appt.* 🏠 🚻 🛗 **Lectures, fan-making workshops** *first Sat of the month.* www.fan-museum.org

One of London's most unlikely museums – the only one of its kind in the world – opened in 1991. It owes its existence and appeal to the enthusiasm of Helene Alexander, whose personal collection of about 3,500 fans from the 17th century onward has been augmented by donations, including several fans that were made for the stage. If there, Mrs Alexander will act as a guide.

Stage fan used in a D'Oyly Carte operetta

FARTHER AFIELD

Many of the great houses originally built as country retreats for London's high and mighty were overrun by sprawling suburbs in the Victorian era. Fortunately several have survived as museums in these now less-rustic surroundings. Most are less than an hour's journey from central London. Richmond Park and Wimbledon Common give a taste of the country, while a trip to the Thames Barrier is an adventure.

SIGHTS AT A GLANCE

Historic Streets and Buildings
Sutton House ⑪
Charlton House ⑲
Eltham Palace ⑳
Hampton Court pp254–5 ㉘
Ham House ㉙
Orleans House Gallery ㉚
Marble Hill House ㉛
Syon House ㉝
Osterley Park House ㉟
PM Gallery and House ㊱
Strand on the Green ㊴
Chiswick House ㊵
Fulham Palace ㊷

Churches
St. Mary, Rotherhithe ⑬
St. Anne's, Limehouse ⑭
St. Mary's, Battersea ㉔

Markets
Camden Market ②

Museums and Galleries
Lord's Cricket Ground ①
Freud Museum ③
The Jewish Museum ⑥
St. John's Gate ⑦
Crafts Council Gallery ⑧
Geffrye Museum ⑩
Bethnal Green Museum of
 Childhood ⑫
William Morris Gallery ⑯
Horniman Museum ㉑
Dulwich Picture Gallery ㉒
Wimbledon Lawn Tennis
 Museum ㉕
Wimbledon Windmill
 Museum ㉖
Musical Museum ㉞
Kew Bridge Steam
 Museum ㊲
Hogarth's House ㊶

Parks and Gardens
Battersea Park ㉓
Richmond Park ㉗
Kew Gardens pp260–61 ㊳

Cemeteries
Highgate Cemetery ⑤

Modern Architecture
Canary Wharf ⑮
The O2 Arena ⑱
Chelsea Harbour ㊸

Historic Districts
Highgate ④
Islington ⑨
Richmond ㉜

Modern Technology
Thames Barrier ⑰

All the sights in this section lie inside the M25 superhighway (see pp12–13).

0 kilometers   5
0 miles   3

KEY
Main sightseeing areas
Superhighway

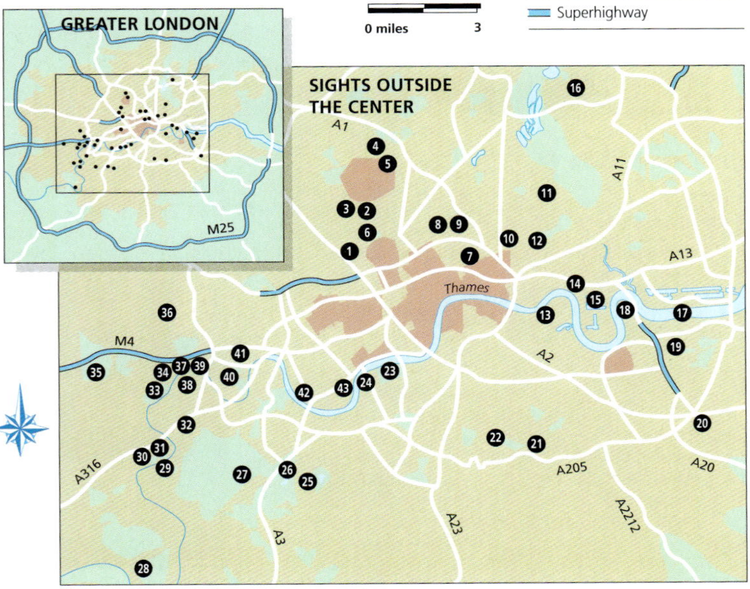

GREATER LONDON

M25

SIGHTS OUTSIDE
THE CENTER

North of the Center

Lord's Cricket Ground ❶

NW8. **Map** 3 A3. **Tel** 020-7616 8595 or 020-7616 8500. ⊖ St. John's Wood. **Open** for guided tours and ticketholders to matches only. **Closed** Jan 1, Dec 25, 26, & 29. **Adm charge**. ♿ 🖎 see website; groups call to reserve in advance. 🎫 See **Entertainment** pp354–5. **www**.lords.org

The headquarters of Britain's chief summer sport contains a museum, including a stuffed sparrow killed by a cricket ball as well as the Ashes (burned wood in an urn), the object of ferocious competition between the English and Australian national teams. The museum explains the history of the game, while paintings and mementos of notable cricketers make it a place of pilgrimage for devotees of the sport. Entrance to the informative museum is included in the tour.

Cricket pioneer Thomas Lord moved his ground here in 1814. The Pavilion (1890), from which women were excluded until 1999, is late Victorian.

The Ashes at Lord's

Camden Market ❷

NW1. ⊖ Camden Town, Chalk Farm. **Open** 10am–6pm daily.

Camden Market is really six markets located close to each other along Chalk Farm Road and Camden High Street. Packed with shoppers at the weekends, most of the shops and some of the stalls are open on weekdays. Many units are housed in restored Victorian buildings alongside Camden Lock and the canal. The first market here was a crafts market at Camden Lock, in 1975. Today all the markets sell a wide range of exciting goods, from arts and crafts and street fashion, to New Age remedies and body piercing.

Sigmund Freud's famous couch

Freud Museum ❸

20 Maresfield Gdns NW3. **Tel** 020-7435 2002. ⊖ Finchley Rd. **Open** noon–5pm Wed–Sun. **Closed** Dec 24–26. **Adm charge**. 📷 no flash. ♿ limited. 🎫 **Events**. **www**.freud.org.uk

In 1938 Sigmund Freud, the founder of psychoanalysis, fled from Nazi persecution in Vienna to this Hampstead house. Making use of the possessions he brought with him, his family recreated the atmosphere of his Vienna consulting rooms. After Freud died in 1939 his daughter Anna (who was a pioneer of child psychoanalysis) kept the house as it was. In 1986 it was opened as a museum dedicated to Freud. The most famous item is the couch on which patients lay for analysis. A series of 1930s home movies shows cheerful moments with his dog as well as scenes of Nazi attacks on his apartment. The bookstore has a large collection of his works.

Highgate ❹

N6. ⊖ Highgate.

There has been a settlement here since at least the early Middle Ages, when an important staging post on the Great North Road from London was established with a gate to control access. Like Hampstead across the Heath (see pp234–5), it soon became fashionable for its unpolluted air, and noblemen built country houses here. It still has an exclusive feel, with a Georgian High Street and expensive houses. It was on Highgate Hill in medieval times that Dick Whittington (a poor young lad) and his pet cat were persuaded by the sound of Bow Bells to turn back and try their fortune in the city. He went on to be Lord Mayor of London three times. A statue of a black cat marks the spot of his epiphany (see p39).

Highgate Cemetery ❺

Swain's Lane N6. **Tel** 020-8340 1834. ⊖ Archway. **Eastern Cemetery Open** Mar–Oct: 10am–5pm Mon–Fri, 11am–5pm Sat & Sun; Nov–Feb: 10am–4pm Mon–Fri, 11am–4pm Sat & Sun. **Western Cemetery open** 🎫 only Mar–Oct: 2pm Mon–Fri, hourly 11am–4pm Sat & Sun; Nov–Feb: hourly 11am–3pm Sat & Sun. No children under 8 years; first come first served. **Closed** Dec 25 & 26 & during funerals (phone to check). **Adm charge**. ♿ Eastern only. **www**.highgate-cemetery.org

The western section of this high-Victorian gem opened in 1839. For many years it lay neglected, until a voluntary group, the Friends of Highgate Cemetery, stepped in to save it from further decline. They have restored the Egyptian Avenue, a street of family vaults styled on ancient Egyptian tombs, and the Circle of Lebanon, more vaults in a ring, topped by a cedar tree. In the eastern section lie Karl Marx, Herbert Spencer, novelist George Eliot, and American artist John Singleton Copley.

George Wombwell's memorial at Highgate Cemetery

Jewish Bakers' Union banner, c.1926,
Jewish Museum, Camden

The Jewish Museum ⑥

129–31 Albert Street, NW1. **Map** 4
E1. **Tel** 020-7284 7384. ⊖ *Camden
Town.* **Open** *10am–5pm Sun–Thu,
10am–2pm Fri.* **Closed** *Sat, Jewish
hols, Dec 25 & 26.* **Adm charge.** ⑤
🖥 📷 www.jewishmuseum.org.uk

When London's Jewish
Museum was founded in 1932,
it was split between two sites
in Finchley and Camden. In
2007, the museum celebrated
its 75th anniversary with the
commencement of works
to bring the two collections
together in a single building.
The project has created
enlarged galleries, educational
facilities, and hands-on
displays for children.

Celebrating Jewish life in
this country from the Middle
Ages, the museum is packed
with memorabilia. It also
has important collections of
Jewish ceremonial art, which
include Hanukkah lamps, a
collection of Jewish marriage
rings, and some illuminated
marriage contracts. The
highlight of this collection
is a 16th-century Venetian
synagogue ark.

St. John's Gate ⑦

St. John's Lane EC1. **Map** 6 F4.
Tel 020-7324 4005. ⊖ *Farringdon.*
Open *10am–5pm Mon–Fri, 10am–
4pm Sat.* **Closed** *Christmas week &
public holiday weekends.* 📷 *11am,
2:30pm Tue, Fri, Sat (donation).* ⑤
limited. www.sja.org.uk/museum

The Tudor gatehouse and parts
of the 12th-century church are
all that remain of the priory of
the Knights of St. John, which
flourished here for 400 years
and was the precursor of the
St. John Ambulance. Over the

years, the priory buildings
have had many uses, such as
offices for Elizabeth I's Master
of the Revels, a pub, and a
coffee shop run by the artist
William Hogarth's father. A
museum of the order's history
has been renovated, with support from the Heritage Lottery
Fund, to create an exhibition
space showing hidden parts of
the gatehouse and a learning
space in the priory church.
To see the rest of the building, join a guided tour.

The Crafts Council

Crafts Council ⑧

44a Pentonville Rd N1. **Map** 6 D2.
Tel 020-7806 2500. ⊖ *Angel.*
📷 *library, 10am–5pm Wed & Thu.*
Closed *Dec 25–Jan 1.* ⑤ 📷
Lectures. www.craftscouncil.org.uk

The Crafts Council is the
national agency for promoting
the creation and appreciation
of contemporary crafts in the
UK. It has a collection of contemporary British crafts, some
of which are loaned to touring
exhibitions, and there is a

library. They also organize
two large craft fairs – one at
the Saatchi Gallery (see *p197*)
in May and the other at
Somerset House (see *p117*)
in September/October.

Islington ⑨

N1. **Map** 6 E1. ⊖ *Angel, Highbury
& Islington.*

Islington was once a highly
fashionable spa, but the rich
began to move out in the late
18th century, and the area
deteriorated rapidly. During
the 20th century, writers such
as Evelyn Waugh, George
Orwell, and Joe Orton lived
here. Now Islington has again
returned to fashion as one of
London's first areas to become
"gentrified," with many young
professionals buying and
refurbishing old houses.

An older relic is Canonbury
Tower, the remains of a medieval manor house converted
into apartments in the 18th
century. Writers such as
Washington Irving and Oliver
Goldsmith lived here and
today it houses the Tower
Theatre. On Islington Green
there is a statue of Sir Hugh
Myddleton, who built a canal
through Islington in 1613 to
bring water to London from
Hertfordshire; today a landscaped walk along its banks
runs between Essex Road and
Canonbury stations. There is a
market, Chapel Market, close
to the Angel station (see *p340*),
antique shops at Camden Passage, and a shopping and cinema complex, the N1 Centre.

St. John's Priory: today, only the gatehouse remains intact

East of the Center

Geffrye Museum's Georgian Room

Geffrye Museum ❿

Kingsland Rd E2. **Tel** *020-7739 9893.* ⊖ *Liverpool St, Old St.* **Open** *10am–5pm Tue–Sat, noon–5pm Sun & public hols.* **Closed** *Jan 1, Good Fri, Dec 24–26.* **Garden open** *Apr–Oct.* ♿ ▯ 🔢 ▯ **Exhibitions & events.** **www**.geffrye-museum.org.uk

This delightful museum is housed in a set of 18th-century almshouses. They were built in 1715 on land bequeathed by Sir Robert Geffrye, a 17th-century Lord Mayor of London who made his fortune through trade. Inside, you take a trip through a series of rooms, chronologically arranged, that have been decorated in different period styles, each one providing an insight into the domestic interiors of the urban middle classes. The historic room settings begin with Elizabethan (which contains magnificent paneling) and run through various major styles, including High Victorian, while an attractive extension houses more modern settings, such as an example of 1990s "loft living."

Each room contains superb examples of British furniture of the period. Outside, there is a series of garden "rooms" that show the designs and planting schemes popular in urban gardens between the 16th and 20th centuries. There is a good café which has a children's menu.

Sutton House ⓫

2–4 Homerton High St E9. **Tel** *020-8986 2264.* ⊖ *Bethnal Green then bus 253.* **Open** *Feb–Dec: 10am–4:30pm Thu–Fri, noon–4:30pm Sat & Sun.* **Adm charge.** ♿ *limited.* ▯ *call first.* ▯ 🔢 **Regular events.** **www**.nationaltrust.org.uk

One of the few London Tudor merchants' houses to survive in something like its original form. Built in 1535 for Ralph Sadleir, a courtier to Henry VIII, it was owned by several wealthy families before becoming a girls' school in the 17th century. In the 18th century the front was altered, but the Tudor fabric remains surprisingly intact, with much original brickwork, large fireplaces, and linenfold paneling.

V&A Museum of Childhood ⓬

Cambridge Heath Rd E2. **Tel** *020-8983 5200.* ⊖ *Bethnal Green.* **Open** *10am–5:45pm daily (to 9pm 1st Thu of month).* **Closed** *Jan 1, Dec 25–26.* 📷 ♿ ▯ 🔢 **Workshop, children's activities.** **www**.vam.ac.uk/moc

This East London branch of the Victoria and Albert Museum *(see pp202–5)* has the largest collection of childhood-related objects in the UK. Its array of toys, games, lavish dolls' houses, model trains, theaters, and costumes dates from the 16th century to the present day, and is well explained and enticingly displayed. The upper floor has lots of fun activities, such as

Tate "Baby" house made in 1760

dressing up, a playable jukebox, and wobbly mirror. There is an excellent store.

The purpose-built museum building was originally erected on the V&A site. In 1872, it was dismantled and reassembled here to bring the light of learning to the East End. The toy collection began in the early 20th century and became a dedicated museum of childhood at Bethnal Green in 1974.

St. Mary, Rotherhithe ⓭

St. Marychurch St SE16. ⊖ *Rotherhithe.* **Open** *9am–6pm daily.* 🔢 *9:30am, 6pm Sun.* 📷 *with permission.* ♿ **www**.stmaryrotherhithe.org

St. Mary, Rotherhithe

This church was built in 1715 on the site of a medieval church. It has nautical connotations, most notably a memorial to Christopher Jones, captain of the *Mayflower*, on which the Pilgrim Fathers sailed to North America. The communion table is made from the timbers of the *Temeraire*, a warship whose final journey to the breaker's yard at Rotherhithe was evocatively recorded in Turner's painting at the National Gallery *(see pp104–7)*. The church also contains a fine example of 18th-century organ building by John Byfield.

William Morris tapestry (1885)

St. Anne's, Limehouse ⑭

3 Colt St E14. **Tel** 020-7987 1502.
⊖ *Westferry (DLR).* **Open**
9:30am–1pm Sun. ⬆ 10:30am Sun.
📷 🎵 *Concerts, lectures* see website for details. **www**.stanneslimehouse.org

This is one of a group of East End churches designed by Nicholas Hawksmoor; it was completed in 1724. Its 130-ft (40-m) tower very soon became a landmark for ships using the East End docks – St. Anne's still has the highest church clock in London. The church was damaged by fire in 1850 and its interior was subsequently Victorianized. It was bombed in World War II and is today in need of further restoration.

Canary Wharf ⑮

E14. ⊖ *Canary Wharf or West India Quay (DLR).* 🚻 🍴 📷 📱
Information center, concerts.
Museum of London Docklands
No. 1 Warehouse, West India Quay
E14 **Tel** 020-7001 9844. **Open**
10am–6pm daily. **Closed** Dec 24–26,
Jan 1. 🚻 🍴 📱 📷 **www**.
museumoflondon.org.uk/docklands

London's most ambitious commercial development opened in 1991, when the first tenants moved into the 50-story Canada Tower, designed by Argentine architect César Pelli. At 800 ft (250 m), it dominates the city's eastern skyline. The tower stands on what was the West India Dock, closed, like all the London docks, between the 1960s and the 1980s, when trade moved downriver to the modern port at Tilbury. Today, Canary Wharf is thriving. A major shopping complex, as well as offices and restaurants, is located in and around Canada Tower. The **Museum of London Docklands**, occupying a late Georgian warehouse, tells the story of the Port of London from Roman times to the present.

William Morris Gallery ⑯

Lloyd Park, Forest Rd E17. **Tel** 020-8496 4390. ⊖ *Walthamstow Central.* **Open** 10am–5pm Wed–Sun. **Closed** Dec 24–26 and public hols. 🚻 *ground floor.* 📱 *Lectures.*
www.walthamforest.gov.uk/wmg

The most influential designer of the Victorian era, born in 1834, lived in this imposing 18th-century house as a youth. It is now a beguiling and well-presented museum giving a full account of William Morris the artist, designer, writer, craftsman, and socialist. It has choice examples of his work and that of other members of the Arts and Crafts movement that he inspired – furniture by A. H. Mackmurdo, tiles by William de Morgan, and paintings by members of the Pre-Raphaelite Brotherhood.

Canada Tower at Canary Wharf

Thames Barrier ⑰

Unity Way SE18. **Tel** 020-8305 4188.
🚇 *Charlton, Silvertown.* **Open** Apr–Sep: 10:30am–4:30pm daily; Oct–Mar: 11am–3:30pm. **Closed** Dec 25–Jan 1.
Adm charge. 🚻 📱 📷 *exhibition*.
www.environment-agency.gov.uk

In 1236 the Thames rose so high that people rowed across Westminster Hall; London flooded again in 1663, 1928, and 1953. Something had to be done, and in 1965 the Greater London Council invited proposals. The Thames Barrier was opened in 1984 and is 1,700 ft (520 m) across. Its 10 gates, which pivot from being flat on the river bed, swing up to 6 ft (1.6 m) above the level reached by the tide in 1953. The barrier has been raised over 100 times since 1984, and can be visited by boat in summer.

Unique structure of the O2 Arena

The O2 Arena ⑱

North Greenwich SE10. **Tel** 020-8463 2000 or 0844-856 0202 (to book tickets). ⊖ *North Greenwich/ The O2 Arena (Jubilee Line).* **Open** 10am–late. **www**.theo2.co.uk

The former Millennium Dome was the focal point of Britain's celebration of the year 2000. Controversial from its earliest days, it is nonetheless a spectacular feat of engineering. Its base is ten times that of St. Paul's Cathedral, and Nelson's Column could stand beneath its roof. Its canopy is made from 109,000 sq yards (100,000 sq m) of Teflon-coated spun glass-fiber, and is held by over 43 miles (70 km) of steel cable rigged to twelve 328-ft (100-m) masts.

Now one of London's most popular concert venues, the O2 boasts an entertainment complex with bars, restaurants, a movie theater, a sports arena, and IndigO2, a smaller venue.

South of the Center

A Jacobean fireplace at Charlton House

Charlton House ⑲

Charlton Rd SE7. **Tel** *020-8856 3951.*
🚊 *Charlton.* **Open** *Main house not open to public. Exhibition area open 8:30am–6pm Mon–Fri. Peace Garden open 10am–5pm daily.* **Closed** *public hols.* 📷 *book ahead.* ♿ *limited.* 📷 *9am–3pm Mon–Fri.*

The house was completed in 1612 for Adam Newton, tutor to Prince Henry. It has good river views and is the best-preserved Jacobean mansion in London – well worth the tricky journey for enthusiasts of that period. It is now used as a community center and library, but many of the original ceilings and fireplaces survive, as does the carved main staircase. Parts of the wood paneling, too, are original, and the ceilings have been restored using the original molds. The summer-house in the grounds was reputedly designed by Inigo Jones, and a mulberry tree (probably the oldest in England) is said to have been planted by James I in 1608 as part of his failed attempt to start an English silk industry.

Eltham Palace ⑳

Court Yard SE9. **Tel** *020-8294 2548.*
🚊 *Eltham, then a 15-minute walk.* **Open** *Sun–Wed. Apr–Oct: 10am–5pm; Nov–Dec & Feb–Mar: 11am–4pm.* **Closed** *Dec 31–Jan 31.* **Adm charge.** ♿ 🚫 🏫 📷 📷 **www.**english-heritage.org.uk

This unique property lets visitors relive the grand life of two very different eras. In the 14th century, English kings spent Christmas in a splendid palace here. The Tudors used it as a base for deer hunting but it fell into ruin after the Civil War (1642–8). In 1935 Stephen Courtauld, of the wealthy textile family, restored the Great Hall which, apart from the bridge over the moat, was the only part of the medieval palace to survive. Next to it he built a house described as "a wonderful combination of Hollywood glamor and Art Deco design." It has been superbly restored and is open, along with the Great Hall, the carp-filled moat, and the 1930s garden.

Horniman Museum ㉑

100 London Rd SE23. **Tel** *020-8699 1872.* 🚊 *Forest Hill.* **Gardens open** *7:30am–sunset Mon–Sat, 8am–sunset Sun.* **Museum & library open** *10:30am–5:30pm daily.* **Closed** *Dec 24–26.* 📷 📷 ♿ **Events & activities.** **www.**horniman.ac.uk

Frederick Horniman, the tea merchant, had this museum built in 1901 to house the curios he had collected on his travels around the world in the 1860s. The museum features a music gallery, aquarium, world culture displays, and a history gallery. There is a good store with toys that represent the popular range of the museum's collections.

Dulwich Picture Gallery ㉒

College Rd SE21. 📞 *020-8693 5254.* 🚊 *West Dulwich, North Dulwich.* **Open** *10am–5pm Tue–Fri, 11am–5pm Sat, Sun, & hol Mon (last adm 4:30pm).* **Closed** *Jan 1, Dec 25 & 26.* **Adm charge.** 📷 📷 *3pm Sat & Sun.* ♿ 📷 📷 **www.**dulwichpicturegallery.org.uk

England's oldest public art gallery, it was opened in 1817 and designed by Sir John Soane (*see pp136–7*). Its imaginative use of skylights

Rembrandt's *Jacob II de Gheyn* at Dulwich Picture Gallery

made it the prototype of most art galleries built since. The gallery was originally commissioned to house the royal collection for the King of Poland. The superb collection has works by Rembrandt (his *Jacob II de Gheyn* has been stolen from here four times), Canaletto, Poussin, Watteau, Claude, Murillo, and Raphael.

The building houses Soane's mausoleum to Desenfans and Bourgeois, who were the original founders of the collection.

Tennis racket and net from 1888, Wimbledon Lawn Tennis Museum

Battersea Park ㉓

Albert Bridge Rd SW11. **Map** 19 C5. **Tel** 020-8871 7530. ⊖ *Sloane Sq then bus 137.* ⊠ *Battersea Pk.* **Open** *8am–dusk daily.* ⬇ ▣ **Sports facilities.** See **Six Guided Walks** pp266–7. www.batterseapark.org

Peace Pagoda, Battersea Park

This was the second public park created to relieve the growing urban stresses on Victorian Londoners (the first was Victoria Park in the East End). It opened in 1858 on the former Battersea Fields – a swampy area notorious for every kind of vice, centered around the Old Red House, a disreputable pub.

The new park immediately became popular, especially for its artificial boating lake, with its romantic rocks, gardens, and waterfalls.

In 1985 a peace pagoda was opened, a 100-ft (35-m) high monument built by Buddhist nuns and monks. There are also an excellent children's zoo (entry fee payable), a children's playground, sports activities, and an art gallery, the Pumphouse.

St. Mary's, Battersea ㉔

Battersea Church Rd SW11. ⊖ *Sloane Sq then bus 19 or 219.* **Open** *daily by arrangement.* ✝ *8:30am, 11am, 6:30pm Sun.* ▣ ⬇ **Concerts.** www.southwark.anglican.org

There has been a church here since at least the 10th century. The present brick building dates from 1775, but the 17th-century stained glass, commemorating Tudor monarchs, comes from the former church.

In 1782 the poet and artist William Blake was married in the church, and J. M. W. Turner later painted some marvelous views of the Thames from the church tower. Benedict Arnold, who served on both sides in the American Revolutionary War, is buried in the crypt.

Wimbledon Lawn Tennis Museum ㉕

Church Rd SW19. **Tel** 020-8946 6131. ⊖ *Southfields.* **Open** *10am–5pm daily (not during championships except to ticket holders).* **Closed** *Dec 24–26, Jan 1.* **Adm charge.** ⬇ ▣ *call for times.* ▣ ▣ www.wimbledon.org/museum

Even those with only a passing interest in the sport will find plenty to enjoy at this museum. It traces tennis's development from its invention in the 1860s as a diversion for country house parties, to the sport it is today. Alongside strange 19th-century equipment are

film clips showing the great players of the past. More recent matches may be viewed in the video theater.

Wimbledon Windmill Museum ㉖

Windmill Rd SW19. **Tel** 020-8947 2825. ⊖ ⊠ *Wimbledon then 30-min walk.* **Open** *Apr–Oct: 2–5pm Sat, 11am–5pm Sun & public hols (Nov–Mar: groups only, by arrangement).* **Adm charge.** ▣ ▣ ▣ www.wimbledonwindmillmuseum.org.uk

The mill on Wimbledon Common was built in 1817. The building at its base was turned into cottages in 1864. Boy Scout founder Lord Baden-Powell lived in the mill house. Today the site is a museum housing model windmills.

St. Mary's, Battersea

West of the Center

Ham House

Richmond Park ②⑦

Kingston Vale SW15. **Tel** 020-8948 3209. Richmond then bus 65 or 71. **Open** daily until dusk. Oct–Feb: from 7:30am; Mar–Sep: from 7am. **www**.royalparks.gov.uk

Deer in Richmond Park

In 1637, Charles I built a wall 8 miles (13 km) round to enclose the royal park as a hunting ground. Today the park is a national nature reserve and deer still graze warily among the chestnuts, birches, and oaks, no longer hunted but still discreetly culled. They have learned to coexist with the thousands of human visitors who stroll here on fine weekends.

In late spring the highlight is the Isabella Plantation with its spectacular display of azaleas, while the nearby Pen Ponds are very popular with optimistic anglers. (Adam's Pond is for model boats.) The rest of the park is heath, bracken, and trees (some of them hundreds of years old). Richmond Gate, in the northwest corner, was designed by the landscape gardener Capability Brown in 1798. Nearby is Henry VIII Mound,

where in 1536 the king, staying in Richmond Palace, awaited the signal that his former wife, Anne Boleyn, had been executed. The Palladian White Lodge, built in 1729, is home to the Royal Ballet School.

Hampton Court ②⑧

See pp254–7.

Ham House ②⑨

Ham St, Richmond. **Tel** 020-8940 1950. Richmond then bus 65 or 371. **Open** Apr–Oct: noon–4pm Sat–Thu. **Closed** Dec 25–26, Jan 1. **Adm charge**. by appt. partial. & 11am–4pm daily (mid-Feb–Oct: to 5pm). **Gardens open** Jan–mid-Feb: 11am–4pm daily; mid-Feb–Oct: 11am–5pm daily; Nov–Dec: 11am–4pm daily. **www**.nationaltrust.org.uk

This magnificent house by the Thames was built in 1610, but

Marble Hill House

its heyday came when it was home to the Duke of Lauderdale, confidant to Charles II and Secretary of State for Scotland. His wife, the Countess of Dysart, inherited it from her father, who had been Charles I's "whipping boy" (punished for the future king's misdemeanors). From 1672 the Duke and Countess modernized the house, and it was regarded as one of Britain's finest. The garden has been restored to its 17th-century form.

On some days in summer, a foot passenger ferry runs from here to Marble Hill House and Orleans House at Twickenham.

Orleans House Gallery ③⓪

Orleans Rd, Twickenham. **Tel** 020-8831 6000. Richmond then bus 33, 90, 290, R68, or R70. **Open** Apr–Sep: 1–5:30pm Tue–Sat, 2–5:30pm Sun & public hols; Oct–Mar:1–4:30pm Tue–Sat, 2–4:30pm Sun & bank hols. **Closed** Dec 24–26, Jan 1, Good Fri. **Gardens open** 9am–dusk daily. limited.

This gallery is located on the site of the original Orleans House, named for Louis Philippe, Duke of Orleans and later King of France, who lived there from 1815 to 1817. Adjacent is the Octagon Room, designed by James Gibbs for James Johnson in 1720. The gallery opened to the public in 1972, and shows temporary exhibitions, including local history displays.

Marble Hill House ③①

Richmond Rd, Twickenham. **Tel** 020-8892 5115. Richmond then bus 33, 90, 290, R68, or R70. **Open** by prebooked guided tour only (phone or access website to check). **Closed** 21 Dec–28 Feb. **Adm charge**. restricted. **Fireworks** at weekends. See **Entertainment** p349. **www**.english-heritage.org.uk

Built in 1729 for George II's mistress, Henrietta Howard, the house and its grounds have been open to the public since 1903. It has now been fully restored to its Georgian appearance. There are paintings by William Hogarth and a view of the river and house in 1762 by Richard Wilson, who is regarded as the father of English landscape painting. The café is especially good.

Richmond ❸❷

SW15. 🚇 ⇄ *Richmond.*

Richmond side street

This attractive London town took its name from the palace that Henry VII built here in 1500. Many early 18th-century houses survive near the river and off Richmond Hill, notably Maids of Honour Row, which was built in 1724. The beautiful view of the river from the top of the hill has been captured by many artists, and is largely unspoiled.

Syon House ❸❸

London Rd, Brentford. **Tel** 020-8560 0881. 🚇 *Gunnersbury then bus 237 or 267.* **House open** mid-Mar–Oct: 11am–5pm Wed–Thu, Sun. **House closed** Nov–mid-Mar. **Gardens open** mid-Mar–Oct: 10:30am–5pm daily; Nov–mid-Mar: 10:30am–4pm Sat & Sun. **Adm charge.** 🚫 🎥 📷 🖥 🅿 ♿ *gardens only.* **www**.syonpark.co.uk

The Earls and Dukes of Northumberland have lived here for 400 years – it is the only large mansion in the London area still in its hereditary ownership. The interior of the house was remodeled in 1761 by Robert Adam, and is considered to be one of his masterworks. The five Adam rooms house original furnishings and a significant collection of Old Master paintings. The 200-acre park was landscaped by Capability Brown, and includes a 40-acre garden with more than 200 species of rare trees. The Great Conservatory inspired Joseph Paxton's designs for the Crystal Palace.

Musical Museum ❸❹

399 High St, Brentford. 📞 020-8560 8108. 🚇 *Gunnersbury, South Ealing then bus 65, 237, or 267.* **Open** 11am–5:30pm Tue–Sun & bank hol Mondays. **Adm charge.** 📷 ♿ 🅿 🖥 🎬 **www**.musicalmuseum.co.uk

The collection is arranged over three floors and comprises chiefly large instruments, including player (or automatic) pianos and organs, miniature, and cinema pianos, and what is thought to be the only surviving self-playing Wurlitzer organ in Europe.

Drawing room: Osterley Park House

Osterley Park House ❸❺

Isleworth. 📞 020-8232 5050. 🚇 *Osterley.* **Open** Mar: noon–3:30pm Wed–Sun, Apr–Oct: noon–4:30pm Wed–Sun, Nov–Dec 18: noon–3:30pm Sat & Sun. **Adm charge.** 🖥 🅿 **Park open** 8am–dusk daily. **www**.nationaltrust.org.uk/osterley

Osterley is ranked among Robert Adam's finest works, and its colonnaded portico and elegant library ceiling are the proof. Much of the furniture is by Adam: the garden and temple are by William Chambers, architect of Somerset House. The garden house is by Adam.

Robert Adam's red drawing room at Syon House

Hampton Court ㉘

Cardinal Wolsey, powerful Archbishop of York to Henry VIII, began building Hampton Court in 1514. Originally it was not a royal palace, but was intended as Wolsey's riverside country house. Later, in 1528, in the hope of retaining royal favor, Wolsey offered it to the king. After the royal takeover, Hampton Court was twice rebuilt and extended, first by Henry himself and then, in the 1690s, by William and Mary, who employed Christopher Wren as architect.

Ceiling decoration from the Queen's Drawing Room

There is a striking contrast between Wren's Classical royal apartments and the Tudor turrets, gables, and chimneys elsewhere. The inspiration for the gardens as they are today comes largely from the time of William and Mary, who created a vast, formal Baroque landscape, with radiating avenues of majestic limes and many collections of exotic plants.

★ The Maze
Lose yourself in one of the garden's most popular features.

Royal tennis court

River boat pier

Main entrance

Thames River

★ The Great Vine
The vine was planted in the 1760s, and, in the 19th century, produced up to 2,000 lbs (910 kg) of black grapes.

Privy Garden

The Pond Garden
This sunken garden was once a pond to store fresh fish for Henry VIII's Court.

★ The Mantegna Gallery
Andrea Mantegna's nine canvases depicting The Triumphs of Caesar (c.1484–1505) are housed here.

VISITORS' CHECKLIST

Surrey KT8 9AU. 📞 0844-482 7777. 🚌 R68 from Kew, Richmond, or Twickenham. 🚆 Hampton Court. 🚢 Hampton Court pier. **Open** Apr–Oct: 10am–6pm daily; Nov–Mar: 10am–4:30pm daily (last adm: 1 hour before closing). **Closed** Dec 24–26. **Adm charge**. 🚻🅿️🖥️🍴🛗 www.hrp.org.uk

Broad Walk
A contemporary print shows the East Front and the Broad Walk during the reign of George II (1727–60).

Long Water
An artificial lake runs parallel to the Thames, from the Fountain Garden across the Home Park.

Fountain Garden
A few of the clipped yews here were planted in the reign of William and Mary.

The East Front
The windows of the Queen's Drawing Room, designed by Wren, overlook the central avenue of the Fountain Garden.

STAR FEATURES

★ The Great Vine

★ The Mantegna Gallery

★ The Maze

Exploring the Palace

Carving on the roof of the Great Hall

As an historic royal palace, Hampton Court bears traces of many of the kings and queens of England from Henry VIII to the present day. The building itself is a harmonious blend of Tudor and English Baroque architecture. Inside, visitors can see the Great Hall, built by Henry VIII, as well as state apartments of the Tudor court. Many of the Baroque state apartments, including those above Fountain Court by Christopher Wren, are decorated with furniture, tapestries, and old masters from the Royal Collection.

Tudor Chimneys
Ornate chimneys, some original, some careful restorations, adorn the roof of the Tudor palace.

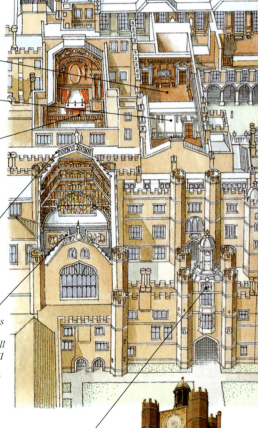

Queen's Presence Chamber

Queen's Guard Chamber

Haunted Gallery

★ Chapel Royal
The Tudor chapel was refitted by Wren except for the carved and gilded vaulted ceiling.

★ Great Hall
The stained-glass window in the Tudor Great Hall shows Henry VIII flanked by the coats of arms of his six wives.

STAR FEATURES

★ Great Hall

★ Fountain Court

★ Clock Court

★ Chapel Royal

★ Clock Court
Anne Boleyn's Archway is at the entrance to Clock Court. The Astronomical Clock, created for Henry VIII in 1540, is also located here.

King's Great Bedchamber
William III bought the crimson bed from his Lord Chamberlain.

Queen's Gallery
This marble chimneypiece by John Nost was moved from the King's Great Bedchamber to the Queen's Gallery.

CARDINAL WOLSEY

Thomas Wolsey (c.1475–1530), simultaneously a cardinal, Archbishop of York, and chancellor, was, after the king, the most powerful man in England. However, when he was unable to persuade the pope to allow Henry VIII to divorce his first wife, Catherine of Aragon, Wolsey fell from royal favor. He died while making his way to face trial for treason.

Wren's east facade

★ **Fountain Court**
The windows of state apartments are visible above the cloisters of Fountain Court.

King's Staircase
Leading to the state apartments, the King's Staircase has wall paintings by Antonio Verrio.

TIMELINE

1514 Construction of palace begins

1532 Henry starts new hall

1528 Wolsey gives the palace to Henry VIII

Henry VIII painted by Hans Holbein

1647 Charles I imprisoned by Cromwell

1689 William and Mary move to Hampton Court

1734 William Kent decorates the Queen's Staircase

c. 1727 Queen's apartments are finally completed

1773 Great Gatehouse reduced by two stories

1838 Public first admitted to the palace

1986 State apartments partly damaged by fire

1992 Damaged apartments are reopened

| 1500 | 1600 | 1700 | 1800 | 1900 |

PM Gallery and House ③⑥

Mattock Lane W5. **Tel** 020-8567
1227. ⊖ Ealing Broadway. **Open**
1–5pm Tue–Fri, 11am–5pm Sat.
Closed public hols. 📷 ♿
Exhibitions. www.ealing.gov.uk/
pmgalleryandhouse

Sir John Soane, architect of
the Bank of England (see
p147), designed this house,
Pitzhanger Manor, on the site
of an earlier one. Completed
in 1803, it was to become his
own country residence. There
are clear echoes of his elaborately constructed town house
in Lincoln's Inn Fields (see
pp136–7), especially in
the library, with its
imaginative use of
mirrors, in the darkly-
painted breakfast room
opposite and in the
"monk's dining room"
which is located on the
basement level.

Soane retained two of
the principal formal rooms:
the drawing room and the
dining room. These were
designed in 1768 by
George Dance the
Younger, with whom
Soane had worked
before establishing his
own reputation.

**Martinware bird at
PM Gallery**

A sympathetic 20th-
century extension has been
refurbished as a gallery offering a wide range of contemporary art exhibitions and
associated events. The house
also contains a large exhibition
of Martinware, highly decorated glazed pottery made in
nearby Southall between 1877

and 1915 and fashionable in
late Victorian times. The gardens of Pitzhanger Manor are
now a pleasant public park
and offer a welcome contrast
to the bustle of nearby Ealing.

Kew Bridge Steam Museum ③⑦

Green Dragon Lane, Brentford. **Tel** 020-
8568 4757. ⊖ Kew Bridge, Gunnersbury then bus 237, 65, or 267. **Open**
11am–4pm Tue–Sun (engines operate
at set times – check website for details).
Closed Mon (except public hols).
Adm charge. 🎫 reserve in advance.
📷 Sat & Sun. 🚻 ♿ www.kbsm.org

The 19th-century water
pumping station, near the
north end of Kew Bridge,
is now a museum of
steam power and water
in London. Its main
exhibits are five giant
Cornish beam engines
that pumped water here
from the river, to be
distributed in London.
The earliest engines,
dating from 1820, are
similar to those built
to pump water out
of Cornish mines.
See them working
on weekends and
public holidays.

Kew Gardens ③⑧

See pp260–61.

City Barge: Strand on the Green

Strand on the Green ③⑨

W4. ⊖ Gunnersbury then bus 237
or 267. 🚆 Kew Bridge.

This charming Thames-side
walk passes some fine 18th-
century houses as well as rows
of more modest cottages once
inhabited by fishermen. The
oldest of its three pubs is the
City Barge (see pp316–19),
parts of which date from the
15th century: the name is
older and derives from the
time when the Lord Mayor's
barge was moored on the
Thames outside.

Chiswick House ④⓪

Burlington Lane W4. **Tel** 020-8995
0508. ⊖ Chiswick. **Open** Apr: 10am–
5pm daily; May–Oct: 10am–5pm Sun–
Wed & bank hols; Nov: pre-booked
visits only. **Closed** end Dec–Mar.
Adm charge. ♿ phone ahead. 📷
🅿 **Gardens Open** 7am–dusk daily.
www.chgt.org.uk

Completed in 1729 to the
design of its owner, the
Earl of Burlington, this is a

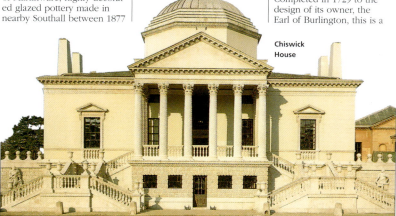

Chiswick House

fine example of a Palladian villa. Burlington revered both Palladio and his disciple Inigo Jones, whose statues stand outside. Built around a central octagonal room, the house and garden are packed with references to ancient Rome and Renaissance Italy.

Chiswick was Burlington's country residence and this house was built as an annex to a larger, older house (since demolished). It was designed for recreation and entertaining – Lord Hervey, Burlington's enemy, dismissed it as "too little to live in and too big to hang on a watch chain." Some of the ceiling paintings are by William Kent, who also contributed to the garden design. The house was a mental home from 1892 to 1928, when a long process of restoration began. The layout of the garden, now a public park, is much as Burlington designed it.

Attractive residential and leisure development in Chelsea Harbour

Plaque on Hogarth's House

Hogarth's House 41

Hogarth Lane, W4. **Tel** 020-8994 6757. ⊖ Turnham Green. **Open** Apr–Oct: 1–5pm Tue–Fri, 1–6pm Sat, Sun; Nov–Dec & Feb–Mar: 1–4pm Tue–Fri, 1–5pm Sat, Sun. **Closed** Jan, Good Fri, Dec 25 & 26. ⬛ ⬛ ⬛ ground floor only. ⬛

When the painter William Hogarth lived here from 1749 until his death in 1764, he called it "a little country box by the Thames" and painted bucolic views from its windows – he had moved from Leicester Square (see p103). Today traffic roars past along the Great West Road, on its way to and from Heathrow Airport – rush hour traffic is also notoriously bad here. In

an environment as hostile as this, and following years of neglect and then bombing during World War II, the house has done well to survive. It has now been turned into a small museum and gallery, which is filled mostly with a collection of engraved copies of the moralistic cartoon-style pictures with which Hogarth made his name. Salutary tales, such as *The Rake's Progress* (in Sir John Soane's Museum – *see pp136–7), Marriage à la Mode, An Election Entertainment*, and many others, can all be seen here.

Fulham Palace 42

Bishops Ave SW6. **Tel** 020-7736 3233. ⊖ Putney Bridge. **Open** 1–4pm Sat–Wed. **Closed** Good Fri, Dec 25 & 26. **Park open** daylight hours daily. ⬛ ⬛ 2–3 times each month, check website for days and times. ⬛ ⬛ **Events, concerts, lectures.** **www**.fulhampalace.org

The home of the Bishops of London from the 8th century until 1973, the oldest surviving parts of Fulham Palace date from the 15th century. The palace stands in its own landscaped gardens northwest of Putney Bridge. A restoration project completed in 2007 revealed a grand, long-hidden Rococo ceiling.

Chelsea Harbour 43

SW10. ⊖ Fulham Broadway. ⬛ **Exhibitions.** ⬛ ⬛

This is an impressive development of modern apartments, shops, offices, restaurants, a hotel, and a marina. It is near the site of Cremorne Pleasure Gardens, which closed in 1877 after more than 40 years as a venue for dances and circuses. The centerpiece is the Belvedere, a 20-story apartment tower with an external glass elevator and pyramid roof, topped with a golden ball on a rod that rises and falls with the tide.

Eyecatching entrance to Fulham Palace dating from Tudor times

Kew Gardens ❸⓿

The Royal Botanic Gardens, Kew are a World Heritage Site and the most complete public gardens in the world. Their reputation was first established by Sir Joseph Banks, the British naturalist and plant hunter, who worked here in the late 18th century. In 1841 the former royal gardens were given to the nation and now display about 40,000 plants. Garden enthusiasts will want a full day to visit. Kew is also a center for scholarly research.

Princess Augusta
King George III's mother established the first garden on a nine-acre (3.6 ha) site here in 1759.

Queen Charlotte's Cottage

Waterlily Pond

River Thames

HIGHLIGHTS

Spring
Cherry Walk ①
Crocus "carpet" ②
Rhizotron and Xstrata
Treetop Walkway ③

Summer
Rock Garden ④
Rose Garden ⑤

Autumn
Autumn foliage ⑥

Winter
Winter Garden ⑦
Witch Hazels ⑧

★ **Pagoda**
Britain's fascination with the Orient influenced William Chambers's pagoda, built in 1762.

Lion Gate entrance

Evolution House
gives a detailed history of plant life on Earth.

★ **Temperate House**
The building dates from 1899. Delicate woody plants are arranged here according to their geographical origins.

Minka House

This minka (traditional wooden Japanese house), built around 1900, was shipped from Japan and reconstructed in the Bamboo Garden in 2001.

White Peaks (exhibition center)

Azalea Garden

Brentford Gate entrance

Princess of Wales Conservatory

Encompassing ten climatic zones, this glasshouse contains cacti, giant waterlilies, and orchids.

Kew Palace

Nash Conservatory

🅿

Main gate entrance

The Orangery

Duke's Garden

Alpine House

Temple of Bellona

Campanile

Victoria Gate entrance and visitor center

★ Palm House

Designed by Decimus Burton in the 1840s, this famous jewel of Victorian engineering houses exotic plants in tropical conditions.

SIX GUIDED WALKS

London is an excellent city for walkers. Although it is much more spread out than most European capitals, many of the main tourist attractions are fairly close to each other *(see pp14–15)*. Central London is full of parks and gardens *(see pp48–51)*, and there are also several walk routes planned by the tourist board and local history societies. These include footpaths along canals and the Thames, and the Silver Jubilee Walk. Planned in 1977 to commemorate the Queen's Silver Jubilee, the walk runs for 12 miles (19 km) between Lambeth Bridge in the west and Tower Bridge in the east; Visit London *(see p362)* has maps of the route, which is marked by silver-colored plaques placed at intervals on the sidewalks.

Statue of boy and dolphin in Regent's Park

Each of the 16 areas described in the *Area by Area* section of this book has a short walk marked on its *Street by Street* map. These walks will take you past many of the most interesting sights in that area. On the following twelve pages are routes for six walks that take you through areas of London not covered in detail elsewhere. These range from the bustling, fashionable King's Road *(see pp266–7)* to the wide open spaces of riverside Richmond and Kew *(see pp268–9)*.

Several companies offer guided walks *(see below)*. Most of these have themes, such as ghosts or Shakespeare's London. Look in listings magazines *(see p342)* for details.

USEFUL NUMBERS The Original London Walks
Tel 020-7624 3978. **www**.walks.com

CHOOSING A WALK

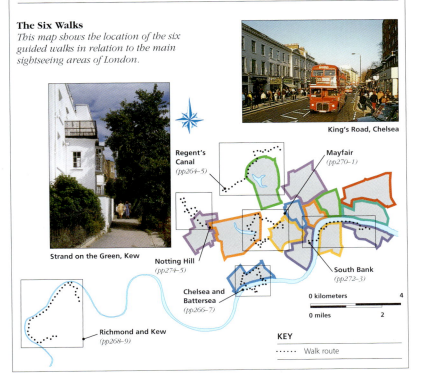

The Six Walks
This map shows the location of the six guided walks in relation to the main sightseeing areas of London.

King's Road, Chelsea

Regent's Canal
(pp264–5)

Mayfair
(pp270–1)

Strand on the Green, Kew

Notting Hill
(pp274–5)

South Bank
(pp272–3)

Chelsea and Battersea
(pp266–7)

0 kilometers 4

0 miles 2

Richmond and Kew
(pp268–9)

KEY

······ Walk route

◁ **Houseboats on Regent's Canal, Little Venice**

A Two-Hour Walk along the Regent's Canal

Master builder John Nash wanted the Regent's Canal to pass through Regent's Park, but instead it circles north of the park. Opened in 1820, it is long defunct as a commercial waterway but is today a valuable leisure amenity. This walk starts at Little Venice and ends at Camden Lock market, diverting briefly to take in the view from Primrose Hill. For more details on the sights near the Regent's Canal, see pages 220–27.

Houseboat on the canal ③

From Little Venice to Lisson Grove

At Warwick Avenue station ① take the left-hand exit and walk straight to the traffic lights by the canal bridge at Blomfield Road. Turn right and descend to the canal through an iron gate ② opposite No. 42, marked "Lady Rose of Regent." The pretty basin with moored narrowboats is Little Venice ③. At the foot of the steps turn left to walk back beneath the blue iron bridge ④. You soon have to climb up to street level again because this stretch of the towpath is reserved for access to the

The Warwick Castle, near Warwick Avenue

barges. Cross Edgware Road and walk down Aberdeen Place. When the road turns to the left by a pub, Crockers ⑤, follow the signposted Canal Way down to the right of some modern apartments. Continue your route along the canal towpath, crossing Park Road at street level. The scenery along this stretch is unremarkable, but it is not long before a splash of green to your right announces that you are now walking alongside Regent's Park ⑥.

Houseboats moored at Little Venice ③

KEY

••••	Walk route
❧	Good viewing point
⊖	Underground station
▤	Rail station

Regent's Park

Soon you see four mansions ⑦. A bridge on huge pillars marked "Coalbrookdale" ⑧ carries Avenue Road into the park. Cross the next bridge, with London Zoo ⑨ on your right, then turn left up a slope. A few steps later, take the right fork, and turn left to cross Prince Albert Road. Turn right before entering Primrose Hill through a gate ⑩ on your left.

Mansion with riverside gardens ⑦

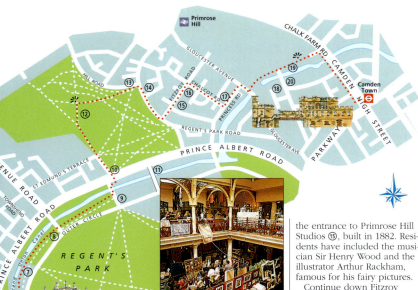

Indoor market, Camden Lock ⑲

Toward Camden

Almost opposite the gate is the Queens ⑬, a Victorian pub, and just to the left is No. 122 Regent's Park Road ⑭. This was for 24 years the home of the communist philosopher Friedrich Engels; he was often visited there by his friend Karl Marx.

Turn right and walk down Regent's Park Road for 150 yd (135 m) then turn left up Fitzroy Road. On the right, between Nos. 41 and 39, is

Primrose Lodge, Primrose Hill ⑩

Primrose Hill

From here there is a view of the Zoo aviary ⑪, designed by Lord Snowdon and opened in 1965. Inside the park, keep to the left-hand path that climbs to the top of the hill. Soon you fork right to the summit, which offers a fine view of the city skyline. A viewing panel ⑫ helps identify the landmarks but it does not include the 1990 skyscraper at Canary Wharf, with its pyramid crown, on the left. Descend on the left, making for the park gate at the junction of Regent's Park Road and Primrose Hill Road.

the entrance to Primrose Hill Studios ⑮, built in 1882. Residents have included the musician Sir Henry Wood and the illustrator Arthur Rackham, famous for his fairy pictures.

Continue down Fitzroy Road past No. 23 ⑯, once home to the poet W. B. Yeats, then go right into Chalcot Road and left down Princess Road, past a Victorian "board school" ⑰. Turn right and rejoin the canal down steps across Gloucester Avenue. Turn left under the railway bridge and past the Pirate Castle ⑱, a watersports center. Cross a hump bridge and enter Camden Lock Market ⑲ *(see p332)* through an arch on your left. After browsing there you can take the water bus ⑳ back to Little Venice or turn right into Chalk Farm Road and walk up to Camden Town Underground station.

Pedestrian bridge over the canal at Camden Lock ⑲

A Three-Hour Walk in Chelsea and Battersea

This delightful circular walk ambles through the grounds of the Royal Hospital and across the river to Battersea Park, with its romantic Victorian landscaping. It then returns to the narrow village streets of Chelsea and the stylish shops on the King's Road. For more details on the sights in Chelsea see pages 192–7.

Royal Hospital ③

Sloane Square to Battersea Park

From the station ①, turn left and walk down Holbein Place. The Renaissance painter's connection with Chelsea stems from his friendship with Sir Thomas More who lived nearby. Pass the cluster of good antique shops ② as you turn on to Royal Hospital Road. Enter the grounds of the Royal Hospital ③, designed by Christopher Wren, and turn left into the informal Ranelagh Gardens ④. The small pavilion by Sir John Soane ⑤ displays a history of the gardens as a Georgian pleasure resort – it was the most fashionable meeting place for London society.

Galleon on Chelsea Bridge

Leave the gardens for fine views of the hospital and Grinling Gibbons's bronze of Charles II ⑥. The granite obelisk ⑦ commemorates the 1849 battle at Chilianwalla, in what is now Pakistan, and forms the center-piece of the main marquee at the Chelsea Flower Show (see p56).

Charles II statue in Royal Hospital ⑥

Battersea Park

When crossing the Chelsea Bridge ⑧ (1937), look up at the four gilded galleons on top of the pillars at each end. Turn into Battersea Park ⑨ (see p251), one of London's liveliest, and follow the main path along the river to enjoy the excellent views of Chelsea. Turn left at the exotic Buddhist Peace Pagoda ⑩ to the main part of the park.

Past the bowling greens lies Henry Moore's carving of *Three Standing Figures* ⑪ (1948) and the lake, a favored spot for wildfowl. (There are boats for rent.) Just beyond the sculpture head northwest and, after crossing the central avenue, fork right and make for the wooden gate into the rustic Old English Garden ⑫. Leave the garden by the metal gate and return to Chelsea via the Victorian Albert Bridge ⑬.

Three Standing Figures by Henry Moore ⑪

KEY

• • •	Walk route
☀	Good viewing point
Ⓤ	Underground station

TIPS FOR WALKERS

Starting point: Sloane Square.
Length: 4 miles (6.5 km).
Getting there: Sloane Square is the nearest subway. There are frequent buses 11, 19, 22, and 349 to Sloane Square and along the King's Road.
Royal Hospital Grounds are open only 10am–6pm Mon–Sat, 2–6pm Sun.
Stopping-off points: There is a café in Battersea Park, by the lake. The Eight Bells, on Cheyne Walk, is a well-known local pub. There are several other pubs, restaurants, and sandwich shops to be found along the King's Road. The Chelsea Farmers' Market on Sydney Street has several cafés.

Old English Garden in Battersea Park ⑫

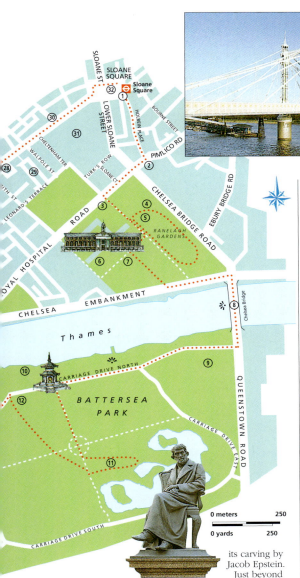

Albert Bridge ⑬

much of its original character. Where Glebe Place meets the King's Road are three pretty, early 18th-century houses ㉓. Cross Dovehouse Green opposite (it used to be a burial ground), to Chelsea Farmers' Market ㉔, an enclave of cafés and craft shops.

The King's Road

Leave the market on Sydney Street and cross into the garden of St. Luke's Church ㉕, where the writer Charles Dickens was married. The walk then winds through pretty backstreets until it rejoins the King's Road ㉖ (see p196), which was very fashionable in the 1960s. On the left is The Pheasantry ㉗. Look down the side-streets on both left and right to see the squares and terraces: Wellington Square ㉘, then Royal Avenue ㉙, intended as a triumphal way to the Royal Hospital, and Blacklands Terrace ㉚, where booklovers will want to visit John Sandoe's shop. The Duke of York's Territorial Headquarters ㉛ of 1803 on the right – now home to the Saatchi Gallery – marks the approach to Sloane Square ㉜ and the Royal Court Theatre (see Sloane Square p197).

Thomas Carlyle statue ⑮

The Back Streets of Chelsea

Over the bridge is David Wynne's sculpture of a boy and dolphin ⑭ (1975). Pass the sought-after residences on Cheyne Walk and the statues of historian Thomas Carlyle ⑮ and Sir Thomas More ⑯. The area was renowned for gatherings of intellectuals. Past Chelsea Old Church ⑰ is Roper's Gardens ⑱ with

its carving by Jacob Epstein. Just beyond these is the old, medieval Crosby Hall ⑲. Justice Walk ⑳ has a nice view of two early Georgian houses – Duke's House and Monmouth House. Turn left to pass the site of the Chelsea porcelain factory ㉑, which used to make highly fashionable (and today very highly collectable) wares in the late 18th century. Glebe Place ㉒ has retained

Royal Court Theatre ㉜

A 90-Minute Walk around Richmond and Kew

This delightful riverside walk begins in historic Richmond by the remains of Henry VII's once-splendid palace and ends at Kew, Britain's premier botanic garden. For more details on the sights in Richmond and Kew, turn to pages 252–8.

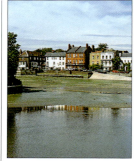

The river at low tide

Richmond Green

From Richmond station ①, proceed to Oriel House ②, which is practically opposite. Take the alleyway beneath it, and turn left towards the red-brick and terracotta Richmond Theatre ③, built in 1899. The remarkable Edmund Kean, whose brief, meteoric career in the early 19th century had a lasting impact on English acting, was closely associated with the previous theater on the site. Opposite is Richmond Green ④. Cross it diagonally and go through the entrance arch ⑤ of the old Tudor palace, which is adorned with the arms of Henry VII.

Old Palace: carving over entrance ⑤

remnants, much modified, of the 16th-century buildings.

Leave Old Palace Yard at the right-hand corner ⑥, following a sign "To the River," and turn left to pass the White Swan pub ⑦. At the river, go right along the towpath under the iron railroad bridge and then the concrete Twickenham Bridge ⑧, completed in 1933, to reach Richmond Lock ⑨, with its cast iron footbridge built in 1894. The Thames is tidal as far as Teddington, some 3 miles (5 km) upstream, and the lock is used to make the river continuously navigable.

The Riverside

Do not cross the bridge but continue along the wooded path by the river to Isleworth Ait ⑩, a large island where herons may be standing warily on the river bank. Just beyond it, on the far shore, is All Saints' Church ⑪, where the 15th-century tower has survived several rebuildings, most recently in the 1960s. Farther round the inlet, Isleworth ⑫, once a small riverside village with a busy harbor, is now a dormitory for central London. Here there is river traffic to watch: barges, yachts, and, in summer, the passenger boats that ply upriver to Hampton Court (see pp254–7). Rowers are out at most times of year, training for races. The most prestigious occasions are the Henley Regatta in July and the Oxford v. Cambridge boat race, every spring from Putney to Mortlake (see p56).

Richmond Theatre ③

Richmond

Richmond owes much of its importance – as well as its name – to Henry, victor of the Wars of the Roses and the first Tudor monarch. On becoming king in 1485 he spent a lot of time at an earlier residence on this site, Sheen Palace, dating from the 12th century. The palace burned down in 1499 and Henry had it rebuilt, naming it Richmond after the town in Yorkshire where he held an earldom. In 1603 his grand-daughter, Elizabeth I, died here. The houses inside the archway on the left contain

Herons fish the river

KEY

• • • Walk route

Good viewing point

Underground station

Train station

Kew

After a while the appearance of iron railings on your right marks where Old Deer Park ⑬ turns into Kew Gardens ⑭ (officially known as the Royal Botanic Gardens – *see pp260–61*). There used to be a riverside entrance for visitors arriving on foot or by water, but the gate ⑮ is now

Kew Palace in Kew Gardens ⑲

Just beyond are modern waterside apartments at Brentford ⑰. This was originally an industrial suburb, sited where the Grand Union Canal runs into the Thames, and its residential potential has only recently been exploited. You can pick out the tall chimney of the waterworks ⑱, now a museum dedicated to steam power. On the right, behind the Kew Gardens parking lot, there is soon a view of Kew Palace ⑲ (1631), now fully restored and open to the public.

Beyond the parking lot, leave the river by Ferry Lane on to Kew Green ⑳. Now you could spend the rest of the day in Kew Gardens or cross Kew Bridge and turn right on to Strand on the Green ㉑, a fine riverside walkway with atmospheric pubs, the oldest of them the City Barge ㉒. Head south down Kew Road if you need to get back, then turn left at Kew Gardens Road to depart from Kew Gardens Underground station (District line).

TIPS FOR WALKERS

Starting point: *Richmond station, District Line.*
Length: *3 miles (5 km).*
Getting there: *Richmond Underground or rail station. Buses 391 and R68 come here from Kew.*
Stopping-off points: *There are many cafés, pubs, and tearooms in Richmond. The famous Maids of Honour tearoom is at Kew, as is Jasper's Bun in the Oven, a good restaurant.*

Steam Museum ⑱

0 meters   500

0 yards   500

closed and the nearest entrance is to the north, near the car park.

Across the river, there are magnificent views of Syon House ⑯, seat of the Dukes of Northumberland since 1594. Part of the present house dates from the 16th century but it was largely redesigned by Robert Adam in the 1760s. You are looking at it across the garden Capability Brown laid out in the 18th century.

The river bank between Richmond and Kew

A Two-Hour Walk Through Mayfair to Belgravia

This walk takes you from Green Park to Hyde Park, through the hearts of Mayfair and Belgravia, two of London's most elegant Georgian residential districts. It includes a bracing stroll through Hyde Park and, if you're feeling energetic, a row on the Serpentine.

L'Artiste Musclé restaurant, Shepherd Market, Mayfair

Green Park to Berkeley Square
Exit Green Park subway station ① following the signs for Piccadilly North. With Green Park opposite you, turn left. Pass Devonshire House ②, a 1920s office block that replaced an 18th-century mansion designed by William Kent. Only Kent's gates survive, now at the park entrance across Piccadilly. Turn left and walk up Berkeley Sreet to Berkeley Square ③. To the south, Lansdowne House by Robert Adam has been replaced by an advertising agency ④.

Berkeley Square statue ③

There are still a few splendid 18th-century houses to the west, including No. 45 ⑤, home of the soldier and governor, Lord Clive of India.

Mayfair
Keep to the south of the square and turn into Charles Street, noting the evocative lampholders at Nos. 40 and 41 ⑥. Turn left into Queen Street and cross Curzon Street to enter Shepherd Market ⑦ (*see p97*) through Curzonfield House alleyway. Turn right up a pedestrian-only street then right onto Hertford Street, passing the Curzon Cinema ⑧ on the corner of Curzon Street. Here you are almost facing Crewe House ⑨, built in 1730 by Edward Shepherd who also laid out the market.

Turn left and walk up Curzon Street, then turn right onto Chesterfield Street. A left turn at Charles Street brings you to Red Lion Yard ⑩, where a pub stands opposite one of the few weatherboarded buildings in the West End. Turn right into Hay's Mews and left up Chesterfield Hill. Cross Hill Street and South Street and head left until you reach an alley leading to the peaceful haven of Mount Street Gardens ⑪. The gardens back on to the Church of the Immaculate Conception ⑫. Cross the garden and turn left

Official supplier to the royal family: royal coat of arms above the door

Berkeley Square, with its ancient plane trees and Georgian houses

0 meters		400
0 yards		400

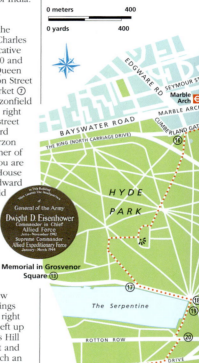

Memorial in Grosvenor Square ⑬

onto Mount Street; then right onto South Audley Street and left at Grosvenor Square ⑬ into Upper Grosvenor Street, passing to the left of the US Embassy. Look out for the statue of Franklin D. Roosevelt. Turn right up Park

Lane and walk past houses that are the remnants of what used to be the city's most desirable residential street before the traffic got so heavy ⑭. At the end you can see Marble Arch (see p211).

Hyde Park

Enter the pedestrian subway ⑮ at exit No. 6 and follow signs for Park Lane West Side, exit No. 5. You will emerge at Speakers' Corner ⑯ (see p211), where on Sundays anyone can make a speech on any topic. Cross Hyde Park (see p211) south-

southwest, enjoying the views on all sides, and make for the boat house ⑰ on the Serpentine (an artificial lake created by Queen Caroline in 1730), where you rent a rowboat. Turn left and follow the path to the Dell Café ⑱ for some refreshments. From there, take the stone bridge ⑲ and cross Rotten Row ⑳, where the very fashionable exercise their horses. Leave the park at Edinburgh Gate ㉑.

Speakers' Corner ⑯

eccentric structure fronted by colossal Doric columns, built in 1830. A path beside it leads to Halkin Arcade ㉔, built in the 1830s and adorned by Geoffrey Wickham's fountain built in 1971.

Belgravia

Turn left out of the arcade onto Kinnerton Street, which boasts one of London's smallest pubs, the Nag's Head ㉕. A street of pretty mews houses runs off to the left of this street at its northern end: look for Ann's Close and Kinnerton Place North. Almost opposite the latter, the street makes a sharp right turn to emerge into Wilton Place opposite St. Paul's Church (1843). Turn right here and follow Wilton Crescent round to the left before turning left into Wilton Row, where there is another small pub, the Grenadier ㉖, once the officers' mess of the Guards' barracks and reputedly frequented by the Duke of Wellington. Up Old Barracks Yard to its right there are some old officers' billets and a worn stone said to have been used by the Iron Duke when mounting his horses. The alley leads to a T-junction. To finish the walk, turn right onto Grosvenor Crescent Mews, then left onto Grosvenor Crescent, which leads you to Hyde Park Corner Underground station.

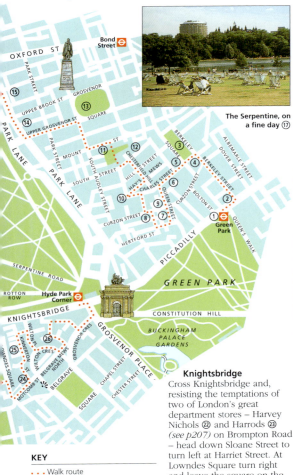

The Serpentine, on a fine day ⑰

Knightsbridge

Cross Knightsbridge and, resisting the temptations of two of London's great department stores – Harvey Nichols ㉒ and Harrods ㉓ (see p207) on Brompton Road – head down Sloane Street to turn left at Harriet Street. At Lowndes Square turn right and leave the square on the far side, turning left into Motcomb Street. On your left is the Pantechnicon, an

KEY

・・・ Walk route

⚜ Good viewing point

⊖ Underground station

Once the officers' mess, now the Grenadier pub, Belgravia ㉖

A 90-Minute Walk Along the South Bank

The Riverside Walk along the South Bank from Westminster Bridge *(see page 187)* via Bankside to Southwark Cathedral is one of the most entertaining excursions in town. From County Hall to Shakespeare's Globe, with the South Bank's well-known music, theater, and movie venues, the stores and galleries of Gabriel's Wharf and the Oxo Tower, there's something for everyone. For more details on the sights in Southwark and Bankside, see pages 173–83.

Cafés and stores at Gabriel's Wharf ⑭

Westminster

Begin at Westminster station ① by the statue of Queen Boudica (or Boadicea), and walk over Westminster Bridge. Once on the south side ②, there is a fine view back over the river to the Houses of Parliament *(see pp72–3)*. The main building on this side is the former County Hall ③, now offering two hotels, several restaurants, and a range of entertainment *(see p188)*, the highlights being the Sea Life London Aquarium ④ to see the vibrant underwater world, and Namco Station, a games hall with computer games, cars, and pool tables. For the

Waterloo Bridge, you reach BFI Southbank ⑪ *(see p347)* where movies are shown throughout the day. Outside its lively café, rows of tables stacked with second-hand books shelter beneath the bridge. The National Theatre ⑫ *(see p188)* also has exhibitions and musical events as well as a good bookstore, while in summer there are free outdoor performances. Several of the theater's restaurants,

best city view, the London Eye ⑤ *(see p189)* is beside Jubilee Gardens ⑥, where buskers and mime artists perform. Walk past Hungerford Bridge ⑦ with its modern walkways and trains to Charing Cross Station, on the site of the former Hungerford market. Ahead is the Southbank Centre ⑧ *(see pp186–7)*, the capital's main arts showcase. Music and exhibitions fill the Royal Festival Hall ⑨ *(see p188)*, created for the Festival of Britain in 1951. Check to see what's showing at the Hayward Gallery ⑩ *(see p188)* too, just beyond, on the level above. Moving on along the Riverside Walk, past

View from the Oxo Tower ⑮

cafés, and bars offer outside seating overlooking the South Bank. Past the London Studios (ITV) ⑬ is Gabriel's Wharf ⑭ *(see p191)*, a pleasant diversion of art and craft stores and lively cafés.

The Oxo Tower

The next landmark you come to is the Oxo Tower ⑮, a red-

TIPS FOR WALKERS

Starting point: *Westminster Bridge.*
Length: *1.75 miles (2.75 km).*
Getting there: *Westminster underground station on the District, Circle, and Jubilee lines.*
Stopping off points: *All the South Bank's art centers have cafés, bars, and restaurants. Also: Gourmet Pizza, Gabriel's Wharf; EAT, Riverside House (snacks and sandwiches); Anchor pub with river terrace (bars and restaurant).*

Art at the Hayward Gallery, South Bank ⑩

Cardinal's Wharf ㉓, where he had a good view of it. Next door to his house is the exhibition and tour center for Shakespeare's Globe ㉔ *(see p177)*. A tour around the theater is the next best thing to attending a performance.

Bankside

Bankside becomes more cramped here, as the historic streets pass The Anchor ㉕ riverside pub and Vinopolis ㉖ to reach the Clink Prison Museum ㉗ *(see p182)*, on the site of one of London's first lockups. At St. Mary Ovarie Dock, climb aboard

KEY

• • • Walk route

🔴 Underground station

🚋 Train station

The Anchor pub, Bankside ㉕

brick industrial building, with contemporary designer stores and galleries, such as gallery@. Take the elevator to the top of the tower for an excellent, free view of the city: the Inner Temple and Fleet Street lie opposite. Once down again, the Riverside Walk passes by Sea Containers House ⑯, with gold trimmings (built as a hotel, but now offices) and Doggett's Coat and Badge pub ⑰ *(see p63)*, then continue under Blackfriars Bridge ⑱, emerging by the remaining piers and railroad emblem of a former bridge. On the right, opposite the Founders Arms ⑲, is the esteemed Bankside Gallery ⑳ *(see p177)*, which has regular exhibitions of its members' work. Behind it, opposite Falcon Point Piazza is Marcus Campbell, an excellent art bookstore, a stone's

throw from Tate Modern ㉑ *(see pp178–81)*, the best free show on the river. Drop in for a coffee if nothing else. The Millennium Bridge ㉒ leads over to St. Paul's *(see pp148–9)* and the City. Its architect Sir Christopher Wren had a house by Cardinal Cap Alley in

a replica (1973) of *Golden Hinde* ㉘, in which the Elizabethan buccaneer Sir Francis Drake became the second man to circumnavigate the world. Southwark Cathedral ㉙ *(see p176)* is a quiet place to end the walk – there is a good tea shop here. Or, if you still feel energetic, browse around Borough Market *(see p176)* and take a look up at London's new landmark, The Shard (www.the-shard.com), before heading to the tube or train at London Bridge station ㉛.

Tate Modern: a vast space for contemporary British art ㉑

A Two-Hour Walk Around Notting Hill

This walk centers around Portobello Road, the city's most famous antiques and bric-a-brac shopping area in one of the ultra-fashionable parts of London. Great for original souvenirs, the neighborhood is fascinating at any time, though the streets are busiest on Fridays and Saturdays, when all the shops are open and the market stalls laid out *(see page 333)*. This is the heart of Notting Hill, renowned for its carnival and also favored as a movie setting and a smart address.

Odd bric-a-brac at a market stall

Sun in Splendour pub frontage ⑤

Portobello Road

Leaving Notting Hill Gate subway station ①, follow the signs to Portobello Road *(see p219)*, taking Pembridge Road ②. Intriguing shops here include Retro Woman ③ (Nos. 20 and 32) and Retro Man ④ (No. 34) for period clothes and accessories. At the Sun in Splendour pub ⑤, turn left into Portobello Road. No. 22, among the attractively painted terraced houses on the right, was where George Orwell lived in 1927 before his writing career began ⑥. Cross Chepstow Villas ⑦ and

the serious antique shops begin. Near the Portobello Arcade ⑧, signposted with a large teapot, is Portobello Gold (Nos. 95–7), a guest house where Bill, Hillary, and Chelsea Clinton dropped in for a beer and a snack in 2000. At No. 115 ⑨ is a plaque to June Aylward,

who opened the first antique shop in the street. At Colville Terrace ⑩ the daily fruit and vegetable market begins. On the left is the Electric Cinema ⑪, said to be Britain's oldest working movie theater (1910),

The Electric Cinema, the UK's oldest working movie theater ⑪

and certainly one of the most delightful. If there is not a movie showing, you can go in and try the comfortable armchair seats and sofas.

The Travel Bookshop

Turn left down Blenheim Crescent to find The Travel Bookshop ⑫, inspiration for the location of the 1999 film *Notting Hill*, in which Hugh Grant was the assistant. Books for Cooks ⑬ (No. 4) is where recipes from the latest books are prepared and sold. Head back to Portobello Road and pass the local Salvation Army center ⑭. Amble for several blocks to Grove Café ⑮ (No. 253a) on the corner (opposite the Market Bar ⑯). If you can find a table on

Notting Hill's Travel Bookshop ⑫

Bevington Road, right along Blagrove Road, and right again into Acklam Road to bring you back to Portobello Road. Continue for several blocks, turning left on Talbot Road, where All Saints' Church ⑲ has a glassed-in shrine to Our Lady of Walsingham – an unusual feature in a Protestant church. Just beyond the red-brick Tabernacle Centre for Arts and Education ⑳, where Pink Floyd made their debut

in 1966, is My Beautiful Laundrette ㉑, named for the successful 1986 film. Turn right into Ledbury Road to find high-fashion shops, and also, at its end, the Westbourne Grove Church ㉒. As you are passing No. 62, try the pastries in Ottolenghi Patisserie ㉓ for a snack to hit the spot. Turn right into Westbourne Grove for more stylish shopping. Nicole Farhi has a shop ㉔ (No. 202) of new and second-hand clothes. Detour to Toms deli and café ㉕ at 127, which claims the best toasted sandwiches in town, and is run by Tom Conran, son of the style guru Terence Conran. The Wild at Heart flower stall on Turquoise Island ㉖ opposite, won awards for its designer, Piers Gough, in 1993. On the far side is the Oxfam thrift shop ㉗, where its bargains reflect the good taste of the locals. Head back to Portobello Road ㉘ and Notting Hill Gate station.

Award-winning Wild at Heart flower stall ㉖

the upstairs terrace, you'll have a good view of the street. All-day breakfasts are a specialty. Excitement dwindles once you pass under the Westway overpass, except on Fridays and Saturdays when Tent City ⑰ and the Golborne Road Flea Market ⑱ are fully active, and the Portuguese cafés (especially the Lisboa at 55) are bustling. From Golborne Road, turn right into

The clock tower on All Saints' Church ⑲

KEY

• • • Walk route

🚇 Underground station

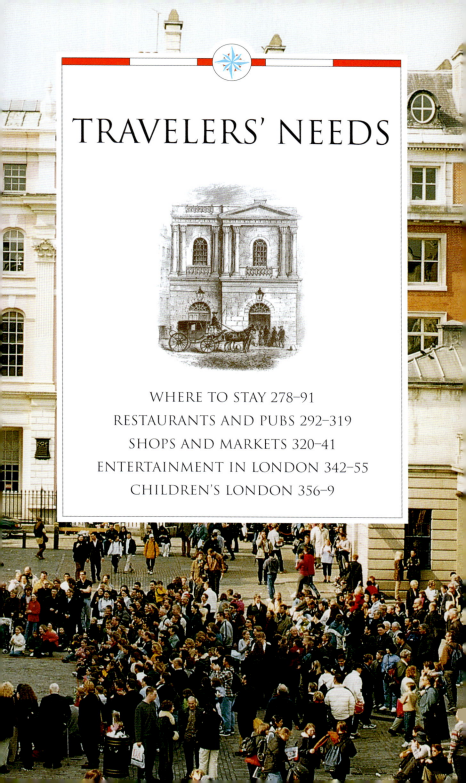

TRAVELERS' NEEDS

WHERE TO STAY

The high cost of accommodations in London is one of the biggest drawbacks for visitors. At the top end of the market, there is no shortage of expensive pedigree hotels, such as the Savoy and the Ritz. Midrange hotels, while there are many, tend to be slightly farther out of the center of town. Sadly, most of the budget hotels are seedy and unappealing, a problem exacerbated by rising land and property prices. However, there are ways to stay in the capital without breaking the bank. Low-cost hotel chains such as Travel Inn, Express by Holiday Inn, and Ibis have been established in many convenient locations throughout the city, and offer good quality if standardized accommodations at affordable prices. We have inspected more than 250 hotels and apartment complexes across a range of price brackets and localities and have more than 120 of the best of their kind. For further details on these, turn to the listings on pages 278–91. Self-contained apartments and private homes *(see pp280–81)* are available at a wide range of prices. Student halls and hostels, even a few camping sites on London's outskirts, are additional possibilities for budget travelers *(see p281).*

Hilton doorman

WHERE TO LOOK

The most expensive hotels tend to be in smart West End areas such as Mayfair and Belgravia. Often large and opulent, with uniformed staff, they are not always the most relaxing places to stay. For smaller, more personal, but still luxurious hotels, try South Kensington or Holland Park.

The streets off Earl's Court Road are full of hotels at the lower end of the price range. Several of the big railroad stations are well served with budget hotels too. Try Ebury Street near Victoria, or Sussex Gardens near Paddington. Close to Euston or Waterloo and in the City and Docklands, well-known hotels chain cater for travelers at a range of prices. The area immediately north of King's Cross is best avoided at night.

There are also inexpensive hotels in the suburbs, such as Ealing, Hendon, Richmond, or Harrow. From here you can get into town on public transportation. Take care not to miss the last train back.

If you get stranded at an airport or have to catch a very early morning flight, consult the list on page 377.

For further information, advice, and reservation services, contact **Visit London**, which publishes several annually updated booklets on accommodations in Greater London.

DISCOUNT RATES

Prices in the capital tend to stay high all year round, but there are bargains. Many hotels, especially the groups, offer reduced rates for weekends and special breaks *(see p280).* Others work on a more ad hoc basis, depending on how busy they are. If a hotel isn't full, it is always worth trying to negotiate a discount, especially if it is low season. Older budget hotels may have rooms without showers or private bathrooms. These usually cost less than those with private facilities.

HIDDEN EXTRAS

Read the small print carefully. Most hotels quote room rates rather than rates per person, but not all. Service charges and VAT are usually included in the quoted price but in some cases they are added on later. Beware of high markups on telephone calls. A hotel with a high room tariff may be even more expensive than at first appears, which means that the final bill can come as a shock to many visitors.

Imaginative design at One Aldwych hotel *(see p289)*

◁ Street entertainer and crowd in Covent Garden Piazza

The Radisson Edwardian Hampshire hotel *(see p287)*

Breakfast may not be included in room rates, though it generally is in cheaper hotels. The definition of breakfast ranges from "full English" (a hearty, traditional fry-up which will see you through the most hectic sightseeing program), to a "Continental" cup of coffee and a roll or croissant. Buffet breakfasts with lavish spreads of fruit, muesli, and yoghurt are increasingly popular with health-conscious visitors.

Tipping is expected in the more expensive hotels, but there is no need to tip staff other than porters, except perhaps a helpful concierge for arranging theater tickets or phoning for taxis.

Single travelers are usually charged a "supplement" and end up paying about 80 percent of the double room rate, even if they are occupying a "single" room – so don't accept anything substandard.

The elegant hallway of The Gore hotel in Kensington *(see p283)*

FACILITIES

Room sizes in London hotels at all price ranges tend to be on the small side, but the majority of hotels now provide telephones, televisions, and private baths or showers in all their rooms. At the top end of the scale, hotels compete to provide the very latest sound-and-video systems, computer equipment, and high-tech gadgetry. Many hotel rooms also come equipped with iPod docks. Whatever the hotel, you will be expected to vacate your room by noon on the day you leave, sometimes earlier.

HOW TO BOOK

It is always advisable to book well in advance, as room availability fluctuates and better quality hotels are in constant demand. Direct bookings can be made by letter, phone, fax, or via the Internet. This generally entails giving some kind of guarantee: either a credit card number from which a cancellation fee can be deducted, or remitting a one-night deposit (some hotels will expect more for longer stays). Don't forget that if you subsequently cancel for any reason, part or all of the room price may be charged unless the hotel can relet the room. Insurance cover is advised.

Travelers can phone the Visit London Accommodation Booking Service on 0870-156 6366 (also at www. superbreak.com). There is no booking fee but customers will need to give a credit card number. During high season there may be a one-night deposit to pay, but that is at the discretion of the hotel. The Booking Service will advise, of course, if there is a deposit to pay. Alternatively, travelers can use a similar booking service on the London Tourist Board's website (www.visitlondon.com) or they can e-mail the service directly at admin@superbreak. com. There is no booking fee if booking online.

Tourists can also book in person at the London Visitor

One of the stylish bathrooms at the Portobello Hotel *(see p283)*

Centre at No. 1 Regent Street, and can order a brochure, "Where to Stay on a Budget," from the Visit London brochure line on 0870-156 6366.

Room reservation services are also available at the British Travel Centre on Regent Street. A number of non-LTB booking agencies operate from booths in the major rail stations, charging a small fee to personal callers. Unidentified touts, who hang around at railroad and bus stations offering cheap accommodations to tourists, should be avoided.

BOOKING ONLINE

The easiest way to book a hotel is online, with the best prices often available only via the Internet. Many hotels have their own online advance purchase rates while Internet travel sites and hotel wholesalers such as Expedia (www. expedia.co.uk) and Travelocity (www.travelocity.co.uk) can also offer good rates, particularly if you book a hotel and flight together. Accommodations agencies more often than not use the Internet as a cost-effective way to do business and, in most cases, at least some of the savings are passed on to customers. Increasingly, the Internet demonstrates the fluidity of many hotel "rack rates" (i.e. the prices printed on the tariff sheet), which, far from being set in stone, fluctuate widely according to the laws of supply and demand.

SPECIAL BREAKS

Many travel agencies carry brochures from the major hotel chains listing special offers, which are usually costed on a minimum two-night stay. Some are extraordinarily good value compared to the usual tariff. For most leisure travelers or families with children, this is the best way to get value for money out of London hotels so that you can spend time in the city without breaking the bank.

City-break packages are organized by specialist operators, ferry companies, and airlines, and some privately owned hotels too. Sometimes the same hotel may be featured in several brochures at widely differing prices and with different perks. It's worth asking the hotel directly what special rates they offer, and checking their websites too.

DISABLED TRAVELERS

Information about wheelchair access is based largely on hotels' own assessments, but travelers with special needs should always confirm when booking whether an establishment is suitable. If forewarned, many hotels will go out of their way to help disabled visitors. The nationwide *Tourism for All* program provides details on accommodations standards and facilities for elderly visitors or those with mobility problems. For information on hotels that meet the three-tier "National Accessible Standard," contact **Visit London** or **Tourism For All**. A guide book for people with access needs, *Open Britain*, can be obtained from **RADAR**.

1920s Savoy poster

TRAVELING WITH CHILDREN

London hotels are no longer the child-free zones they used to be. Many now make a concerted effort to cater to the needs of people traveling with children, providing cribs, highchairs, babysitting services (always ensure sitters have had a Criminal Records Bureau check), and special meal arrangements. Ask whether the hotel offers special deals for children – some have special rates, or allow children to stay free of charge in their parents' room.

APARTMENTS

Many agencies offer self-contained accommodations in furnished apartments, usually for stays of a week or more. Prices, depending on size and location, start at about £300 per week. Some luxury complexes are fully serviced, so you don't need to cook, shop, or clean. **Bridge Street**

Worldwide has over 550 London apartments in smart locations. It caters mainly for corporate and professional travelers, but its properties can be rented for short-term stays whenever they are available.

The **Landmark Trust** rents apartments in historic or unusual buildings. These include apartments in Hampton Court *(see pp254–7)* and in a pretty 18th-century terrace in the City: one of them was the home of the late poet laureate, Sir John Betjeman. A handbook of Landmark Trust properties is available for a charge.

STAYING IN PRIVATE HOMES

A number of agencies organize stays in private homes; several are registered with Visit London. Credit card reservations can be made through Visit London's telephone booking service *(see box)*. Several agencies have minimum stays of anything up to a week. Prices depend on location, starting at around £20 per person per night. Sometimes you will enjoy family hospitality, but this isn't guaranteed, so enquire when you book. Deposits may be requested and cancellation fees imposed. The **Bed & Breakfast and Homestay Association (BBHA)** is an umbrella organization for several reputable agencies whose properties are inspected regularly. Several BBHA members are listed in the Directory *(see box)*.

Uptown Reservations arranges upscale B&B in interesting, well-located London homes which have been inspected for their welcome, security, and comfort. Prices start at £95 per night for a double room. It works in tandem with **Wolsey Lodges**, a nationwide consortium of distinctive private homes, often of historic or architectural interest, offering individual hospitality and a good dinner. Wolsey Lodges lists a couple of charming London properties.

Classical opulence at Claridge's Hotel *(see p286)*

CHAIN HOTELS

Chain hotels are an important feature of the London hotel market. Though they can lack character, they offer some of the best value accommodations in town. Some also offer particular facilities; Novotel, for example, caters for both business guests and families. Other good-value chains include Express by Holiday Inn and easyHotel.

BUDGET ACCOMMODATIONS

Despite the high cost of many London hotels, budget accommodations do exist, and not only for young travelers.

Dormitory accommodations and youth hostels

These can be booked through the LTB's information center at Victoria Station for a small fee plus a refundable deposit. Some private hostels near Earl's

City of London Youth Hostel

Court charge little more than £10 a night for a dormitory bed with breakfast. The **London Hostel Association** has a selection of reasonably priced accommodations throughout central London. The **Youth Hostels Association (YHA)** runs seven hostels in London. There is no age limit, though nonmembers pay a small joining fee and adults also

pay a little more. Of the seven, two are located in the heart of London. The Oxford Street hostel is actually in nearby Noel Street, Soho, and the City hostel is in an atmospheric street near St. Paul's Cathedral *(see pp148–51)*.

There is an online booking service, the **International Booking Network**, run by the International Youth Hostel Federation, that is the easiest way to book a bed. One of the most popular hostels is Holland House, a Jacobean mansion in Holland Park.

Residence halls

Many student rooms are available at Easter and from July to September. Some of these are in central locations such as South Kensington and places are sometimes available at short notice. Try **City University**, or, if you need a room in a hurry, **King's College** or **Imperial College** may be able to find you one.

DIRECTORY

RESERVATIONS AND INFORMATION

British Hotel Reservation Centre
Victoria Rail Station,
East Concourse,
SW1V 1JU.
Tel 020-7592 3055.
www.bhrc.online.com

Visit London
1 Warwick Row
SW1E 5ER.
Tel 0870-156 6366.
www.visitlondon.com

DISABLED TRAVELERS

RADAR
Unit 12,
City Forum,
250 City Road EC1V 8AF.
Tel 020-7250 3222.
www.radar.org.uk

TOURISM FOR ALL
c/o Vitalise,
Shap Road Industrial
Estate, Shap Road,
Kendal, Cumbria
LA9 6NZ.
Tel 0845-124 9971.
www.tourismforall.org.uk

APARTMENT AGENCIES

Bridge Street Worldwide
Compass House,
22 Redan Place W2 4SA.
Tel 020-7792 2222.
www.bridgestreet.com

Landmark Trust
Shottesbrooke, Maidenhead, Berks SL6 3SW.
Tel 01628 825925.
www.landmarktrust.org.uk

AGENCIES FOR STAYS IN PRIVATE HOMES

At Home in London
70 Black Lion Lane W6 9BE.
Tel 020-8748 1943.
www.athomeinlondon.co.uk

Bed & Breakfast & Homestay Assoc.
8 Kelso Place W8 5OP.
Tel 020-7937 2001.
www.bbha.org.uk

Host & Guest Service
103 Dawes Road SW6 7DU
Tel 020-7385 9922.
www.host-guest.co.uk

London Bed and Breakfast Agency
71 Fellows Road NW3 3JY
Tel 020-7586 2768.
www.londonbb.com

Uptown Reservations
8 Kelso Place W83 5QD.
Tel 020-7937 2001.
www.uptownres.co.uk

Wolsey Lodges
9 Market Place, Hadleigh,
Ipswich, Suffolk, IP7 5DL.
Tel 01473-822058.
www.wolseylodges.com

HOSTEL BOOKING

Hosteling International
Tel 01707-324170.
www.hihostels.com

London Hostels Association
54 Eccleston Sq
SW1V 1PG.
Tel 020-7727 5665.
www.london-hostels.co.uk

Youth Hostels Association
Dimple Rd, Matlock,
Derbyshire DE4 3YH.
Tel 01629-592700.
www.yha.org.uk

BOOKING ADDRESSES FOR RESIDENCE HALLS

City University Accommodation & Conference Service
Northampton Sq
EC1V 0HB.
Tel 020-7040 8037.
www.city.ac.uk

Imperial College Summer Accommodation Centre
Sherfield Building, Level 3,
SW7 2AZ. *Tel* 020-7594 9507. www.imperial-accommodationlink.com

King's Conference & Vacation Bureau
26–29 Drury Lane,
1st floor, WC2B 5RL.
Tel 020-7848 1700.
www.kcl.ac.uk/kcvb

Choosing a Hotel

These hotels have been selected across a wide price range for their good value, facilities, and location; they are listed by area. Starting with west and southwestern districts of London, the guide moves through central parts of the city and on to eastern districts, eventually looking at hotels further outside the city.

PRICE CATEGORIES
For a standard double room per night, inclusive of breakfast, service charges, and any additional taxes such as VAT.

£ under £90
££ £90–£140
£££ £140–£200
££££ £200–£250
£££££ over £250

BAYSWATER, PADDINGTON

Best Western Mornington
££   Map 10 F2

12 Lancaster Gate, W2 **Tel** *020 7262 7361* **Fax** *020 7706 1028* **Rooms** *70*

This reliable, good-value midrange hotel just off Hyde Park was refurbished in 2010. Rooms are comfortable and well equipped, enjoyable English breakfasts are served, and there's a cozy bar for sitting and chatting at the end of the day. Discount offers are often available and Wi-Fi use is complimentary. **www.bw-morningtonhotel.co.uk**

Garden Court Hotel
££   Map 10 D2

30–31 Kensington Gardens Square, W2 **Tel** *020 7229 2553* **Fax** *020 7727 2749* **Rooms** *32*

An antique beefeater guards the lobby of this good-value hotel on a lovely garden square. The hotel celebrated its 50th anniversary in 2004 with a facelift; rooms have tasteful modern wallpaper and wooden furniture. To keep the cost down even further, you can opt for shared facilities. Charge for Wi-Fi use. **www.gardencourthotel.co.uk**

Pavilion Hotel
££   Map 11 B1

34–36 Sussex Gardens, W2 **Tel** *020 7262 0905* **Fax** *020 7262 1324* **Rooms** *30*

The conventional Bayswater exterior shields one of London's most special hotels. Each room (some of them very small) has its own extravagant theme decor, from Moroccan-palace in *Casablanca Nights* to 1970s TV in *Honky Tonk Afro*. It's beloved by the rock and fashion world, but rates remain low. Free Wi-Fi in all rooms. **www.pavilionhoteluk.com**

Prince's Square
££   Map 10 D2

23–25 Prince's Square, W2 **Tel** *020 7229 9876* **Fax** *020 7229 4664* **Rooms** *50*

Behind the grand Victorian façade is a friendly, modern hotel. The refurbished pastel rooms may have standard hotel furnishings, but they are neat and cheerful, and the bathrooms are spotless. There's a handy bar in the lobby, and special deals bring the price down considerably. Charge for Wi-Fi use. **www.princessquarehotel.co.uk**

Stylotel
££   Map 11 A2

160–162 Sussex Gardens, W2 **Tel** *020 7723 1026* **Fax** *020 7262 2983* **Rooms** *40*

Offering some of the cheapest rates in central London, Stylotel is true to its name, although the high-tech style may not suit all tastes. Rooms have wooden floors, aluminium walls, light-box bedside tables and futuristic bathrooms. There's a groovy lounge with curved stainless steel bar and blue leather seats. Wi-Fi in public areas (charged). **www.stylotel.com**

The Delmere
££   Map 11 A2

130 Sussex Gardens, W2 **Tel** *020 7706 3344* **Fax** *020 7262 1863* **Rooms** *36*

Part of the Best Western chain, the Delmere offers accommodation a stone's throw away from Paddington Station. Rooms are well proportioned and attractively decorated, bathrooms are small yet stylish, and there's a pleasant dining room and lounge where you can relax with the day's papers. Free Wi-Fi available. **www.delmerehotels.co.uk**

The Royal Park
£££   Map 10 F2

3 Westbourne Terrace, W2 **Tel** *020 7479 6600* **Fax** *020 7479 6601* **Rooms** *48*

This townhouse hotel near Hyde Park has a discreet luxury, which has attracted celebrity guests. Classic, unfussy rooms are furnished with exquisite fabrics, original prints and stone-tiled bathrooms. All the usual gadgetry, plus complimentary welcome drink and evening champagne in the drawing room. Free Wi-Fi in all rooms. **www.theroyalpark.com**

Vancouver Studios
£££   Map 10 D2

30 Prince's Square, W2 **Tel** *020 7243 1270* **Fax** *020 7221 8678* **Rooms** *47*

These stylishly decorated studios in three 19th-century terraced houses have fully equipped kitchenettes, flatscreen TVs and DVD players. Resident cat Panther presides over the living room with a view onto the secluded garden. Laundry and free Wi-Fi complete the home-from-home package. **www.vancouverstudios.co.uk**

The Hempel
£££££   Map 10 E2

31–35 Craven Hill Gardens, W2 **Tel** *020 7298 9000* **Fax** *020 7402 4666* **Rooms** *50*

Fans of the minimalist aesthetic will be in their element in Anouska Hempel's serene white hotel. Each room, complete with candles and all the requisite gadgetry, including free Wi-Fi, is special. There is a striking geometric landscaped garden and a European restaurant called Number 35. Conference rooms available. **www.the-hempel.co.uk**

Key to Symbols *see back cover flap*

KENSINGTON, EARL'S COURT

base2stay
25 Courtfield Gardens, SW5 **Tel** *020 7244 2255* **Fax** *020 7244 2256* **Rooms** *67*   **Map** *18 E2*

An original hotel with an imaginative combination of sleek boutique-hotel-style minimalist design and accessible prices. Rooms are in different sizes, from singles to suites, but all have mini-kitchens and an exceptional range of high-quality electronics (including free Wi-Fi) and other extras. Staff are very helpful. **www.base2stay.com**

Mayflower Hotel
26–28 Trebovir Road, SW5 **Tel** *020 7370 0991* **Fax** *020 7370 0994* **Rooms** *48*   **Map** *18 D2*

This beautifully furnished, budget boutique hotel is a cut above the rest. The spacious, contemporary rooms have wooden floors and Eastern elements such as elaborately carved beds and rich silks, as well as marble bathrooms, ceiling fans, CD players, and free Wi-Fi. There are also 35 tasteful apartments nearby. **www.mayflowergroup.co.uk**

Rushmore
11 Trebovir Road, SW5 **Tel** *020 7370 3839* **Fax** *020 7370 0274* **Rooms** *22*   **Map** *17 C2*

Like the nearby Mayflower, the Rushmore is proof that accommodation doesn't have to be expensive to be stylish. Each room in this Victorian townhouse has been designed in a different style; even the bathrooms have been customized to fit in with the mood. Breakfast is served in a chic conservatory. Lower floors have free Wi-Fi. **www.rushmore-hotel.co.uk**

Twenty Nevern Square
20 Nevern Square, SW5 **Tel** *020 7565 9555* **Fax** *020 7565 9444* **Rooms** *20*   **Map** *17 C2*

This townhouse overlooking a private garden square combines unique decor with reasonable rates. Rooms are furnished with gorgeous silks and spectacular beds such as Eastern-carved wooden styles or four-posters. Widescreen TVs, CD players, and 24-hour room service are further attractions. Free Wi-Fi throughout. **www.twentynevernsquare.co.uk**

The Gore
190 Queen's Gate, SW7 **Tel** *020 7584 6601* **Fax** *020 7589 8127* **Rooms** *50*   **Map** *10 F5*

The Gore has been in operation for more than 100 years and, while it has been refurbished, it preserves the atmosphere of a bygone age. Rooms feature four-poster beds, antiques, luxurious draperies, and opulent fabrics. There's an oak-paneled bar and casual bistro as well. Free Wi-Fi. **www.gorehotel.com**

The Milestone Hotel
1 Kensington Court, W8 **Tel** *020 7917 1000* **Fax** *020 7917 1010* **Rooms** *56 + 6 apartments*   **Map** *10 E5*

This plush hotel opposite Kensington Palace features originally designed rooms, from the smart "Savile Row" to the Colonial-style "Safari Suite." Extras include gym and resistance pool, broadband Internet and Penhaligon's toiletries in rooms, 24-hour butler, and use of the hotel Bentley. **www.milestonehotel.com**

NOTTING HILL, HOLLAND PARK

New Linden Hotel
59 Leinster Square, W2 **Tel** *020 7221 4321* **Fax** *020 7727 3156* **Rooms** *51*   **Map** *10 D2*

Warm, subtle color schemes and chic modern design are features of this very stylish, renovated hotel. Rooms combine a fresh, bright feel with sumptuous comforts, and TVs and other equipment (including free Wi-Fi) are state of the art. Breakfasts include plenty of fresh fruit. **www.newlinden.co.uk**

The Main House
6 Colville Road, W11 **Tel** *020 7221 9691* **Rooms** *4*   **Map** *9 B2*

In the heart of Notting Hill, this chic guesthouse features airy suites – one per floor. The decor combines modern elements and antiques. Thoughtful extras include the loan of mobile phones and bikes, and morning coffee brought to your room on a silver tray. Free Wi-Fi and use of off-site gym. No single-night stays. **www.themainhouse.com**

Miller's Residence
111a Westbourne Grove, W2 **Tel** *020 7727 6934* **Fax** *020 7243 1064* **Rooms** *8*   **Map** *10 D2*

Owned by antiques expert Martin Miller and a short stroll from Portobello Road's famous market, this hotel is a bric-a-brac-hunter's fantasy. Rooms are individually furnished with his finds, and free drinks are served in the eccentrically cluttered drawing room, which is candlelit in the evening. Free Wi-Fi available. **www.millershotel.com**

Portobello Hotel
22 Stanley Gardens, W11 **Tel** *020 7727 2777* **Fax** *020 7792 9641* **Rooms** *21*   **Map** *9 B2*

This long-running, popular hotel combines Victorian coziness with sumptuous extravagance in its individually decorated bedrooms, with special features like Moroccan lamps and antique bed-heads. Facilities (including free Wi-Fi) are high-standard. The same owners run Julie's Restaurant next door. Use of nearby health club. **www.portobellohotel.com**

KNIGHTSBRIDGE, BROMPTON, BELGRAVIA

The Rembrandt
£££

11 Thurloe Place, SW7 **Tel** *020 7589 8100* **Fax** *020 7225 3476* **Rooms** *192 + 1 suite*   **Map** *19 A1*

This hotel offers contemporary style mixed with original Edwardian features in a great location for visiting the V&A and other museums. After a day exploring the sights, guests can unwind in the swimming pool and spa or relax on the luxurious sofas in the bar. Not all rooms are air conditioned. Wi-Fi in lobby. **www.sarova.com/rembrandt**

Knightsbridge Green Hotel
££££

159 Knightsbridge, SW1 **Tel** *020 7584 6274* **Fax** *020 7225 1635* **Rooms** *31*   **Map** *11 C5*

A shopaholic's dream, this well-kept hotel is right on Knightsbridge and rates are reasonable for more spending power in Harrods and Harvey Nichols. The tidy, modern rooms (some facing Hyde Park) are regularly upgraded and feature air conditioning, Wi-Fi, and satellite TVs. There's also a small business center on-site. **www.thekghotel.com**

The Cadogan
££££

75 Sloane Street, SW1 **Tel** *020 7235 7141* **Fax** *020 7245 0994* **Rooms** *64*   **Map** *19 C1*

Opened in 1888, the Cadogan has welcomed such famous guests as Lillie Langtry and Oscar Wilde. The latter was arrested in room 118. It has a traditional British character, and guests have access to the private Cadogan Place gardens and tennis courts across the road. Free Wi-Fi throughout. **www.cadogan.com**

The Berkeley
£££££

Wilton Place, SW1 **Tel** *0808 238 0245* **Fax** *020 7235 4330* **Rooms** *214*   **Map** *12 D5*

Not the best-known of London's luxury hotels, rebuilt in the 1970s, but the Berkeley offers an exceptional range of opulent services (including free Wi-Fi) – with the rooftop pool and spa as a crowning glory. An equally impressive choice of restaurants includes Marcus Wareing at the Berkeley, showcase for one of Britain's finest chefs. **www.the-berkeley.co.uk**

The Capital
£££££

22 Basil Street, SW3 **Tel** *020 7589 5171* **Fax** *020 7225 0011* **Rooms** *49*   **Map** *11 C5*

A more intimate variation on the luxury hotel, with just 49 individually designed rooms and suites, all traditionally styled but with superior Wi-Fi and other modern equipment. Service throughout is excellent, and under chef Jérôme Ponchelle the Capital restaurant is superb. Good discounts available online. **www.capitalhotel.co.uk**

The Halkin
£££££

5 Halkin Street, SW1 **Tel** *020 7333 1000* **Fax** *020 7333 1100* **Rooms** *41*   **Map** *12 D5*

Modern comforts meet Eastern serenity at this gracious luxury hotel. Warm wood, curving lines, and creamy bed linen are accented by Southeast Asian art handpicked by the Singaporean owner. Be sure to have a meal at Nahm, the excellent Thai restaurant. Free Wi-Fi access throughout. **www.halkin.como.bz**

The Knightsbridge
£££££

10 Beaufort Gardens, SW3 **Tel** *020 7584 6300* **Fax** *020 7584 6355* **Rooms** *44*   **Map** *19 B1*

With its book-lined library and drawing room full of modern artworks, the Knightsbridge feels like the home of a well-traveled intellectual. A bit cheaper than the other Firmdale hotels, this one offers the same lovely, updated English-style bedrooms and faultless attention to detail. Wi-Fi is available at a charge. **www.firmdalehotels.com**

SOUTH KENSINGTON, CHELSEA

easyHotel
£

14 Lexham Gardens, W8 **Rooms** *34*   **Map** *18 D1*

Some of the cheapest rates in London for en suite double rooms can be found at the easy group's bright budget hotels. Rooms and service are basic, but clean and well maintained. There are extra charges for using towels and TVs. There are three more easyHotels around London and one at Heathrow. Book via website. **www.easyhotel.com**

Aster House
£££

3 Sumner Place, SW7 **Tel** *020 7581 5888* **Fax** *020 7584 4925* **Rooms** *13*   **Map** *19 A2*

Three-time winner of the Tourist Board's best B&B award, this friendly hotel in a grand white stucco house has immaculate rooms in a typical English country style. A superior breakfast served in the palm-filled conservatory and a garden complete with pond and ducks attract guests. Free Wi-Fi and access to off-site gym. Minimum 3-night stay. **www.asterhouse.com**

Sydney House
£££

9–11 Sydney Street, SW3 **Tel** *020 7376 7711* **Fax** *020 7376 4233* **Rooms** *21*   **Map** *19 A2*

This small hotel is just steps away from the chic shops of Brompton Cross. Airy rooms are furnished with blond wood furniture, Frette linens, contemporary art, and thoughtful features such as American wall sockets and water softener in the ultramodern bathrooms. Free Wi-Fi in rooms. **www.sydneyhousechelsea.com**

Key to Price Guide *see p282* **Key to Symbols** *see back cover flap*

The Rockwell
181–183 Cromwell Road, SW5 **Tel** *020 7244 2000* **Fax** *020 7244 2001* **Rooms** *40*
Map *18 D2*
£££

Housed in a beautifully restored Victorian terrace, The Rockwell is owned by an architect, and it shows in the stunning decor and the glass bridge that links the hotel to its courtyard garden. Other features include 24-hour room service, free Internet access, perfectly fluffy bathrobes, and plenty of original English charm. **www.therockwell.com**

myhotel Chelsea
35 Ixworth Place, SW3 **Tel** *020 7225 7500* **Fax** *020 7225 7555* **Rooms** *45*
Map *19 B2*
££££

Very deliberately hip design – in line with feng shui – and chic luxury are hallmarks of the myhotel group. Their Chelsea hotel has a slightly more traditional look to match the location. High-standard electronics, naturally including free Wi-Fi, are also a feature. The smart mybar restaurant offers varied menus through the day. **www.myhotels.com**

Blakes Hotel
33 Roland Gardens, SW7 **Tel** *020 7370 6701* **Fax** *020 7373 0442* **Rooms** *42*
Map *18 F2*
£££££

Blakes is the original "boutique hotel," created by designer Anouska Hempel over two decades ago. Rooms range in style from baronial manor to opulent Oriental and contain pieces collected on her travels. The discreet residential location has made it a favorite celeb hideaway. Only some suites are air conditioned. Wi-Fi is charged. **www.blakeshotels.com**

San Domenico House
29–31 Draycott Place, SW3 **Tel** *020 7581 5757* **Fax** *020 7584 1348* **Rooms** *15*
Map *19 C2*
£££££

In the wealthy heart of Chelsea, this intimate boutique hotel offers privacy and opulence, with just 15 rooms and suites decorated with antique furniture and paintings. Hidden away there are modern electronics (including free Wi-Fi) and a gym. Personal service is another trademark. Room service available. **www.sandomenicohouse.com**

VICTORIA, WESTMINSTER, PIMLICO

Dover Hotel
42–44 Belgrave Road, SW1 **Tel** *020 7821 9085* **Fax** *020 7834 6425* **Rooms** *34*
Map *20 F2*
£

This well-maintained hotel is terrific value for money. It may not be luxurious once past the grand stucco façade, but the decor is refreshingly modern and every room has satellite TV and pristine en suite shower and WC. It's handy for Victoria Station and Pimlico's many pubs and cafés and it has free Wi-Fi. **www.dover-hotel.co.uk**

Morgan Guest House
120 Ebury Street, SW1 **Tel** *020 7730 2384* **Rooms** *11*
Map *20 E2*
£

This comfortable guesthouse in a listed Georgian building offers excellent value for money, especially if you opt for a room without facilities, or one of the spacious family rooms that sleeps four. The decor is light and airy and many rooms contain original fireplaces. There is also a pretty garden and free Wi-Fi. **www.morganhouse.co.uk**

Vandon House
1 Vandon Street, SW1 **Tel** *020 7799 6780* **Fax** *020 7799 1464* **Rooms** *32*
Map *13 A5*
£

A great location within easy walking distance of Westminster and Buckingham Palace is one reason for the popularity of this budget hotel. Rooms – singles, twins with or without en suite facilities, and family rooms – are simple but good value. Continental breakfast is included. There is a charge for Wi-Fi. **www.vandonhouse.com**

B&B Belgravia
64–66 Ebury Street, SW1 **Tel** *020 7259 8570* **Fax** *020 7259 8591* **Rooms** *17*
Map *20 E2*
££

This award-winning townhouse B&B set out to revamp the bed and breakfast concept and has succeeded with 17 contemporary designed bedrooms (ground-floor room has wheelchair access). It provides outstanding value for money, with free Internet access and Wi-Fi, and cooked breakfasts made to order. **www.bb-belgravia.com**

Windermere
142–144 Warwick Way, SW1 **Tel** *020 7834 5163* **Fax** *020 7630 8831* **Rooms** *20*
Map *20 E2*
££

This Victorian house has a long history of hospitality – it was the site of one of the area's earliest B&Bs in 1881. Rooms are spacious with large windows and done in tasteful, traditional chintz, with extras such as satellite TV, free Wi-Fi, and safe; all have en suite facilities. The basement restaurant serves evening meals. **www.windermere-hotel.co.uk**

Mint Hotel Westminster
30 John Islip Street, SW1 **Tel** *020 7630 1000* **Fax** *020 7233 7575* **Rooms** *460*
Map *21 B2*
£££

There's no great character to this big, modern tower-block hotel near Tate Britain, but the attractions are high-quality services at reasonable rates, especially for online deals. All rooms have computers, free Wi-Fi, and other extras, and many have superb views from floor-to-ceiling windows. Rooms are well equipped for disabled guests. **www.minthotel.com**

The Trafalgar
2 Spring Gardens, SW1 **Tel** *020 7870 2900* **Fax** *020 7870 2911* **Rooms** *129*
Map *13 B3*
££££

A boutique-style departure for the Hilton group, boasting one of London's best locations – right on Trafalgar Square. There's a roof garden with fabulous views, and the chic Rockwell bar-restaurant offers a global menu. Light, spacious rooms are in luxury-minimalist style, with free Wi-Fi and other fittings. **www.thetrafalgar.com**

41

41 Buckingham Palace Road, SW1 **Tel** *020 7300 0041* **Fax** *020 7300 0141* **Rooms** *28*   **Map** *12 5F*

A boutique hotel with the feel of a private club. Guests are assigned a personal butler for their stay. The classic rooms have a smart, black-and-white color scheme, state-of-the-art technology (including free Wi-Fi), and marble bathrooms. Some have views of the Royal Mews, where the Queen's horses and carriages are kept. Gym access. **www.41hotel.com**

The Goring

Beeston Place, SW1 **Tel** *020 7396 9000* **Fax** *020 7834 4393* **Rooms** *71*   **Map** *20 E1*

The Goring family have been running this snug luxury hotel since it opened in 1910. It boasts special assets such as a lovely garden, London's most sumptuous family rooms and children's facilities, and access to an off-site gym. The style is English traditional but all rooms have state-of-the-art electronics. Internet access is charged. **www.thegoring.com**

MAYFAIR, ST. JAMES'S

Brown's Hotel

Albemarle Street, W1 **Tel** *020 7493 6020* **Fax** *020 7493 9381* **Rooms** *117*   **Map** *12 F3*

This historic hotel, composed of 11 Georgian townhouses, has undergone extensive refurbishment, which respects its heritage while introducing contemporary furniture, British art, and the latest technology (rooms have broadband; Wi-Fi is payable). There is a bar, English Tea Room, and restaurant as well as a health club. **www.brownshotel.com**

Chesterfield

35 Charles Street, W1 **Tel** *020 7491 2622* **Fax** *020 7491 4793* **Rooms** *107*   **Map** *12 E3*

A welcoming luxury hotel near Berkeley Square, the Chesterfield offers a variety of rooms (all with free Wi-Fi), from the understated pinstriped "Savile Row" to the fun-themed "Garden Suite" with trellises and wicker furniture. There's underfloor heating in the marble bathrooms and free use of a nearby health club. **www.chesterfieldmayfair.com**

Claridges

Brook Street, W1 **Tel** *020 7629 8860* **Fax** *020 7499 2210* **Rooms** *203*   **Map** *12 E2*

Favored by the European aristocracy in the 19th century (Empress Eugenie wintered here), Mayfair's Art Deco jewel attracts showbusiness, glitterati, and corporate guests. Rooms range from Victorian to contemporary by way of fabulous Art Deco suites. Gordon Ramsay's fêted restaurant and a smart bar are further draws. Free Wi-Fi. **www.claridges.co.uk**

Haymarket Hotel

1 Suffolk Place, SW1 **Tel** *020 7470 4000* **Fax** *020 7470 4004* **Rooms** *50*   **Map** *13 A3*

A boutique addition to the West End's luxury hotels, the Haymarket has subtly colorful, very well-equipped rooms and suites designed with panache. Another seductive plus – rare in central London – is a superb indoor pool. The stylish Brumus bar-restaurant serves imaginative Modern European cuisine. Wi-Fi is charged. **www.firmdale.com**

Metropolitan

Old Park Lane, W1 **Tel** *020 7447 1000* **Fax** *020 7447 1100* **Rooms** *150*   **Map** *12 E4*

The Metropolitan redefined the London luxury hotel when it opened in the 1990s with its blond wood, subtle colors, and cleanly elegant modern lines. Equally chic are the spa, the Met Bar, and the ever-fashionable Nobu Japanese restaurant *(see p302)*. Services and electronics (complimentary Wi-Fi) are naturally first-class. **www.metropolitan.como.bz**

No. 5 Maddox

5 Maddox Street, W1 **Tel** *020 7647 0200* **Fax** *020 7647 0300* **Rooms** *12*   **Map** *12 F2*

Beautiful, contemporary one- to three-bedroom suites, complete with kitchens, hidden in an unmarked townhouse off Regent Street. Many have terraces or balconies. Among the many treats are welcome trays of goodies, linen kimonos, CD and DVD library, and in-room holistic treatments. Charge for Wi-Fi and use of off-site gym. **www.living-rooms.co.uk**

Stafford

16–18 St James's Place, SW1 **Tel** *020 7493 0111* **Fax** *020 7493 7121* **Rooms** *105*   **Map** *12 F4*

This long-established townhouse hotel near Green Park has won a slew of awards and spends more than £1 million a year keeping up its refined period-style interior. Guests can stay in the main house or the atmospheric restored 17th-century stable yard. The American Bar is a cozy favourite. Free Wi-Fi available. **www.kembinski.com/london**

The Connaught

Carlos Place, W1 **Tel** *020 7499 7070* **Fax** *020 7495 3262* **Rooms** *121*   **Map** *12 E3*

One of Mayfair's historic grand hotels, the Connaught has undergone an imaginative renovation, combining its historic features with contemporary gadgets, refined modern design, and the luxurious Aman Spa. All guests have a personal butler. The celebrated main restaurant is on a high under admired chef Hélène Darroze. **www.the-connaught.co.uk**

The Dorchester

Park Lane, W1 **Tel** *020 7629 8888* **Fax** *020 7409 0114* **Rooms** *250*   **Map** *12 D3*

The epitome of the glamorous luxury hotel, with an outrageously lavish lobby and a star-studded history, the Dorchester has revamped its tasteful floral bedrooms. The Art Deco-style marble baths are probably the deepest in London. For even more pampering, pop down to the fabulous Art Deco spa. **www.thedorchester.com**

The Ritz

150 Piccadilly, W1 **Tel** *020 7493 8181* **Fax** *020 7493 2687* **Rooms** *137*   **Map** *12 F3*

A byword for pampering luxury since it opened in 1906, the Ritz continues to win awards for superior all-round service. Bedrooms and the dazzling dining room are in ornate Louis XVI style, but include every modern extra (Wi-Fi is charged). Afternoon tea at The Ritz is a great London institution and booking is essential. **www.theritzlondon.com**

OXFORD STREET, SOHO

Edward Lear

28–30 Seymour Street, W1 **Tel** *020 7402 5401* **Fax** *020 7706 3766* **Rooms** *31*   **Map** *11 C2*

This characterful small hotel is in the former home of Victorian poet and artist Edward Lear. Rooms are tidy and spacious with satellite TVs. Opt for en suite or shared facilities to keep the cost down. There's a computer with free Internet access (Wi-Fi is also available) and leather seating in the pleasant guests' lounge. **www.edlear.co.uk**

Radisson Edwardian Hampshire

31–36 Leicester Square, WC2 **Tel** *020 7839 9399* **Fax** *020 7930 8122* **Rooms** *127*   **Map** *11 C2*

Colorful Leicester Square is a good base if you want to make the most of London's nightlife, as it's well placed for the theater district, bars, clubs, restaurants, and movie theaters. This luxurious Radisson has designer bedrooms with Philippe Starck bathrooms and Bose sound systems in the suites. Free Wi-Fi access. **www.radissonedwardian.com**

The Cumberland

Great Cumberland Place, W1 **Tel** *0871 376 9014* **Fax** *0871 376 9114* **Rooms** *1000*   **Map** *11 C2*

This giant hotel near Marble Arch has been transformed into something of a design showcase, with elegantly stylish lounges and rooms fitted with the latest technology and decorated with original artwork. The exceptional choice of bars and dining areas include the hip Carbon bar and chef Gary Rhodes' flagship Rhodes W1 restaurant. **www.guoman.com**

The Sumner

54 Upper Berkeley Street, W1 **Tel** *020 7723 2244* **Fax** *0870 705 8767* **Rooms** *20*   **Map** *11 C1*

This boutique hotel has been carefully designed to combine contemporary styling, natural fabrics, and state-of-the-art electronics (complimentary Wi-Fi) with the original features of the 1820s building. Each bedroom is different, and the lounges and breakfast room are particularly chic. **www.thesumner.com**

Durrants Hotel

26–32 George Street, W1 **Tel** *020 7935 8131* **Fax** *020 7487 3510* **Rooms** *92*   **Map** *12 D1*

Privately owned, the Durrant maintains a cozy, very traditional style, in a row of Georgian townhouses north of Oxford Street. Bedrooms are in English country-house style – but now incorporate Wi-Fi (charged) and other extras – and staff are very welcoming. The George Bar and the restaurant are full of old-world charm. **www.durrantshotel.co.uk**

The Leonard

15 Seymour Street, W1 **Tel** *020 7935 2010* **Fax** *020 7935 6700* **Rooms** *48*   **Map** *11 C2*

Rooms at this intimate hotel are seductively comfortable, with traditional decor featuring high-quality materials. Occupying four 18th-century townhouses, it now incorporates Wi-Fi (charged) and other modern musts. As well as standard rooms, the Leonard also has magnificent suites and five fully equipped apartments. **www.theleonard.com**

Hazlitt's

6 Frith Street, W1 **Tel** *020 7434 1771* **Fax** *020 7439 1524* **Rooms** *30*   **Map** *13 A2*

The 19th-century essayist William Hazlitt was just one of the interesting figures to have resided here. Hazlitt's is as close to time travel as you can get: its period rooms feature fireplaces, antique beds, and claw-footed baths, with mod cons such as DVD players hidden discreetly away. Free Wi-Fi in the meeting room. **www.hazlittshotel.com**

Sanderson

50 Berners Street, W1 **Tel** *020 7300 1400* **Fax** *0207 300 1401* **Rooms** *150*   **Map** *12 F1*

The Sanderson's witty decor – red lips sofa and a framed portrait that seems to hang in mid-air – is like a surreal stage set. Rooms have every comfort (Wi-Fi is charged), and the Suka restaurant and two sophisticated cocktail bars are destinations in their own right. Agua spa offers holistic pampering. **www.sandersonlondon.com**

The Soho Hotel

4 Richmond Mews, W1 **Tel** *020 7559 3000* **Fax** *020 7559 3003* **Rooms** *85 + 4 apartments*   **Map** *13 A2*

Firmdale Hotels' venture combines the light and space of a warehouse-style building with its signature modern English style. Two screening rooms, gym with personal trainer, and exclusive Miller Harris products in the granite walk-in showers complete the sophisticated urban experience. Wi-Fi is charged. **www.firmdalehotels.com**

W Hotels Leicester Square

10 Wardour St, W1 **Tel** *020 7758 1000* **Rooms** *192*   **Map** *13 A2*

With its translucent glass exterior and glamorous interior, this trendy hotel is a luxurious escape from the Soho bustle. Rooms combine high-end modern design with cutting-edge technology. Hang out in the stylish Wyld bar or try the tantalizing southeast Asian cuisine in the Spice Market restaurant. Wi-Fi is charged. **www.starwoodhotels.com**

REGENT'S PARK, MARYLEBONE

22 York Street · W · ££

22 York Street, W1 **Tel** *020 7224 2990* **Fax** *020 7224 1990* **Rooms** *10* · **Map** *3 C5*

This beautiful property is a cut above most B&Bs. Liz and Michael Callis ensure rooms in these two immaculately preserved Georgian houses are spotless and stylishly furnished with antiques and French quilts. A gourmet Continental breakfast is served in the rustic kitchen. Free Wi-Fi access and meeting rooms. **www.22yorkstreet.co.uk**

Hotel La Place · ££

17 Nottingham Place, W1 **Tel** *020 7486 2323* **Fax** *020 7486 4335* **Rooms** *20* · **Map** *4 D5*

Located a short walk from Regent's Park, this popular small hotel works hard to keep customers happy with regularly improved facilities and extras such as free Wi-Fi. Spacious bedrooms have opulent traditional decor, and include suites and family rooms. The pretty bar-restaurant is open for breakfast and dinner. **www.hotellaplace.com**

Hart House Hotel · W · £££

51 Gloucester Place, W1 **Tel** *020 7935 2288* **Fax** *020 7935 8516* **Rooms** *15* · **Map** *11 C1*

A well-maintained Georgian townhouse hotel with huge windows and high ceilings in some rooms. The dark wood furniture and bold tartan curtains make a refreshing change from frills and florals. The modern tiled bathrooms are spotless. Gloucester Place is a busy road, so you may prefer a back-facing room. Wi-Fi is charged. **www.harthouse.co.uk**

Park Plaza Sherlock Holmes · £££

108 Baker Street, W1 **Tel** *020 7486 6161* **Fax** *020 7958 5211* **Rooms** *119* · **Map** *3 C5*

Though the name hints at a tacky Sherlock Holmes-theme hotel, this large establishment has been given an elegant modern makeover, with light, fresh rooms with delicate color schemes. The split-level loft suites are especially impressive, and the Sherlock Grill restaurant is similarly smart. Wi-Fi is charged. **www.parkplazasherlockholmes.com**

No. Ten Manchester St · ££££

10 Manchester St, NW1 **Tel** *020 7378 2499* **Fax** *020 7378 2460* **Rooms** *45* · **Map** *12 D1*

At this elegant, stylishly designed hotel in an Edwardian townhouse rooms are glamorous, well-equipped, and feature the lastest technology, including free Wi-Fi. Aveda toiletries and Egyptian cotton linens are luxurious extras. The Ten lounge bar serves food all day – indulge with a Champagne afternoon tea. **www.tenmanchesterstreethotel.com**

The Marylebone Hotel · ££££

47 Welbeck Street, W1 **Tel** *020 7486 6600* **Fax** *020 7486 7492* **Rooms** *256* · **Map** *12 D1*

A classically furnished modern hotel in the heart of Marylebone village, the hotel offers spacious accommodation and great facilities, including its own health club with a swimming pool, whirlpool, and sauna, a bar, and a restaurant. Very cheap seasonal offers are advertised on the website. **www.doylecollection.com**

The Langham, London · £££££

1C Portland Place, W1 **Tel** *020 7636 1000* **Fax** *020 7323 2340* **Rooms** *382* · **Map** *12 E1*

The Langham was Europe's first grand hotel when it opened in 1865 and still offers an ultraluxurious experience behind its sprawling Victorian façade. Rooms achieve a tasteful middle ground between modern and traditional and there are extensive spa facilities including a swimming pool. Near Regent's Park. **www.langhamhotels.com**

BLOOMSBURY, FITZROVIA

Clink 261 Hostel · £

261–265 Grays Inn Road, WC1 **Tel** *020 7833 9400* **Fax** *020 7833 9677* **Rooms** *34* · **Map** *5 C3*

This Kings' Cross favorite is mainly a backpackers' hostel with dorm-style rooms, but it also has low-cost single and double rooms that are in great demand so they must be booked well ahead. Rooms and common spaces are bright and stylish, and there's an Internet room with Wi-Fi access (charged). **www.clink261.co.uk**

Arosfa Bed & Breakfast · W · ££

83 Gower Street, WC1 **Tel** *020 7636 2115* **Fax** *020 7636 2115* **Rooms** *15* · **Map** *5 A5*

The rooms are plainly furnished, but pristine, in this Georgian townhouse near London University. Every room has a tiny but spotless en suite shower and WC, making this one of the best deals in central London. True to its name, which means "resting place" in Welsh, there's a lounge with books and comfy sofas. Free Wi-Fi, too. **www.arosfalondon.com**

Euston Square Hotel · ££

152–156 North Gower Street, NW1 **Tel** *020 7388 0099* **Fax** *020 7788 9699* **Rooms** *75* · **Map** *5 A4*

An imaginative take on the budget hotel, combining a bit of boutique style with low rates that make it one of London's best bargains. Rooms are small, but bright and smartly designed, with good TVs, Wi-Fi (complimentary), and other extras. At ground level, the bar-restaurant offers an enjoyable global food range. **www.euston-square-hotel.com**

Key to Price Guide *see p282* **Key to Symbols** *see back cover flap*

Hotel Cavendish

[W] £££

75 Gower Street, WC1 **Tel** *020 7636 9079* **Fax** *020 7580 3609* **Rooms** *33*

Map *5 A5*

This characterful B&B near London University has a fascinating history – D. H. Lawrence and the Beatles stayed here once. Rooms are simple yet comfortably furnished, and some have original fireplaces. Original artworks brighten up the breakfast room, and there's a pretty garden as well. Shared facilities available and free Wi-Fi. **www.hotelcavendish.com**

myhotel Bloomsbury

££

11–13 Bayley Street, W1 **Tel** *020 7667 6000* **Fax** *020 7667 6044* **Rooms** *78*

Map *5 A5*

East meets West at this stylish contemporary hotel designed according to feng shui principles. The simple, serene rooms have low, Oriental-style beds and Aveda products. On-site facilities include a branch of Yo! Sushi, a buzzy public bar plus guests' library with Internet access and free Wi-Fi, and holistic spa treatments. **www.myhotels.com**

The Academy

£££

21 Gower Street, WC1 **Tel** *020 7631 4115* **Fax** *020 7636 3442* **Rooms** *49*

Map *5 A5*

Five Bloomsbury townhouses were linked together to create this discreet boutique hotel. Rooms have modern fittings (including free Wi-Fi) and soft, often sumptuous traditional decor to maximize comfort. Below there are attractive lounges full of cozy sofas, a bar, and a garden that's ideal for a drink in summer. **www.theetoncollection.com**

The Bloomsbury Hotel

£££

16–22 Great Russell St, WC1 **Tel** *020 7347 1000* **Rooms** *153*

Map *13 B1*

In a magnificent neo-Georgian listed building designed by renowned British architect Sir Edwin Lutyens, this grand hotel combines traditional elegance with high-end contemporary design. Rooms feature queen-size beds, power showers and free Wi-Fi access. The restaurant serves classic British dishes and there's a club-style bar. **www.doylecollection.com**

The Montague on the Gardens

££££

15 Montague Street, WC1 **Tel** *020 7637 1001* **Fax** *020 7612 8430* **Rooms** *100*

Map *5 B5*

This traditional townhouse hotel near the British Museum has high-tech amenities and refurbished bathrooms in its classic, predominantly floral-print rooms and a well-equipped gym with sauna. There are two restaurants, a conservatory, and a terrace bar on the secluded gardens. Wi-Fi is free. **www.montaguehotel.com**

Charlotte Street Hotel

£££££

15 Charlotte Street, W1 **Tel** *020 7806 2000* **Fax** *020 7806 2002* **Rooms** *52*

Map *13 A1*

The ground floor bar is always buzzing with local workers as well as guests in this exquisitely designed hotel in a street full of restaurants. Reflecting the area's history, its decor nods to the Bloomsbury set period with original artworks by Vanessa Bell and others. Weekend films in the screening room and charged Wi-Fi. **www.firmdale.com**

COVENT GARDEN, STRAND, HOLBORN

Citadines London Holborn-Covent Garden

£££

94–99 High Holborn, WC1 **Tel** *020 7395 8800* **Fax** *020 7395 8799* **Rooms** *192*

Map *13 C1*

The French Citadines *aparthotel* chain has a clever concept. All the well-equipped rooms – single/double studios or larger flats – are full apartments, with kitchens, but maid and other hotel services are offered. Mainly directed at business people, they can be great value for anyone staying more than a few days in London. **www.citadines.com**

Covent Garden Hotel

£££££

10 Monmouth Street, WC2 **Tel** *020 7806 1000* **Fax** *020 7806 1100* **Rooms** *58*

Map *13 B2*

This exquisite hotel's Covent Garden location is one reason why it's popular with thespians. Part of the Firmdale chain, it is decorated in contemporary-English style with antiques and fresh fabrics. Brasserie Max is a popular meeting spot and films are shown in the luxurious screening room at weekends. Wi-Fi is charged. **www.firmdalehotels.com**

One Aldwych

£££££

1 Aldwych, WC2 **Tel** *020 7300 1000* **Fax** *020 7300 1001* **Rooms** *105*

Map *13 C2*

A grand contemporary hotel in former Edwardian newspaper offices. Impressive details include original art and tarazzo-stone bathrooms with heated floors and mini TVs. There's a spacious health club with a swimming pool, several chic restaurants, and the buzzing, high-ceilinged Lobby Bar. Free Wi-Fi is available. **www.onealdwych.co.uk**

St. Martin's Lane

£££££

45 St Martin's Lane, WC2 **Tel** *020 7300 5500* **Fax** *020 7300 5501* **Rooms** *204*

Map *13 B2*

An outpost of New York-based Morgans Hotel Group, the St. Martins has been a flagship of the boutique-hotel wave, with eye-popping design by style guru Philippe Starck. Rooms are in minimalist white, while public spaces are playfully colorful: the Light Bar and Asia de Cuba restaurant are celebrity hot spots. Wi-Fi is charged. **www.stmartinslane.com**

Savoy

£££££

Strand, WC2 **Tel** *020 7836 4343* **Fax** *020 7240 6040* **Rooms** *263*

Map *13 C2*

This legendary hotel was an afterthought. Richard D'Oyly Carte capitalized on the success of his Savoy Theatre by providing a place to stay. The rest is history. Monet painted the Thames from his window; the dry martini was made popular in the bar. The hotel has had a multimillion-pound refurbishment. Charged Wi-Fi. **www.fairmont.com/savoy**

SOUTHWARK, LAMBETH

Comfort Inn 🄯 P ♿ W ££

87 South Lambeth Road, SW8 **Tel** *020 7735 9494* **Fax** *020 7735 1001* **Rooms** *115* **Map** *21 5C*

The interior of this modern low-rise chain hotel is surprisingly cool and there are often very cheap offers on the website. Simple, contemporary rooms have en suite power showers and satellite TVs with pay Internet, Wi-Fi, and games, while executive suites come with fridge, microwave, and Jacuzzi. **www.comfortinnvx.co.uk**

London Bridge Hotel 🄯 ᚷ 📺 ☰ W £££

8–18 London Bridge Street, SE1 **Tel** *020 7855 2200* **Fax** *020 7855 2233* **Rooms** *141* **Map** *15 B4*

This contemporary, urban hotel near foodies' paradise Borough Market has stylish executive rooms. Guests have a choice of two dining options, with the Londinium restaurant and the Borough restaurant and bar, and are given free entry to the adjoining Fitness First health club. Free Wi-Fi available. **www.londonbridgehotel.com**

Southwark Rose Hotel 🄯 P ᚷ ☰ ♿ W £££

47 Southwark Bridge Road, SE1 **Tel** *020 7015 1480* **Fax** *020 7015 1481* **Rooms** *84* **Map** *15 A3*

The name may conjure up images of an old-English inn, but this is a budget version of a modern luxury hotel near Tate Modern and Shakespeare's Globe. Rooms, in a different color scheme on each floor, are kitted out with modern leather headboards, slick mosaic-tiled bathrooms, and Wi-Fi (charged). **www.southwarkrosehotel.co.uk**

Travel Inn London County Hall 🄯 ᚷ ♿ W £££

Belvedere Road, SE1 **Tel** *0870 238 3300* **Fax** *020 7902 1619* **Rooms** *314* **Map** *14 D5*

This branch of the budget premier Travel Inn chain is housed in the massive former County Hall on the Thames. The more expensive Marriott, which shares the building, has all the river views, but it's a good-value option next to the London Eye, near Waterloo and the Southbank arts complex. Wi-Fi is available but is charged. **www.premierinn.com**

Novotel London City South 🄯 P ᚷ 🛗 📺 ☰ ♿ W ££££

53–61 Southwark Bridge Road, SE1 **Tel** *020 7089 0400* **Fax** *020 7089 0410* **Rooms** *182* **Map** *15 A3*

Novotel hotels (of which there are nine around London) may not seem to have great character but they have plenty of pluses: attractive modern rooms with many extras (Wi-Fi for an extra charge), enjoyable restaurants, and excellent facilities for families and disabled guests. Frequent online offers ensure good-value prices. **www.novotel.com**

Marriott County Hall 🄯 P ᚷ 🛗 📺 ☰ ♿ W £££££

Westminster Bridge Road, SE1 **Tel** *020 7928 5200* **Fax** *020 7928 5300* **Rooms** *200* **Map** *13 C5*

Housed in the vast former County Hall building on the Thames, this Marriott is on a grand scale, with a magnificent library, gym, and spa, and one of the largest pools in London. Rooms are in keeping with the period style; some boast four-poster beds and amazing views of Big Ben. There is a charge for Wi-Fi use. **www.marriottcountyhall.com**

Shangri-La Hotel, at The Shard 🄯 ᚷ ⛲ 📺 🛗 ☰ ♿ W ££££££

32 London Bridge Road, SE1 **Tel** *020 8747 8484* **Fax** *020 8747 8591* **Rooms** *195* **Map** *15 B4*

Spread over floors 34–52 of The Shard, London's tallest building, is this luxury hotel, which opens in 2012. Rooms and suites are spacious, luxurious, and well-equipped, and many areas of the hotel feature spectacular city views. Facilities include an indoor infinity pool, fitness center, and a range of bars and dining options. **www.shangri-la.com**

CITY, CLERKENWELL

The Hoxton 🄯 ᚷ 🛗 ♿ W £££

81 Great Eastern Street, EC2 **Tel** *020 7550 1000* **Fax** *020 7550 1090* **Rooms** *208* **Map** *7 C4*

Hoxton is one of the trendiest areas in London, and it fittingly has the city's hippest hotel, with small but inventively styled rooms with plenty of technology (free Wi-Fi), still at reasonable rates. There's cutting-edge work by local artists in the public areas, and a lively bistro. **www.hoxtonhotels.com**

ANdAZ 🄯 ᚷ 📺 ☰ ♿ ££££

40 Liverpool Street, EC2 **Tel** *020 7961 1234* **Fax** *020 7961 1235* **Rooms** *267* **Map** *15 C1*

This magnificent 19th-century railway hotel was formerly the Great Eastern Hotel. It is now a concept hotel with boutique-inspired credentials. There's no check-in desk, the traditional hotel lobby is replaced with a living room, and a dedicated team member oversees your stay. **www.london.liverpoolstreet.andaz.com**

The Zetter 🄯 ᚷ ☰ ♿ W ££££

86–88 Clerkenwell Road, EC1 **Tel** *020 7324 4444* **Fax** *020 7324 4456* **Rooms** *59* **Map** *6 F4*

In this loft hotel, in a 19th-century warehouse, rooms have exposed brick, quirky 1970s furniture, old Penguin books, hot-water bottles, and high-tech extras (including Internet access), while vending machines on each floor dispense necessities. Bistro Bruno serves award-winning French cuisine. **www.thezetter.com**

Key to Price Guide *see p282* **Key to Symbols** *see back cover flap*

Malmaison

Charterhouse Square, EC1 **Tel** *020 7012 3700* **Fax** *020 7012 3702* **Rooms** *97* **Map** *6 F5*

The London outpost of this chic chain is in a red-brick Victorian building on a historic cobbled square; inside is a striking modern, art-filled interior and trendy brasserie. Rooms are spacious and comfortable with upholstered headboards, CD players, Internet access, and French wines. **www.malmaison-london.com**

Rookery

12 Peter's Lane, Cowcross Street, EC1 **Tel** *020 7336 0931* **Fax** *020 7336 0932* **Rooms** *33* **Map** *6 F5*

Occupying six Georgian houses and shops (with faded butchers' and bakers' signs still visible on some), this Dickensian hideaway retains many original features, such as flagstone floors in the hall and ceiling beams in some of the rooms. Decorated with antiques throughout, it also offers all the latest technology, including free Wi-Fi. **www.rookeryhotel.com**

FURTHER AFIELD

The Mitre

291 Greenwich High Road, SE10 **Tel** *020 8293 0037* **Fax** *020 8355 6761* **Rooms** *16* **Map** *23 B2*

Bustling pub with rooms close to sights and transport links. The protected 18th-century building was originally a coffee house, and interior-designed, en suite rooms are traditional in pastel color schemes. There's a weekday bar menu and carvery meals at weekends and bank holidays in the pub. Free Wi-Fi available. **www.mitregreenwich.com**

Church Street Hotel

29–33 Camberwell Church Street, SE5 **Tel** *020 7703 5984* **Fax** *020 7358 4110* **Rooms** *30*

A hotel unlike any other in London, decorated by its much-traveled, very friendly Spanish owners with rich Cuban-Mexican colors and quirky Mexican artifacts, brings a breath of Latin America to unexotic Camberwell. There's a lovely, atmospheric bar, and generous organic breakfasts. Free Wi-Fi, too. **www.churchstreethotel.com**

Hampstead Village Guesthouse

2 Kemplay Road, NW3 **Tel** *020 7435 8679* **Fax** *020 7443 5009* **Rooms** *9* **Map** *1 B5*

This Victorian home, in the picturesque village and a short walk from the heath, is intriguingly cluttered with antiques and curios. Breakfast is served in the garden in summer, English weather permitting. Rooms are equipped with a hot-water bottle and fridge. The rates are cheaper if you forgo en suite facilities. Free Wi-Fi. **www.hampsteadguesthouse.com**

Hilton London Docklands

265 Rotherhithe Street, SE16 **Tel** *020 7231 1001* **Fax** *020 7231 0599* **Rooms** *365*

A modern hotel with great views of Canary Wharf, the Hilton is both family friendly and geared up for business travelers. Many of the spacious rooms have balconies, there's a fitness center with a pool and a restaurant on the hotel's terrace overlooking the river. Cheap rates are often available. Internet access and Wi-Fi are charged. **www.hilton.co.uk/docklands**

Cannizaro House

West Side, Wimbledon Common, SW19 **Tel** *020 8879 1464* **Fax** *020 8879 7338* **Rooms** *46*

This Georgian mansion on the edge of Wimbledon Common is an ideal base for keen tennis fans. Rooms are decorated in a country-house style; some have four-poster beds and air conditioning. There is a restaurant, cocktail bar, and extensive grounds, where you can play croquet. There is also free Wi-Fi. **www.cannizarohouse.com**

Colonnade

2 Warrington Crescent, W9 **Tel** *020 7286 1052* **Fax** *020 7286 1057* **Rooms** *43*

Near the picturesque canals of Little Venice, this hotel in two Victorian mansions has been operating since the 1930s. Freud stayed here while his house was being redecorated, and JFK paid a visit in the 60s. The interior is grand yet unintimidating and every luxurious room has a different feel. Wi-Fi is free. **www.theetoncollection.co.uk**

K West

Richmond Way, W14 **Tel** *020 8008 6600* **Fax** *020 8008 6650* **Rooms** *220*

Off the beaten track near BBC HQ, this striking steel and glass hotel is popular with high-profile guests, and often offers amazingly cheap deals on the website. Sleek rooms are soothingly neutral, there's a cool bar and, best of all, a luxurious spa with gym, marble Jacuzzi room, and E'SPA treatments. There is a charge for Wi-Fi. **www.k-west.co.uk**

Novotel Greenwich

173–185 Greenwich High Road, SE10 **Tel** *020 8312 6800* **Fax** *020 8312 7810* **Rooms** *151* **Map** *23 A3*

This modern hotel is conveniently located next to Greenwich station. It is light and airy and has a stylish decor created from wood, stone, and richly colored furnishings. 24-hour room service is available. There are conference rooms, computers, and Wi-Fi (charged). **www.novotel.com**

The Petersham

Nightingale Lane, Richmond, Surrey, TW10 **Tel** *020 8939 1010* **Fax** *020 8939 1098* **Rooms** *58*

This sprawling Victorian hotel perches on Richmond Hill overlooking the Thames. The elegant rooms are in keeping with the building's period grandeur, while integrating modern elements; some have spectacular views of the Thames. Unsurprisingly given its romantic location, it's popular for weddings. Free Wi-Fi available. **www.petershamhotel.co.uk**

RESTAURANTS AND PUBS

Hailed as the world's dining capital, London thrives on an extraordinary culinary diversity. From a traditional forte of Indian, Chinese, French, and Italian restaurants, eating out in London now enables your palate to take a gastronomic journey around the world, from America to Africa, taking in a pan-European tour, as well as the Middle East, Asia, and the Pacific Rim.

A pre-theater menu board

main tourist areas, although some that merit a special trip farther afield are also included.

London's café scene has become much more dynamic over the past few years, with good coffee and snacks readily available throughout the day. Good-quality chains have also sprung up all over the capital and include Ask (pizza), Giraffe (for families), and Leon (healthy fastfood). London's pubs have evolved and are now some of the most popular places to eat. "Gastropubs" have become an accepted part of the food scene and offer a wide range of fare. For a selection of mainly informal places to eat and drink, including pubs, see pages 312–19.

CHOOSING YOUR TABLE

The restaurants on pages 296–311 of this guide represent a comprehensive range of styles and prices. They are listed alphabetically within each price category and are spread across the

LONDON RESTAURANTS

The broadest choice of restaurants can be found in Covent Garden, Piccadilly, Mayfair, Soho, and Leicester Square. Knightsbridge, Kensington, and Chelsea also offer a good range of restaurants. Central London has few riverside restaurants, but there is a cluster along Chelsea Harbour, in Chelsea, and at Butler's Wharf on the south bank of the Thames. While traditional British food can be enjoyed, the style is not so readily available. Chefs such as Fergus Henderson at St.

John are revitalizing British dishes, but the emphasis is on Modern British cooking which combines a variety of culinary influences and techniques from around the world. Home-grown chefs such as Sally Clarke, Alastair Little, and Marco Pierre White have been instrumental in helping to elevate restaurant dining over the past two decades.

Alongside great improvements in cuisine, the standard of service has risen, and there has never been so much focus on interior design. This has added to the "diversity" of London's restaurants, which offer anything from classically ornate and romantic decor, to modern and postmodern minimalism. London has long been a paradise for Indian, Chinese, French, and Italian food, with more restaurants specializing in regional cuisine. Asian food is increasingly popular, particularly Thai and Japanese, with Soho offering plenty of choice.

Most restaurants provide at least one vegetarian option, and some have a separate vegetarian menu. A growing number of specialist vegetarian restaurants offer more adventurous dishes. Fish and seafood is another speciality, with both traditional and modern-style restaurants.

Great Eastern Dining Room (see p309)

OTHER PLACES TO EAT

Many hotels have excellent restaurants open to non-residents, which in some cases include a menu composed by, or even the actual dishes prepared by, a star chef. These restaurants range from the very formal to the fun and flamboyant, and prices tend to be at the top end of the scale. There are also increasing numbers of pizza, pasta, and brasserie chains serving reliable, good-value food across the city.

Among these dramatic improvements are also "gastro-pubs" and wine bars that serve anything from standard staples to Thai curries, accompanied by global wine lists. Otherwise, you can grab a quick snack from one of the many sandwich bars or cafés.

Commissionaire at the Hard Rock Café (see p315)

Hakkasan *(see p306)*

TIPS ON EATING OUT

Most London restaurants serve lunch between noon and 2:30pm, with dinner from 6:30pm until 11pm, which usually means that last orders are taken at 11pm. Ethnic restaurants may stay open longer, until midnight or later. Some restaurants may close for either lunch or dinner during the weekend, and it is always best to check opening times first. All-day cafés and brasseries may serve alcohol without restriction during licensing hours (11am–11pm).

The traditional British Sunday lunch appears in many pubs and restaurants, although more informal brunches are increasingly popular. It is worth checking beforehand, however, unless traditional Sunday lunch is what you particularly want, as even high-class restaurants may suspend their normal menu on Sundays.

Some of the most formal restaurants insist on a jacket and tie, or a jacket. Booking is advisable, especially at gourmet restaurants and from Friday through Sunday.

Smoking is banned in all London pubs and restaurants.

PRICE AND SERVICE

As London is one of the world's most expensive cities, restaurant prices can often seem exorbitant to visitors, with an average three-course meal and a few glasses of house wine, at a medium-priced central London restaurant costing around £25–35 per person. Many restaurants have set-price menus which are generally significantly less expensive than ordering à la carte and, in some instances, the price includes coffee and service.

Similarly, various West End restaurants serve pre-theater set menus (typically from around 5:30–6pm). Although geared toward a quick turn-around, this provides an opportunity to eat at quality restaurants at a competitive price. Lower prices (around £10–15 a head) apply at smaller, more modest ethnic and vegetarian restaurants, wine bars, and pubs, where the food can nevertheless be well prepared and offer good value. However, some of these establishments will only accept cash or checks, not credit cards.

Before ordering, check the small print at the bottom of the menu. Prices will include Value Added Tax (VAT) and may add an optional service charge (between 10 and 15 percent). Some restaurants may also impose a cover charge (£1–2 a head), or a minimum charge during the busiest periods, while some do not accept certain credit cards. Beware of the old trick where service is included in the bill but staff leave the "total" box on your credit slip blank, hoping you will add another 10 per cent. Expect different types of service in different types of restaurant. This can range from cheerful and breezy in fast-food joints to discreet yet attentive in more expensive venues. At peak dining times you will usually have to wait longer to be served.

St. John *(see p309)*

EATING WITH CHILDREN

Except in Italian restaurants, fast-food establishments, branches of Wagamama and a few other venues such as The Rainforest Café on Shaftesbury Avenue (a tropical haven for young diners), children tend to be simply tolerated in London restaurants rather than warmly welcomed.

However, with the growing trend for a more informal style of dining, more and more restaurants are learning to become child-friendly, offering a special children's menu or smaller portions and highchairs, while some provide coloring books and even put on live entertainment to keep the little diners happy. See page 357 for suggested places that cater for children of a wide range of ages.

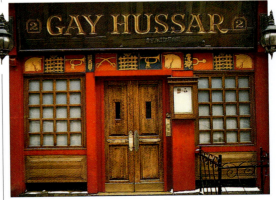

London's top Hungarian restaurant *(see p304)*

The Flavors of London

"Modern European cooking" describes much of what's on offer in London, a reflection of the British capital's cosmopolitan nature. However, as competitive restaurateurs vie for customers, they often look to traditional foods, from once-unfashionable beetroot to pig's trotters and offal, while increasing concern about what goes into the growing and rearing of food is also reflected on London menus. Even pub food, once limited to Sunday roasts, the ubiquitous "ploughman's lunch" (cheese or ham with bread and pickles), or sandwiches has been given fresh slant by "gastropubs" and a new breed of sandwich bars offering fresh, top-quality snacks.

Chef and customer at Clerkenwell's St. John restaurant

LONDON'S LARDER

Nowhere better exemplifies the city's blossoming love affair with good food than Borough Market *(see p339)*. Its busy stalls of both regional and continental food are a microcosm of what Londoners today like to eat. There is produce from all over the British Isles – English and Irish cheeses; Scottish beef; Welsh lamb; Devon cider; Suffolk oysters – as well as from the rest of the world. Visitors can snack as they browse, on anything from Cornish scallops to grilled Spanish chorizo.

MODERN BRITISH FOOD

London menus increasingly detail the provenance of ingredients with obvious pride. Ancient or "rare" breeds of cattle are name-checked, such as Gloucester Old Spot pork. Once-overlooked, old-fashioned ingredients like rhubarb and black (blood) pudding are being used in creative new ways. Seasonal and organic produce is also taking more of a center stage. The new breed of "gastropubs" were among the first to adopt these trends, offering good, imaginative, well-prepared,

Dorstone (Dorset)   Waterloo (Berkshire)   Blue Stilton

Ashdown (Sussex)   Golden Cross (Sussex)

Selection of superb English farmhouse cheeses

TRADITIONAL ENGLISH FOOD

You can still find traditional dishes, such as jugged hare, roast beef, or brown Windsor soup, but even fish 'n' chips can be harder to hunt down than tapas, pizza, or chicken tikka masala. A "full English breakfast" is a fry-up of sausages, eggs, bacon, tomatoes, mushrooms, and toast, perhaps with black (blood) pudding. Baked beans and fried potatoes may be included, as can bubble and squeak (re-fried cabbage and potato). There is an English heritage of heavy "nursery" puddings. These are a favorite of gentlemen's clubs and include such treats as treacle tart, jam roly-poly (suet and jam) pudding, spotted dick (suet and currants), and fruit crumbles with custard. Teatime may be a thing of the past but some top hotels still offer "cream teas" with scones, cakes, and perhaps cucumber sandwiches.

Celery and Stilton soup *The king of English cheeses makes an excellent winter soup when combined with celery.*

Bountiful vegetable stall at south London's Borough Market

sensibly-priced food, as well as fine wines and beers, in the relaxed surroundings of the traditional London pub.

Chef Fergus Henderson of St. John *(see p308)* is a pioneer of "head-to-toe" eating, espousing anything from ox cheek and tail to entire roast suckling pig.

London's historic seafood favorites, such as cockles and whelks, are increasingly hard to find at present but, as capital of an island nation, the city offers many fine fish restaurants. Concerns about overfishing and farmed fish means that you are likely to see more of such local catches as bream, bass, sole, and gurnard alongside cod and haddock, as well as salmon being billed as wild, and scallops as diver-caught.

EASTERN FLAVORS

Britain has long had a love affair with both Oriental and Indian food, and some of the best examples of each can be found in London. While

A mouthwatering pint of traditional London bitter beer

chicken tikka masala has been voted the nation's favorite dish (invented here, the legend goes, to satisfy the national passion for gravy by pairing tandoori dry-roasted meat with a mild, creamy sauce), regional Indian food is now to the fore, notably southern cuisine strong on coconut, fish, and fruits. The balti is another British take on the food of the subcontinent – named for the bowl-shaped dish in which they are cooked and served, fresh-tasting stews are served alongside vast naan breads for dunking.

In Chinatown, you can enjoy everything from a simple bowl of noodles to gourmet dishes featuring rare ingredients such as razorshell clams and sea urchins.

WHAT TO DRINK

Beers There are two large brewers in London – Young's and Fuller's – and some microbrewers, too. The main varieties found in Britain are:
Bitter Brewed from malted barley, hops, yeast, and water; drunk at room temperature.
Mild ale Sweeter than bitter.
Lager Hundreds of varieties of this pale carbonated beer are available. Served chilled.
Stout Thick, dark, creamy Guinness is the most famous.

Cider English cider has undergone a revival, with producers often featuring single old English apple varieties and using traditional methods.

Dover sole *This is the most tasty flatfish, best served simply grilled with lemon, spinach, and new potatoes.*

Roast beef *Horseradish sauce is a traditional accompaniment, as are crisp Yorkshire puddings made of batter.*

Summer pudding *Lightly cooked fruits fill a basin lined with bread, which absorbs the sweet juices.*

Choosing a Restaurant

These restaurants have been selected for their good value or exceptional food and are listed alphabetically within each price category. Starting with west and southwestern districts of London, the guide moves through central parts and onto eastern districts, eventually looking at restaurants farther outside the city.

PRICE CATEGORIES
For a three-course meal per person including tax, service, and half a bottle of house wine (unless required to supply your own).

£ under £20
££ £20–£35
£££ £35–£55
££££ £55–£75
£££££ over £75

BAYSWATER, MARYLEBONE

Alounak Kebab £
44 Westbourne Grove, W2 5SH **Tel** 020 7229 0416
Map 10 D2

A typical Iranian restaurant, which means it isn't exactly the same as Persian or any other related cuisine. The food is a little lighter and less rich. The style verges on a bazaar café, with simple bare wood tables, no wine on sale, and soft drinks served in a can. The price reflects this simplicity, and the presence of so many Iranians proves the authenticity.

Aphrodite Taverna ££
15 Hereford Road, W2 4AB **Tel** 020 7229 2206
Map 10 D2

Small and unpretentious, this little tavern tries hard and succeeds. Halloumi, kleftiko, moussaka, baklava, and all the Greek greats are delicious and their stuffed vine leaves aren't bathed in vicious brine. If not homemade, they are at least made by someone who cares. Aphrodite excels at appetizers and is popular with guests from nearby hotels.

Busaba Eathai ££
8–13 Bird Street, W1U 1BU **Tel** 020 7518 8080
Map 12 D2

One of a small chain of restaurants by Alan Yau, its communal and casual Thai dining is reasonable, and it meets demand for value and speed of service. As a result, there can be a line of legendary length after 7pm, so get there early. Tables are shared whatever time you arrive, so not the best choice for a romantic occasion.

Caffe Caldesi ££
118 Marylebone Lane, W1U 2QF **Tel** 020 7935 1144
Map 12 D1

This airy Italian bistro with bar offers a frequently changing seasonal menu of classic dishes and a very reasonable all-Italian wine list. The dining space upstairs offers a slightly more formal atmosphere. Dig into a traditional home-cooked dinner. The café also plays host to La Cucina Caldesi – an Italian cooking school.

Ishtar ££
10–12 Crawford Street, W1U 6AZ **Tel** 020 7224 2446
Map 3 C5

Modern Turkish, so no plate throwing and no exotic dancers. You can dine on two levels, including under some romantic cellar arches, and the dishes are familiar but updated. Go for panfried sea bass with potatoes and saffron sauce or some well-marinated kebabs. Leave room for some pastries, too!

Queen's Head & Artichoke ££
30–32 Albany Street, NW1 4EA **Tel** 020 7916 6206
Map 4 E4

Handily located between Regent's Park and Euston Road, this friendly gastropub is rightly popular. You can eat outside, in the bustling, wood-paneled bar, or in a quieter dining room. Fare includes Mediterranean-inspired tapas, steaks, seafood, and other dishes, created using high-quality ingredients. There is an excellent wine selection.

Reubens ££
79 Baker Street, W1U 6RG **Tel** 020 7486 0035
Map 3 C5

A wonderful dining experience is in store at this Jewish restaurant, with all the Jewish classics on the menu like latkes and salt beef sandwiches. It is, of course, officially kosher (all meat is glatt kosher) and the portions are big and well priced. Takeout is available from the deli on the ground floor. Closed Saturday.

Tawana ££
3 Westbourne Grove, W2 4UA **Tel** 020 7229 3785
Map 10 D1

A restaurant that has been established in the area for many years. A commitment to authentic Thai cuisine means it has a loyal clientele. Ingredients are fresh and the balance of hot and sour is always perfect. Dishes include *tom ka gai* (chicken, lemongrass, and coconut milk soup) and red curry with roast duck.

Galvin Bistrot de Luxe £££
66 Baker Street, W1U 7DJ **Tel** 020 7935 4007
Map 3 C5

Brothers Chris and Jeff Galvin run their restaurants with a blend of originality and a thorough French culinary training. The Baker Street restaurant summons up the atmosphere of a traditional Paris bistro, with a menu of flavor-rich, robust, but very sophisticated dishes, including wonderful versions of classics like chicken pot roast *landaise*.

Key to Symbols *see back cover flap*

Island Restaurant & Bar
📋 ♿   £££
Royal Lancaster Hotel, Lancaster Terrace, W2 2TY **Tel** *020 7551 6070*   **Map** *10 F2*

The north side of Hyde Park is not well supplied with restaurants but inside the Royal Lancaster Hotel there's a bright, attractive contemporary bar-brasserie with friendly, fast-moving staff. Menus feature an enjoyable mix of modern European dishes, from steaks to fresh seafood, and salads and pasta as lighter options. Cheaper lunch menu available.

Royal China Club
📋 ♿   £££
40–42 Baker Street, W1U 7AJ **Tel** *020 7486 3898*   **Map** *12 D1*

Much more refined than the standard neighborhood Chinese, the award-winning Royal China serves superior Cantonese food in a beautiful, calm setting. Lunchtime dim sum is exquisite, an irresistible array of little delicacies prepared with great skill. The full menu includes specialties such as razor clams stir-fried with lilies.

Defune
📋 ♿   ££££
34 George Street, W1U 7DP **Tel** *020 7935 8311*   **Map** *12 D1*

Top-class sushi at a high price, which the experts say is well worth it. A charming minimalist decor is matched by an atmosphere that some find austere but is really just a cool appreciation of the food. This is a decent place and the service is superb. When you're eating raw fish you expect the highest standards and you pay for them.

Locanda Locatelli
📋 ♿ 🍴   ££££
8 Seymour Street, W1H 7JZ **Tel** *020 7935 9088*   **Map** *11 C10*

Giorgio Locatelli is a star among London chefs, producing some of the most refined Italian cuisine in the city. The seasonally based menus change frequently, and subtle use of Mediterranean herbs and truffles is a hallmark. The dining room is sleekly elegant and service very smooth. Reservations need to be made well ahead.

Orrery
📋 ♿ 🍴 🍴 ▸   ££££
55–57 Marylebone High Street, W1U 5RB **Tel** *020 7616 8000*   **Map** *4 D5*

A special-occasion restaurant in the heart of Marylebone village, with elegant contemporary decor, abundant staff, a huge wine list, and high prices. On the French-inspired menu are luxurious modern haute-cuisine dishes featuring first-rate ingredients. In summer, you can dine on the roof terrace, with lovely views of the old Marylebone churchyard.

Providores & Tapa Room
📋 ♿ 🍴   ££££
109 Marylebone High Street, W1U 4RX **Tel** *020 7935 6175*   **Map** *4 D5*

This stylish, much-praised restaurant is almost a showcase for global fusion cooking. Executive chef Peter Gordon is from New Zealand and his dishes combine Pacific Rim, Mediterranean, and many other influences, often using rare, delicate ingredients. As an alternative to the restaurant, try equally hip snacks in the ground-floor Tapa Room.

KENSINGTON, HOLLAND PARK, NOTTING HILL

Cibo
📋 🍴 ▸   ££
3 Russell Gardens, W14 8EZ **Tel** *020 7371 6271*   **Map** *9 A5*

You get plenty of bread and olives to pack in while you wait for excellent regional Italian food here. It's been on this site so long it's an institution, while its clever mix of tried and trusted Italian favorites combined with more adventurous dishes never fails to satisfy a young crowd. A good wine list and fixed-price lunch complete its appeal.

Kitchen W8
📋 ♿   ££
11 Abingdon Road, W8 6AH **Tel** *020 7937 0120*   **Map** *17 C1*

Designed with comfort in mind is this relaxed, welcoming Michelin-starred Kensington restaurant. The modern European menu is prepared with the highest quality ingredients and features such dishes as pan-fried sea bream with a risotto of chanterelles. Set-price menus are a great bargain, as is Sunday lunch.

Maggie Jones
📋 ▸   ££
6 Old Court Place, W8 4PL **Tel** *020 7937 6462*   **Map** *10 D5*

A quirky ambience and the intimate dining atmosphere make this a peculiarly British dining experience. Huge portions mean no one has left Maggie's hungry for over 45 years now. Service can be eccentric, so just sit back and enjoy. The steak and kidney pie is a must.

Utopia
🎵 🍴 ▸   ££
1 Kensington High Street, W8 5NP **Tel** *020 7937 0393*   **Map** *10 E5*

Persian and Greek food par excellence with perfect kebabs grilled to smoky brilliance over a real coal barbecue. Try their tasty, moist pieces of marinated lamb and/or chicken over saffron-scented, buttery rice. Friendly staff are happy to advise on choice of dishes and to stop you from over-ordering, which you may be tempted to do. Good value.

Assaggi
📋   £££
39 Chepstow Place, W2 4TS **Tel** *020 7792 5501*   **Map** *9 C2*

Near to Notting Hill and Bayswater tube station is this small restaurant. The menu is in Italian, but you can guess most dishes and the waiters will explain the rest. It's all smiles from the staff, but then they know you might easily break your bank. Good food, but be careful what you spend.

Geales

⊞ ⊞ ▸   **£££**

2 Farmer Street, W8 7SN **Tel** *020 7727 7528*

Map *9 C3*

One of London's classic fish-and-chip cafés, Geales has evolved into a chic, upscale fish restaurant to match its wealthy neighborhood. Exceptional-quality fish and chips remain the specialty, but you can have fish cooked many other ways. This is a great place for a long lunch, with a fixed-price lunch menu. Good range of wines, too.

Rodizio Rico

⊞ ⊞   **£££**

111 Westbourne Grove, W2 4UW **Tel** *020 7792 4035*

Map *9 D2*

Brazilian-style eating and great fun. Go for the buffet where you pick up your salad yourself and let the waiters bring you different bits of variously grilled meats at regular intervals. *Rodizio* is a concept in Brazil, which translates pretty much as "all you can eat." Really not a place for noncarnivores, but those who are will never leave hungry.

The Cow

⌂ ⊞   **£££**

89 Westbourne Park Road, W2 5QH **Tel** *020 7221 5400*

Map *9 C1*

A hub of the Notting Hill social scene, this hugely popular gastropub regularly hosts celebrities among the crowds thronging the bar or climbing the narrow staircase to the dining room. Opulent seafood platters are the big specialty, but steaks also hit the spot. Drinks include a global fine wine collection.

Whits

⊞ ⌂   **£££**

21 Abingdon Road, W8 6AH **Tel** *020 7938 1122*

Map *17 C1*

A neighborhood restaurant on a side lane off busy Kensington High Street. Because of its position it does not attract the masses. Serves dishes such as citrus-cured salmon with potted crab brûlée and sourdough bread and duck confit with honey and cumin jus. Food is consistently good and very seasonal, but always very affordable.

Clarke's

⊞ ⌂   **££££**

124 Kensington Church Street, W8 4BH **Tel** *020 7221 9225*

Map *9 C4*

Sally Clarke learned her cooking skills in California and pioneered global and Pacific-Rim cuisine in London in the 1980s. Her pretty, tranquil restaurant has stayed true to its style, which now seems more conventional compared to other fusion experiments elsewhere. Superb fresh ingredients are a mainstay, and the breads are delicious.

The Belvedere

⊞ ⌂ ⊞ ▸   **££££**

Holland Park, off Abbotsbury Road, W8 6LU **Tel** *020 7602 1238*

Map *9 B5*

Once the ballroom of Holland House, the aristocratic mansion around which Holland Park was created, This is one of London's most charming restaurants, whether you dine inside or on the garden terrace. Service is very smooth; on the menu are enjoyable versions of mostly French and British dishes, beautifully presented. Cheaper set lunch menu.

SOUTH KENSINGTON, CHELSEA, FULHAM

Bugis Street Brasserie

⊞ ⌂ ⊞   **££**

The Millennium Gloucester Hotel, Ashburn Place, SW7 4LH **Tel** *020 7331 6211*

Map *18 E2*

It's called a brasserie but it's not French food. The Chinese and Singaporean dishes are robust, extremely tasty, and come in gigantic portions. Plus, it's not very expensive for the area. For appetizers, the salt and pepper squid is exceptional. A fixed-price menu is available.

Buona Sera at the Jam

⊞ ▸   **££**

289a King's Road, SW3 5EW **Tel** *020 7352 8827*

Map *19 A4*

It can be a Jam by name and nature at this popular Chelsea Italian café: two floors of intimately sized tables have been squeezed into an amazingly snug space, but this all adds to the fun and friendly atmosphere. Fans also enjoy the no-nonsense traditional Italian pasta, pizza, and other favorites. Robust wines and beers.

Lots Road Pub & Dining Room

⊞ ⌂   **££**

114 Lots Road, SW10 0RJ **Tel** *020 7352 6645*

Map *18 E5*

A chic take on gastropub style: one side of this old pub has been turned into a light, stylish modern dining area, decorated with fresh flowers, but there's still a relaxed bar for sampling the excellent beers. Regulars on the menu include lively salads and gastropub favorites like braised lamb shank and superior-quality burgers.

Pig's Ear

£££

35 Old Church Street, SW3 5BS **Tel** *020 7352 2908*

Map *19 A4*

Affluent Chelsea locals appreciate this traditional-looking pub, with comfy bar and wood-paneled upstairs dining room. The French-influenced menu highlights powerful choices like pork cheeks and wild mallard with buttered cabbage, and there's a great cheese selection. Try the Pig's Ear bitter, brewed in Gloucestershire. Also bar menu.

Racine

⊞ ⌂ ▸   **£££**

239 Brompton Road, SW3 2EP **Tel** *020 7584 4477*

Map *19 B1*

A restaurant that sets out to showcase French cuisine (*racine* also means "root") and succeeds very well. Genuine French food, French waiters, and great atmosphere all combine to keep locals coming back for more. The venison, when in season, is excellent and the menu changes regularly. It includes vegetarian options.

Key to Price Guide *see p296* **Key to Symbols** *see back cover flap*

The Ebury

11 Pimlico Road, SW1W 8NA **Tel** 020 7730 6784

Map 20 D2

This beautifully converted gastropub is a welcome option in this rather upmarket neighborhood. The high-quality modern British cuisine includes tempting choices for everyone, from burgers and fries to roast English partridge and black bream fillet. Bar menu also available. A great place to stop for lunch.

The Painted Heron

112 Cheyne Walk, SW10 0DJ **Tel** 020 7351 5232

Map 19 A5

A nice bistro serving modern Indian cuisine in a pleasant part of Chelsea. Flavors at this award-winning restaurant are fresh, with meat and poultry scoring highly for complex spices without overpowering chili burn. It's a good deal classier than many Indian places in every way. Closed Sunday.

Bibendum

Michelin House, 81 Fulham Road, SW3 6RD **Tel** 020 7581 5817

Map 19 B2

Bibendum's location in the 1930s former Michelin tire building, with spectacular Art Deco tiles and stained glass showing Michelin Men riding bicycles, makes any meal here a special occasion. Service is charming, and the creative modern cuisine is consistently impressive. Save space for a scrumptious dessert. There's also an oyster bar and a café.

Cambio de Tercio

163 Old Brompton Road, SW5 0LJ **Tel** 020 7244 8970

Map 18 F2

Compact but comfortable, with a vibrant Spanish color scheme, Cambio is a London showcase for sophisticated modern Spanish cooking. Dishes are refined and very enjoyable, with delectable combinations of flavors, whether in classic dishes (suckling pig) or new creations. There's a superb Spanish wine list, too.

Gordon Ramsay

68 Royal Hospital Road, SW3 4HP **Tel** 020 7352 4441

Map 19 C4

A tasting menu here costs around £120 per person, but this is probably the best restaurant in London, the UK, and, Ramsay might tell you, the world. Everything is perfect from place settings to service. This place deserves all three of its Michelin stars. As a souvenir of London, your meal memories here will last a lifetime. Closed weekends.

L'Etranger

36 Gloucester Road, SW7 4QT **Tel** 020 7584 1118

Map 18 E1

A gem of a place serving excellent French food with Asian influences in very stylish surroundings. People rave about the caramelized black cod with miso for good reason. But then every dish on this menu is delectable, including the vegetarian options. A massive wine list has been created with passion. And you can dance in the club downstairs.

Tom Aikens

43 Elystan Street, SW3 3NT **Tel** 020 7584 2003

Map 19 B2

Chef Aikens prepares incredible modern French food at his flagship restaurant, which has been awarded a Michelin star. Dishes are lovingly constructed and beautifully plated with flavors finely balanced with a watchmaker's care. Special lunch and seven-course tasting menus are available, as are vegetarian dishes. Reserve in advance.

KNIGHTSBRIDGE, BELGRAVIA

Il Convivio

143 Ebury Street, SW1W 9QN **Tel** 020 7730 4099

Map 20 E2

It's a cliché to say that an Italian restaurant is "welcoming," but this one really is. Plus it has that aroma that makes you feel extra hungry. Couples, groups, children, and everyone else cram in to fill up on very good and honest Italian food such as Tuscan black (squid ink) spaghetti with lobster. There are vegetarian dishes, too, and 150 Italian wines.

La Poule au Pot

231 Ebury Street, SW1W 8UT **Tel** 020 7730 7763

Map 20 D2

Belgravia residents have been frequenting this French bistro for years. There's a sidewalk terrace in summer while inside it looks like a slice of old France. Menus accordingly stick mainly with French classics – hearty cassoulet, mussels, steak au poivre, good cheeses, and fruity desserts. The set-price menus are great value.

Mu

Millennium Knightsbridge, 17–25 Sloane Street, SW1X 9NU **Tel** 020 7201 6330

Map 19 C1

In this location you expect style and at this evening-only restaurant you get it. The food at Mu is hard to categorize. The best way to appreciate it is to go for the tasting menu. Each small dish is assembled with a smart precision. Try seared fillet of red mullet with tomato confit and basil foam or foie gras terrine, braised oxtail, and Madeira jelly.

Noura

16 Hobart Place, SW1W 0HH **Tel** 020 7235 9444

Map 20 E1

This is one of three Noura restaurants in London offering award-winning Lebanese cuisine. You can try a little of everything with the hot and cold mezzes, which include plenty of vegetarian options, or order the signature tabbouleh. An extensive wine list offers a good selection of Lebanese wines.

Amaya
📖♿ ££££

Halkin Arcade, 15 Motcomb Street, SW1X 8JT **Tel** *020 7823 1166*

Map 12 D5

A very different Indian restaurant, indeed. Spacious, stylish, and with the kitchen on honest display. The specialty here is grills and you can see the three stations – tandoori, sigra, and tawa – in action all evening. The range of meats and vegetables is brilliant and the presentation and service faultless. Expensive, but worth dining here.

Fifth Floor at Harvey Nichols
📖♿🍴 ££££

Harvey Nichols, Knightsbrige, SW1X 7RJ **Tel** *020 7235 5250*

Map 11 C5

Harvey Nichols has a special place among London's big stores, and its top-floor restaurant has a special verve. All white, and loved by the fashion crowd, it has wonderfully refined, intricate, delicious modern cuisine. Extravagantly subtle desserts are worth a visit by themselves. À la carte prices are high while the market menu is more affordable.

Nahm
📖♿❯ ££££

The Halkin, 5 Halkin Street, SW1X 7DJ **Tel** *020 7333 1234*

Map 12 D5

A remarkable Thai restaurant where Executive Chef David Thompson creates fresh, original flavors. The set menu offers not a dull moment. Try the appetizer *ma hor* – minced shrimp and chicken simmered in palm sugar with deep fried shallots, garlic, and peanuts, served on pineapple and mandarin orange. The wine list is extensive.

Zafferano
📖♿🍴 ££££

15 Lowndes Street, SW1X 9EY **Tel** *020 7235 5800*

Map 20 D1

Zafferano has long been recognized as one of the capital's premier Italian restaurants. It's a discreet place, where the emphasis is firmly on the food. Dishes such as rack of lamb with black olives and artichokes and the white truffle tasting menu, in season October to Christmas, allow the quality of the ingredients to shine through.

Dinner by Heston Blumenthal
📖♿🍴 £££££

Mandarin Oriental Hyde Park, 66 Knightsbridge, SW1X 7LA **Tel** *020 7201 3833*

Map 11 C5

This fantastic fine-dining restaurant offers uninterrupted views of Hyde Park, but don't let that distract you from the food created by Executive Head Chef Ashley Palmer-Watts. The menu focuses on simple, modern dishes inspired by traditional British recipes and includes scallops with cucumber ketchup and peas and slow-cooked rib of beef.

One 0 One
📖♿🍴 £££££

101 William Street, SW1X 7RN **Tel** *020 7290 7101*

Map 11 C5

Fish and shellfish are the specialty here. Dishes include confit of Norwegian salmon with green pea *velouté* and surf and turf combos like red king crab with roasted Anjou squab pigeon. Meals are reasonably priced, considering the quality of the ingredients and the commitment to sourcing sustainable foods.

Zuma
📖♿🍴 £££££

5 Raphael Street, SW7 1DL **Tel** *020 7584 1010*

Map 11 C5

Very cool, very trendy, and one block opposite Harrods. Celebrities can be spotted here but they come for the great food just like everyone else. Great sashimi, nigiri, sushi, and tempura with fancy service and fancy prices. Try the Zuma tasting menu. A visit is definitely an experience, but be prepared to dig deep into your vacation money.

WESTMINSTER, TRAFALGAR SQUARE, VICTORIA

Mekong
🍴❯ £

46 Churton Street, SW1V 2LP **Tel** *020 7630 9568*

Map 20 F2

This long-standing Vietnamese eatery still fills up on account of its wallet-friendly food. The ground-floor dining area can seem cramped, and the rustic walls painted in clashing pink and green leave something to be desired. But the kitchen delivers some tasty treats. Delightful staff and sought-after alfresco tables add to the experience of it all.

London Showboat – Hispaniola
📖♿🎵🍴 £££

Victoria Embankment, WC2N 5DJ **Tel** *020 7839 3011*

Map 13 C5

Something different: a four-course Mediterranean-influenced meal or tapas and a Thames boat trip combined. As you sail out majestically past London's landmarks you'll be entertained with a cabaret performance of songs from London's top shows. On the way back, the decks are cleared for dancing. Open noon–11pm Tue–Sat, noon–6pm Sun.

National Dining Rooms
📖♿❯ £££

Sainsbury Wing, National Gallery, Trafalgar Square, WC2N 5DN **Tel** *020 7747 2525*

Map 13 B3

Museum and gallery cafés traditionally tend to be dull and functional, but the National Gallery has improved things with this lively modern brasserie. It's open for breakfast, lunch, and dinner, so at different times you can try cakes, teas, steaks, pasta, nicely prepared fish grills, or cocktails. There's also a generous children's menu.

The Atrium
📖♿🎵 £££

4 Millbank, SW1P 3JA **Tel** *020 7233 0032*

Map 21 B1

The name says it all; this is a vast glass-covered space that has a real "wow" factor. The menu changes four times a year, mixing and matching to largely good effect – try seared scallop with pea purée, parma ham and mint oil, or braised lamb shank with swede and turnip mash and rosemary jus. Bright and modern in a conservative area.

Key to Price Guide *see p296* **Key to Symbols** *see back cover flap*

Cinnamon Club 🗎 ♿ ££££

30–32 Great Smith Street, SW1P 3BU **Tel** *020 7222 2555*   **Map** *21 B1*

London has hundreds of Indian restaurants, but the Cinnamon Club is not just one of the crowd. It occupies a grand old former library in the heart of Westminster, with an atmosphere of hushed elegance. Under head chef Hari Nagaraj it offers diners very refined, subtle North Indian cuisine, made with the finest ingredients and rare spicings.

MAYFAIR, PICCADILLY, ST. JAMES'S

Al Duca 🗎 ♿ 🍴 ▸ £££

4–5 Duke of York Street, SW1Y 6LA **Tel** *020 7839 3090*   **Map** *13 A3*

Just off Piccadilly, this bright, modern Italian restaurant offers great value in an expensive area, with set-price menus. Classic North Italian dishes are nicely presented, especially grilled fish, pestos, and richly flavored risottos. An excellent wine list and a great range of Italian liqueurs for after your meal. Closed Sun.

Chor Bizarre 🗎 ▸ £££

16 Albemarle Street, W1S 4HW **Tel** *020 7629 9802*   **Map** *12 F3*

Serving dishes from regional India, this restaurant is always busy. Try the lamb with fenugreek, spinach, and ginger and the aubergine (eggplant) with peanut sauce. Waiters can lose interest so keep them on their toes if you don't want to be forgotten. But they are friendly and willing to help you choose from the large menu.

Green's Restaurant & Oyster Bar 🗎 ▸ £££

36 Duke Street, SW1Y 6DF **Tel** *020 7930 4566*   **Map** *12 F3*

Wonderful old-world ambience and extensive champagne list, this is a great establishment. Excellent lobster salads, first-class fish and chips with pea purée, and, of course, a nice choice of oysters, most of them down from Scotland that very day. Daily lunch specials include hearty favorites like fish pie. Closed on Sundays from May to September.

Langan's Brasserie 🗎 🎵 £££

6 Stratton Street, W1J 8LB **Tel** *020 7491 8822*   **Map** *12 F3*

The original and perhaps still the best Langan's. The eponymous owner went to see the great chef in the sky a while back now, but his style lives on. Service is discreetly attentive and the staff are friendly. The menu changes weekly and includes dishes like soufflé with anchovy sauce.

Momo 🗎 ♿ 🎵 ▸ £££

25 Heddon Street, W1B 4BH **Tel** *020 7434 4040*   **Map** *12 F2*

Momo has been credited with giving a hip, fashionable appeal to North African food. Tagine stews and couscous are infused with cumin, mint, lemon, and coriander, and there are less well-known dishes, too. The design evokes old Marrakesh with style. Tables are snug, but you might rub elbows with celebrities. Afternoon tea also available.

Rasa W1 🗎 ▸ £££

6 Dering Street, W1S 1AD **Tel** *020 7629 1346*   **Map** *12 E2*

Restaurants of the Rasa chain are among the foremost exponents – in India or abroad – of the distinctive, mainly vegetarian cuisine of Kerala, in South India. They serve some of London's most interesting vegetarian food as well as seafood dishes. Seasonings are more subtle than hot, and the flavor palette is full of delicious surprises. Closed Sun.

The Criterion 🗎 ♿ 🎵 ▸ £££

224 Piccadilly, W1J 9HP **Tel** *020 7930 0488*   **Map** *13 A3*

A monument of a restaurant, right on Piccadilly Circus. Dating from the 1870s, the giant Criterion has fantastic Arabian-fantasy decor, with a glittering mosaic ceiling, and now has food to match. There are few more impressive places to sit and escape the city outside, enjoying fine wines and succulent, sophisticated, Franco-British cuisine.

Wild Honey 🗎 ♿ ▸ £££

12 St. George's Street, W1S 2FB **Tel** *020 7758 9160*   **Map** *12 F2*

Oak paneling and striking contemporary art combine to create the look of this elegant modern bistro. Prices are lower than many in the area, but the inventive food is first-rate, and made with the best fresh British and European ingredients. Try Scottish dived scallop and oyster tartare followed by roast English rose veal and polenta. Very popular.

Le Caprice 🗎 🎵 🍴 ▸ ££££

Arlington House, Arlington Street, SW1A 1RJ **Tel** *020 7629 2239*   **Map** *12 F4*

Opened in the 1980s, the Caprice instantly became a media and music-world hangout and still maintains its buzzy feel. Service is famously superb whether or not you're a famous face; fans often come for brasserie standards like superior burgers and grills but there are many other options, and an exceptional vegetarian menu.

The Wolseley 🗎 ♿ ▸ ££££

160 Piccadilly, W1J 9EB **Tel** *020 7499 6996*   **Map** *12 F3*

London never had many 19th-century *grands cafés*, but in 2003 this fine Piccadilly building was made into a great modern version of one. The decor is glamorous, with chandeliers hanging from lofty ceilings, and the atmosphere always buzzing. Menus offer plenty of variety, from salads to grills and seafood platters. Open for breakfast and tea.

Hélène Darroze at the Connaught
🝙 ♿ 🕴   £££££

Connaught Hotel, Carlos Place, W1K 2AL **Tel** *020 3147 7200*

Map *12 E3*

Restaurants in the Connaught have enjoyed an august reputation ever since the hotel opened in the early 1900s. In 2007 it hit a new high with the arrival of renowned, Michelin-starred French chef Hélène Darroze. Her cooking is endlessly inventive, blending French traditions with intricate spicings. Very expensive, but a real gourmet experience.

Le Gavroche
🝙 ♿ 🕴   £££££

43 Upper Brook Street, W1K 7QR **Tel** *020 7408 0881*

Map *12 D2*

Brothers Michel and Albert Roux have been synonymous with fine dining in Britain for decades, and the Gavroche is their flagship London restaurant. The head chef is now English, but the restaurant remains true to its traditions of timeless luxury and superb French haute cuisine, with every detail taken care of.

Maze Inside Marriott Hotel
🝙 ♿ 🕴   £££££

10–13 Grosvenor Square, W1K 6JP **Tel** *020 7107 0000*

Map *12 D2*

Part of the Gordon Ramsay empire, and run by El Bulli veteran Jason Atherton, Maze has been awarded a Michelin star for its highly creative and impeccably presented menus. Dishes such as honey and soy roasted quail, Landes *foie gras*, and spiced pear chutney showcase international influences. Highly recommended tasting menu.

Nobu
🝙 ♿ 🕴   £££££

Metropolitan hotel, Old Park Lane, W1K 1LB **Tel** *020 7447 4747*

Map *12 E4*

London's sleekest, hippest Japanese restaurant was one of the chain's first international ventures. At times it's been more famous for its celebrity diners than its food, but it's also a benchmark for quality: fresh fish and seafood are of supreme quality, and tempura, sashimi, and modern Japanese dishes are prepared with immense skill.

Umu
🝙 ♿ ⤐   £££££

14–16 Bruton Place, W1J 6L **Tel** *020 7499 8881*

Map *12 E3*

Seriously expensive (especially the tasting menu) but extremely stylish as well – the futuristic front door will make you gasp. The beautiful interior and impeccable service provided by great staff will also impress. As for the food, this is one of the few places in London where you can find genuine Japanese kaiseki. Vegetarian options available.

Wiltons
🝙 ♿ 🕴   £££££

55 Jermyn Street, SW1Y 6LX **Tel** *020 7629 9955*

Map *13 A3*

A landmark institution, there has been a Wiltons in London since 1742. A quintessential expensive club-dining experience. Whitstable Bay potted shrimp, grilled Dover sole, Scottish lobster thermidor, and West Mersey oysters are the main attractions here, but you will also want to bask in the atmosphere and in the attentive service.

SOUTH BANK, SOUTHWARK

Canteen
🝙 ♿ 🔲 ⤐   ££

Royal Festival Hall, Belvedere Road, SE1 8XX **Tel** *0845 686 1122*

Map *14 D4*

Conveniently located for theatergoers, Canteen is open all day, serving delicious and reasonably priced British dishes from breakfast to dinner. Daily specials include roasts and pies, and there's a selection of hearty British desserts such as treacle tart with Jersey cream. Weekend brunch is popular and is well complemented by a Bloody Mary.

Giraffe
🝙 ♿ 🔲 ⤐   ££

Riverside Level 1, Royal Festival Hall, SE1 8XX **Tel** *020 7928 2004*

Map *14 D3*

Giraffe restaurants form one of London's best something-for-everyone chains. Globetrotting menus have plenty to please kids – burgers, pasta – and grownups – Malay noodles, enchiladas, great bargain salads. Speedy, friendly staff ensure a fun feel. The South Bank branch has a terrace near the river: there are 14 more Giraffes around London.

Kennington Tandoori
🝙 ♿ ⤐   ££

313 Kennington Road, SE11 4QE **Tel** *020 7735 9247*

Map *22 E3*

One of the best Indian curry houses in London, according to many. Since it is a short drive from Westminster, many curry-loving Members of Parliament can be found debating policy over a chicken jalfreezi. There are classic dishes and quite a few unique ones with nice innovations such as their own Nilgiri murgh. Reliable food in a calm oasis.

Mar I Terra
🝙 ♿ 🔲   ££

14 Gambia Street, Waterloo, SE1 0XH **Tel** *020 7928 7628*

Map *14 F4*

Described as a little gem by its fans, this local Spanish tapas restaurant and bar has been steadily building custom from people living and working miles away. The quality of the ingredients is one of its secrets, as is its location off the main drag. This means the diners are discerning gourmets who have come for the food and the cheerful atmosphere.

Tapas Brindisa
🝙 ♿ 🔲 ⤐   ££

18–20 Southwark Street, SE1 1TJ **Tel** *020 7357 8880*

Map *15 B4*

Brindisa, based in the adjacent Borough Market, has led the way in importing the finest Spanish foods into the UK – superb Serrano hams, cheeses, piquillo peppers, and more. Their tapas bar showcases these delights in a fabulous array, all prepared with as much skill as grand cuisine. Very popular and no reservations, so come prepared to wait.

Key to Price Guide *see p296* **Key to Symbols** *see back cover flap*

Tate Modern Café2

Level 2, Tate Modern, Sumner Street, SE1 9TG **Tel** *020 7401 5014*

Map *14 F3*

The airy café in the Tate Modern (open to nongallery visitors) is an excellent port of call on the South Bank. Choose between sandwiches, snacks, salads, or larger dishes like pan-roasted chicken with puy lentils; all are finely presented, with fresh ingredients. Kids eat free with accompanying adult. On Level 7 there is a fancier, more expensive restaurant.

Tito's Peruvian Restaurant

4–6 London Bridge Street, SE1 9SG **Tel** *020 7407 7787*

Map *15 B4*

A favorite lunch spot for City workers, Tito's serves Peruvian staples such as seafood, fish soups, and fried *yuca* and rice, and its portions are extremely generous. Try the king prawn *chupe*, which is milky soup with rice, peas, and egg, or one of the restaurant's *pisco*-based cocktails.

Troia Bar and Restaurant

3F Belvedere Road, County Hall, SE1 7GQ **Tel** *020 7633 9309*

Map *14 D4*

Covering a lot more of Turkey's national dishes than many similar restaurants in London, Troia lets you explore on your own or you can let the set menus do all the hard work. *Kisir*, a cold appetizer of nuts, bulgar wheat, herbs, and green onions feels healthy and allows you the space to dig into the very hearty main dishes on offer.

Baltic Restaurant & Bar

74 Blackfriars Road, SE1 8HA **Tel** *020 7928 1111*

Map *14 F4*

Beetroot vodka-cured salmon? Well that's eastern European for sure. This restaurant exudes charm and is located inside a former coach house, which gives it exciting high ceilings. There's a massive range of vodkas, and the food constantly surprises with dishes such as roast guinea fowl kiev with spring greens, chestnuts, and cranberries.

Bermondsey Kitchen

194 Bermondsey Street, SE1 3TQ **Tel** *020 7407 5719*

Map *15 D5*

A great place for brunch, with dishes such as eggs Florentine. There's a Portuguese flavor to many of the options, with fresh ingredients from nearby Borough Market, and tapas also on the menu, which changes on a daily basis. Global wines and an easygoing atmosphere complete its appeal. The large front windows open in summer.

Cantina del Ponte

Butlers' Wharf Building, 36C Shad Thames, SE1 2YE **Tel** *020 7403 5403*

Map *16 E4*

The riverside terrace tables here have one of the best possible views of Tower Bridge, and are understandably in demand. To eat, there are all the Italian standards – salads, pizza from a wood-fired oven, pasta with plenty of sea-food – made with perky fresh ingredients, nicely washed down with decent wines. Set lunch menus are great value.

Cantina Vinopolis

1 Bank End, SE1 9BU **Tel** *020 7940 8333*

Map *15 B3*

This is next to the massive wine museum *(see p182)* so you know the wine list will be good. The food isn't bad, either, with a wide choice to suit most tastes. Try the monkfish and sea bass or panfried scallops with herb salad. Can be a little lacking in atmosphere, but if you're visiting the museum, it's an ideal place to lunch. Closed Sun.

Delfina Studio Café

50 Bermondsey Street, SE1 3UD **Tel** *020 7357 0244*

Map *15 C4*

Don't let the word "café" put you off. A former chocolate factory, it has a light gallery space, charming service, and an interesting, balanced menu. Fish of the day might be from Australia, or you may see springbok. The menu is short but changes every two weeks and is always interesting. There is a good wine list as well. Closed weekends.

Fish!

Cathedral Street, Borough Market, SE1 9AL **Tel** *020 7407 3803*

Map *15 B3*

Occupying a prime location in London's foodie mecca, Borough Market, this restaurant prepares fine ingredients bought directly from the suppliers on the market floor. It has a strong commitment to sustainable fish, fairly priced. Main courses include classic fish pie and the best of the morning's catch served simply. Daily vegetarian special.

Ozu

County Hall, Riverside Building, Westminster Bridge Road, SE1 7PB **Tel** *020 7928 7766*

Map *14 D5*

French owner, whose classic taste in Japanese food has been inspired by the Japanese director Yasujiro Ozu. Simple, contemporary decor and great views over the Thames and Westminster combine with exquisite attention to detail. Ozu serves sushi and sashimi, as well as a full à la carte menu.

The Lobster Pot Restaurant

3 Kennington Lane, SE11 4RG **Tel** *020 7582 5556*

Map *22 F2*

A remarkable little restaurant in an unprepossessing location. The French owners set out to recreate Brittany (even down to seagull soundtracks) and succeed brilliantly. The eight-course "surprise" menu is fantastic and the fish is always superbly fresh. Reserve in advance since it's not very big. Vegetarians should call ahead, too. Closed Mon & Sun.

Roast

Floral Hall, Borough Market, Stoney Street, SE1 1TL **Tel** *0845 034 7300*

Map *15 B4*

The grand Victorian Borough Market is the place to find much of the best meat, fish, and fresh produce in London, and Roast, with a sleek modern dining room inside the restored old structure, makes full use of them in its British-inspired menu. It opens early for fabulous breakfasts, and later there are delicious roasts and grills. Closed Sun dinner.

The Oxo Tower Restaurant & Brasserie 🔳♿🔳🎵 ££££
8th Floor, Oxo Tower Wharf, Barge House Street, SE1 9PH **Tel** *020 7803 3888*   **Map** *14 E3*

There are plenty of reasonably priced chains along this stretch of the South Bank, all offering river views, but to enjoy a really special evening's dining reserve a window table at this eighth-floor restaurant. It combines well-executed modern European food (including excellent vegetarian and vegan options) and slick service with great river views.

SOHO, CHINATOWN

Tokyo Diner 🧍🔳🌙♿ £
2 Newport Place, WC2H 7JJ **Tel** *020 7287 8777*   **Map** *13 B2*

This small Japanese eatery boasts an extensive range of dishes, from sushi to curry and soba noodles, at unbeatable prices. The attentive staff will provide complimentary green tea and rice crackers on arrival, but there's no tipping – the menu explains that this is not customary in Japan. Try one of the bento boxes or lunchtime set meals.

Cha Cha Moon 🔳♿🔳 ££
15–21 Ganton Street, W1F 9BN **Tel** *020 7297 9800*   **Map** *12 F2*

Since it opened in 2008, this popular, canteen-style noodle bar has been regularly winning awards. Owned by Hong Kong-born restaurateur Alan Yau, of Wagamama fame, the menu features an eclectic mix of Chinese, Taiwanese, Singaporean, and Malaysian cuisine and includes signature noodle broths with old favorites such as duck or wonton.

Harbour City 🔳🌙 ££
46 Gerrard Street, W1D 5QH **Tel** *020 7439 7859*   **Map** *13 B2*

The pedestrianized center of Chinatown is home to many restaurants and wonderful grocers. This restaurant doesn't have staff outside trying to lure you in; it relies on regulars. And on the food, which is consistently good. The decor is bright, colorful, and cheerful.

Jen Café ££
4–8 Newport Place, WC2H 7JP   **Map** *13 B2*

A busy Chinatown café near Leicester Square tube. One corner of the window is usually occupied by a member of staff hand-rolling the house specialty – Beijing dumplings – at an incredible speed. Barbecued meat and rice dishes and noodle soup also feature on the menu. Prices reflect the humble decor. No alcohol and no credit cards.

Masala Zone 🔳🌙 ££
9 Marshall Street, W1F 7ER **Tel** *020 7287 9966*   **Map** *12 F2*

An award-winning restaurant offering exceptional value combined with a healthy, delicious meal. Masala Zone features home-style Indian cooking, with dishes ranging from street food to burgers, noodle bowls to thalis. Service is fast and you can order food to go.

New Mayflower 🔳🌙 ££
68–70 Shaftesbury Avenue, W1D 6LY **Tel** *020 7734 9207*   **Map** *13 A2*

This genuine Cantonese restaurant proves Shaftesbury Avenue is not just for theatergoers. Dishes such as bean curd stuffed with shrimp and deep-fried crab are appetizing and fresh. There are vegetarian choices, too. Service is efficient, and free juicy oranges are given at the end of your meal (a Hong Kong tradition). Open until 4am.

Princi 🔳♿🌙 ££
135 Wardour Street, W1F 0UT **Tel** *020 7478 8888*   **Map** *13 A2*

Another Alan Yau establishment, this lively café/restaurant is in the heart of Soho and is a great spot for a quick bite to eat or a relaxed dinner. Seating is at communal tables or counters, and the menu contains good examples of standard Italian fare; breads, pizzas, and pasta. Breakfast and take-out are also available.

Andrew Edmunds 🔳🔳 £££
46 Lexington Street, W1F 0LW **Tel** *020 7437 5708*   **Map** *13 A2*

Small and romantically snug, with a secluded conservatory at the back, this feels almost like a country restaurant lost in the middle of Soho. It has gained many fans with its light, creative modern cooking – seen particularly in original, nicely balanced fish and seafood dishes. Be sure to reserve ahead since there are only a few tables.

Arbutus 🔳🌙 £££
63–64 Frith Street, W1D 3JW **Tel** *020 7734 4545*   **Map** *13 A2*

The award-winning Arbutus has established itself as a landmark on the London dining scene. The simple, elegant decor offsets the excellent, seasonal cooking perfectly and brings a touch of class to this rowdy street. Menus make the most of top quality British ingredients. Many excellent wines are available in smaller carafes.

Gay Hussar 🔳 £££
2 Greek Street, W1D 4NB **Tel** *020 7437 0973*   **Map** *13 A1*

Once the place of choice for cherry-nosed old journalists to meet and gossip and enjoy (on expenses) second-rate food that reminded them of their private schools. However, now it provides a proper insight into authentic Hungarian cuisine, wines, and spirits, and is a charming, cozy restaurant with welcoming staff.

Key to Price Guide *see p296* **Key to Symbols** *see back cover flap*

Haozhan

8 Gerrard Street, W1D 5PJ **Tel** 020 7434 3838

Map 13 B2

Haozhan's cool interior continues to entice Chinatown visitors away from standardized sweet-and-sour pork toward more innovative flavors. Prices are reasonable, though the dining experience can feel rushed. The set-lunch deal and fine-wine specials add to Haozhan's appeal. The chef's recommendations are often the best thing on the menu.

L'Escargot

48 Greek Street, W1D 4EF **Tel** 020 7437 6828

Map 13 B2

One of Soho's historic restaurants and a favorite of the media-theatrical crowd. It's owned by chef-entrepreneur Marco Pierre White. Menus offer refined modern cuisine, such as a lovely tian of crab and avocado, or scallops with tarragon risotto. Choose between the main dining room or the more luxurious Picasso Room upstairs.

Little Italy

21 Frith Street, W1D 4RN **Tel** 020 7734 4737

Map 13 A2

The name says it all. A busy and vibrant place with late hours until 4am. A page full of pasta dishes is always a safe bet, but if you feel like splashing out, the main courses are good, too. You might miss the unassuming doorway so back up and look again, it's there. Some live music and dancing most nights.

Vasco & Piero's Pavilion

15 Poland Street, W1F 8QE **Tel** 020 7437 8774

Map 13 A2

Most of the dishes on the menu are Italian and the owner's Umbrian heritage ensures that garbanzo beans and lentils feature frequently. The pasta is made in-house, with the finest quality ingredients and the menu changes twice daily. If you like truffles come visit – in season black or white truffles are imported from Umbria.

Zilli Fish

36–40 Brewer Street, W1F 9TA **Tel** 020 7734 8649

Map 13 A2

Aldo Zilli has brought a new touch to Italian food in London by showcasing Italian fish and seafood cuisine. The style is bright and unfussy: contented diners dig into platters of tasty grilled squid, spaghetti with lobster or clams, monkfish in pancetta, and more. There are two more Zillis around Soho, including a dedicated vegetarian restaurant.

Quo Vadis

26–29 Dean Street, W1D 3LL **Tel** 020 7437 9585

Map 13 A2

Another Soho restaurant with a long history – it first opened in 1926, but earlier, Karl Marx had lived in the house upstairs. Under its present owners the spacious, elegant dining room presents a fresh, modern British menu, emphasizing superior steaks but with excellent fish and lighter dishes, too. A place with a guaranteed metropolitan buzz.

Veeraswamy

99–101 Regent Street, W1B 4RS **Tel** 020 7734 1401

Map 12 F3

A touch of the old Empire. Slide into London's oldest Indian restaurant (open since 1926) and try some rather unique and genuine Indian cuisine from the "noble houses of India." It is elegant and expensive but the presence of so many people from the subcontinent clearly enjoying themselves speaks for itself.

Corrigan's

28 Upper Grosvenor Street, W1K 7EH **Tel** 020 7499 9943

Map 12 D3

Irishman Richard Corrigan is not London's best-known chef, but one of its most admired. His Michelin-starred restaurant is intimate and discreet (you ring a bell to be let in) and the creative, robustly flavored British-Irish dishes are prepared with immense flair. Service is perfect, and the wine list is renowned. Excellent-value lunch menu.

FITZROVIA, BLOOMSBURY

Bam-Bou

1 Percy Street, W1T 1DB **Tel** 020 7323 9130

Map 13 A1

The "red" bar upstairs in this Georgian town house lures you to a few drinks before you descend to the restaurant proper. Seated at a table with just candlelight playing off dark wood, you feel a million miles from London. This is not your average Southeast Asian restaurant. The food is excellent and the atmosphere relaxed and warm.

Salt Yard

54 Goodge Street, W1T 4NA **Tel** 020 7637 0657

Map 5 A5

Given modern London's international flavor, it is no surprise the city has its own take on the traditional Spanish tapas bar. Instead of using only Spanish ingredients, the award-winning Salt Yard also uses first-rate Italian and British produce in irresistible small delights like salt cod fritters with orange *allioli*, or duck and spinach *gnocchetti*.

Thai Metro

38 Charlotte Street, W1T 2NN **Tel** 020 7436 4201

Map 5 A5

Top-class Thai cuisine that won't break the bank. Go for green curry but be warned: if you aren't used to chilies, you could break out in a sweat. The zingy flavors that characterize Thai food are all here in abundance, and if the weather is warm you can enjoy your food in the fresh air. Service is fast, which may not be to everyone's taste.

Elena's L'Etoile

30 Charlotte Street, W1T 2NG **Tel** *020 7636 7189*

£££

Map *13 A1*

Another local institution, at lunchtime it fills up with media people from surrounding ad agencies and TV companies. They know what they want and Elena's delivers classic French bistro food under the gaze of celebrity pictures that cover the walls. It's not cheap but you get what you pay for and that indefinable extra – real atmosphere. Closed Sun.

Elysee

13 Percy Street, W1T 1DT **Tel** *020 7636 4804*

£££

Map *13 A1*

A legend among London's Greek restaurants, this is a noisy place that's not ideal for romantic couples. That said, it's great fun for a night out with belly dancers, bands, and singers all delivering an impressive show. The food does take second billing to the entertainment, but it's perfectly good food at a fair price. Roof terrace. Open until 3:30am.

Pescatori

57 Charlotte Street, W1T 4PD **Tel** *020 7580 3289*

£££

Map *5 A5*

The cooking always smells great when you pass this place, and because patrons try to sit outside in just about any weather, you get to gaze jealously at their food, too. It's easy to go a bit crazy and end up with a large bill. Grilled squid is always good and garlicky, while pasta and seafood dishes are consistently tasty. Closed Sat lunch and Sun.

Hakkasan

8 Hanway Place, W1T 1HD **Tel** *020 7927 7000*

££££

Map *13 A1*

A very expensive, Michelin-starred modern Chinese restaurant that has had no problems filling its tables from day one. The basement dining room has a DJ from 9pm each evening. The decor is superbly stylish and the food even more so. It's busy, but if you have the money and love good food you won't leave disappointed. Closed Sunday dinner.

Pied à Terre

34 Charlotte Street, W1T 2NH **Tel** *020 7636 1178*

£££££

Map *5 A5*

Plush, discreetly elegant decor sets the tone for this celebrated gourmet haven presided over by Michelin-starred chef Shane Osborn. The haute cuisine menus offer all kinds of rare delights, often using rich ingredients as in poached sea bass in a truffle crust. Desserts, such as chestnut mousse in a chocolate pancake, are fabulously seductive.

COVENT GARDEN, HOLBORN

Food for Thought

31 Neal Street, WC2H 9PR **Tel** *020 7836 9072*

£

Map *13 B2*

This relaxed little café has been serving London's vegetarians for decades. The basement dining room is down a narrow staircase: it's packed every lunchtime, but regulars cooperate to make the most of the space. Lasagnes, quiches, salads, fruity desserts, and more are full of good flavors. Takeout options are upstairs.

Belgo Centraal

50 Earlham Street, WC2H 9LJ **Tel** *020 7813 2233*

££

Map *13 B2*

Flagship of a small chain, this remains popular every night. Cool young staff whip up a great variety of mussels dishes, from *moules marinières* to more exotic creations featuring Belgium's famous beers. Meat-eaters are also catered for. Eat at the long refectory tables and enjoy the fun. Very cheap set menu deals, and kids eat for free.

Café Mode

57 & 59 Endell Street, WC2H 9AJ **Tel** *020 7240 8085*

££

Map *13 C2*

Always great value and very popular, Café Mode's great salads, pasta, and vegetarian dishes, and warm, friendly staff all contribute to a winning formula. Lone diners don't feel out of place, and the downstairs Moroccan-themed lounge is a cool retreat from the hustle and bustle of Covent Garden.

Café Pacifico

5 Langley Street, WC2H 9JA **Tel** *020 7379 7728*

££

Map *13 B2*

If you like a lively night, you'll like it here. Occasional Mexican live music, a buzzy atmosphere, and, if you're young or young at heart, a few cocktails followed by some filling and reasonably priced food such as burritos will send you singing out into the piazza.

Kulu Kulu Sushi

51–53 Shelton Street, WC2H 9HE **Tel** *020 7240 5687*

££

Map *13 C2*

Fresh raw fish at a price that's right. Simple decor belies the attention to detail that goes into the creation and presentation of dishes. Salmon sashimi comes recommended by regulars and there's always a line forming at lunchtime as health-conscious office workers choose fish over sandwiches. Closed on Sundays.

Porter's English Restaurant

17 Henrietta Street, WC2E 8QH **Tel** *020 7836 6466*

££

Map *13 C2*

Porter's serves up warm, hearty, traditional British "grub" with savory pie dishes such as steak and Guinness, cod, and salmon and prawn. Desserts are equally large and not for anyone dieting. You'll get a proper fish and chips here, too, and all served by cheerful staff and at a good price for the location. There's a cheap two-course theater menu.

Key to Price Guide *see p296* **Key to Symbols** *see back cover flap*

Wahaca
66 Chandos Place, WC2N 4HG **Tel** *020 7240 1883*

Map 13 C3

A roaring success since it opened in 2007, Wahaca is a great place for a cheap meal in this touristy part of town. The innovative menu, designed by Thomasina Miers who won the television Masterchef title in 2005, brings authentic Mexican flavors to London diners using a mix of imported and British ingredients. Excellent mojitos and tasty desserts.

Bertorelli's
1 Plough Place, Fetter Lane, EC4A 1DE **Tel** *020 7842 0510*

Map 14 E1

An Italian institution in Covent Garden, Bertorelli's Roman empire now extends farther afield with this branch near Holborn Circus. You always feel looked after here and the cooking is regional Italian kept simple to bring out the flavors. Good value, too. There is also a sophisticated bar area.

Chez Gérard Opera Terrace
The Market, Covent Garden Piazza, WC2E 8RF **Tel** *020 7379 0666*

Map 13 C2

The 11 Chez Gérard branches in London all follow the same formula – evoking the classic French brasserie in look and menu. Steak-frites served many different ways is the specialty, but other Gallic classics are on offer, too. On the upper level of Covent Garden market, this branch has the bonus of irresistible views from its spacious terrace.

Christopher's The American Grill
18 Wellington Street, WC2E 7DD **Tel** *020 7240 4222*

Map 13 C2

Rather more formal than you might expect from an American grill, but then this is a superior establishment. And there are plenty of other American favorites to choose from, including delicious prime rib chops, excellent lobster, and New York cheesecake. Good value and unpretentious.

Joe Allen
13 Exeter Street, WC2E 7DT **Tel** *020 7836 0651*

Map 13 C2

This atmospheric basement has been a favorite with pre-and post-theater crowds – actors and audiences – for over 30 years, and is often busiest after 11pm. American classics are Joe Allen mainstays – freshly made burgers, crisp Caesar salads – but there are more varied modern dishes, too. Service is always on the ball. Great breakfasts too.

Le Deuxieme
65a Long Acre, WC2E 9JD **Tel** *020 7379 0033*

Map 13 C2

Special pre-theatre meals mean you can enjoy your food confident you'll be on to your coffee in plenty of time before the curtain is raised. A large dining area and a warm team contribute to family-friendly dining. A good choice of dishes, with tuna steak being a popular item. The set menu is good value for the area.

Navajo Joe
34 King Street, WC2E 8JD **Tel** *020 7240 4008*

Map 13 B2

A lively atmosphere, a busy bar, and a good mix of spicy food under the umbrella "Pacific Rim street food" make this a popular Covent Garden eatery. Dishes come from South of the Border (down Mexico way) as well as from the heartland, so it's hard not to find something to enjoy on the menu. Biggish portions and fairly speedy service.

Sarastro
126 Drury Lane, WC2B 5QG **Tel** *020 7836 0101*

Map 13 C2

Not any old restaurant: entertainment at this "opera restaurant" includes opera singers – students and professionals – and string quartets. The extravagant decor is just as operatic, with ornate booths covered in velvet, gilt, and drapes. To eat, there's a varied Turkish and Mediterranean menu. Don't expect a quiet time, but it's great fun.

The Chancery
9 Cursitor Street, EC4A 1LL **Tel** *020 7831 4000*

Map 14 E1

A little gem of a restaurant tucked away down a side street. Adventurous, modern, and very good cooking in a stylish establishment. Try the terrine of *foie gras*, goose confit, and piquant sauce or crisp fillet of sea bass with seared scallops, risotto of herbs, and basil oil. It's all very good and well priced. Closed Saturday lunch and Sunday.

The Terrace
Lincoln's Inn Fields, WC2A 3LJ **Tel** *020 7430 1234*

Map 14 D1

One of London's special oases located in a summer house in the middle of Lincoln's Inn Fields gardens. Chef Patrick Williams combines British and Caribbean cuisine, producing vibrant but subtle original dishes. A delightful place for summer lunch; last orders are taken by 7pm. Great breakfasts available from 9–11am Monday to Friday.

Tom's Kitchen at Somerset House
Somerset House, The Strand, WC2R 1LA **Tel** *020 7845 4646*

Map 14 D2

Neoclassical Somerset House is one of London's most imposing spaces, around a magnificent courtyard. It is now the setting for Michelin-starred chef Tom Aiken's restaurant. The menu offers the freshest of British produce with highlights including the signature seven-hour confit lamb with balsamic onions and slow roast pork belly.

White Swan Pub & Dining Room
108 Fetter Lane, EC4A 1ES **Tel** *020 7242 9696*

Map 14 E1

With so many restaurants to choose from around Covent Garden, there's perhaps been less interest in the "gastro-pub" idea. The bar at the White Swan still looks like a proper pub, but above it is a chic modern dining area, with a sophisticated menu of such enticing options as a smoked trout salad and delicious roast pork. Good wine list, too.

Indigo

1 Aldwych, WC2B 4RH **Tel** *020 7300 0400*

Map 13 C2

This is a calm, modern, and stylish restaurant with an eclectic mixture of dishes beautifully presented and attentively served. Enjoy a drink in the stunning lobby bar before moving to the plush dining room, where they serve modern European cuisine. The informal Cinnamon bar is also a great place for snacks.

J. Sheekey

32–34 St. Martin's Court, WC2N 4AL **Tel** *020 7240 2565*

Map 13 B2

Sheekey's fish restaurant first opened near Leicester Square in 1896. It was sadly neglected for years, but since 1998, under the same owners as Le Caprice, its wonderful Victorian interior is again thronged with Theaterland crowds. British fish classics such as a celebrated fish pie are finely done, and the fresh catch-of-the-day fish are superb.

Rules

35 Maiden Lane, WC2E 7LB **Tel** *020 7836 5314*

Map 13 C2

London's oldest restaurant, here since 1798, has retained its fascinating historic decor, and its standards: it remains a temple of fine British cooking. The roast beef is definitive, served with fabulous horseradish sauce. Game is another specialty (freshly brought from Rules' own hunting estate). Service is very smooth. A great institution.

Simpson's-in-the-Strand

100 The Strand, WC2R 0EW **Tel** *020 7836 9112*

Map 13 C2

Simpsons' wood-paneled Grand Divan dining room is a Victorian monument, and a perfect setting for what the restaurant is famous for: true English roast beef, theatrically carved at your table on a silver trolley. Sadly, Simpson's legendary quality and service have been more erratic lately, but eating here is still an event. Also open for breakfast.

The Gaucho Grill

125 Chancery Lane, WC2A 1PU **Tel** *020 7242 7727*

Map 14 E1

There are a few Gauchos around London and they remain consistent value. Of course the thing to eat is the steak – big ones, but there's also lobster and hot and cold seafood platters. A large wine list helps wash down your enormous meal, and the cocktails aren't bad, either. Closed Saturday lunch and Sunday.

Asia de Cuba

4–5 St. Martin's Lane, WC2N 4HX **Tel** *020 7300 5588*

Map 13 B2

Perhaps fusing Cuban and Asian-American food is an experiment too far, but Asia de Cuba seems to be doing well on it. It's not cheap but the portions are massive and the service and attention to detail justify the cost. Calamari salad is popular as are the honey-glazed belly pork ribs. The aptly named "Bay of Pigs" dessert will finish you off!

L'Atelier de Joël Robuchon

13–15 West Street, WC2H 9NE **Tel** *020 7010 8600*

Map 13 B2

Being dubbed France's greatest living chef is no small accolade: having done it all, Joël Robuchon has radically departed from traditional styles in his restaurants. In the Atelier bar, you're encouraged to sample small dishes, almost sushi-style, instead of conventional courses; a luxurious full menu can be had in the dining room above.

Pearl Restaurant & Bar

252 High Holborn, WC1V 7EN **Tel** *020 7829 7000*

Map 14 D1

Pearl's seasonal menu features exquisite modern French cuisine. Go for the multicourse tasting menu and you won't go wrong. They also score high by offering a very large selection of wines by the glass. The decor is glamorous, with pearl chandeliers and walnut paneling. The two- and three-course fixed-price menus offer good value.

CLERKENWELL, HOXTON, SPITALFIELDS

East is East

230 Commercial Road, E1 2NB **Tel** *020 7702 7222*

A very decent Indian restaurant that doesn't serve Bangladeshi dishes like some do. Of course you are spoiled for choice in this part of London for "an Indian," but this one seems to get top marks every time for its authentic cuisine and friendly service. And it's very low priced, which is always a bonus.

Bengal Cuisine

12 Brick Lane, E1 6RF **Tel** *020 7377 8405*

Map 8 E5

Just about every building in Brick Lane is an Indian restaurant, but the quality varies. It's certainly a lot cleaner and more modern here than some we daren't mention. Very good value and the cook goes easy on the chili to suit the more Western customers. Staff are happy to advise on dishes if asked. Good Sunday buffet as well.

Cantaloupe

35–42 Charlotte Road, EC2A 3PD **Tel** *020 7613 4411*

Map 7 C4

One of the most hip bar-restaurants in one of London's trendiest districts, with DJs in the bar several nights each week. In such a party venue food can be neglected, but Cantaloupe's kitchen keeps up a high standard: the pan-Latin menu is full of fun dishes such as Brazilian stews, Argentinian steaks, and Spanish tapas. Great cocktails.

Key to Price Guide *see p296* **Key to Symbols** *see back cover flap*

The Eagle
159 Farringdon Road, EC1R 3AL **Tel** *020 7837 1353*

££

Map 6 E4

Credited with being the original "gastropub" and popular with journalists based in offices nearby, The Eagle serves hearty Mediterranean-inspired food from a tiny open kitchen. There's no à la carte menu, just a range of tapas and eight main courses on a chalkboard. Pub-style features include bar service and no reservations. Closed Sunday dinner.

The Real Greek
14–15 Hoxton Market, N1 6HG **Tel** *020 7739 8212*

££

Map 7 C3

Join the crowd in Hoxton and take in a massive selection of Greek dishes. They're all very tempting but keep an eye on the prices or you could end up with financial indigestion. The food is home-style cooking so many of the dishes on the menu have never been seen in the UK before. The wine bar serves Greek wines as well. Closed Sundays.

Vinoteca
7 St. John Street, EC1M 4AA **Tel** *020 7253 8786*

££

Map 6 F5

This is a relaxed, European-style wine bar and store, serving simply prepared, good food made from high quality ingredients. The constantly evolving wine list is displayed on chalk boards and features a wide variety of wines by the glass. Each of these is paired with one of the dishes on the menu. In summer, tables spill out onto the street.

Acorn House
69 Swinton Street, WC1X 9NT **Tel** *020 7812 1842*

£££

Map 5 C3

Laid back café by day, grown up restaurant by night, Acorn House takes every care to create a wholly ethical dining experience – the interior was built from 100 per cent recycled materials and the kitchen uses sustainable Fairtrade ingredients to create first class dishes such as chargrilled mackerel fillet with cardamom and ginger. Closed Sun dinner.

Great Eastern Dining Room
54–56 Great Eastern Street, EC2A 3QR **Tel** *020 7613 4545*

£££

Map 7 C4

Very tasty and popular, Great Eastern has been a raging success since day one. It serves Pan-Asian food such as phad thai, Singapore noodles, sushi, dim sum, and curries. Dim sums are filling and the curries balanced and spicy. And for once, service is impeccable and friendly. DJ sets on Friday and Saturday nights.

Moro
34–36 Exmouth Market, EC1R 4QE **Tel** *020 7833 8336*

£££

Map 6 E4

A restaurant that has been hugely influential. Inspired by Mediterranean travels, Sam and Samantha Clark create succulent dishes blending Spanish, Portuguese, and Moroccan influences, with wonderful fresh ingredients. You can also try equally irresistible tapas at the bar. It's noisy and very popular, so reserve well ahead. Closed Sunday.

The Peasant
240 St. John Street, EC1V 4PH **Tel** *020 7336 7726*

£££

Map 6 F4

This giant old pub, with its own Wat Tyler beer, has been successfully turned into a great gastropub. You can eat great British food in the pub downstairs or superb fine dining in the restaurant upstairs. Don't leave without trying the delightfully tasty, fresh, and fruity desserts.

Smiths of Smithfield
67–77 Charterhouse Street, EC1M 6HJ **Tel** *020 7251 7950*

££££

Map 6 F5

This lofty, post-industrial converted warehouse answers several needs. On the ground floor is a buzzy bar, with snacks and DJs; above is a wine bar. The middle floor is the main dining space where owner John Torode presents lively dishes using the best British produce. The Top Floor is his pricier fine-dining restaurant, with a great rooftop terrace.

St. John
26 St. John Street, EC1M 4AY **Tel** *020 3301 8069*

££££

Map 6 F5

Here they like to eat the bits of animals you barely hear about so don't bring squeamish eaters. Set in a converted smokehouse near the meat markets, the food is fantastic if you want to try something different, like the pigs' tongue with dandelion. Feasting menus for large groups can be reserved in advance and include whole roast suckling pig.

CITY OF LONDON

Café Below
St. Mary-le-Bow Church, EC2V 6AU **Tel** *020 7329 0789*

£

Map 15 A2

A rare find among the chains and power-lunching restaurants of the Square Mile, this relaxed, friendly café serves hearty vegetarian fare such as quiches, salads, and sandwiches on homemade bread. Open from breakfast until 9pm, make the most of "off-peak" deals from 11:30am to noon and 1:30 to 2:30pm. Closed weekends.

Leon
86 Cannon Street, EC4N 6HT **Tel** *020 7623 9699*

£

Map 15 B2

Allegra McEvedy and her team have hit the spot with their bright modern cafés. Eat in or take out and choose from a range of mostly Mediterranean-inspired dishes (with plenty of vegetarian options) such as grilled halloumi, salmon fish-cakes, "superfood salads," and more. Several branches around the city, including a big one at Spitalfields.

Haz Premier Place
      ⑤   ££

9 Cutler Street, E1 7DJ **Tel** *020 7929 7923*
      Map *16 D1*

Lively, fun, and a little posh, too, this is a touch of true Turkey in the city. Go for a mixed *meze* appetizer. They just keep coming and they're all delicious. Go for the well-marinated meat dishes and kebabs and mop up the juice with the lovely flatbread. The office workers throng into Haz at lunchtime so get here before noon.

Wagamama
      目 ⑤   ££

1A Ropemaker Street, EC2Y 9AW **Tel** *020 7588 2688*
      Map *7 B5*

Popular with suited diners, this City branch of the popular chain of Japanese noodle restaurants serves fast-food noodle and rice dishes to an appreciative crowd. Wagamama's specialty is the ramen noodle bowl, served in soups with delicious topping or teppan fried, offering a nutritionally complete meal.

The Don
      目   £££

The Courtyard, 20 St. Swithin's Lane, EC4N 8AD **Tel** *020 7626 2606*
      Map *15 B2*

This used to be a wine warehouse so it's no surprise that it has an excellent wine list. It also has very attentive staff, who go out of their way to be helpful. A good sommelier and a range of interesting and unique dishes from a modern European menu make this a very popular restaurant, indeed, and reservations are a must. Closed Sat & Sun.

Sauterelle
      目 ⑤   ££££

Royal Exchange, Threadneedle Street, EC3V 3LR **Tel** *020 7618 2483*
      Map *15 B2*

Location is the great attraction here. Sauterelle occupies a mezzanine level beside the magnificent courtyard of the Neoclassical Royal Exchange, which, no longer used for trading, is now a luxury shopping mall. The French-based cuisine is rich, inventive, and satisfying; the wine list is carefully chosen. A chic hideout in the City.

HAMPSTEAD

Base
      目 🔲   ££

71 Hampstead High Street, NW3 1QP **Tel** *020 7431 2224*
      Map *1 B5*

During the day Base is a gourmet bar offering fresh Mediterranean cuisine and an à la carte menu. In the evening it becomes a fine-dining Mediterranean fusion restaurant, offering sumptuous food with an emphasis on fresh ingredients. The menu changes regularly and is complemented by an extensive wine list. Closed Sunday dinner.

Weng Wah House
      目 ▶   ££

240 Haverstock Hill, NW3 2AE **Tel** *020 7794 5123*

Highly regarded by locals for reliably good Chinese food at great prices. Be warned that there is karaoke, which isn't everyone's cup of tea, but it's not too intrusive and can actually be a lot of fun. Families will feel at home here. The food is actually very tasty, so it's worth listening to the amateur Frank Sinatras accompanying it. Take-out available.

The Wells
      ⑤ 🔲   £££

30 Well Walk, NW3 1BX **Tel** *020 7794 3785*
      Map *1 B4*

A few steps away from Hampstead Heath, this superior gastropub is a great stop for an indulgent meal after a walk. The bar, with tables outside in summer, has an easy-going pub feel; the delicately decorated upstairs dining rooms are more tranquil, and the menu is both sophisticated and ultraenjoyable. Plan to take your time and settle in.

Villa Bianca
      🎵 ▶   £££

1 Perrin's Court, NW3 1QS **Tel** *020 7435 3131*
      Map *1 B5*

Tucked away from the crowd, this welcoming Italian restaurant seems to make most visitors happy. The charming bow windows are inviting, and the place has a traditional feel about it. There are set menus, dishes such as beef fillet with truffles, and a great wine list. Business lunch served Monday to Friday.

The Gaucho Grill
      目 ⑤ 🔲 🎵 ▶   ££££

64 Heath Street, NW3 1DN **Tel** *020 7431 8222*
      Map *1 A4*

Part of a group serving hearty steaks for the larger appetite. A good family place with a lively atmosphere, too. Can get a little boisterous when large groups come in, but you can normally have a pleasant, calm meal here. The outside seating is worth making an effort to secure.

GREENWICH

Greenwich Union
      🔲   ££

56 Royal Hill, SE10 8RT **Tel** *020 8692 6258*
      Map *23 B3*

This old pub is now the main outlet for the small Meantime Brewery, so its range of fine beers is unique: as well as their own seven original varieties, there are fine bottled beers from around the world. Wines and spirits are out of the ordinary, too, and to eat with all this drink there are generous modern menus. Lunch here is a great bargain.

Key to Price Guide *see p296* **Key to Symbols** *see back cover flap*

Inside
🔲 ♿ ➡️   ££

19 Greenwich South Street, SE10 8NW **Tel** *020 8265 5060*   **Map** *23 B3*

Modern European cuisine in a clean minimalist setting and ideally placed to enjoy a pre-theater meal. The menu keeps fresh by constantly changing and the staff exudes confidence in their kitchen. Vegetarian options are available. This is a restaurant that could comfortably charge more for your meals, but which so far thankfully doesn't.

Rivington Bar & Grill
🔲 ➡️   £££

178 Greenwich High Road, SE10 8NN **Tel** *020 8293 9270*   **Map** *23 B3*

Back-to-basics British cooking in a comfortable dining room with further tables on a mezzanine floor. The menus feature seasonal British produce. Try potted Morecambe Bay shrimp on toast, followed by whole roasted Devon red chicken, or go along for breakfast.

The North Pole
🔲 🔲 🎵 ➡️   £££

131 Greenwich High Road, SE10 8JA **Tel** *020 8853 3020*   **Map** *23 A3*

One of Greenwich's trendier spots, this old pub now has three distinct spaces. The North Pole bar has snacks, funky decor, and cocktails; the much quieter Piano restaurant above has a menu of modern European cuisine. The basement is the South Pole, a club with DJs on weekends and live bands some nights. Open evenings only Thursday to Sunday.

The Spread Eagle
🔲 🔲 🎵 🍴   £££

1–2 Stockwell Street, SE10 9JN **Tel** *020 8853 2333*   **Map** *23 B2*

Fiercely championed by locals, this place radiates confidence with its innovative French cuisine. Small, cozy booths to dine in and a real, roaring fire in winter all conspire to make you want to stay long after the coffee has been cleared away. The food is rich and satisfying and the whole experience is a lot better than the West End, at half the price.

FARTHER AFIELD

Brown's West India Quay
🔲 ♿ 🔲 🎵 ➡️   ££

Hertsmere Road, E14 8JJ **Tel** *020 7987 9777*

From its beginnings in Brighton, the Brown's empire has spread out. It's solid British cooking with some European classics. Sitting amid dark wood café chairs and palms and whirling fans, you get quite a colonial feel. This branch is housed in a sugar warehouse – overlooking the dock at the front there is alfresco dining.

Song Que
➡️   ££

134 Kingsland Road, E2 8DY **Tel** *020 7613 3222*

In a large room with plastic tables and chairs, an extensive laminated menu offers all the standard Vietnamese dishes and a few Chinese ones, too. For a bargain price, pho – a noodle soup with beef, shrimp, or pork – is served up in large steaming bowls, accompanied by fresh chilies, beansprouts, Asian basil, and lemon wedges. Closed Sunday.

Fig Bistro
🔲 ➡️   £££

169 Hemingford Road, N1 1DA **Tel** *020 7609 3009*

A charming neighborhood restaurant set among the Regency terraces and leafy squares of Barnsbury in Islington. Fig has earned a solid reputation with the well-heeled, local clientele for serving sophisticated, seasonal food in an unpretentious environment. The wine list is well balanced and moderately priced. Summer dining under the fig tree.

Manna
🔲 🔲   £££

4 Erskine Road, NW3 3AJ **Tel** *020 7722 8028*

Manna is a delight for many London vegetarians. In place of the tired meat-free choices served up in many vegetarian cafés, it has a ground-up approach to vegetarian cooking, producing dishes full of tantalizing flavors like yam and black bean fajitas. Salads and desserts are invigorating, and it's a very comfortable spot. Closed Monday.

Chez Bruce
🔲   ££££

2 Bellevue Road, Wandsworth Common, SW17 7EG **Tel** *020 8672 0114*

The menu is modern British, and after 10 years here, Bruce has got it right. Lots of emphasis on offal, so not a vegetarian paradise, but it also offers a good range of fish choices. Great flavor combinations and a sure hand at the stove means it's worth the money.

Morgan M
🔲 🍴   ££££

489 Liverpool Road, N7 8NS **Tel** *020 7609 3560*

A converted old pub in Islington can seem an odd place to find a superb French gourmet restaurant, but this is where chef Morgan Meunier has set up shop. The atmosphere is quiet, calm, and formal; menus – great value for this quality – present a gorgeous range of flavors, with every detail outstanding. Reservations are essential.

The River Café
🔲 ♿ 🔲   £££££

Thames Wharf, Rainville Road W6 9HA **Tel** *020 7386 4200*

This restaurant set on the Thames River rarely disappoints. The River Café's ethos is first-rate seasonal ingredients cooked simply, and the menus change daily. Dishes such as pumpkin soup with mascarpone, whole Anjou pigeon, and linguine with crab, combined with friendly staff, make dining here worth every penny.

Light Meals and Snacks

When you want to make the most of the available sightseeing time, it doesn't always make sense to sit down for a lengthy restaurant meal. Or, perhaps you don't have the budget or the appetite for a full-course affair. London has several eateries for every taste and occasion – many of them unmissable institutions – from traditional fish-and-chip and pie-and-mash stores to elegant tea rooms and cool cafés.

BREAKFAST

A good breakfast prepares you for a solid day's sight-seeing, with the traditional British breakfast including staples such as bacon and eggs, smoked salmon, and grilled kippers. Many hotels (*see pp282–91*) serve traditional breakfasts to non-residents, but to start the day like a 19th-century lord, head for **Simpson's-in-the-Strand**, which on weekdays offers an old-fashioned breakfast menu (as well as classic lunchtime and dinner roasts) in a historic paneled dining room. Oatmeal, lamb's kidneys, Cumberland sausage, and black pudding are just part of the multicourse "10 deadly sins" set breakfast.

Several pubs around Smithfield serve the all-night meat market workers. The most famous of these is the **Cock Tavern**, dishing up good-value fare from 6am onward. Traditional cafés also fry up artery-clogging working-men's morning meals including egg, sausage, mushrooms, and baked beans.

For Continental breakfasts such as pastries and a cappuccino, there are many cafés to choose from. **The Wolseley** serves croissants, brioches, and cooked breakfasts in opulent surroundings. Brunch has become increasingly popular in London. The spacious, modern restaurant in the back of popular French grocer/delicatessen, **Villandry**, serves one of the best on Saturday and Sunday. American restaurants such as **Joe Allen** and **Christopher's** also offer brunch, or head for well-heeled Westbourne Grove, where it's a weekend ritual at relaxed eateries such as **202** and **Tom's** delicatessen.

COFFEE AND TEA

For a cappuccino or espresso at any time of day, step into round-the-clock Soho stalwart **Bar Italia**, which also serves a range of pastries and paninis. It's a legendary late-night pitstop, full of colorful characters (but do keep a hand on your purse/wallet). There is no shortage of coffee-bar chains, but one of the best is **Caffè Nero**, which dispenses authentic Italian coffee at reasonable prices across town.

If you're out shopping, many of London's department stores have their own cafés; Harvey Nichols' is one of the most stylish, while Selfridges has a branch of the cool Moroccan tearoom **Momo** among its many eating options. Designer stores such as Emporio Armani, Nicole Farhi, and Joseph have trendy cafés – from the outside **202** looks like a chic French-style café, but it showcases Nicole Farhi's fashion and home designs downstairs. **Joe's Café**, surrounded by Joseph's three boutiques at Brompton Cross, is a small yet slick refreshment option; there are a few branches around town. In Portobello Market, quaint tearoom **Still Too Few**, below the antique kitchenalia store of the same name, serves tea, sandwiches, and cakes to bric-a-brac hunters on Saturdays.

Patisseries such as **Maison Bertaux** and **Patisserie Valerie** are a delight, with mouth-watering window displays of French pastries. **Richoux** in Piccadilly is another popular refreshment spot. Chic French bakery/patisserie **Paul** offers delicious tarts and other treats in a Parisian-café atmosphere. The elegantly old-world **The Wolseley** in Piccadilly has an all-day café menu of sandwiches and salads. If you're strolling in picturesque Little Venice, **Café Laville** commands a spectacular view over Regent's Canal. **Bluebird**, Terence Conran's multi-faceted food center in the converted 1920s Bluebird motor garage on the King's Road, has a café with tables on its cobbled forecourt as well as a more formal restaurant, bar, and market.

No visit to London would be complete without taking afternoon tea. Top hotels such as the **Ritz** and **Brown's** (*see p286*) offer pots of your choice of tea, scones with jam and cream, delicious, thin cucumber sandwiches, and cakes galore. For a relaxed place in beautiful Kensington Gardens, there's nothing to beat **The Orangery**. Its selection of English teas and cakes tastes even better in the elegant surroundings of Sir John Vanbrugh's 18th-century building. Good coffee (and cakes) can also be found at the **Monmouth Coffee House** in Covent Garden. **Fortnum and Mason** (*see p321*) serves both afternoon and high teas. In Kew, the **Maids of Honour** tearoom offers pastries, reputedly enjoyed by Henry VIII. For a more modern experience, **Sketch** offers exquisite contemporary confections in a restyled Georgian room.

TRADITIONAL CAFÉS

These basic greasy spoons all over the city are a London institution, serving up fried breakfasts and such British staples as sausages, savory pies, and grills. They are usually only open until about 5pm; some close earlier. Granddaddy of them all is East End legend **E Pellicci**, with its wonderful Art Deco interior. A vogue for simple British fare has spawned some modern versions of the "caff", including the mini chain **S&M Café** – sausage and mash, before you get any funny ideas.

MUSEUM AND THEATER CAFÉS

Most museums and galleries have cafés, including the Royal Academy, Tate Modern (with wonderful views over the Thames), the National Portrait Gallery, and the British Museum. The National Film Theatre on the South Bank has a buzzing bar/café frequented by film fanatics, while St. Martin-in-the-Fields church in Trafalgar Square, famous for its concerts, has a capacious self-service café in its vaulted crypt.

SANDWICH BARS

A leading sandwich chain in London is **Prêt à Manger**, with branches throughout the center decked out with metalwork features and serving a range of delicious pre-packed sandwiches, salads, cakes, and soft drinks. Another popular sandwich chain is **Eat**, which offers a daily changing menu of innovative soups and salads using seasonal ingredients as well as sandwiches made with homemade breads and tortilla wraps. Quality Italian sandwich fillings in focaccia and ciabatta breads can be had at Soho's **Carlton Coffee House**. For a quick bite in Fitzrovia, **Squat & Gobble** makes great freshly made doorstep sandwiches, healthy salads, and home-cooked dishes, as well as breakfasts.

DELIS

With Londoners becoming more and more interested in high-quality foods from small producers in Britain and abroad, there has been a boom in stylish delis, many of which provide seating so that you can sample their wares on site. **Tom's** is a one-stop deli and café. The chic **Grocer on Warwick Café** offers breakfast and light Oriental-influenced dishes as well as ready-prepared foods to take out, while deli/cheese shop **La Fromagerie** has a large communal table in the back for light bites. Nearby, is the 100-year-old family-run delicatessen/lunchroom **Paul Rothe & Son**, which serves sandwiches and soups among the shelves of "British and foreign provisions."

DINERS

London is full of American-style fast-food joints, serving burgers, fries, fried chicken, apple pie, milk shakes, and cola, particularly around Soho, Leicester Square, Shaftesbury Avenue, and Covent Garden. Some time-honored establishments include family favorite **Maxwell's**, in Covent Garden, the **Hard Rock Café**, and the fun, 1950s-kitsch **Ed's Easy Diner**, but thanks to the continuing vogue for retro burger restaurants, new ones keep popping up. **Hamburger +**, where you order at the grill before sitting down, is one of the best, while the **Lucky 7** near Notting Hill serves up burgers and breakfasts in a dice-and-cards-themed diner, complete with vinyl-seated booths and blaring rock 'n' roll.

PIZZA AND PASTA

Italian food has now become a staple of the British diet. Street-side stands offer variable quality, while there are well-established chains with several branches, including **Ask**. **Pizza Express** offers thin-crust pizzas that are a step up from the norm. Try the elegant Georgian townhouse outlet on Chelsea's King's Road, or the branch in a converted dairy in Soho where there's also live jazz. **Kettners**, also part of the group, offers casual, inexpensive eating in a legendary old dining room (there's also a champagne bar). The **Carluccio's Caffè** chain, which has a branch with al fresco tables in pedestrianized St. Christopher's Place, serves good-quality, freshly made pastas and salads. **Marine Ices** near Camden Market serves great pizza and pasta in addition to its famous ice cream (see Street Food pp314–5). Other reliable pasta chains are **Spaghetti House** and **Café Pasta**. Inexpensive pasta is also served at bustling trattorias such as **Pollo** in Soho.

FOOD IN PUBS

Perhaps the biggest – and most popular – change in the London dining scene in the last 15 years has been the transformation in the food found in pubs. Before the early 1990s, most pubs that provided food at all offered a pretty simple range of salads and sandwiches, put together with no great imagination. The last two decades, though, have seen the rapid rise of the "gastropub," in which the food range is treated with as much care as the beer selection. Grilled steaks, fresh fish, or English classics like sausage and mash have been reinvigorated by the use of first-rate, organic ingredients and the menus have become increasingly sophisticated, mixing Mediterranean, Oriental, and other global influences.

The neighborhood gastro-pub has become an essential London institution. Some have separate dining rooms while others have stayed more pub-style, where you order at the bar from a chalked-up menu. All tend to be more relaxed than formal restaurants but they can get busy so reserve in advance. Among the best are **The Eagle**, **The Engineer**, **The Lansdowne**, **The Queen's Head & Artichoke**, and **The Wells** in Hampstead. (See also pp316–9).

FISH AND CHIPS

Fish and chips is typically considered the national dish of Britain, with a "chippy" serving a choice of fish (typically cod or plaice) deep-fried in batter, accompanied by chips (thicker cut than French fries). A range of accompaniments includes bread baps (rolls) for a "chip buttie" (a chip sandwich), mushy peas, pickled eggs, or onions. Four of the best places for such fare are the **North Sea Fish Restaurant**, **Rock & Sole Plaice**, **Faulkner's**, and **Fish Central**. Fish and chips is now considered very "trendy" and is increasingly available on the menu in various stylish restaurants and chains such as **Fish!**

BARS AND WINE BARS

The range and quality of London's bars has grown over the past five years. There are numerous wine bars in the center, such as **Café des Amis du Vin** in Covent Garden (downstairs from its ground-floor brasserie), and the legendary **El Vino**, as well as chains such as **Corney & Barrow** and **Balls Bros**, which also serve good food. The cozy **Tapa Room** on the ground floor of acclaimed **The Providores** restaurant serves globally influenced tapas. Good-value food is also part of the success of such chain bars as **All Bar One**. Capitalizing on young Londoners' habit of spending an entire evening out drinking, many style-conscious, modern bars serve food, such as the sleek **Eagle Bar Diner** off Oxford Street, which has a wide-ranging menu encompassing breakfast, burgers, pasta, and grills, and the **Alphabet Bar** in Soho. *(See also pp317–9.)*

BRASSERIES

Now that informal dining is an integral aspect of life in London, brasseries have become part of the landscape. These are based on the classic French blueprint, with its Parisian ambience and decor, serving such favorites as steak frites and seafood platters – a classic example is long-established **La Brasserie** in South Kensington. Among the chains is **Café Rouge**. **Randall & Aubin**

is a buzzy oyster and lobster (plus champagne) bar in a former delicatessen that has retained its period charm and overlooks Soho's lively Brewer Street. Relative newcomer **The Electric Brasserie**, next to Portobello's luxurious art-house movie theater of the same name, is a popular update on the traditional model.

JUICE BARS AND ORGANIC CAFÉS

The healthy-diet trend has made juice bars and organic food stores very popular. Longstanding Lebanese favorite **Ranoush Juice** has added outlets to its original Edgware Road location, and chains such as **Crussh** have branches all over London. Organic food chains such as **Planet Organic** and **Whole Foods Market** do a roaring trade in hot and cold fare and freshly squeezed juices alongside their groceries, baked goods, and vitamins. With tables on the premises, you can enjoy the freshly prepared food and drinks immediately.

NOODLE BARS

Popular chain **Wagamama** still draws long lines for its good-value noodles and other Oriental dishes in airy yet basic environs; customers sit at long communal tables. **Dim T Café** serves dim sum and mix-and-match noodles, meat, and toppings in a modern café setting. **Taro** is a busy Japanese diner offering cheap sushi, ramen, and teriyaki.

STREET FOOD

During summer, many parks have ice-cream vans parked by the entrances, with **Marine Ices** serving some of the town's best ice cream. Hot roasted chestnuts, made on mini-barbecues, are a winter delight found along Oxford Street. Shellfish stalls, selling ready-to-eat potted shrimp, crab, whelks, and jellied eels are a feature of many street markets. At Camden Lock and Old Spitalfields Market, you can wander among the stalls choosing from falafel, satay chicken, vegeburgers, and honey balls. In the East End, Jewish bakeries such as **Brick Lane Beigel Bake** are open 24 hours a day. Fresh plain bagels as well as ones with a wide range of fillings are available here.

The East End also has the largest number of pie and mash shops, which provide an inexpensive and satisfying "nosh-up" of jellied eels and potatoes, or meat pie with mash and liquor (green parsley sauce). Two classic venues, both on Bethnal Green Road, are **G. Kelly** and **S. & R. Kelly**. Or try **Manze's** on Tower Bridge Road. For the real East End experience, you should drench your food in vinegar and wash it all down with a couple of mugs of strong, hot tea. Modern pie-maker **The Square Pie Company** sells superior pies with gourmet fillings in Old Spitalfields Market and Selfridges.

DIRECTORY

BREAKFAST

202
202 Westbourne Grove W11.
Map 9 C2.

Christopher's
18 Wellington St WC2.
Map 13 C2.

Cock Tavern
East Poultry Avenue, Smithfield Market EC1.
Map 6 F5.

Joe Allen
13 Exeter St WC2.
Map 13 C2.

Simpson's-in-the-Strand
100 Strand WC2.
Map 13 C2.

Tom's
226 Westbourne Grove W11. **Map** 9 B2.

Villandry
170 Great Portland Street W1. **Map** 4 F5.

The Wolseley
160 Piccadilly W1.
Map 12 F3.

COFFEE AND TEA

Bar Italia
22 Frith St W1.
Map 13 A2.

Bluebird Café
350 King's Rd SW3.
Map 19 A4.

Café Laville
Little Venice Parade, 453 Edgware Rd W2.

Emporio Armani Caffè
191 Brompton Rd SW3.
Map 19 B1.

Joe's Café
126 Draycott Ave SW3.
Map 19 B2.

Maids of Honour
288 Kew Rd Richmond, Surrey.

DIRECTORY

Maison Bertaux
28 Greek St W1.
Map 13 A1.

Monmouth Coffee House
27 Monmouth St WC2.
Map 13 B2.

The Orangery
Kensington Palace,
Kensington Gardens W8.
Map 10 D3.

Patisserie Valerie
17 Motcombe St, Belgravia
SW1. **Map** 12 D5.

Paul
29 Bedford St WC2.
Map 13 B2.

Richoux
172 Piccadilly W1.
Map 12 F3.

Sketch
9 Conduit St W1.
Map 12 F2.

Still Too Few
300 Westbourne Grove
W11. **Map** 9 B2.

TRADITIONAL CAFÉS

E Pellicci
332 Bethnal Green Rd E2.

S. & M. Café
268 Portobello Rd W11.
Map 9 A1.

MUSEUM AND THEATER CAFÉS

Café in the Crypt
St. Martin-in-the-Fields,
Duncannon St WC2.
Map 13 B3.

Riverfront Bar & Kitchen
BFI Southbank, South
Bank SE1. **Map** 14 D3.

SANDWICH BARS

Carlton Coffee House
41 Broadwick St W1.
Map 13 A2.

Eat
12 Oxo Tower Wharf,
Barge House St SE1.
Map 14 E3.

Prêt à Manger
421 Strand WC2.
Map 13 C3.

Squat & Gobble
69 Charlotte Street W1.
Map 5 A5.

DELIS

La Fromagerie
2–4 Moxon St W1.
Map 4 D5.

Grocer on Warwick Café
21 Warwick St W1.
Map 12 F2.

Paul Rothe & Son
35 Marylebone Lane W1.
Map 12 D1.

DINERS

Ed's Easy Diner
12 Moor St W1.
Map 13 B2.

Hamburger +
4–6 Garrick St WC2.
Map 13 B2.

Hard Rock Café
150 Old Park Lane W1.
Map 12 E4.

Lucky 7
127 Westbourne Park Rd
W2. **Map** 9 C1.

Maxwell's
8 James St WC2.
Map 13 C2.

PIZZA AND PASTA

Ask
56–60 Wigmore St W1.
Map 12 D1.

Café Pasta
184 Shaftesbury Avenue
WC2.
Map 13 2B.

Carluccio's Caffè
St Christopher's Place W1.
Map 12 E2.
One of several branches.

Kettner's
29 Romilly St W1.
Map 13 A2.

Pizza Express
30 Coptic St WC1.
Map 13 B1.
One of many branches.

Pollo
20 Old Compton St W1.
Map 13 A2.

FISH AND CHIPS

Faulkner's
424–426 Kingsland Rd E8.

Fish!
Borough Mkt SE1.
Map 15 B4.

Fish Central
149–151 Central St EC1.
Map 7 A3.

North Sea Fish Restaurant
7–8 Leigh St WC1.
Map 5 B4.

Rock & Sole Plaice
47 Endell St WC2.
Map 13 B1.

WINE BARS

All Bar One
103 Cannon St EC4.
Map 15 A2.

Alphabet Bar
61 Beak Street W1.
Map 12 F2.

Balls Bros
Hays Galleria Tooley Street
SE1. **Map** 15 B3.

Café des Amis du Vin
11–14 Hanover Place
WC2. **Map** 13 C2.

Corney & Barrow
19 Broadgate Circle EC2.
Map 7 C5.

Dickens Inn
St Katharine's Dock E1.
Map 16 E3.

Eagle Bar Diner
3–5 Rathbone Place W1.
Map 13 A1.

Providores Tapa Room
109 Marylebone High St
W1. **Map** 4 D5.

El Vino
47 Fleet Street EC4.
Map 14 E1.

BRASSERIES

La Brasserie
272 Brompton Rd SW3.
Map 19 B2.

Café Rouge
27 Basil St SW3.
Map 11 C5.
One of many branches.

The Electric Brasserie
191 Portobello Rd W11.
Map 9 B2.

Randall & Aubin
16 Brewer St W1.
Map 13 A2.

JUICE BARS AND ORGANIC CAFÉS

Crussh
Unit 1, 1 Curzon Street
W1. **Map** 12 E3.

Fluid Juice Bar
208 Fulham Rd SW3.
Map 19 A2.

Planet Organic
22 Torrington Place WC1.
Map 5 A5.

Ranoush Juice
43 Edgware Rd W2.
Map 11 C2.

Whole Foods Market
69–75 Brewer St.
Map 13 A2.

NOODLE BARS

Dim T Café
32 Charlotte St W1.
Map 13 A1.

Taro
59–61 Brewer St W1.
Map 13 A2.

Wagamama
101 Wigmore Street W1.
Map 12 D1.

STREET FOOD

Brick Lane Beigel Bake
159 Brick Lane E1.
Map 8 E5.

G. Kelly
S. & R. Kelly
Bethnal Green Road E1.
Map 8 D4.

Manze's
87 Tower Bridge Road
SE1.
Map 16 D5.

Marine Ices
8 Haverstock Hill NW3.

London Pubs and Bars

Affectionately known as a "pub" as well as "boozer" and "the local," a public house was originally just that – a house in which the public could eat, drink, and even stay the night. Large inns with courtyards, such as The George Inn, were originally stopping points for horse-drawn coach services. Some pubs stand on historic public house sites, for instance the Ship, the Lamb and Flag, and the City Barge. However, many of the finest ones date from the emergence of "gin palaces" in the late 1800s, where Londoners took refuge from the misery of their poverty amid lavish interiors, often with stunning mirrors (The Salisbury) and elaborate decorations. Since the 1990s cocktail-bar boom, the traditional pub has been given an image makeover, restoring the British institution's popularity with a fashionable crowd.

RULES AND CONVENTIONS

Visitors to London have long been bemused by early pub closing times, which made a night out a bit tricky – an after-theater nightcap, for example, was usually out of the question outside of your hotel. In theory, reforms to the licensing laws, which came into effect in 2005, mean pubs can now stay open up to 24 hours, as long as they obtain permission from their local authority, and many extend their hours beyond the 11am–11pm standard. Some may close in the afternoon or early evening and also on weekends. You must be at least 18 to buy or drink alcohol, and at least 14 to enter a pub without an adult. Children can be taken into pubs that serve food, or can use outside areas. Order at the bar and pay when you are served; tips are not customary unless you are served food and drink at a table. "Last orders" are usually called 10 minutes before closing, then "time" is called, and a further 20 minutes is then allowed for finishing up drinks. Since July 2007, smoking has been banned from all pubs and clubs.

BRITISH BEER

The most traditional beers are available in various different strengths and styles, and are flat (not fizzy), and served only lightly cooled. The spectrum of bottled beers goes from "light" ale, through "pale," "brown," "bitter," and the strong "old." A sweeter, lower alcohol alternative is shandy, a classic mixture of draft beer or lager and lemonade. Many traditional methods of brewing and serving beer have been preserved over the years, and there is a great variety of "real ale" in London pubs. Serious beer drinkers should look for "Free Houses," pubs that are not tied to any particular brewery. The main London brewers are Young's (try their strong "Winter Warmer" beer) and Fuller's. The **Orange Brewery** serves a good pint and excellent food, and offers tours of the brewery.

OTHER PUB DRINKS

Cider is another traditional English drink found in every pub. Made from apples, it comes in a range of strengths and degrees of dryness. Blended Scotch whisky and malt whiskies are also staples, together with gin, usually drunk with tonic water. During the winter, mulled wine (warm and spicy) or hot toddies (brandy or whisky with hot water and sugar) may be served. Nonalcoholic drinks are also always available.

HISTORIC PUBS

Many pubs have a fascinating history and decor, whether it is a beamed medieval snug, Victorian fantasy, or an extraordinary Arts-and-Crafts interior, as at the **Black Friar**, a must-see temple to imbibing, featuring bronze bas reliefs, and an intimate, marble-and-mosaic chamber at the back. While many of the "gin palaces" of the 19th century have been revamped or abandoned, there are some notable survivors. At the **Prince Alfred** in Maida Vale the bar is divided by "snobscreens," a feature that enabled the upper set to enjoy a drink without mixing with their servants. The semi-circular **Viaduct Tavern**, opposite the Old Bailey, is a suitably stately setting for distinguished barristers and judges, ablaze with mirrors, chandeliers, and etched glass, while the **Princess Louise** retains its magnificent central mahogany bar, complete with original clock, moulded ceiling, and vivid wall tiles. Less grand but just as lovingly decorated is the tiny, tiled **Dog & Duck** in Soho – but you may have to battle for a seat or (in warm weather) stand outside with its many devotees.

Many pubs have strong literary associations, such as the **Fitzroy Tavern**, a meeting place for writers and artists in the 1930s and 40s, including Dylan Thomas, George Orwell, and Augustus John, **Ye Olde Cheshire Cheese** is associated with Dr. Johnson, Charles Dickens frequented the **Trafalgar Tavern**, while Oscar Wilde often went to **The Salisbury**. Samuel Pepys witnessed the Great Fire of London from the **Anchor**, on the river at Bankside. The less literary **Old Bull and Bush** in north London was the subject of a well known old music-hall song, while the 17th-century **Lamb and Flag** – one of central London's few surviving timber-framed buildings down an alleyway – was known as the Bucket of Blood because it was the venue for bare-knuckle prize fights. Some pubs have sinister associations, for example some of Jack the Ripper's victims were found near the **Ten Bells**. Dick

Turpin, the 18th-century highwayman, took refreshment at the **Spaniards Inn** in north London, and the **French House** in Soho was a meeting point for the French Resistance during World War II.

PUB NAMES

Signs have hung outside public houses since 1393, when King Richard II decreed they should replace the usual bush outside the door. As most people were illiterate, names that could easily be illustrated were chosen, such as the Rose & Crown, coats of arms (Freemasons' Arms), historical figures (Princess Louise), or heraldic animals (White Lion).

PUB ENTERTAINMENT

Fringe theater productions (see p346) are staged at the **King's Head**, the **Latchmere**, and at the **Gate Theatre** above the Prince Albert. Some pubs have live music: there is excellent modern jazz at the **Bull's Head** in Barnes and a wide variety of music styles at the popular **Mean Fiddler** (see pp351–3). The diminutive **Golden Eagle**, on a winding backstreet in Marylebone, is a rare central London piano pub with nostalgic singalongs a few nights a week.

OUTDOOR DRINKING

Most pubs with outdoor seating tend to be located slightly outside the city center. The **Freemason's Arms** for example, near Hampstead Heath, has a very pleasant garden. Some pubs enjoy riverside locations with fine views, from the **Prospect of Whitby** in Wapping and the **Grapes** in Limehouse to the **White Cross** in Richmond.

MICROBREWERIES

Delicious beer is brewed on the premises at microbreweries such as **Mash** where a space-age interior makes you forget that real ale tends to be the domain of older drinkers. This bar is frequented by a young and

trendy crowd. Huge orange vats indicate where the actual brewing takes place. The **Bünker Bier Hall Bar and Kitchen** in Covent Garden has three signature beers, and a good atmosphere.

THEMED PUBS AND BARS

Big, brash Irish pubs such as **Filthy McNasty's** and **Waxy O'Connor's** (mocked up like a Catholic church, complete with confessional) attract a young, fun-loving crowd, as does Australian bar chain **Walkabout**. Sports bars are popular as well. The **Sports Café**, near Piccadilly, has three bars, a dance floor, and 120 television sets showing global sporting events on satellite TV. More low-key is "footie" (soccer) bar **Kick** in Shoreditch (there's a smaller sister establishment, **Café Kick**, in Exmouth Market), which features tablesoccer games and organic food in a relaxed setting. Pool players can take their cue at a branch of slick pool-bar chain the **Elbow Room**.

GASTROPUBS

Since the early 1990s, many old pubs have been given gleaming makeovers and kitchens turning out superior fare. Among the first "gastropubs" was the **Eagle**, which offers gourmet dishes from the open kitchen that occupies half of the bar. Many, like **The Lansdowne** and **The Engineer** have dedicated dining rooms as well as laid-back pub rooms where you can eat, drink, or do both. TV foodie Roxy Beaujolais serves simple bistro dishes in tiny, quirky old pub the **Seven Stars** near the Royal Courts of Justice. **The Cow** is known for its oysters and Guinness, while the **Chapel**, the **Fire Station**, and the **Dusk** are popular with both drinkers and diners. (See also pp313–15).

BARS

London's bar scene has been gradually transformed since the mid-1990s; up till then, the choice was limited to either hotel bars, wine bars,

or pubs (see pp314–15). Propelled by a cocktail revival, as well as the fact that eating and drinking out is now deeply ingrained in daily London life, new bars are opening all the time.

Eagerly sought out by style-conscious connoisseurs, the latest watering holes are now as much a talking point as new restaurants. Soho and Covent Garden are brimming with bars, but to sample the hottest nightspots, head either east or west. In the past decade, Shoreditch has been transformed from no-go area to an evening destination, which is spilling into neighbouring Bethnal Green.

Two of the earliest pioneers – basement lounge **Home** and the no-frills **The Shoreditch Electricity Showrooms** – are still hopping. They've since been joined by, among others, the 1970s-styled warehouse space **T**, which is so vast it will never get too crowded, and, slightly farther afield, the gloriously camp **Loungelover**, decorated with crystal chandeliers, vintage handbags, and stuffed animals.

Across town in Notting Hill, sip good-value Scorpion Bowls and Zombies in the kitsch tiki-lounge ambience of **Trailer Happiness** or go for classic or more inventive cocktails at the **Lonsdale** with its bronze bubble-studded walls and hazy violet lighting. The area's style bars are in contrast with down-to-earth pubs frequented by the market traders, such as the bustling **Portobello Star**.

If you want to stick to the center of town, fashionable options include the **Lab Bar**, which serves excellent cocktails, especially Central American drinks such as caprinhas and mojitos, or **Match**, which has a branch in Oxford Circus as well as Clerkenwell. Heading south, the **Fridge Bar** in Brixton has DJs playing decent hip hop and deep house with lots of dancing and drinking.

Many restaurants feature excellent bars. The bar at **Green's Restaurant and Oyster Bar** (see p301) is a very special place to go, to

SHOPS AND MARKETS

L ondon is still one of the most lively shopping cities in the world. Here ultramodern stores sit alongside the old-fashioned emporia presided over by tailcoated staff. You can buy anything here, as long as you're prepared to pay. Luxury goods are expensive, although bargain-hunters will find a wealth of cheap goods in the thriving markets, which simply exude a carnival atmosphere. Explore the famous department stores, which encompass a huge breadth of merchandise, or seek out specialist shops.

Bags from two of the most famous West End shops

In general, you'll find upmarket designer stores around Knightsbridge, Regent Street, and Bond Street, while Oxford Street is the frenetic center for mid-priced labels as well as for mainstream department stores. Notting Hill, Islington, Soho, and the vicinity of Covent Garden are all rich in small, independent shops. Specialties include clothes, from raincoats and traditional tweeds to cutting-edge design and catwalk copies; books and records; toiletries; art and antiques; and craft goods such as jewelry, ceramics, and leather.

WHEN TO SHOP

In central London, most stores open around 10am and close between 5:30pm–6pm from Monday to Saturday, and are also open 11am–4pm Sunday. Many department stores have longer hours. The "late night" shopping until 7 or 8pm is on Thursdays and Fridays in Oxford Street and the rest of the West End, and on Wednesdays in Knightsbridge and Chelsea. Some shops in tourist areas, such as Covent Garden (see pp110–19) and the Trocadero, are open until 7pm or later every day and on Sundays. Some street markets (see pp339–41) are usually open on Sundays as well.

HOW TO PAY

Most stores accept all major credit cards, including Master-Card, AmericanExpress, Diners Club, Japanese Credit Bureau and Visa. However, smaller shops and street markets do not. A few of the stores also accept traveler's checks, especially if they're in sterling; for other currencies the rate of exchange is less favorable than in a bank. You need your passport. Most stores no longer accept payment by personal check, and their use is likely to be phased out completely by 2018. Debit cards are accepted in many major stores, as are Euros.

RIGHTS AND SERVICES

On a defective purchase, you usually get a refund, if proof of purchase is produced and the goods are returned. This isn't always the case with sales goods, so inspect them carefully. Most large stores, and some small ones, will pack goods up for you and send them anywhere in the world.

VAT EXEMPTION

VAT (Value Added Tax) is a sales tax of 20% which is charged on virtually all goods sold in Britain. The exceptions are books, food and children's clothes. VAT is mostly included in the advertized or marked price, although business suppliers, including some stationers and electrical goods shops, often charge separately.

Non-European Union visitors to Britain who stay no longer than three months may claim back VAT. If you plan to do so, carry your passport when shopping. You must complete a form in the store when you buy the goods and then give a copy to Customs while leaving the country. The tax refund may be returned by check or attributed to your credit card, but then a service charge will be deducted and most stores have a minimum purchase threshold (often £50 or £75). If you arrange to have your goods shipped directly home from the store, VAT should be deducted before you pay.

Harrods' elaborate Edwardian tiled food halls

TWICE-YEARLY SALES

The traditional sale season starts from after Christmas to February and again in June to July, when shops slash their prices and sell off unwanted stock. The department stores have some of the best reductions; for the famous **Harrods** *(see p211)* lines form outside long before opening.

BEST OF THE DEPARTMENT STORES

The king of London's department stores, by tradition is **Harrods**, with over 300 departments and a staff of 5,000. The spectacular food hall with Edwardian tiles displays fish, cheese, fruit, and vegetables. The specialties also include fashions for all ages, china and glass, kitchenware, and electronics. **Harvey Nichols**, aims to stock the best of everything. Clothes are particularly strong on high fashion, with emphasis on talented British, European as well as American names. There's also an impressive menswear section. The food hall, opened in 1992, is one of London's most stylish.

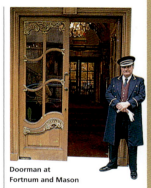
Some well-known names in British clothes design

Selfridges, on Oxford Street, has a wide choice of labels, a great lingerie department, and a section devoted to emerging designers. A melange of high-street concessions on the first floor caters to young women. It also has a food hall featuring global delicacies.

The original **John Lewis** was a draper, and even today his shop has a good selection of fabrics and haberdashery. Its china, glass and household items make John Lewis, and its popular Sloane Square partner, Peter Jones, equally popular with Londoners. **Liberty** *(see p109)* near Carnaby Street still sells beautiful silks and other Oriental goods, for which it was famed after opening in 1875. Look out for the famous scarf department.

Fortnum and Mason's first-floor food department is so engrossing that the upper floors of classic fashion and luxury items often remain free of crowds. The food section has everything from Fortnum's tins of biscuits and tea to the lovely wicker hampers.

The latest addition to the retail scene is **Westfield London**, an impressive, upscale shopping destination with over 250 retailers, as well as several restaurants.

MARKS AND SPENCER

Marks and Spencer has come a long way since 1882, when the Russian emigré Michael Marks had a single stall in the Kirkgate market, Leeds, with the sign, "Don't ask the price – it's a penny!" It now has more than 690 stores worldwide and most stock is "own label" – Marks and Spencer's underwear in particular is a staple of the British wardrobe. The food department mostly stocks convenience foods. The main Oxford Street branches at the Pantheon (near Oxford Circus) and Marble Arch are best for clothes and household goods.

SHOPPING AREAS

As well as offering a wealth of delights for the discerning bargain hunter, London's thriving markets also provide an atmospheric glimpse into the past, with many dating back to Medieval times.

Soak up the rich colors, aromas, and flavors at specialist food stalls, browse quaint antique shops for curios, or pick up a retro bargain at one of the many vintage clothes outlets that spill out onto the streets. Early risers have a better chance of finding a bargain *(see also pp339–41).*

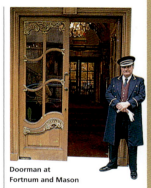

Doorman at Fortnum and Mason

DEPARTMENT STORES

Fortnum and Mason
181 Piccadilly W1. **Map** 12 F3.
Tel 020-7734 8040.

Harrods
87–135 Brompton Rd SW1.
Map 11 C5. *Tel 020-7730 1234.*

Harvey Nichols
109–125 Knightsbridge SW1.
Map 11 C5. *Tel 020-7235 5000.*

John Lewis
300 Oxford St W1. **Map** 12 E1.
Tel 020-7629 7711.

Liberty
210–220 Regent St W1.
Map 12 F2. *Tel 020-7734 1234.*

Selfridges
400 Oxford St W1. **Map** 12 D2.
Tel 0870-837 7377.

Westfield London
http://uk.westfield.com/london

Penhaligon's for scents *(see p333)*

London's Best: Shopping Streets and Markets

London's best shopping areas range from the elegance of Knightsbridge, where porcelain, jewely, and *couture* clothes come at the highest prices, to colorful markets such as Brick Lane, Spitalfields, and Portobello. Meccas for those who enjoy searching for a bargain, London's markets also reflect the vibrant street life engendered by its enterprising multi-ethnic community. The city is fertile ground for specialist shoppers: there are streets crammed with antique shops, antiquarian booksellers, and art galleries. Turn to pages 324–38 for more details of shops, grouped according to category.

97B ANTIQUES

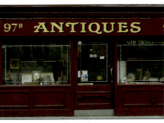

Kensington Church Street
Home to over 60 antique dealers with one of the largest selections of art and antiques in London. (See p215.)

The Royal Borough of Kensington
and Chelsea
PORTOBELLO
ROAD, W.11.

Portobello Road Market
Over 1,000 stalls sell objets d'art, *jewelry, medals, paintings, and silverware – plus fresh fruit and vegetables.* (See p341.)

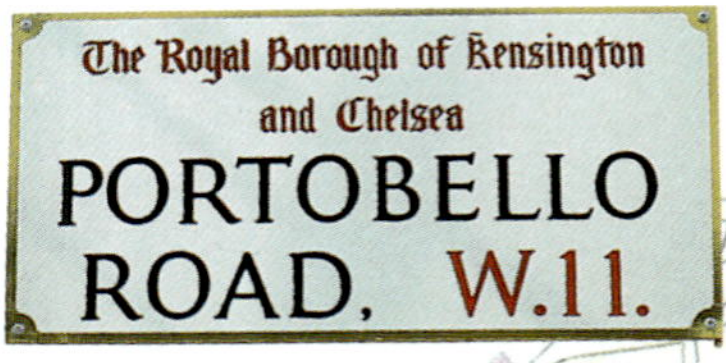

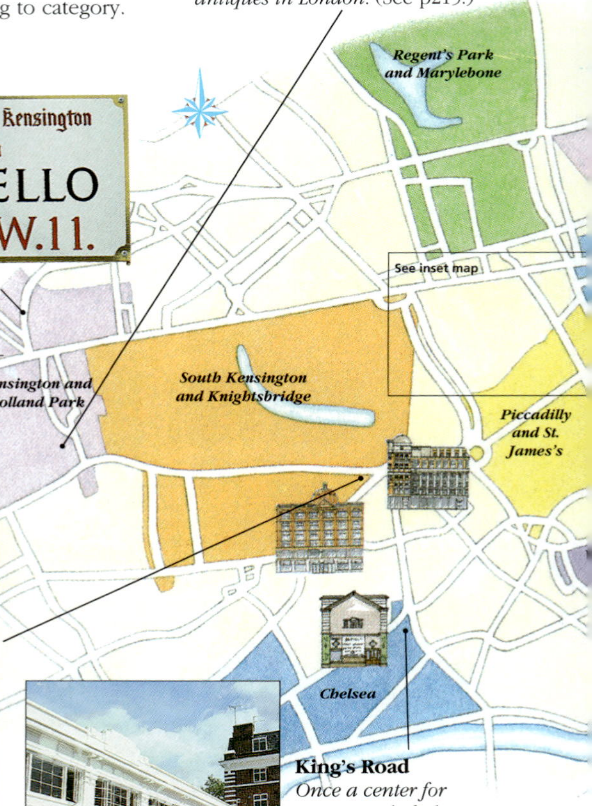

Regent's Park
and Marylebone
See inset map
Kensington and
Holland Park
South Kensington
and Knightsbridge
Piccadilly
and St.
James's
Chelsea

ESCADA

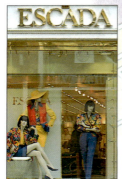

Knightsbridge
Exclusive designer-wear is on sale here, at Harrods as well as smaller stores. (See p211.)

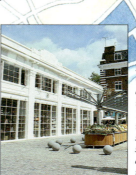

King's Road
Once a center for avant-garde fashion in the 1960s and 1970s, the street is now home to chain-stores and designer shops. There is also a good antiques market. (See p196.)

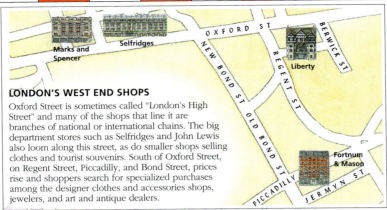

LONDON'S WEST END SHOPS

Oxford Street is sometimes called "London's High Street" and many of the shops that line it are branches of national or international chains. The big department stores such as Selfridges and John Lewis also loom along this street, as do smaller shops selling clothes and tourist souvenirs. South of Oxford Street, on Regent Street, Piccadilly, and Bond Street, prices rise and shoppers search for specialized purchases among the designer clothes and accessories shops, jewelers, and art and antique dealers.

Brick Lane Market
In this East End street, everything from old books to new sneakers is on sale. (See p339.)

Petticoat Lane
London's most famous market has leather, clothes, watches, jewelry, and toys. (See p341.)

Gabriel's Wharf
The wharf has been converted into small shops selling art, jewelry and crafts. (See p191.)

Charing Cross Road
Crammed shops selling old and new books line this long street. (See p330.)

Covent Garden and Neal Street
Street entertainers perform in this lively and historic market. The specialty shops of Neal Street are nearby. (See p115.)

0 kilometers 1

0 miles 0.5

Clothes

London has never been better for clothes shopping, offering a virtually inexhaustible range of styles, price levels, and quality, across a far-reaching and varied geographical area. Besides the traditional British-style famous the world over, you'll also find international designers, global and home-grown chains, and an ever increasing number of independent boutiques catering to every taste. While old-fashioned tailors, shirt-makers, and cobblers still thrive, often in their original premises, stores are increasingly design-led. The hugely popular chain stores have perfected the art of producing good-quality catwalk knock-offs, while a new generation of British design talent has revitalized the fashion scene.

TRADITIONAL CLOTHING

British tailoring and fabrics are world-renowned for their high quality. In Savile Row, you can follow in the sartorial footsteps of Winston Churchill and the Duke of Windsor, among other dapper luminaries, and have a suit made to measure or buy one off the peg. Established in 1806, **Henry Poole** was the first tailor in the Row. At **H. Huntsman & Sons**, you can choose from three options – bespoke, custom-made, and ready-to-wear. The bespoke suits are painstakingly hand-stitched on the premises, which partly explains the exorbitant £3,000-plus price tag. In addition to making suits to order, **Gieves & Hawkes** has two ready-to-wear lines.

A new generation of fashion-conscious tailors, known for modern cuts and vibrant fabrics, has joined the distinguished and traditional line-up, including **Ozwald Boateng** and **Richard James**. Jermyn Street is famous for smart shirts. At venerable stores such as **Turnbull & Asser** or the family-run **Harvie & Hudson**, you can either have them custom-made or choose the less expensive standard-sized options. Many manufacturers, including the popular shirt chain **Pink**, now also sell a wide variety of classic women's blouses.

In the past few years, several bastions of classic British style have completely reinvented themselves as fashion labels. **Burberry** is the best example of this, although it still does a brisk trade in its famous trenchcoats, checkered clothing (for children too), and distinctive accessories. **Aquascutum** is also a good choice for classic raincoats, suits, and accessories for both sexes, as is **Daks**, which produces high-fashion takes on traditional British looks. **Dunhill** specializes in immaculate, if expensive, menswear and accessories, while at the **Crombie** outlet, you can buy the famous fitted overcoat which came to be known by the company's name. The famous menswear emporium, **Hackett**, caters to a younger, yet still conservative, clientele. Designers **Margaret Howell** and **Nicole Farhi** create updated versions of relaxed British country garments for men and women, such as knitwear, tweeds, and sheepskin coats. You can still find a more traditional, smart country look in the Regent Street, Piccadilly, or Knightsbridge areas. Waxed Barbour jackets are on sale at Harrods (see p321). **Cordings**, established 1839, is good for country-gent/-lady gear, such as checkered shirts, moleskin trousers, and Covert coats.

While **Liberty** (see p109) now has a good selection of contemporary designers, it still uses its famous patterned prints to make blouses and stylish men's shirts as well as scarves and ties. Floral print "English rose" dresses and feminine blouses can be found

---

SIZE CHART

For Australian sizes follow British and American convention

Children's clothing

British	2–3	4–5	6–7	8–9	10–11	12	14	14+ (years)
American	2–3	4–5	6–6X	7–8	10–12	14	16 (size)	
Continental	2–3	4–5	6–7	8–9	10–11	12	14	14+ (years)

Children's shoes

British	7½	8	9	10	11	12	13	1	2
American	7½	8½	9½	10½	11½	12½	13½	1½	2½
Continental	24	25½	27	28	29	30	32	33	34

Women's dresses, coats and skirts

British	6	8	10	12	14	16	18	20
American	4	6	8	10	12	14	16	18
Continental	32	34	36	38	40	42	44	46

Women's blouses and sweaters

British	30	32	34	36	38	40	42
American	6	8	10	12	14	16	18
Continental	34	36	38	40	42	44	46

Women's shoes

British	3	4	5	6	7	8
American	5	6	7	8	9	10
Continental	36	37	38	39	40	41

Men's suits

British	34	36	38	40	42	44	46	48
American	34	36	38	40	42	44	46	48
Continental	44	46	48	50	52	54	56	58

Men's shirts

British	14	15	15½	16	16½	17	17½	18
American	14	15	15½	16	16½	17	17½	18
Continental	36	38	39	41	42	43	44	45

Men's shoes

British	7	7½	8	9	10	11	12
American	7½	8	8½	9½	10½	11	11½
Continental	40	41	42	43	44	45	46

at **Laura Ashley**, although the store has introduced more contemporary looks as well.

MODERN BRITISH DESIGN AND STREET FASHION

London designers are known for their eclectic, irreverent style. Grand dames Vivienne Westwood and Zandra Rhodes have been on the scene since the 1970s – the latter opened the **Fashion and Textile Museum** in southeast London in 2003. It features 3,000 of her own garments as well as examples by other influential fashion figures. Many British designers of international stature have their flagship stores in the capital, including the popular **Paul Smith** and **Stella McCartney**, both of whom showcase their collections in fabulous townhouses. **Matthew Williamson** and the late **Alexander McQueen** also have stand-alone stores. Young home-grown talent such as Alice Temperley, whose feminine frocks are beloved of the London party set, Eley Kishimoto, characterized by bold prints, and avant-garde design duo Boudicca, can be found in most of the capital's boutiques.

Selfridges *(see p321)* also has an impressive selection of emerging designers. **Dover Street Market**, conceived by Comme des Garçons' Rei Kawakubo, revives the age-old London tradition of the covered clothes market, but in a much more upmarket milieu. Its four minimalist floors showcase a varied array of goods, from glitzy shoes by king of the platform, Terry de Havilland, to cool art books and vintage and contemporary designer clothes.

If you want to take home a bit of British design, but can't afford the high prices, it's worth visiting **Debenhams**, which has harnessed the talents of numerous leading designers, including Jasper Conran, Julien Macdonald, and Ben De Lisi, to create cheaper collections exclusive to the store. Young designers often start out with a stall on Portobello Road or Old Spitalfields Market *(see p341)*, both

good sources of interesting clothing. There are also a few good designer sale stores: **Paul Smith Sale Shop** and **Browns Labels for Less** are both in central London. While those looking for **Burberry** bargains at its factory outlet will have to travel a bit farther afield to the East End.

BOUTIQUES

London is home to an extensive variety of boutiques – hot new stores crop up and, it must be said, close down with dizzying regularity. The mother of them all is **Browns**. Established in the 1970s, it occupies several storefronts in South Molton Street and stocks a wide selection of international labels. But the highest concentration of boutiques is in Notting Hill, near the intersection of Westbourne Grove and Ledbury Road. Because of the numerous cafés in the area, and the relaxed, affluent atmosphere away from the crowded West End shopping districts, it's an extremely pleasant place to browse.

J. W. Beeton embodies quirky British style, while **Matches**, which also has outposts in Richmond and Wimbledon, dominates Ledbury Road with three separate stores – one for both sexes, another just for women plus one specializing in frocks by Diane von Furstenberg. Like Browns in the West End, **Matches** stocks international designer labels, including Balenciaga, Prada, and Chloé, interspersed with a variety of British talent such as Temperley, Bella Freud, Matthew Williamson, and Georgina Goodman. **Question Air** and **Feathers** also stock designer labels, while **Aimé** specializes in French clothes and homewares. A short walk away in a quiet residential street, celebrity favorite, **The Cross** is a delightfully understated little store, packed with women's fashion, cute children's clothes and toys, toiletries, and varied displays of unusual accessories. **Cross The Road**, located opposite, caters to chic interiors while

The Dispensary in Kensington Park Road is much loved by locals for its Notting Hill style. Primrose Hill, Islington, Soho and the streets radiating off Seven Dials near Covent Garden are also dotted with independent fashion stores. Some, such as **Labour of Love** in Islington, combine clothes with a careful selection of interior items, art books, and CDs. **Diverse**, also in Islington, caters for both sexes with a great selection of labels.

CHAIN STORES AND STREET FASHION

In Britain, designer looks are no longer, as they once were, the exclusive preserve of the rich. National fashion chains – or "high-street" stores – have never been better, both in terms of quality and design. Moreover, the cheaper versions of all the latest styles appear in the stores, almost as soon as they have been sashayed down the catwalk. **Oasis** and **Topshop** have both won celebrity fans for their up-to-the-minute, young womenswear. The latter, which proudly claims to be "the world's largest fashion store," is a complete mine of inexpensive clothes and beautiful accessories; there is even an in-store "boutique" with latest collections by hip designers, and a vintage section as well.

Vintage fashion *(see p326)* has become so popular, many high-street chains either sell it or feature collections that recreate the style.

The upmarket chains, **Jigsaw** and **Whistles** are more expensive with the emphasis on beautiful fabrics and shapes which, while stylish, don't slavishly copy the catwalk. **Jigsaw Junior**, available in larger branches, offers delectable mini versions of its designs for little girls. **Reiss** and **Ted Baker** are more popular with the trend-conscious young men, though they also have good women's collections. More streetwise stores can be found in and around Newburgh Street, behind Carnaby Street. **Cecil Gee** in Covent Garden is among the trail-blazers for men.

VINTAGE FASHION

The city offers a vast hunting ground for the aficionados of vintage style, from market stalls to the exclusive stores showcasing immaculately preserved designerwear. Head east for funky emporia such as **Rokit**, which also has other branches in Camden and Covent Garden, in addition to the huge warehouse, **Beyond Retro**. Grays Antique Market *(see p340)* covers all the bases with the award-winning Vintage Modes, spanning the styles of the past century as well as fashion-conscious Advintage, run by a former department-store personal shopper. Glamorous evening gowns and pin-up lingerie for the girls, flashy Hawaiian shirts and novelty bar accessories for the guys, can be found at Sparkle Moore's gloriously kitsch string of stalls, **The Girl Can't Help It** in Alfies Antique Market, which also houses excellent vintage store **Persiflage**.

For mint-condition 1930s bias-cut silk slips and 1920s flapper dresses, head to **Annie's Vintage Clothes** in Camden Passage. Those looking for old designer gems should pay a visit to **Appleby** in West London, which is pretty much strong on the 1950s through 80s. Be warned, neither of these excellent stores is cheap, they both charge quite handsomely.

KNITWEAR

From the sought-after Fair Isle sweaters to Aran knits, the traditional British knitwear is famous. The best places for these are in Piccadilly, Regent Street, and Knightsbridge. Heritage labels **Pringle** and **Ballantyne** have been revitalized with more contemporary shapes and vivid colors. Luxurious, casual label **Joseph** features modern chunky knits, while **John Smedley** concentrates on more simple designs in fine-gauge wool and sea island cotton. For cashmere, **N. Peal**, which has both men's and women's stores at opposite ends of the Burlington Arcade, has a great selection – including a fairly cheaper, fashion-conscious line, npealworks. While the popular chain, **Brora** offers an affordable range of contemporary, Scottish cashmere for the entire family. **Marilyn Moore**, designs hip interpretations of classic knitwear.

UNDERWEAR AND LINGERIE

Marks & Spencer *(see p321)* is the most popular source of reasonably priced basics, it now has several fashionable lingerie lines as well. **Agent Provocateur**, owned by the famous designer, Vivienne Westwood's son and his wife, oozes retro pin-up glamor, from the slightly kinky, pink-uniforms worn by the staff to its nostalgically seductive bra sets. **Myla** sells contemporary lingerie and designer sex toys that can pass for objets d'art. **Miss Lala's Boudoir** located in Primrose Hill, is an exquisitely feminine store. Its collection includes, wispy negligées and hand-made, frilled undergarments, mixed in with items of clothing such as kitsch sequinned T-shirts, pretty tutu skirts, and some vintage pieces.

CHILDREN'S CLOTHES

You can get traditional hand-smocked dresses and romper suits from Liberty, **Young England**, and **Rachel Riley**, which stock smocks, gowns, and tweed coats. Burberry's New Bond Street store has a children's section showcasing adorable mini macs, kilts, and other items featuring the famous check. **Trotters** offers everything from shoes and clothes to haircuts, while **Their Nibs** sells eclectic designer children's clothing. For the very special, quintessentially English girls' clothes in pretty, patterned vintage fabrics, as seen on Madonna's daughter, visit the **Bunny London** concessions in Harrods and Harvey Nichols.

SHOES

Some of the most famous names in the footwear industry are based in Britain. If you have a few thousand pounds to spare, you can have a pair custom-made by the Royal Family's shoemaker, **John Lobb**. In the East End, ex-Lobb shoemaker, **Jason Amesbury** creates a bespoke range of footwear for considerably less, but you will still end up paying over £1,500. Ready-made, traditional brogues and Oxfords are the mainstay of **Church's Shoes**, while **Oliver Sweeney** gives classics a contemporary edge. For traditional, bench-made shoes at bargain prices, it's worth traveling farther afield to Battersea, and splurge at the **Shipton & Heneage** outlet. It offers an exceptionally wide range of Oxfords, Derbys, loafers, and boots crafted in the same Northamptonshire factories as some of the most celebrated names, for considerably lower prices, the out-of-the-way location keeps costs down.

Fans of the Fab Four can step into their idols' shoes; **Anello & Davide** designed the original Beatle Boot and still sells bespoke shoes in a range of materials. **The British Boot Company** in funky Camden has the widest range of Dr. Martens, which were originally designed as hard-wearing work boots and appropriated by the rock 'n' rollers. **Jimmy Choo** and **Manolo Blahnik** are certainly two beloved designers of most fashionable women worldwide. Their sophisticated high heels and cutting-edge designs are much sought-after.

While **Gina** emulates its namesake, Gina Lolobrigida with super-sexy designs, such as jeweled stiletto sandals, **Emma Hope** in Sloane Square is best known for simple, timeless shapes embellished with embroidery or beadwork. Less expensive, yet good quality designs can be found in **Hobbs** or **Pied à Terre**, while **Faith** and **Office** turn out young fashion-led styles, the latter also sells men's shoes. If you are on a look out for something that's a bit different, it's worth visiting London designer, **Georgina Goodman's** store in the picturesque Shepherd Market, where she showcases her unique ready-to-wear range.

DIRECTORY

TRADITIONAL CLOTHING

Aquascutum
100 Regent St W1.
Map 12 F3.
Tel 020-7675 8200.

Burberry
21–23 New Bond St W1.
Map 12 F2.
Tel 020-7930 3343.

Cordings
19–20 Piccadilly W1.
Map 13 A3.
Tel 020-7734 0830.

Crombie
48 Conduit St W1.
Map 12 F2.
Tel 020-7434 2886.
One of two branches.

Daks
10 Old Bond St W1.
Map 12 F3.
Tel 020-7409 4000.

Dunhill
48 Jermyn St W1.
Map 12 F3.
Tel 0845-458 0779.

Gieves & Hawkes
1 Savile Row W1.
Map 12 E3.
Tel 020-7434 2001.

H. Huntsman & Sons
11 Savile Row W1.
Map 12 F3.
Tel 020-7734 7441.

Hackett
87 Jermyn St SW1.
Map 13 A3.
Tel 020-7930 1300.
One of several branches.

Harvie & Hudson
77 Jermyn St SW1.
Map 12 F3.
Tel 020-7930 3949.
One of three branches.

Henry Poole & Co.
15 Savile Row W1.
Map 12 F3.
Tel 020-7734 5985.

Jaeger
200–206 Regent St W1.
Map 12 F2.
Tel 020-7979 1100.

Laura Ashley
House of Fraser, 318
Oxford St W1. **Map** 12 F1.
Tel 0871-223 1425.
One of several branches.

Liberty
Regent St W1.
Map 12 F2.
Tel 020-7734 1234.

Margaret Howell
34 Wigmore St W1.
Map 12 E1.
Tel 020-7009 9006.

Nicole Farhi
158 New Bond St W1.
Map 12 E2.
Tel 020-7499 8368.
One of several branches.

Ozwald Boateng
12a Savile Row &
9 Vigo St W1.
Map 12 F3.
Tel 020-7437 0620.

Pink
85 Jermyn St SW1.
Map 12 F3.
Tel 020-7930 6364.
One of several branches.

Richard James
29 Savile Row W1.
Map 12 F2.
Tel 020-7434 0605.

Turnbull & Asser
71–72 Jermyn St SW1.
Map 12 F3.
Tel 020-7808 3000.

MODERN BRITISH DESIGN AND STREET FASHION

Alexander McQueen
4–5 Old Bond St W1.
Map 12 F3.
Tel 020-7355 0088.

Browns Labels for Less
50 South Molton St W1.
Map 12 E2.
Tel 020-7514 0052.

Burberry Factory Shop
29–53 Chatham Place E9.
Tel 020-8985 3344.

Debenhams
334–348 Oxford St W1.
Map 12 E2.
Tel 08445-616 161.

Dover Street Market
17–18 Dover Street W1.
Map 12 F3.
Tel 020-7518 0680.

Fashion and Textile Museum
83 Bermondsey St SE1.
Map 15 C4.
Tel 020-7407 8664.

Matthew Williamson
28 Bruton St W1.
Map 12 E3.
Tel 020-7629 6200.

Paul Smith
Westbourne House
120 & 122 Kensington
Park Rd W11.
Map 9 B2.
Tel 020-7727 3553.
One of several branches.

Paul Smith Sale Shop
23 Avery Row W1.
Map 12 E2.
Tel 020-7493 1287.

Stella McCartney
30 Bruton St W1.
Map 12 E3.
Tel 020-7518 3100.

Vivienne Westwood
6 Davies St W1.
Map 12 E2.
Tel 020-7629 3757.

BOUTIQUES

Aimé
32 Ledbury Rd W11.
Map 9 C2.
Tel 020-7221 7070.

Anna
126 Regent's Park Rd
NW1.
Tel 020-7483 0411.

b Store
24a Saville Row W1.
Map 12 F2.
Tel 020-7734 6846.

Browns
23–27 South Molton
St W1.
Map 12 E2.
Tel 020-7514 0016.

The Cross
141 Portland Rd W11.
Map 9 A3.
Tel 020-7727 6760.

Diverse
286 & 294 Upper St,
Islington N1. **Map** 6 F1.
Tel 020-7359 8877.

Feathers
176 Westbourne Grove
W11.
Map 9 C2.
Tel 020-7243 8800.

J. W. Beeton
48–50 Ledbury Road W11.
Map 9 C2.
Tel 020-7229 8874.

Koh Samui
65–67 Monmouth St
WC2.
Map 13 B2.
Tel 020-7240 4280.

Labour of Love
193 Upper St N1.
Map 6 F1.
Tel 020-7354 9333.

Matches
60–64, 83 & 85
Ledbury Rd W11.
Map 9 C2.
Tel 020-7221 0255.

Question Air
229 Westbourne Grove
W11.
Map 9 C2.
Tel 020-7221 8163.

CHAIN STORES AND STREET FASHION

Cecil Gee
36 Long Acre WC2.
Map 13 B2.
Tel 020-7379 0456.

The Dispensary
200 Kensington Park Rd
W11. **Map** 9 B2.
Tel 020-7727 8797.

Hobbs
84–88 King's Rd SW3.
Map 19 C2.
Tel 020-7581 2914.
One of many branches.

Jigsaw
6 Duke of York Sq, Kings
Rd SW3. **Map** 19 C2.
Tel 020-7730 4404.
One of many branches.

Karen Millen
262–264 Regent St W1.
Map 12 F1.
Tel 020-7629 1901.
One of several branches.

DIRECTORY

Oasis
12–14 Argyll St W1.
Map 12 F2.
Tel 020-7434 1799.
One of several branches.

Reiss
Kent House, 14-17 Market
Place W1.
Map 12 F1.
Tel 020-7637 9112.
One of several branches.

Ted Baker
9–10 Floral St WC2.
Map 13 C2.
Tel 020-7836 7808.
One of several branches.

Topshop
Oxford Circus W1.
Map 12 F1.
Tel 0844-848 7487.
One of several branches.

Whistles
12–14 St Christopher's
Pl W1.
Map 12 D1.
Tel 020-7487 4484.
One of several branches.

VINTAGE FASHION

**Annie's Vintage
Clothes**
12 Camden Passage N1.
Map 6 F1.
Tel 020-7359 0796.

Appleby
95 Westbourne Park Villas
W2.
Map 9 C1.
Tel 020-7229 7772.

Beyond Retro
110–112 Cheshire St E2.
Map 8 E4.
Tel 020-7613 3636.

**The Girl Can't
Help It**
Alfies Antiques Market,
13–25 Church Street NW8.
Map 3 A5.
Tel 020-7724 8984.

Persiflage
Alfies Antiques Market,
13–25 Church St NW8.
Map 3 A5.
Tel 020-7724 7366.

Rokit
101 & 107 Brick Lane E1.
Map 8 E4.
Tel 020-7375 3864.
One of three branches.

KNITWEAR

Ballantyne
153a New Bond St
W1.
Map 12 F2.
Tel 020-7495 6184.

Brora
81 Marylebone High St
W1.
Map 4 D5.
Tel 020-7224 5040.
One of several branches.

John Smedley
24 Brook St W1.
Map 12 E2.
Tel 020-7495 2222.

Joseph
77 Fulham Rd SW3.
Map 19 B2.
Tel 020-7823 9500.
One of several branches.

Marilyn Moore
7 Elgin Crescent W11.
Map 9 B2.
Tel 020-7727 5577.

N. Peal
Burlington Arcade,
Piccadilly, W1.
Map 12 F3.
Tel 020-7499 6485.

Pringle Scotland
112 New Bond St W1.
Map 12 E2.
Tel 020-7297 4580.

UNDERWEAR AND LINGERIE

Agent Provocateur
6 Broadwick St W1.
Map 13 A2.
Tel 020-7439 0229.
One of several branches.

**Miss Lala's
Boudoir**
148 Gloucester Ave NW1.
Map 4 D1.
Tel 020-7483 1888.

Myla
77 Lonsdale Rd W11.
Map 9 B2.
Tel 020-7221 9222.
One of several branches.

Rigby & Peller
22A Conduit St W1.
Map 12 F2.
Tel 0845-076 5545.

CHILDREN'S CLOTHES

Bunny London
Tel 020-7627 2318.

Rachel Riley
82 Marylebone High St
W1. **Map** 4 D5.
Tel 020-7935 7007.
One of two branches.

Their Nibs
214 Kensington Park
Road W11. **Map** 9 A1.
Tel 020-7221 4263.

Trotters
34 King's Rd SW3.
Map 19 C2.
Tel 020-7259 6920.

Young England
The Old Imperial
Laundry, 71 Warrior
Gardens SW11.
Tel 0845-055 9722.

SHOES

**Anello &
Davide**
15 St Alban's Grove,
Kensington W8.
Map 10 E5.
Tel 020-7938 2255.

**The British Boot
Company**
5 Kentish Town Rd
NW1. **Map** 4 F1.
Tel 020-7485 8505.

Church's Shoes
201 Regent St W1.
Map 12 F2.
Tel 020-7734 2438.

Emma Hope
53 Sloane Sq SW1.
Map 19 C2.
Tel 020-7259 9566.
One of three branches.

Faith
192–194 Oxford St W1.
Map 12 F1.
Tel 020-7580 9561.
One of several branches.

**Georgina
Goodman**
12–14 Shepherd St W1.
Map 12 E4.
Tel 020-7499 8599.

Gina
189 Sloane St SW1.
Map 19 C1.
Tel 020-7235 2932.

Hobbs
47–48 South Molton St
W1.
Map 12 E2.
Tel 020-7629 0750.
One of several branches.

**Jason
Amesbury**
32 Elder St E1.
Map 8 D5.
Tel 020-7377 2006.

Jimmy Choo
27 New Bond St W1.
Map 12 F2.
Tel 020-7493 5858.

John Lobb
88 Jermyn St SW1.
Map 12 F3.
Tel 020-7930 8089.

Kate Kuba
22 Duke of York Square,
King's Rd SW3.
Map 19 C2.
Tel 020-7259 0011.

**Manolo
Blahnik**
49–51 Old Church St,
Kings Road SW3.
Map 19 A4.
Tel 020-7352 8622.

Office
57 Neal St WC2.
Map 13 B1.
Tel 020-7379 1896.
One of several branches.

**Oliver
Sweeney**
66 New Bond St W1.
Map 12 E2.
Tel 020-7355 0387.

Pied à Terre
19 South Molton St W1.
Map 12 E2.
Tel 020-7629 1362.

Shelly's
14–18 Neal St WC2.
Map 13 B2.
Tel 020-7240 3726.
One of several branches.

Shipton & Heneage
117 Queenstown Rd SW8.
Map 20 E5.
Tel 020-7738 8484.

Specialist Stores

London may be famed for the grand department stores such as Harrods, but there are many specialist stores that should also figure on the visitor's itinerary. Some have expertise built up over a century or more, while others are new and fashionable or cater to the whims of eccentric collectors. Whether you are looking for traditional British products and food, high-tech gadgets, or the latest trends in music, London has a wide range of stores to suite everyone's tastes.

FOOD

Britain's reputation for terrible food is proving hard to shake off, but over the past decade, not only has the national cuisine improved immeasurably, London has become one of the culinary capitals of the world. There is an unprecedented interest in local and organic produce as well as delicacies imported from all over Europe. This is reflected in the growing number of food markets, the main one being Borough Market (see p339). Specialties that are well worth sampling include a variety of chocolates, cookies, preserves, cheeses, and teas (see pp294–5).

The food halls of Fortnum & Mason, Harrods, and Harvey Nichols (see p321) are good outlets for all of these, but it's also worth visiting the gastronomic gems dotted around town. Of these, **A. Gold**, housed in an atmospheric old milliner's store near Spitalfields Market, specializes in traditional foods from across Britain. Its wares, including cheeses, sausages, jams, baked goods, English wines and mead, are advertised on chalkboards. **Paxton & Whitfield**, a delightful store dating from 1797, stocks more than 300 cheeses, including baby Stiltons and Cheshire truckles, along with pork pies, cookies, oils, and preserves.

The shelves of tiny **Neal's Yard Dairy** groan with huge British farmhouse cheeses. **Paul Rothe & Son** is a family-run deli that has hardly changed since it opened more than a century ago. Besides selling "British and foreign provisions," such as preserves, old-fashioned sweets, and cookies, the white-coated proprietors also serve morning toast and sandwiches on proper china. For traditional English chocolates, such as violet or rose creams and after-dinner mints in beautiful gift boxes, head for **Charbonnel et Walker** in Royal Arcade off Old Bond Street. It has been in business for more than 100 years, and holds Royal warrants. True chocoholics will be in their element at **The Chocolate Society's** store/café, where only the finest pure chocolate is available. Also committed to "real" chocolate, **Rococo** is well-known for its unique blue-and-white Victorian-esque packaging.

DRINKS

Tea, the most British of drinks, comes in all kinds of flavors. Fortnum & Mason's traditional teas come in appealingly refined gift selections. **The Tea House** is packed with myriad varieties from classic to creative (such as "summer pudding"), colorful tourist-oriented tins and teapots. **Postcard Teas** is another specialist retailer of high-quality teas.

The quaint 19th-century **Algerian Coffee Stores** manages to pack more than 140 varieties of coffee and 200 teas into its small shop. Family business **H. R. Higgins**, sells fine coffees and teas from around the world. There are many attractive gift boxes and you can try before you buy in the coffee room downstairs.

For whisky lovers, **The Vintage House** displays the widest array of single malts in England, including some very old bottles. **Berry Bros & Rudd** is one of the oldest wine merchants in the world, still trading in wines, fortified wines, and spirits from its ancient, paneled shop in St. James's. In contrast, **Vinopolis** (see p182), Bankside's "wine city," which charges admission, has a vast range of wines to choose from once you been on their interactive world wine tour and enjoyed five tastings. You can continue to imbibe in the restaurant or wine bar.

ONE-OFFS

Sadly, many of London's quirky old specialist stores have closed, but there are still some fascinating anachronisms, as well as interesting newcomers, to be found across the city. A large number of specialist traders operate from stalls in antiques markets such as Alfies and Portobello Road (see p341), where you can find everything from old military medals to commemorative china and vintage luggage. A notable survivor is **James Smith & Sons**, the largest and oldest umbrella store in Europe. It first opened for business in 1830. Behind its mahogany and glass-paneled facade lies an array of high-quality umbrellas and walking sticks, including the once ubiquitous city gent brolly.

Halcyon Days specializes in little enameled copper boxes, the delightful products of a revived English 18th-century craft. Top-quality wooden chess sets and boards, including an ornamental design featuring Sherlock Holmes characters, are available at **Chess & Bridge Ltd. V. V. Rouleaux**, on the other hand, is festooned with every imaginable type of ribbon and flamboyant trimming.

For serious collectors of model-making kits and historic TV character dolls and toys, **Comet Miniatures** has the largest selection in London. **Honeyjam** sells traditional toys and games for all ages. Without a Gameboy in sight, **Benjamin Pollock's Toyshop** does a nifty line in miniature self-assembly paper theaters as well as other traditional toys and antique teddies. **Flower Space** specializes in

1960s and 1970s furniture and classic movie prints.

At **The Bead Shop** in Covent Garden you will find two floors stocked with everything from Swarovski crystals to semi-precious beads and sterling silver. The tasteful erotic boutique **Coco de Mer**, banishes the seedy sex shop cliché with its exquisite hand-made lingerie and aesthet-ically pleasing sex toys.

Fans of Doctor Who and all things science fiction will love **ScifiCollector**, on the Strand. It stocks a huge range of Doctor Who, Red Dwarf, and other collectible toys and merchandise. There is also a section for first day covers, stamp sheets, and signed items. Special events held at the store include appearances by science fiction authors, artists, and actors.

BOOKS AND MAGAZINES

Bookstores are high among London's specialties. Charing Cross Road (see p108) is undoubtedly the focal point for those searching for new, antiquarian and second-hand volumes. Although film buffs won't be able to browse in the store that inspired the book and film, *84 Charing Cross Road*, they will be consoled by a commemorative plaque marking the site of the now defunct Marks & Co, which bore the celebrated address.

On the strip there are plenty of other antiquarian book-sellers, shelves groaning with dusty finds. **Francis Edwards** here has a good selection covering travel, natural history, naval and military history, and art and literature. Many stores offer a book-finding service if the title you want is no longer in print.

Charing Cross Road is famously the home of **Foyles**, known for its massive but notoriously badly organized stock; however, it was given a facelift and is now much easier to navigate. Here, you'll find everything from the latest bestsellers to academic tomes.

London's largest women's interest bookstore, **Silver Moon**, is on the third floor,

there's a jazz shop and a cool café (*see below*), plus an art gallery and real live piranhas in the children's department. As well as large branches of chains **Waterstone's** and **Blackwell**, many specialist bookstores are based here. A popular one is **Magma**, which is excellent for design subjects and avant-garde illustrated books.

Stanfords (*see p112*), which stocks maps and guides to cover the globe, is in Long Acre; more travel books can be found at the **Travel Bookshop** in Notting Hill. Nearby is **Books for Cooks**, complete with café and test kitchen.

The beautiful Edwardian **Daunt Books** in Marylebone has a soaring, galleried back room devoted entirely to travel titles and, unusually, related fiction organized by country. Graphic novels and American and European comics are the specialty at **Gosh!** and **Orbital Comics**, while fantasy and science fiction abound at **Forbidden Planet**. For gay writing, visit the pioneering **Gay's The Word**, near Russell Square. The best selection of books on movies is found at the **Cinema Store**.

London's oldest bookstore, **Hatchards** in Piccadilly, is also one of the best, offering a well-organized and extensive choice. **Grant & Cutler** is an unrivaled source of foreign books and videos, while **The Banana Bookshop** in Covent Garden must be London's most endearing remainder shop, artistically decorated with jungle murals.

Cecil Court (*see p101*) is a charming pedestrian alleyway lined with dealers specializing in everything from illustrated children's books to modern first editions. There are also stores selling old prints covering every theme – great for gifts – and especially theatrical memorabilia. **The French Bookshop** in South Kensington is stocked full of best-selling French titles. If you are looking for newspapers and magazines from abroad, **Capital News-agents** stocks among others,

American, Italian, French, Spanish, and Middle Eastern publications. **Gray's Inn News** is also worth a visit for European press. For those with a keen interest in vintage magazines, there are more than 200,000 in the basement of **Vintage Magazines** in Soho, dating from the early 1900s all the way through to the present day. There are also all manner of movie and popular-culture memorabilia and gifts on the ground floor of the store.

CDS AND RECORDS

As one of the world's greatest centers of recorded music, London has a huge and excellent selection of record stores catering to fans of all musical styles. Stores in the **HMV** chain are a reliable source of mainstream platters from pop to punk to peaceful easy listening, and their Oxford Circus branch stocks a comprehensive range of classical music.

Small specialist stores tend to cater to the more esoteric tastes. **Rough Trade** was at the center of the emerging punk scene and still sniffs out interesting indie talent today, found in both East and West London. For jazz, check out **Ray's Jazz**, which is now housed in Foyle's bookstore along with a cool café where you can chill out to the vibe.

Even if you're not a collector of rare vinyl, if you happen to be in the area, it's worth having a look at the kitsch Hawaiian hut interior of **Intoxica!**. It offers almost everything, from the 1960s surf pop to funk, punk, and independent rock.

Stern's has long been without an equal when it comes to exclusive collection of African music, and has recently broadened its scope to cover all world music.

There is a high concen-tration of indie vinyl and CD shops in and around Berwick Street. For 12-inch singles, the medium of club and dance music, **Vinyl Junkies** and **Black Market** are certainly two of the most central places to visit.

DIRECTORY

FOODS

A. Gold
42 Brushfield St E1.
Map 8 D5.
Tel 020-7247 2487.

Charbonnel et Walker
1 Royal Arcade, 28 Old Bond St W1. **Map** 12 F3.
Tel 020-7491 0939.

The Chocolate Society
36 Elizabeth St SW1.
Map 20 E2.
Tel 020-7259 9222.

Neal's Yard Dairy
17 Short's Gardens WC2.
Map 13 B2.
Tel 020-7240 5700.

Paul Rothe & Son
35 Marylebone Lane W1.
Map 12 E1.
Tel 020-7935 6783.

Paxton & Whitfield
93 Jermyn St SW1.
Map 12 F3.
Tel 020-7930 0259.

Rococo
321 King's Rd SW3.
Map 19 A4.
Tel 020-7352 5857.

DRINKS

Algerian Coffee Stores
52 Old Compton St W1.
Map 13 A2.
Tel 020-7437 2480.

Berry Bros & Rudd
3 St James's St SW1.
Map 12 F4.
Tel 0870-900 4300.

H. R. Higgins
79 Duke St W1.
Map 12 D2.
Tel 020-7629 3913.

Postcard Teas
9 Dering St W1.
Map 12 E2.
Tel 020-7629 3654.

The Tea House
15A Neal St WC2.
Map 13 B2.
Tel 020-7240 7539.

Vinopolis
1 Bank End SE1.
Map 15 B3.
Tel 0870-241 4040.

The Vintage House
42 Old Compton St W1.
Map 13 A2.
Tel 020-7437 2592.

ONE-OFFS

Benjamin Pollock's Toyshop
44 The Market, Covent Garden Piazza WC2.
Map 13 C2.
Tel 020-7379 7866.

Chess & Bridge Ltd
44 Baker St W1.
Map 12 D1.
Tel 020-7486 8222.

Coco de Mer
23 Monmouth St WC2.
Map 13 B2.
Tel 020-7836 8882.

Comet Miniatures
44–48 Lavender Hill SW11.
Tel 020-7228 3702.

Flower Space
301 Portobello Rd W10.
Map 9 A1.
Tel 020-8968 9966.

Halcyon Days
14 Brook St W1. **Map** 12 E2. *Tel 020-7629 8811.*

Honeyjam
267 Portobello Rd W11.
Map 9 A1.
Tel 020-7243 0449.

James Smith & Son
53 New Oxford St W1.
Map 13 B1.
Tel 020-7836 4731.

ScifiCollector
79 Strand, WC2.
Map 13 C3.
Tel 020-7836 2341.

The Bead Shop
21a Tower St WC2.
Map 13 B2.
Tel 020-7240 0931.

V. V. Rouleaux
102 Marylebone Lane W1.
Map 4 D5.
Tel 020-7224 5179.

BOOKS AND MAGAZINES

The Banana Bookshop
Unit 42 The Market, Covent Garden Piazza WC2.
Map 13 C2.
Tel 020-7836 0561.

Blackwell
100 Charing Cross Rd WC2. **Map** 13 B2.
Tel 020-7292 5100.

Books for Cooks
4 Blenheim Crescent W11.
Map 9 B2.
Tel 020-7221 1992.

Capital Newsagents
48 Old Compton St W1.
Map 13 A2.
Tel 020-7437 2479.

Cinema Store
Unit 4B, Upper St Martin's Lane WC1. **Map** 13 B2.
Tel 020-7379 7838.

Daunt Books
83–84 Marylebone High St W1. **Map** 4 D5.
Tel 020-7224 2295.

Forbidden Planet
179 Shaftesbury Ave W1. **Map** 13 A2.
Tel 020-7420 3666.

Foyles
113–119 Charing Cross Rd WC2. **Map** 13 B1.
Tel 020-7437 5660.

Francis Edwards
72 Charing Cross Rd WC2.
Map 13 B1.
Tel 020-7379 7669.

The French Bookshop
28 Bute St SW7. **Map** 18 F2. *Tel 020-7581 2840.*

Gay's The Word
66 Marchmont St WC1.
Map 5 B4.
Tel 020-7278 7654.

Gosh!
39 Gt Russell St WC1.
Map 13 B1.
Tel 020-7636 1011.

Gray's Inn News
50 Theobalds Rd WC1.
Map 6 D5.
Tel 020-7405 5241.

Hatchards
187 Piccadilly W1.
Map 12 F3.
Tel 020-7439 9921.

Magma
8 Earlham St WC2.
Map 13 B2.
Tel 020-7240 8498.

Orbital Comics
8 Great Newport St,
WC2. **Map** 13 B2.
Tel 020-7240 7672.

Stanfords
12–14 Long Acre WC2.
Map 13 B2.
Tel 020-7836 1321.

Travel Bookshop
13 Blenheim Crescent W11. **Map** 9 B2.
Tel 020-7229 5260.

Waterstone's
421 Oxford St W1.
Map 11 D2.
Tel 020-7495 8507.

Vintage Magazines
39–43 Brewer St W1.
Map 13 A2.
Tel 020-7437 8525.

CDS AND RECORDS

Black Market
25 D'Arblay St W1.
Map 13 A2.
Tel 020-7437 0478.

Fopp
1 Earlham St WC2.
Map 13 B2.
Tel 020-7845 9770.

HMV
150 Oxford St W1.
Map 13 A1.
Tel 020-7631 3423.

Intoxica!
231 Portobello Rd W11.
Map 9 B2.
Tel 020-7229 8010.

Ray's Jazz
(See Foyles).
Tel 020-7437 5660.

Rough Trade West
130 Talbot Rd W11.
Map 9 C1.
Tel 020-7229 8541.

Rough Trade East
91 Brick Lane E1.
Map 8 E5.
Tel 020-7392 7788.

Stern's
42 Theobald's Rd WC1.
Map 6 D5.
Tel 020-7831 6608.

Vinyl Junkies
94 Berwick St W1.
Map 13 A1.
Tel 020-7439 2923.

Gifts and Souvenirs

London is a wonderful place to shop for gifts. It presents an impressive array of original ceramics, jewelry, perfume, and glassware, exotic merchandise from around the world including jewelry from India and Africa, stationery from Europe, and kitchenware from France and Italy. The elegant, Regency-period Burlington Arcade *(see p91)*, the largest of several covered shopping arcades in the area, is popular for its high-quality clothes, antique and new jewelry, leather goods, and other items, many of which are made in the UK. It is also a real boon when the famously unpredictable weather turns nasty.

The stores at big museums, such as the Victoria and Albert *(see pp202–5)*, the Natural History *(see pp208–9)*, and the Science Museum *(see pp212–13)* often have unusual items to take home as mementoes, while Contemporary Applied Arts and the market in Covent Garden Piazza *(see p114)* sell a range of British pottery, knitwear, pictures, clothing, and other crafts. To buy all your gifts under one roof, go to Liberty *(see p109)*, where beautiful stock from the world over fills every department, and the classic Liberty print features on many goods.

GIFT STORES

If the phrase "gift store" conjures up images of tacky tourist souvenirs, think again. A number of interesting stores bringing together a variety of present-friendly goods under one roof, has sprung up in the capital. Just off Brick Lane, one-room **Shelf** showcases stationery, prints, ceramics, and other objects by local and European artists and designers. It's only open Thursday to Sunday; call to check hours before making a special trip. There are several other quirky, small stores in this street good for gift-hunting, including **Labour & Wait**.

A short walk away, **Story**, in a beautifully preserved 18th-century residential street looks more like a gallery space than a shop. The fascinating mix of wares unites vintage dresses, organic bath products, and modern and classic furnishings.

Across town in Notting Hill, **Coco Ribbon** is a girly emporium, furnished with antique armoires and chandeliers, selling everything from 1950s-influenced embroidered cushions and scented candles to prettily packaged toiletries, hand-made lingerie, and Australian designer fashion. The **Design Museum Shop** is a museum gift store with a difference. It displays post-modern toys, games, and innovative – and in some cases surprisingly affordable – accessories for home and office by big design names such as Arne Jacobsen, Tord Boontje, and Eames. There are some wonderfully witty items, such as shoe-shaped shoe brushes and a doorstop in the form of a figure holding it open. Boutiques **Saloon** and **Labour of Love** *(see p327)* also sell an eclectic range of items.

JEWELRY

There are styles to suit every taste, from the fine, traditional jewelry found in the exclusive shops of Bond Street to unusual pieces by independent designers in areas like Covent Garden *(see pp110–19)*, Gabriel's Wharf *(see p191)*, and Camden Lock *(see p339)*. Antique jewelry can be found in Hatton Garden and the Silver Vaults *(see p141)*. The Crown Jeweler, **Garrard** in Albemarle Street, has been brought bang up-to-date under creative director Jade Jagger. Be warned, the spectacular creations have pricetags to match. Its former business partner, **Asprey** sells updated classics. While **Butler & Wilson** specializes in reproductions of vintage jewelry and accessories, **Electrum Gallery** next door showcases striking contemporary pieces. **Kabiri**, with stores in Covent Garden and Marylebone and a concession in Selfridges, aims to bring works of previously unseen jewelry designers to London. Popular London design house **Erickson Beamon**, which is also sold in Harrods *(see p321)*, typically features dramatic chokers and earrings dripping with beads. The husband and wife duo, **Wright & Teague** design covetable modern silver and gold charm bracelets and necklaces, among other things.

The **Victoria & Albert store** sells modern replicas of ancient British designs, as does the store at the British Museum *(see pp126–9)*. The **Lesley Craze Gallery**, which also deals in other handmade accessories and crafts, sells jewelry by designers from around the globe. Liberty *(see p109)* stocks a wide range of attractive jewelry as well.

HATS

Traditional men's headgear, from flat caps to trilbies and toppers, can be found at **Edward Bates**. Venerable hatter **Lock & Co**, established in 1672, caters for both men and women, while Swaine Adeney Brigg sells hats for both sexes by well-known name **Herbert Johnson**.

Philip Treacy is Britain's most celebrated milliner and his fabulous creations are on display at his store on Elizabeth Street and in upmarket department stores. Established name **Stephen Jones** also has some very eye-catching looks, while **Rachel Skinner's** beautifully made, slightly nostalgic designs range from cute cloches to extravagant Ascot confections, which are less expensive than more famous names. **Fred Bare's** funky, affordable designs can be bought from the store in Columbia Road on Sundays when the weekly flower market is in bloom, or from high-end department stores.

BAGS AND LEATHER GOODS

Traditional British luggage, bags, and small leather goods can be found in the streets and arcades off Piccadilly. **Swaine Adeney Brigg** sells umbrellas, hats, classic bridle-leather bags, old-fashioned walking sticks, and other accoutrements for the country gent and lady. Well known for its classic, hard-wearing bags and luggage is upmarket **Mulberry**. Established in 1971, its modern interpretations of English country clothes and accessories are sought after by fashion folk as well as anyone who appreciates fine quality.

The ultimate luxury is **Connolly**, a name famous for crafting sleek leather interiors for Rolls-Royce. Its two swish shops sell items that hark back to the golden age of motoring, such as leather driving jackets and shoes, magnificent tool cases and chic luggage, bound diaries, and other extravagant home accessories and clothes.

J. & M. Davidson, owned by an Anglo-French couple, produces beautifully crafted, slightly retro bags, belts, and small leather goods, often in unusual colors or skins. The store in Notting Hill also stocks a line of clothes and interior items. In Piccadilly, **Bill Amberg's** store sells simple, contemporary bags in various types of leather, suede, and other skins, plus gloves, wallets, leather boxes, and unusual items such as a stylish leather and sheepskin baby "papoose."

Lulu Guinness and **Anya Hindmarch** both bring British wit and eccentricity to their handbags. Guinness's elaborate designs include a bag in the shape of a flowerpot topped with red roses and a circular purse resembling an old-fashioned rotary telephone dial and there are also many London-themed items. Hindmarch is famous for personalized, digitally printed photo bags, but also produces classic leather ones. For less expensive but high quality unique bags, try **Radley**.

SCARVES

Ginka by Neisha Crosland is a tiny store crammed with items bearing the designer's signature colorful, graphic prints; besides scarves there are bags, gloves, hats, clothes, and stationery. Of course, Liberty's famous print scarves are perennially popular. Small, stylish **Fenwick** is also known for its accessories department, which includes a wide array of interesting scarves by the likes of Pucci and Missoni, as well as bags, hats, and a huge range of hair decorations. The **V&A Museum** store has a good selection of scarves, including William Morris print silk scarves and stunning replica scarves inspired by V&A collections. N. Peal *(see p328)* has an extensive choice of cashmere scarves and shawls.

PERFUMES AND TOILETRIES

Many British perfumeries use recipes that are hundreds of years old. **Floris** and **Penhaligon's**, for example, still manufacture the same flower-based scents and toiletries for men and women that they sold in the 19th century. The same goes for men's specialists **Truefitt & Hill** and **George F. Trumper**, where you can buy some wonderful reproductions of antique shaving equipment as well. Chemist and perfumer **D. R. Harris** has been making its own range of toiletries for over two centuries; it's worth stopping in just to see the old-fashioned store.

Neal's Yard Remedies employs traditional herbal and floral remedies as bases for its natural, therapeutic products. Former facialist **Jo Malone** uses such delicious aromas as herbs, fruit, even coffee, as well as traditional floral essences in her fragrances, skincare, and candles, which come in simple yet sophisticated packaging. If you're looking for an unusual scent, head for **Miller Harris**; young Grasse-trained perfumer Lyn Harris creates fragrances with remarkable depth, which come in boxes decorated with botanical prints.

Scent Systems is a contender for the smallest store in the capital, but its fragrances are worn by some of London's biggest names. The tiny store near Carnaby Street brings together an exclusive selection of marvelously packaged perfumes from Europe and the US, including Mandy Aftel's Pink Lotus, which was specially commissioned for Madonna.

Space NK stocks the best and the most up-to-date collection of beauty products from around the world, along with its popular own-brand range. **The Body Shop** uses recyclable plastic packaging for its affordable natural cosmetics and toiletries, and encourages staff and customers alike to take an interest in environmental issues. **Molton Brown** sells a range of natural cosmetics, body and haircare products in branches throughout London. **The Studio Perfumery** stocks a selection of luxury brand fragrances and beauty products.

STATIONERY

For luxurious writing paper and desk accessories, try the Queen's stationer, **Smythson** of Bond Street. The little bound notebooks and address books embossed with a wide selection of amusing and practical titles, such as "Travel Notes" and "Blondes, Brunettes, Redheads" make great gifts and souvenirs. Fortnum and Mason *(see p321)* sells handsome leather-bound diaries, blotters and pencil holders, while Liberty *(see p109)* embellishes desk accessories with its famous Art Nouveau prints. For personal organizers covered in anything from vinyl to iguana skin, try **The Filofax Centre**. **Asprey** also sells a chic line of pocket diaries, organizers, key fobs and jewelry boxes in a variety of eye-catching skins.

Tessa Fantoni's attractive, paper-covered photo albums used to be sold at the Conran Shop and Harrods, but nowadays they are only available from her store in

Clapham, where you will also find an appealing selection of gifts, cards, and wrapping paper. Neisha Crosland's striking contemporary prints adorn a wide range of stationery items, including wrapping paper, cards and notebooks, as well as photograph albums.

Shepherd's Bookbinders stocks a range of handmade and decorative papers. Its marbled paper, can make a glorious giftwrap for that very special present. Finally, for greeting cards, pens, gift wrapping paper, and general stationery, pop into one of the branches of **Paperchase**.

INTERIORS

Wedgwood still makes the famous pale blue Jasper china that Josiah Wedgwood designed in the 18th century. You can buy this and the Irish Waterford crystal, at **Waterford Wedgwood** on Piccadilly. For a fine variety of original pottery, visit **Contemporary Ceramics**, the gallery of the Craft Potters Association, or go to **Contemporary Applied Arts**. **Mint's** hand-picked selection of unique furniture, home accessories, china and glassware by established names and up-and-coming design talent is a pleasure to browse. Large interior stores,

Heal's and the **Conran Shop**, have a great display of stylish, modern accessories for the home. Those with more traditional tastes may prefer **Thomas Goode**, presided over by courteous tail-coated staff, which sells exquisite china, glassware, crystal, linen, and gifts, including some antique pieces. The **Nicole Farhi Home** line exudes the same laid-back luxury as her clothes. If you're on a tighter budget, check out **Graham & Green**, which stocks a huge array of attractive items from around the globe, ranging from Moroccan tea glasses to Mongolian cushions and pretty nightwear.

Labour & Wait is a wonderful source of solid, functional British items for home and garden, such as old-fashioned stainless steel kettles, Welsh blankets and Guernsey sweaters. **David Mellor** is famous for his streamlined modern cutlery designs, while **Divertimenti** sells all manner of kitchen equipment and has a pleasant cafe at the back.

Bridgewater Pottery has chunky mugs, crockery, and kitchen towels, which are decorated with traditional motifs and amusing mottoes. The **Irish Linen Company** has everything from lacy hankies and appliquéd guest towels to kitchen towels and

tablecloths. **Cath Kidston** designs fresh, nostalgic, English-style prints that adorn everything from humble household items to fashion accessories. There's a huge range of pretty, giftable goods such as toiletries, ironing-board covers, laundry bags, bedspreads, clothes for women and children, bags, china, and stationery.

Several interiors stores on Upper Street in affluent Islington offer an impressive cache of gifts. **After Noah** is a big warehouse-like space bursting with vintage and retro-look items also include Bakelite rotary telephones, nostalgic toiletries, old metal tins and street signs, classic board games, and a huge assortment of children's toys. There is another branch in King's Road and a concession in Harvey Nichols *(see p321)*.

The modern interiors emporium **Aria** has two stores in the same vicinity. One of these concentrates entirely on furniture and housewares by designers such as Alessi and Philippe Starck, while its satellite across the street sells gifts, including stationery, frames, bags, and jewelry. Also on the same stretch is the contemporary-design heavyweight **twentytwentyone**.

DIRECTORY

GIFT STORES

Coco Ribbon
21 Kensington Park Rd W11.
Map 9 B2.
Tel 020-7229 4904.

Design Museum Shop
Shad Thames SE1.
Map 16 E4.
Tel 020-7940 8753.

Labour & Wait
18 Cheshire Street, Brick Lane.
Map 8 E4.
Tel 020-7729 6253.

Shelf
40 Cheshire St E2.
Map 8 E4.
Tel 020-7739 9444.

Story
4 Wilkes St E1. **Map** 8 E5.
Tel 020-7377 0313.

JEWELRY

Asprey
167 New Bond St W1.
Map 12 F3.
Tel 0870-905 0767.

Butler & Wilson
20 South Molton St W1.
Map 12 E2.
Tel 020-7409 2955.

Electrum Gallery
21 South Molton St W1.
Map 12 E2.
Tel 020-7629 6325.

Erickson Beamon
38 Elizabeth St SW1.
Map 20 E2.
Tel 020-7259 0202.

Garrard
24 Albemarle St W1.
Map 12 F3.
Tel 0870 871 8888.

Kabiri
37 Marylebone High St W1. **Map** 4 D5.
Tel 020-7317 2150.

Lesley Craze Gallery
33–35a Clerkenwell Green EC1. **Map** 6 E4.
Tel 020-7608 0393.

Wright & Teague
14 Grafton St W1. **Map** 12 F3. *Tel 020-7629 2777.*

HATS

Edward Bates
21a Jermyn St SW1.
Map 13 A3.
Tel 020-7734 2722.

Fred Bare
118 Columbia Rd E2.
Map 8 E3.
Tel 01904-624 579.

Herbert Johnson
54 St James's Street.
Map 12 F3.
Tel 020-7409 7277.

Lock & Co
6 St James's St SW1.
Map 12 F4.
Tel 020-7930 8874.

Philip Treacy
69 Elizabeth Street SW1.
Map 20 E2.
Tel 020-7730 3992.

Rachel Skinner
13 Princess Rd NW1.
Map 4 D1.
Tel 020-7209 0066.

DIRECTORY

Stephen Jones
36 Great Queen St WC2.
Map 13 C1.
Tel 020-7242 0770.

BAGS AND LEATHER GOODS

Anya Hindmarch
15–17 Pont St SW1.
Map 20 D1.
Tel 020-7838 9177.

Bill Amberg
14 Burlington Arcade W1.
Map 12 F3.
Tel 020-7499 0962.

Connolly
32 Grosvenor Crescent
Mews SW1. **Map** 12 D5.
Tel 020-7235 3883.

J. & M. Davidson
97 Goldborne Rd W10.
Tel 020-8969 2244.

Lulu Guinness
3 Ellis St SW1. **Map** 19 C2.
Tel 020-7823 4828.

Mulberry
41–42 New Bond St W1.
Map 12 E2.
Tel 020-7491 3900.

Radley
37 Floral St WC2. **Map** 13
B2. **Tel** *020-7379 9709.*

Swaine Adeney Brigg
54 St James's St SW1.
Map 12 F3.
Tel 020-7409 7277.

SCARVES

Fenwick
63 New Bond St W1.
Map 12 E2.
Tel 020-7629 9161.

Ginka by Neisha Crosland
137 Fulham Rd SW3.
Map 19 B2.
Tel 020-7978 4389.

V&A Enterprises
V & A Museum, Cromwell
Rd SW7. **Map** 19 A1.
Tel 020-7942 2696.

PERFUMES AND TOILETRIES

The Body Shop
64, 360 & 374, Oxford St
W1. **Map** 12 D2–F1.
Tel 020-7631 0027.

D. R. Harris
29 St James's St SW1.
Map 12 F3.
Tel 020-7930 3915.

Floris
89 Jermyn St SW1.
Map 13 A3.
Tel 0845-702 3239.

George F. Trumper
9 Curzon St W1.
Map 12 E3.
Tel 020-7499 1850.

Jo Malone
23 Brook St W1.
Map 12 E2.
Tel 0870-192 5181.

Molton Brown
58 South Molton St W1.
Map 12 E2.
Tel 020-7499 6474.

Miller Harris
21 Bruton St W1.
Map 12 E3.
Tel 020-7629 7750.

Neal's Yard Remedies
15 Neal's Yard WC2.
Map 13 B1.
Tel 020-7379 7222.

Penhaligon's
41 Wellington St WC2.
Map 13 C2.
Tel 020-7836 2150.

Scent Systems Studio
13 Rugby St WC1.
Map 6 D5.
Tel 0780-943 3153.

Space NK
131 Westbourne Grove
W2. **Map** 9 C2.
Tel 020-7727 8002.

The Studio Perfumery
170 Regent's Park Rd
NW1. **Map** 3 C1.
Tel 020-7722 1478.

Truefitt & Hill
71 St James's St SW1.
Map 12 F3.
Tel 020-7493 8496.

STATIONERY

Asprey
167 New Bond St W1.
Map 12 F3.
Tel 020-7493 6767.

The Filofax Centre
21 Conduit St W1.
Map 12 F2.
Tel 020-7499 0457.

Paperchase
213 Tottenham Court Rd
W1. **Map** 5 A5.
Tel 020-7467 6200.

Shepherd's Bookbinders
76 Southampton Row
WC1. **Map** 5 C5.
Tel 020-7831 1151.

Smythson
40 New Bond St W1.
Map 12 E2.
Tel 020-7629 8558.

Tessa Fantoni
73 Abbeville Rd SW4.
Tel 020-8673 1253.

INTERIORS

After Noah
121 Upper Street N1.
Map 6 F1.
Tel 020-7359 4281.

Aria
Barnsbury Hall,
Barnsbury St N1.
Map 6 F1.
Tel 020-7704 6222.

Bridgewater Pottery
81a Marylebone High St.
Map 4 D5.
Tel 020-7486 6897.
Also: 739 Fulham Road
Map 17 C5.
Tel 020-7371 5264.

Cath Kidston
51 Marylebone High St
W1. **Map** 4 D5.
Tel 020-7935 6555.

Conran Shop
Michelin House, 81
Fulham Rd SW3.
Map 19 A2.
Tel 020-7589 7401.

Contemporary Applied Arts
2 Percy St WC1.
Map 13 A1.
Tel 020-7436 2344.

Contemporary Ceramics
Somerset House,
Strand WC2.
Map 14 D2.
Tel 020-7845 4600.

David Mellor
4 Sloane Sq SW1.
Map 20 D2.
Tel 020-7730 4259.

Divertimenti
33–34 Marylebone High St
W1. **Map** 4 D5.
Tel 020-7935 0689.

Graham & Green
4 Elgin Crescent W11.
Map 9 B2.
Tel 020-7243 8908.

Heal's
196 Tottenham Court Rd
W1. **Map** 5 A5.
Tel 020-7636 1666.

Irish Linen Company
Burlington Arcade W1.
Map 12 F3.
Tel 020-7493 8949.

Mint
2 North Terrace SW3.
Map 19 A1.
Tel 020-7225 2228.

Nicole Farhi Home
17 Clifford St W1.
Map 12 F3.
Tel 020-7494 9051.

Thomas Goode
19 South Audley St W1.
Map 12 D3.
Tel 020-7499 2823.

twentytwentyone
274 Upper St N1.
Map 6 F1.
Tel 020-7288 1996.

Waterford Wedgwood
173–174 Piccadilly W1.
Map 12 F3.
Tel 020-7629 2614.

Art and Antiques

London's art and antique stores are spread across the length and breadth of the capital city. While the more fashionable and more expensive dealers are mainly concentrated in a relatively small area bounded by Mayfair and St. James's, other stores and galleries catering to a relatively modest budget are scattered over the rest of the city. Whether your taste is for Old Masters or young modern artists, Boule or Bauhaus, you are bound to find something of beauty in London that is within your financial means.

MAYFAIR

Cork Street is the center of the British contemporary art world. The huge line-up of galleries offers work in varying degrees of the avant-garde. The biggest name to look out for is **Waddington Galleries**, and if you want to discover the flavor of the month, a stop here is a must. However, purchasing is only for the serious and rich collector. The **Mayor Gallery**, famous for Dada and Surrealism, was the first gallery to open in the street. **Redfern Gallery** shows mainstream modern art while **Flowers Central**, part of a growing modern-gallery chain, has some unusual British pieces. A couple of doors down, **Browse and Darby Gallery** sells 19th- and 20th-century British and French paintings as well as contemporary works.

Also look into Clifford Street, where **Maas Gallery** excels in Victorian masters, and Sackville Street for **Henry Sotheran's** rare books and prints. Walk down Dover Street toward Piccadilly and, on your right you'll see a discreet sign for the **Piccadilly Gallery**, which sells modern British pictures. Although it's tucked away in the building's basement, casual visitors are always welcome.

Nearby, New Bond Street is the center of the fine antiques trade in London. If it's Turner watercolors or Louis XV furniture you're after, this is the place. A walk up from Piccadilly takes you past the lush portals of **Richard Green** (which also has a gallery in Dover Street) and the **Fine Art Society**, among other extremely smart galleries. For jewelry and objets d'art visit **David Aaron Ancient Art** and **Grays Antique Market**; for silver go to **S. J. Phillips**; and for 18th-century British furniture and art, try **Mallet Antiques**.

Even if you are not a buyer, these galleries are fascinating places to visit, so don't be afraid to walk in – you can learn more from an hour spent here than you can from weeks of studying text books. Also on New Bond Street are two of the big London auction houses, Bonhams and Sotheby's.

ST. JAMES'S

South of Piccadilly lies a maze of 18th-century streets. This is gentlemen's club country (see Pall Mall p92) and the galleries mostly reflect the traditional nature of the area. The center is Duke Street, home of Old Master dealers, **Johnny van Haeften** and **Derek Johns**. Nearby, on King Street, you will find the main salerooms of **Christie's**, the well-known auction house where Van Goghs and Picassos change hands for millions. On the corner of Bury Street, celebrating past masculine pleasures is the sophisticated **Pullman Gallery**, which specializes in automobile art and collectables, vintage cocktail shakers, racy cigarette cases, and other bar accessories.

Walk back up Bury Street past several interesting galleries, including the **Tryon Gallery** for traditional British sporting pictures and fine sculptures. Also duck into Ryder Street to take in **Chris Beetle's** gallery of works by illustrators and caricaturists.

KNIGHTSBRIDGE

If you walk around to the back of **Harrods** (see p321), you'll find the beginning of pretty Walton Street, which is lined with art galleries, traditional interior stores, and boutiques. As you would expect in this exclusive area, prices are high. On nearby Brompton Road the **Crane Kalman** gallery shows an enticing variety of contemporary art. Not far away is **Harvey Nichols** (see p321), Knightsbridge's other swish department store. Motcomb Street houses some notable galleries, including the fascinating **Mathaf Gallery**, which features 19th-century British and European paintings of the Arab world.

PIMLICO ROAD

The antique stores that line this road tend to cater predominantly to the pricey requirements of the interior decorator. This is where to come if you are searching for an Italian leather screen or a silver-encrusted ram's skull. Of particular fascination is **Westenholz**. While he doesn't deal in antiques, the Queen's nephew, furniture designer **Viscount Linley**, produces some beautiful pieces that could pass as such, as well as contemporary designs. The finely crafted accessories, such as inlaid wooden boxes and frames, make great gifts.

EAST AND WEST

London's East End is a growth area for contemporary art. In addition to the famous **White Cube Gallery** in Hoxton Square and **Flowers East** in Kingsland Road, there is a cluster of art dealers and galleries in **The Tea Building** on nearby Shoreditch High Street. **The Approach** combines an upstairs gallery with a good pub, frequented by local artists.

On the other side of the river in southeast London, **Purdy Hicks**, based in a converted warehouse near Tate Modern, is great for contemporary British painting. Over in Mayfair, **Eyestorm** is a gallery that shows the work of both leading and emerging artists.

The **Oxo Tower Wharf**, in a landmark Thameside building topped by a good restaurant, is a hive of creativity, housing over 30 design and craft studios. You can find everything from handwoven textiles and jewelry to homewares and fashion. Among the highlights are Black + Blum's innovative, affordable interior designs – for example, a lamp in the shape of a reading figure, made up of a lightbulb "holding" a book shade. Bodo Sperlain's delicate modern china and Studio Fusion's striking enamel pieces are also a draw for the visitors.

There are also some very interesting contemporary galleries in the vicinity of Portobello Road and Westbourne Grove. Some of the popular names include, **East West Gallery** for contemporary art, **Themes & Variations**, which combines striking post-war and contemporary furniture and decorative art, and **The State of the Art**, selling works ranging from pop art and graffiti to fine art and photography.

A browse along Kensington Church Street in west London will reveal everything from Arts and Crafts furniture to Staffordshire dogs in a concentration of small antiques emporia.

NORTH

High-profile American dealer Larry Gagosian has been at the forefront of the regeneration of famously sleazy King's Cross by opening his second gallery here, in a capacious former garage. Expect world-class contemporary names as well as lesser-known artists at **Gagosian Gallery**. **Victoria Miro's** massive Victorian warehouse in Islington is a showcase for British as well as young international talent. At its two spaces in the same quiet Marylebone Street, the **Lisson Gallery** often features cutting-edge installations. **Thompson's Gallery** has locations in

Marylebone and the City, selling a diverse mix of appealing if somewhat mainstream current British art.

AFFORDABLE ART

For the chance to acquire a work by what could become one of the big names of the future, visit the **Contemporary Art Society**. Its annual ARTFutures market showcases the work of more than 100 artists, their prices run from £100 into the thousands.

Open seven days a week all year round, **Will's Art Warehouse** in Putney sells pieces from £50–£3,000. This friendly gallery offers a wide variety of art to choose from and holds a new exhibition every six weeks. The owner founded the aptly named Affordable Art Fair, which takes place twice a year in Battersea Park.

PHOTOGRAPHY

The largest collection of original photographs for sale in the country is at the **Photographers' Gallery**. **Special Photographers Company** is well known for selling top-quality work by unknown artists as well as some famous photographic names. **Hamiltons Gallery** is worth visiting, especially during its major exhibitions.

Michael Hoppen's new three-floor space in Chelsea shows both vintage and current works. If you want to take home a piece of London's rock n' roll heritage, the **Rock Archive**, near Camden Passage in Islington, is a great source of limited-edition prints of British music legends such as Paul Weller posing with Pete Townshend or Mick Jagger jamming with Ronnie Wood.

To pick up an interesting work on a budget, head to **55 Max**, where limited-edition framed prints often cost £55. It showcases a range of subjects and styles by young photographers and photojournalists, from moody London cityscapes and abstractions to fashion and celebrity shots.

BRIC-À-BRAC AND COLLECTABLES

For smaller, more affordable pieces, it's worth going to one of the established London markets, such as Portobello Road, Alfies Antique Market, Camden Passage (see p340), or Bermondsey (see p339), which is the main antiques market, catering to the trade. Conveniently situated in the city's main shopping district, Grays Antique Markets (see p340) have some great specialist dealers, but the prices are a bit higher than elsewhere given the location, while farther afield, Greenwich Market (see p340) is well worth a rummage and may unearth some bargains. Many high streets out of the center of town have covered markets of specialist stalls.

Cary Grant's small store hidden on a side street near Sadlers Wells contains a collector's cache of immaculate post-war ceramics by the modern designers of the day, including the young Terence Conran.

AUCTIONS

If you are confident enough, auctions are a much cheaper way to buy art or antiques, but be sure to read the small print in the catalog, which usually costs around £15. Bidding is simple – you need to register, take a number, then raise your hand when the lot you want comes up. The auctioneer will see your bid. It's as easy as that, and can be great fun.

The main auction houses in London are **Christie's Fine Art Auctioneers**, **Sotheby's Auctioneers**, and **Bonhams**. Don't forget Christie's sale room in Kensington, and Sotheby's premises in Olympia, which both offer art and antiques for the modest budget. Bonhams' second London saleroom in Knightsbridge holds weekly auctions of affordable antiques and collectables.

DIRECTORY

MAYFAIR

Browse and Darby Gallery
19 Cork St W1.
Map 12 F3.
Tel 020-7734 7984.

David Aaron Ancient Art
22 Berkeley Square W1.
Map 12 E3.
Tel 020-7491 9588.

Fine Art Society
148 New Bond St W1.
Map 12 E2.
Tel 020-7629 5116.

Flowers Central
21 Cork St W1.
Map 12 F3.
Tel 020-7439 7766.

Grays Antique Markets
58 Davies St & 1-7 Davies Mews W1. **Map** 12 E2.
Tel 020-7629 7034.

Henry Sotheran
2–5 Sackville St W1.
Map 12 F3.
Tel 020-7439 6151.

Maas Gallery
15a Clifford St W1.
Map 12 F3.
Tel 020-7734 2302.

Mallet Antiques
141 New Bond St W1.
Map 12 E2.
Tel 020-7499 7411.

Mayor Gallery
22a Cork St W1.
Map 12 F3.
Tel 020-7734 3558.

Piccadilly Gallery
43 Dover St W1.
Map 12 F3.
Tel 020-7629 2875.

Redfern Gallery
20 Cork St W1.
Map 12 F3.
Tel 020-7734 1732.

Richard Green
33 & 147 New Bond St.
Also: 39 Dover St W1.
Map 12 E2.
Tel 020-7493 3939.

S. J. Phillips
139 New Bond St W1.
Map 12 E2.
Tel 020-7629 6261.

Waddington Galleries
11, 12, 34 Cork St W1.
Map 12 F3.
Tel 020-7851 2200.

ST. JAMES'S

Chris Beetle
8 & 10 Ryder St SW1.
Map 12 F3.
Tel 020-7839 7551.

Derek Johns
12 Duke St SW1.
Map 12 F3.
Tel 020-7839 7671.

Johnny van Haeften
13 Duke St SW1.
Map 12 F3.
Tel 020-7930 3062.

Pullman Gallery
14 King St SW1.
Map 12 F4.
Tel 020-7930 9595.

Tryon Gallery
7 Bury St SW1.
Map 12 F3.
Tel 020-7839 8083.

KNIGHTSBRIDGE

Crane Kalman
178 Brompton Rd SW3.
Map 19 B1.
Tel 020-7584 7566.

Mathaf Gallery
24 Motcomb St SW1.
Map 12 D5.
Tel 020-7235 0010.

PIMLICO ROAD

Viscount Linley
60 Pimlico Rd SW1.
Map 20 D2.
Tel 020-7730 7300.

Westenholz
80–82 Pimlico Rd SW1.
Map 20 D2.
Tel 020-7824 8090.

EAST AND WEST

The Approach
1st Floor, 47
Approach Rd E2.
Tel 020-8983 3878.

East West Gallery
8 Blenheim Cres W11.
Map 8 D4.
Tel 020-7229 7981.

Eyestorm
27 Hill St W1.
Map 12 E3.
Tel 0845-643 2001.

Flowers East
82 Kingsland Rd E2.
Tel 020-7920 7777.

Oxo Tower Wharf
Bargehouse St SE1.
Map 14 E3.
Tel 020-7021 1600.

Purdy Hicks
65 Hopton St SE1.
Map 14 F3.
Tel 020-7401 9229.

The State of the Art
281 Portobello Rd W10.
Map 9 A1. *Tel 0770 868 932, 0184-428 1812.*

The Tea Building
56 Shoreditch High St E1.
Map 8 D4.
Tel 020-7729 2973.

Themes & Variations
231 Westbourne Grove W11. **Map** 9 B2.
Tel 020-7727 5531.

White Cube Gallery
Hoxton Square N1.
Map 7 C3.
Tel 020-7930 5373.

NORTH

Gagosian Gallery
6–24 Britannia St WC1.
Map 5 C3.
Tel 020-7841 9960.

Lisson Gallery
29 & 52-54 Bell St NW1.
Map 3 B5.
Tel 020-7724 2739.

Thompson's Gallery
76 Marylebone High St W1.
Map 4 D5.
Tel 020-7935 3595.

Victoria Miro
16 Wharf Rd N1.
Map 7 A2.
Tel 020-7336 8109.

AFFORDABLE ART

Contemporary Art Society
11–15 Emerald St WC1.
Map 6 D5.
Tel 020-7831 1243.

Will's Art Warehouse
180 Lower Richmond Rd SW15.
Tel 020-8246 4840.

PHOTOGRAPHY

Hamiltons Gallery
13 Carlos Place London W1. **Map** 12 E3.
Tel 020-7499 9493.

55 Max
6 Lonsdale Rd,
Queen's Park NW6.
Tel 020-7625 3774.

Michael Hoppen
3 Jubilee Place SW3.
Map 19 B3.
Tel 020-7352 3649.

Photographers' Gallery
16–18 Ramilies St W1.
Map 12 F1.
Tel 0845-262 1618.

Rock Archive
110 Islington High St N1.
Map 6 F2.
Tel 020-7704 0598.

Special Photographers Company
236 Westbourne Park Rd W11. **Map** 9 B1.
Tel 020-7221 3489.

BRIC-À-BRAC AND COLLECTABLES

Cary Grant
18 Arlington Way EC1.
Map 6 E3.
Tel 020-7713 1122.

AUCTIONS

Bonhams, W. & F.C., Auctioneers
Montpelier St SW7.
Map 11 B5.
Tel 020-7393 3900.
Also: 101 New Bond St W1. **Map** 12 E2.
Tel 020-7447 7447.

Christie's Fine Art Auctioneers
8 King St SW1. **Map** 12 F4.
Tel 020-7839 9060.
Also: 85 Old Brompton Road SW7. **Map** 18 F2.
Tel 020-7930 6074.

Sotheby's Auctioneers
34–35 New Bond St W1.
Map 12 E2.
Tel 020-7293 5000.
Also: Hammersmith Rd W14.
Map 17 A1.
Tel 020-7293 5555.

Markets

Even if you're not looking for cut-priced cabbages or a silk sari, it's worth paying a visit to one of London's crowded, colorful markets. Many mix English traditions with those of more recent immigrants, creating an exotic atmosphere and a fascinating patchwork quilt of merchandise. At some, the seasoned cockney hawkers have honed their sales patter to an entertaining art, which reaches fever pitch just before closing time as they advertise ever-plummeting prices. Keep your wits about you and your hand on your purse and join in the fun. For details go to www.visitlondon.com.

Archway Market

Holloway Rd N19. ⊖ *Archway.*
🚌 *4, 17, 41, 43, 143, 271.* **Open** *10:30am–6pm Thu, 10am–5pm Sat.*

This young and growing market is one of North London's best kept secrets. Its specialty traders are committed to offering shoppers things that can't be bought anywhere else, including organic cheeses, breads, and cakes, gourmet pickles and chutneys, farm-pressed juices and much more. Tasty lunch options include Breton crêpes, spicy curries, and organic hot dogs. Several craft stalls sell unusual objects and gifts.

Bermondsey Market (New Caledonian Market)

Long Lane and Bermondsey St SE1. **Map** 15 C5. ⊖ *London Bridge, Borough.* **Open** *4am–1pm Fri. Starts closing midday. See p182.*

Bermondsey is the gathering point for London's antique traders every Friday. Serious collectors start early and scrutinize the paintings, the silver and the vast array of old jewelry. Browsers might uncover some interesting curiosities but most bargains go before 9am.

Berwick Street Market

Berwick St W1. **Map** 13 A1. ⊖ *Piccadilly Circus, Leicester Sq.* **Open** *9am–6pm Mon–Sat. See p108.*

The spirited costermongers of Soho's Berwick Street sell some of the cheapest and most attractive fruit and vegetables in the West End. Spanish black radish, star fruit, and Italian plum tomatoes are among the produce you might find here, in addition to the various nuts and sweets. The market is good for fabrics and cheap household goods, too, as well as for leather handbags and delicatessen items. Separated from Berwick Street by a seedy passageway is the quieter Rupert Street market, where stallholders sell cheap street fashion.

Borough Market

Southwark St SE1. **Map** 14 F3. ⊖ *London Bridge.* **Open** *11am–5pm Thu, noon–6pm Fri, 8am–5pm Sat. See p176.*

On one of London's most ancient trading sites, Borough has for many years been a wholesale market catering to the restaurant and hotel trade. Now open to the public from Thursday to Saturday, the award-winning market has a reputation as London's premier center for fine foods, selling a vast array of British and international foodstuffs. Among the cornucopia is organic meat, fish, and produce, top-quality handmade cheeses, breads, sweets, chocolates, coffees and teas, and also soaps. It's a favorite foraging ground for the city's celebrity chefs.

Brick Lane Market

Brick Lane E1. **Map** 8 E5. ⊖ *Shoreditch, Liverpool St, Aldgate East.* **Open** *11am–6pm Sat, 10am–5pm Sun. See pp170–1.*

This massively popular East End jamboree is at its best around its gloriously frayed edges. Pick through the mish-mash of junk sold on Bethnal Green Road or head east on Cheshire Street, past the new outcrop of fashionable home-design and gift stores, to explore the indoor stalls, packed with tatty furniture and old books. Much of the action takes place in cobbled, Sclater Street and the lots on either side. Here you'll find everything from fresh shellfish and trainers to old power tools and new bicycles. Farther south on Brick Lane itself, the trendy boutiques and cafés give way to spice shops and curry restaurants in this center for London's Bangladeshi community.

Brixton Market

Electric Ave SW9. ⊖ *Brixton.* **Open** *8am–6pm Mon, Tue, Thu–Sat; 8am–3pm Wed.*

This market offers a wonderful assortment of Afro-Caribbean food, from goats' meat, pigs' feet, and salt fish to plantain, yams, and breadfruit. There is an abundance of produce in the large Brixton Village and Market Row arcades, where exotic fish are a highlight. You'll also find Afro-style wigs, strange herbs and potions, traditional African ensembles and fabrics, and children's toys. From record stalls, the bass of raw reggae pounds through this cosmopolitan market like a heartbeat.

Broadway Market

Broadway Market, between Andrews Rd & Westgate St E8. 🚌 *394.* **Open** *8am–6pm Sat.*

Although this market is a bit tricky to get to because it's not served by the tube, it's worth getting a bus from Islington or walking from Bethnal Green tube. One of London's oldest, Broadway Market had gone into decline until its rebirth as a popular organic farmers' market. On Saturdays the historic street running between London Fields and the Regent's Canal, comes alive with around 40 stalls selling fruit and vegetables, cheeses, baked goods, meats, and confectionery. Also lining Broadway Market are some interesting, arty stores catering to the young creative types who have been colonizing this part of Hackney over the past couple of decades. Black Truffle (No.74), owned by shoemaker Melissa Needham, stocks a range of accessories made by independent designers – both local and international – while textile designer Barley Massey sells her own unusual designs and those of others at Fabrications (No.7). L'Eau à la Bouche (No.49) is a superior deli offering everthing from charcuterie to fruit tarts. There are also a couple of contemporary galleries such as Flaca (No.69) and Seven Seven (No.75–77). When it's time to refuel, duck into the Dove pub (No.24–28) for a choice of Belgian beers.

Camden Lock Market

Chalk Farm Road NW1. ⊖ *Camden Town.* **Open** *10am–5:30pm Mon–Fri, 10am–6pm Sat and Sun.*

Camden Lock Market has grown swiftly since its opening in 1974, spreading along Chalk Farm Road and Camden High Street. Crafts, new and second-hand street fashion, organic foods, books, records, and antiques form the bulk of the goods that a shopper can choose from. Often, thousands of young people come here simply to enjoy the vibrant atmosphere, especially at weekends when Camden Lock is abuzz with activity *(see p246).*

Camden Passage Market

Camden Passage N1. **Map** 6 F1. 🚇 *Angel*. **Open** 9am–6pm Wed, Sat.

Camden Passage is a quiet walk-way where cafés nestle among bijou antique stores. Prints, silver-ware, 19th-century magazines, jewelry, and toys are among the many collectables that are on show. Don't miss the tiny stores tucked away in the atmospherically poky Pierrepont Arcade; one is precari-ously stacked with 18th and 19th-century porcelain; another spe-cializes in antique puzzles and games. Jubilee Photographica deals in photographs from the 19th century onward. The passage is also lined with stores – Annie's Vintage Clothes is known for pristine 1920s–40s frocks, while Origin sells classic 20th-century furniture. There's a specialist book market on Thursdays.

Chapel Market

Chapel Market N1. **Map** 6 E2. 🚇 *Angel*. **Open** 9am–3:30pm Tue, Wed, Fri, Sat; 9am–1pm Thu, Sun.

This is one of London's most traditional and exuberant street markets. Weekends are best; the fruit and vegetables are varied and cheap, the fish stalls are the finest in the area, there are also stalls sell-ing European delicacies and cheeses and a wealth of bargain household goods and clothes.

Church Street Market

Church St NW8 and Bell St NW1. **Map** 3 A5. 🚇 *Edgware Rd*. **Open** 8am–6pm Mon–Sat.

Like many of London's markets, Church Street reaches a crescendo on the weekends. On Friday and Saturday, stalls selling cheap clothes, household goods, fish, cheese, and antiques join the everyday fruit and vegetable stalls. Alfies Antique Market (No.13–25) houses around 100 dealers selling everything from jewelry to furniture.

There is also a cluster of interesting stand-alone antique furniture stores, plus the fascinating Gallery of Antique Costume and Textiles (No.2), which showcases immaculate garments dating back as far as the 17th century.

Columbia Road Market

Columbia Rd E2. **Map** 8 D3. 🚇 *Shoreditch, Old St*. **Open** 8am–3pm Sun. See p171.

This is the perfect place to come to buy greenery and blossoms, or just to enjoy the fragrances and colors. Cut flowers, plants, shrubs, seedlings, and pots are all sold at about half their normal prices on a Sunday morning in this charming Victorian street. (During December, as you might expect, there's a brisk trade in Christmas trees.) There are also some lovely stores that keep market hours, such as Angela Flanders' pretty perfumerie (No.96), Salon for vintage jewelry and cufflinks (No.142), and hip hatter, Fred Bare (No.118).

When you're shopped out, have tea at Treacle (No.160), which turns out cute retro cupcakes and classic jam sponge cakes, plus cups of proper tea to wash them down. There is also a selection of vintage and modern china for sale. People with a sweet tooth can snack on deep-fried prawns from hole in the wall, Lee's Seafoods (No.134).

Earlham Street Market

Earlham St WC2. **Map** 13 B2. 🚇 *Covent Garden*. **Open** 10am–4pm Mon–Sat.

Situated on a short road just off Shaftesbury Avenue, this market is a small affair. Several stalls sell a range of items from exotic flowers and secondhand clothes to fashion jewelry and accessories.

East Street Market

East St SE17. 🚇 *Elephant and Castle*. **Open** 8am–5pm Tue–Fri, 8am–6.30pm Sat; 8am–2pm, Sun.

East Street Market's high spot is Sunday, when more than 250 stalls fill the narrow street and a small plant and flower market is set up on Blackwood Street. The majority of traders sell clothes, accessories, and household goods, although there is plenty of British and Afro-Caribbean produce, fish, and other delicacies. Charlie Chaplin (see p37) was born in this street and sought inspiration for his characters in the area.

Gabriel's Wharf and Riverside Walk Markets

56 Upper Ground and Riverside Walk SE1. **Map** 14 E3. 🚇 *Waterloo*. **Gabriel's Wharf Open** 11am–6pm Tue–Sun; **Riverside Walk open** noon–7pm Sat, Sun. See p191.

Little stores filled with ceramics, paintings, and jewelry surround a bandstand in Gabriel's Wharf where jazz groups sometimes play in the summer. A few stalls are set up around the courtyard, selling ethnic clothing and handmade jewelry and pottery. The book market under Waterloo Bridge includes a good selection of new and old Penguin paperbacks.

Grays Antique Markets

58 Davies St & 1–7 Davies Mews W1. **Map** 12 E2. 🚇 *Bond Street*. **Open** 10am–6pm Mon–Fri; 11am–5pm Sat.

Conveniently placed in the West End, Grays probably isn't the place to bag a bargain – the liveried doorman is a tip-off that this place is posh – but it makes a pleasant place to browse. There are some lovely pieces here, from costume jewelry and fabulous vintage fashion to enamel boxes and modern first editions from Biblion bookseller.

Greenwich Market

College Approach SE10. **Map** 23 B2. 🚆 *Greenwich*. 🚇 *Cutty Sark DLR*. **Open** 10am–5:30pm Wed–Sun.

At weekends, the area west of Hotel Ibis accommodates dozens of trestle tables piled with coins, medals, banknotes, second-hand books, Art Deco furniture, assorted bric-à-brac, and vintage clothing. The covered crafts market specializes in wooden toys, clothes made by young designers, hand-made jewelry, and accessories.

Jubilee and Apple Markets

Covent Gdn Piazza WC2. **Map** 13 C2. 🚆 *Covent Gdn*. **Open** 9am–5pm daily.

Covent Garden has become the center of London streetlife, with some of the capital's best busking. Both these markets sell crafts and designs. The Apple Market, inside the Piazza where the famous fruit and vegetable market was housed (see p114), has knitwear, jewelry and novelty goods. Jubilee Hall sells antiques on Monday, crafts on the weekend, and a large selection of clothes, handbags, cosmetics, and tacky mementoes in between. During the first weekend of November, the Covent Garden Market is the venue for renowned food writer, Henrietta Green's Food Lovers' Fair. During that time it comes alive with around 100 speciality food producers from all over Britain. The event also features cookery demonstrations and celebrity chefs.

Leadenhall Market

Whittington Ave EC3. **Map** 15 C2. 🚇 *Bank, Monument*. **Open** 7am–4pm Mon–Fri. See p159.

There has been a marketplace on this site since medieval times, but the present spectacular, glass-roofed structure was built in 1881. Leadenhall Market was traditionally famous for fish, meat, and poultry, but only fishmonger

H. S. Linwood & Sons remains. The smart, red and green facades now bear the names of upmarket clothing chains, restaurants, pubs, and gift stores. Leadenhall does, however, retain something of its reputation as a center of fine food. More than a dozen stalls set up store on the cobblestones beneath this dramatic structure Monday to Friday from 11am to 4pm. Wares include European cheeses, cured meats, baked goods, condiments, and other gourmet goods as well.

Leather Lane Market

Leather Lane EC1. **Map** 6 E5.
🚇 *Farringdon, Chancery Lane.*
Open *10:30am–2pm Mon–Fri.*

This ancient street, originally called Leveroun Lane, has played host to a market for over 300 years. The history of the Lane, however, has nothing to do with leather. Stalls here sell cut-price high-street clothes, plus shoes, bags, jewelry, and accessories. All are well worth having a browse through.

Marylebone Farmers' Market

Cramer St parking lot, behind Marylebone High St W1. **Map** 4 D5.
🚇 *Baker Street, Bond Street.*
Open *10am–2pm Sun.*

In response to Britain's interest in local organic produce, weekly markets have sprung up all over the city. This enables farmers and other producers to sell directly to the public. Marylebone is the largest and most central, offering seasonal fruit and vegetables, dairy products, fish, meat, breads, preserves, and sauces. There is also a lineup of excellent gourmet stores in adjacent Moxon Street, including a renowned rare-breed pork butcher, the Ginger Pig, and La Fromagerie delicatessen with its extensive cheese cave. Other locations include Islington Green and the parking lot behind Waterstone's, Notting Hill.

Old Spitalfields Market

Commercial St E1. **Map** 8 E5.
🚇 *Aldgate East, Liverpool Street.*
Open *10am–4pm Mon–Fri,
9am–5pm Sun. See p170.*

The main market is on a Sunday, and is a mecca for those interested in the latest street fashion trends. Many young designers have stalls, and prices are also reasonable. The stalls are of mixed quality, so you have to really search for the gems. The organic food stalls and a selection of cafés make it a good brunch venue any day. A varying number of stalls are open during the week.

Petticoat Lane Market

Middlesex St E1. **Map** 16 D1.
🚇 *Liverpool St, Aldgate, Aldgate East.* **Open** *9am–2pm Sun
(Wentworth St 10am–2:30pm
Mon–Fri). See p169.*

Probably the most famous of all London's street markets, Petticoat Lane continues to attract many thousands of visitors and locals every Sunday. The prices may not be as cheap as some of those to be found elsewhere, but the sheer volume of leather goods, clothes (the Lane's traditional strong point), watches, cheap jewelry and toys more than make up for that. A variety of fast-food sellers do a brisk trade catering for the bustling crowds that throng the market on a weekend.

Piccadilly Crafts Market

St. James's Church, Piccadilly W1.
Map 13 A3. 🚇 *Piccadilly Circus,
Green Park.* **Open** *Antiques:
10am–6pm Tues. Arts and crafts:
10am–6pm Wed–Sat.*

Many of the markets in the Middle Ages were held in churchyards and Piccadilly Crafts Market is rekindling that ancient tradition. It is aimed mostly at visitors rather than locals, and the merchandise on display ranges from tacky T-shirts to wooden toys. All are spread out in the shadow of Wren's beautiful church *(see p90).*

Portobello Road Market

Portobello Rd W10. **Map** 9 C3.
🚇 *Notting Hill Gate, Ladbroke
Grove.* **Open** *antiques and junk:
5:30am–5:30pm Sat. General market:
9am–5pm Mon–Wed, Fri, Sat;
9am–1pm Thu. See p219.*

Portobello Road is really three or four markets rolled into one. The Notting Hill end has more than 1,000 stalls in numerous arcades and on the street, displaying a compendium of objets d'art, jewelry, old medals, paintings, and silverware. Most stalls are managed by experts, so bargains are very rare. Farther down the gentle hill, antiques give way to fruit and vegetables.

The next transformation comes under the Westway flyover, where young fashion designers sell inexpensive creations alongside second-hand clothes, record, and food stalls on Fridays and Saturdays. It's also worth venturing into the covered Portobello Green market, which has an interesting mix of small stores selling everything from avant-garde fashion to kitsch cushions and lingerie. From this point on, the market becomes increasingly shabby.

Ridley Road Market

Ridley Rd E8. 🚋 *Dalston.* **Open**
*9am–3pm Mon–Wed, 9am–noon
Thu, 9am–5pm Fri, Sat.*

Early last century Ridley Road was a center of the Jewish community. Since then, Asians, Greeks, Turks, and West Indians have also settled in the area and the market is a lively celebration of this cultural mix. Highlights include the 24-hour bagel bakery, shanty-town shacks selling green bananas and reggae records, colorful drapery stalls, and cheap fruit and vegetables.

Roman Road Market

Roman Rd, between Parnell Rd and St Stephen's Rd E3. 🚇 *Bethnal Green.*
🚌 *8.* **Open** *10am–3pm Tue & Thu;
9am–4pm Sat. Farmers' market 1st
Sat of month.*

This lively market established in the 19th century has a real East End flavor and traditionally sells everything from cheap bedding and fashion to cut-price cleaning products and fruit and vegetables. Chances are that you'll be treated to some colorful cockney patter from the stallholders trying to drum up business. Recently, some more unusual vendors have been added to the mix, thus offering a unique variety to please the customers.

When you pay a visit to the Roman Road Market, you may just be tempted to buy some of the handmade jewelry, vintage clothes, or antiques being sold at the stalls.

Shepherd's Bush Market

Goldhawk Rd W12.
🚇 *Goldhawk Road, Shepherd's
Bush.* **Open** *9am–6pm Mon–Sat.*

A focal point for many of the local ethnic communities, this rambling market contains an impressive volume of eclectic wares.

West Indian food, Afro wigs, Asian spices, exotic fish, rugs, and other household goods are just some of the major attractions. There are acres of cheap clothing for every occasion, from floral flannel nighties and men's suits to clubwear and elaborately beaded wedding gowns. Cheap fabric stalls are a highlight of the Shepherd's Bush Market, and there is even an on-site tailor and barber, if you please.

ENTERTAINMENT IN LONDON

London has the enormous, multilayered variety of entertainment that only the great cities of the world can provide, and, as always, the city's historical backdrop adds depth to the experience. While few things could be more contemporary than dancing the night away in style at a famed nightclub such as Café de Paris or Heaven, you could also

Café sign advertising free live music

choose to spend the evening picturing the ghosts of long-dead Hamlets pacing ancient boards in the shadow of one of the living legends that grace the West End theaters today. There's a healthy, innovative fringe theater scene, too, plus world-class ballet and opera in fabled venues such as Sadler's Wells, the Royal Opera House, and the Coliseum. In London you'll be able to hear the best music, ranging from classical, jazz, and rock to rhythm and blues, while dedicated movie buffs can choose from hundreds of different films each night, both in large, multiscreen complexes and excellent small independent movie theaters. Sports fans can watch a game of cricket at Lords, cheer on oarsmen on the Thames, or eat strawberries and cream at Wimbledon. Should you be feeling adventurous and sporty yourself, you could try going for a horse ride along Rotten Row in Hyde Park. There are festivals, celebrations, and sports to attend, and there's plenty for children to do, too – in fact, there's plenty for everyone to do. Whatever you want, you'll be sure to find it on offer in London; it's just a question of knowing where to look.

Cultural classics: a concert at Kenwood House *(top)*; open-air theater at Regent's Park *(above left)*; performers at the Coliseum *(above right)*

INFORMATION SOURCES

For details of events in London, check the comprehensive weekly listings and review magazine *Time Out* (published every Tuesday), sold at most newsagents and many bookstores. The commuter newspaper *Metro* (weekdays) and London's evening newspaper, the *Evening Standard*, are both free and give brief daily listings. The *Independent* has daily listings and also reviews a different arts sector every day, plus a weekly round-up section, "The Information"; the *Guardian* has arts reviews in its G2 section every day and weekly listings in "The Guide" on Saturday. The *Independent, Guardian*, and *The Times* all have lists of ticket availability.

Specialized news sheets, brochures, and advance listings are distributed free in the foyers of theaters, concert halls, movie theaters, and arts complexes such as the South Bank and Barbican. Tourist information offices and hotel foyers often have the same publications. Fly posters advertise forthcoming events on billboards everywhere.

The Society of London Theatre (SOLT) publishes an informative free broadsheet every two weeks, available in many theater lobbies. It tends to concentrate on mainstream theaters, but does provide invaluable information about what's on. The National Theatre and the Royal Shakespeare Company also publish free broadsheets detailing future performances, distributed at the theaters.

SOLT's website (www.officiallondontheatre.co.uk) provides full details of current productions. It also has news, interviews, access information and online ticket booking. Many theaters operate a faxback service which enables you to see a seating plan showing the unsold seats for any performance.

Line-up from the Royal Ballet, on stage at Covent Garden

BUYING TICKETS

Some of the more popular shows and plays in London's West End – the latest Lloyd Webber musical for instance – can be totally sold out for weeks and even months ahead and you will find it impossible to purchase any tickets. This is not the norm, though, and most tickets will be available on the night, especially if you would be prepared to wait in line in front of the theater for returns. However, for a stress-free vacation it helps to purchase tickets in advance; this will ensure that you get the day, time, and seats that you want. You can purchase tickets from the box office in person, by telephone, online, or by mail. Quite a few hotels have concierges or porters who will give advice on where to go and arrange tickets for you.

Box offices are usually open from about 10am–8pm, and accept payment by cash, credit card, traveler's check or else a personal UK check

Palace Theatre plaque

when supported by a check guarantee card. Many venues will now sell unclaimed or returned tickets just before the performance; ask at the box office for the time to get in line. To reserve seats by telephone, call the box office and either pay on arrival or send payment – seats are usually held for three days. Some venues now have separate phone numbers for your credit card purchases – check before you call. Reserve your seat, and always take your credit card with you when you collect your ticket. Some smaller venues do not accept credit cards.

DISABLED VISITORS

Many London venues are old buildings and were not originally designed with disabled visitors in mind, but

many facilities have been updated, particularly to give access to those using wheelchairs, or for those with hearing difficulties.

Telephone the box office prior to your visit to reserve the special seating places or equipment, which are often limited. Special discounts may be available: for details and information on facilities call Artsline (020-7388 2227, www.artsline.org.uk).

TRANSPORTATION

Night buses (see p383) are now the preferred late-night mode of transportation, or phone for a cab from the venue. If you find yourself outside the city center late at night, do not rely on being able to hail a black taxi quickly in the street. Never take an unlicensed mini-cab. The Underground usually runs until just after midnight, but check the timetables in the stations (see pp380–81).

TICKET AGENCIES

The major listings magazines

Tickets are also available from agencies. Try the theater box office first; if no seats are available there, find out the standard prices before going to an agency. Most, but not all, are reputable. Agencies advertising top show tickets for "tonight" may really have them, and they may be a fair price. If you order by phone, tickets will be mailed to you or sent to the theater for you to collect. Commission should be a standard 22%. Some shows waive the agency fee by paying the commission themselves; this is usually advertised, and agencies should then charge standard box office prices. Always compare prices, try to avoid agencies in bureaux de change, and do not be tempted to buy from ticket touts or unofficial Internet sources.

Ticket booth in Leicester Square

London's Theaters

London offers an extraordinary range of theatrical entertainment – this is one of the world's great stages, and, at its best, standards of quality are extremely high. Despite their legendary reputation for reserve, the British are passionate about theater and London's theaters reflect every nuance of this passion. You can stroll along a street of West End theaters and find a somber Samuel Beckett, Brecht, or Chekhov play showing next door to some absurdly frothy farce like *No Sex Please, We're British!* Amid such diversity there is always something to appeal to everyone.

WEST END THEATER

There is a distinct glamor to the West End theaters. Perhaps it is the glittering lights of the foyer and the impressively ornate interiors, or maybe it is their hallowed reputations – but whatever it is, the old theaters retain a magic all of their own.

The West End billboards always feature a generous sprinkling of world-famous performers such as Judi Dench, Kenneth Branagh, John Malkovich, and Kevin Spacey.

The major commercial theaters cluster along Shaftesbury Avenue and the Haymarket and around Covent Garden and Charing Cross Road. Unlike the national theaters, most West End theaters survive only on profits; they do not receive any state subsidy. They rely on an army of ever-hopeful "angels" (financial backers) and producers to keep the old traditions alive.

Many theaters are historical landmarks, such as the classic **Theatre Royal Drury Lane**, established in 1663 (*see p115*), and the elegant **Theatre Royal Haymarket** – both superb examples of early 19th-century buildings. Another to note is the **Palace** (*see p108*), with its terra cotta exterior and imposing position right on Cambridge Circus.

NATIONAL THEATRE

The **National Theatre** is based on the Southbank Centre (*see p188*). Here, the large, open-staged Olivier, the proscenium-staged Lyttelton and the small, flexible Cottesloe offer a range of size and style, making it possible to produce every kind of theater from large, extravagant works to miniature masterpieces. The complex is also a lively social center. Enjoy a drink with your friends before your play begins; watch the crowds and the river drift by; wander around the many free art exhibitions; relax during the free early evening concerts in the foyer or browse through the theater bookstore.

The **Royal Shakespeare Company** is Britain's national theater company, one of the world's great theater ensembles, with an unparalleled reputation for its dramatic interpretation of Shakespeare and other leading dramatists. Although its official home since the 19th century has been in Stratford-upon-Avon, the company has maintained a regular London presence since the 1960s. Its London base used to be the Barbican Centre, but now the RSC enjoys regular London seasons in the West End, at the Novello Theatre and other smaller venues. If you want to find out where the RSC is performing in London, call their ticket hotline.

NATIONAL THEATRE TICKET OFFICES

National Theatre
(Lyttelton, Cottesloe, Olivier)
South Bank SE1. **Map** 14 D3.
Tel 020-7452 3000.
www.nationaltheatre.org.uk

Royal Shakespeare Company
Tel 01789-403 4444 (information).
Tel 0844-800 1110 (tickets).

PANTOMIME

Should you happen to be visiting London between December and February, one unmissable experience for the whole family is pantomime. "Panto" is an absurd tradition in which major female characters are played by men and male characters by women, and the audience has to participate, shouting encouragement according to a set formula. Whatever adults may think of it, children love the experience.

OPEN-AIR THEATER

A performance of one of Shakespeare's airier creations, such as *A Midsummer Night's Dream,* takes on an atmosphere of pure enchantment among the green vistas of **Regent's Park** (*see p224*). Lavish opera productions are staged during the summer months in **Holland Park** (*see p218*). Wear warm clothing, take a blanket, and, to be safe, an umbrella. Refreshments are available, or you can bring a picnic.

Open-air performances of a different kind can be experienced at **Shakespeare's Globe** on Bankside (*see p177*). This authentic reproduction of an Elizabethan playhouse, open to the skies – but with protected seating – is open to visitors all year round but only puts on performances in the summer months.

OPEN-AIR THEATER TICKET OFFICES

Holland Park Theatre
Holland Park. **Map** 9 B4.
Tel 0845-230 9769. **Open** Jun–Aug.
www.operahollandpark.com

Open Air Theatre
Inner Circle, Regent's Park NW1.
Map 4 D3. **Open** Jun–Sep.
Tel 0844- 826 4242.
http://openairtheatre.org

Shakespeare's Globe
New Globe Walk SE1. **Map** 15 A3.
Tel 020-7401 9919.
Performances Apr–Oct.
www.shakespeares-globe.org

WEST END THEATERS

Adelphi 13
Strand WC2.
Tel 0844-412 4651.

Aldwych 18
Aldwych WC2.
Tel 0844-847 2330.

Ambassadors 26
West St WC2.
Tel 0844-811 2334.

Apollo 32
Shaftesbury Ave W1.
Tel 0844-579 1971.

Cambridge 24
Earlham St WC2.
Tel 0844-412 4652.

Comedy 8
Panton St SW1.
Tel 0844-871 7612.

Criterion 7
Piccadilly Circus W1.
Tel 0844-847 1778.

Dominion 23
Tottenham Court Rd.
Tel 0844-847 1775.

Duchess 16
Catherine St WC2.
Tel 0844-412 4659.

Duke of York's 3
St Martin's Lane WC2.
Tel 0844-871 7623.

Fortune 20
Russell St WC2.
Tel 0844-871 7626.

Garrick 4
Charing Cross Rd WC2.
Tel 0844-579 1974.

Gielgud 31
Shaftesbury Ave W1.
Tel 0844-482 5141.

Her Majesty's 10
Haymarket SW1.
Tel 0844-482 5158.

Lyceum 15
Wellington St WC2.
Tel 0844-844 0005.

Lyric 33
Shaftesbury Ave W1.
Tel 0844-412 4661.

New Leicester Square Theatre 5
Leicester Pl W1.
Tel 0844-847 2475.

New London 21
Drury Lane WC2.
Tel 020-7907 7090.

Noel Coward 1
St Martin's Lane WC2.
Tel 0844-482 5120.

Novello 17
Aldwych WC2.
Tel 0844-482 5170.

Palace 28
Shaftesbury Ave W1.
Tel 0844-755 0016.

Phoenix 27
Charing Cross Rd WC2.
Tel 0844-871 7627.

Piccadilly 34
Denman St W1.
Tel 0844-412 6666.

Playhouse 12
Northumberland Ave WC2.
Tel 0870-060 6631.

Prince Edward 29
Old Compton St W1.
Tel 0844-482 5151.

Prince of Wales 6
Coventry St W1.
Tel 0844-482 5115.

Queen's 30
Shaftesbury Ave W1.
Tel 0844-482 5160.

Shaftesbury 22
Shaftesbury Ave WC2.
Tel 020-7379 5399.

St. Martin's 25
West St WC2.
Tel 0844-499 1515.

Theatre Royal Drury Lane 19
Catherine St WC2.
Tel 0844-412 2955.

Theatre Royal Haymarket 9
Haymarket SW1.
Tel 0845-481 1870.

Trafalgar Studios 11
Whitehall SW1.
Tel 0844-871 7632.

Vaudeville 14
Strand WC2.
Tel 0844-412 4663.

Wyndham's 2
Charing Cross Rd WC2.
Tel 0844-482 5138.

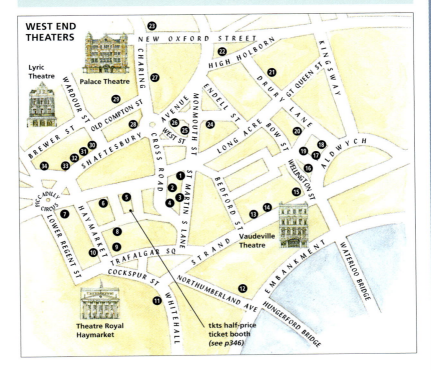

WEST END THEATERS

tkts half-price ticket booth
(see p346)

FRINGE THEATER

London's fringe theater acts as an outlet for new, adventurous writing and for writers from other cultures and lifestyles – works by Irish writers appear regularly, as do plays by Caribbean and Latin American authors and feminist and gay writers.

The plays are usually staged in tiny theaters based in pubs, such as the **Gate Theatre** above the Prince Albert pub in Notting Hill, the **King's Head** in Islington, and the **Latchmere** pub in Battersea, or in warehouses and spare space in larger theaters, such as the **Donmar Warehouse** and the **Lyric**.

Venues like the **Bush Theatre**, the **Almeida**, and the **Jerwood Theatre Upstairs** at the Royal Court have earned their reputations for discovering outstanding new works, some of which have subsequently transferred successfully to the West End.

Foreign-language plays are sometimes performed at national cultural institutes; for example you might be able to catch Molière at the **Institut Français** or Brecht at the **Goethe Institute**; check the listings magazines.

For alternative stand-up comedy and cabaret, where you can encounter the sharp edge of satire with its brash, newsy style, try the **Comedy Store**, the birthplace of so-called "alternative" comedy, or the **Hackney Empire**, a former Victorian music hall that showcases local talent and hosts theater, music, and comedy events.

BUDGET TICKETS

There is a wide range of prices for seats in London theaters. The cheaper West End tickets, for example, can cost under £10, whereas the best seats for musicals hover around £35–50. However, it is usually quite possible to obtain cheaper tickets.

"tkts" (see p345) is the only official discount theater ticket shop in London, and sells tickets on the day of the performance for a wide range of mainstream shows. Located on the south side of Leicester Square, the booth is open Monday to Saturday (10am–7pm) for matinee and evening shows, and Sunday (noon–3:30pm) for matinees only. Payment is by cash or credit card, and there is a strict limit of up to four tickets per purchase, and a small service charge.

You can sometimes get reduced price seats for matinee performances, press, and preview nights – it is always worth checking with the box office to see what they currently have on offer.

CHOOSING SEATS

If you go to the theater in person, you will be able to see its seating plan and note where you can get a good view at an affordable price. If you reserve by telephone, you should note the following: stalls are in front of the stage and expensive. The back stalls are slightly cheaper; dress, grand, or royal circles are above the stalls and cheaper again; the upper circle or balcony are the cheapest seats but you will have to climb several flights of stairs; the slips are seats that run along the edges of the theater; boxes are the most expensive option.

It is also wise to bear in mind that some of the cheap seats have a restricted view.

THEATER-RELATED ACTIVITIES

If you are curious about theater mechanics, you would probably enjoy a backstage tour. The National Theatre organizes tours (contact the box office – see p344 – for details). The tour includes the Lyttleton, Olivier, and Cottesloe auditoria, as well as the workshops and dressing rooms. The London Palladium also offers a backstage guided tour of the theater's history.

IRATE GHOSTS

Many London theaters are reputed to have ghosts; however, the two most famous specters haunt the environs of the Garrick and the Duke of York's (see p345). The Garrick is heavily atmospheric and the ghost of Arthur Bourchier, a manager at the turn of the 20th century, is reputed to make fairly regular appearances. He hated critics and many believe he is still trying to frighten them away. The ghost occupying the Duke of York's theater was Violet Melnotte, an actress manager during the 1890s, who was famed for her extremely fiery temper.

FRINGE THEATER	Donmar Warehouse	Hackney Empire	Lyric
Almeida	41 Earlham St WC2.	291 Mare St E8.	King St, Hammersmith
Almeida St N1.	**Map** 13 B2.	**Tel** 020-8985 2424.	W6. **Tel** 0871-221 1729.
Tel 020-7359 4404.	**Tel** 0844-871 7624.		
		Institut Français	**Theatre 503**
Bush Theatre	**Gate Theatre**	17 Queensberry Pl SW7.	The Latchmere Pub, 503
Shepherds Bush Green	The Prince Albert Pub,	**Map** 18 F2.	Battersea Park Rd SW11.
W12.	11 Pembridge Rd W11.	**Tel** 020-7073 1350.	**Tel** 020-7978 7040.
Tel 020-8743 5050.	**Map** 9 C3.		
	Tel 020-7229 0706.	**King's Head**	**Royal Court**
Comedy Store		115 Upper St N1.	Sloane Sq SW1.
28a Leicester Sq WC2.	**Goethe Institute**	**Map** 6 F1.	**Map** 19 C2.
Map 13 B3.	50 Prince's Gate, Exhibition	**Tel** 020-7226 8561.	**Tel** 020-7565 5000.
Tel 0844-847 1728.	Rd SW7. **Map** 11 A5.		
	Tel 020-7596 4000.		

Movie Theaters

If you can't find a movie you like in London, then you don't like movies. The huge choice of British, American, foreign-language, new, classic, popular, and special-interest movies makes London a major international movie center, with about 250 different films showing at any one time. There are about 50 movie theaters in the central district of London alone, many of them ultra-modern multiscreen complexes. The big commercial chains show current blockbusters and a healthy number of independent movie theaters offer inventive programs drawing on the whole history of film. London's listings magazines carry full details of what's on where.

WEST END MOVIE THEATERS

West End is a loose term for the main theaters in the West End of London that show new releases, such as the **Odeon Leicester Square** and the **Cineworld** Shaftesbury Avenue at the Trocadero, but it also includes the theaters found in Chelsea, Fulham, and Notting Hill. Programs begin around noon and are repeated every two or three hours, with the last show around 8:30pm; there are often late-night screenings on Fridays and Saturdays.

West End movie theaters are very expensive, but admission is often cheaper for afternoon performances or on Mondays. Reserve your seats well in advance for screenings of the more popular movies on Friday and Saturday evenings and Sunday afternoon.

BFI LONDON IMAX

The largest IMAX screen in Britain shows specially created movies accompanied by surround sound. Subjects like spaceflight or the undersea world suit this breathtaking format well, as do animations.

REPERTORY THEATERS

These theaters often show foreign-language and slightly more "off-beat" art films and sometimes change programs daily or even several times each day. Some theaters show two or three movies, often on the same theme, for one entrance charge.

These include the **Prince Charles**, which is situated centrally, close to Leicester Square, the **Everyman** in locations across north London, the ICA in the Mall, the **Ritzy** in Brixton, South London, and the BFI Southbank.

BFI SOUTHBANK

Formerly known as the National Film Theatre, BFI Southbank is located in the Southbank Centre, near Waterloo Station. It has two theaters of its own, which together offer a huge and diverse selection of movies, both British and international. The BFI Southbank also holds regular screenings of rare and restored films and television programs. It is absolutely essential for movie buffs to pay a visit.

FOREIGN-LANGUAGE FILMS

These are screened at a number of repertory and independent movie theaters, including the **Renoir**, the **Prince Charles**, the **Curzon Soho** in Shaftesbury Avenue, the **Screen** theater chain and the **Ciné Lumière**. Movies are shown in the original language, with English subtitles.

FILM CERTIFICATES

Children are allowed to go to a movie theater unaccompanied by an adult to films that have been awarded either a U (universal) or a PG (parental guidance advised) certificate for viewing. Children must be accompanied by an adult to view a film rated 12A.

With other films, the numbers 12, 15, or 18 quite simply denote the minimum ages allowed for admission to the movie theater.

LONDON FILM FESTIVAL

The most important cinematic event in Britain is held every November, when over 100 movies – some of which will have already won awards abroad – from a number of countries are screened. The BFI Southbank, several of the repertory theaters and some of the big West End theaters have special showings of these movies. Details are published in the listings magazines. Tickets are quite hard to come by but some "stand-by" tickets will generally be available to the public 30 minutes before a screening.

CINEMA ADDRESSES

BFI London IMAX
Waterloo Rd SE1.
Map 14 D4.
020-7199 6000.

BFI Southbank
Southbank Centre, SE1.
Map 14 D3.
Tel 020-7928 3232.

Ciné Lumière
Institut Français, 17 Queensberry Pl SW7. **Map** 18 F2. **Tel** 020-7073 1350.

Cineworld (at the Trocadero)
Coventry St W1. **Map** 13 A3. 0871-200 2000.

Curzon Soho
93–107 Shaftesbury Ave W1. **Map** 13 B2.
0871-703 3988.

Everyman
Hollybush Vale NW3.
Map 1 A5.
0870-066 4777.

Odeon Leicester Sq
Leicester Sq, WC2.
Map 13 B2.
0871-224 4007.

Prince Charles
Leicester Pl, WC2.
Map 13 B2
Tel 020-7494 3654.

Renoir
Brunswick Sq WC1.
Map 5 C4.
020-7837 8402.

Ritzy
Coldharbour Lane SW2.
Tel 0871-704 2065.

Screen Cinemas
96 Baker St NW1.
Map 3 C5.
Tel 0871-906 9060.

Opera, Classical, and Contemporary Music

Opera has always been tarred with a somewhat elitist reputation in Britain. However, televised concerts and free outdoor concerts in Hyde Park and the Piazza, Covent Garden, have greatly increased its popularity. London is home to five world-class orchestras and a veritable host of smaller music companies and contemporary music ensembles; it also houses three permanent opera companies and numerous smaller opera groups and leads the world with its period orchestras. It is a major center for the classical recording industry, which helps to support a large community of musicians and singers. Mainstream, obscure, traditional, and innovative music are all to be found in profusion. *Time Out* magazine *(see p342)* has the most comprehensive listings of the classical music on offer around the capital.

Royal Opera House

Floral Street WC2. **Map** 13 C2.
Tel 020-7304 4000. See p115.
www.roh.org.uk

The building, with its elaborate red, white, and gold interior, is opulent; it looks, and is, expensive. It is the home of the Royal Opera and the Royal Ballet, but visiting opera and ballet companies also perform here. Many productions are shared with foreign opera houses, so check that you haven't already seen the same production at home. Works are always performed in the original language, but English translations are flashed up above the stage.

Seats are usually reserved well in advance, particularly if major stars such as Placido Domingo or Anna Netrebko are performing. The sound is best in the seats center of stage, right in the front. Tickets range from about £5 to £200 or more for a world-class star. The cheapest seats tend to go first, although a number of these tickets are reserved for sale on the day. Some of the cheaper seats have extremely restricted views. Standing passes can often be obtained right up to the time of a performance. Standby information is available on the day, and there are often concessions on tickets. It is worthwhile waiting in line for last-minute returns.

London Coliseum

St Martin's Lane WC2. **Map** 13 B3.
Tel 0871-911 0200 (24 hrs).
See p119. **www**.eno.org

The Coliseum, home of the English National Opera (ENO), was founded in 1961. The company's hallmarks are performances in English, high musical standards, and a permanent ensemble complemented by guest appearances. Productions range from the classic to the adventurous. They are often praised for their contemporary interpretations. The audiences tend to be younger than at the Royal Opera House, the seats are much cheaper, and there is less corporate entertaining. For weekday performances, there are 500 prereserved seats at £10 and under.

Southbank Centre

Southbank Centre SE1. **Map** 14 D4.
Tel 0844-875 0073. See pp186–7.
www.southbankcentre.co.uk

The Southbank Centre includes the **Royal Festival Hall (RFH)**, the **Queen Elizabeth Hall**, the **Purcell Room**, and the **Hayward Gallery**. There are nightly performances, mostly of classical music, interspersed with opera, jazz, ballet, and modern dance seasons, as well as festivals of contemporary and ethnic music. The largest concert hall on the South Bank is the RFH. Built in the 1950s, it is now considered one of the best modernist structures in London. The RFH is ideal for major orchestras and large-scale choral works. The airy halls outside the auditorium are also used to house exhibitions, a number of cafés, a book and music store, and the occasional free performance.

The Purcell Room is comparatively small and tends to host chamber and contemporary music in addition to many debut recitals of young artists. The Queen Elizabeth Hall lies somewhere in between. It stages medium-sized ensembles whose audiences, while too large for the Purcell Room, would not fill the Festival Hall. Jazz and ethnic music are performed here and the innovative and often controversial Opera Factory makes several appearances throughout the year. It performs a range of modern interpretations of the classics, and often commissions new works. The London

(see p349)

LONDON MUSIC FESTIVALS

The BBC-run Promenade concerts are mostly held at the Royal Albert Hall *(see p349)* between July and September. More than 70 concerts feature soloists, orchestras and conductors from around the world, performing a wide repertoire from much-loved classics to newly commissioned pieces. Every concert is broadcast live both on the radio and online. Tickets are best bought in advance, but 500 standing or "promming" places are sold on the day, one and a half hours before the performance. The City of London Festival is held annually in June and July, when churches and public buildings in the City host a range of varied musical events. Venues such as the Tower of London *(see p154)* and Goldsmiths' Hall lend a special atmosphere to the events. Many concerts are free. For more details, apply to the information office (020-7583 3585) from May onward.

Philharmonic Orchestra and the Philharmonia are resident at the South Bank. The Royal Philharmonic and the BBC Symphony Orchestra are frequent visitors, along with leading ensembles and soloists such as Angela Gheorghiu, Mitsuko Uchida, Stephen Kovacevich, and Anne-Sofie von Mutter. Visiting international musicians cover a wide repertoire of music from the Kronos Quartet to the Vienna Symphony Orchestra. World-class conductors who have played here include Daniel Barenboim, Kurt Masur, and Simon Rattle.

The Academy of St. Martin-in-the-Fields, the London Festival Orchestra, Opera Factory, the London Classical Players, and the London Mozart Players all have regular seasons. There are also frequent free foyer concerts, and throughout the summer the center is well worth visiting since musical events take place on the terraces when the weather permits.

Barbican Concert Hall

Silk Street EC2. **Map** 7 A5.
Tel 020-7638 4141. See p165.
www.barbican.org.uk

The Barbican is the home of the London Symphony Orchestra (LSO). Classical concerts are performed by the resident LSO and the BBC Symphony Orchestra, as well as many other visiting orchestras and ensembles, as part of the Barbican's own international concert seasons. The concert hall is also renowned for its perform-ances of contemporary music, including jazz, blues, and world music, which attract the top musicians in their field.

Royal Albert Hall

Kensington Gore SW7. **Map** 10 F5.
Tel 020-7589 8212. See p207.
www.royalalberthall.com

Each year the Royal Albert Hall hosts over 300 concerts, from ballet to rock, pop, opera, and national events. From mid-July to mid-September it is devoted to the Henry Wood Promenade Concerts, the "Proms." Organized by the BBC, the season features the BBC Symphony Orchestra performing modern symphonies and other works as well as classics. Visiting orchestras make up a varied pro-gram. Tickets for the Proms can be bought on the day of performance or purchased in advance, but long lines form early in the day, so experienced Promenaders take cushions to sit on. Tickets sell out weeks ahead for the "Last Night of the Proms," which has become a national institution.

The hall is also open for tours that take you on a journey of its extraordinary history, and give you the chance to experience the workings of this performing arts venue.

Handel House Museum

25 Brook St W1. **Map** 12 E2.
Tel 020-7495 1685. **Open** 10am–6pm Tue–Sat (until 8pm Thu), noon–6pm Sun.
www.handelhouse.org

Located in the finely restored Georgian house where George Frideric Handel lived from 1723 until his death in 1759, the Handel House Museum provides an intimate venue for performances. Thursday night recitals of baroque music on period instruments are held in the paneled rehearsal and performance room, where Handel himself would have entertained his guests. Concert tickets include access to the museum. Check the website for more concerts, lectures, and workshops.

OUTDOOR MUSIC

London has many outdoor musical events in summer. At Kenwood House on Hampstead Heath (see p234), a grassy hill leads down to a lake, beyond which is the concert platform. Arrive early since the concerts are popular, particularly if fireworks are to accompany the music. Deck chairs tend to be taken early, so most people sit on the grass. Take a sweater and a picnic. Purists beware – people walk around, eat, and talk throughout and the music is amplified so it can be a little distorted. You don't get your money back if it rains, since they have never abandoned a performance yet.

Other venues include Marble Hill House in Twickenham (see p252), with practices similar to Kenwood, Crystal Palace Park, and Holland Park.

Wigmore Hall

36 Wigmore St W1. **Map** 12 E1.
Tel 020-7935 2141. See p226.
www.wigmore-hall.org.uk

Because of its excellent acoustics the Wigmore Hall is a favorite with visiting artists, and attracts international names such as Andreas Scholl and András Schiff for a wide-ranging program of events. It presents seven evening concerts a week, BBC Monday lunchtime concerts, and a Sunday morning concert from September to July.

St. Martin-in-the-Fields

Trafalgar Sq WC2. **Map** 13 B3.
Tel 020-7766 1100. See p102.
www.smitf.org

This elegant Gibbs church is where the famous Academy of St. Martin-in-the-Fields and the famous choir of the same name began life. Orchestras as disparate as the Delmont Ensemble and the London Oriana Choir provide evening concerts. The choice of each pro-gram is partly dictated by the reli-gious year; for example, Bach's *St. John Passion* is played at Ascen-siontide. Free lunchtime concerts are held on Mondays, Tuesdays, and Fridays by young artists.

St. John's, Smith Square

Smith Sq SW1. **Map** 21 B1.
Tel 020-7222 1061. See p81.
www.sjss.org.uk

This converted Baroque church has good acoustics and comfortable seating. It hosts varied concerts by groups such as the Academy of Ancient Music, the London Mozart Players, the Monteverdi Choir, and Polyphony. The concert period runs from September to mid-July.

Broadgate Arena

3 Broadgate EC2. **Map** 7 C5.
Tel 020-7505 4068. See p169.

This open-air venue in the City offers a summer season of lunch-time concerts, with varied pro-grams, frequently from up-and-coming musicians.

MUSIC VENUES

Orchestral

Barbican Concert Hall
Broadgate Arena
Queen Elizabeth Hall
Royal Albert Hall
Royal Festival Hall
St. Martin-in-the-Fields
St. John's, Smith Square

Chamber and Ensemble

Barbican Concert Hall
Broadgate Arena
Handel House Museum
LSO St. Luke's
Purcell Room
Royal Festival Hall foyer
St. Martin-in-the-Fields
St. John's, Smith Square
Wigmore Hall

Soloists and Recitals

Barbican Concert Hall
Handel House Museum
Purcell Room
Royal Albert Hall
St. Martin-in-the-Fields
St. John's, Smith Square
Wigmore Hall

Children's

Barbican Concert Hall
Royal Festival Hall

Free

Barbican Concert Hall
Royal Festival Hall foyer
Royal National Theatre foyer (see p344)
St. Martin-in-the-Fields (lunchtime)

Early Music

Purcell Room
Wigmore Hall

Contemporary Music

Barbican Concert Hall
Southbank Centre

Dance

London-based dance companies present a range of styles from classical ballet to mime, jazz, experimental, and ethnic dance. London is also host to visiting companies as diverse as the classic Bolshoi Ballet and the innovative Jaleo Flamenco. Most dance companies (with the exception of the resident ballets) have short seasons that seldom last longer than two weeks and often less than a week – check the listings magazines for details *(see p342)*. Theaters that regularly feature dance are the **Royal Opera House**, the **London Coliseum, Sadler's Wells**, and **The Place Theatre**. There are also performances at the **Southbank Centre** and other arts centers throughout the city.

BALLET

The **Royal Opera House** *(see p115)* and the **London Coliseum** in St. Martin's Lane are by far the best venues for classical ballet, providing the stage for foreign companies when they visit London. The Opera House is home to the Royal Ballet, which usually invites major international guest artists to take up residence. Purchase well in advance for classics such as *Swan Lake* and *Giselle*. The company also has an unusual repertoire of modern ballet; triple bills provide a mixture of new and old and seats are normally quite readily available.

The English National Ballet holds its summer season at the **London Coliseum**. It has a similar repertoire to the Royal Ballet and stages some very popular productions.

Visiting companies also perform at **Sadler's Wells**, which, although it is London's premier venue for contemporary dance, also hosts a few companies with a classical repertoire.

CONTEMPORARY

A plethora of new and young companies is flourishing in London, each one with a distinctive style. **Sadler's Wells** in Islington, near Angel, has a proud reputation as the host of contemporary dance companies from around the world. There are regular visits from such luminaries of dance as the Nederlands Dance Theatre and the Alvin Ailey Company from New York. The innovative English ensemble, the Rambert Dance Company, have a regular, twice-a-year slot at the theater – usually in May and November. A stunning modern theater was built on the historic site of the Sadler's Wells Ballet in 1998. The **Peacock Theatre** (the West End home of Sadler's Wells) also features contemporary dance as part of its program.

The **Place** is the home of contemporary and ethnic dance companies and has a year-round program of performances from these and a number of visiting dancers.

A purpose-built space in Deptford, south London, the **Bonnie Bird Theatre**, presents a rich and diverse mix of dance, music, and physical theater. Other venues include the **Institute of Contemporary Arts** (ICA) *(see p92)* and the **Chisenhale Dance Space**, a center for small companies currently regarded as being on the experimental fringes.

ETHNIC

There is a constant stream of visiting groups coming to perform traditional dance from all over the world. Both **Sadler's Wells** and the **Riverside Studios** are major venues, while classical ethnic dance companies, including Indian and Far Eastern, have seasons at the Southbank Centre, often in the **Queen Elizabeth Hall**. Check the listings magazines for details.

DANCE FESTIVALS

There are two major contemporary dance festivals each year in London, featuring many different companies. Spring Loaded runs from February to April, while Dance Umbrella runs from early October to early November. The listings magazines carry all details.

Other smaller festivals include Almeida Dance, from the end of April to the first week of May at the **Almeida Theatre**, and The Turning World, a festival running in April and May offering dance from all over the world.

DANCE VENUES

Almeida Theatre
Almeida St N1.
Tel 020-7359 4404.

Bonnie Bird Theatre
Creekside SE8. **Map 23 A2. Tel** 020-8691 8600.

Chisenhale Dance Space
64 Chisenhale Rd E3.
Tel 020-8981 6617.

ICA
Nash House,
Carlton House Terrace,
The Mall SW1.
Map 13 A4.
Tel 020-7930 3647.

London Coliseum
St Martin's Lane WC2.
Map 13 B3.
Tel 0871-911 0200.

Peacock Theatre
Portugal St WC2.
Map 14 D1.
Tel 0844-412 4322.

The Place
17 Duke's Rd WC1.
Map 5 B3.
Tel 020-7121 1100.

Queen Elizabeth Hall
Southbank Centre SE1.
Map 14 D4.
Tel 020-7960 4200.

Riverside Studios
Crisp Rd W6.
Tel 020-8237 1111.

Royal Opera House
Floral St WC2.
Map 13 C2.
Tel 020-7304 4000.

Sadler's Wells
Rosebery Ave EC1.
Map 6 E3.
Tel 0844-412 4300.

Rock, Pop, Jazz, Reggae, and World Music

You will find the whole range of popular music being strummed and hummed, howled, growled, or synthesized in London. There may be as many as 80 listed concerts on an ordinary weeknight, featuring rock, reggae, soul, folk, country, jazz, Latin, and world music. In addition to the gigs, there are music festivals in the summer at parks, pubs, halls, and stadiums throughout the capital *(see p353)*. Check the listings magazines and keep your eyes open for publicity posters *(see p342)*.

MAJOR VENUES

The largest venues in London are host to an extraordinary variety of music.

Places where pop idols hope to draw enormous crowds of adoring fans include the **O2 Arena** in Greenwich, the indoor **Wembley Arena**, the **Hammersmith Apollo**, or, if they take themselves seriously, the grand **Royal Albert Hall**.

The **O2 Academy Brixton** and the **Town and Country Club** are next in prominence and size. Each can take well over 1,000 people, and for many Londoners these former movie theaters are the capital's best venues, with seating upstairs, large dance floors downstairs, and accessible bars.

ROCK AND POP

Indie music is one of the mainstays of London's live music output. Following the leads of Manchester and Bristol, the capital has a healthy, cross-fertilized rock scene: venues all over town offer Britpop, bratpop, hip-hop, trip-hop, and the many other variations on pop which have yet to be labelled for the mass market. The **Union Chapel** in Islington hosts a variety of bands. Kentish Town's **Bull and Gate** is good for goth, and rock is the order of the day at venues such as **The Bullet Bar** and **The Shepherd's Bush Empire**, among others.

The **Underworld** in Camden is a famous live venue for up and coming bands as well as big name artists such as Sheryl Crow, Radiohead, and The Darkness. The venue is also home to two nightclubs.

London is the home of pub-rock, which is a vibrant blend of rhythm and blues, rock, and punk that has been evolving since the 1960s as a genre in which bands frequently develop before finding their real musical identity. Such diverse bands as the Clash, Dr. Feelgood and Dire Straits all started as pub rockers. While there's usually no entrance fee to pub gigs, drinks tend to be surcharged.

New bands have a popular showcase at the **Betsey Trotwood** in Clerkenwell most week nights, while **Borderline**, near to Leicester Square, is frequented by record company talent scouts.

The **Barfly** in Chalk Farm delivers a good range of indie acts. **Koko** in Camden is a great intimate venue in a restored theater dating from 1900. Here you can listen to the finest established artists such as Madonna or Coldplay and live performances from up-and-coming indie bands. Another good venue for stimulating rock bands in North London is **The Relentless Garage** at Highbury Corner.

JAZZ

The number of jazz venues in London continues to grow – both the music and the lifestyle that are romantically imagined to go with it are officially hip once again. **Ronnie Scott's** in the West End is still the pick of the vintage crop, and since the 1950s many of the finest performers in the world have come to play here. The **100 Club** in Oxford Street is another very popular venue for confirmed jazzniks.

Jazz and food have formed a partnership at venues such as the **Palookaville** in Covent Garden, the **Dover Street Wine Bar and Club**, and the largely vegetarian **Jazz Café**. Others include the **Pizza Express** on Dean Street and the **Pizza on the Park**, by Hyde Park Corner.

The **Southbank Centre** *(see pp186–7)* and also the **Barbican** *(see p165)* feature formal jazz concerts and free jazz in the foyers.

REGGAE

London's large West Indian community has made the city the European reggae capital. At the **Notting Hill Carnival** *(see p57)*, late in August, many top bands perform free.

Reggae has now become integrated with the mainstream rock music scene, and bands appear at most of London's rock venues.

WORLD MUSIC

Musicians from every corner of the globe live in London. "World music" includes African, Latin, South American, anything exotic, and its popularity has sparked a revitalization of British and Irish folk music. **Cecil Sharp House** has regular shows for folk purists, while the **ICA** *(see p92)* hosts innovative acts. **Cargo** in Shoreditch has an eclectic program of live music that includes African beats and Latin funk. Hot Latin nights can be found at **Cuba Libre** in Islington, and laid-back vibes pervade the **Notting Hill Arts Club**. For all French Caribbean and African sounds you could check **Le Café de Piaf** inside Waterloo Station; and for the widest selection of African sounds and food in town, try visiting the **Africa Centre** in Covent Garden. The **Barbican Centre**, the **Royal Festival Hall**, and the **Queen Elizabeth Hall** at the Southbank Centre all offer plenty of world music.

Clubs

The old cliché that London dies when the pubs shut no longer holds true. Europe has long scoffed at Londoners going to bed at 11pm when the night is only just beginning in Paris, Madrid, and Rome, but London has caught on at last and you can revel all night if you want to. The best clubs are not all confined to the city's center – initial disappointment that your hotel is a half-hour tube-ride from Leicester Square can be offset by the discovery of a trendy club right on your doorstep.

ETIQUETTE

Fashions and club nights change very rapidly and nightspots open and close down all the time. Some of the best club nights are one-nighters – check the listings magazines *(see p342)*. Be aware that there are some-times bouncers on the door, enforcing a variety of dress or other appearance codes for a particular club. If you are set on visiting one of these, do some research before you go.

A few clubs require that you arrange membership 48 hours in advance, and you may also find that you have to be introduced by a member. Again, check these details in the listings magazines. Groups of men may not be welcome, so split up and find a woman to go in with; expect to wait in line to get in. Entrance fees may seem reasonable, but drinks tend to be over-priced.

Opening times are usually 10pm–3am Monday to Saturday, although many clubs stay open until 6am on the weekend and some open on Sunday from about 8pm to midnight.

MAINSTREAM

London offers a broad selection of nightclubs that cater for all musical tastes and budgets.

Most of the more upmarket nightclubs in London, for example **Annabel's**, have a strict members-only policy; they require nominations by current members and have long waiting lists, so unless you mix in privileged circles you are unlikely to get in.

Traditional disco-type clubs that are easier to enter include the **Café de Paris**,

where you can dine and boogie the night away. For those with a lust for samba and Latin beats, **Guanabara** in Covent Garden is friendly, unpretentious, and fun.

Farther north, the **Forum** hosts popular club nights, which feature classic soul, funk, and rhythm and blues. Similar clubs are **East Village** in Shoreditch and the **Tattershall Castle**, a disco boat moored on the bank of the Thames.

FASHIONABLE VENUES AND CLUB NIGHTS

Over the last few years London has become one of the most innovative and sought-after club capitals in the world. It is now a major stage where trends are set. **Heaven** hosts England's premier "house" night. With its huge dance floor, excellent lasers, sound systems, and lightshows it's very popular, so start lining up early. **Punk** in Soho is a trendy spot playing a mixture of sounds (you might even spot a celebrity). The **Ministry of Sound** is a New York-style club that set the pattern for others to follow, hosting some of the world's best-known DJs. If you are feeling energetic, club nights are also run at the **Queen of Hoxton** in Shoreditch. Try **Envy Nightclub** for funky house, electro, and old skool, and for die-hard clubbers there's always the music-loving **Fabric**.

As with many clubs, **Bar Rumba** has different themes on different evenings, but if you like your dancing with a dash of spice and a lot of sauce, sashay along to its salsa night with dance classes also available. **Cargo**, the

pioneering live/mixed music venue, features some of London's funkiest sounds. **93 Feet East** showcases a variety of live music and club nights from indie and rock to techno beats. Dress in uniform for the "School Disco Night" with 70s, 80s, and 90s sounds. It takes place on Saturdays in the **HMV Forum**, but check listings – it moves sometimes.

In Kensington, **The Roof Gardens** is London's only rooftop private members club. It opens on Friday and Saturday nights, admits over 21s only, and has a "no effort, no entry" dress code. Apply for entry via the website at www.roofgardensclub.com.

GAY

London has a number of gay nightclubs. The best-known and most popular is **Heaven**, with its huge dance floor and bar and video lounge under the arches of Charing Cross station. The **Fridge** and the **Queen of Hoxton** host mixed gay nights, and the Fridge holds women-only nights.

TRANSVESTITE

Watch for the occasional "Kinky Gerlinky" night in the listings magazines, an outrageously kitsch collection of drag queens and assorted exotica. In Soho, **Madame Jojo's** revue is a fabulous whirl of glittering color and extreme high camp.

CASINOS

To gamble in London you must be a member, or at least the guest of a member, of a licensed gaming club. Most clubs are happy to let you join but membership must be arranged 48 hours in advance. Many will let you in to use facilities other than the gambling tables until about 4am, when most close. Try the excellent restaurants and bars, which are often subject to the usual licensing laws *(see p318)*. Many clubs also have "hostesses" – beware of the cost of their company.

DIRECTORY

MAJOR MUSIC VENUES

Hammersmith Apollo
Queen Caroline St W6.
Tel 020-8563 3800.

HMV Forum
9–17 Highgate Rd NW5.
Tel 020-7284 1001.

O2 Academy Brixton
211 Stockwell Rd SW9.
Tel 020-7771 3000.

Royal Albert Hall
See p203.

Wembley Arena
Empire Way, Wembley, Middlesex HA9.
Tel 0844-815 0815
(tickets), 020-8782 5500
(inquiries).

ROCK AND POP VENUES

Barfly
49 Chalk Farm Rd NW1.
Map 4 F1.
Tel 0844-847 2424.

Betsey Trotwood
56 Farringdon Rd
EC1. **Map** 6 E4.
Tel 020-7253 4285.

Borderline
Orange Yard, Manette St
WC2. **Map** 13 B1.
Tel 020-7734 5547.

Bull and Gate
389 Kentish Town Rd
NW5.
Tel 020-8826 5000.

The Bullet Bar
147 Kentish Town Rd
NW1.
Tel 020-7485 6040.

Envy Nightclub
41–43 Woodfield Rd W9.
Tel 020-7266 3030.

Koko
1a Camden High St NW1.
Map 4 F2.
Tel 0870-432 5527.

The Relentless Garage
20–22 Highbury Corner,
N5. *Tel* 020-7619 6720.

Shepherd's Bush Empire
Shepherd's Bush Green
W12.
Tel 0905-020 3999.

The Underworld
174 Camden High St
NW1.
Map 4 F1.
Tel 020-7482 1932.

Union Chapel
The Vestry, Compton
Ave N1.
Tel 020-7226 1686.

JAZZ VENUES

100 Club
100 Oxford St W1.
Map 13 A1.
Tel 020-7636 0933.

Barbican Hall
See p165.

Dover Street Wine Bar and Club
8–10 Dover St W1.
Map 12 F3.
Tel 020-7629 9813.

Jazz Café
5 Parkway NW1.
Map 4 E1.
Tel 020-7485 6834.

Pizza Express
10 Dean St W1.
Map 13 A1.
Tel 0845-602 7017.

Pizza on the Park
11 Knightsbridge SW1.
Map 12 D5.
Tel 020-7235 7825.

Ronnie Scott's
47 Frith St W1.
Map 13 A2.
Tel 020-7439 0747.
www.ronniescotts.co.uk

Royal Festival Hall
See p348.

Vortex Jazz Club
Dalston Culture House
Gillett St, N16.
Map 8 1D.
Tel 020-7993 3643 or
020-7254 4097.

WORLD MUSIC

Africa Centre
38 King St WC2.
Map 13 C2.
Tel 020-7836 1973.

Barbican Centre
See p349.

Cargo
83 Rivington St EC2.
Map 7 C3.
Tel 020-7749 7840.

Cecil Sharp House
2 Regent's Park Rd NW1.
Map 4 D1.
Tel 020-7485 2206.

Cuba Libre
72 Upper St N1.
Map 6 F1.
Tel 020-7354 9998.

ICA
See p350.

Notting Hill Arts Club
21 Notting Hill Gate W11.
Map 9 C3.
Tel 020-7460 4459.

Queen Elizabeth Hall
Southbank Centre SE1.
Map 14 D4.
Tel 020-7960 4200.

Royal Festival Hall
See p348.

CLUBS

93 Feet East
150 Brick Lane,
Shoreditch E1.
Map 8 E4.
Tel 020-7770 6006.

Annabel's
44 Berkeley Sq W1.
Map 12 E3.
Tel 020-7629 1096.

Bar Rumba
36 Shaftesbury Ave
WC2. **Map** 6 E2.
Tel 020-7287 6933.

Café de Paris
3 Coventry St W1.
Map 13 A3.
Tel 020-7734 7700.

Cargo
89 Rivington St EC2.
Map 7 C3.
Tel 020-7749 7840.

East Village
89 Great Eastern St EC2.
Map 7 C4.
Tel 020-7739 5173.

Fabric
77a Charterhouse St EC1.
Map 6 F5.
Tel 020-7336 8898.

Fridge
Town Hall Parade,
Brixton Hill SW2.
Tel 020-7326 5100.

Guanabara
Drury Lane WC2.
Map 13 C1.
Tel 020-7242 8600.

Heaven
Under the Arches,
Villiers St WC2.
Map 13 C3.
Tel 020-7930 2020.

Madame Jojo's
8–10 Brewer St W1.
Map 13 A2.
Tel 020-7734 3040.

Ministry of Sound
103 Gaunt St SE1.
Tel 0870-060 0010.

Punk
14 Soho St W1.
Map 13 A1.
Tel 0871-223 1242.

Queen of Hoxton
1 Curtain Rd EC2.
Map 7 C3.
Tel 020-7422 0958.

Tattershall Castle
Victoria Embankment,
SW1.
Map 13 C3.
Tel 020-7839 6548.

The Roof Gardens
99 Kensington High St
W8.
Map 10 D5.
Tel 020-7937 7994.

Sports

The range of sports on offer in London is phenomenal. Should you feel the urge to watch a game of medieval tennis or go scuba diving in the city center, you've come to the right place. More likely, you'll just want to watch a football (soccer) or rugby match, or play a set of tennis in a park. With far more public facilities than most European capitals, London is the place to enjoy cheap, accessible sports. Wembley Stadium, the national stadium for football (soccer), is located in northwest London. The Olympic Stadium, Aquatics Centre, and other venues have been built in Stratford for the 2012 Olympic Games. Events are also being held at venues across the city.

ATHLETICS

Athletes will find a good choice of running tracks, often with free admission. **Linford Christie Stadium** has good facilities; **Regent's Park** is free; try also **Parliament Hill Fields**. For a sociable jog, meet the Bow Street Runners at **Jubilee Hall** on Tuesdays at 6pm.

CRICKET

Five-day test matches and one-day internationals are played in summer at **Lord's** *(see p246)* and the **Brit Oval**, near Vauxhall. Tickets for the first four days of tests and for one-day games are hard to get, but you may get in on the last day and see a thrilling finish. When Middlesex and Surrey play county games at these grounds there are always seats.

FOOTBALL (SOCCER)

This is the most popular spectator sport in Britain, its season running from August to May, with matches on weekends and weekday evenings. It is the most common topic of conversation in pubs, where games are often shown live on TV. Premier League and FA Cup games are frequently sold out in advance. London's top clubs include **Arsenal, Chelsea, West Ham**, and **Tottenham Hotspur**.

GOLF

There are no golf courses in central London, but a few are scattered around the outskirts. The most accessible public courses are **Hounslow Heath, Chessington** (nine holes, train from Waterloo), and **Richmond Park** (two courses, computerized indoor teaching room). If you didn't pack your clubs, sets can be rented at a reasonable price.

GREYHOUND RACING

At a night "down the dogs," you can follow the races on a screen in the bar, stand by the track, or watch from the comfort of the restaurant (reserve in advance) at **Romford Stadium or Wimbledon Stadium**.

HORSE RACING

High class flat racing in summer and steeplechasing in winter can be seen at **Ascot, Kempton Park**, and **Sandown Park**, which are all less than an hour from central London by train. Britain's most famous flat race, the Derby, is run at **Epsom** in June.

HORSE-RIDING

For centuries, fashionable riders have exercised their steeds in Hyde Park; **Ross Nye** will provide you with a horse so that you can follow a long tradition.

ICE-SKATING

Ice-skaters should head for London's best-known rink, **Queens**. The most attractive ice rinks, open only in winter, are in the **Broadgate** complex in the City, and at **Somerset House** *(see p117)*.

RUGBY FOOTBALL

Rugby union, or rugger, is a 15-a-side game, once played only by amateurs, but now a professional sport. International matches are played at **Twickenham Rugby Football Ground**. The season runs from September to April and you can watch "friendly" weekend games at local grounds. Top London teams **Saracens** and **Rosslyn Park** can be seen at their own grounds outside the center of town.

SQUASH

Squash courts tend to be busy, so try to reserve at least two days ahead. Many sports centres have squash facilities and will rent equipment, including **Swiss Cottage Sports Centre** and the **Oasis Sports Centre**.

SWIMMING

The best indoor pools include **Chelsea Sports Centre**, the **Oasis**, and **Porchester Baths**; for outdoor swimming, try **Highgate and Hampstead Ponds** (two separate ponds for men and women and one mixed), **Hampstead**, and the **Oasis**.

TENNIS

There are hundreds of tennis courts in London's public parks, most of them cheap to rent and easily reserved. It can be busy in the summer, so reserve your court two or three days ahead. You must supply your own racquet and balls. Good public tennis courts include **Holland Park** and **Parliament Hill**.

Tickets for the Centre Court of the **All England Lawn Tennis Club** at Wimbledon are hard to obtain – it is possibly easier to enter the tournament as a player than to obtain tickets for Centre Court; try waiting in line overnight, or line up for return tickets after lunch on the day – for a bargain price, you can still enjoy a good four hours of tennis *(see p57)*.

TRADITIONAL SPORTS

An old London tradition is the University Boat Race, held in March or April, when teams from Oxford and Cambridge row from Putney to Mortlake (see p56); a newer tradition is the London Marathon, which is run from Greenwich to The Mall at Westminster (see p56) on an April Sunday. You can watch croquet at **Dulwich Croquet Club** and medieval (real) tennis at **Queen's Club**.

WATER SPORTS

There are facilities for a wide variety of water sports at the **Docklands Sailing & Water Sports Centre**. You can choose from sports such as windsurfing, dinghy sailing, motorboating, waterskiing, and canoeing. Rowboats are also available for rent by the hour on the calmer, central London waters of the **Serpentine** in Hyde Park and **Regent's Park Lake**.

WORKING OUT

Most sports centers have gymnasiums, workout studios, and health clubs. If you are a member of the YMCA, you'll be able to use the excellent facilities at the **Central YMCA**. **Jubilee Hall Clubs** and the **Oasis Sports Centre** both offer a variety of aerobics and keep-fit classes, and weight training. For those who have overdone it, the **Chelsea Sports Centre** has a sports injury clinic.

DIRECTORY

London 2012
Tel 020-3 2012 000.
For general enquiries.
www.london2012.com

All England Lawn Tennis and Croquet Club
Church Rd, Wimbledon SW19. *Tel 020-8946 2244.*

Arsenal (Emirates) Stadium
Ashburton Grove N7.
Tel 020-7704 4000.

Ascot Racecourse
Ascot, Berkshire.
Tel 0870-727 1234.

Brit Oval
Kennington Oval SE11.
Map 22 D4.
Tel 08712-461100.

Broadgate Ice Rink
Broadgate Circle EC2.
Map 7 C5.
Tel 020-7505 4120.

Central YMCA
112 Great Russell St WC1.
Map 13 B1.
Tel 020-7343 1844.

Chelsea Football Club
Stamford Bridge SW6.
Tel 0871-984 1955.

Chelsea Sports Centre
Chelsea Manor St SW3.
Map 19 B3.
Tel 020-7352 6985.

Chessington Golf Course
Garrison Lane, Surrey.
Tel 020-8391 0948.

Docklands Sailing & Watersports Centre
235a Westferry Rd, E14.
Tel 020-7537 2626.
www.dswc.org

Dulwich Croquet Club
Giant Arches Rd, Off Burbage Rd SE24.
Tel 020-7928 9834.
www.dulwichcroquet.com

Epsom Racecourse
Epsom Downs, Surrey.
Tel 01372-470047.

Hampstead and Highgate Ponds
Mixed: off East Heath Rd NW3. **Map** 1 C4.
Men's and Women's:
Millfield Lane N6. **Map** 2 E3.
Tel 020-7482 7073.

Holland Park Public Tennis Courts
1 Ilchester Place W8. **Map** 9 B5. *Tel 020-7602 2226.*

Hounslow Heath Golf Course
Staines Rd, Middlesex TW4.
Tel 020-8570 5271.

Jubilee Hall Clubs
30 The Piazza, Covent Garden WC2. **Map** 13 C2.
Tel 020-7836 4007.

Kempton Park
Sunbury on Thames, Middx.
Tel 01932 782292.

Linford Christie Stadium
Du Cane Rd W12.
Tel 020-8749 6758.

Lord's Cricket Ground
St. John's Wood NW8.
Map 3 A3.
Tel 020-7289 1611.

Oasis Swimming Pool & Sports Centre
32 Endell St WC2.
Map 13 B1.
Tel 020-7831 1804.

Parliament Hill
Highgate Rd NW5.
Map 2 E5.
Tel 020-7485 4491.

Porchester Centre
Queensway W2.
Map 10 D1.
Tel 020-7792 2919.

Queen's Club (Real Tennis)
Palliser Rd W14.
Map 17 A3.
Tel 020-7385 3421.

Queens Ice Skating Club
17 Queensway W2.
Map 10 E2.
Tel 020-7229 0172.

Regent's Park and Lake
Regent's Park NW1.
Map 3 C3.
Tel 020-7486 7905.
Tel 020-7724 4069 (boat rental).

Richmond Park Golf
Roehampton Gate, Priory Lane SW15.
Tel 020-8876 3205.

Romford Stadium
London Road, Essex RM7.
Tel 01708-762 345.

Rosslyn Park Rugby
Priory Lane, Upper Richmond Rd SW15.
Tel 020-8876 1879.

Ross Nye Stables
8 Bathurst Mews W2.
Map 11 A2.
Tel 020-7262 3791.

Sandown Park Racecourse
Esher, Surrey.
Tel 01372 464348.

Saracens Rugby Football Club
5 Vicarage Rd, Watford, Hertfordshire, WD1.
Tel 01727-792 800.

Serpentine
Hyde Park W2. **Map** 11 B4.
Tel 020-7298 2100 (boat rental).

Somerset House Ice Rink
Strand WC2. **Map** 14 D2.
Tel 020-7845 4600.

Tottenham Hotspur FC
White Hart Lane, 748 High Rd N17.
Tel 0844-499 5000.

Twickenham Rugby Ground
Whitton Rd, Twickenham, Middlesex.
Tel 0871-222 2120.

West Ham United
Boleyn Ground, Green St, Upton Park E13.
Tel 0871-222 7000.

CHILDREN'S LONDON

London offers children a potential goldmine of fun, excitement, and adventure. Each year finds new attractions and sights opening up and older ones being updated.

First-time visitors may want to watch traditional ceremonies (*see pp52–5*) or visit famous buildings (*see p37*), but these are merely the tip of the iceberg. While London's parks, zoos, and

Humpty Dumpty doll

adventure playgrounds provide outdoor activities there are also loads of workshops, activity centers, and museums providing quizzes, hands-on experiments and interactive displays. A day out need not be costly: children under 11 are entitled to free tube, bus, and DLR travel provided they are traveling with an adult who has a valid ticket or Oystercard. Most London museums are free.

PRACTICAL ADVICE

A little planning is the key to a successful outing. You may want to check the opening hours of the places you plan to visit in advance, by telephone or online via the venue's website. Work out your journey thoroughly using the subway map at the end of this book.

If you are traveling with very young children remember that there are very likely to be lines at subway stations or at bus stops near popular sights. These will be long during peak hours, so buy your tickets, Travelcard, or Oyster card in advance (*see p378*).

Children under 11 can travel free on buses and tubes and child fares operate for all children between the ages of 11 and 15. Children very often enjoy using public transportation, especially when it's a novelty, so plan

Punch and Judy show in the Piazza, Covent Garden

your outing carefully using one form of transportation on the way there and another for the journey home. You can get around London easily by bus, Underground, taxi, train, and riverboat (*see pp378–85*). Visiting all the exhibitions and museums as a family doesn't have to be as expensive as it

Covent Garden clowns

sounds. The majority of London's principal museums have no entry charge. For those where you do have to pay, an annual family season ticket, usually for two adults and up to four children, is available at many of the museums and often costs only marginally more than the initial visit.

In some cases you can buy a family ticket that covers a group of museums. Being able to visit a sight more than once means that you won't exhaust your children and put them off museums for life by trying to see absolutely everything over one long, tiring day.

If your children want a break from sightseeing, most borough councils provide information on activities for children such as playgroups, theaters, funfairs, and activity centers in their area. Leaflets are usually available from libraries and leisure centers, as well as local town halls. During the long summer school holidays (July through the beginning of September) there are organized activity programs all over London.

CHILDREN AND THE LAW

Children under 14 are not allowed into British pubs and wine bars (unless there is a special family room or garden) and only people over 18 can drink or buy any alcohol. In restaurants, the law is a little more relaxed. Those over 16 can drink wine or beer with their meal, but you

EATING OUT WITH CHILDREN

Restaurants are becoming more welcoming of tiny patrons. Italian eateries are often the friendliest, but even the traditional British pub, once resolutely child-free, has relented, with beer gardens and family rooms. As long as your offspring are reasonably well-behaved, most informal restaurants will be happy to serve a family. Some can also provide highchairs and booster cushions, as well as coloring mats to keep children entertained while waiting for their food to arrive. Many will also offer special children's menus with small helpings, which will cut the cost of your meal.

Over the weekend some restaurants (such as **Smollensky's** and **Sticky Fingers**) provide live entertainment for children in the form of clowns, face painters, and magicians. A number accept bookings for children's parties. It is worth trying to book in advance (especially for Sunday lunch), so that you don't have to hang around waiting with tired and hungry children.

Coming up for air at Smollensky's

London has a number of restaurants ideal for older children. Among these are the **Rainforest Café** and the **Hard Rock Café** on Old Park Lane.

For budget eating, try the Café in the Crypt, St. Martin-in-the-Fields *(see p102)*.

Dine with the elephants at the Rainforest Café

USEFUL ADDRESSES

Hard Rock Café
150 Old Park Lane W1. **Map** 12 E4.
Tel 020-7514 1700.

Rainforest Café
20 Shaftesbury Ave W1. **Map** 13 A2.
Tel 020-7434 3111.

Smollensky's
105 Strand WC2. **Map** 14 D2.
Tel 020-7497 2101.

Sticky Fingers
1a Phillimore Gdns, W8. **Map** 9 C5.
Tel 020-7938 5338.

still have to be over 18 to be served spirits. In general, young children are rarely welcome anywhere they might create a nuisance. Some movies are classed as unsuitable for children *(see p347)*.

If you want to take your children by car, you must use seat belts wherever they are provided. Babies will need a special child seat. If you are in doubt, ask at any police station.

GETTING THEM OFF YOUR HANDS

Many of London's museums *(see pp40–43)* and theaters *(see pp344–6)* provide weekend and holiday activities and workshops where you can leave children over a certain age for a few hours or even for a whole day, and the children's theaters are a great way to spend a rainy afternoon. A day at the fair is always a success – try Hampstead fair on summer holiday Mondays. London has a great many sports centers

(see pp354–5), that often have special clubs and activities to occupy children of every age.

If you want a total break, call **Nannies Unlimited**, **Sitters**, **Kensington Nannies**, or **Pippa Pop-Ins**, a nursery school offering full-day childcare. All registered child minders will have been verified by the Criminal Records Bureau.

BABYSITTING

Kensington Nannies
3 Hornton Place W8.
Map 10 D5. *Tel 020-7937 2333.*
www.kensington-nannies.com

Nannies Unlimited
11 Chelverton Rd, Putney SW615
Tel 020-8788 9640.

Pippa Pop-Ins
430 Fulham Road SW6. **Map** 18 D5.
Tel 020-7731 1445.
Also at 233 New King's Rd SW6.

Sitters
126 Rickmansworth Rd, Watford
WD18. *Tel 0800-389 0038.*

Airborne at the Hampstead fair

Holiday fun at Pippa Pop-Ins

SHOPPING

All children love a visit to **Hamleys** toy store or Harrods toy department (see p321). **Davenport's Magic Shop** and **The Disney Store** are smaller and more specialized.

Both the **Early Learning Centre** (many branches) and **The Cat and the Fiddle** have good selections of books. Some stores organize readings and signings by children's authors, especially during Children's Book Week in October.

USEFUL NUMBERS The Cat and the Fiddle **Tel** 020-8989 8100; Davenport's Magic Shop **Tel** 020-7836 0408; The Disney Store **Tel** 020-7491 9136; Early Learning Centre **Tel** 020-7581 5764; Hamleys **Tel** 0844-855 2424.

Bears at Hamleys toy shop

MUSEUMS AND GALLERIES

London has a wealth of museums, exhibitions, and galleries; more information on those listed here is to be found on pages 40–43. Most have been updated over the last few years to incorporate some exciting modern display techniques. It's unlikely that you'll have to drag reluctant children around an assortment of lifeless, stuffy exhibits.

The V&A Museum of Childhood (p248), the children's branch of the

V&A in East London, and Pollock's Toy Museum (p131) are both especially good for young children.

For older children try one of London's Brass Rubbing Centres: the great Brass Rubbing Centre in the Crypt of St. Martin-in-the-Fields (p102) or at St. James's Church on Piccadilly (p90). Madame Tussauds (p224) and Tower Bridge (p153) are firm favorites with children.

The British Museum (pp126–9) has fabulous treasures from all over the world, and the Horniman Museum (p250) has colorful displays from many different cultures. The Science Museum (pp212–13), with over 600 working exhibits, is one of London's best attractions for children – its hands-on galleries in the basement, including the much-loved Launch Pad, will help keep them amused for hours. The interactive displays in the high-tech Wellcome Wing are also entertaining. If you have the stamina, the Natural History Museum (pp208–9) next door contains hundreds of amazing objects and animals from the world of nature. Included is a Dinosaur Exhibition. Suits of armor built for knights and monarchs can be seen at the

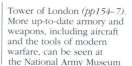

Shirley Temple doll at Bethnal Green Museum

Tower of London (pp154–7). More up-to-date armory and weapons, including aircraft and the tools of modern warfare, can be seen at the National Army Museum (p197) and the Imperial War Museum (pp190–91). Also worth a visit is the Guards' Museum (p80) located on Birdcage Walk. London's colorful past is brought alive at the Museum of London. The superb London Aquarium (p188), on the bank of the Thames, offers close-up encounters with sea life from starfish to sharks.

THE GREAT OUTDOORS

London is fortunate in having many parks and open spaces (see pp48–51). Most local parks contain conventional playgrounds for children, many with modern, safe equipment. Some parks also have One O'Clock Clubs (enclosed areas for children under 5 with activities supervised by play-workers) as well as adventure playgrounds, nature trails, boating ponds, and athletic tracks for older children and energetic adults.

Puppets at the Little Angel Theatre, Islington

Playground at Gunnersbury Park

A delightful children's park in Bloomsbury is Coram's Fields (p125), where grassy areas, sandpits and playgrounds make it perfect for picnics. Kite-flying on Blackheath (p243), Hampstead Heath, or Parliament Hill can be fun, as can boating in Regent's Park. A trip to Primrose Hill (pp266–7) can be combined with a visit to the Zoo and Regent's Canal (p227). The large parks are one of London's greatest assets for parents who have energetic children. For a good walk or cycle ride, there are parks all over London. For instance, there's Hyde Park in the city center; Hampstead Heath up in the north; Wimbledon Common in southwest London; and Gunnersbury Park in west London. Cyclists should be sure to watch out for pedestrians and remember thatsome paths may be out of bounds.

Battersea Park has a children's zoo and Crystal Palace Park (Penge SE20) has a dinosaur park. Richmond Park has a deer herd. For a relaxing trip, go feed the ducks in St. James's Park.

Tuojiangasaurus skeleton at the Natural History Museum

CHILDREN'S THEATER

Introducing children to the theater can be great fun for adults too. Get involved at the **Little Angel Theatre,** or the **Puppet Theatre Barge** in Little Venice. The **Unicorn Theatre** offers the best range of children's theater and the **Polka Children's Theatre** has some good shows.
USEFUL NUMBERS Little Angel Theatre **Tel** 020-7226 1787. Polka Children's Theatre **Tel** 020-8543 4888. **www**.polkatheatre.com Puppet Theatre Barge Marionette Performers **Tel** 020-7249 6876. **www**.puppetbarge.com Unicorn Theatre **Tel** 020-7645 0560. **www**.unicorntheatre.com

Deer in Richmond Park

SIGHTSEEING

For seeing the sights of London you can't beat the top of a double-decker bus (see pp382–3). It's a cheap and easy way of entertaining children, and if they get restless you can always jump off the bus at the next stop. London's colorful ceremonies are detailed on pages 52–5.

Children will also enjoy such spectacles as the summer funfairs in London's parks, the firework displays throughout London

Boating lake near Winfield House in Regent's Park

on Guy Fawkes Night (every November 5), the Christmas decorations in Oxford Street and Regent Street, and Trafalgar Square's Christmas tree.

BEHIND THE SCENES

Older children in particular will love the opportunity to look "behind the scenes" and see how famous events or institutions are run.

If you have a brood of sports enthusiasts, you should visit Twickenham Rugby Football Ground (see p355), Lord's Cricket Ground (p246), the Wimbledon Lawn Tennis Museum (p251), and Chelsea soccer stadium (p355).

For budding theater buffs, the Royal National Theatre (p188), the Royal Opera House (p115), Sadler's Wells (p350), and the Theatre Royal Drury Lane (p115) all offer tours.

Other good buildings for children to visit include the Tower of London (pp154–7), the Old Bailey courthouse, (p147) and the Houses of Parliament (pp72–3).

If none of the above satisfies the children, the London Fire Brigade (020-7587 4063) offers more unusual guided tours.

SURVIVAL
GUIDE

PRACTICAL INFORMATION 362–71

GETTING TO LONDON 372–7

GETTING AROUND LONDON 378–85

PRACTICAL INFORMATION

London has responded well to the demands of modern tourism. The range of facilities on offer to travelers, from ATM machines and medical clinics to boutique hotels and late-night transportation, continues to expand. Whether you find London an expensive city will depend on the exchange rate between the pound and your own currency. It is known for high hotel prices, but even here there are good mid-range and budget options (see pp278–81). Nor need you spend a lot on food, if you choose carefully and make the most of the range London has to offer; for the price of a single meal at some West End restaurants you could eat enjoyably for several days (see pp312–15). The following tips will help you make the most of your visit.

Crossing the Millenium Bridge

WHEN TO GO

London's weather is famously changeable, but in general it is chilly from November to February, and warmest from June to August (see p59). It can rain at any time of year, so pack accordingly. Extremes of temperature – whether of cold in winter or heat in summer – are rare, so there is no time of year when London "closes down" and everyone goes on vacation. Events and cultural programs run throughout the year. Many major concert series and exhibitions take place in winter and spring, but there are plenty of cultural events during the summer too, such as the BBC Proms season of classical concerts, and open-air theater seasons. In short, there's plenty to see all year round (see pp56–9).

VISAS AND PASSPORTS

Citizens of European Union countries may enter the UK for an unlimited period with a passport or national identity card. Visitors from the United States, Canada, Australia, and New Zealand need only a full passport for tourist and business stays of up to six months, but on arrival they must fill in an Immigration Card, which is given out on incoming flights. Citizens of some countries may require a visa; details can be found in the "Visa Services" section of the **UK Border Agency** (UKBA) website. The UK is not signed up to the Schengen open-borders agreement operated by most EU countries. Hence, visitors arriving from France or any other Schengen country must still pass through immigration checks when entering the UK.

The UKBA has a strict points-based visa system under which anyone from any non-EU country (including the USA, Canada, Australia, and New Zealand) entering Britain for any purpose other than pure tourism or short business trips (this includes students on short study-abroad programs) must obtain a visa before traveling. The visa system is complicated and detailed, so check well in advance; details are on the UKBA website.

CUSTOMS INFORMATION

EU residents may carry any amount of goods between EU countries without paying duty, as long as the goods are for their personal use. Customs officers can still question whether large amounts of any item are genuinely for your own use. Examples of amounts usually accepted are: up to 3,200 cigarettes and up to 90 liters of wine. For travelers arriving from outside the EU, stricter allowances apply – for example, 200 cigarettes. Visitors not resident in the EU can reclaim the Value Added Tax (VAT) on many goods when they leave Britain, but note that the items must have been bought from a store operating the VAT Retail Export Scheme (which should be indicated in the store window). Ask the retailer for the correct form, which has details on how to obtain your refund; these can also be found on the UKBA website under "Travel and Customs."

TOURIST INFORMATION AND TOURS

Visit London is the city's central tourism service and is a key source of information. The main tourist office is the **Britain and London Visitor Centre** (see p365); there are also Tourist Information Centres in the City (by St. Paul's Cathedral), at main rail stations and at several other locations (visitlondon.com has a full list). The centers sell travelcards and **London Pass** (see p363) discount cards, provide currency exchange, and distribute Visit London's handy free monthly magazine, *London Planner*.

For comprehensive listings information – including art, movies, music, theater, and nightlife – visit the websites of **LondonNet** and *Time Out*

Signposted directions

ROYAL OPERA HOUSE
COVENT GARDEN MARKET
THEATRE MUSEUM
LONDON TRANSPORT MUSEUM

Double-decker sightseeing boat on the Thames

London, London's leading listings magazine.

Guided tours are an effective way to explore the city; a trip in an open-topped double-decker bus makes a good introduction. **Original London Sightseeing Tours** and **Big Bus Tours** are the main companies offering hop-on, hop-off services, with tickets valid for 24 or 48 hours. Other tour companies include **London Walks**, which offers over 40 different routes, and **London Duck Tours**, for tours in a World-War-II-era amphibious vehicle. To find a private tour guide to suit your interests, contact the **Association of Professional Tourist Guides**. For river cruises and commuter services, *see page 61*.

Major sights in London are often crowded and lines are likely. Museums and galleries get particularly busy on weekends and on late-opening nights, so try to visit midweek and earlier in the day.

ADMISSION PRICES

Admission to the main collections of London's major public museums and galleries is free, but you will pay to see temporary exhibits. Private museums and other attractions have admission charges; they vary greatly, but for adults most are between £5 and £15. There are often reduced prices for seniors, students, and children.

If you aim to do lots of sightseeing, you can cut costs with a **London Pass**, a card that gives you free entry and fast-track admission at many attractions. Cards are valid for 1, 2, 3, or 6 days and can be combined with a bus and Underground travelcard. A London Pass can be bought in advance from visitlondon.com and mailed to your home or collected from a tourist center.

OPENING HOURS

Opening times for individual sights are listed in the *Area by Area* section of this book. Core visiting times are 10am to 5pm or 6pm daily; last admission is usually 1 hour before closing time. Most of the big museums have at least one late-opening day each week. Opening hours are often shorter on Sundays and public holidays. Some smaller attractions are closed on Mondays.

SOCIAL CUSTOMS AND ETIQUETTE

Londoners are traditionally renowned for waiting in line – whether for theater tickets, taxis, or takeouts. Things aren't quite as genteel as they used to be, but in general, anyone barging in will still encounter frosty glares.

Casual clothing is accepted in most restaurants, and only a few upscale establishments still require men to wear a jacket and tie.

The religious pattern of London reflects the city's huge ethnic diversity; all of the world's major faiths are represented here.

Smoking is forbidden in all public indoor spaces. Some hotels still designate bedrooms for smokers, but it's best to double check when reserving.

TIPPING

It is usual to tip in restaurants, hotels, hairdressers, taxis, and minicabs, but not for bar service in pubs. Many restaurants add a service charge – usually 12.5 percent – to the bill, in which case an extra tip is not necessary. Be wary of places that add a service charge, then encourage you to add a "gratuity" when you pay by credit card. In taxis and cabs, tip around 10 percent; for hotel porters, £1 is usually sufficient.

TRAVELERS WITH SPECIAL NEEDS

Access to transportation, attractions, and services for wheelchair users and others with mobility problems is continually improving. The Visit London website has a guide to access and services. **Transport for London** (TfL) produces a *Getting around London* guide, which can be downloaded from the TfL or Visit London websites, and is available free from Underground stations. **Artsline** gives information on facilities at cultural events and venues.

Nearly all London buses have wheelchair-access ramps, and all licensed taxis and some minicabs are wheelchair-accessible. The huge task of improving access to the entire Underground network is ongoing. Underground maps show accessible stations. Most museums and theaters have access facilities, but hotels with fully adapted rooms are scarce.

Disabled drivers with a blue badge allowing free parking should note that in four London boroughs – the City, Westminster, Kensington & Chelsea, and Camden – it allows you to park only in designated blue-badge bays.

London bus with ramp for easy wheelchair access

The Natural History Museum, a great day out for the whole family

TRAVELING WITH CHILDREN

Under Transport for London's "Kids Go Free" scheme, travel is free on buses, the Underground, DLR, and trains within London for all children aged under 11 accompanied by an adult (up to four children per adult). Children aged 11–15 can also travel free, with or without an adult, on all buses, and for reduced prices on the Underground and DLR (see p378); also available is a Zip Oyster 11–15 Identity Card, which can be ordered online and collected at a tourist information center on arrival in London; see the Visit London and Transport for London websites.

Most museums and attractions have reduced prices for children under 11; at several, entry is free for under-5s. Many also offer good-value family tickets. Plenty of restaurants welcome children, and a number of hotels have family rooms; the Novotel chain represents particularly good value for families.

London is a child-friendly city. A huge variety of entertainment and activities are laid on for children, and many museums have special kids' programs. There are dozens of parks, many of them with playground facilities. The Visit London website's "Family" pages are a useful source of information. Time Out London's "Kids" pages are good for current attractions.

SENIOR TRAVELERS

Older visitors enjoy fewer benefits than younger ones, but there are reduced admission prices for over-60s at most museums, exhibitions, and other attractions. You may be asked to show photo ID. Free travel on public transportation is only available to residents.

GAY AND LESBIAN TRAVELERS

London has a huge and diverse gay scene. Its core is Soho – it even has a (non-official) **LGBT Tourist Office**, which offers advice on everything from the best gay bars to accommodations. It's hard to keep track of everything going on, but the **Pink Paper** and **Gay London** websites, as well as the gay pages of Time Out London, are all useful and up-to-date sources of information.

TRAVELING ON A BUDGET

London can be a very expensive city, but sightseeing costs can be cut with the London Pass (see p363), and remember that admission to London's

International Student Identity Card (ISIC)

largest museums is free. To get around by public transportation, always buy a travelcard rather than single tickets; for trips out of town, coach (long-distance bus) is much cheaper than train, especially when bought in advance. Discounted theater tickets can be bought at the **tkts** booth in Leicester Square, and many theaters have cheap-ticket nights.

London has plenty of budget restaurants and cafés, and even quite grand restaurants offer accessibly priced lunch menus. As well as dorm-style hostels, there are no-frills budget hotels with private rooms, some ensuite, for under £50 (see p281). There's also a growing trend for spare-room lets and "couch surfing" via the **Crashpadder** website.

Students pay lower admission to many exhibitions, and holders of an **ISIC** (International Student Identity Card) or IYTC (International Youth Travel Card) are eligible for a range of other discounts. A **Hostelling International** card is also handy for lower rates at hostels and other discounts.

ELECTRICITY

The voltage in London is 240V AC, and plugs have three square pins. Visitors will need plug adaptors for appliances, and with any older North American 110V equipment you may also need a current transformer.

CONVERSION CHART

Officially the metric system is used, but imperial measures are still common.

Imperial to metric
1 inch = 2.5 centimeters
1 foot = 30 centimeters
1 mile = 1.6 kilometers
1 ounce = 28 grams
1 pound = 454 grams
1 pint = 0.6 litre
1 gallon = 4.6 liters

Metric to imperial
1 millimeter = 0.04 inch
1 centimeter = 0.4 inch
1 meter = 3 feet 3 inches
1 kilometer = 0.6 mile
1 gram = 0.04 ounce
1 kilogram = 2.2 pounds

TIME

London is on Greenwich Mean Time (GMT) during the winter months, 5 hours ahead of Eastern Standard Time and 10 hours behind Sydney. From late March to late October, clocks are set forward 1 hour to British Summer Time (equivalent to Central European Time). At any time of year you can check the correct time by dialing 123 on a BT landline to contact the 24-hour automated Speaking Clock service (note that there is a charge).

RESPONSIBLE TOURISM

London has set ambitious targets for improving the urban environment and reducing energy use. **Thames 21**, for example, is an evironmental charity that involves the local community in programs to help keep the river Thames clean and clear.

The **Green Tourism Business Scheme** awards "Green Tourism" badges to businesses in the

Green Tourism badge

UK that meet the highest environmental standards. These standards ensure that each business is committed to sustainable tourism and dedicated to minimising its damage to the environment. See the website for green accommodations details.

Recycling bins, which separate paper and plastic, are widely available and many shoppers carry reusable cloth bags to avoid using plastic bags.

DIRECTORY

VISAS AND PASSPORTS

UK Border Agency
www.ukba.homeoffice.gov.uk

EMBASSIES AND CONSULATES

Australian High Commission
Australia House, The Strand, WC2.
Map 13 C2.
Tel 020-7379 4334.
www.uk.embassy.gov.au

Canadian High Commission
1 Grosvenor Square, W1.
Map 12 D2. *Tel 020-7258 6600.* www.unitedkingdom.gc.ca

New Zealand High Commission
80 Haymarket, SW1.
Map 13 A3.
Tel 020-7930 8422.
www.nzembassy.com/united-kingdom

United States Embassy
24 Grosvenor Square, W1.
Map 12 D2.
Tel 020-7499 9000.
www.usembassy.org.uk

TOURIST INFORMATION

Association of Professional Tour Guides
Tel 020-7611 2545.
www.touristguides.org.uk

Big Bus Tours
Tel 020-7233 9533.
www.bigbustours.com

Britain and London Visitor Centre
1 Lower Regent St, Piccadilly Circus, SW1.
Map 13 A3. Piccadilly Circus. **Open** Daily.

London Duck Tours
Tel 020-7928 3132.
www.londonducktours.co.uk

LondonNet
www.londonnet.co.uk

London Pass
www.londonpass.com

London Walks
Tel 020-7624 3978.
www.walks.com

Original London Sightseeing Tour
Tel 020-8877 1722.
www.theoriginaltour.com

Time Out London
www.timeout.com/london

Transport for London
www.tfl.gov.uk

Visit London
www.visitlondon.com

RELIGIOUS SERVICES

Anglican (Episcopalian)
St. Paul's Cathedral EC4.
Map 15 A2.
Tel 020-7246 8357.
www.stpauls.co.uk

Catholic
Westminster Cathedral, Victoria St SW1.
Map 20 F1.
Tel 020-7798 9055.
www.westminstercathedral.org.uk

Evangelical Alliance
Whitefield House, 186 Kennington Park Rd SE11.
Map 22 E4.
Tel 020-7207 2100.
www.eauk.org

Jewish
Liberal Jewish Synagogue, 28 St. John's Wood Rd NW8.
Map 3 A3.
Tel 020-7286 5181.
www.ljs.org.

United Synagogue (Orthodox), 735 High Rd, N12.
Tel 020-8343 8989.
www.theus.org.uk.

Muslim
Islamic Cultural Centre, 146 Park Rd NW8.
Map 3 B3.
Tel 020-7724 3363.
www.iccuk.org

TRAVELERS WITH SPECIAL NEEDS

Artsline
www.artsline.org.uk

Transport for London
Tel 0843 222 1234 (24 hours).
www.tfl.gov.uk

GAY & LESBIAN TRAVELERS

Gay London
www.gaylondon.com

LGBT Tourist Information Office
130 Lisle St, WC2.
Map 13 B2.
Tel 020-7437 0003.
www.gaytouristoffice.co.uk

Pink Paper
www.pinkpaper.com

TRAVELING ON A BUDGET

Crashpadder
www.crashpadder.com

Hostelling International
www.hihostels.com

ISIC (International Student Identity Card)
www.isiccard.com

tkts (Discount Theatre Tickets)
Leicester Square, WC2.
Map 13 B2.
www.tkts.co.uk

RESPONSIBLE TOURISM

Thames 21
www.thames21.otg.uk

Tourism Business Scheme
Tel 01738-632 162.
www.greenbusiness.co.uk

Personal Security and Health

London is a large city which, like any other, has had its share of urban problems. It has also been a terrorist target, and London life is sometimes disrupted by security alerts. Nearly all of these turn out to be false alarms, but they should always still be taken seriously. Never hesitate to approach one of London's many police constables for assistance – they are trained to help the public with problems.

Mounted police

POLICE

If you are robbed, or are the victim of any other kind of crime, report it to the police as soon as possible. Patrolling police officers are generally fairly easy to find in central London, but if you cannot find one, call or go to the nearest police station – these are listed on the **Metropolitan Police** website; alternatively your hotel should be able to help advise. Note that the **City of London Police** is a separate force, with its own website. Police stations are also shown on the Street Finder maps toward the end of this book (pp386–423).

When you report a crime, police will take a statement from you, and you will need to list any lost or stolen items.

WHAT TO BE AWARE OF

It is unlikely that your stay in London will be blighted by crime. Even in run-down parts of town, the risk of having your pocket picked or bag stolen is not particularly great. It is actually more likely to happen in the middle of heaving shopping crowds in areas like Oxford Street or Camden Lock, or perhaps on a packed Underground platform.

As in any big city, the risk of being a victim of street crime can be further reduced by following a few sensible precautions. Make sure your possessions are adequately insured before you travel. Do not carry all your valuables around with you but take only as much cash as you need, and leave the rest in a hotel safe or a locked suitcase. Avoid poorly lit or isolated places like backstreets, parks, and unmanned train stations at night, and don't use ATMs after dark. To be extra careful, try to travel around in a group at night.

In crowds, be aware of anyone standing especially close. Keep bags zipped up; keep a hand on your bag when walking; and never leave bags unattended in any public place – they may be stolen or considered a security threat. When you sit at a table, especially outdoors, always keep your bag within reach and in sight – preferably on your lap or on the table – and never leave it on the ground or hanging on the back of a chair.

IN AN EMERGENCY

In a serious emergency you can call 999 – or the European emergency number 112 – to summon police, fire, or ambulance services. Note that this is only for genuine emergencies, so if you have a lesser problem it is better to contact a police station or hospital directly.

LOST AND STOLEN PROPERTY

Although you should report thefts, or loss of any property, to the police, be warned that it's unlikely that they will be able to recover any of it for you. However, they will give you a copy of your police statement, which you will need to make an insurance claim.

If you lose anything on buses, Underground and DLR trains, or in taxis (black cabs), it should eventually reach the **Transport for London Lost Property Office** in Baker Street. You can also inquire about lost items online, through the TfL website (under "Help & Contact" or "Useful Contacts"). It will usually take a few days for items to reach the office, so if you notice the loss the same day, try to inquire about it at the station nearest to where you lost it, or at the nearest police station. Items lost on river boats or in minicabs should be held by the individual companies.

HOSPITALS AND PHARMACIES

All European Union nationals with a European Health Insurance Card (EHIC), as well as citizens of some other countries with special agreements with the UK (Australia and New Zealand among them), can obtain free treatment from the British **National Health Service (NHS)**. Visitors from other non-EU countries should have full medical cover as part of their travel insurance, and if necessary make use of an NHS or private hospital (such as **Medical Express**) on a paying basis. In case of emergency, anyone – EU or non-EU – will be treated free of charge.

If you have an accident or other problem needing medical attention, ask your hotel to recommend a doctor,

Traffic police officer

Typical London police car

London ambulance

London fire engine

or go to the nearest NHS health center (doctor's surgery) or hospital Accident & Emergency (A&E) department. Not all hospitals have A&E departments, but those that do are listed on the NHS and Visit London websites, and in local phone books. In many cases the simplest thing may be to call **NHS Direct**, a free advice service that will give you immediate health advice and also direct you to the nearest hospital A&E department.

If you have a dental problem, you can also call NHS Direct for addresses of emergency dentists. Dental treatment through the NHS is not entirely free, so it may make more sense to arrange private treatment (again, hotels should be able to recommend a dentist) and claim on your insurance policy.

Pharmacies (also known as chemists) are plentiful around London, and staff are trained to dispense and advise on a wide range of medications. Some medicines are only available with a prescription. It is worth noting that prescription drugs are not not free even if you are entitled to NHS treatment; if you are not, you will be charged the full price, and so will need to make an insurance claim. The **Boots** company is the largest chain of pharmacies in the UK. Most pharmacies are closed on Sundays, but those listed in the Directory, below, have extended hours.

TRAVEL AND HEALTH INSURANCE

All visitors to London should have a comprehensive travel insurance policy providing adequate cover for all eventualities including potential legal expenses, theft, lost luggage or other property, accidents, cancellations, travel delays, and medical cover.

Even if you are entitled to use the NHS for medical needs, it can be a good idea to have private medical insurance included too, as a backup, since this may allow you to get quicker treatment with fewer formalities. Your insurance company should provide you with a 24-hour emergency number in case of need.

Pharmacy sign

DIRECTORY

EMERGENCIES

Police, Fire, & Ambulance services
Tel 999 or 112.
Calls are free.

POLICE

City of London Police
Tel 020-7601 2222.
www.cityoflondon.
police.uk

Metropolitan Police
Tel 0300-123 1212.
www.met.police.uk

West End Central Police Station
27 Saville Row, W1.
Map 12 F2.
Tel 0300-123 1212.

LOST PROPERTY

Transport for London Lost Property Office
200 Baker St, NW1.
Map 3 C5.
Tel 0845-330-9882.
www.tfl.gov.uk. *Open* 8:30am–4pm Mon–Fri.

HEALTH SERVICES

Medical Express (Private)
117A Harley St, W1.
Tel 0800-9800 700.
www.medicalexpress clinic.com

NHS
www.nhs.uk
To locate a hospital, look under "Find and choose services."

NHS Direct

Tel 0845-4647.
www.nhsdirect.nhs.uk
(24-hr health information and nurse-led advice).

University College Hospital
Accident and Emergency,
235 Euston Road NW1.
Map 5 A4.
Tel 0845-155 5000.

DENTISTS

24-Hour Emergency Dental Clinic
8F Gilbert Place WC1.
Map 13 B1. *Tel* 020-8123 3132. **www**.24hour-london-emergencydentist.
co.uk

LATE-OPENING PHARMACIES

Bliss Chemist
5–6 Marble Arch W1.
Map 11 C2. *Tel* 020-7723 6116. *Open* 9am until midnight daily.

Boots the Chemist
44–46 Regent St, W1.
Map 13 A3. *Tel* 020-7734 6126. **www**.boots.
com *Open* 8am–midnight Mon–Fri, 9am– midnight Sat, noon–6pm Sun.

Superdrug
508–520 Oxford St, W1.
Map 11 C2. *Tel* 020-7629 1649.
www.superdrug.com
Open 7am–11pm Mon–Fri, 8am–10pm Sat, 12:30–6:30pm Sun.

Banking and Local Currency

Visitors to London will find that banks usually offer the best rates of exchange, but care should be taken to check the small-print details relating to commission and other charges before completing any transaction. Privately owned exchange bureaus have variable exchange rates and commissions – some, in particular, charge more for changing smaller amounts of money – but they do stay open long after the banks have closed.

ATM (cashpoint machine)

BANKS AND EXCHANGE BUREAUS

Banking hours vary. The minimum opening hours for all banks are 9:30am–3:30pm Mon–Fri, but many branches now stay open till 5 or 5:30pm, especially in central London; some also open on Saturdays from about 10am–4pm. All banks are closed on Sundays and public holidays *(see p59).* The commission charged on currency exchange will vary from bank to bank.

When banks are closed, there are plenty of other facilities for changing cash and traveler's checks across the city. You will find exchange bureaus

(bureaux de change) at airports, main train stations, in large stores, and at many other locations. **Chequepoint, Thomas Cook**, and **Travelex** are some of the largest companies. The central London (Piccadilly) branch of **Money Corporation** is open 24 hours daily.

CREDIT CARDS AND TRAVELER'S CHECKS

Major credit cards such as Visa and MasterCard, and debit cards such as Delta, Maestro, and Cirrus, are widely accepted all over London. Fewer businesses accept the American Express card, because of their high charges.

British credit and debit cards operate on a chip-and-PIN security system; you must enter your PIN number into a card reader to validate the purchase. If you have a North American or other card that does not use chip-and-pin technology, your card will have to be swiped in the more traditional way.

It may also be useful to have some currency with you in traveler's checks, in case you lose your cards. Traveler's checks cannot be used to pay for goods directly in stores in the UK, but must be

exchanged for cash at a bank or exchange bureau. US dollar and Euro traveler's checks are easily exchanged at all banks and change desks. Again, check the latest commission rates and conditions before cashing your checks.

ATMS

There are ATM cash machines (also known as cashpoints), from which you can obtain cash with any of the major credit or debit cards, at all bank branches, many post offices, and many other locations such as stations. The cards accepted by each ATM are indicated on the machine, which usually gives instructions in several languages. Given the high commission rates sometimes charged by banks and exchange bureaus for exchanging traveler's checks, the most economical, as well as most convenient, way to get cash can be to withdraw it from an ATM with a debit card.

MAIN BANKS IN LONDON

These are some of the main banks with branches all over London. Many will offer currency-exchange facilities, but proof of identity may be required.

Santander logo

National Westminster logo

HSBC logo

Barclays Bank logo

Lloyds TSB logo

Avoid using the independent ATMs found in some small stores, as they often carry expensive extra charges. There is also a certain risk of crime at some ATMs. Avoid using any in dark streets at night, and don't use an ATM if any part of it looks damaged or as if it has been tampered with, especially the card slot. Be aware of anyone standing close to you when using an ATM, and shield the numbered keypad with your hand as you enter your PIN.

CURRENCY

Britain's currency is the pound sterling (£), which is divided into 100 pence (p). Since there are no exchange controls in Britain, there is no limit to how much cash you may import or export. Many large stores in London accept payments in US dollars and Euros, but often at a poor exchange rate.

English bank notes of all denominations always feature the Queen's head on one side

Bank Notes
English notes used in the UK are £5, £10, £20 and £50. Scotland has its own notes which, despite being legal tender throughout the UK, are not always accepted.

£50 note

£20 note

£10 note

£5 note

Coins of the Realm
Coins in circulation are £2, £1, 50p, 20p, 10p, 5p, 2p, and 1p (they are shown here slightly smaller than actual size). They all have the Queen's head on the other side.

2 pounds (£2) 1 pound (£1) 50 pence (50p) 20 pence (20p)

10 pence (10p) 5 pence (5p) 2 pence (2p) 1 pence (1p)

Communication and Media

British Telecom logo

The telecommunications systems in Britain are efficient and inexpensive. Most static landline phones and public phoneboxes are operated by British Telecom (BT), and there are many other mobile (cell) phone operators and Internet service providers. Charges on BT lines depend on when, where, and for how long you talk. National calls are most expensive from 9am to 1pm on weekdays. A cheap rate applies before 7am or after 7pm on weekdays, and all day on weekends. Cheap times for overseas calls vary, but tend to be on weekends and in the evening.

INTERNATIONAL AND LOCAL TELEPHONE CALLS

All London landline telephone numbers have 11 digits and begin with the code 020. Phone numbers in central London continue with 7, and in outer London with 8, although some business numbers continue with 3. If you are calling from another London number you do not need to dial the 020, but only the remaining eight digits. Every other part of Britain has its own area code, beginning with 01 or 02.

Whenever possible, avoid making calls from hotels – above all, long-distance – since most add hefty surcharges, and some even charge for toll-free calls. There are several special-rate numbers within the UK. Phone numbers beginning 03 are low-cost numbers used mostly by public agencies, such as the police. All 0800 or 0808 numbers are free to call from UK landlines (but not from cell phones). 0844, 0845, 0870, and 0871 numbers are reduced-rate lines that are used by many companies and organizations for information services. Numbers beginning 09 are premium-rate and so particularly expensive.

To call Britain from abroad, dial 011 44, but then omit the initial zero from the UK area code. So to call a London number 020 7123 4567 from abroad, you would dial 011 44 20 7123 4567. To call abroad from London, dial 00 and then the usual country code (for example, Australia: 61; USA and Canada: 1).

CELL PHONES

All UK mobile (cell) phone numbers begin with 07. Calling a cell phone from a landline is considerably more expensive than calling another landline. There is a very high level of cell phone ownership in London and signal coverage is good all over the city. UK cell phones use the European-standard 900 and 1900 MHz frequencies, so cell phones from other European countries work easily here so long as they have their roaming facility enabled. North American and Asian cell phones will not operate here unless they have a tri- or quad-band facility (which is increasingly standard on current phones). Before using a cell phone while traveling, always check with your own service provider on the current level of roaming charges, which can be high. Many companies offer "packages" of foreign calls to cut costs.

If you anticipate using the phone a great deal, it may well be more economical to buy a cheap "pay-as-you-go" British mobile (a basic phone can cost as little as £10, or less) from one of the main local providers such as **O2**, **Orange**, **T-Mobile**, or **Vodafone**, all of which have stores all over the city.

PUBLIC TELEPHONES

You will find a **BT** phonebox on many streets in central London, and in every train station. Some are the old-style red ones, others are much more modern in appearance;

but whichever type, they generally have the same technology inside. Some have multimedia terminals allowing Internet and email access. You can pay with coins, or by credit or debit card. Payphones accept 10p, 20p, 50p, £1, and £2 coins; some also accept Euro coins (50c, €1, and €2). The minimum call cost is 40p for the first 20 minutes to a UK landline; and 10p for each 10 minutes after that. For a short call, use 10p or 20p pieces, since payphones only return unused coins. For credit-card calls, the minimum charge is £1.20.

Old BT phonebox

Modern BT phonebox

USEFUL DIALING CODES

- The area code for London is 020.
- Phone numbers in central London start with 7 or 3, and in outer areas with 8. The 020 prefix must be used if dialing from outside these two areas.
- British Telecom directory inquiries is 118 500.
- If you have any problems contacting a number, call the operator on 100.
- To make an international call, dial 00 followed by the country code (USA and Canada: 1; Australia: 61; New Zealand: 64), the area code and the number. The international operator number is 155 (freephone).
- A phonecard needs at least £2 credit for an international call.
- **In an emergency, dial 999 or 112. All emergency calls are free.**

INTERNET AND EMAIL

Internet access is very easy to find in London. Public libraries, tourist information centers, and some other public buildings have free terminals. Internet cafés are common in every part of the city, and rates per hour are often very low.

Many hotels and a growing number of budget B&Bs and hostels offer Wi-Fi access. Some hotels charge, but this is increasingly rare. There are also many free Wi-Fi hotspots across London, in public libraries, arts centers, cafés, restaurants, and pubs.

POSTAL SERVICES

Standard mail in the UK is handled by the **Royal Mail**. There are main post offices providing all postal services in every London district, as well as many smaller sub-post offices attached to newsagents and other small stores – these can handle all normal mail. Main post offices are usually open from 9am to 5:30pm Monday to Friday, and to 12:30pm on Saturday. **Trafalgar Square Post Office** has extended hours: 8am–8pm Monday to Saturday. Post offices also exchange money and handle international money transfers.

Mail within the UK can be sent by first- or second-class mail. First-class costs a little more and is quicker. Stamps can be bought from post offices or any store with a "Stamps sold here" sign. Newsagents usually sell them, but may only have UK first- and second-class stamps, so for international mail you may need to find a Post Office.

Old-style pillar mailbox

Hotels nearly always sell stamps, and larger ones may have mailboxes. Public post boxes come in different shapes and sizes – some are sunk into walls – but are always red, and can

Newsagent stocking a range of international newspapers

be found throughout the city. There are several collections a day (Mon–Sat); collection times are indicated on the box.

International letters and cards sent from London take about three days to reach European destinations, and four to six days to North America, Japan, or Australasia. A competitively priced Airsure service is available for express deliveries (2–4 days worldwide), as well as a much slower but cheaper surface mail option.

NEWSPAPERS AND MAGAZINES

London's main local paper is the *Evening Standard*, distributed free in the center of town from noon on weekdays. *Time Out London* magazine, published each Thursday, is London's most comprehensive listings guide.

A range of international newspapers and magazines, including *USA Today*, *International Herald Tribune*, and major European papers, is on sale at many newsstands and newsagents around central London. For more specialist foreign press, one of the best places to go is Old Compton Street in Soho, where newsagents regularly carry an extraordinary global variety.

TV AND RADIO

The UK is gradually changing from analog to digital TV channels, although five TV channels are available throughout the UK through a traditional signal: two run by the publicly-owned BBC; the independent ITV; and Channel 4 and Five. In addition, many hotels also have digital or satellite systems. Extra channels available include BBC3 (youth-oriented), BBC4 (arts-oriented), various movie, shopping, and music channels, and CNN. If you want to be able to view a wide range of US and other international channels (such as ESPN), ask whether a hotel has Sky Plus or an enhanced Freeview package.

The BBC also has a large number of radio stations, of which Radios 1 (97–99 FM) and 2 (88–91 FM) focus on pop music of different kinds, Radio 3 (90.2 FM) on classical and jazz, Radio 4 (92–96 FM) on speech and drama, and Radio 5 (909/693 AM) on news and sports. BBC London (94.9 FM) is good for keeping up with local issues and interests.

GETTING TO LONDON

London is one of Europe's central hubs for international air and rail travel. By air, travelers face a bewildering choice of carriers from Europe, North America, Australasia, the Far East, and every other part of the globe. Stiff competition on some routes, especially from major European countries and North America, means that low-fare deals can often be found, so it's always worth shopping around. Since 1995, the Channel Tunnel has provided an efficient high-speed train link – Eurostar – between France and Belgium and the UK, as well as a fast, weatherproof Channel crossing for drivers. Eurostar trains depart from St. Pancras International Station in London's King's Cross. Many European cruises sail from or finish at ports not far from London, such as Southampton, Dover, or Tilbury, and there are efficient passenger and car ferry services from Europe, using large ferries and faster jetfoils and catamarans, across the North Sea and the English Channel.

Station concourse at St. Pancras International

ARRIVING BY RAIL

Eurostar runs frequent daily trains to London from Paris, Brussels, and Lille, where the Paris and Brussels lines meet. Nonstop trains from Paris (Gare du Nord) take 2 hours 15 minutes; from Brussels, 1 hour 50 minutes. Some trains also stop at Calais before entering the Channel Tunnel on the French side, and at Ashford and Ebbsfleet on the English. If you travel by train from any other part of Europe and want to connect with Eurostar, it's best to do so at Lille, since you change trains in the same station – quicker and far easier than doing so in Paris. Check-in on Eurostar is only 30 minutes before departure, so it's generally far quicker than flying.

Eurostar trains arrive in London at St. Pancras International, on the northern edge of central London, next to King's Cross Underground station. The station is a junction of six Underground lines, so is well-connected with every part of the city. Eurostar fares vary a good deal according to flexibility and the time of day you travel (early morning trains are often the cheapest), so check current rates on the website when booking. Information and reservations for connecting trains from other parts of Europe can be found on the **Rail Europe** website.

London has eight mainline rail stations at which trains from different parts of Britain terminate: Paddington serves the West Country, Wales, and the South Midlands; Liverpool Street serves East Anglia and Essex; King's Cross, St. Pancras, and Euston cover northern Britain; and Charing Cross, Victoria, and Waterloo cover southern England, and also the main Channel ferry ports.

The current UK railroad system is complicated and can be confusing. Lines are run by several different companies, but they are coordinated by **National Rail**, which operates a joint information service.

Fare structures are especially complex: tickets can be very expensive or surprisingly cheap, depending on whether you grasp how the system operates. Going to a station the same day you want to travel and buying a ticket over the counter is always the most expensive way to travel. Whenever possible book trains in advance and check alternative fares, bearing in mind that the best fares may only be available online. The National Rail website has a useful "cheapest fare finder" feature, which then links you to the relevant company site to make the purchase. Also helpful is **Trainline**, an independent reservation agency that often has discounted tickets. Tickets bought online can usually be collected at the station.

Fares on suburban rail services around London are less complex, so there is no need to reserve ahead. Rail lines within London accept the Oyster Card (see p378).

Rail information point at a London station, for help and advice

Cross-channel ferry heading to Calais

ARRIVING BY COACH

International and national coach (long-distance bus) services from every part of Europe and the UK arrive in London at Victoria Coach Station on Buckingham Palace Road, about 5 minutes' walk from Victoria rail and Underground stations, and with several local bus stops outside. If you're planning to travel to any UK destinations outside of the London area, it's slower but nearly always cheaper to do it by coach than by train, with fares as low as £1 on some London–Oxford services (although some train companies try to offer lower fares on the same routes).

National Express operates the most extensive UK coach network, with around 1,000 destinations covered, and is also associated with Eurolines international coach services. **Megabus** has especially low fares to many UK destinations, and also discount train offers. **Green Line** runs buses between London and the surrounding counties, and has a service to Luton Airport *(see p377)*.

ARRIVING BY SEA AND TUNNEL

The **Eurotunnel** shuttle – the other train service using the Channel Tunnel – is a drive-on, drive-off service for cars between Calais and Folkestone, where the Tunnel connects with the M20 motorway to London. There are usually four shuttles per hour, with a journey time of about 35 minutes.

If you prefer to brave the elements, there are still plenty of ferry services between southeast England and Continental ports. Harwich in Essex has ferries from Esbjerg in Denmark, with **DFDS**; and from Hook of Holland in the Netherlands, with **Stena Line**. Dover is the busiest port, with frequent services from France: from Dunkerque with **Norfolk Line**; from Calais with **P&O Ferries** and **Seafrance**; and from Boulogne with **LD Lines**. Newhaven–Dieppe ferries are operated by **LD/Transmanche**.

There are also several routes in the western Channel, which take longer, but may leave you better located for visiting the west of England: to Portsmouth from Caen, Cherbourg, and St. Malo with **Brittany Ferries**, or from Le Havre with LD Lines; to Poole from Cherbourg with Brittany Ferries; or to Poole or Weymouth from St. Malo and the Channel Islands with **Condor Ferries**.

Crossing times to Dover are around 1 hour 15 minutes; in the western Channel it takes more like 5-6 hours, although in summer, fast jetfoils and catamarans cut this to 2–3 hours.

There are also ferry services from Spain: from Santander to Plymouth or Portsmouth with Brittany Ferries; and from Bilbao to Portsmouth with P&O. Crossings take around 24 hours, on comfortable "mini cruise ships."

Driving time from Dover or the Channel Tunnel to central London is usually around 2 hours; from Portsmouth, 2½–3 hours. If you bring a car to London, always try to arrange a place to stay with free parking, otherwise this can become extremely expensive.

DIRECTORY

RAIL SERVICES

Eurostar
London St. Pancras International.
Tel 08432-186 186.
www.eurostar.com

National Rail
Tel 0845-748 4950.
www.nationalrail.co.uk

Rail Europe
Tel 1-800-622 8600 (USA),
08448-484 064 (UK).
www.raileurope.com

Trainline
Tel 0871-244 1545.
www.thetrainline.com

COACH SERVICES

Green Line
Tel 0844-801 7261.
www.greenline.co.uk

Megabus
Tel 0900-160 0900.
http://megabus.com/uk

National Express
Tel 08717-818 181.
www.nationalexpress.com

TUNNEL AND FERRIES

Brittany Ferries
Tel 0871-244 0744.
www.brittany-ferries.com

Condor Ferries
Tel 01202-207 216.
www.condorferries.co.uk

DFDS Seaways
Tel 0871-522 9955.
www.dfdsseaways.co.uk

Eurotunnel
Tel 08443-353 535.
www.eurotunnel.com

LD Lines/Transmanche Ferries
Tel 0844-576 8836.
www.ldlines.co.uk

Norfolk Line
Tel 0844-847 5042.
www.norfolkline.com

P&O Ferries
Tel 0871-664 5645.
www.poferries.com

Seafrance
Tel 0871-423 7119.
www.seafrance.com

Stena Line
Tel 0844-770 7070.
www.stenaline.co.uk

Arriving by Air

London's two main airports, Heathrow and Gatwick, are augmented by smaller facilities at Luton, Stansted, and London City *(see pp376–7)*. Check which airport you will land at, and plan your journey from there. All the airports have train or bus links; Heathrow is also connected to central London by Underground. Because the airports are so far apart from each other, traveling between them is best avoided. Further details can be found online.

Access to the underground in the arrival terminal at Heathrow

British Airways passenger jet at Heathrow airport

AIRLINES AND FARES

Heathrow and Gatwick have long-haul connections with every part of the world, on scores of airlines. The main United States airlines offering scheduled flights to London include **Delta**, **United**, **American Airlines**, and **US Airways**, while from Canada there are frequent services with **Air Canada**. **British Airways** and **Virgin Atlantic** also fly from many North American cities. The flight time from New York is about 6½ hours; from Los Angeles, about 10 hours. The choice of carriers from Australasia and Asia is enormous too: **Qantas**, **Air New Zealand**, and British Airways may be the obvious first choices, but operators such as **Singapore Airlines** and **Emirates** offer interesting alternatives.

All the main carrier airlines, such as British Airways, Air France, **Iberia**, and **Lufthansa**, offer frequent European connections, mostly to Heathrow or Gatwick, but they now carry less traffic than the low-cost airlines. **Ryanair** has budget flights to all of Europe, Ireland, and the UK, mostly from Stansted, while **easyJet** runs almost as extensive a European and British network from Stansted, Luton, and Gatwick.

Very few airlines now offer reduced prices for children. Low-cost flights can normally be booked only through each airline's own website. Note that low-cost airlines regularly add "extra" charges on top of the fare – such as one for checking in luggage. Ryanair in particular, charges £40 if you cannot download and print your own boarding card, and need one issued by ground staff at the airport.

SECURITY

Security is tighter than ever at London airports. Allow at least two hours to check in and get through security before your flight, especially – because of its size – at Heathrow. Allow ample time also (2 hours again) to catch low-cost flights if you are checking in a bag, since in the interests of keeping costs down there are not many check-in staff, so lines move slowly.

HEATHROW (LHR)

Heathrow in west London is one of the world's busiest airports. It has five terminals, so it's important to know which one your flight will arrive at or depart from. Terminals 1, 2, and 3, the oldest, share an Underground station and Heathrow Central rail station; Terminal 4 has its own Underground station; Terminal 5, which opened in 2008, has Underground and rail stations. A free shuttle bus runs between the Terminals. Most British Airways flights use Terminal 5; most other long-haul airlines use Terminals 3 or 4. There are shops and other facilities in every terminal.

There are several ways into London from Heathrow. The fastest rail service is the **Heathrow Express**, with trains every 15 minutes from around 5am to 11:30pm daily to Paddington station on the west side of central London. Journey time is about 15 minutes, and trains also stop at Terminal 5. To get to Terminals 1, 2, and 3, take the shuttle bus from Terminal 4. Fares are quite high, at around £18 single, £32 return (slightly less if you buy online).

Heathrow Terminal 5, used exclusively by British Airways

Heathrow Connect trains run on the same lines but with several stops, and take 25–30 minutes to reach Paddington. Fares are around £8 single.

The Underground (tube) offers a much cheaper way of getting into London, but is also much slower. Trains run frequently, calling at all Heathrow Terminals from around 5am to midnight Monday to Saturday; 5:50am–11:30pm Sunday. Unlike the Heathrow Express, the tube runs right into the city center; allow about 45 minutes to get to Leicester Square. As on all London public transport, it's cheaper with an Oyster Card *(see p378)*; the adult fare from Heathrow into the city center is around £4.50.

National Express and other companies run a number of bus routes from Heathrow to Oxford, London, other London airports, and other destinations. The main bus station is at Terminals 1, 2, and 3, but

London City Airport, within sight of the city's Docklands area

buses also stop at 4 and 5. A taxi to central London costs about £40. Driving time is from 30 minutes to 1 hour. Local minicab companies offer much cheaper rates *(see p385)*.

LONDON CITY AIRPORT (LCY)

London City is the closest airport to central London, in the Docklands business area just east of London's financial district (the City). Unlike the low-cost airports, it was created primarily for business travelers, so flights are quite expensive. It offers flights to many European destinations, and a luxury service to New York.

London City has its own station on the Docklands Light Railway (DLR), which connects with the Underground network at Tower Hill and Bank. An Express Shuttle Bus runs every 30 minutes to Canary Wharf, for £7 single fare. A taxi to the City costs about £20 and takes 30 minutes; to the West End £30, taking around 45 minutes.

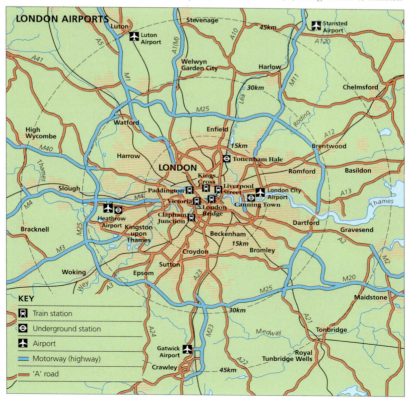

LONDON AIRPORTS

KEY

- 🚆 Train station
- Ⓔ Underground station
- ✈ Airport
- ▬ Motorway (highway)
- ▬ 'A' road

GATWICK (LGW)

Gatwick airport lies due south of central London, and handles long-haul, European, and low-cost flights. There are two terminals – North and South – so as at Heathrow, you need to be clear on which you need. The train station and main bus stops are at the South Terminal, from where there is a free shuttle train to the North. Allow around 20 minutes to transfer between terminals. There are banks, stores, cafés, and other facilities at both.

There is a choice of three rail services from Gatwick into London, all from the same station. The **Gatwick Express** is the fastest, with trains every 15 minutes to Victoria Station. It runs from around 4:30am to midnight daily and takes about 30 minutes (a little longer on Sundays), but it isn't cheap; the fare is around £17 single, £29 return. Tickets can be bought online. **First Capital Connect** runs around four trains per hour over the same period to St. Pancras International via several stops, including East Croydon and London Bridge. Journey time is about an hour, and single fare around £9. **Southern Railway** has several trains each hour to London Victoria, with a journey time of 30–50 minutes and a single fare of around £11.

Entrance to Stansted's spacious modern passenger terminal

National Express and other companies run buses from the South Terminal to Heathrow and many towns in southern England (including central London), and **easyBus** runs frequently from the North Terminal to Fulham Broadway Underground in London. Buses are not limited to easyJet passengers, and fares begin at £2. A taxi into central London will set you back around £90, and can take 1–2 hours. As at Heathrow, minicab companies offer better rates to Gatwick.

STANSTED (STN)

Around 40 miles northeast of London, Stansted is the airport in southeast England most popular with the low-cost airlines, and so has a huge number of flights to destinations in every part of Europe.

The rail link into London is the **Stansted Express** train, which runs every 15 minutes from around 6am to 12:30am, with variations on weekends. Trains run to Liverpool Street, on the east side of central London, with a stop at Tottenham Hale (where you can transfer to the Victoria Underground line). Trains from Liverpool Street to Stansted run from approximately 4:40am to 11:30pm daily. The full journey takes 45 minutes. Adult fares to Liverpool Street are £19 single, £28.70 return (cheaper online). **National Express East Anglia** trains also run roughly once an hour to London Stratford station in East London's Olympic Park, with several stops, taking 1 hour for a fare of about £17.

Several bus services run from Stansted to London. National Express runs to Victoria Coach Station (£10.50) and many other destinations around the region, but easy-Bus is again the cheapest,

Gatwick's free monorail service linking the two terminals

AIRPORT	FROM CITY CENTER	AVERAGE JOURNEY TIME	AVERAGE TAXI FARE
London City	6 miles (10 km)	Tube and DLR: 40 minutes	£20
Heathrow	14 miles (23 km)	Rail: 15 minutes Tube: 45 minutes	£40
Gatwick	28 miles (45 km)	Rail: 30 minutes Bus: 70 minutes	£90
Luton	32 miles (51 km)	Rail: 35 minutes Bus: 70 minutes	£60
Stansted	34 miles (55 km)	Rail: 45 minutes Bus: 75 minutes	£90

with tickets to Baker Street Underground station from £2. A taxi to central London can take 1 hour 30 minutes and cost £90–100.

LUTON (LTN)

Luton airport lies northwest of London near the M1 motorway, and is used almost exclusively by charter flights and low-cost airlines, especially easyJet. A shuttle bus connects the terminal with Luton Airport Parkway train station (about a 5-minute drive), from around 5am to midnight daily. First Capital Connect has about four trains each hour to London St. Pancras – a journey of around 25–40 minutes for an adult single fare of £13.50. **East Midlands Trains** operate on the same route, and are a little cheaper, at £11.90. Green Line buses (route 757) run every 15 minutes almost 24 hours daily between the airport and London Victoria Coach station, with adult fares around £11 (*see p373*); easyBus has frequent services to Victoria via Baker Street, with tickets from £2. National Express runs from Luton to Heathrow, Gatwick, Stansted, and other destinations. A taxi into London will cost around £60, and take about 45 minutes.

AIRPORT HOTELS

Given the long check-in times at the main airports, it can be a good idea – or even necessary – to stay nearby the night before departure, especially if you have an early-morning flight. There is a large number of hotels in the vicinity of Heathrow and Gatwick; many of these frequently have discount offers. All of them provide shuttle buses to the

Relaxing bar of the popular Sheraton Skyline hotel

airport terminals – in budget hotels this may be charged extra. The **Premier Inn**, **Travelodge**, and **Holiday Inn** chains have cheap, functional rooms close to the airports. A selection of airport hotels is listed below, but there are many more to choose from.

DIRECTORY

MAJOR AIRLINES

Air Canada
www.aircanada.com

Air New Zealand
www.airnewzealand.com

American Airlines
www.aa.com

British Airways
www.britishairways.com

Delta Airlines
www.delta.com

easyJet
www.easyjet.com

Emirates
www.emirates.com

Iberia
www.iberia.com

Lufthansa
www.lufthansa.com

Qantas
www.qantas.com.au

Ryanair
www.ryanair.com

Singapore Airlines
www.singaporeair.com

United Airlines
www.united.com

US Airways
www.usairways.com

Virgin Atlantic
www.virgin-atlantic.com

Travel Websites
www.bestfares.com
www.cheapflights.com
www.ebookers.com
www.expedia.com
www.flights.com
www.orbitz.com
www.priceline.com
www.travelnow.com
www.travelocity.com

AIRPORT INFORMATION

Gatwick
Tel 0844-335 1802.
www.gatwickairport.com

Heathrow
Tel 0844-335 1801.
www.heathrowairport.com

London City Airport
Tel 020-7646 0088.
www.londoncityairport.com

Luton
Tel 01582-405 100.
www.london-luton.co.uk

Stansted
Tel 0844–335 1803.
www.stanstedairport.com

AIRPORT TRANSPORT

easyBus
www.easybus.co.uk

East Midlands Trains
Tel 0845-712 5678.
www.eastmidland trains.co.uk

First Capital Connect
Tel 0845457-484 950.
www.firstcapitalconnect.co.uk

Gatwick Express
Tel 0845-850 1530.
www.gatwickexpress.com

Heathrow Connect
Tel 0845-678 6975.
www.heathrowconnect.com

Heathrow Express
Tel 0845-600 1515.
www.heathrowexpress.com

National Express East Anglia
Tel 0845-600 7245.
www.nationalexpresseast anglia.com

Southern Railway
Tel 0845-127 2920.
www.southernrailway.com

Stansted Express
Tel 0845-850 0150.
www.stanstedexpress.com

HOTELS

Holiday Inn London Heathrow Ariel
Tel 0871-942 9040.
www.ichotelsgroup.com

Premier Inn Heathrow (Bath Road)
Tel 0870-607 5075.
www.premierinn.com

Sofitel London Gatwick
Tel 01293-567 070.
www.sofitel.com

Travelodge Gatwick Airport
Tel 0871-984 6031.
www.travelodge.co.uk

GETTING AROUND LONDON

London has one of the busiest and most extensive public transportation systems in Europe; it also has all the problems of overcrowding. A program is underway to upgrade the Underground (tube) train system, and the extension of the East London Line offers a direct link to the Olympic sites. Within London

"Heritage" bus

and its suburbs, most of the public transportation systems – the Underground, city buses, overground rail lines, river buses – are coordinated by Transport for London (TfL), which operates a common ticketing system centered on the Oyster Card, a "smartcard" that is rapidly replacing the need for paper tickets.

GREEN TRAVEL

Traveling around London by foot, tube, bus, train, or river bus is more energy-efficient than taking your own vehicle or a taxi. The Congestion Charge helps to discourage driving in the city center (see p379). London has improved conditions for bicyclists, and this can be the fastest way to get around the city – **Transport for London's** website has a dedicated cycling page. Many of London's black cabs now run on alternative fuels. There are several "green" minicab companies that use hybrid or alternative-fuel vehicles, such as **Gogreencar** and **Climatecars**.

THE TRANSPORTATION SYSTEM

The Underground railroad (or "tube") is generally the fastest, most convenient way to get around the city. The Docklands business district and some other areas of east London and Greenwich are served by the Docklands Light Railway (DLR), which connects with the tube network principally at Bank, Tower Hill, Canary Wharf, and Stratford. Tube and DLR lines do not run to every part of the city, however; in particular, large parts of south London are reliant on overground rail connections. Bus routes cover every part of London. There are also several riverbus boat services (see p61).

Avoid traveling on public transportation during morning and evening "rush hour" – 7–10am and 4–7pm Monday to Friday – if at all possible.

For detailed information on every aspect of transportation in London, call Transport for London information or check the TfL website, which has an invaluable "Journey Planner" feature. TfL also has several Travel Information Centres, at Heathrow and Piccadilly Circus Underground stations and Euston, King's Cross, Liverpool Street, and Victoria mainline stations, which provide free maps and other information.

OYSTER CARDS & TRAVELCARDS

London's public transit is relatively expensive compared to that of many European cities, but if you use one of the multijourney cards available to visitors you will cut your costs considerably. For tube, DLR, and local train fares, London is divided into six main fare zones radiating out from Zone 1 in the center (on buses, there is a flat fare for each trip, no matter how far you travel). If you aim to pack all your sightseeing into one or two days, the best ticket to get will be a one-day off-peak Travelcard, which gives unlimited travel on all systems after 9:30am on weekdays (or any time on Saturday and Sunday) within your chosen zones for a flat fee (currently £6.60 for an adult card for Zones 1 and 2, which covers most of the main sights in London).

A London Underground sign outside a station

If you expect to travel more freely, it will be better to get a pay-as-you-go Oyster Card, which you can charge up with as much credit as you wish. Whenever you use public transportation, you "touch in" with your card on a yellow Oyster Card reader, and the corresponding amount is deducted. On Underground, DLR, and overground trains you must also remember both to "touch out" at the station where you finish your journey, or you will be charged the maximum fare for the line.

Travelcards and Oyster Cards can be bought at tube and local rail stations, Travel Information Centres, and hundreds of small stores that have the TfL "Ticket Stop" sticker in the window. You can also obtain them before arriving in London, on Eurostar, Gatwick Express, or Stansted Express trains, or online, with advance delivery to 63 countries, through the Visit London and TfL websites.

Travel is free on all buses for under-16s; the Underground and DLR are free for under-11s, and have reduced fares for 11–15-year-olds. A one-day Travelcard for 11–15s costs only £2 for main fare zones, 1 to 6. Details of all current fares and tickets can be found on www.tfl.gov.uk.

Prepaid Oyster card being placed on a card reader

A pedestrian zebra crossing

WALKING

Once you get used to traffic driving on the left, London can be enjoyably explored on foot, but take care crossing the road. There are two types of pedestrian crossing in London: striped "zebra" crossings, marked by beacons; and push-button crossings at traffic lights. Traffic should stop if you wait at a zebra crossing, but at push-button crossings, cars will not stop until they have a red light. Look out for instructions printed on the road, telling you from which direction you can expect traffic to appear.

DRIVING IN LONDON

For visitors, driving is usually the worst way of getting around town. Traffic moves at an average of 11 mph (18 kmh) for much of the day, parking is scarce and expensive, and in the city center there is the added cost of the Congestion Charge – a £10-a-day fee for private vehicles entering the central charging zone (roughly: the City, the West End, Mayfair, and south as far as Elephant & Castle) between 7am and 6pm Monday to Friday. If you are determined to drive, remember always to drive on the left.

All the well-known car-rental firms are represented in London. Renting a car in advance through a site such as **Auto Europe**, or as an add-on with your flight, will get the best rates. To drive right out of London from the center takes about 1 hour in any direction; if you want to tour the countryside, it can be less tiring to take a train to a city like Oxford and rent there.

PARKING

Parking is prohibited at all times wherever the street is marked with red or there are double yellow lines by the curb. If there is a single yellow line, parking is usually allowed from 6:30pm–8am Monday to Saturday and all day Sunday, but exact hours vary so always check the signs along each street. Where there is no line at all, parking is free at all times, but this is rare in central London. Note that rental car drivers are still liable for parking fines.

BICYCLING

The TfL "Cycling" page is an invaluable source of information on bicycling around the city. Bike routes – sometimes even separate bike lanes – are signposted around the city.

Barclays Cycle Hire, London's bike hire scheme, has 6,000 bikes available at docking terminals across the city. Visit the website for details on how to access the bikes. The **London Bicycle Tour Company** both delivers and collects bikes to and from your location. With your rented bike you should be given a helmet, lock, and other accessories.

A bicycle path in one of London's parks

Traveling by Underground

The underground system, known as the "tube" to Londoners, has some 270 stations, each identified by the Underground logo. Trains run every day except Christmas Day, from about 5:30am till midnight Monday to Thursday; 5:30am till 1am on Friday and Saturday; and 6:30am to 11:30pm on Sunday. Exact times of first and last trains are posted at stations and on the Transport for London website: www.tfl.gov.uk. The Docklands Light Railway (DLR), with some 40 stations in east and southeast London, connects with the tube and also runs to London City Airport. For schedules and all other information, call 0843-222 1234 or check the TfL website.

London Underground train

PLANNING YOUR JOURNEY

There are 12 tube lines, all named and color-coded (red for Central, blue for Victoria, and so on), which intersect at various stations. Some lines, like the Jubilee, have a single branch; others, like the Northern, have more than one, so it's important to check the digital boards on the platform and the destination on the front of the train. The Circle Line is a continuous loop around central London but now extends to Hammersmith. Maps of the entire Tube system *(see inside back cover)* are posted at each station. Note that the tube map is topological, not geographical; it isn't to scale, nor can it be relied upon for directions. From it, you can work out where to change lines to travel to any station on the system. All eight of London's mainline rail stations *(see p372)* have associated Tube stations. Due to the ongoing tube improvement program, services are sometimes suspended, usually on weekends. When this happens, replacement buses are provided. Check for line closures before traveling.

BUYING A TICKET

All tube and DLR stations fall within one of six main fare zones *(see p378)*. The zones you travel through determine the cost of your journey. Unless you plan on making very few journeys by tube, it will usually be best to travel with a multi-journey Travelcard or an Oyster Card *(see p378)*. However, you can also buy single or return tickets from ticket offices and ticket machines. All Underground and DLR stations have touch-screen machines that give step-by-step instructions in a variety of languages. They accept coins, bills, and credit and debit cards, and you can also use them to top up your credit on an Oyster Card. To check on current fares, select the ticket type you need, choose the station you wish to travel to, and the fare will be displayed on screen.

HOW TO READ THE JOURNEY PLANNER MAPS
(see inside back cover)

Station for changing between lines or to British Rail train

Double circle, meaning two stations are linked

Station serving two lines

TUBE ARCHITECTURE

The underground's reputation for exciting architecture was established in the 1930s. In 1999 the Jubilee Line Extension opened to great acclaim, with six imposing and elegant stations designed by a group of top architects including Will Alsop (North Greenwich), Norman Foster (Canary Wharf), and Matthew Hopkins (Westminster). A similar light, spacious style has been adopted in the impressive tube, DLR, bus, and mainline rail hub at Stratford, which is the gateway to the Olympic Park.

Concourse at Canary Wharf Station, Jubilee Line

MAKING A JOURNEY BY UNDERGROUND

1 When you first enter the station, check which line, or lines, you need to take. If you have any difficulty planning your route, ask the clerk at the ticket office for help.

Journey planner

Feed your ticket into the slot at the front of the machine; retrieve it from the slot at the top.

2 Buy your ticket, Travelcard, or Oyster Card from a ticket office or ticket machine at the station. Keep your ticket; you will need it to exit at your destination. For return trips, you will usually be given one ticket that you must keep for both journeys. Oyster Cards can be topped up for later trips.

oyster

If you have an Oyster Card, just touch it on the yellow card reader.

The ticket office is near the ticket barriers in most stations.

3 The platforms are on the other side of the ticket barriers. These are easy to use if you follow the instructions above.

Central line →

4 Follow the directions to the line on which you need to travel. In some cases this can be a complicated route, but it will be well sign-posted.

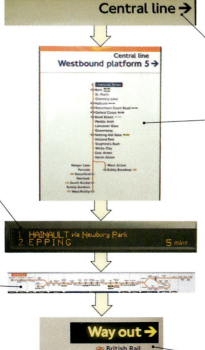

Central line
Westbound platform 5 →

5 You will eventually find yourself with a choice of platforms for the line you want. Look at the list of stations if you are not sure which direction to take.

6 All platforms have electronic indicators displaying the final destination of the next two or three trains and how long you will have to wait before they arrive. On lines with branches, they also indicate the route of each train.

1 HAINAULT via Newbury Park
2 EPPING   5 mins

DOOR BUTTON
PUSH
TO OPEN

On all DLR and some tubes, push a button to open the carriage doors.

7 Once you have begun your journey, you can check on your progress using the line chart displayed in every carriage. On many trains, the name of the next station is announced before you arrive, and as you pull into each station you will see its name posted along the walls.

Way out →
⇌ British Rail

Hammersmith & City →
Metropolitan and Circle lines

8 After leaving the train, look for signs giving directions to exits or to platforms for any connecting lines.

Traveling by Bus and Boat

Distinctive logo used on London bus stops

The red double-decker bus is one of London's most recognizable symbols, but the design of London buses has changed a great deal over the years. The old, classic, open-backed Routemaster buses have been withdrawn (with the exception of two "heritage" routes), and in their place there are modern, square-sided double-deckers, single-deckers for less busy routes, and a modernized Routemaster bus that allows passengers to hop on and hop off. Traveling by bus is an enjoyable, easy way to see London, especially in the middle of the day, and much cheaper than going by tube or DLR if you have an Oyster Card. On the minus side, bus journeys can be slow, especially during rush hour (7–10am and 4–7pm Monday to Friday).

FINDING THE RIGHT BUS

Bus maps showing all the main routes are available free from Travel Information Centres, or can be downloaded from the Visit London and Transport for London websites. All London bus stops have bus route signs displaying the routes that run from that stop, with lists of their main destinations. On streets that are used by several bus routes – notably Oxford Street in the West End – routes are "bunched together" at different stops

Bus Stops
If you are boarding a bus at a yellow stop (below), you must buy a ticket at the adjacent machine before boarding. At some stops, called request stops, the driver will not halt unless asked. If you want to board, raise your arm as the bus approaches the stop; when you want to get off, ring the bell once before your stop.

near each other, so make sure you find the right one. Stops also have local area maps showing which of the adjacent bus stops, identified by a letter, you need for buses to a particular area. If in doubt, check with the bus driver when boarding.

USING LONDON'S BUSES

Buses halt at stops marked with the London bus logo. Some stops are "request"

stops, where drivers will not stop unless they are waved down by a passenger. Destinations are displayed clearly on the front of the bus, and on many buses the next upcoming stop is indicated on electronic information boards, or announced by an automatic voice system. However, if you are unsure which stop you need, ask the driver to alert you, and stay on the lower deck.

Board buses at the front, so that you can touch in your Oyster Card on the yellow Oyster reader by the driver's seat, show your Travelcard, or buy a single ticket. In central London, single tickets cannot be bought on board the bus, but must be bought in advance from ticket machines at the bus stop, and then shown to the driver. Fares are the same for each bus trip no matter how far you travel, at £2.20 for a single ticket or £1.30 with an Oyster Card – so the Oyster saving is considerable. Inspectors often check whether passengers have valid tickets or passes.

USEFUL BUS ROUTES

Several of London's bus routes are particularly convenient for the capital's main sights and stores. If you arm yourself with an Oyster Card or Travelcard and are in no particular hurry, sightseeing or shopping by bus can be great fun. The cost of a journey by public transportation is far less than any of the charges levied by tour operators, although you won't have the commentary that tour companies give you as you pass sights *(see p362–3).*

There are also some sights or areas in London that are either hard to get to by Underground, or can be reached much more directly by bus. Buses run regularly from the city center to, for instance, the Albert Hall *(see p207)* and Chelsea *(see pp192–7).*

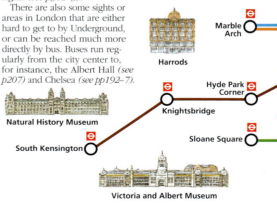

Harrods

Marble Arch

Natural History Museum

Hyde Park Corner

Knightsbridge

South Kensington

Sloane Square

Victoria and Albert Museum

Thames Clipper boat on the river heading toward Waterloo Bridge

minutes from 6am to 1am daily in both directions, on a route between Waterloo and Woolwich, via the London Eye, Tower Bridge, Greenwich, and other stops at the various river piers. They also operate the **Tate Boat**, a direct boat between the Tate Britain and Tate Modern museums (every 40 minutes in each direction, 10am to 5pm), as well as special services for events at the O2 Arena. Oyster Cards can be used on board, and Travelcard holders get discounted tickets. For all details check with Thames Clippers or www.tfl.gov.uk.

NIGHT BUSES

Some main bus routes run 24 hours a day. Night bus services (indicated by the letter "N" added before the route number) also run on many popular routes from 11pm until 6am, generally 3–4 times per hour up to 2–3am, but often only once an hour after that. Many night bus routes originate in or pass through Trafalgar Square, then run out into the suburbs. In the center they are often very crowded, especially on weekends, but empty out quickly as they move farther out. Plan your journey carefully; London is so big that even if you board a bus going in the right direction, you can still be a long walk from your accommodations. As always, be aware of your personal security when traveling at night.

RIVERBOATS

Some of London's most spectacular views can only be seen from the River Thames. River trips have also been integrated into London's general transportation service. **Thames Clippers** has a riverbus service with catamarans running every 20

DIRECTORY

RIVERBOAT SERVICES

Tate Boat
Tel 020-7887 8888.
www.tate.org.uk/tatetotate

Thames Clippers
Tel 020-7001 2222.
www.thamesclippers.com

For more information on river cruises see "Cruise Highlights" on p61.

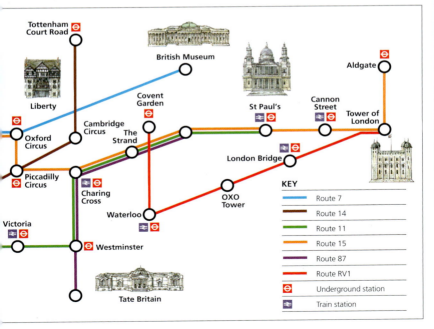

KEY

▬▬▬	Route 7
▬▬▬	Route 14
▬▬▬	Route 11
▬▬▬	Route 15
▬▬▬	Route 87
▬▬▬	Route RV1
⊖	Underground station
≋	Train station

Traveling by Train

Railway sign

London's local and suburban train lines (also known as the "overground") are used by hundreds of thousands of commuters every day. For visitors, rail services are most useful for trips to the outskirts of London and areas of the city without nearby Underground connections (especially in south London). If you are planning to travel outside of the capital, always try to purchase train tickets in advance, and check to see what alternative fares are available; for more on train tickets see p372.

USEFUL ROUTES

Two of the most popular rail lines for visitors to London are those from Charing Cross (via London Bridge) and, on weekdays, Cannon Street to Greenwich *(see pp237–43)*; and Waterloo to Hampton Court *(see pp254–7)*. A First Capital Connect line runs right through London, north to south, from Luton via St. Pancras International to Gatwick. The North London line makes a loop around north London all the way from the East End to Kew *(see pp260–61)* and Richmond.

USING THE TRAINS

London has eight main rail terminals serving different parts of Britain. Each terminal is also the starting point for local and suburban lines that cover the whole of southeast England. There are over one hundred smaller London stations. Rail services travel overground and vary between trains that stop at every station, faster suburban trains, and express trains that run nonstop to major destinations. Some train doors will open automatically; others at the touch of a button.

RAIL TICKETS

Travelcards and Oyster Cards are valid on nearly all overground rail services that fall entirely within the London area (defined as Transport for London fare zones 1–6, plus three more suburban zones), so using one or the other will generally be much more economical, and a lot quicker, than buying individual tickets. Be aware, though, that on most overground trains, peak travel times include the evening rush hour (4–7pm Monday–Friday) as well as the morning one (before 9:30am), so with an Oyster you will be charged more during these times. Many small stations do not have staffed ticket counters, just machines.

Return tickets for rail travel

DAY TRIPS

Southern England has a lot to offer visitors besides London. By rail or by bus *(see p373)*, getting out of the city is fast and easy. For details of sights contact Visit Britain (www.visitbritain.com; 020-8846 9000). National Rail (0845-748 4950) has details of all rail services.

Boating on the River Thames at Windsor Castle

Audley End
Village with a stunning Jacobean mansion nearby.
≷ *from Liverpool Street.*
40 miles (64 km); 1 hr.

Bath
Beautiful Georgian city, with Roman baths, which has escaped redevelopment.
≷ *from Paddington.*
107 miles (172 km); 1 hr 25 mins.

Brighton
Lively and attractive seaside resort. See the Royal Pavilion.
≷ *from Victoria. 53 miles (85 km); 1 hr.*

Cambridge
University city with fine art gallery and ancient colleges.
≷ *from Liverpool Street or King's Cross. 54 miles (86 km); 1 hr.*

Canterbury
Its cathedral is one of England's oldest and greatest sights.
≷ *from Victoria.*
62 miles (100 km); 1 hr 25 mins.

Hatfield House
Elizabethan palace with remarkable contents.
≷ *from King's Cross or Moorgate to Hatfield station.*
21 miles (33 km); 20 mins.

Oxford
Like Cambridge, famous for its ancient university.
≷ *from Paddington.*
56 miles (90 km); 1 hr.

St. Albans
Cathedral and Roman theater.
≷ *from King's Cross or Moorgate.*
25 miles (40 km); 30 mins.

Salisbury
Famous for its cathedral, and close to Stonehenge.
≷ *from Waterloo.*
84 miles (135 km); 1 hr 40 mins.

Windsor
Riverside town with Britain's grandest royal castle.
≷ *from Paddington, change Slough.*
20 miles (32km); approx. 30 mins.

Traveling by Taxi

London's well-known black cabs are as much of an institution as its red buses. Black cabs (some of which, it should be pointed out, are not actually black – you will often see blue, green, red, or even white cabs) are the only cabs licensed to pick up passengers who hail a cab on the street, and their drivers have to take a stringent test on their knowledge of London and its traffic routes before they are awarded a license. Minicabs, which by law must be ordered in advance, not hailed, are a cheaper alternative for specific journeys.

London taxi stand

FINDING A CAB

Licensed London taxis, or "black cabs," are large, distinctive vehicles – of which there are now several models – whose yellow "Taxi" sign is lit up whenever the taxi is free. You can hail them on the street, phone for them, or find them at taxi stands, especially at airports, main train stations, and major hotels. Raise your arm and wave purposefully. If a cab stops, it must take you anywhere within a radius of 6 miles (9.6 km), as long as it is in the Metropolitan Police district, which includes most of the Greater London area and Heathrow Airport.

TAXI FARES

All black cabs have meters that start ticking at around £2.20 as soon as the driver accepts your custom. The fare then increases by the minute, or for each 340 yds (311 m) traveled. There are also three tariff time bands: the cheapest is 6am–8pm Monday–Friday; the next-most expensive, 8–10pm Monday–Friday and 6–10pm Saturday–Sunday; the most expensive, 10pm–6am nightly. The meter must be clearly visible in the vehicle. It is usual to tip taxi and minicab drivers. If you lose anything in a licensed taxi, contact Transport for London's lost property office *(see p367)*. You will need the driver's cab license number, displayed in the back of the taxi.

MINICABS

Licensed minicabs are badged with a blue-and-white Transport for London sticker, usually on the back window. Do not use the unlicensed cabs that sometimes cruise for business in the street. Transport for London's Cabwise service is a good way of finding a safe cab: text "CAB" to 60835 and you will be sent phone numbers for one black cab office and two reliable minicab companies in the area. If your cell phone is international, text your location (street name and postal district) to 011-44-7797 800 000 to access the same service (international charges will apply).

DIRECTORY

Complaints (Public Carriage Office)
Tel 0845-300 7000.
www.tfl.gov.uk

Computer Cabs
Tel 020-7908 0000.
www.computercab.co.uk.

Dial-a-Minicab
Tel 0800-019 6768.
www.dialaminicab.com

Lady Minicabs (women-only drivers)
Tel 020-7272 3300.
www.ladyminicabs.com

Radio Taxis
Tel 020-7272 0272.
www.radiotaxis.co.uk

The light, when lit, shows the cab is available.

The meter displays your fare as it increases, and surcharges for extra passengers, luggage, or unsocial hours. Fares are the same in all licensed black cabs.

Fare   Surcharges

Licensed Taxi Cabs
London's cabs are a safe way of traveling around the city. They can carry a maximum of five passengers, are all accessible for wheelchair users, and have ample luggage space.

STREET FINDER

The map references given with all sights, hotels, restaurants, shops, and entertainment venues described in this book refer to the maps in this section only *(see* How Map References Work *opposite)*. A complete index of street names and all the places of interest marked on the maps can be found on the following pages.

The key map shows the area of London covered by the *Street Finder*, with the postal codes of all the various districts. The maps include the sightseeing areas (which are color-coded), as well as the whole of central London with all the districts important for hotels, restaurants, pubs, and entertainment venues.

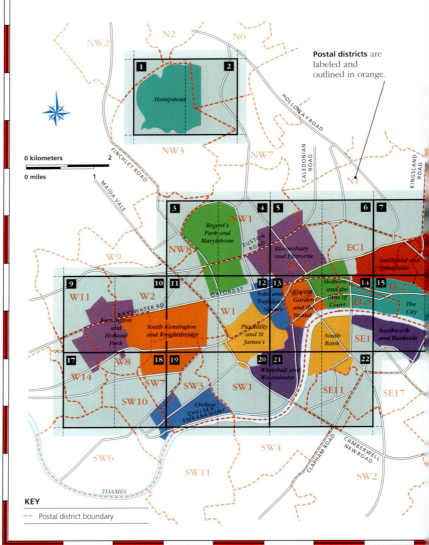

Postal districts are labeled and outlined in orange.

0 kilometers 2

0 miles 1

KEY

- - - Postal district boundary

HOW THE MAP REFERENCES WORK

The first figure tells you which Street Finder map to turn to.

Wesley's Chapel–Leysian Mission ⑫

49 City Rd EC1. **Map 7** **B4**. **Tel** 020-7253 2262. ⊖ Old St. **Open** 10am–4pm Mon–Sat, 12:30–1:45pm Sun. ♿ not house. ✝ 9:45am (not 1st Sun of month), 11am Sun, 12:45pm Thu. ⛪ groups book ahead. ⬚ www.wesleyschapel.org.uk

A letter and number give the grid reference – letters along the map's top and bottom, figures down the sides.

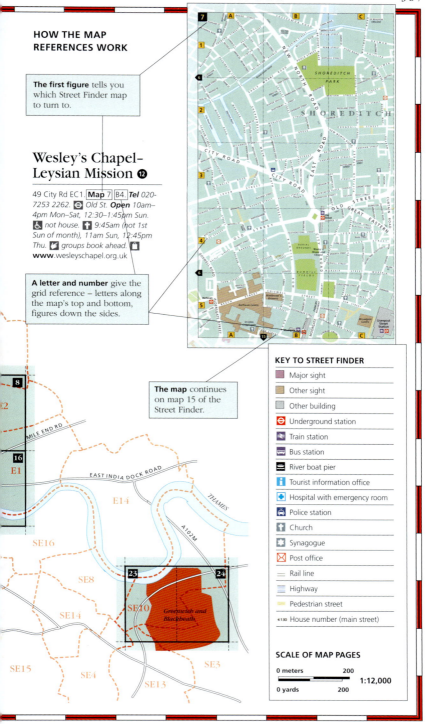

The map continues on map 15 of the Street Finder.

KEY TO STREET FINDER

▨	Major sight
▨	Other sight
▨	Other building
⊖	Underground station
⭻	Train station
🚌	Bus station
⛴	River boat pier
ℹ	Tourist information office
✚	Hospital with emergency room
👮	Police station
✝	Church
✡	Synagogue
⊠	Post office
=	Rail line
=	Highway
=	Pedestrian street
◂130	House number (main street)

SCALE OF MAP PAGES

0 meters   200
0 yards   200

1:12,000

Street Finder Index

Each place name is followed by its postal district, and then by its Street Finder reference

Each place name is followed by its postal district, and then by its Street Finder reference

Each place name is followed by its postal district, and then by its Street Finder reference

Each place name is followed by its postal district, and then by its Street Finder reference

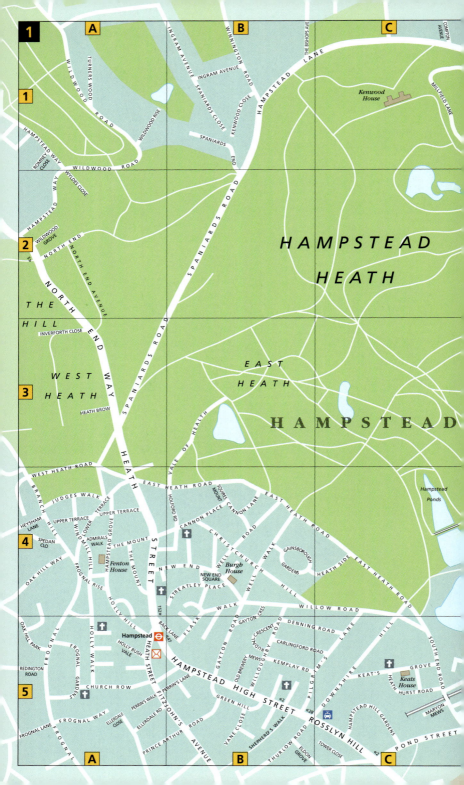

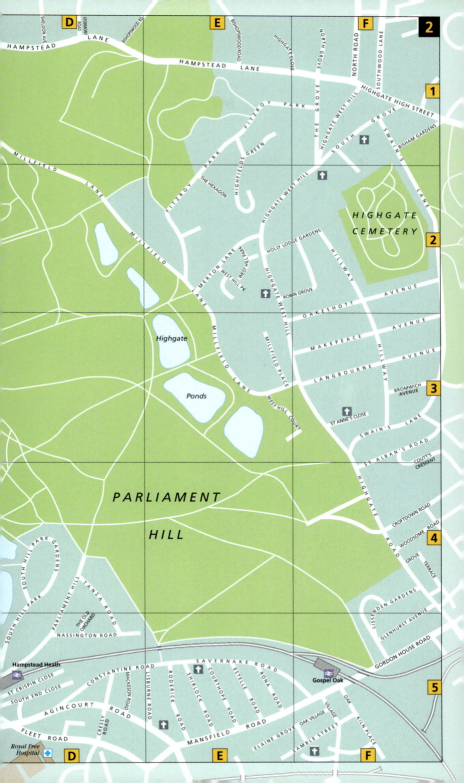

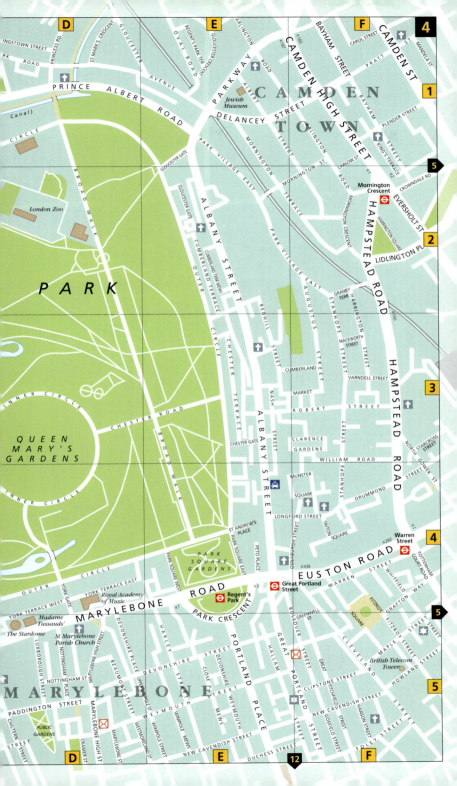

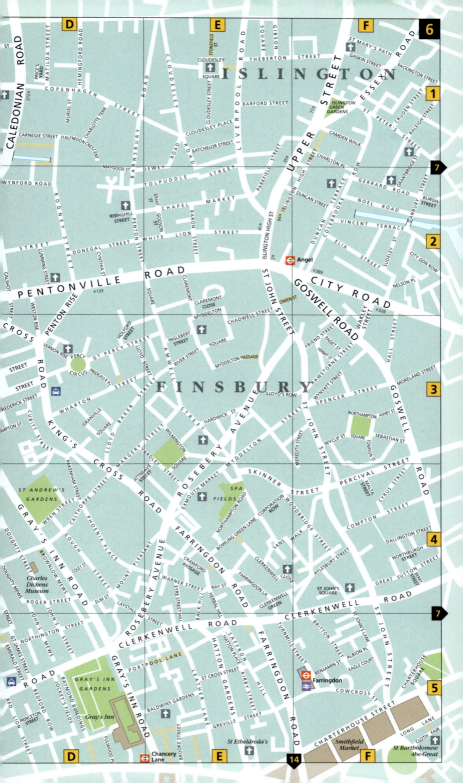

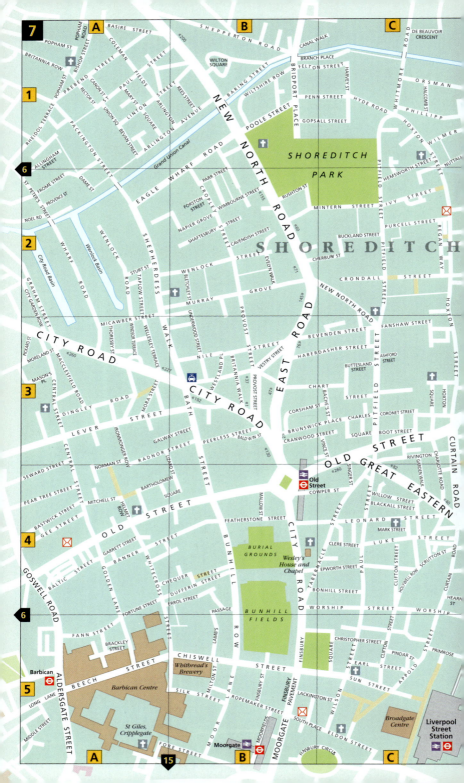

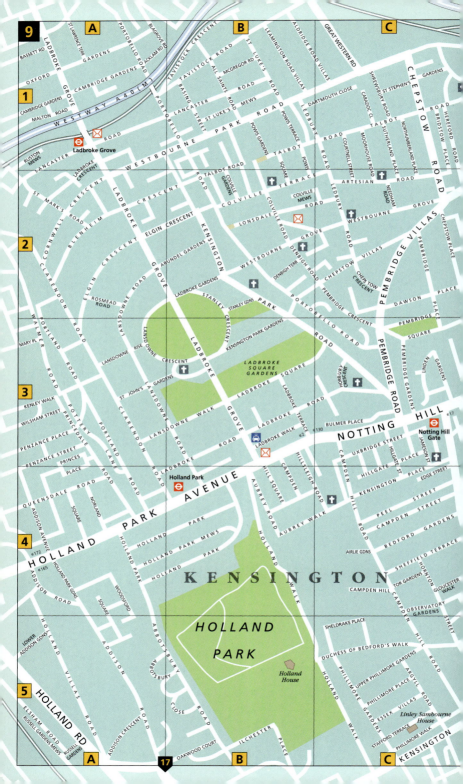

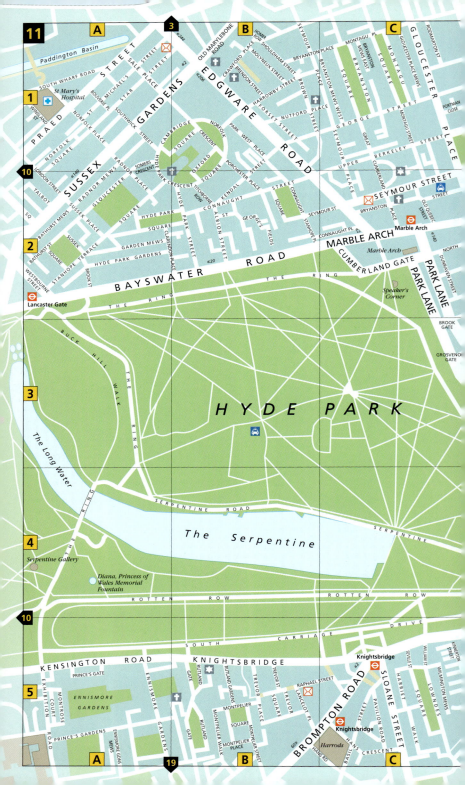

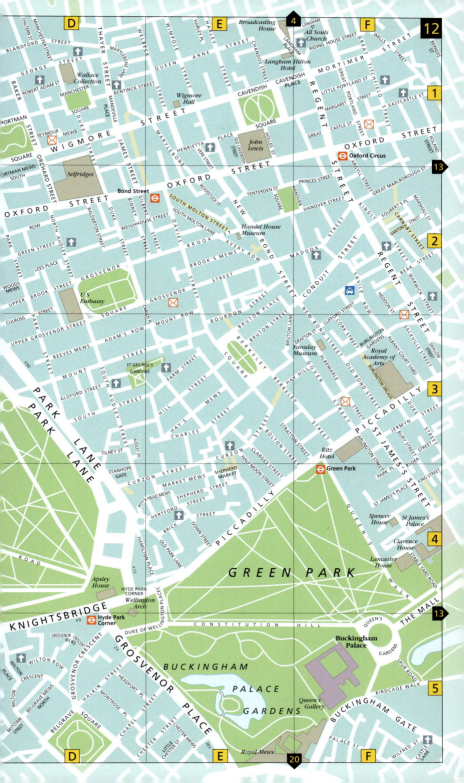

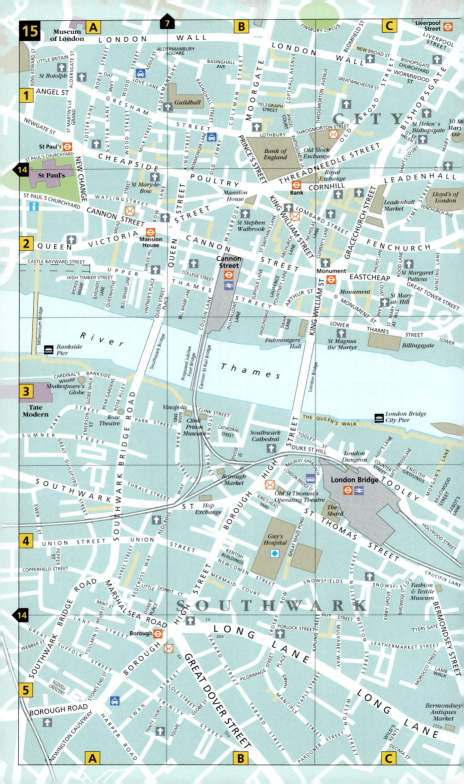

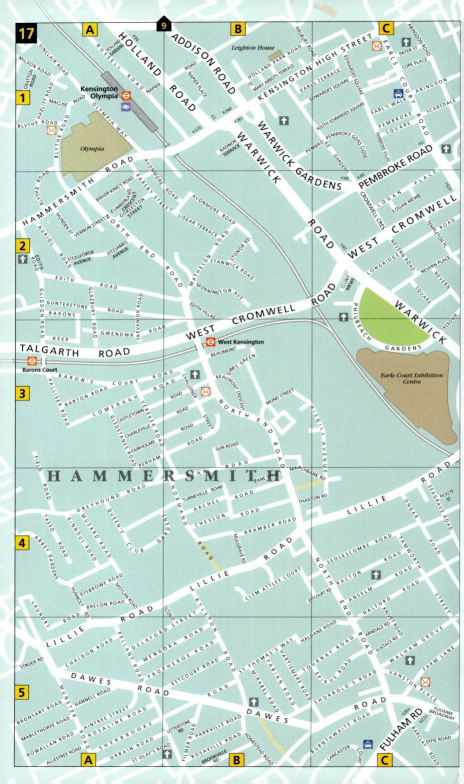

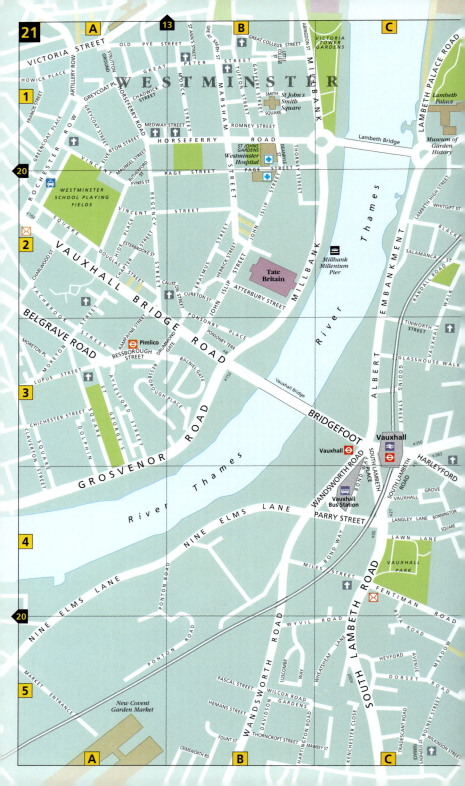

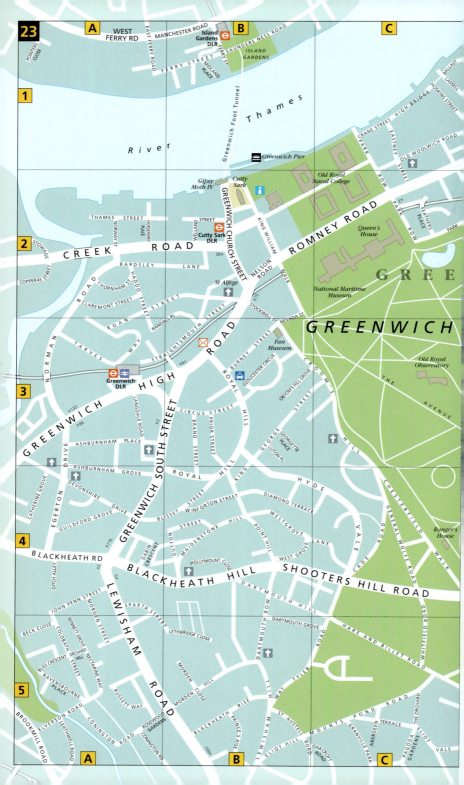

General Index

Acknowledgments

Dorling Kindersley would like to thank the following people whose help and assistance contributed to the preparation of this book.

Main Contributor

Michael Leapman was born in London in 1938 and has been a journalist since he was 20. He has worked for most British national newspapers and writes about travel and other subjects for several publications, among them *The Independent, Independent on Sunday, The Economist,* and *Country Life.* He has written ten books, including *London's River* (1991) and the award-winning *Companion Guide to New York* (1983, revised 1991). In 1989 he edited the acclaimed *Book of London.*

Contributors

James Aufenast, Yvonne Deutch, Guy Dimond, George Foster, Iain Gale, Fiona Holman, Phil Harriss, Lindsay Hunt, Christopher Middleton, Steven Parissien, Christopher Pick, Bazyli Solowij, Matthew Tanner, Mark Wareham, Jude Welton, Ian Wisniewski.
DORLING KINDERSLEY wishes to thank the following editors and researchers at Webster's International Publishers: Sandy Carr, Matthew Barrell, Siobhan Bremner, Serena Cross, Annie Galpin, Miriam Lloyd, Ava-Lee Tanner.

Additional Photography

Max Alexander, Peter Anderson, Stephen Bere, June Buck, Peter Chadwick, Michael Dent, Philip Dowell, Mike Dunning, Philip Enticknap, Andreas Einsiedel, Rhiannon Furbear, Steve Gorton, Christi Graham, Alison Harris, Peter Hayman, Stephen Hayward, Roger Hilton, Sean Hunter, Ed Ironside, Colin Keates, Dave King, Bob Langrish, Neil Lukas, Neil Mersh, Nick Nichols, Robert O'Dea, Ian O'Leary, Vincent Oliver, John Parker, Tim Ridley, Ellen Root, Rough Guides/Viktor Borg, Kim Sayer, Chris Stevens, James Stevenson, James Strachan, Doug Traverso, David Ward, Mathew Ward, Steven Wooster, Nick Wright.

Additional Illustrations

Ann Child, Gary Cross, Tim Hayward, Arghya Jyoti Hore, Fiona M Macpherson, Janos Marffy, David More, Chris D Orr, Richard Phipps, Rockit Design, Michelle Ross, John Woodcock.

Cartography

Andrew Heritage, James Mills-Hicks, Chez Picthall, John Plumer (DK Cartography). Advanced Illustration (Cheshire), Contour Publishing (Derby), Euromap Ltd (Berkshire). Street Finder maps: ERA Maptec Ltd (Dublin) adapted with permission from original survey and mapping from Shobunsha (Japan).

Cartographic Research

James Anderson, Roger Bullen, Tony Chambers, Ruth Duxbury, Jason Gough, Ailsa Heritage, Jayne Parsons, Donna Rispoli, Jill Tinsley, Andrew Thompson, Iorwerth Watkins.

Design and Editorial

MANAGING EDITOR Douglas Amrine
MANAGING ART EDITOR Geoff Manders
SENIOR EDITOR Georgina Matthews
EDITORIAL DIRECTOR David Lamb
ART DIRECTOR Anne-Marie Bulat
PRODUCTION CONTROLLER Hilary Stephens
PICTURE RESEARCH Ellen Root, Rhiannon Furbear
DTP EDITOR Siri Lowe

REVISIONS Keith Addison, Emma Anacootee, Elizabeth Atherton, Sam Atkinson, Lydia Baillie, Chris Barstow, Oliver Bennett, Julie Bowles, Chloe Carleton, Michelle Clark, Carey Combe, Vanessa Courtier, Lorna Damms, Hannah Dolan, Jessica Doyle, Nicola Erdpresser, Jane Ewart, Simon Farbrother, Gadi Farfour, Fay Franklin, Simon Hall, Marcus Hardy, Sasha Heseltine, Paul Hines, Phil Hunt, Stephanie Jackson, Gail Jones, Laura Jones, Nancy Jones, Stephen Knowlden, Priya Kukadia, Esther Labi, Michelle de Larrabeiti, Chris Lascelles, Jude Ledger, Jeanette Leung, Carly Madden, Hayley Maher, Ferdie McDonald, Alison McGill, Caroline Mead, Jane Middleton, Rebecca Milner, Sonal Modha, Fiona Morgan, Catherine Palmi, Louise Parsons, Marianne Petrou, Andrea Powell, Leigh Priest, Rada Radojicic, Mani Ramaswamy, Marisa Renzullo, Nick Rider, Liz Rowe, Simon Ryder, Sadie Smith, Susannah Steel, Kathryn Steve, Anna Streiffert, Rachel Symons, Andrew Szudek, Hugh Thompson, Karen Villabona, Diana Vowles, Matthew Walder, Andy Wilkinson.

Special Assistance

Christine Brandt at Kew Gardens, Sheila Brown at The Bank of England, John Cattermole at London Buses Northern, the DK picture department, especially Jenny Rayner, Pippa Grimes at the V&A, Emma Healy at the V&A Museum of Childhood, Alan Hills at the British Museum, Emma Hutton and Cooling Brown Partnership, Gavin Morgan at the Museum of London, Clare Murphy at Historic Royal Palaces, Ali Naqei at the Science Museum, Patrizio Semproni, Caroline Shaw at the Natural History Museum, Gary Smith at National Rail, Monica Thurnauer at Tate, Simon Wilson at Tate, Alastair Wardle.

Photographic Reference

The London Aerial Photo Library, and P and P F James.

Photography Permissions

DORLING KINDERSLEY would like to thank all the museums, galleries, churches and other sights that allowed us to photograph at their establishments.

Picture Credits

a = above; b = below/bottom; c = center; f = far; l = left; r = right; t = top.

Works of art have been reproduced with the permission of the following copyright holders: *Three Studies for Figures at the Base of the Crucifixion*, (1944, detail), Francis Bacon © Estate of Francis Bacon/DACS, London 2011 83b; *The Bath*, 1925, Pierre Bonnard © ADAGP, Paris and DACS, London 2011 181b; *Maman*, 2000 © Louise Bourgeois/VAGA, New York/DACS, London 2011 181cr; Fish 1926, Constantin Brancusi © ADAGP, Paris and DACS, London 2008 178tr; *After Lunch*, 1975 © Patrick Caulfield. All rights Reserved, DACS 2011 180t; *Spatial Concept "Waiting"*, 1960, © Fondazione Lucio Fontana, 179cr; *Lobster Telephone*, 1936 © Salvador Dali, Gala-Salvador Dali Foundation/DACS 2011 41cr; 2011*The First Marriage (A Marriage of Styles I)* 1962 Oil on Canvas 72 x 60″ David Hockney 85t; Bust of *Lawrence of Arabia* © The Family of Eric H. Kennington, RA 151bl; *Skydiver VI* 1964 Oil on canvas support 2032 x 1467mm © Gerald Laing; *Whaam!* 1963, Roy Lichtenstein © The Estate of Roy Lichtenstein/DACS, London 2008 178cla; Mario Merz 178la; *The Snail*, 1953, Henri Matisse © Succession H. Matisse/DACS, London 2008 179tl; The works by Henry Moore illustrated on the following pages have been reproduced by kind permission of the Henry Moore Foundation: 45c, 85c, 266cb. *Soft Drainpipe – Blue (Cool) version*, 1967 © Claes Oldenburg 179c; *Summertime: Number 9A*, 1948, Jackson Pollock © ARS, New York and DACS, London 2011 181; *Quattro Stagioni* 1993–4, © Cy Twombly 178cl.

The Publishers are grateful to the following individuals, companies, and picture libraries for permission to reproduce their photographs: ALAMY IMAGES: Martyn Goddard 367tl; Robert Harding World Imagery 100clb; BIANKA KADIC: 364tl; THE ALBERMARLE CONNECTION: 91t; ARCAID: Richard Bryant, Architect Foster and Partners 126t; Richard Bryant 249cr; ARCBLUE: Peter Durant 189cl; THE ART ARCHIVE: 21bl, 28c, 28bc, 29bl, 30br, 31cra, 31clb, 35tc, 35cr, 188b, 188bl; British Library, London 20cr; Imperial War Museum, London 32bc; Museum of London 17b, 29br, 30bl; Science Museum, London 29cla; Stoke Museum Staffordshire Polytechnic 25bl, 27cl, 35bc; Victoria and Albert Museum, London 22c, 23bc, 27tr; AXIOM: James Morris 164tl.

GOVERNOR AND COMPANY OF THE BANK OF ENGLAND: 145tr; BRIDGEMAN ART LIBRARY, London: 23t, 30t; British Library, London 16, 21tr, (detail) 23br, 26cb, (detail) 34tl, 34bl; Courtesy of the Institute of Directors, London 31cla; Guildhall Art Gallery, Corporation of London (detail) 28t; Guildhall Library, Corporation of London 26br, 76c; ML Holmes Jamestown – Yorktown Educational Trust, VA (detail) 19bc; Master and Fellows, Magdalene College, Cambridge (detail) 25clb; Marylebone Cricket Club, London 246c; William Morris Gallery, Walthamstow 21tl, 249tl; Museum of London 24–5; O'Shea Gallery, London

(detail) 24cl; Royal Holloway & Bedford New College 157bl; Russell Cotes Art Gallery and Museum, Bournemouth 38tr; Thyssen-Bornemisza Collection, Lugano Casta 257b; Westminster Abbey, London (detail) 34bc; White House, Bond Street, London 30cb. BRITISH AIRWAYS: Adrian Meredith Photography: 372t, 374tl; reproduced with permission of the BRITISH LIBRARY BOARD: 125b; © THE BRITISH MUSEUM: 18t, 18ca, 19tl, 40t, 91c, 126–7 all pics, 128–9 all pics; BRITTANY FERRIES 373tl; BT GROUP PLC: 370tl.

CAMERA PRESS, London: P. Abbey - LNS 73cb; Cecil Beaton 79tl; HRH Prince Andrew 95bl; Allan Warren 33cb; COLLECTIONS: Oliver Benn 60b; John Miller 163bl; COLORIFIC!: Steve Benbow 55t; David Levenson 66–7; CONRAN RESTAURANTS 293cl, 322bc; CORBIS: 259t; Bruce Burkhardt 289c; Tim Graham 3br, 95bl; Angelo Hornak 61c, 183b; London Aerial Photo Library 189bl, 189t; Kim Sayer 2br; Patrick Ward 61t; Courtesy of the CORPORATION OF LONDON: 55c, 146t; COURTAULD INSTITUTE, London: 41c, 117b; CUTTY SARK TRUST: 238cla.

COPYRIGHT: Dean & Chapter of Westminster 78bl, 79tr; DEWYNTERS LTD.: 117t; Courtesy of the GOVERNORS AND THE DIRECTORS DULWICH PICTURE GALLERY: 43bl, 250bl.

FRANCIS EDWARDS: 323clb; ENGLISH HERITAGE: 252b, 258b; Jonathon Bailey 241clb; ENGLISH LIFE PUBLICATIONS LTD: 252b; PHILIP ENTICKNAP: 255tr; MARY EVANS PICTURE LIBRARY: 18bl, 18br, 19bl, 19br, 22bl, 24bl, 26t, 27bc, 27br, 29t, 29cb, 29bc, 32bl, 34br, 35tl, 35cl, 35bl, 35br, 38tl, 39bl, 72cb, 72b, 90b, 112b, 114b, 135t, 139t, 155bl, 159t, 162ca, 174ca, 177l, 207b, 216t, 226b.

Courtesy of FAN MUSEUM (Helene Alexander Collection) 243b; FREUD MUSEUM, LONDON: 246t. GATWICK EXPRESS: 375t; GORE HOTEL, London: 279b; GEFFRYE MUSEUM, London: 248tl; GETTY IMAGES: 33br; SUPERSTOCK 107br; GREEN TOURISM BUSINESS SCHEME: 365tr; GREENWICH INC: 238bc; GREENWICHMARKET.NET: 238cl.

ROBERT HARDING PICTURE LIBRARY: 33ca, 42c, 52ca, 169tl, 343t, 367cl, 384b; Philip Craven 210t; Nigel Francis 376tr; Sylvain Gradadam 289tl; Brian Hawkes 23clb; Michael Jenner 23cra, 242t; 58t, 227t; Mark Mawson 113tl; Nick Wood 63bl; HARRODS (printed by kind permission of Mohamed al Fayed): 320b; HAYES-DAVIDSON (computer generated images: 174bl; HAYWARD GALLERY: Richard Haughton 273tl; Reproduced with permission of HER MAJESTY'S STATIONERY OFFICE (Crown Copyright): 156 all pics; JOHN HESELTINE: 51tr, 63br, 98, 124b, 132, 172, 220; FRIENDS OF HIGHGATE CEMETERY: 244, 246b; HISTORIC ROYAL PALACES (Crown Copyright): 5ca, 7t, 37tc, 154cla, 254–255 all except 254br, 256–7 all except 257b; THE HORNIMAN MUSEUM, London: 256br; HOVERSPEED LTD: 377b; HULTON GETTY: 26bl, 124tl, 135cr, 232t. THE IMAGE BANK, London: Gio Barto 55b; Derek Berwin 33t, 272t; Romilly Lockyer 12bl, 13br,

72t, 94br; Leo Mason 56t; Terry Williams 139b; Courtesy of ISIC, UK: 370t. iSTOCKPHOTO.COM: Alan Crawford 374br, peterspiro 379. PETER JACKSON COLLECTION: 26–7; JEWISH MUSEUM, London: 247tl.

LEIGHTON HOUSE: 216b; LITTLE ANGEL MARIONETTE THEATRE: 359tl; LONDON AMBULANCE SERVICE: Tim Saunders 367cla; LONDON AQUARIUM 3c, 188c, 188r; LONDON CITY AIRPORT: 375tr; LONDON DUNGEON: 183t; LONDON PALLADIUM: 103; LONDON REGIONAL TRANSPORT: 380t; LONDON TRANSPORT MUSEUM: 30ca, 380–81 all maps and tickets.

MADAME TUSSAUDS: 222c, 224t; MANSELL COLLECTION: 21br, 22t, 22br, 23bl, 24t, 24cl, 25br, 29ca, 34tr; METROPOLITAN POLICE SERVICE: 365t; ROB MOORE: 115t; MUSEUM OF LONDON: 15crb, 18cb, 19tr, 19cb, 20t, 23crb, 41tc, 166–7.

NATIONAL EXPRESS LTD: 376; Reproduced by courtesy of the TRUSTEES, THE NATIONAL GALLERY, London: (detail) 37c, 104–5 all except 104t, 106–7 all except 107t and 107br; NATIONAL PORTRAIT GALLERY, London: 4t, 41tl, 101cb, 102br; NATIONAL POSTAL MUSEUM, London: 28bl; By permission of the KEEPER OF THE NATIONAL RAILWAY MUSEUM, York: 30–31; NATIONAL TRUST PHOTOGRAPHIC LIBRARY: Wendy Aldiss 25ca; John Bethell 252t, 253t; Michael Boys 38b; NATURAL HISTORY MUSEUM, LONDON: John Downs 12clb, 209t, 209cr; Derek Adams 208b, 208cl; NEW SHAKESPEARE THEATRE CO: 342bl.

PA PHOTOS LTD: 33cr; PALACE THEATRE ARCHIVE: 108t; PERETTI COMMUNICATIONS: Chris Gascoigne & Lifschutz Davidson 292cr; PICTOR INTERNATIONAL, London: 60cl, 174br; PICTURES COLOUR LIBRARY: 54br; PIPPA POP-INS CHILDREN'S NURSERY, London: 357b; PITZHANGER MANOR MUSEUM: 258c; POPPERFOTO: 31tl, 31crb, 32tl, 32tr, 32c, 35tr, 39br; THE PORTOBELLO HOTEL: 279TR; POST HOUSE HEATHROW: Tim Young 377t; PRESS ASSOCIATION LTD: 31bl, 31br; PUBLIC RECORD OFFICE (Crown Copyright): 20b.

BILL RAFFERTY: 342br; RAINFOREST CAFE: 357cl; RBS GROUP: 366c, 366cb; REX FEATURES LTD: 53tl; Peter Brooker 53tr; Andrew Laenen 54c; Jonathon Player 288cla; THE RITZ, London: 91b; ROYAL ACADEMY OF ARTS, London: 90tr; THE BOARD OF TRUSTEES OF THE ROYAL ARMOURIES: 41tr, 155tl, 157t, 157br; ROYAL BOTANIC GARDENS, KEW: Andrew McRob 48cl, 56b, 260–61 all pics except 260t & 260br; THE ROYAL COLLECTION © 2010 HER MAJESTY

QUEEN ELIZABETH II: 8–9, 53b, 88t, 93t, 94–5 all pics except 94br & 95bl, 96t, 254br; Derry Moore 95cra; ROYAL COLLEGE OF MUSIC, London: 200c, 206c.

ST PAUL'S CATHEDRAL: Sampson Lloyd 148cl, 150cla, 151tr. GRUPO SANTANDER: 368cb; THE SAVOY GROUP: 116cr, 274t, 274b; SCIENCE MUSEUM, London: 212–13 all pics; SCIENCE PHOTO LIBRARY: Maptec International Ltd 12b; SOCIETY OF LONDON THEATRE/tkts: 343br; SOMERSET HOUSE: Peter Durant/arcblue.com 117tr; SPENCER HOUSE LTD: 88b; SOUTHBANK PRESS OFFICE: 186bl; Stephen Cummiskey 186cla; Graeme Duddridge 272cla; STA TRAVEL GROUP: 364cb; SYNDICATION INTERNATIONAL: 33bl, 37tr, 52cb, 53c, 58bl, 59t, 136; Library of Congress 27bl.

TATE LONDON 2001: 12br, 41cr, 43br, 82–3 all pics, 84–5 all pics, 178–9 all pics, 180–81 all pics; 273br. TRANSPORT FOR LONDON: 364br, 378bl, 382bl, 383tl; THE ROYAL COLLECTION © 2010 HER MAJESTY QUEEN ELIZABETH II Courtesy of the BOARD OF TRUSTEES OF THE VICTORIA AND ALBERT MUSEUM: 12cl, 37br, 40b, 201cl; 202–3 all pics, purchased with the assistance of the NACF and the Goldsmith's Company 203cra, 204–5 all pics, 254b, 358t; VIEW PICTURES: Dennis Gilbert 380br. THE WALDORF, London: 272b; By kind permission of the trustees of THE WALLACE COLLECTION, London: 40ca, 226cl; PHILIP WAY PHOTOGRAPHY: 64lb, 150clb, 177b; Courtesy of the TRUSTEES OF THE WEDGWOOD MUSEUM, Barlaston, Stoke-on-Trent, Staffs, England: 28br; VIVIENNE WESTWOOD: Patrick Fetherstonhaugh 33br; THE WIMBLEDON LAWN TENNIS MUSEUM: Micky White 251t; Photo © WOODMANSTERNE: Jeremy Marks 37tl, 149t; GREGORY WRONA 267r. YOUTH HOSTEL ASSOCIATION: 277; ZEFA: 12t, 52b, 342c; Bob Croxford 57t; Clive Sawyer 57b. ZWEMMER MEDIA: David Bennett 323bl.

Front Endpaper: All special photography except JOHN HESELTINE: Left page tr. Right page tr.

JACKET Front – GETTY IMAGES: The Image Bank/Scott E Barbour; Back – ALAMY IMAGES: David Pearson cla; AWA IMAGES: Travel Pix Collection bl, DORLING KINDERSLEY: Rough Guides/Victor Borg clb, Matthew Ward tl. Spine – GETTY IMAGES: The Image Bank/ Scott E Barbour t.

MAP COVER – GETTY IMAGES: The Image Bank/Scott E Barbour.

All other images © DORLING KINDERSLEY
For further information see www.DKimages.com

The London Underground

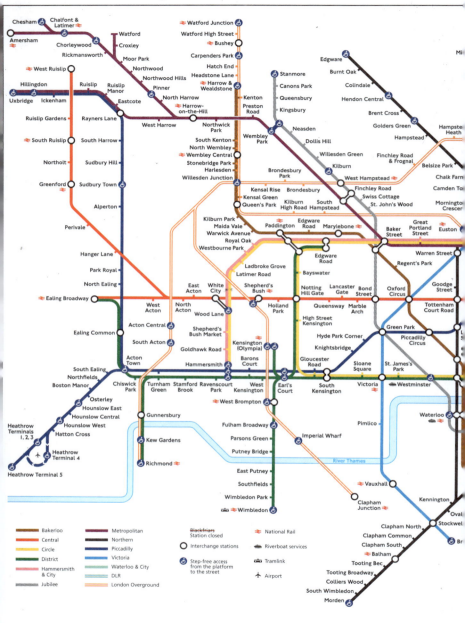

Legend:

Bakerloo	Metropolitan		Blackfriars Station closed
Central	Northern		
Circle	Piccadilly		National Rail
District	Victoria		Riverboat services
Hammersmith & City	Waterloo & City		Tramlink
	DLR		Airport
Jubilee	London Overground		

Interchange stations

Step-free access from the platform to the street